W9-BEX-800

LANGUAGE, MEMORY, AND THOUGHT

THE EXPERIMENTAL PSYCHOLOGY SERIES

Arthur W. Melton · Consulting Editor

LANGUAGE, MEMORY, AND THOUGHT

John R. Anderson
YALE UNIVERSITY

 LAWRENCE ERLBAUM ASSOCIATES, PUBLISHERS

1976   Hillsdale, New Jersey

DISTRIBUTED BY THE HALSTED PRESS DIVISION OF
JOHN WILEY & SONS
New York   Toronto   London   Sydney

Copyright © 1976 by Lawrence Erlbaum Associates, Inc.
All rights reserved. No part of this book may be reproduced in
any form, by photostat, microform, retrieval system, or any other
means, without the prior written permission of the publisher.

Lawrence Erlbaum Associates, Inc., Publishers
62 Maria Drive
Hillsdale, New Jersey 07642

Distributed solely by Halsted Press Division
John Wiley & Sons, Inc., New York

Library of Congress Cataloging in Publication Data
Anderson, John Robert, 1947–
   Language, memory, and thought.

   (The Experimental psychology series)
   Includes bibliographical references and indexes.
   1. Human information processing.   2. Languages–
Psychology.   3. Memory.   4. Thought and thinking.
BF455.A52   001.53   76-21791
ISBN 0-470-15187-0

Printed in the United States of America

Contents

Preface

This book presents a theory about human cognitive functioning, a set of experiments testing that theory, and a review of some of the literature relevant to the theory. The theory is embodied in a computer simulation model called ACT. The ACT model consists of two major components. There is an associative network model of long-term memory that encodes the model's propositional knowledge about the world, and a production system that operates on the propositional network to perform various cognitive tasks. The model is a theory of "higher-mental processes." It is very consciously not concerned with perception or other nonsymbolic aspects of cognition. However, within the domain of "higher-mental processes" this is a very general theory and is proveably capable of all specifiable behaviors. The principal empirical areas of concern are indicated by the title of this book—there are chapters dealing with retrieval from long-term memory, inference making, learning and retention of prose, language understanding and generation, induction, and language acquisition. An attempt is made in these chapters to provide ACT models for these tasks.

The theory presented in this book represents a continuation of my efforts to understand the nature of human intelligence by building models of cognitive processes and testing them. In 1973 Gordon Bower and I published a book describing a model of human memory called HAM, which represented the outcome of our four years of collaboration at Stanford. Gordon Bower and I were agreed that the HAM model had a number of serious deficiencies. ACT evolved as an attempt to produce a model that would deal with HAM's problems. Unfortunately, the end of my graduate career meant an end to the close collaboration I had with Gordon Bower. So, while he agrees as to what these problems are, it is not so clear that he would want to endorse all the solutions adopted in ACT.

The central problem with HAM was that, while there was a well worked out theory of how memory operates, there was no well-defined theory of the processes that used this component. The consequence was that it was difficult to know how to apply HAM to many empirical domains and as a result difficult to perform definitive empirical tests of the model. Our primary goal in the HAM project was to develop a model for prose memory. However, an adequate model required that we specify processes of language comprehension and inference making. The HAM framework seemed rather bankrupt in providing us with ideas about these processes. There were also serious problems with HAM because its propositional network lacked a formal semantics. In addition to the general problems, over the period of the three years since the formulation of HAM we and other researchers have found a great many specific empirical inadequacies with that model.

There are a number of ways to deal with the inadequacies found in HAM. One is to give up the attempt to develop a large scale general theory and focus on tractible subproblems. Another is to take a more artificial intelligence bent, and to begin to develop large and complex models to deal with the richness and complexity of human cognition. For reasons set forth in Chapter 1, I rejected both of these approaches and instead attempted to find a small set of basic mechanisms that would provide adequate building blocks for human cognition. To provide some focus to my efforts I decided to concentrate on inference making and language acquisition. My efforts to understand inference making led me into modern logic, mechanical theorem proving, and into research on human inferential processes. My attempts to deal with language acquisition led me much more directly to a new computer model. This model was called LAS (see Chapters 11 and 12 of this book). It used an augmented transition network (ATN) grammar like that advocated by Ron Kaplan, Eric Wanner, and William Woods. The LAS model had moderate success in simulating the learning of simple languages. At first it seemed that the ATN model had some promise as a general model for cognitive processing, not just language processing.

Meanwhile empirical work by myself and others on memory processes had indicated some serious defects in the HAM conception of memory, particularly with respect to how memory was searched. Rather than HAM's logical serial search, the data seemed to indicate that memory was searched by means of a parallel activation process, somewhat along the line suggested earlier by Ross Quillian. This was the state of affairs when I first considered writing this book in the summer of 1974. The HAM model was beginning to crumble under empirical onslaught, and headway was being made in developing an ATN model for cognitive procedures. It seemed that there was a potential for integrating an ATN model with a revised memory model. Such a model had the promise of being very powerful. The book writing enterprise seemed like the ideal means for disciplining this theoretical endeavor.

However, as soon as I had begun to set the theory down, I encountered two stumbling blocks. The first occurred when I tried to apply an ATN model to deal with the set of ideas and data I had been collecting about inference making. The model did not seem to have any natural application to this domain. Moreover, the problems uncovered in the application of ATNs to inference making made me reassess their suitability as models for language processing. As will be detailed in Chapter 11, I came to the conclusion that ATNs were too powerful as models of human language processing, particularly with respect to their potential for recursive self-embedding. These difficulties led me to consider carefully the production system models of Allen Newell, which had some similarities to ATNs but did not have their excessive power. It seemed that Newell's notions could be transformed to serve my purposes. So ACT acquired production systems as its procedural component.

The second stumbling block occurred as I tried to gather data in support of the basic assumptions underlying the ACT model. It seemed that there was no way to discriminate empirically the ACT assumptions from certain other possibilities. One could show that some possibilities like HAM were wrong, but there seemed no way to discriminate ACT from others. This led to a very extensive set of ruminations about the nature and purpose of a cognitive theory. The outcome was a reassessment of my goals, which is presented in Chapter 1.

The first version of the ACT simulation model was developed in the fall of 1974. That model, ACTA, resides on tape but there is no other documentation of it, and I have since lost all memory of it. A second model, ACTB, was developed in the first two months of 1975. Jim Greeno has taken that model, made some changes and additions to it, and it is currently running on the Michigan computer. A third version of ACT, ACTC, was written for the Michigan machine, and some small simulations of language acquisition have been performed with that version. The summer of 1975 was spent at Stanford, and a fourth version of the ACT program, ACTD, was developed for the SUMEX computer. Upon my return to Michigan in the fall of 1975, Paul Kline and I developed the fifth and current version of the ACT program, ACTE. This is currently running on the SUMEX computer.

This history of program writing and rewriting reflects a tumultous period of interaction between book writing, experimentation, and programming. Each version of the program was an attempt to set forth the current best conception of the ACT theory. The process of experimentation and theory development (in the course of book writing) would indicate problems with the program. The process of writing another program would lead to new ideas for empirical investigation and new theoretical studies. The book itself has gone through three drafts. The first draft was completed April, 1975, the second October, 1975, and the third January, 1976. Parts of the first draft were distributed to a seminar I taught at Michigan in the Winter term, and parts of the second draft were distributed to a seminar taught in the summer at Stanford. The participants in these two seminars were very helpful in pointing out the many inadequacies of the first two versions. Each version of the book was a drastic revision of the previous as theoretical ideas underwent wholesale revamping.

I hope that the ACT theory has emerged from its period of great turmoil. Paul Kline, Clayton Lewis, and myself are currently engaged in a research project trying to further develop the program as a model for language processing and language acquisition. It remains to be seen how much of the current ACT will survive these efforts. Some of our early discussions have already resulted in changes in the theory as it is presented in this book.

The research reported here has considerable similarity to a great many research projects. Almost any of current work in psychology on semantic memory and language comprehension has a relation to the ACT theory. Similarly, the work in artificial intelligence on language processing, question answering, "intelligent" programming languages, etc., is relevant. There are three research efforts that are particularly close and deserve special acknowledgement. There is the work of Donald Norman and David Rumelhart on their computer model of cognition, LNR. This research seems closest to ACT in its scope, goals, and methods. There is the work of Walter Kintsch, which is closest in its use of empirical data. Finally, there is the work of Allen Newell and Herbert Simon from which the production-system model is taken. The relevant aspects of these various theories are reviewed at the appropriate places in the book. There are some attempts to contrast these theories with ACT, but the extent to which such similar theories are complementary and do not permit contrasts is surprising.

I have acquired a great many debts in the writing of this book. There are many people who have read and commented on portions of the book. During my summer at Stanford, Gordon Bower went through the first half of the book and provided his broad and penetrating perspective on the issues. The exchanges we had over the book were pleasant reminders of the wonderful days when we were developing the HAM theory. Clayton Lewis at Michigan read many portions of the book in various drafts. His abilities to comprehend, evaluate, and criticize have been invaluable. I have long since lost track of how many important ideas have evolved out of my discussions with him. Reid Hastie reviewed the entire second draft and provided comments and suggestions that have been of great help in writing the final draft. David Kieras also read large portions of the second draft and provided many helpful reactions to the conceptual issues and suggestions for better exposition of the technical developments. Lynne Reder labored many hours with me throughout the writing of the book and providing badly needed help at all levels—spelling, grammar, organization, theory, and philosophy. In addition she provided me with the love, understanding, and encouragement needed to get through the rigors of book writing. She did all this at a period where she needed the time to develop her own professional career. My debt to her is enormous. There have been a number of others who have read portions of the book and provided comments that resulted in improvements—John Black, Herbert Clark, Walter Kintsch, Paul Kline, Donald Norman, Rebecca Paulson, Edward Smith, and Robert Sternberg.

The Society of Fellows of the University of Michigan deserves special thanks for their support of me. Three years of complete freedom from all academic responsibility and complete freedom to devote oneself to research is indeed a golden opportunity. Without this freedom I would only have been able to finish a fraction of the work on ACT. They were also a major source of funds for the early simulation work. The Psychology Department at Michigan and the Human Performance Center have proved to be valuable resources of colleagues and graduate students. The intellectual climate here has been sufficiently different from Stanford and Yale to provide a very broadening experience. Rebecca Paulson, my research assistant at Michigan, has been fabulous in her ability to take responsibility for the design and execution of the many experiments reported in this book. Without Becky and the resources of the Human Performance Center, my experimental research program would either have been much stunted or would have drained my time away from theory development.

Experimentation, development of theory, and the writing of the book was also critically dependent on the support from federal granting agencies. The research testing the HAM theory and the early development of ACT was supported by Grant GB-40298 from the National Science Foundation. The National Science Foundation is continuing to support experimentation on ACT through Grant BMS76-00959. The research on development of computer simulation model is being supported by Grant MH26383 from the National Institutes of Mental Health. The SUMEX-AIM project has provided me with marvelous computing facilities that have greatly helped the development of ACT in the last six months and promise to facilitate future development.

A final thanks goes to those who have helped with the physical preparation of the book and manuscript. Many secretaries typed chapters of this manuscript. I won't try to name them all. A special thanks is due to Carolyn Hohnke on whose shoulders fell the principal responsibility over these last few hectic months. I appreciate her ability to deal with all the many issues that arose so that I would have time to think as I must in writing a final draft. The staff of LEA deserves the highest praise for their efforts to bring this book out as expeditiously as possible.

JOHN R. ANDERSON

To My Parents

Adeline Landgraff Anderson
John Leonard Anderson

1

Preliminary Considerations

I believe that parsimony is still inappropriate at this stage, valuable as it may be in later phases of every science. There is room in the anatomy and genetics of the brain for much more mechanism than anyone today is prepared to propose, and we should concentrate for a while more on sufficiency and efficiency rather than on necessity.

MARVIN MINSKY

1.1 INTRODUCTION TO THIS BOOK

This century has seen an amazing intellectual blossoming. Psychology at the beginning of this century was largely a parlor room avocation. Today it is approaching a mature science. There have been momentous developments in many of the disciplines adjacent to psychology—mathematics, philosophy, logic, linguistics, and computer science. We in psychology are still trying to digest the implications of these developments for the practice of our own science.

The computer revolution of the past 25 years has been particularly important to me. When researchers in artificial intelligence began to apply themselves seriously to the task of reproducing human intelligence on a machine, it became clear in a very concrete way how remarkable is human cognitive functioning. Despite the impressive advances in artificial intelligence, current computer programs do not approach the power and generality of human intelligence. Today we really have little idea about how humans perceive, remember, process language, or reason. This respect for the power of human cognitive functioning is reinforced by the more abstract analyses coming out of philosophy, logic, and linguistics.

All this poses an intellectual challenge. How is the power of human cognitive functioning possible? There have been two main approaches to this question. Those in artificial intelligence have tried to program machines to be as intelligent or more intelligent than man. There is a range of justifications for the artificial intelligence approach (see Newell, 1970, for a review). One justification asserts that the abstract logical character of a program which matches feats of human intelligence must be very similar to that of the human mind. This is asserted despite the fact a computer and a human brain are very different. It is argued that feats of human intelligence are so difficult that there can be only one way of accomplishing them on any physical device. Another justification is more modest. It simply asserts that it is interesting to know how a machine could be intelligent. This knowledge would improve our perspective on the nature of human intelligence, and also has obvious practical applications.

The approach of cognitive psychology, on the other hand, has been to build models of human information processing which predict features of human behavior. In some respects this is easier and in others it is harder than the artificial intelligence approach. It is easier because there is no requirement that the model be translatable into an intelligent computer program. The model certainly must be specified well enough so that it can be simulated on a computer, but that simulation can be so inordinately slow and inefficient as to disqualify it as an intelligent program. The cognitive psychology approach is more difficult because its models must predict the specifics of human behavior and not just reproduce the global intelligent aspects of that behavior.

Purpose of the Book

In this book I present a model in the cognitive psychology tradition. Various aspects of the model have received computer implementation, but these implementations are in no way artificial intelligence programs. This model is an attempt to provide an integrated account of certain linguistic activities—acquisition, comprehension, and generation of language, reasoning with linguistic material, and memory for linguistic material. Perhaps this model could be extended to deal with other areas of human cognitive processing—in particular, perception. At this time, I do not know whether such extentions will be possible.

This book is greatly concerned with the construct of memory, which has undergone drastic change in the last decade in Cognitive Psychology. It used to refer to the facility for retaining information over time. Now it more and more refers to the complex structure that organizes all our knowledge. In its concern with memory the book is an extension of the HAM model that I developed with Gordon Bower (Anderson & Bower, 1973). However, the model developed here is remarkably different from the HAM model. Research subsequent to formulation of the HAM model indicated there were some mistakes in that theory, which have been corrected in the new model. Other theoretical changes have been introduced, not because HAM made incorrect predictions, but because it seemed that a more parsimonious theory could be achieved if changes were made.

The theory has also changed because it has been extended to account for more than just memory. I have been concerned extensively with problems of inference making and language comprehension. In recognition of all these change the theory has been given a new name—ACT. We claimed in the HAM book that we really were not committed to that theory. We had developed that theory because it

provides a concrete realization of a certain theoretical position. It provides something definite for research workers to discuss, examine, criticize, and experiment upon. It is hoped that some resolution will be eventually achieved with respect to the fundamental theoretical questions. We hope that others will be encouraged to provide and motivate other explicit models of fundamentally different theoretical positions [p. 7].

In completing the HAM book we had the feeling that we had more or less defined the HAM theory once and for all and that the major task ahead of us was to test its empirical consequences. I feel less certain that ACT has achieved its final shape as a theory. There remains much exploration to be done as to the potential of the theory and variations on it, largely because ACT is a theory of much broader generality than HAM and consequently has more potential to explore. In this book I have caught the ACT theory in a stage of development and presented that. As this book goes to press new developments are occurring. However, it is unlikely that these new developments will be radical departures from the concepts set forth here. Therefore, this book will provide a comprehensive statement of the ACT theory. It also provides evidence for why this theory constitutes a real advance. Later publications will use this book as a reference for expositions of important ACT concepts.

I would like to emphasize that I do not think that ACT, at any stage in its evolution, will constitute the final shape of a theory of human cognitive functioning, any more than did HAM. In my perception of science it is critical to develop models like ACT. One needs to have explicit models that seem compatible with a wide range of data. Once formulated, such a model can be subject to intensive study and its range of performance understood. Having obtained a firm grasp on the character of the theory, one can then begin to explore its weak points and the potential of variations on the model. One can also explore the differences between this theory and others. All this rumination about the theory serves to increase one's sophistication about the significant issues. It is only after such rumination that one can confidently formulate a different and better model.

Contents of This Book

Despite the fact that a somewhat different theory is being offered in this book, it has a similar structure to the old HAM book. In addition to this chapter there are two general survey chapters in which issues relevant to the theory are considered. In the other three sections of this chapter I discuss some general questions about what the limitations of a cognitive theory are, and what its goals and strategies should be, with special attention to the role of computer simulation in a cognitive theory. The ACT model involves the integration of a memory network with a production system. The memory network is intended to embody one's propositional knowledge about the world. The production system is intended to embody one's procedural knowledge about how to perform various cognitive tasks. As a form of background, in Chapter 2, I review other propositional theories of knowledge. In Chapter 3, I consider production system models of procedural knowledge and how they are an advance over the older, but remarkably similar, stimulus–response theories.

The next four chapters present the main body of the ACT theory. In Chapter 4 I present an overview of the model, in Chapter 5 a detailed development of the propositional network, and in Chapter 6 a detailed development of ACT's production system. In Chapter 7 I present a formal semantics for the ACT representational system and an analysis of the expressive power of that system.

The next five chapters attempt to apply the ACT model to various content areas. In Chapter 8 I will consider the ACT model for fact retrieval; in Chapter 9, inference making; in Chapter 10, the learning and retention of prose material; in Chapter 11, language comprehension; and in Chapter 12, induction of production systems. Parts of these five chapters would be incomprehensible without an understanding of the theory set forth in Chapters 4–6. On the other hand, Chapters 8–12 can be read in almost any order as they have relatively little dependence on one another. A final short chapter provides an attempt to evaluate the ACT model. The reader might want to skip ahead and read that chapter to get a sense of how the book "will end."

Various sections of this book differ greatly in the formal and technical prerequisites they assume of the reader. I have tried to make the general substance of my arguments accessible to all. However, there were occasions when there was no choice but to plunge into formal analysis which I fear will be obscure to many. These sections are starred in the book as a warning to the reader, and are difficult for anyone to comprehend without the appropriate technical background.

1.2   LIMITATIONS OF A COGNITIVE THEORY

The goal of a cognitive theory might be stated as the understanding of the nature of human intelligence. One way to achieve such an understanding would be to identify, at some level of abstraction, the structures and processes inside the human head. Unique identification of mental structures and processes was once my goal and it seems that it is also the goal of other cognitive psychologists. However, I have since come to realize that unique identification is not possible. There undoubtedly exists a very diverse set of models, but all equivalent in that they predict the behavior of humans at cognitive tasks. Realization of this fact has had a sobering influence on my research effort, and caused me to reassess the goals of a cognitive theory and the role of computer simulation. The third and fourth sections of this chapter present the outcomes of these reassessments.

The purpose of this section is to show that it is not possible to uniquely identify internal structures and processes. Some find this assertion immediately obvious and have complained this section is unnecessary. Others, however, resist this claim and want to believe that the data available to a cognitive psychologist is so rich that he can uniquely determine the internal structures of the mind or that, if there is an equivalence class of models, all amount to slight variations on the same model. This section is intended to dissuade the second group. First, an argument is given from the theory of automata that there are many different models which generate the same behavior. Then two examples from the current mileau of cognitive psychology are presented. The first example shows that there is no way to tell if processes are occurring in parallel or in serial. Second, it will be shown that there is no way to uniquely determine the internal representation of knowledge.

Ignoring for the time being the possibility of physiological data, our data base consists of recording the stimuli humans encounter and the responses they emit. Nothing, not even introspective evidence, escapes this characterization. Thus, basically we have the behaviorist's black box into which go inputs and out of which come outputs. The goal is to induce the internal structure of that black box. We may not be behaviorists, but we can neither deny that we work with a behavioral data base nor deny that our cognitive theory must account for that data base. The difficulty with this data base is that it does not allow us to directly observe the mental objects and processes. We must infer their existence and their properties indirectly from behavior, which makes this induction problem a difficult one. Its logical character will be examined more carefully in Section 12.1.

The set of possible cognitive theories is not well defined. However, it presumably can include all the types of machines that are studied in formal automata theory (see Minsky, 1967). Therefore, if there are problems of uniqueness in the formal automata subspace, there will be even greater problems in the full space of cognitive theories. For any well-specified behavior (presumably including cognitive behavior) there exist many different automata which can reproduce that behavior. Any well-specified behavior can be modeled by many kinds of Turing Machines, register machines, Post production systems, etc. These formal systems are clearly different, and in no way can they be considered to be slight variations of one another. The machines are sufficiently different that it would be very hard to judge whether a theory specified in one was more or less parsimonious than a theory specified in another. Moreover, within a class of machines like the Turing Machines there are infinitely many models that will predict any behavior. Such equivalence classes are also known to exist in certain more standard cognitive formulations like stochastic models. Within such a class, parsimony could probably serve to select some model. However, suppose our goal is not to find the simplest model but rather the "true" model of the structures and processes in the human brain. How much credibility can we give to the claim that nature picked the simplest form?[1]

The preceding argument is the basic justification for the claim that it is not possible to obtain unique identifiability of mental structures and processes. That

[1]The identifiability problem is even worse when we consider the fact there are models that make different predictions but that the differences in the predictions are so small relative to the noise in the data that they cannot be tested. I argue (Section 10.4) that this is part of the problem with certain issues of network representation. Of course, one might argue that differences which are too small to be tested are not interesting.

is, we know from automata theory that, for any behavior, there are many "black boxes" (i.e., specifications of automata) that will reproduce it.[2] I fear that this argument will not convince some cognitive psychologists because they will either not understand it or not accept correspondence between different automata and different cognitive theories. Therefore, I have provided the following two examples of reasonably well-defined issues in cognitive psychology where one can prove nonidentifiability. These examples, however, do not establish the general thesis of this section. That follows simply from the fact that for any well-specified behavior one can produce many models that will reproduce it. These examples are only meant to illustrate the general thesis.

Serial versus Parallel Processing

One of the most fundamental issues that a psychologist would want to be able to decide about information processing is whether a number of operations is occurring in serial or in parallel. There has been a great deal of research trying to decide this issue. However, it has turned out that a little more thought should have been given to the question of whether it is really possible to decide the issue on the basis of behavioral data. Townsend (1971, 1972, 1974) has given a formal analysis of this question, and the outcome of his work has been quite sobering. In this section I present a slightly stronger case than Townsend has been willing to argue—I will argue that it is never possible to decide whether a process is parallel or serial.

Consider the simple case in which there are two mental processes that must occur, a and b. Assume that we can observe when both processes have been completed—although we are usually not so lucky in psychology. We might think of a subject being presented with two items, either nonsense syllables or words, on the right and left of his screen. He must press a button to his right if the right item is a word and similarly he must press the left button if the left item is a word. Deciding the right item is a word corresponds to process a and deciding the left item is a word corresponds to process b. Consider only the trials on which both items are words. We will have the following data after completing the experiment:

1. The probability p of pressing button a first.
2. The distribution of times of button a presses when it is pressed first.

[2]One might wonder what effect time information might have in producing identifiability. For instance, it is known that there exist different automata which generate the same output but which take different amounts of time to compute that output. There are two reasons to doubt that such time information can help. First, while such time information will separate some automata otherwise not distinguishable, for any one automaton there will always be others which generate the same behavior in the same time. So time information will reduce the size of the equivalence class of machines but will not make any machine uniquely identifiable. Second, one need not regard the time it takes for a machine to compute an output as its prediction about a human's processing time. Rather, one can have the automaton generate as part of its output a predicted time. In that case, all considerations about number of processing steps for the automaton model would be irrelevant.

3. The distribution of times of button a presses when it is pressed second.
4. The distribution of times of button b presses when it is pressed first.
5. The distribution of times of button b presses when it is pressed second.

The question is whether this data is adequate to tell us if the subject processed one item first and then the other or whether he processed them in parallel. The probability, p, tells us nothing in and of itself. This serial model would just assume that the subject has a probability p of starting on a first. The parallel model would assume the process a has a probability p of finishing first. Therefore, if there is going to be any information it must be in the distribution of response times.

Consider the situation where a completes first and b completes second. The ways this would happen in the serial and the parallel systems are illustrated in Fig. 1.1. In the serial system, a is started and takes time Z_{a1} before completion and then b is started and takes time Z_{b2}. In the parallel system a and b start simultaneously, a taking t_{a1} until completion and b taking t_{b2} until completion with $t_{b2} > t_{a1}$.

Suppose we had a parallel system. How could we construct a serial system to mimic it? Let $P_{a1}(t_1)$ and $P_{b1}(t_1)$ be the distributions of times in the parallel model when a and b complete first. Let $S_{a1}(t_1)$ and $S_{b1}(t_1)$ be the corresponding distributions of completion times in the serial case of a and b when they start first. To get the serial model to mimic the parallel we need to make

$$S_{a1}(t_1) = P_{a1}(t_1) \tag{1}$$

$$S_{b1}(t_1) = P_{b1}(t_1) \tag{2}$$

There is a difference in status between these serial and parallel distributions. One can think of the serial distribution as directly reflecting the distributions of the

SERIAL SYSTEM

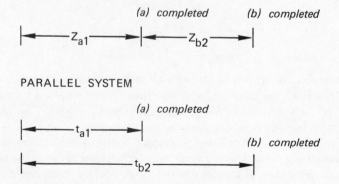

PARALLEL SYSTEM

FIG. 1.1 Schemes showing the total time spent processing a and b in a serial or parallel system when a is completed first.

underlying processes. However, it is much more natural to think of the parallel distributions $P_{a1}(t_1)$ and $P_{b1}(t_1)$ as deriving from different underlying distributions $\tilde{P}_{a1}(t_1)$ and $\tilde{P}_{b1}(t_1)$. For instance, theories often propose that a race takes place between independent underlying distributions $\tilde{P}_{a1}(t_1)$ and $\tilde{P}_{b1}(t_1)$. Then

$$P_{a1}(t_1) = [\tilde{P}_{a1}(t_1) \int_{t_1}^{\infty} \tilde{P}_{b1}(t) \, dt]/P$$

where

$$P = \int_0^{\infty} \tilde{P}_{a1}(t_1) \, [\int_{t_1}^{\infty} \tilde{P}_{b1}(t) \, dt] \, dt_1$$

However, there are other ways in which the observed parallel distributions might arise from underlying distributions. Therefore, I am referring to the observed distributions. These can be translated to different underlying distributions depending on the assumptions about the relation between the underlying and observed distributions.

Let $P_{a2}(t_2|t_1)$ be the distributions of completion times, t_2, for a second in the parallel model, conditional on the time, t_1, for b to complete first. Similarly, define $P_{b2}(t_2|t_1)$. For the serial model define $S_{a2}(t_2|t_1)$ to be the distribution of times for a to complete when it follows b, given that b took t_1. Similarly define $S_{b2}(t_2|t_1)$. A simpler case would be where the second times were not conditional on the first, but I want to consider the more general possibility. To make the serial model mimic the parallel we simply require

$$S_{a2}(t_2|t_1) = P_{a2}(t_1 + t_2|t_1) \tag{3}$$

$$S_{b2}(t_2|t_1) = P_{b2}(t_1 + t_2|t_1) \tag{4}$$

By defining the processes in the serial model according to Eqs. (1)–(4) we can obtain perfect mimicry. It is no more difficult to get the parallel system to mimic the serial system. Equations (5)–(8) guarantee this:

$$P_{a1}(t_1) = S_{a1}(t_1) \tag{5}$$

$$P_{b1}(t_1) = S_{b1}(t_1) \tag{6}$$

$$P_{a2}(t_2|t_1) = S_{a2}(t_2 - t_1|t_1) \tag{7}$$

$$P_{b2}(t_2|t_1) = S_{b2}(t_2 - t_1|t_1) \tag{8}$$

In general, it always is possible to create such equivalences between serial and parallel processes. As Townsend points out, in some of the equivalences one of the models is much more intuitive and compelling than the other. Consider an unlimited capacity parallel model where the mean time to process an item is independent of the number of items being processed. In the case considered above, two items were being processed, but imagine an experiment in which the number of items was varied, always keeping a as one item. In an unlimited capacity parallel model the mean time to process a would not vary with the number of other items being processed. A serial model might be able to mimic this by always processing *a* first, but suppose we had evidence that other items were completed before *a* and that any order of completing items was equally likely. The serial model could still mimic the parallel model according to equations like (1)–(4) but this would require assuming the serial model processed *a* faster the more other elements were present. As Townsend points out, this is a rather nonintuitive assumption.

There are also circumstances under which mimicry of the serial model by the parallel model would be bizarre. One might suppose in a serial model that the subject selects an algorithm which dictates the order in which the items should be processed. Moreover, the speed with which the first of *n* items is processed might depend upon which order (that is, algorithm) is chosen. It is possible to incorporate into a parallel model this dependence on processing rate for the first item on the processing order, but it gives the model a clairvoyant quality.[3] For instance, if there are three items being processed, the speed with which the first is processed can depend upon which is completed last. It seems hard to imagine how the first of three parallel processes to finish can know which of the remaining two will finish last and adjust its processing rate accordingly.

Sometimes there are pairs of equivalent parallel and serial models where one of the pairs seems to clearly contradict our intuitions about possible physical models. However, very often there is no such basis for selecting between members of a pair. In practical applications it usually seems that there are equivalent models which are almost equally acceptable.

An example is the Sternberg task (e.g., Sternberg, 1969). Subjects in a typical experiment are given a set of digits varying in number from 1 to 4. These they commit to short-term memory and they are then shown a probe digit. They must decide if that digit is part of the target set committed to memory. Subjects take approximately an additional 35 msec in making this judgement for each additional digit that is in the target set. This systematic increase in reaction time suggests a serial model in which the probe digit is serially compared to each digit in the target set, with each comparison taking 35 msec. However, a perfectly natural parallel model will also account for this data (see Atkinson, Holmgren, & Juola, 1969). This assumes the subject simultaneously compares the probe digit to all digits in the memory set. However, the speed at which a subject can make a comparison depends on how many other comparisons he is making. The idea is that the subject has a fixed amount of energy which he must distribute among all comparisons. Specifically, if the subject is making *n* comparisons it will take him mean time $n\alpha$ to make a comparison. The time for each of the *n* comparison processes is assumed to be distributed as an independent exponential. Therefore, the first completed comparison will be the fastest of *n* independent exponentials, each with mean $n\alpha$. The distribution of the fastest is known to be also an exponen-

---

[3]Townsend considers this to be a much more serious violation than the previous example of a serial model mimicking an unlimited capacity parallel model. I find this violation very upsetting but no more so than the first. So, there is clearly a variation in people's intuitions about such matters.

tial but with mean α. Upon completing this comparison, the energy assigned to it can be redistributed among the remaining $n - 1$ processes. With this added energy, they will behave now like exponentials with mean time $(n - 1)\alpha$. The fastest of these will complete in mean time α. In general, all n comparisons will complete at intervals that are on the average α time units apart. The mean time for all n to complete is $n\alpha$. So, by setting $\alpha = 35$ msec we can get the parallel model to look like the serial model.

These serial and parallel models are only two of many that have been offered for the Sternberg paradigm. It is one of the most researched and theorized-about paradigms in experimental psychology (Anderson, 1973; Anderson & Bower, 1973; Baddeley & Ecob, 1973; Corballis, Kirby, & Miller, 1972; Kirsner, 1972; Murdock, 1971; Sternberg, 1969; Theios, Smith, Haviland, Traupmann, & Moy, 1973—to name but a few). The fact that so many theories have been proposed consistent with the basic facts should also serve to indicate that behavioral data cannot uniquely determine the internal structure of the black box that generated it. It is also true that most of these models do not predict all the available facts. However, when a model is found that does, there will be many models equivalent to it.

Internal Structure

Equally fundamental as the parallel-versus-serial issue is the issue of what is the internal representation of information. Is it verbal? imaginal? propositional? or some combination of these? There have been a wide variety of propositional representations, some of which are reviewed in Chapter 2. If the representation is propositional, how do we decide which propositional representation is correct? It can be shown that these questions about internal representation cannot be answered. One cannot test issues just about the representation in the abstract, one must perform tests of the representation in combination with certain assumptions about the processes that use the representation. That is, one must test a representation-process pair. Given any representation-process pair it is possible to construct other pairs equivalent to it. These pairs assume different representations but make up for differences in representation by assuming compensating differences in the processes.

The problem is, again, that we cannot inspect directly the internal structure of the information representation. We must infer that structure from behavior. The situation might be characterized abstractly as follows: At any point in time, t, an input, I_t, enters and creates internal structure, S_t. Let us refer to this encoding of the input by the operater E. Thus

$$S_t = E(I_t) \tag{9}$$

The encoding function E constitutes our theory of internal representation. Some response, R_t, is determined by the internal structure, S_t. Let us denote this dependency by the operation D. Thus

$$R_t = D(S_t) \tag{10}$$

The data we have are a sequence of pairs $\langle I_t, R_t \rangle$. The question is whether they are sufficient to determine E and D. Note that we cannot address the question of internal structure (i.e., E) without addressing ourselves to the question of the process (i.e., D) that operates on that structure to generate behavior.

Concretely, we might think of this situation in terms of a paraphrase task. Then I_t would be a sentence to be paraphrased, E would represent the process of comprehending, S_t would represent the comprehension of the sentence, D would represent processes of generating a paraphrase, and R_t would represent the paraphrase.

Suppose we have a model M consisting of E and D. Then given certain other E^* (i.e., a different theory of representation), one can construct a D^* to yield a different model M^* that perfectly mimics M. If this is true, there is no way to distinguish one theory of internal representation, E, from the other theory of internal representation, E^*.

It remains to be shown for what E^* there exists the potential to mimic M. To do this requires that we define the concept of an *equivalence class under E* for an encoding function E. We will say two inputs, I_1, and I_2, are in the same equivalence class, $[I_1]_E$, under E if $E(I_1) = E(I_2)$. That is to say, they have the same internal representation.

THEOREM: *A model M using an encoding function E can be mimicked by some model M^* using E^* if, for all input I, $[I]_E{}^* \subset [I]_E$.*

This theorem asserts that mimicry is possible if the mimicking model, M^*, does not fail to discriminate in its representation any inputs that M discriminates. The simplest case of this would be where M^* gave a distinct representation to each distinct input. Since this can always be done, there always exists a mimicking M^* for any M.

PROOF: Let E^{*-1} represent the inverse mapping from a representation S^* to an input.[4] If a number of inputs could have given rise to S^*, then E^{*-1} would have selected one of these. Given a model M consisting of E and D, and given an E^* subject to the constraint above, a model M^* can be created to mimic M by setting $D^* = D \cdot E \cdot E^{*-1}$ where this denotes the operation created by applying E^{*-1} to S^*, applying E to the output of this operator, and applying D to the output of this. This would transform S^* to an input I, then to an internal structure S, and

---

[4]Under very general conditions, it is possible to compute the inverse. For instance, one procedure would be to enumerate all the possible inputs until one is found that E^* maps into S^*. This would not be a very efficient procedure, but it serves to show that at least one procedure exists, if it is possible to enumerate the inputs.

finally to a response. Clearly, if $S^* = E^*(I)$, $S = E(I)$, and $R = D(S)$, then $R = D^*(S)$. So, as stated, M^* mimics the behavior of M.

One might protest, however, that D^* was created by the very involved construction $D \cdot E \cdot E^{*-1}$. It might be thought that D is more simple than D^* and to be preferred on grounds of parsimony. However, it is actually not so simple. The above argument was only intended to show that equivalent models do exist with different representations. It does not prove that the only way to get M^* to mimic M is by constructing D^* in this complicated way. There may be a very simple specification of D^*—perhaps simpler than D.

It would be useful to have a concrete example of this abstract argument. Consider an experimental paradigm used by Weisberg (1969) to show that a sentence had a deep structure memory representation. Subjects had to memorize sentences like *The man who chased the cat is old*. After learning the sentences, subjects were given a word from the sentence and were asked to free associate another word from the sentence. Subjects tended to give as associates words that were close in the deep structure rather than physically close in the sentence. So, for instance, given *old* they would tend to associate *man* and not *cat*. We can cast Weisberg's model in terms of the preceding abstract characterization. That is, S would be the deep structure representation. The encoding function, E, would be some parsing routine. Finally, D would be some graph-searching algorithm, which, given one word, would retrieve the nearest word to it in the deep structure.

It is quite easy to construct a model, M^*, to mimic Weisberg's model, M. Suppose one simply assumed that the representation for a sentence was the sentence itself. Thus, E^* would be just the identity transformation. This encoding function has the desired feature of preserving all the distinctions among the input that E does. Then the D^* that would yield mimicry would be $D^* = D \cdot E \cdot E^{*-1}$. Since E^* is the identity transformation, this may be written more simply: $D^* = D \cdot E$.

As specified above it would seem that D^* would apply the parsing routine E to the sentence representation in M^* to retrieve the deep structure, and then apply the graph-searching routine D to the deep structure. Thus, M^* would just be postponing the computation of a deep structure until test. However, D^* need not be the procedure D concatenated on E. It can be any procedure equivalent to $D \cdot E$ in input–output characteristics. A much simpler procedure would be some surface scanning routine which identified the major constituents of the sentence and retrieved elements within these constituents. Such a routine would never have to compute explicitly a deep structure. Given that there is some parsing routine which can retrieve a complete deep structure from the surface string, there would certainly be a simpler scanning routine which would retrieve the element closest to a word in the deep structure.

This alternate model, which just stores the input sentence and performs a surface scan on it at test, may actually be simpler than the Weisberg model. It is also not implausible to me. It seems quite likely that subjects in Weisberg's experiment would commit the surface string to memory. At the time of test, they might also perform some series of surface tests to retrieve a response semantically related to the stimulus. This scanning routine would be used because the subjects perceived the task demands of the experiments as indicating that a semantically related response was required.

The general point is that any psychological theory is a representation-process pair. One can take two different theories about representations (as embodied by two encoding functions E and E^*) and generate equivalent predictions from them by appropriately choosing the processes that operate on the representations (as embodied by the decoding functions D and D^*). Realizing this, a number of current efforts in cognitive psychology seem mistaken. For instance, in the HAM book (also Thorndyke & Bower, 1974) we performed many experiments in an effort to show that the HAM propositional representation was superior to other representations. What we were really showing was that the HAM representation, with certain processing assumptions, was superior to other representations, again with certain processing assumptions. However, there were other processing assumptions that would have made these other representations equivalent in predictions to HAM.

There is currently considerable effort underway to determine whether information is represented only in a digital, symbolic, propositional mode or whether there is also an imaginal, perceptual, analog mode (Anderson & Bower, 1973, Section 14.5; Kosslyn, 1975; Moran, 1973; Paivio, 1975; Pylyshyn, 1973; Shepard, 1975). One criticism against imagery representations is that the concept of an image is not very well defined, relative to current ideas about propositional representations and other symbolic representations. However, one could make it precise—perhaps as a topologically structured array of information. Another criticism is that it is unnecessary to propose an imagery representation in addition to a propositional one since the former can be used to explain all the phenomena. This is presumably true, but it may be that a propositional representation can only handle certain phenomena with great awkwardness and lack of parsimony. Much of the current experimental research performed in defense of imagery representations is an attempt to produce phenomena that seem "naturals" for an imagery explanation (e.g., the mental rotation experiments of Metzler & Shepard, 1974). It seems that these phenomena would require contorted explanations in the case of a propositional system. However, given that there is no well-specified theory of imagery, it is hard to judge whether such a theory would really give a more parsimonious account of the phenomena than a propositional theory.

At best, however, this is what the imagery-versus-propositional controversy will reduce to—that is, a question of which gives the more parsimonious account of which phenomena. Given the earlier results, there is no way to prove one is correct and the other wrong. Moreover, even if parsimony could yield a decision between propositional and imagery theories, there would still remain the possibility that there are other, fundamentally different, representations which are as parsimonious as the preferred member of the propositional-imagery pair.

Physiological Data

Given behavioral data, it is not possible to decide uniquely internal structures and processes. This naturally brings up the potential for physiological data. Why not just open up the black box and see what is going on? There are more problems with this approach than just the ethical. First of all, the brain is a notoriously difficult object to inspect. Second, the terms in which brain processes and structures are described do not make direct contact with the issues that concern the cognitive psychologist. Suppose we wanted to decide whether comparisons in the Sternberg task are made in parallel or serial. What would correspond, physiologically, to a comparison? It seems that it is much harder to make contact between physiological data and cognitive constructs than it is to make contact between behavioral data and these constructs. Witness the almost nonexistent theory today about the physiological basis of higher mental processes. This difficulty is not unique to the brain. A knowledge of the circuitry of the computer is of little use in determining how it executes a program. Obviously, one would be foolish to claim that physiological data will never be of use to the cognitive psychologist. However, one would be equally foolish to expect that physiological data will help decide current issues about internal structure and process.

Influence of Preconception on Theory

The conclusion so far is that there are many different models for specifying the same behavior. Given that this is so, it becomes an interesting question how one theory out of the many equivalent to it is selected for a particular set of behaviors. I think if we observe how theories are chosen, we will see that a great many preconceived biases held by the theorist determine the structure of the theory. Certain assumptions are taken as inviolable and serve as the framework for the theory. Other assumptions are added to flesh out the theory and make it fit with the data. This is clearly what has happened in my construction of ACT. I have taken some ideas about the representation of propositions and productions and their interrelation as initial givens. To this I added assumptions, as necessary, to build a viable model. There is nothing wrong with letting such biases govern theory construction. However, one should be prepared for the fact that some other theorist with different biases might happen to construct a different theory that makes the same predictions. Often, too much effort is expended trying to discriminate between positions that are not discriminable on the basis of empirical data. Chapter 10 will argue that this is the case for the Gestalt–associationist contrast. Rather than trying to discriminate among basically nondiscriminable theories one ought to try to arrive at some theory which can account for the available data. That is hard enough, and much more important.

There is another sense in which the choice of a theory is strongly relative to the biases of the theorists. Its choice depends upon the behavioral measures selected as important. For instance, I make much of the speed with which a subject presses a button but ignore the force with which he responds. Another theorist could, conceivably, regard my interest in differences of a few hundred milliseconds as silly and insist that what is important is pounds pressure. Very different theories about structures and process can be developed by attempting to predict different behavioral indices.

All this has led me to the conclusion that a cognitive theory is very much a servant of behavioral data. It provides a way to understand and deal with that data. However, the theory does not have a unique status with respect to the data. It could be replaced by another equivalent theory. Moreover, if we decided other behavioral indices were more important, the theory might have to be abandoned.

These considerations should serve to defuse some of the controversy over whether computer simulation models of cognition are adequate. On one hand, there are those (Dreyfus, 1972; Ortony, 1974) who are struck by the enormous physical differences between the computer and the brain and refuse to believe that any model based on analogy with the computer could be correct. However, their arguments seem too strong because it is futile to try to find a "correct" model. Our aspiration must be the correct characterization of the data. If a computer simulation model provides it, fine. On the other hand, there are those (for example, Newell & Simon, 1972) who seemed committed to arguing that at an abstract level, the human and the computer are the same sort of devices. This may be true but the problem is that a unique abstract characterization of man's cognitive functioning does not exist. So it is somewhat pointless to try to decide what kind of device he is.

It would be a shame if this section were interpreted as asserting that theories about mental structures and processes are uninteresting or that we should return to hard-core behaviorism. Data without a theoretical interpretation constitutes just a confusing mass of particulars. There may be other ways of theorizing in cognitive psychology, but the success of the past twenty years would seem to indicate that the best way to theorize is by proposing a model of internal structure and process. The purpose of this book is to provide such a model. However, the point of this section is that such models, including ACT, are not unique. One knows, in the abstract, that there are other, different models, equivalent in their prediction and probably equivalent in parsimony and intuitiveness.

1.3   GOALS FOR A COGNITIVE THEORY

The fact that it is not possible to uniquely determine cognitive structures and processes poses a clear limitation on our ability to understand the nature of human intelligence. The realization of this fact has also led to a shift in my personal goals. I am less interested in defending the exact assumptions of the theory and am more interested in evolving some theory that can account for important empirical phenomena. By a theory that accounts for "important empirical phenomena" I mean one that addresses real world issues as well as laboratory phenomena. Such real world issues for ACT would include how to improve people's ability to learn and use language, to learn and remember text, to reason, and to solve problems. This reflects my belief that the final arbiter of a cognitive theory is going to be its utility in practical application. Thus, I am proposing a change in our interpretation of what it means to understand the nature of human intelligence. I once thought it could mean unique identification of the structures and processes underlying cognitive behavior. Since that is not possible, I propose that we take "understanding the nature of human intelligence" to mean possession of a theory that will enable us to improve human intelligence.

Even if this practical application is taken as an ultimate goal, cognitive theories must evolve, to some degree, abstracted from real world issues and focused on controlled laboratory experiments. The reader will see little in this book to indicate the practical applications of ACT. The complexity of the real world is too great to tackle head on. Nonetheless, there are a number of criteria that seem useful to keep in mind in evolving a theory from the laboratory in order to maximize the probability of its eventually being capable of practical application. Four such criteria are parsimony, effectiveness, broad generality, and accuracy. These four criteria are very traditional and can be found in elementary texts on philosophy of science (e.g., Quine & Ullian, 1970). However, it may be useful to reassert the obvious. It may also be worthwhile to show how these criteria naturally follow from the requirement that one's theory ultimately prove to be practical.

Parsimony

A theory must be sufficiently simple that it is conceptually tractible, so that one can understand it and reason about its implications. If there are two theories, equally adequate on all other grounds, the more parsimonious will be preferred. However, a theory which is so complex that it cannot be understood (even by its authors) is useless, regardless of whether there is any other adequate theory that is simpler. So the criterion of parsimony provides both a relative and an absolute standard for evaluating theories. It is particularly important if one has in mind practical applications. The real world problems that demand practical applications are quite complex. While a more complex theory might serve to generate predictions for a simple laboratory experiment, it could prove hopelessly intractible when faced with real world complexity. Also, the users of theories in practical applications are unlikely to have the training or the patience to attempt to deal with excessive complexity.

It should, of course, be emphasized that parsimony is a subjective concept. It would be foolish to propose a metric for measuring the simplicity of a theory or to expect that there will always be consensus about which of two theories is the simpler. However, there is considerable consensus in extreme cases. Despite its subjective nature, no one can deny the importance of parsimony to the acceptance of a theory.

There is a rather alarming growth in the complexity of current theories in cognitive psychology. In part, this is perhaps unavoidable given an organism as complex as man. This growth in complexity is also aided by the advent of computer simulation which has made theories tractable that formerly were not. However, it is easy to become deluded about how complex a computer-based theory can become before it is intractable. There are a number of problems associated with attempts to shore up complex theories with the computer. First, theories are often not accompanied by simulation proofs of their tractability, only the claim that it is in principle possible to simulate them, which is less than reassuring (e.g., see the discussion of recent language understanding attempts in Section 11.1). Second, simulations are often only partially implemented. Different parts of the theory are simulated but the whole theory is never put together in one program. This was partly the problem with HAM. Third, even when the total theory is in some sense realized as a program, that program may be useless as a predictive device. That is, it is often too complicated to introduce the effects of basic parameters of human limitation such as short-term memory or speed of processing (for example, see the discussion of LNR in Section 2.4 and ATNs in Section 11.2). Fourth, complex theories can sometimes be made tractable with great effort in a special experiment, but it is impossible as a practical matter to use it as a general predictive model. This is a current difficulty with the ACT model and with some of the protocol matching programs.

Suppose some scientist presented a program consisting of 30,000 lines of LISP code which successfully simulated a large array of human behavior. Would anyone consider that he had a real psychological theory? I think this example brings home the fallacy in the argument that the complexity of man justifies the complexity of a psychological theory. The goal of a scientific theory is to reduce the complexity found in nature to a few general laws. If human behavior is not amenable to treatment in terms that are much simpler than the behavior, it is not really amenable to scientific analysis. It is better to have a simpler theory that is incorrect in some details than a theory that is too complex to handle.

Another problem with relaxing the criterion of parsimony is that it eliminates the potential to falsify the theory. A basically wrong theory could survive forever. In response to each embarrassing piece of data the theorist could introduce some additional assumption that would accommodate the discrepancy. We clearly need to be able to respond to such post hoc attempts when they have gone too far and call for a new, simpler approach to the problem.

Effectiveness

The term *effectiveness* refers to the requirement that there should be explicit procedures for deriving predictions from the theory. Clearly a theory must be effective if it is to be of practical use. One of the great problems with the verbal theories of the past is it was not clear how to derive predictions from them. However, even in the case of rigorous mathematical theories there may be no way to derive by hand the predictions of the theory. This is particularly true if the theory proposes any dynamic interactions in the processes underlying a behavior. Computer simulation can be of considerable aid in such situations because it is possible to simulate the proposed processes and obtain predictions by Monte Carlo means.

Broad Generality

One would like to have a theory which addresses as broad a range of phenomena as possible. This is clearly a goal for ACT which deals with memory, language processes, and inference making. If a theory does predict a broad range of phenomena we are more likely to believe it and to believe that its predictions will hold up in situations we have not investigated. It is also the case that such a theory is more likely to prove to be successful in practical applications. A frequent feature of practical problems is that they do not observe the narrow borders we set up in our laboratory paradigms. For instance, question answering in the real world involves a combination of language processing, retrieval from memory, and inferential reasoning.

The typical approach in experimental psychology has been to focus theories on constrained paradigms. The theories that evolve are of limited generality, but they are naturally much easier to produce. The rationale behind this approach is that if enough small-scale theories are produced it should be possible to merge them into one very general theory. The principle criticism of this approach (for example, Newell, 1973) is that it does not seem to be getting anywhere. Theoretical interpretations of the limited paradigm never seem to be settled; endless experiments occur in a paradigm with no end in sight; new paradigms keep evolving to complicate the picture; there seems to be little convergence of the small-scale theories. These criticisms may just reflect a lack of patience, a failure to appreciate how long it will take for this divide-and-conquer strategy to work. Certainly, there is no reason why it should not work, nor is there any necessary reason why a more ambitious approach like ACT will work. However, whichever approach is taken, a theory of broad generality should be the final outcome.

Accuracy

There is not much that needs to be said about the requirement that the predictions of a theory need to be accurate. However, combined with parsimony, effectiveness, and broad generality, it makes the burden of the cognitive theorist a heavy one. No available theory—certainly not ACT—properly satisfies the intersection of these four requirements. However, I think it is a mistake to focus on any one requirement to the exclusion of the others. In particular, one should be willing to sacrifice a little accuracy if it permits a considerable gain in the other dimensions. This conclusion clearly follows from the desire for the theory to serve as a practical tool. We are willing to give up some accuracy in a tool for the sake of getting something that is easy to use and which can be used over a wide range of situations.

Importance of Temporal Relations

In terms of the practicality of a theory it is important that it focus on the temporal relations in the behavior. This contrasts with the emphasis in many research paradigms. For instance, in free recall concern frequently is on what is recalled and the order of recall, but not on the time to recall to or how the amount of recall depends on study time. Similarly, protocol matching attempts (for example, Newell & Simon, 1972) are concerned with having the simulation program mimic the moves of the subject but not the temporal relations among the moves. Any theory which does not ultimately address temporal features has little hope of providing a useful theory for dealing with problems of intelligence. Humans are thought intelligent not just because they make the correct response but because they make the correct response in time to be useful. The concept of time is inextricably part of the notion of intelligence. Computer programs in artificial intelligence (AI) that would come up with the correct behavior but would take centuries to do so are not considered intelligent.

As anyone who has written a few computer programs quickly realizes, there are many different programs which are identical in their input–output characteristics but which differ grossly in the time they take to perform various tasks. What is interesting about human behavior is how long it takes to perform certain tasks. It would not have been very interesting if Ebbinghaus had reported to the world that he could learn a list of nonsense syllables. His research was thought interesting because he reported how long it took him to learn the material and reported his retention over time.

There is a natural time measure associated with a simulation program, which is the time it takes to run. However, usually the psychologist does not want to take this measure seriously; there are deep problems in coordinating psychological time with computer time. Suppose the psychologist has good motivation for proposing that time for processing a sentence increases linearly with the length of the sentence, but it is a fact about his program that processing time is a function of the square of the sentence's length. Then there is no way he can mimic the purported real time behavior of the human by the real time behavior of the program. In my work, similar situations occur because I must compute serially operations that I claim occur in parallel. I calculate the theoretical time associated with a step in the simulation and print this out along with the response. I can disregard, then, the actual time for a response to be emitted by the program. The cost, of course, is that I lose the attractive feature of mimicry. However, it may still be an accurate predictive model.

This emphasis on time has produced a major shift in my research strategy which will be manifested in later portions of the book. Reaction time is my favorite dependent measure. There is another reason for focusing on time measures with a model like ACT. ACT can be shown to be computationally universal. That is to say, with important caveats about memory limitations and random errors, ACT is capable of the same behavior as that of a Turing Machine. A popular thesis (Church's thesis) is that a Turing Machine can perform any well-specified behavior. If so, it follows that there is no behavior that ACT could not produce. This is a desirable property of the model because it seems true of humans (again with important caveats about memory limitations and random errors). However, it means that one cannot test the model by seeing if it generates the same responses as humans. The critical test is whether it can predict the time relations in human behavior—which responses are rapid and which are slow.

Learning

Another major shift in my research concerns a renewed interest in the process of learning—not the learning of facts or lists, but rather the learning of procedures that underlie our ability to understand language, answer questions, make inferences, etc. Most of the serious unanswered questions in the ACT system can be laid at the door of such learning. Interest in the mechanisms of procedural learning seems to have died in cognitive psychology with the demise of stimulus–response theories. The lack of learning programs has long been acknowledged to be a serious gap in artificial intelligence.

It is important that cognitive psychology concern itself more with the issue of learning, both because of its important practical implications and because it serves to place important constraints on cognitive theories. Suppose one could construct a model of language understanding that adequately predicted what we would understand when we heard a sentence and how long it would take us to reach that understanding. Then certainly, at the level of explaining adult performance, it would be adequate. However, one could further require that a learning theory be added that would explain how that comprehension system initially evolved and what would happen to it if given additional learning history. It might be shown that there was no sensible way for the proposed comprehension system to have evolved. Or it might be shown that the way for such a system to evolve did not match child language development. Therefore, it is important that cognitive psychologists who propose models of adult competence give attention to the question of how such systems might develop.

1.4   STRATEGIES FOR THEORETICAL ADVANCE

Taking the goals of the previous section as desiderata for a theory, the next question concerns how they can be achieved. One obvious strategy is not to try to achieve the goals by oneself. There exist in the literature many useful theoretical ideas which I have blissfully incorporated into ACT. The most transparent case of this is the production system model of Newell, but there are many others. I have also made some other strategic decisions that may not be so obviously wise. Therefore, I have devoted this section to defending certain of these strategic decisions.

Need for Abstraction

There seems to be a belief in some quarters (e.g., Newell & Simon, 1972) that a theory should account for all aspects of behavior. This belief is sometimes used to promote computer simulation models. Since computer models actually mimic the behavior they predict, they are supposed to specify all aspects of the behavior and to leave nothing unsaid. However, there is no reason why a science should feel compelled to specify all aspects of a behavior or to deliver working models of the object of its study. I know of no other science where this is seriously attempted. The reason is that a science usually deals in data that are to some degree abstractions. So, for instance, meterologists in simulating weather patterns do not feel compelled to specify each drop of rain in their simulation. So, too, traditional theories of memory do not feel compelled to specify the actual items a subject will recall but only patterns and probabilities of recall.

Science progresses because of decisions to abstract out and focus on certain measures of the phenomena at hand. This abstraction reflects the scientist's judgement about what is important and what is tractable. Other scientists may differ with him in their judgment on this matter, but all must agree that abstraction is necessary. There are other ways to achieve abstraction in addition to one's selection of dependent measures. One means is the assumption that certain processes are probabilistic. For instance, in ACT it is assumed that there is a certain probability of forming an association. While I am quite unalarmed about the possibility that some of the basic processes in the universe may be random, I do not mean to imply that the process of forming a link is purely random or that one should not perform further analysis of the processes underlying link formation. I am only asserting that for my purposes I want to ignore such subprocesses and will summarize their behavior with a probability.

Another way of achieving an abstraction is to look at average subject behavior and to regard individual differences as random variations. While it is certainly the case that important characterizations can be missed by ignoring individual differences, it is also the case that simple observations on how subjects are different provide no theoretical gain. Whether it is profitable to invest time on individual differences is really a question that varies from task to task. I feel that it is not important in the experiments I perform, although I can always be proved wrong.

Role for Computer Modeling

The computer model has a number of advantages to offer in developing a cognitive theory. As already noted, it can provide an effective means for deriving predictions from an otherwise intractible theory. It also helps in many ways the creative task of theory development. One can use a computer simulation to try out one's ideas about how some subprocess (for example, retrieval from long-term memory) might function. In attempting this one is often likely to discover "bugs" in his theory from malfunctions of the simulation program. Simulation also often serves to suggest ideas that might not occur otherwise. In fact a profitable strategy for developing a psychological theory of a process is to simply try to write a program that performs the task and not worry about whether the program simulates the human. The outcome of this endeavour is often a set of useful constructs for developing a psychological theory. This evolutionary process for a psychological theory has happened in the case of language understanding systems (see Section 11.2).

However, there are also drawbacks to computer simulation. As noted earlier, there are dangers of the program becoming too complex. Also there is the risk of taking too much advantage of the computational power of the computer and endowing the program with unrealistic powers. There is also the danger of allowing what is easy to simulate in a serial computer determine the shape of a theory.

One positive feature of computer models, but which is not unique to them, is that they provide mechanistic models of the phenomena. Mechanistic theories are not required to satisfy the criteria set forth in the previous section for a cognitive theory, nor any of the other criteria that are normally set forth for a scientific theory. One could have a set of axioms embodying a theory of a phenomenon with no reference to internal mechanism (Newton's laws of motion, a set of equations describing serial position curves, etc.). However, for some reason we seem to prefer mechanistic theories. I am particularly fond of them within psychology. It is very interesting intellectually to know some mechanism that would mimic human behavior, even if it is found that there is more than one mechanism that will do so. In addition to satisfying an intellectual curiosity such mechanisms have the potential of contributing to the development of useful artificial intelligence programs.

Role for Formal Analysis

This book contains a number of analyses of formal properties of ACT and other models. For instance, in Section 4.4. I show that ACT can simulate (with qualifications) an arbitrary Turing Machine. Such formal analyses are relatively novel in cognitive psychology and the point of them is lost on some. These analyses serve the role of providing a test of the model. By means of a sometimes involved analysis of the model, one can derive very general predictions (for example, it can simulate an arbitrary Turing Machine). Then we can ask whether that property is true of humans (in this case I will argue it is). If it is, the model is vindicated and if it is not, the model is falsified.

This procedure differs from more traditional testing only in degree. That is, in a traditional experimental test there is only minimal formal analysis of the model and extensive gathering of experimental data. In the more formal analyses, one appeals to empirical facts that can be confirmed by common observation without extensive investment in methodology. The classic example of the application of formal analyses in psychology was the demonstration of the failure of stimulus–response (S–R) theory to account for the learning of natural language (for example, see Section 3.2). Natural language was asserted to have a certain complexity and it was shown S–R theories could not acquire language that complex. As in the S–R example, formal analyses can often have far-reaching consequences. It is often not possible to introduce a simple ''patch'' to the theory to repair the deficit detected by a formal analysis. One can challenge the accuracy of particular empirical facts claimed from common observation and one can challenge the correctness of a particular formal analysis, but one cannot challenge the use of the general logic behind such formal analyses.

I think such formal analyses can go a long way to direct theory construction. Their great advantage is that the data they require are cheaply obtained. The trick is to see how to make contact between common observation about human cognition and the constructs of one's theory. In some cases that is not very difficult. For instance, in Section 11.3 I use many ''common facts'' about language comprehension as tests of ACT's model for language comprehension. It seems unnecessary to perform experiments if there is a wealth of already known facts about language.

Role for Negative Arguments

One way to make progress in science is to discover the inadequacies of existing theories. This means that one must submit his theories and those of others to critical analysis. The progression from HAM to ACT was accomplished largely under the stimulus of faults discovered by others and myself in HAM. This book contains many critical analyses of my past work and that of others. It should be obvious that these analyses, if correct, are a contribution to cognitive psychology.

However, this last ''obvious'' conclusion is not obvious to all. It has been argued that one should be positive and supportive of work similar to his own, that one should not try to find and point out faults because this disrupts an impression of consensus in the field and of continuous progress in understanding of cognitive phenomena. Undoubtedly there is a role for praise in science, but to avoid criticism would seem to promote intellectual stagnation.

SUMMARY OF CHAPTER 1

This book introduces a new theory of human cognition, ACT, which combines a propositional network representation of declarative knowledge with a production system model of procedural knowledge. It is concerned with memory, inferential reasoning, language processing, and language acquisition. An argument is made from automata theory that it is not possible to determine uniquely the mental structures and processes underlying cognitive performances. This general thesis is illustrated with respect to two current issues in cognitive psychology. It is shown that it is not possible to decide whether processes are occurring in parallel or in serial. It is also not possible to decide uniquely the representation of information. It is argued that an ultimate goal of a cognitive theory is that it be capable of practical applications. Eventual practical applications seem more likely if one tries to produce theories that meet the criteria of parsimony, effectiveness, broad generality, and accuracy. Cognitive theories should try to predict the temporal relations in behavior and should concern themselves with how cognitive procedures are acquired. To successfully develop a cognitive theory, one needs to abstract certain features from cognitive phenomena and avoid trying to explain all details. There are useful roles to be played in theory development by computer modeling, formal analyses, and negative arguments.

REFERENCES

Anderson, J. A. A theory for the recognition of items from short memorized lists. *Psychological Review*, 1973, **80**, 417–438.

Anderson, J. R., & Bower, G. H. *Human associative memory*. Washington: Winston & Sons, 1973.

Atkinson, R. C., Holmgren, J. E., & Joula, J. F. Processing time as influenced by number of items in a visual display. *Perception and Psychophysics*, 1969, **6**, 321–326.

Baddeley, A. D., & Ecob, J. R. Reaction time and short-term memory: Implications of repetition effects for the high-speed exhaustive scan hypothesis. *Quarterly Journal of Experimental Psychology*, 1973, **25**, 229–240.

Corballis, M. C., Kirby, J., & Miller, A. Access to elements of a memorized list. *Journal of Experimental Psychology*, 1972, **94**, 185–190.

Dreyfus, H. L. *What computers can't do*. New York: Harper & Row, 1972.

Kirsner, K. Naming latency facilitations: An analysis of the encoding component in recognition time. *Journal of Experimental Psychology*, 1972, **95**, 171–176.

Kosslyn, S. M. Information representation in visual images. *Cognitive Psychology*, 1975, **7**, 341–370.

Metzler, J., & Shepard, R. N. Transformational studies of the internal representation of three-dimensional objects. In R. L. Solso (Ed.), *Theories of cognitive psychology: The Loyola Symposium*. Hillsdale, New Jersey: Lawrence Erlbaum Assoc. 1974.

Minsky, M. L. *Computation: finite and infinite machines*. Englewood Cliffs, New Jersey: Prentice-Hall, 1967.

Moran, T. P. *The symbolic imagery hypothesis: A production system model*. Unpublished doctoral dissertation, Carnegie-Mellon University, 1973.

Murdock, B. B. Jr. A parallel-processing model for scanning. *Perception and Psychophysics*, 1971, **10**, 289–291.

Newell, A. Remarks on the relationship between artificial intelligence and cognitive psychology. In R. B. Banerji & M. D. Mesarovic (Eds.), *Theoretical approaches to non-numerical problem solving*. Berlin: Springer-Verlag, 1970.

Newell, A. You can't play 20 questions with nature and win: projective comments of the papers of this symposium. In W. G. Chase (Ed.), *Visual information processing*. New York: Academic Press, 1973.

Newell, A., & Simon, H. *Human problem solving*, Englewood Cliffs, New Jersey: Prentice-Hall, 1972.

Ortony, A. Review of human association memory. *Journal of Educational Research*, 1974, **68**, 396–401.

Paivio, A. Perceptual comparisons through the mind's eye. *Memory and Cognition*, 1975, **3**, 635–647.

Pylyshyn, Z. W. What the mind's eye tells the mind's brain: A critique of mental imagery. *Psychological Bulletin*, 1973, **80**, 1–24.

Quine, W. V., & Ullian, J. S. *The web of belief*. New York: Random House, 1970.

Shepard, R. N. Form, formation, and transformation of internal representations. In R. L. Solso (Ed.), *Information processing and cognition*. Hillsdale, New Jersey: Lawrence Erlbaum Assoc. 1975.

Sternberg, S. Memory-scanning: Mental processes revealed by reaction time experiments. *Acta Psychologica*, 1969, **30**, 276–315.

Theios, J., Smith, P. G., Haviland, S. E., Traupmann, J., & Moy, M. C. Memory scanning as a serial, self-terminating process. *Journal of Experimental Psychology*, 1973, **97**, 323–336.

Thorndyke, P. W., & Bower, G. H. Storage and retrieval processes in sentence memory. *Cognitive Psychology*, 1974, **5**, 515–543.

Townsend, J. T. A note on the identifiability of parallel and serial processes. *Perception and Psychophysics*, 1971, **10**, 161–163.

Townsend, J. T. Some results on the identifiability of parallel and serial processes. *British Journal of Mathematical and Statistical Psychology*, 1972, **25**, 168–199.

Townsend, J. T. Issues and models concerning the processing of a finite number of inputs. In B. H. Kantowitz (Ed.), *Human information processing: Tutorials in performance and cognition*. Hillsdale, New Jersey: Lawrence Erlbaum Assoc. 1974.

Weisberg, R. W. Sentence processing through intrasentence word association. *Journal of Experimental Psychology*, 1969, **82**, 332–338.

2
Propositional Theories of Knowledge

Other theorists have proposed networks of descriptive propositions and abstract semantic entities as the common substrate of both verbal and nonverbal knowledge. These alternatives are open to the criticisms that the descriptive representations themselves cry out for psychological interpretation, they do not solve the problem of memory capacity, and their implications are too restrictive. Recent empirical evidence is more consistent with the view that verbal and nonverbal knowledge are represented in independent but interconnected symbolic systems, and that our memorial knowledge of the world is functionally equivalent to perceptual knowledge.

ALLAN PAIVIO

ACT involves a propositional representation for knowledge. This has become a particularly popular idea in the last five years. This chapter will review four recent theories that propose propositional representations—those of Clark (1974), Anderson and Bower (1973), Kintsch (1974), and Norman, Rumelhart, and the LNR Research Group (1975). The ACT theory involves a representation similar to the HAM model of Anderson and Bower. Therefore the section of this chapter dealing with HAM will serve to introduce some representational ideas that will be used throughout the book. The principal goal of this chapter, however, is to identify the common features of the propositional approach, its motivation, and the principal dimensions of variation within the approach. This should provide a background for evaluating ACT's theory of representation.

2.1   CLARK'S LINGUISTIC THEORY

The oldest of the propositional theories is that of Herbert Clark (Clark, 1971, 1974; Clark & Chase, 1972; Haviland & Clark, 1974). Clark claims his theory is concerned with sentence comprehension, but as we shall see, it is really concerned with the propositional representation of sentences and the utilization of these representations. Clark has developed explicit process models for a considerable variety of tasks. His theory is the most extensively tested of the theories to be reviewed here, and consequently rather more detailed criticisms can be made of his theory than of the others.

Clark's theory is the most strongly influenced by the neo-Chomskian transformational linguistics of the late 1960s and early 1970s. His principal concern is with representing the meaning of a single sentence and he assumes that each unambiguous sentence has but one meaning representation. He has developed a representation that attempts to both capture our linguistic intuitions about sentences and predict the subject latencies displayed in verifying sentences against pictures, answering questions, and following commands.

To satisfy the linguistic criteria for a sentence representation, Clark (1974) calls upon the current linguistic theory: "The semantic representation of a sentence, I assume, is equivalent to, or closely related to, the linguistic deep structure of the sentence [p. 1292]." The problem is that current linguistic theories have not and probably never will agree on the exact details of deep structure representation. Therefore, Clark needs some representation that will blur the differences in detail of the various linguistic representations and extract what is common to them. To do this he opts for a bracketing notation in which each level of bracketing corresponds to a relatively atomic proposition. So, for instance, *John isn't happy* is represented ((John is happy) is false). In the outer proposition *is false* is predicated of the inner proposition, *John is happy*.

Deep structures differ from Clark's propositional bracketings in that they commit themselves to many additional details. Figure 2.1 illustrates a possible deep structure for *John isn't happy*. Every symbol and branch in such a phrase

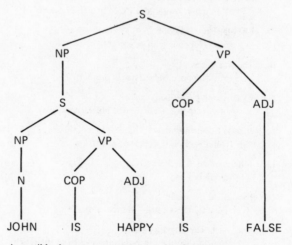

FIG. 2.1   A possible deep structure representation for the sentence *John isn't happy*.

structure tree is an attempt to capture some linguistic intuition and hence is a potential source of linguistic controversy. By choosing a representation that is a level of abstraction above such details, Clark successfully frees himself of such controversy.

A criticism of Clark is that he never specifies formally what are the permissible propositional structures. Rather he provides us with illustrations of how a wide variety of sentences might be represented and we are left to induce from his

TABLE 2.1
Sentences and Their Propositional Representations
à la Clark

---

1. John isn't happy
    ((John is happy) is false)

2. The star is above the plus
    (star above plus)

3. John killed Harry
    (John caused (Harry die))

4. Cross out all even numbers.
    (you cross out X (if (X is even)))

5. Many men aren't leaving
    (false (suppose (men (men are many) leave)))

6. Few men are leaving
    (Men (false (suppose (men are many))) leave)

7. A few men are leaving
    (Men (suppose (false (man are many))) leave)

8. Mark all numbers except 1, 2, 5, 6
    (You mark X (if (false (X is (1 or 2 or 5 or 6)))))

9. The star isn't present
    (false (suppose (star is present)))

10. The star is absent
    (true (suppose (false (star is present))))

11. Exactly one player isn't male
    (false (suppose (exactly one player is male)))

12. John is better than Pete
    ((John is good +) (Pete is good))

13. John is as good as Pete
    ((John is good =) (Pete is good))

14. Fats killed the roach
    (Fats did (Fats cause (the roach die)))

15. The roach was killed by Fats
    ((Fats cause (the roach die)) happened to the roach)

---

examples the principles they exemplify. Table 2.1 gives a series of sentences and their representations à la Clark. In addition to failing to specify the formal properties of his representations, Clark fails to specify the principles by which one goes from a sentence to its propositional representation. He calls upon his intuition to decide what representation to assign to a sentence, and his intuitions generally agree with those of others, but not always. The failure to specify a procedure for assigning representations to sentences is common to all current propositional theories and has serious consequences for all of the theories. For instance, Clark wants to use his representation to make predictions about the processing of sentences. However, because he is not formally constrained as to what representation he will use for a sentence he has unknown degrees of freedom in predicting the data. Thus, his model is not as falsifiable as one would like it to be.

The Comprehension Process

Clark attempts to test his representational ideas by building models to predict subject latencies and errors in various comprehension tasks. He has been principally concerned with a paradigm in which a subject reads a sentence, sees a picture, and must confirm whether the sentence is true of the picture. Clark proposes a four-stage schema for this comprehension task. The subject first encodes the sentence into a propositional representation. Second, he encodes the picture. The third stage involves a comparison of the two representations, and the fourth stage the output of a response. One of Clark's strong claims is that the picture is encoded into the same propositional format as the sentence. This is intended to facilitate the process of comparison by having the picture and the sentence in a common format.

Presumably, a theory of sentence comprehension should be concerned with Stage 1. However, Clark's theory focuses principally on the comparison processes that occupy Stage 3. Since these processes operate on the output of Stage 1 and 2, a study of the comparison processes allows one to make indirect inferences about the structure of the representation produced by the Stages 1 and 2 encoding processes. However, it does not allow one to infer much about the comprehension processes used in deriving those representations.[1] Therefore, Clark's theory might be better described as a theory about the utilization of sentence representations rather than a theory of comprehension. As Clark and Chase (1972) write, "We have made no attempt in the present theory to account for how subjects actually construct semantic representations from the printed sentences they encounter. . . . This omission has been quite deliberate both because the rest of the theory does not

---

[1] A good question is what experimental tasks would tap the comprehension process. An appropriate paradigm would have to take measurements of the subject in the process of encoding the sentence. It would seem unwise to wait until the subject has finished the sentence and presumably comprehended it. In Sections 11.2 and 11.3 I will review some of the existing research that uses transient processing measures. Not surprisingly, it is not easy to perform such experiments.

seem to depend on how this process is carried out and because too little can be said about it at the present time [p. 511]."

Clark claims that his analysis of the Stage 3 comparison process is determined by the *Principle of Congruence*. That principle asserts that the comparison operations serve to make the picture and sentence representations completely congruent with each other. To illustrate, consider one task studied by Clark and Chase (1972) where subjects saw pictures and then saw sentences. The subject's task was to decide whether the sentence was true of the picture. If the picture was of *a star above a plus,* it is assumed to be encoded as (star above plus) and not as (plus below star). This is because *above* is the unmarked, less complex relational term. If the sentence was *The plus is below the star,* it would be encoded (plus below star) which is not congruent with the picture representation. Therefore, the picture code would have to be transformed to (plus below star). The two codes could then be compared and found identical, so a true response would be emitted. However, the subject was slowed because he had to transform the picture. In general, subjects were slower, as predicted, when the proposed code for the picture mismatched the proposed code for the sentence.

Processing Negatives

One of Clark's most carefully worked out cases involves the procesing of negation (Chase & Clark, 1972; Clark & Chase, 1972). A discussion of his model for negation will serve to illustrate his general theory and also his experimental paradigm. In the Clark and Chase experiment the subject has to verify sentences about the spatial location of stars and pluses. The sentence might be something like *The star isn't below the plus,* and the subject is to decide as rapidly as possible whether the sentence is true or false of the picture. The sentence can take one of the eight forms: the preposition can be "above" or "below," the subject of the sentence can be "star" or "plus" and the statement can be positive or negative ("is" or "isn't"). The picture can also be one of the two forms (star above plus, or plus above star). Crossed with the eight sentence types, the two pictures yield 16 trial types.

I will consider the situation where the picture comes after the sentence. Clark assumes that subjects will encode the picture using the same preposition that was used in the sentence. This facilitates the comparison stage and also reduces the number of distinct cases to be handled theoretically to four. These four paradigmatic cases are shown in Table 2.2. The same predictions would apply for sentences involving the *below* preposition except that an additional *a* msec is required for encoding *below.* The procedures for verification are illustrated in the flow chart of Fig. 2.2. The representation of the picture is compared to that of the sentence in a series of steps to decide whether the sentence is true or false. During the comparisons the executive is said to keep track of a truth index. This index starts out with the value true in it but can be changed by Operations 3a

TABLE 2.2
Latency Components for the Sentence–
Picture Verification Task

Sentence type	Stage 1: Sentence representation	Stage 2: Picture representation	Latency components	Actual latencies
True positive	(A above B)	(A above B)	t_0	1744
False positive	(B above A)	(A above B)	$t_0 + c$	1959
True negative	(false (B above A))	(A above B)	$t_0 + c + (b + d)$	2624
False negative	(false (A above B))	(A above B)	$t_0 + (b + d)$	2470

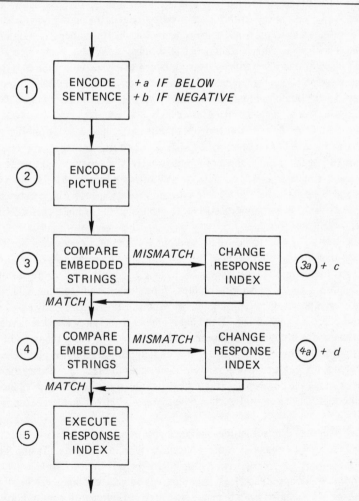

FIG. 2.2   A flow chart of the operations in the Clark and Chase sentence verification paradigm.

or 4a (see Fig. 2.2) during the comparison stage. The final value of the index at the end of the comparison stage determines whether the response is true or false.

The various cases will be enumerated to illustrate the quantitative predictions of the model. The true positive sentence is most quickly verified, in a basic time of t_0 msec because it occasions no mismatches. The false positive statement causes a mismatch at Step 3, so Branch 3a is taken and the truth index is changed. This branch requires an additional time of c msec. The negative statements in lines 3 and 4 of Table 2.2 require a time of b msec longer to encode (box 1) than the positive sentences. The false negative statement produces a match at Step 3, the comparison of the two inner strings; but causes a mismatch at Step 4, when the two outer predicates, false ( ) and ( ), are compared. This causes a branch to Step 4a to change the truth index to false. This extra operation is assumed to take d msec. Thus, the total excess time for the false negative statement is $b + d$. The true negative sentence is the most complex: first, it requires an extra b msec of encoding time because it is negative; second, in Step 3, the inner strings mismatch, so the 3a branch is taken, requiring an extra c msec; third, in Step 4, the outer predicates mismatch, so the 4a branch changes the index back to true, requiring an extra d msec.

This model fits the reaction-time (RT) data extremely well. It predicts quantitatively that the RT increment (of $b + d$) between true positives and false negatives should be the same as the increment between false positive and true negatives. A typical estimate of c, for Step 3a, is 187 msec; while for $b + d$, for negation setup and Step 4a times, a typical estimate is 685 msec. These estimates fall consistently in this range across several experiments of this type (see Chase & Clark, 1972).

Clark has been able to postulate sequences of mental operations like those in Fig. 2.2 that do excellent jobs of predicting many comprehension experiments. However, there are no explicit methods in Clark's theory for deriving a flow chart like Fig. 2.2 from the general principles of the theory. For instance, Clark (1974) identifies the principle of congruence as central to his theory. However, it plays no part in the structure of Fig. 2.2. That is, the two encodings are being compared and mismatches noted but no attempt is being made to bring the encodings into congruence. However, in a slightly different situation (where the picture precedes the sentence), Clark proposes that the subject tries to bring the picture into partial congruence with the sentence. Thus, the principle of congruence serves the role of an extra degree of freedom which can be evoked when needed to get the model to fit the data.

Clark proposes that sometimes subjects will transform a negative sentence into a positive code to make it more congruent with the picture. Thus, they will transform *The A isn't above the B* into (*A below B*). In contrast to the previous model, this model predicts that false negatives should take longer than true negatives. Data which satisfy neither model, Clark attributes to a combination of the two strategies. Thus, Clark permits his model on occasion to compute transforma-

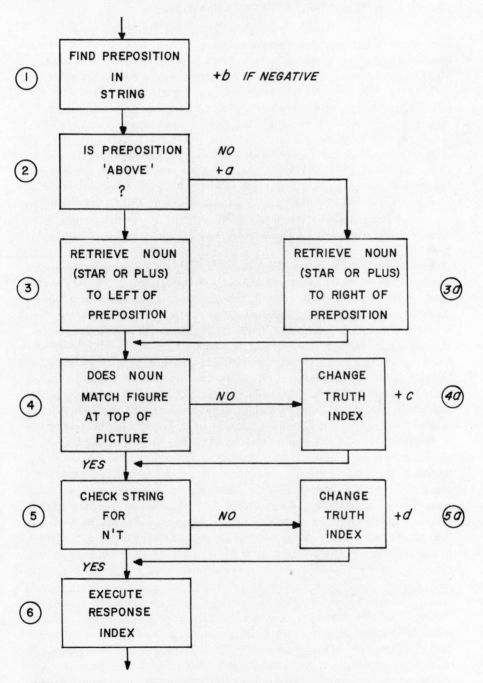

FIG. 2.3 A flow chart of an alternative procedure for the Clark and Chase sentence verification paradigm.

tions of the picture code and the sentence code, and on other occasions, not to transform. This allows his model considerable freedom in accounting for the data. That Clark can produce an additive model for one of his comprehension tasks is, in itself, trivial. It is only necessary to estimate a different parameter for every significant effect and interaction and assign that parameter to some hypothetical process. The model is only interesting if it can specify in advance of data what the significant effects will be.

There is, however, a point that needs to be made in defense of Clark's model. Chase and Clark (1972) explicitly instructed subjects to follow the various strategies ascribed to uninstructed subjects. When so instructed, subjects behaved as would be predicted by the Chase and Clark model for that strategy. This is important because it shows that subjects are capable of the postulated conversion operations and that when operating under a specified strategy they behave as predicted by the model.

Another difficulty with the Clark research is that it failed to produce any compelling evidence for the representation claimed to be central to the theory. Clark has shown that his representation plus some process assumptions can deliver accurate predictions for the paradigm. However, as argued in Chapter 1, one should be able to take a radically different representation and a different process and derive the same predictions. Figure 2.3 shows a concrete realization of this claim for the Clark paradigm (suggested by Richard Schweickert). It assumes the sentence is encoded as a string of words and the only encoding of the picture is the raw percept. The reader is invited to inspect for himself the exact operations in this flow chart and confirm that their predictions agree exactly with those of the *true model* in Fig. 2.2. In Chapter 9 I present an ACT model for this paradigm. It involves another different representation and different procedure that also yield similar predictions. Anderson and Bower (1973, Section 13.2) proposed yet another representation. So it is clear that there is not a unique representation-process pair for the Clark paradigm. Moreover, it is not the case that any representation is really more parsimonious than the others. It has been argued that the Clark model is more general than a string-processing model like Fig. 2.3, but this is not so. A string processing model of a similar variety could be produced for any of Clark's paradigms.

Semantic Decomposition

One way in which Clark's representation differs from standard deep structure is that he decomposes many lexical items into semantic primitives (see Clark, 1971). For instance, Clark argues that *The plus is absent* should be represented (*false* (*plus present*)) and thus should behave like a negative. Thus, under the *true model* (i.e., no transformations) Clark would predict that the subjects should take longer to respond to a true sentence involving *absent* than a false sentence involving *absent*—a prediction which is confirmed. The difference between *true absent* and *false absent* should correspond to the amount $b + d$ in Table 2.2. In his experiment on *absent* that amount was 232 msec, which is considerably less than 685 msec reported earlier. This difference is attributed to a phenomenon known as scope of negation. Clark assumes that there is a difference between the "suppositions" of the explicit negative *The plus isn't present* and the implicit negative, *The plus is absent*. *The plus is absent* affirms the supposition that the plus is not present, whereas *The plus isn't present* denies the supposition that the plus is present. Thus, if we expand our notation to include these suppositions, Clark would represent *The plus isn't present* as (false (suppose (plus present))), whereas *The plus is absent* is represented (true (suppose (false (plus present)))). Note that the negation (that is, "false") is more external in the representation of the explicit negative than the implicit negative. In general, Clark finds that the more external a mismatching element, the longer it takes to deal with the mismatch. An intriguing suggestion for why this might be so has been offered by Carpenter and Just (1975).

Subject–Object Asymmetry

Clark analyzes three types of binary sentences—that is, sentences with pairs of noun arguments. These are locative sentences like *The star is above the plus,* comparative sentences like *The baker is taller than the butcher,* and transitive verb sentences like *The boy hit the girl.*

   The comparative and the locative expressions have much in common. In both, two terms are to be located with respect to one another on a particular dimension. The presuppositions of such expressions are that the location of the second term is known and the first term is being placed with respect to the second. Thus, Sentences (3) and (6) are appropriate answers for Questions (1) and (4) but not Questions (2) and (5).

   (1)   Where is the star?
   (2)   Where is the plus?
   (3)   The star is above the plus.
   (4)   How tall is the baker?
   (5)   How tall is the butcher?
   (6)   The baker is taller than the butcher.
   (7)   The star is in the middle of the page.
   (8)   The plus is in the middle of the page.
   (9)   The star is above the plus.
   (10)   The butcher is six feet tall.
   (11)   The baker is six feet tall.
   (12)   The butcher is taller than the baker.

Similarly, Sentences (9) and (12) seem easier to comprehend when preceded by Sentences (8) and (11) than when preceded by Sentences (7) and (10). Clark suggests that these asymmetries can be captured by tagging the second term as known. So he would represent Sentence (12) as ((The butcher is tall +) (known (baker is tall))) in which it is asserted (a) both butcher and baker are tall; (b) the butcher's tallness is greater than the baker's (indicated by the plus sign); and (c) the baker's tallness is known.

Clark provides a somewhat different analysis of the asymmetries in transitive verb sentences. Clark argues that the two sentences *Fats killed the roach* and *The roach was killed by Fats* presuppose the same underlying fact but the first asserts that it is something that Fats did while the second asserts that it is something that happened to the roach. Thus, he represents these two sentences as

(13)   (Fats did (Fats cause (the roach die))).

(14)   ((Fats cause (the roach die)) happened to the roach).

Thus, the active sentence is a more appropriate answer to the question *What did Fats do?* whereas the passive sentence is a more appropriate answer to *What happened to the roach?* Clark considers a series of experiments in which subjects affirm active and passive sentences against pictures. In one experiment (Olson & Filby, 1972) subjects were induced to encode a picture actively by instructions to focus on the subject and passively by instructions to focus on the object. Subjects were slower when induced to encode a picture in a way that is different from the voice of the sentence. Clark proposes that subjects first attempt to match the embedding strings of the picture and sentence. If the picture and sentence have been encoded in different voices these embedding strings will mismatch—that is, *Fats did* versus *happened to the roach*. The subject must transform one of the embedding strings to make them congruent. This is the source of the extra time for a voice mismatch. However, it is unclear why the subject should compare these embedding strings at all since they do not contribute to the truth judgment. This proposal is also contrary to Clark's proposal for negatives where embedded strings are compared first and where no attempt to achieve congruence is made. Further, in his model for negatives, mismatches of the embedding strings contribute to a change of the truth index and not a transformation of the string.[2]

These points aside, one significant aspect of Clark's representation is that it does identify asymmetries between subject and object nouns. These asymmetries are not preserved in the *n*-ary relational representations of Kintsch or Norman and Rumelhart.

Pattern Matching

The manipulations performed by Clark's model on the propositional representations in sentence verification are really pattern matching operations of

[2]A somewhat different analysis of the active and passive sentences is to be found in the more recent work of Clark and Haviland (1976) on the given-new contract. They propose that subjects comprehend an active or passive sentence by committing the subject of the sentence to memory and then adding the information in the predicate to the subject information. I am not able to see in detail how this analysis would explain why subjects are slower when there is a voice mismatch.

various sorts. He proposes similar pattern matching operations to perform question answering. For instance, suppose a subject hears *The star is above the plus* and must answer *Where is the star?* The sentence is represented (star above plus) and the question is represented (star at X). The question code would be matched to the picture code and in this process the variable X would be bound to the *above plus,* and this value of X would be generated as the answer.

This pattern matching analysis of question answering would seem to demand more compliance to the congruence principle than in the sentence verification paradigm. This is because the question code must be put in correspondence to the code that contains the answer so that the variable can be bound. Suppose the subject hears the sentence *The star is not below the plus*—represented (false (star below plus))—and was asked the question *Where is the plus?*—represented (plus at X). The code for the first sentence would have to be transformed to (plus below star) to make it congruent with the question. In contrast, under Clark's true model for sentence verification such congruence transformations do not necessarily occur—the subject needs only to keep track of mismatches.

Clark provides a similar analysis of following instructions. Suppose a child is confronted with a red truck on the ground, and is given a blue truck and is told to "make it so the blue truck is ahead of the red truck." Clark proposes the subject represents the command as (blue truck ahead red truck) and his task as (blue truck at X). That is, he must determine X, or where to place the mobile blue truck. The variable X matches *ahead red truck* and the subject uses this information to determine the location of the blue truck. Note the subject would have considerable difficulty in responding if he were told "Make it so the red truck is ahead of the blue truck." This would be represented (red truck ahead blue truck) and would not match the other encoding—(blue truck at X). Huttenlocher (1968) finds children have more difficulty responding when the subject of the sentence does not match the mobile, to-be-placed object.

Summary Evaluation

Clark's theoretical analyses have served to generate and integrate a great many studies. These facts are clear testimony to the contribution of his ideas to the understanding of language comprehension. However, two detracting points need to be emphasized. First, he does not provide any succinct statement of his representational assumptions or what processes may operate on his representations. Consequently he often seems to be making contradictory assumptions in trying to explain different phenomena. The second major weakness of the Clark theory is that he has not assumed the responsibility of proving the generality of the phenomena he has discovered. It is quite conceivable that subjects develop special processing strategies to deal with the rather limited range of sentences they encounter. We might not observe the same effects if the sentences were presented in the context of other sentences of different structure or in a prose passage. If Clark wants to establish the relevance of his research to language comprehension, then it is critical that he show that the same processes are occurring when subjects have no advance knowledge about the class of sentences they will see.

The question of the generality of the Clark results seems sufficiently important that I have performed an experiment to test it. The experiment compared subjects verifying sentences under two conditions. The first condition was the standard Clark paradigm. Subjects saw two objects (in this case a plus above a dash) and a sentence describing the picture. The sentence always used the preposition *above* and was either a true positive, true negative, false positive, or a false negative. Subjects went through a block of 80 trials on this material. The expectation was that if subjects were likely to develop special strategies these would be developed and used in this blocked testing procedure.

In the unblocked condition subjects saw 8 tests of this variety intermixed randomly with 88 unrelated tests. These unrelated tests included verification of different types of sentences against pictures (for example, *There are more pluses than dashes*), semantic memory questions, syllogisms, and arithmetic problems.

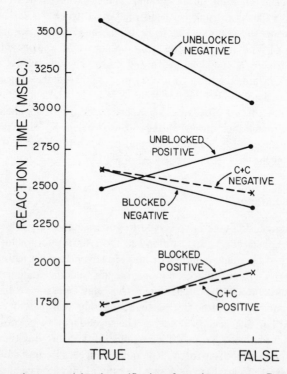

FIG. 2.4 An experiment examining the verification of negative sentences. Contrasted are verification latencies when a subject is set to process that class of sentences (blocked) and when he is not (unblocked). Also data is reported from Clark and Chase (1972).

Subjects were presented with a sentence and possibly some information (for example, a picture) above the sentence. They were just told to verify the truth of a conclusion given the above information. It is important to emphasize that in the critical eight trials involving pluses above dashes or vice-versa, the physical display presented to the subject was identical to that in the blocked condition. However, it was thought that the subject might not implement a special strategy in the unblocked condition. Therefore, if the Clark verification procedures were not general, we might expect to see a different pattern of data.

Figure 2.4. presents the data from 41 subjects in the blocked and unblocked conditions, and the data reported by Clark and Chase. The data in the blocked condition is remarkably similar to the data from Clark and Chase. So I have managed to replicate their basic result. Subjects are 801 msec slower in the unblocked condition, which is an enormous difference. So clearly they do employ a more efficient strategy in the blocked condition. However, what is remarkable is how similar are the patterns of the four points under these two testing conditions. One can estimate the parameters c and $b + d$ in these two conditions. In the blocked condition these estimates are $c = 302$ msec and $b + d = 644$ msec, and in the unblocked condition, $c = 413$ and $b + d = 693$. The parameters are somewhat smaller in the blocked condition but are remarkably similar. This would seem to give support to the generality of Clark's model for comprehension experiments. Whatever the subjects did to be more efficient in the blocked condition did not seem to affect the basic comparison steps, as reflected by the interrelation of the four points. While this experiment indicates the generality of the results from the Clark paradigm, it does not give evidence for the uniqueness of the Clark theory over other possible equivalent theories for the paradigm.

2.2 SUMMARY OF HAM

I will not try to enumerate exhaustively the strengths and weaknesses of the HAM theory. The function of this section is to summarize the theory for subsequent chapters and to provide the reader with a basis for comparing HAM with other propositional theories. For critical remarks, I refer the reader to the reviews of HAM (Abrahamson, 1974; Collins, 1974; Martin, 1975; Ortony, 1974; Polson, 1975; Posner, 1974; Wanner, 1974; Wicklegren, 1975). A number of critical remarks will also be made about HAM in subsequent chapters. A brief listing of some of these will be given at the end of this section.

Strategy-Free Long-Term Memory

The highest level decision made in developing the HAM theory was the specification of a strategy-free long-term memory system which could be separated from other cognitive systems. We proposed that long-term memory had a fixed manner of encoding input and a fixed manner of retrieving answers to probes. It operated in the same way independent of circumstance and task demand. Behavior could still be adaptive because other cognitive processes which used long-term memory would modify their requests of it depending on the situation. The obvious analogy is to memory systems in various programming languages which have fixed principles of organization, fixed procedures for inputting information, fixed procedures for searching the memory, and fixed procedures for taking information out. Still programs in these languages can be quite variable and adaptive because of the logical character of the program's control structure (that is, the instructions) which is separate from the memory. Of course, it is possible to have computer systems in which the distinction between memory and program is not clear-cut or almost nonexistent. HAM, however, was the former type of system.

The motivation for a strategy-free memory was largely that it offered the promise of simplifying the analysis of behavior. The idea was that a subject's performance in a particular task could be divided into two subprocesses: the long-term memory component and task-specific processes. If the memory component were understood and if it was strategy free, then the problem of understanding a particular task would reduce to that of understanding the nonmemory, task-specific processes. Intuitively, it seems that there are basic memory processes that are invariant over tasks, but this intuition cannot be put to direct, rigorous experimental test. Like the issue of serial versus parallel processing or the issue of internal representation, the question of whether there is a strategy-free memory component cannot be decided on the basis of a behavioral test. Any model with a strategy-variant memory could be mimicked by a model with a strategy-free memory by putting the effects of strategy into the control processes that use the memory.

Abstract Propositional Representation

Another important decision made in creating HAM was to abstract the memory system from behavior. Nothing like direct stimulus–response pairs resided in memory. Rather, we proposed that memory consisted of abstract propositions which had no necessary relation to the sensory qualities of the stimulus input that was the original cause of the memory. These propositions also bore no necessary relation at all to possible behaviors. However, through the mediation of other cognitive processes these memory propositions could affect the response of a subject to environmental events.

The decision to choose an abstract propositional representation was motivated by both empirical and logical concerns. There was the considerable evidence that subjects, in remembering prose material, were more likely to remember the gist of what was said than the exact wording (Anderson, 1974; Bransford, Barclay, & Franks, 1972; Fillenbaum, 1966, Gomulicki, 1956; Kintsch, 1974; Sachs,

1967). As evidence of this, subjects tend to confuse, in a recognition memory test, sentences which have the same meaning. Subjects also suffer confusion about whether they read a sentence describing a fact or saw a picture depicting it (Rosenberg & Simon, 1974). These results suggest that subjects retain in memory the abstract, propositional import of what they learn. It also seemed that information would have to be structured propositionally to permit rapid, successful inference making.[3] Certainly, question-answering computer programs are of this nature. HAM's propositional representation was much less motivated by the concern for capturing linguistic intuitions, in contrast to Clark's theory. Nonetheless, it also claimed that justification.

None of these arguments compel one to accept a propositional representation. As argued in Chapter 1 other representations could be interfaced with process assumptions that would mimic the predictions of the propositional representation. In particular, I think that more sensory-based representations should be able to mimic propositional representations. They impose the same equivalence classes or finer equivalence classes on their input. The theories of Chapter 1 identified this as the sufficient condition for mimicry. The above arguments clearly, then, do not exclude other representations. Rather, they are meant to suggest that sensory-based representations would provide a less intuitive, less parsimonious account of some basic data.

Nonobservability of the Theory

The strategy-free memory component did not directly respond to external stimuli, nor did it directly affect behavior. We proposed that linguistic and perceptual parsers would convert various environmental stimuli into propositional memory representations. The nature of the perceptual parser was never really specified although we had more definite ideas about the linguistic parser. A parsing program was written for a limited subset of English. While we acknowledged that the parser was much too simple to be a realistic model of human language comprehension, we still used its output to predict the representation of sentences in various memory tasks.

A complete analysis was never made of how the memory system would affect other cognitive components or observable behavior. The experimental tasks under study were of two varieties—either the subject had to report whether a particular sentence had been studied (that is, a recognition task) or he would be cued with part of the sentence and had to retrieve the remainder (that is, a cued recall task). It was assumed that if the memory system could retrieve the information, the subject would display successful memory performance in these tasks. Thus these tasks were taken to directly tap the strategy-free memory component. Some dis-

[3] I am not so sure any more how important propositional structuring is to inference making.

cussion was offered of how information in memory might be used in languge comprehension and inference making, but no detailed models were presented for these tasks.[4]

Memory Structures and Processes

A computer simulation model was constructed as a partial embodiment of the assumptions in HAM. It operated in a question-answering task domain. One could assert facts to it which it would parse and store in its data base. One could also ask questions of it and, if the information was stored in the data base, it would generate the answer. The program's inference capacities were almost nonexistent; it could not infer anything that involved creatively combining independently asserted facts.

The structures and processes of HAM can be described by following its computer simulation as it processed a sentence. When a sentence was received, for example, "In a park a hippie touched a debutante," it was analyzed by a linguistic parser into a binary graph structure (see Fig. 2.5). This graph structure was initially held in a working memory. A separate tree structure was composed for each proposition in the sentence. Because our example sentence involved only one proposition, the graph structure in Fig. 2.5 is a simple tree. It is composed of nodes interconnected by labeled arrows. The nodes are represented by lower case letters and the labels on the arrows by upper case letters. The letters representing nodes are arbitrarily chosen and simply facilitate reference to a particular node. (More often nodes will simply be indicated by circles.) In contrast, the labels indicate specific semantic relations holding among the nodes. There is a small finite set of these relations. Note also that function words like "a" are not maintained in HAM's representation. Any semantic information conveyed by choice of function words is expressed in graph-structure configuration and by the choice of labels.

Each propositional tree is divided into two subtrees—a *context* subtree and a *fact* subtree. The arrow labeled with a C points to the context subtree and the arrow with an F to the fact subtree. Intuitively, the nodes in the tree represent *ideas* and the links *relations* or *associations* between the ideas. Therefore, in Fig. 2.5 node *a* represents the idea of the proposition, *b* represents the idea of the context, and *c* the idea of the fact. Effectively, the proposition is asserting that fact *c* is true in context *b*. The context node *b* is further subdivided into a *location* node *d* and a *time* node *e*. The arrows leading to these nodes are labeled L and T, respectively. Similarly, the fact node *c* leads by an arrow S to a subject node *f* and by an arrow P to a *predicate* node *g*. That is, the fact is composed of a predicate *g* being asserted about a subject *f*. Finally, the predicate node *g* leads by an arrow R to a relation

---

[4]The ACT model, unlike HAM, provides a theoretical framework for the translation between the basic memory processes and behavior. However, the notions of a strategy-free memory component and of an abstract propositional data base are maintained in ACT.

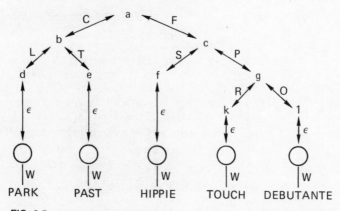

FIG. 2.5 An example of a propositional representation generated by HAM.

node k and by an arrow O to an object node l. So, what is being predicated of f is that it has relation k to l.

This completes the binary division in the proposition. The node d represents a particular park, e a particular past time, f a particular hippie, k a particular touching, and l a particular debutante. These are connected by a *membership* relation, ϵ, to the general concepts of *park, past, hippie, touch,* and *debutante*. These general nodes already exist in memory and represent our ideas of each concept. Connected to each is an associative structure giving the meaning of the general idea. Note in Fig. 2.5 that there is a distinction between the words and the concepts to which they refer. The words are connected to the concepts by links labeled W.

The concept nodes, in which the tree structure is anchored, were assumed to be preexisting in memory before receipt of the sentence. However, all the structure above the concept nodes is new and records the novel information in the sentence. To encode this sentence each of the 13 working-memory links above the concept nodes must be transformed into long-term memory associations. A stochastic model describing this encoding process was developed and tested in Chapter 10 of the HAM book.

Besides the associative relations revealed in Fig. 2.5, there are two more that are important to developing the logical structure of memory. First, there is the subset relation (labeled⊆) which permits a hierarchical nesting of concepts. For instance, the fact that a *dog* is a *pet* would be encoded by a subset relation from the *dog* node in memory to the *pet* node. The other relation is the generic (labeled ∀) which was used to encode defining features of a particular concept.

These generic and subset links gave some of the power of universal and existential quantification. Figure 2.6 shows how HAM would represent *Some philosophers read all books*. A subset of the philosophers is represented by node X, and of this subset is predicated, via the generic (∀) link, that all members read all

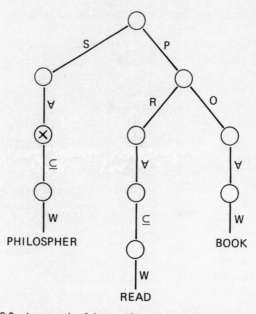

FIG. 2.6   An example of the use of generic and subset links in HAM.

books. Note in Fig. 2.6 there is no context subtree. In HAM the context modification was omitted for such sentences purported to be true in all contexts.

The Match Process

This graph representation of a proposition seemed useful for describing how a subject searched memory for information about a concept. When a subject received a question like "What did the hippie do?", he would enter memory from *hippie* and perform a graph search from that node looking for the requisite information. Of particular interest was a task we called *fact retrieval*. This task required the subject to recognize a proposition like *The hippie touched the debutante*. It was assumed that the subject built up a probe tree to represent this sentence (see Fig. 2.7) and attempted to see whether the probe tree already matched a graph structure in memory. This was performed by a process known as the MATCH process. This was basically a pattern-matching and pattern-completion process. A similar process will play an important role in the ACT model.

The MATCH process always matched the terminal nodes of the probe tree to the appropriate long-term memory nodes. This match of terminal nodes always succeeded because HAM could access these nodes directly from the words in the sentence (an assumption of content addressability). Once the terminal nodes had been accessed, HAM tried to serially match paths through the probe tree to associative paths in long-term memory. An associative path in memory was assumed to match a probe path if and only if the following two conditions were satisfied: (a) the paths connected the same terminal nodes; and (b) the labels or relations on the segments occurred in identical sequence for both paths. To illustrate: For a memory path to match the path between *hippie* and *debutante* in Fig. 2.7 it would be necessary that (a) the memory path connect *hippie* and *debutante* and (b) the relational labels on that path be W, ϵ, S, P, O, ϵ, and W in just that order. By concatenating a number of these path-matching operations, the MATCH process was able to achieve a complete match between memory and the probe tree. A prediction of this model is that subjects should be slowed down in making a match according to the number of paths leading out of a terminal node in memory. This is because the more alternative paths there are the longer it would take MATCH to retrieve the target path. This prediction was confirmed in a series of experiments that manipulated the number of propositions learned about a concept (see Chapter 8).

One issue concerning the MATCH process is how to guide the search through the giant long-term memory network of associations in homing in on the desired pattern of associations. Even confining the search to paths leading from the terminal nodes of the probe tree (for example, *past, hippie, touch,* and *debutante* in Fig. 2.7) may not restrict the search sufficiently, since there are many facts involving *past, hippie, touch,* and *debutante.* In HAM two additional devices were used to curtail the search. First, it used the labeled relations of the probe tree to search selectively from the terminal nodes. Thus, if it was looking for an ϵ-labeled association from *hippie* it did not need to spend time considering any other labeled associations that led from the *hippie* node in long-term memory. (There are in HAM a number of other types of possible labels for associations leaving *hippie.*)

However, there are still probably a large number of ϵ associations with *hippie* in our memories, each corresponding roughly to a different hippie that we once knew. As a second means of facilitating search, these ϵ associations were ordered on a list (called the ''GET list'') according to their recency of usage. In searching

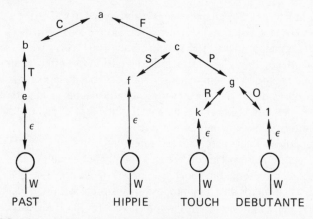

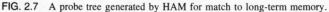

FIG. 2.7   A probe tree generated by HAM for match to long-term memory.

for the desired association HAM scanned *serially* through the GET list, testing one association after another to see if any led to a successful match. Since the GET list was constantly updated according to recency of occurrence, HAM would consider the most recently encountered hippie instances first. Since the desired association was more likely than not to be recent, this recency-updating mechanism should significantly curtail mean search time.

The MATCH process in HAM was used to perform a number of functions in processing linguistic input:

1. Decide whether incoming information should be stored. If the graph structure encoding the sentence is already in memory then nothing need be stored. If it is partially in memory, then only the new part is stored. Otherwise, the total structure must be encoded.

2. It can be used in question answering. If one is asked a yes–no question (for example, Did John give Mary Fido?), HAM can respond positively if the information is stored in memory. This matching procedure is also used to determine the answer to wh-questions (What did John give to Mary?).

3. It can be used to determine the referent of noun phrases like *The boy who gave Fido to Mary*. A representation is built up for *X is a boy and X gave Fido to Mary*. This representation is then matched to memory with X allowed to match any node. The node X matches is taken as the referent of the noun phrase.

The MATCH process was given a highly serial nature because it seemed the obvious algorithm to use in a serial computer. This reflects a strategy we adopted in theory construction. It was assumed that if a particular process was an efficient computer algorithm for performing a cognitive task it should be made part of the psychological model for the task. We were aware that this need not be true, but it provided a good start for generating ideas.

Clark's Theory versus HAM

Given the structure of this chapter one is naturally led to want to compare Clark's theory with HAM. Clark usually avoids discussion of long-term memory whereas this was the principal focus of HAM. In some of his recent work (for example, Clark & Haviland, 1976) he is beginning to consider the effect of information in long-term memory on the comprehension process, but he has yet to commit himself to any ideas about the organization of information in long-term memory. On the other hand, HAM provides no model of the type of mental operations that Clark identifies in his comprehension task.

Clark proposes a linear parenthesized representation for propositions and HAM a network representation. This difference is purely notational. Clark's embedding could be easily represented in network terms. For instance, Fig. 2.8 offers a network representation for the Clark propositional structure (false (star above plus)). Conversely, one might represent the information in the HAM structure of Fig.

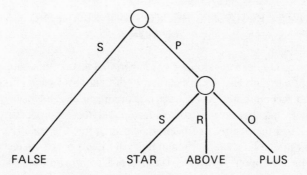

FIG. 2.8   A network representation of a Clark propositional structure.

2.5 by the linear expression ((past park) (hippie (touch debutante))). One of the principal motivations in HAM for network representations is to provide a convenient notation for analyzing search of long-term memory. As Clark never considers memory tasks, he has no need for network representations. Such networks are clearly more cumbersome than linear expressions and should only be used when they contribute something to the analysis or exposition. In Chapter 5 I propose a linearization of the ACT propositional networks that will be used when more convenient.

Detracting Remarks about HAM

As already noted, HAM was incomplete in that there was no explicit theory of the processes that used the memory. The production system of ACT is designed to deal with this source of incompleteness. However, there are some more specific problems with HAM that should be pointed out.

1. HAM can be shown to deal inadequately with quantification and other aspects of language. Also the HAM representation has some unnecessary complications. These problems arose partly because there was no formally specified semantics for HAM's representation. These matters are dealt with in Chapters 5 and 7.

2. Many aspects of the process by which long-term memory is searched seem wrong. In particular, it seems that the search process does not take advantage of relations labeling links. The search process also seems better characterized as a parallel strength process rather than a serial all-or-none process. These points are dealt with in Chapter 8.

3. In HAM the process of acquiring information was conceived of as depending simply upon probabilities of encoding of associations. This ignored the important contributions of elaborative and encoding processes to performance in memory tasks. These issues are discussed in Chapter 10.

2.3 KINTSCH'S PROPOSITIONAL THEORY OF MEMORY

Walter Kintsch has been developing a propositional theory of memory. In 1970 he proposed a theory principally concerned with recall and recognition of words. However, to account for effects of semantic organization, and for logical reasons, he elaborated that theory with some ideas about the semantic structure of the lexion. By 1972 that theory had been transformed into a distinctly propositional representation, and Kintsch had begun to study issues of sentence and paragraph memory. His 1974 book, *The Representation of Meaning in Memory,* is a comprehensive report of the current state of his theory and of the impressive variety of experiments it has generated.

The Theory

The principal object of analysis for Kintsch is a text which is a series of one or more sentences. A text is represented as a list of atomic propositions. So, for instance, Kintsch proposes to represent the sentence *Cleopatra's downfall lay in her foolish trust in the fickle political figures of the Roman world* as the list of eight propositions in Table 2.3 Note that one proposition may be part of another proposition. So Propositions (2) and (3) (α and β) are part of Proposition 1. In this way Kintsch can create hierarchical nestings of propositions.

Kintsch gives considerable care to explicating the structure of propositions. He uses an n-ary relational structure. This representational system is quite powerful and similar systems are also used by such researchers as Frederiksen (1972), Rumelhart, Lindsay, and Norman (1972), Simmons (1972), and Winograd (1972). In his representation relational terms (for example, verbs) and predicates (for example, adjectives) are written first, and are followed by a list of their arguments. For instance, in proposition 3 *trust* is the relational term and *Cleopatra*

TABLE 2.3
Kintsch's Representation of "Cleopatra's Downfall Lay
in Her Foolish Trust in the Fickle Political Figures of the
Roman World"

---

1. (BECAUSE, α, β)
2. (FELL DOWN, CLEOPATRA) = α
3. (TRUST, CLEOPATRA, FIGURES) = β
4. (FOOLISH, TRUST)
5. (FICKLE, FIGURES)
6. (POLITICAL, FIGURES)
7. (PART OF, FIGURES, WORLD)
8. (ROMAN, WORLD)

---

and *Figures* are the arguments. The arguments are either nouns or other propositions.

Most aspects of his representation seem adequate, but I find Kintsch's decision to use nouns as arguments unsatisfactory. Consider his representation of *The old man smiled:* (OLD, MAN) & (SMILED, MAN). This identified only two propositions underlying the sentence. However, the predicate calculus analysis of this sentence identifies a third proposition: $(\exists x)$ (old(x) and man(x) and smile (x)), that is, there exists someone (x) who was old, a man, and smiled. There is a separate proposition that *x is a man*. Thus, we can negate the original sentence by saying *No, you're mistaken, the old thing that smiled wasn't a man.* Thus, the noun *man* is not the argument of the predicates *old* and *smile*. Rather, it is also a proposition about an unspecified individual (represented by the x in predicate calculus). Kintsch might represent this in his notation as (MAN, X). I think Kintsch would have been wiser to use nouns as predicates as is done in predicate calculus. Actually in Kintsch's theory nouns can sometimes serve as predicates. For instance, he represents *A robin is a bird* as (BIRD, ROBIN). In this representation, the noun bird is a predicate and robin is an argument.

Another reason for using nouns as predicates is that the distinction between nouns and adjectives is not clear-cut. The same term will be used as noun or adjective in different contexts. For instance, *square* is an adjective when referring to picture frames whereas it is a noun in a geometry text. *Red,* too, is usually an adjective but it can be a noun in Las Vegas. Given that Kintsch (1974, p. 15) is only trying to represent the logical-semantic structure of language, and not the pragmatic considerations that determine a word's usage as a noun or adjective in a particular context, it seems that he should represent both nouns and adjectives identically.

Note that Kintsch's propositional notation is different from that of Anderson and Bower (1973) or Norman, Rumelhart, and the LNR Research Group (1975) but like that of Clark's in that it is linear and not a network structure. He argues that there is good reason for preferring linear structures because they more easily represent long and complex paragraphs than a network notation. Network structures, when they become large, tend to get messy and unwieldly, with crossing branches, etc. This point is purely notational, but still important.

Kintsch wants to establish the expressive power of his formalism. To do this, he reviews such problematic features of natural language as definite versus indefinite description, quantification, modality, implication, presupposition, location, time, and tense. For each such feature he attempts to show that the problems can be properly handled within his system. I think Kintsch is fairly successful with respect to most of these features, but his treatment of quantification is inadequate. He proposes to treat quantifiers as predicates. So he will represent *All men die* as (DIE, MAN) & (ALL, MAN). Similarly, *some citizens complained* is represented (COMPLAIN, CITIZEN) & (SOME, CITIZEN). However, this will not deal with a phenomenon known as *scope of quantification*.

Consider the following two sentences:

(13)   All philosophers read some books.
(14)   Some books are read by all philosophers.

The most common interpretation of Sentence (13) is that every philosopher reads some books although not necessarily the same ones as other philosophers, while the most common interpretation of (14) is that are is a specific set of books, each of which is read by all philosophers. Kintsch would represent both sentences as (READ, PHILOSOPHER, BOOK) & (SOME, BOOK) & (ALL, PHILOSOPHER). Thus, his representation does not have the facility to represent the potential difference in meaning of these two sentences.

He offers a procedural analysis of many features of language. One example Kintsch gives is the difference between the indefinite and definite article. That is, the first time a particular woman is mentioned in a text we will refer to her as *a woman* but on later appearances as *the woman*, e.g., *A woman bought steak yesterday. The woman was shocked by the price.* Thus, Kintsch states that the meaning of *a* versus *the* resides in the procedures that use these terms to decide reference in language comprehension or the procedures that choose between *a* and *the* in text generation.

Pattern Matching

Kintsch proposes a pattern-matching and pattern-completion model to describe how current episodes make contact with events in memory. These pattern-matching processes serve for his model the same role as the MATCH process in HAM. He proposes that each episode in memory is stored as a set of elements. "Elements" can refer to abstract propositions or to sensory events. One question Kintsch addresses is how an input Y will be recognized as old. Kintsch proposes that Y is encoded as a set of elements and this set is simultaneously matched to all episodes in memory. Let χ be the set of all episodes in memory and let X_j be a particular episode. Then Kintsch proposes that the probability of recognition will be a function of the maximum overlap between Y and elements in χ. He writes

$$\Pr(\text{match } Y \text{ to } \chi) = \max_{X_j \in \chi} \left[\frac{N(X_j \cap Y)}{N(Y)} \right]$$

where $N(X_j \cap Y)$ is the number of elements in the intersection of X_j and Y and where $N(Y)$ is the number of elements in Y. Note that Kintsch is measuring overlap solely in terms of set intersection. This equation specifies that the probability of recognition is a function of the amount of overlap. If the input Y is recognized it will be recognized as corresponding to the memory episode X_j with the maximum overlap. Of course, if the maximum overlap is small, Y is unlikely to be recognized.

A pattern-matching model is essential to a theory of memory that is going to deal with prose. Kintsch has made a good beginning here, but his formulation runs into difficulties because it does not make reference to the structure of the episodes. That is, Kintsch only measures how many elements in two sets are the same. He does not consider whether they are in the same structural relation.

Kintsch considers propositions as elements to be matched. Presumably, one proposition must perfectly match another. So (GIVE, JOHN, MARY, BALL, YESTERDAY) would completely mismatch (GIVE, JOHN, MARY, BAT, YESTERDAY). This seems wrong. The pattern-matching process should have access to the internal structure of propositions and be able to detect overlap. Another problem with Kintsch's structureless notion of pattern matching can be seen by considering Sentences (1)–(3) along with their propositional representations:

1. The man who teased the young dog hit the woman.

    (TEASE, MAN, DOG) & (YOUNG, DOG) & (HIT, MAN, WOMAN).

2. The man who liked the beautiful girl hit the woman who teased the young dog.

    (LIKE, MAN, GIRL) & (BEAUTIFUL, GIRL) & (HIT, MAN, WOMAN) & (TEASE, WOMAN, DOG) & (YOUNG, DOG).

3. The man who teased the young dog hit the woman who liked the beautiful girl.

    (TEASE, MAN, DOG) & (YOUNG, DOG) & (HIT, MAN, WOMAN) & (LIKE, WOMAN, GIRL) & (BEAUTIFUL, GIRL).

Consider Sentence (3) as an input and contrast its match with Sentences (1) and (2) in memory. It overlaps with each in three propositions and so has the same overlap with both as measured by Kintsch's equation. But surely Sentence (2) is a poorer match to (3) than (1) is to (3). The proposition (BEAUTIFUL, GIRL) occurs as part of the modification of *man* in Sentence (2) but *woman* in (3). Similarly, the location of the proposition (YOUNG, DOG) is reversed from modifying *woman* to *man*. However, the overlap measures are insensitive to these differences in the location of propositions in the overall structure.

The Experiments

Kintsch (1974) reports a large number of experiments in an attempt to illustrate the usefulness of the concepts of his theory. These are not really tests of the theory. As he concludes at the end of his experimental section:

The reader has surely realized by now that the experiments are not tests of strict deductions from the theory. The theory is not specified completely enough to permit such strict deductions.

It merely sketches in the relevant logical-linguistic background, but lacks a detailed processing component. Linguistic-logical considerations are powerful enough to constrain our ideas about how knowledge can or must be represented in memory, but they fail to provide us with more than the most general notions about psychological processing. The experiments reported here are studies in search of a processing theory rather than tests of one [p. 243].

What is impressive about Kintsch's research is the variety of experiments he has performed to obtain evidence for his theory. However, his experiments like many on memory for linguistic material have methodological problems. In reviewing these experiments I feel compelled to point out the methodological problems.

One of the features of propositions is that they are abstractions from text. So two different texts can assert the same set of propositions. In one series of experiments Kintsch has subjects study two types of paragraphs, one syntactically simple and one complex, but both assert the same set of propositions. He reasons that it should take longer to read and comprehend the complex paragraphs because it is harder to extract the underlying abstract propositions. However, once comprehended, it should make no difference what was the original paragraph in a task where the subject has to make an inference from the material he has comprehended. The reason is that the inference is made from the identical set of abstract propositions in both cases.

Kintsch does find reading time greater for complex paragraphs, but once the paragraph is comprehended there is no difference in time to make an inference. However, Kintsch finds that across four experiments subjects make more errors in inferences from complex paragraphs. While none of the differences in error rates is significant, the pattern is suspicious. Given the dangers of speed–accuracy tradeoff (see Pachella, 1974), Kintsch seems too willing to accept the null hypothesis here. He seems to fall prey to the representativeness error (Tverksy & Kahneman, 1971) of equating no significant difference with no difference.

Kintsch in a later chapter looks at another, similar prediction about inference making. He has subjects study paragraphs such as *A burning cigarette was carelessly discarded. The fire destroyed many acres of virgin forest.* Kintsch argues that in comprehending such a paragraph a subject must make the inference *A discarded cigarette caused a fire.* This would be stored with the propositions explicitly affirmed in the paragraph. Then, in a later test of the truth of the inference, subjects should be just as fast as if the inference had been actually stated. This would be another example of the abstract nature of the memory representation in that the same representation will be set up for different texts (that is, with or without the inference explicitly stated).

Kintsch contrasted verifying propositions which were explicitly stated with propositions which had to be inferred. He found, contrary to prediction, that subjects were quicker to verify sentences when they were actually stated. In a later experiment he found that when he delayed his test 20 min or 48 hr, the difference between the two types of sentences became insignificant. Therefore, he argued that the advantage of the explicit sentences in an immediate test was due to a surface representation of the sentence that was still available. Surface representations can be accessed more rapidly than the propositional representation and so permit rapid verification.

There are problems with Kintsch's data analysis for this experiment. In the crucial experiment he contrasts verification of explicit versus implicit statements at delays of 0 sec, 30 sec, 20 min, and 48 hr. He finds significant differences between explicit and implicit at 0- and 30-sec delay but nonsignificant differences at 20-min or 48-hr delay. However, explicit statement verifications are still made somewhat faster than implicit at 20-min and 48-hr delays. Once again Kintsch regards failure to reject the null hypothesis as evidence for no difference. What he should have done to provide evidence for his theory is show that the difference at the 20-min and 48-hr delays is significantly less than at the 0- and 30-sec delays. This he does not do. Also, there are many more errors (17%) in the implicit delayed conditions than the explicit conditions (4%). Once again one should be concerned about a speed–accuracy tradeoff.

Tests of Representation

In addition to showing that the idea of abstract propositions is useful, Kintsch wants to show that the details of his propositional representation are useful in understanding data. He provides a number of demonstrations of this point. He shows that reading time for a text is a function of the number of propositions that his analysis assigns to the text. That is, when the number of words in a text is held constant, it takes subjects longer to read texts that contain more propositions. Another predictive variable uncovered by his analysis is the position of the proposition in a heirarchical representation of the text. The higher propositions display greater probability of recall. In another demonstration, Kintsch shows that with the number of content words controlled, sentences based upon two or three propositions are recalled less as a unit than sentences based on a single proposition. This is again taken as evidence for the psychological reality of the proposition as a unit of analysis.

A constant problem in all his research derives from the fact that Kintsch is contrasting different types of sentences under different conditions. Differences he ascribes to the structural variables in the sentences may actually be due to other uncontrolled differences in his texts. For instance, he contrasts recall of sentences like *The settler built the cabin by hand* with *The crowded passengers squirmed uncomfortably*. Although both have four content words, according to Kintsch's analysis the first has just one underlying proposition and the second three. Therefore, as explained above, subjects should tend to recall the former more as a unit and the second in a more fragmentary fashion. However, the differences between these sentences are confounded with lexical choice. The first sentence consists of three nouns and a verb; the second sentence consists of an adjective, a noun, a verb, and adverb. Adjectives, verbs, and adverbs tend to be less imagable than nouns and as a consequence are probably harder to recall (Paivio, 1971). If they are being more poorly recalled one would expect to see more fragmentary recall of the sentences in which they occur.

Related to this problem is Kintsch's decision not to apply the statistics advocated by Clark (1973) for testing whether effects are consistent across all text material. As Clark demonstrated, apparent differences can be due to peculiarities of the particular sentences under study and would not replicate with other text material. Clark advocates procedures which test whether the effects may be generalized over all text material as well as subjects. As it stands Kintsch seems to too often "accept" the null hypothesis, whereas if he had used Clark's procedure most of his remaining effects would also have become insignificant (as he admits). The obvious solution would be for him to have performed more powerful experiments with larger samples of material and subjects. However, this would have been extremely expensive, working with his paragraph material, in which he frequently gets one observation per paragraph. This is much less efficient than verbal learning research in which one gets one observation per word.

Semantic Decomposition

A currently appealing idea both in generative semantics and computational linguistics is that complex words are decomposed into semantic primitives. So, for instance, Lakoff (1970) analyzes *persuade* as *cause to come about to intend*. There have been suggestions (for example, Anderson & Bower, 1973; Clark, 1974; Norman & Rumelhart, 1975; Schank, 1972) that when we hear *John persuaded Bill to hit Mary* we store in memory something on the order of *John caused Bill to come about to intend to hit Mary* in which there was no remnant left of the term *persuade*. Both Anderson and Bower and Norman and Rumelhart were a bit cautious in their advocacy of semantic decomposition, suggesting that it is an option that the subject may use if he wants a deep, detailed representation of the meaning of the sentence.

Kintsch (1974) acknowledges some of the linguistic arguments for decomposition and admits it might have advantages in a computer implementation, but he argues against semantic decomposition as a psychological model. Intuitively it seems to him "a poor hypothesis to assume that in memory and comprehension processes all concepts are decomposed into some small set of features, given that language has evolved to where we use complex word concepts [p. 12]." He wonders whether decomposition would ever stop—whether the final atomic primitives would ever be reached.

He puts to test a hypothesis which he sees as deriving from the semantic decomposition position. The hypothesis is that it should be more difficult to process sentences that contain semantically complex words, i.e., words that require considerable decomposition. In various experiments Kintsch looks at sentence initiation times, sentence completion times, phoneme monitoring, and sentence memory, but in none of these does he find evidence that semantically complex words like *convince* are more difficult to comprehend than less complex words like *believe*. These results present something of a challenge to theorists proposing semantic decomposition. It seems incumbent upon them to show that there are differences in the processing of complex words versus simple words. As reviewed in Section 2.1, Clark has shown in a picture verification that certain words (for example, absent) tend to behave according to their semantically decomposed representation (that is, *not present*) but he has not shown that they are harder to comprehend in a pure test of comprehension. There is no way of knowing in his experiments whether the total effect is in the comparison stage.

Summarizing Kintsch's Experiments

Kintsch's research contains a number of technical problems which I have tried to point out. The purpose of these technical criticisms was to highlight issues which it seemed that researchers should heed when designing experiments in this area. However, these technical criticisms should not detract from the force of his experimental work—which is that he has performed a large body of research which is loosely consistent with his general theory. It is particularly impressive just how wide a range of data Kintsch tries to address with his theory. In more recent research (e.g., Kintsch, Kozminsky, Streby, McKoon, & Keenan, 1975; Kintsch & van Dijk, 1976) he has begun to be concerned with representing the structures and processes unique to large-scale passages like folk stories. Kintsch's efforts range from single words to 1600 word passages. On the dimension of broad generality set forth in Section 1.3 his work scores highly.

2.4   THE LNR PROJECT

Donald Norman, David Rumelhart, and Peter Lindsay began a research project on memory and cognition in 1971 which has continuously grown, developed, and transformed. An early version of that theory was published in Tulving and Donaldson (1972). It is apparently still an active research project in 1976 although it bears only a minimal resemblance to the 1971 theory. This review of that theory will focus principally on their 1975 book, *Explorations in Cognition,* by Norman, Rumelhart, and the LNR Research Group.

   Of all the theories examined in this chapter, the LNR project is the most oriented to developing computer models. The goal of translating theoretical ideas into computer implementation is clearly more important in this project than is the goal of putting these theoretical ideas to experimental test. That is, the concern is to develop a computer model that can comprehend linguistic input, integrate that input with its knowledge base, store it in memory, retrieve it, reason with it, and otherwise operate effectively with linguistic information. A clear goal for such a model is to have it answer questions and obey commands. As the work in artificial intelligence (AI) has shown us, it is very difficult to build programs that can successfully deal with linguistic material.

One should not get the impression that the LNR Research Group shuns psychological data. They are concerned that their mechanisms simulate the performance aspects of human behavior in these linguistic tasks, and report attempts to see whether correlations exist between constructs in their model and human behavior. However, nowhere in their research will one find attempts to develop detailed process models, like those of Clark or Anderson and Bower, which interface the model's constructs with the quantitative aspects of human performance. What they are trying to do is to develop a theory which can perform a task (for example, question answering) without being overly concerned that it display the same behavior as a human at the task. However, they do not let the program adopt just any solution to the task. The solution must strike them as a plausible psychological mechanism. The goal of the project is to eventually derive a set of theoretical mechanisms which can form the basis of explicit process models. In my opinion this will prove to be a very profitable strategy for theory construction. However, this can be a relatively slow and drawn out process, and until such a project can deliver a true psychological model, it is difficult to judge the progress that is being made.

In addition to delivering a psychological model, the LNR project has the promise of producing important artificial intelligence programs. However, again we cannot expect the rapid development of impressive programs such as seen in other AI work. Norman and Rumelhart are sometimes prevented from using easily implemented mechanisms by their requirement that the mechanisms satisfy psychological intuitions. However, computer programs that do take the expedient roads often run into dead ends after initial rapid progress. One might argue that if the programs were modeled in the human image there would be greater long-term progress. This potential for long-term progress is the unique AI promise of work like that of Norman and Rumelhart.

MEMOD

The computer implementation of the LNR Group's ideas is called MEMOD. It has served the function of providing a medium for developing and testing the LNR theory, and consists of three major components. There is the active structural network which encodes the information within human memory. The properties of this network representation will be of principal concern in this section. Second, there is an augmented transition network parser which converts sentences into network representations. The augmented transition aspect of MEMOD will be largely ignored in this section. (A discussion of augmented transition networks is to be found in Section 11.2.) The third component of MEMOD is the interpreter which uses procedural knowledge encoded in the active structural network to direct the behavior of the system. The interpreter will be examined in this section since it is the mechanism that is assumed to translate the network information into behavior and hence testable predictions.

Active Structural Network

The LNR Group (1975) uses a network representation like HAM, but it is called an *active structural network* because of the emphasis on representing procedures like "how to bake a cake." They emphasize that the format for representing propositional knowledge like "Fred kicked Mary" be the same as the format for representing the procedural knowledge:

> It is important that we be able to store our plans and programs in this manner, for then they can be examined, modified, or performed. Because a sequence of instructions is both a program and data, it can be changed in the same way as other information stored in memory can be modified. Just as a person can modify his knowledge of concepts and of events, so too can one modify actions [p. 30].

While the LNR representation is intended to encode much more than the information conveyed by sentences, a good deal of the discussion in the LNR book concerns sentence representation. There is a rather shallow representation which maintains many surface features of the sentence, and is referred to as the level of the surface proposition. This can undergo various levels of deeper analysis until a level of semantic primitives is reached. At this level, the representation is quite abstract and maintains only indirectly the features of the sentence. The early LNR representation (Rumelhart, Lindsay, & Norman, 1972) was of the surface variety only. The deeper representations evolved later as they tackled various problems of language comprehension. So we have another case of ontogeny recapitulating phylogeny.

Figure 2.9 illustrates their surface level representation for the sentence *The ball hit by John hit the same house that Mary hit*. The words *ball, hit, house, John,* and *Mary* reside in the vocabulary and they are connected to their corresponding concepts by links labeled *name*. Connected to the various concepts are tokens. There are four tokens of the concept *hit*, two tokens for *house*, and one token for *ball, John,* and *Mary*. The connection between the concept or type node and the token is indicated by an arrow labeled *type*. The relational term *hit* connects various arguments. The connecting links are labeled with case relations (for example, *agent, object,* and *instrument*) to indicate their semantic function.

Figure 2.10a shows the LNR representation for *Mary gave a dollar to John* and Fig. 2.10b shows the representation for *John took a dollar from Mary*. It introduces us to a shorthand notation that is used in which the words themselves are put in the token slots. It is certainly more readable, but it should be kept in mind that it stands for a more complicated representation like Fig. 2.9. This shorthand notation is quite similar to the *n*-ary relational structures used by

VOCABULARY

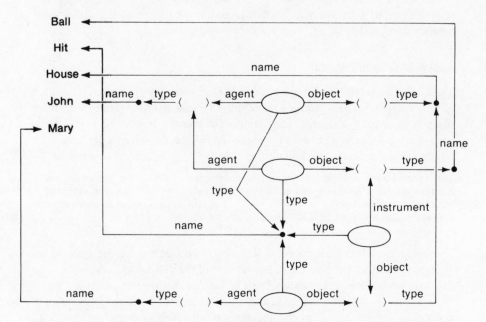

FIG. 2.9   An example of a surface LNR representation. (From *Explorations in Cognition* by Donald A. Norman and David E. Rumelhart. W. H. Freeman and Company. Copy © 1975.)

Kintsch—except that he uses a linearized structure whereas LNR uses network notation. Such simple *n*-ary representations are extremely convenient, even if they do not expose all the complications one might wish. I will have occasion to resort to an LNR-like structure when I want to illustrate the graph structure of interconnections among concepts (for example, in Chapter 10). In my case, like that of Norman and Rumelhart, representations like Fig. 2.10 are being used as convenient approximations.

Primitive Meaning Structures

Rumelhart and Norman argue that representations like Figs. 2.9 and 2.10 do not adequately reflect the meaning of the sentences they are supposed to represent. Therefore, they introduce another, deeper, level of representation in which only semantic primitives are used. They argue that these *primitive meaning structures* more directly express the meaning of a sentence. A good portion of the LNR deep representational system concerns conventions for representing states, state changes, and causal relations.

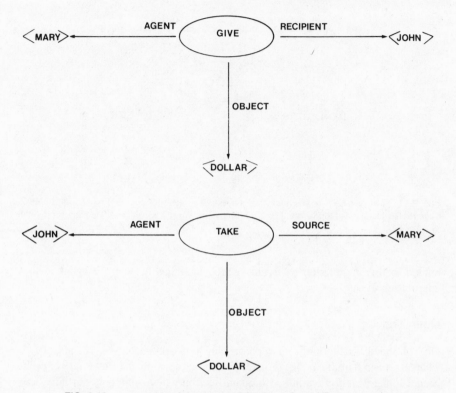

FIG. 2.10   An example of the shorthand for the surface LNR representation.

According to Rumelhart and Norman a simple kind of sentence is one that asserts that an object was in a certain state. It can have an optional specification of time and location. So, Fig. 2.11 shows the deep LNR representation for *A stadium was located in the park from 1956 to 1963*. A token of the primitive relation LOC is built up with arguments consisting of tokens of *stadium, park, 1956,* and *1963*. According to Rumelhart and Norman, nouns and adjectives should also be treated as states. Thus, when we assert that something is a red ball we are asserting that it is in the state of being *red* and being a *ball*.

More complex sentences involve the specification of a change from one state to another. For instance, Fig. 2.12 shows the representation for the sentence *The train moved out of the station at 3 o'clock*. Note that *change* is a primitive relation that may connect two states.

State changes are one kind of *event*. Other events can be created by connecting two events together through a *cause* relation. Figure 2.13 shows the representation for the sentence *A cowboy woke up Ambrose by putting water on him*. Note the dummy *do* in this representation. It stands for an unspecified event. *Cowboy* is

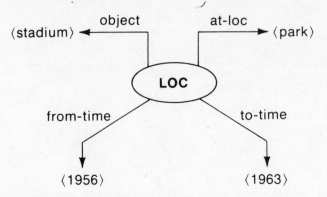

FIG. 2.11 The deep LNR representation information for state information. (From *Explorations in Cognition* by Donald A. Norman and David E. Rumelhart. W. H. Freeman and Company. Copyright © 1975.)

related to this *do* relation by *agent,* which indicates he was the agent in that unspecified event.

Quantification

One of the difficult things to represent in network form (see Woods, 1975; Chapters 5 and 6 of this book) is quantification. Anderson and Bower (1973) suggested some ideas for dealing with quantification which were only partially adequate (detailed criticisms are forthcoming in Chapter 5). Kintsch, too, has difficulty handling quantification, as discussed earlier. The LNR active network offers a somewhat better solution. For instance, Fig. 2.14 shows how LNR would

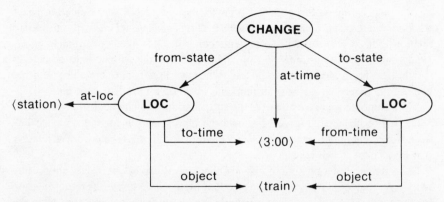

FIG. 2.12 The deep LNR representation for change of state information. (From *Explorations in Cognition* by Donald A. Norman and David E. Rumelhart. W. H. Freeman and Company. Copyright © 1975.)

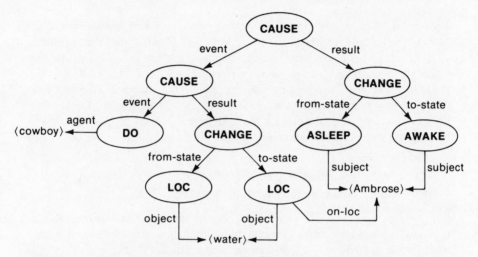

FIG. 2.13   The deep LNR representation for causal information. (From *Explorations in Cognition* by Donald A. Norman and David E. Rumelhart. W. H. Freeman and Company. Copyright © 1975.)

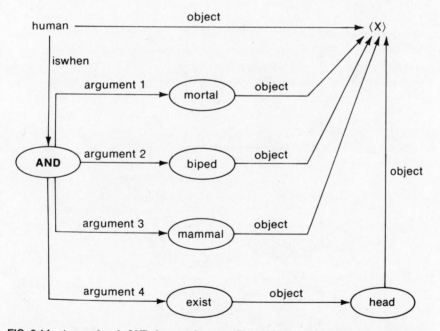

FIG. 2.14   A procedure in LNR that encodes quantificational information. (From *Explorations in Cognition* by Donald A. Norman and David E. Rumelhart. W. H. Freeman and Company. Copyright © 1975.)

represent *All humans are mortal, biped, mammals, and have heads*. That structure is to be regarded as basically a procedure. It asserts that whenever an object, *x,* is a human it is also mortal, biped, mammal, and has a head. I gather that whenever *human* is asserted of some particular *x,* say *Ford,* then all these other predicates will also be added by this procedure. Unfortunately, the technical details of how such procedures are evoked and applied are not developed in the LNR book. Another problem with the LNR representation of quantification is that it is not clear how it would represent the different scope relations of the two sentences:

(15)   All philosophers read some books.
(16)   Some books are read by all philosophers.

So, on this score, LNR may be no better than the Kintsch representation. In Chapter 7 I will offer a procedural interpretation of quantification, somewhat similar to LNR, but which does not suffer this drawback.

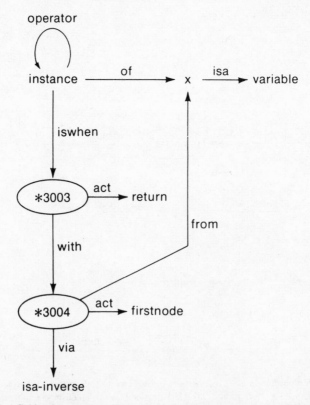

FIG. 2.15   A definition for an action. (From *Explorations in Cognition* by Donald A. Norman and David E. Rumelhart. W. H. Freeman and Company. Copyright © 1975.)

The Interpreter

As noted earlier, the LNR network not only encodes declarative knowledge, it also encodes procedures. In fact, it is a strong claim of Norman and Rumelhart that there is no real difference between declarative and procedural knowledge. They have constructed an interpreter which will translate the procedural information contained in a network into action. The interpreter examines information connected to nodes in the network and executes the action specified by the node. There are certain primitive actions which the interpreter can execute directly. These actions include creating a new node, connecting some node *a* to some node *b* with relation *R*, forgetting particular relations between two nodes, finding the first or last link on a node, finding the next or previous link on a node, or testing whether part of the structure on one node is the same as the structure on another node. However, it is also possible for the interpreter to execute complex actions which are defined in the network as combinations of these more primitive actions. For instance, MEMOD can create an action *instance-of* which will retrieve the first instance attached to a concept. Figure 2.15 shows the definition built up in the memory network for this concept. This definition is framed in terms of primitive actions which the system already knows—*return, firstnode,* and other primitive concepts like *isa-inverse*. The interpreter in executing the action *instance-of* would retrieve and execute all the defining primitive actions.

Language Comprehension

The interpreter uses procedural information encoded in the network to help derive a representation of a sentence's meaning. Such procedural information is particularly important in translating from surface propositions to primitive meaning structures. Consider the sentence *John gave Mary Fido.* This is analyzed by the parser into a structure like Fig. 2.16a. This is the surface proposition level of the LNR representation. However, the verb *give* has a definition which basically asserts that *give* means *The agent did something which caused the recipient to get the object.* The interpreter takes this definition of *give,* applies it to the representation in Fig. 2.16a, and derives the representation in Fig. 2.16b. This is a semiprimitive representation. There is a definition of *get* which asserts that *get* means "The state changed from the agent possessing the object to the subject possessing the object." Application of this definition to Fig. 2.16b results in the representation of Fig. 2.16c. This is a primitive representation and the elements cannot be decomposed further.

The Procedural–Declarative Distinction

Norman and Rumelhart argue that there is no distinction in representation between our knowledge of procedures and our declarative knowledge of facts about the world. This contrasts with ACT where a production system representation will be offered for the procedural knowledge and a propositional network representa-

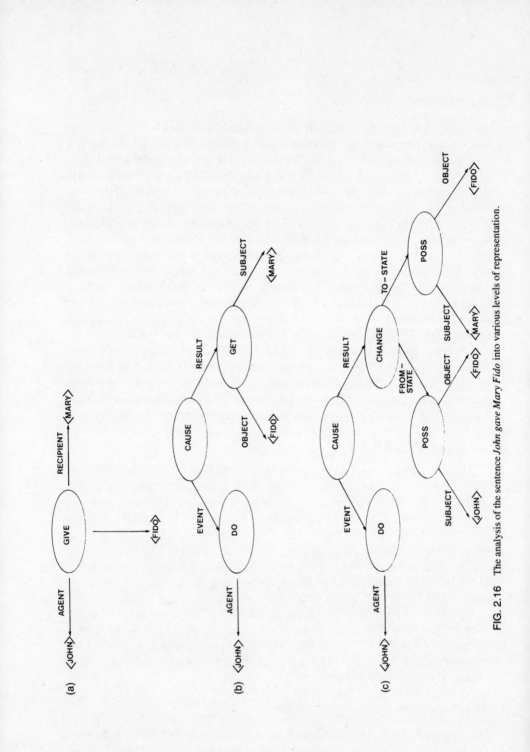

FIG. 2.16 The analysis of the sentence *John gave Mary Fido* into various levels of representation.

tion for the declarative knowledge. Arguments for the ACT option will be given in Chapter 4. Here, however, I would like to note one particular drawback of the LNR system on this score. Procedural knowledge exists in a network. It is difficult to see how one could prevent LNR from inspecting and reporting the contents of networks that encode procedural information since it can presumably inspect and report networks set up to encode declarative information like that contained in sentences. However, it is well known that certain types of procedural information are not reportable—such as how we comprehend a sentence or ride a bike. It may be possible for LNR to explain the nonreportability of certain procedures by assuming that the subject has not acquired verbal labels for certain terms defining these procedures. However, one would still think a subject could give a partial report of the procedure. It seems incumbent on the LNR group to provide in the context of their model an explicit mechanism that could report declarative knowledge but not be able to give any report of certain procedural knowledge.

Evaluation of LNR

I have found it extremely difficult to review the LNR research because it is unclear how to form an evaluation of the theory. The purpose of the research program is clear: to create a theory of broad generality capable of dealing with many (perhaps all) issues of cognitive psychology. They want to unify this theory within a single theoretical framework about the nature of human memory. This is certainly a commendable goal, but how does on evaluate how much progress they have made towards this goal. I will apply to the LNR research the measures of the A.I. quality of the computer program and the traditional psychological measure of empirical adequacy. I feel somewhat guilty in doing this because it is clear that these are not the principal measures Norman and Rumelhart (1975) feel should be applied. Rather they see their main accomplishment as the creation of "an analytical tool with which to approach the study of the problems of cognition [p. 405]." While they obviously intend this tool to be applicable to generating empirical predictions, they have largely postponed the development of an interface between their theory and data. The problem is that one cannot evaluate a set of theoretical constructs in the abstract. It is incumbent upon Norman and Rumelhart to propose some explicit criteria for evaluation. It is in the nature of a scientific theory that its evaluation is essential, and that this evaluation cannot rest solely on one's intuition about how good the ideas of the theory are.

LNR as Artificial Intelligence

It is worth considering how the set of ideas and programs fare relative to other work in the artificial intelligence community. The computer implementations of LNR are principally concerned with language comprehension. What is the status of LNR as a working language comprehension program? How does it compare with other programs such as Kaplan (1973), Kay (1973), Schank (1975), Winograd (1972), and Woods, Kaplan, and Nash-Webber (1972)? One must conclude that LNR does not fare well on this dimension. It really does little that is concrete and of interest in the way of language comprehension. I may be missing something in my reading of the book, but it seems there are no novel ideas about computer processing of language. Moreover, there is no evidence that MEMOD can process any of the aspects of natural language generally considered problematical for language systems. The only application of MEMOD to a concrete problem is reported by Scragg in a system called LUIGI which answers questions about a kitchen. Besides an interesting sample dialogue, Scragg's chapter contains an informative discussion of some of the technical problems that arise when one tries to implement MEMOD in a kitchen world. The discussion of noun phrases and the use of procedural knowledge to obtain facts for question answering is particularly good. However, Scragg's implementation does not use many of the important ideas proposed in other chapters. For instance, he does not appear to use the levels of analysis for verbs that was illustrated in Fig. 2.16. It is hard to assess the AI worth of such ideas until they are put to the test in an implementation like Scragg's, which has a reasonably well-defined task domain.

Despite the fact that it is largely lacking in demonstration programs, Norman and Rumelhart assert that their computer system has great potential. That is, the representation, parsing schemes, interpretative schemes, etc., are so structured that, given sufficient investment of programming time, they could form the basis for a very powerful language system. Such claims for a system's potential rather than for a system's actual performance are frequently made in artificial intelligence (AI) and can carry considerable weight in the AI community. It is argued that it would be a waste of artificial intelligence researchers to require them to spend the years of hack programming required to translate potential into reality. This would be an eminently reasonable argument if there were objective criteria for evaluating the potential of a language system other than its actual performance as a concrete program. But there are no such objective criteria.

Psychological Contributions

One would willingly excuse LNR from the requirement of having to make an AI contribution. However, it is less easy to excuse it from the standard psychological requirement of helping us understand empirical data. In the abstract, Norman and Rumelhart (1975) agree: "One of the more important aspects of our research effort has been an emphasis on broad generality. It has been of critical importance that we be able to understand a wide variety of cognitive phenomena within a single theoretical framework [p. 405]." The book does contain reports of a number of experimental efforts. These are of two kinds: The first are attempts to establish the psychological reality of various aspects of the model and the second are attempts to apply the model to various empirical phenomena that are of interest, independent of the model.

The experimental tests performed generally support predictions of the model but these experimental outcomes could be predicted by many other models. Of course, there are also many theories that would not predict these results. Therefore, these experiments constitute real tests of the model. It is just that we again have another case of the nonuniqueness of ideas about internal representation and process (see Section 1.3). For instance, Stevens and Rumelhart show that augmented transition networks (ATNs) are useful in predicting the sorts of errors people will make in reading paragraphs. That is, these errors are largely substitutions of other linguistic forms and these substitutions tend to satisfy the syntactic constraints posed on that portion of the passage by an ATN. However, these are also constraints that would be specified by many other grammatical formalisms. It does not seem that this evidence justifies all the complications of an ATN. Section 11.2 will consider some experimental evidence by Kaplan and Wanner that is aimed at testing mechanisms more uniquely associated with ATNs.

Dedre Gentner (in Rumelhart & Norman, 1975) puts the LNR analysis of verbs of possession to test. The LNR analysis identified certain verb pairs like *receive* and *borrow* as having considerable overlap in meaning. She finds subjects tend to be confused and recall for one verb a grammatical object that they learned for another overlapping verb. She also examines the order in which various verbs of possession are acquired. The more rapidly acquired ones are those identified by LNR as less complex in representation.

There have been attempts to extend the LNR model to deal with issues beyond language comprehension. Palmer in his chapter deals with issues of visual perception. He argues in favor of a network representation for the products of perception. This idea has been advocated by a number of others (Anderson & Bower, 1973; Baylor & Gascon, 1974; Pylyshyn, 1973; Winston, 1970). Unfortunately, no one has shown such a representational system to be feasible except in terms of the most simple geometric objects. To demonstrate feasibility for more interesting domains of perception would require that one construct an operating computer implementation that can deal with these propositional networks in the same way humans handle their percepts. Palmer does not provide such an implementation, but he does provide an informative discussion of the problems inherent in creating such an implementation.

Eisenstadt and Kareev see Go and Gomoku as task domains for developing the problem-solving abilities of the LNR program. They report an interesting series of experiments that show the weaknesses players have in these games—of a perceptual nature, a strategic nature, and arising from information processing limitations. They provide the outlines of a model for such game playing situations. A working memory is proposed, with a limited capacity for representing such information as the current position in a sequence of hypothetical moves. They propose a control mechanism that operates on this working memory which is similar to the production systems of Newell (1973; see Section 3.3) or of ACT.

Conclusion

The LNR project is a theoretical enterprise with much potential but relatively little to show for it. Perhaps more work should be devoted to translating theoretical ideas into computer implementations that succeed in well-specified task domains. Certainly more effort should be given to planting the theoretical model in a firm empirical base. As they attempt to translate the computer program into a model that will predict specifics of human behavior, they will probably find many of their assumptions to be wrong and discover new ideas for cognitive mechanisms.

The LNR project was initiated on the assumption that better progress could be made if more attention was paid to the general accomplishments of human cognition and not to the details of its specific manifestation in a particular experimental paradigm. It is important to have some idea of what kinds of mechanisms could succeed at the complex cognitive tasks man performs with such ease. A greater concern with human competence is a wise research strategy. However, it is to err in the opposite direction when this means abandoning the classical principles of scientific accountability.

It is disappointing that Norman and Rumelhart have not specified and tested more psychological properties of their abstract model. I will name just a few properties that could have been specified and tested: What is the rate at which information can be written into long-term memory? What is the probability of encoding information in memory and what are the retention characteristics of that information? What are the information-processing limitations on their model and what happens when these limitations are exceeded? What are the variables that control the speed at which information can be retrieved from long-term memory? How does one relate the number of steps taken by the interpreter to psychological time? It would be extremely informative to see the LNR model address some questions like these.

2.5 SUMMARY CONCLUSIONS ABOUT PROPOSITIONAL THEORIES

After having reviewed four propositional theories one naturally wants to come to some summary evaluation. Which are the good representations? Which is the best? I will go through various criteria that have been offered for evaluating such models. My general thesis will be that there is little basis for making discriminations among the four propositional representations.

Psychological Validity

The most obvious criteria to bring to bear about these representations is the question whether predictions derived from them conform to what is known about cognitive behavior. As argued in Chapter 1 (page 10) it is meaningless to ask this question without specifying the processes that operate on these representations. Clark's model seems to maintain the most distinctions between sentences in its representation. The Kintsch model and HAM collapsed some distinctions (for example, active–passive). The LNR model tended to map any paraphrase onto the same representation and so collapsed the most distinctions between sentences. Thus, by the theorem in Section 1.2, the Clark model which preserves the most distinctions should be able to mimic the predictions of any of the other models, but not vice versa. However, it is clear that none of these other models wants to endorse the claim that subjects cannot encode any indication of what the original sentence was. Both Kintsch and Anderson and Bower explicitly allow their systems to encode information about the surface features of the sentences as well as an abstract memory representation which is free of some of these features. Thus, it seems unlikely that one representation will generate a prediction which the other representations cannot mimic. It is the case, however, that each representation is shaped to fit a particular set of empirical phenomena. Clark has concerned himself with the processes of sentence verification, whereas Anderson and Bower were concerned with the storage and retrieval of single sentences. Kintsch has focused principally on memory for larger multiple-proposition texts and inferences from such texts. While each model could be made to accommodate the data reported for the others, it would probably only be possible with a certain amount of difficulty.

Linguistic Intuitions

Herbert Clark suggests as a special goal that a theory of sentence representation be shown to account for linguistic intuitions. While linguistic intuitions are certainly an acceptable form of data there is no reason why they should have special status relative to other kinds of data. Thus, they can no more constrain a propositional representation than any other data. Because of the indeterminacy introduced through the representation-process tradeoff, it is unlikely that any of these four models will fail to explain various linguistic intuitions.

Completeness

Anderson and Bower, Kintsch, and Norman and Rumelhart all subscribe to a completeness criterion for a propositional representation. This criterion is basically that the representation be able to encode any conception of which a human is capable, which is certainly a desirable property if one wants a theory of broad generality. As noted, none of the representations of the above authors seemed to be able to adequately represent the various types of quantificational distinctions which we seem capable of making.[5] In Chapters 5 and 7 I show that these quantificational nuances can be handled in ACT only by augmenting the propositional network with information stored in the production system. See Schubert (1974) and Woods (1975) for some additions to the networks themselves which will yield adequate power to express quantificational relationships.

There are some serious difficulties with using the criterion of completeness. Note that to apply this criterion implies that we be able to decide for a particular representation whether it actually encodes a particular conception. However, in past work there has been no attempt to formalize the semantics of propositional representations. As a consequence there is no rigorous way of evaluating a theorist's claim about whether a representation actually captures some test conception. This is a point that Woods (1975) has also complained about. For instance, Anderson and Bower (1973, pp. 167–169) claimed HAM was able, in a general way, to represent scope of quantification, and gave some examples of how various scope relations could be represented by HAM networks. I am now of the opinion that we were wrong and these networks did not represent what we claimed they did. However, since the HAM network did not have a formal semantics it is really not possible to decide for sure one way or the other. In Chapter 7 I will provide a formal semantics for the ACT network.

Even if the propositional representation does have a formal semantics, it can be difficult to establish the completeness of the representation. The typical strategy of theorists has been to boldly assert that their representation was complete and challenge others to find counterexamples. If no counterexamples are immediately forthcoming, their claim is taken as proven. Clearly the logic of this verification strategy leaves something to be desired. There is a better procedure to follow. One can take a well-defined and rich formal language like the predicate calculus and attempt to show that all distinctions in the language can be mirrored in the psychological representation. This is done for ACT in Chapter 7.

It has been argued (R. Schank, personal communication) that another way to establish completeness is by computer implementation. That is, if a computer program using a certain representation is capable of all of human behavior, then certainly the representation must be complete. This argument would work but for the fact that there is no way to prove that a computer implementation is capable of *all* the behavior of a human. All we can observe is that some behaviors of a human are replicated in the implementation. In a typical implementation this is a very limited subset. One would not want to be in the position, if he could help it, of reasoning from this biased set of particular observations to a general conclusion.

---

[5]Clark's representation is too ill specified to be able to address the question of its completeness.

Invariance under Paraphrase

Another criterion offered by Anderson and Bower (1973), Schank (1975), Norman and Rumelhart (1975), and others is that semantic representations should be invariant under paraphrases of the same information. For instance, active and passive sentences should have identical representations. Another example is that a sentence like *The star is above the plus* should be represented identically as the *The plus is below the star*. The various theories reviewed here differ in the amount of invariance under paraphrase they achieve. Clark seldom represents paraphrases identically. Kintsch and Anderson and Bower are able to give identical representations to some paraphrases (like the active–passive example) but would seem to fail on others (like the above–below example).Norman and Rumelhart (and Schank) make invariance under paraphrase an absolute goal.

The motivation for the criterion of invariance under paraphrase is both that of efficiency and of psychological plausibility. It is more efficient when trying to retrieve information at the time of test if that information is only stored in one form and it is not necessary to consider the possibility of many paraphrases of that information. Also there is the psychological evidence that subjects do not seem to discriminate very well in their memories between paraphrases of the same information. (However, they can usually be shown to be able to discriminate better than chance.)

There is good reason to suspect that invariance under paraphrase is not realizable as an absolute goal for a representational system. If this is true, invariance under paraphrase stands, at best, as a feature that one would want to maximize in his representation. To argue against the absolute position it is important to recognize that it comprises two distinct subclaims. First, it is claimed that it is not possible for the representational formalism to have two distinct constructions with the same meaning. Second, it is claimed that a parser can be constructed which will assign all same-meaning sentences the same internal representation.

First, let us consider why the first subclaim seems unlikely. Any interesting and powerful formal system developed so far (for example, the predicate calculus) has multiple ways of representing the same assertion. It is not possible to ask whether this is the case for the propositional representations in this chapter because they do not have a formal semantics. However, if their semantics were formalized so this question could be asked, it would probably be easy to show that there exist different representations equivalent in meaning. This fact can be shown for ACT's representation which has a formal semantics. It seems unlikely that one can have a representation rich in expressive power which avoids duplication of meanings. Woods (1975) has argued convincingly for the same conclusion.

The second claim of the absolute position is that it is possible to assign all same-meaning sentences the same representation. Besides being a claim about the character of the representation this is a claim about the character of the parser. The problem with exploring this possibility rigorously is that there is no explicit criterion for what it means for two sentences to have the same meaning. It would be circular to say two sentences S_1 and S_2 are paraphrases if they have the same underlying representations. It is uninformative to simply use judged synonymity by a sample population because this does not give an analysis of why two sentences are synonymous. Besides, such ratings are notoriously unstable.

One explicit definition for paraphrase would be logical equivalence. That is, two sentences S_1 and S_2 would be considered paraphrases if and only if the sentence "S_1 *if and only if* S_2" were true. Thus, clearly, *John hit Mary* and *Mary was hit by John* are paraphrases. Presumably, so are *John gave Fido to Mary* and *Mary received Fido from John*. The sentences *John has nine wives* and *The number of John's wives is the second power of 3* are also paraphrases. Under this criterion somewhat bizarre pairs of sentences are considered paraphrases. *Either John hit Mary or John did not hit Mary* is synonymous with *If Rome is burning then Rome is burning* since both are logically true. Adopting this criterion for want of a better one, it can be shown that invariance under paraphrase is impossible. That is, it can be shown that a contradiction is implied by the assumption that an effective parser exists which can achieve invariance of representation under this definition of paraphrase. If such a parser existed it would be possible to effectively decide the truth of formulas in the predicate calculus for which it is known that there exists no effective decision procedure.

PROOF: Suppose there were an effective procedure that would give synonymous sentences identical meaning representation. Then this procedure could be used to decide if a predicate calculus expression of the form P_1 *iff* P_2[6] were true. It is known that no such procedure exists for the predicate calculus. Let S_1 and S_2 be the English translation of P_1 and P_2. (There should be no difficulty in translating from statements in the predicate calculus to English although there is often much difficulty in going in the reverse direction.) It is possible to decide if S_1 and S_2 are synonymous by determining if the proposed procedure gives them identical meaning representations. They are synonymous if and only if S_1 *iff* S_2 is true or equivalently if and only if P_1 *iff* P_2 is true.

This argument shows that invariance under paraphrase is impossible if we equate paraphrase with logical equivalence. However, it exposes the general problem of invariance under paraphrase—whatever the definition of paraphrase. It is not always easy to decide whether two sentences are paraphrases. Consider the following pair of sentences:

(17)   Psychology, like economics, is a science concerned with interdependence among certain events rather than with their physical nature.

(18)   Neither psychology nor economics is concerned with events, rather they are concerned with relations among the events.

[6]The term *iff* is shorthand for *if and only if*.

Are these sentences true paraphrases? I think it is a very hard decision to make and certainly I wondered about the question long after comprehending the two sentences. If the comprehended representation of these sentences maintained invariance under paraphrase, it would not be so difficult to make decisions about paraphrase.

This brings up another point made by Woods (1975) and others. Achieving invariance under paraphrase puts enormous strain on the parser. Requiring absolute invariance would seem to put an impossible strain on the parser. The more cases there are where one wants to achieve invariance the more work it seems the parser will have to do. Recall that one motivation for invariance was that it reduced the amount of work one has to do at retrieval. However, it seems that one is trading off more work at input for less work at output. The optimal strategy would seem to be one where there is an intermediate amount of invariance achieved by the parser. Therefore, the fact that Clark, Anderson and Bower, and Kintsch only produce partial invariances does not put them at a disadvantage compared with Norman and Rumelhart and Schank whose models aspire to absolute invariance.

The Overlap and Continuity Criteria

Rumelhart and Norman suggest a couple of additional criteria as extensions of the invariance criterion. They propose the *overlap criterion* which is that sentences which have overlap in meaning should have overlap in their representation. Thus, there should be overlap in the representations for the following two sentences:

   (19)   Henry strolled to a store.
   (20)   Henry sauntered to a store.

Their second additional criterion is the *continuity criterion* which is that small changes in meaning should cause small changes in representation. Given that invariance is not possible absolutely, it seems unlikely that there could be any absolute and precise enforcement of these criteria. Moreover, it is unclear that any advantage is gained by the enforcement of these criteria. Norman and Rumelhart point out that one could explain judgement of similarity of meaning with a representation that had this property. However, one does not need this feature to explain such judgements. One could postulate procedures which would compare very different representations with similar meanings and recognize the similarity. Once again it is a question of whether one wants to do the work at input or at test. Probably, some tradeoff between the two extremes would be optimal.

Semantic Decomposition

An issue related to, but independent of, the invariance question is whether one wants to decompose sentence representations into primitive meaning elements. Kintsch

has taken a position against semantic decomposition whereas Norman and Rumelhart came out strongly in favor of it. Clark, while a clear advocate of decomposition, does not seem to practice it to the same extent as Norman and Rumelhart.
The HAM model is least clear on this issue. Generally, HAM avoids semantic
decomposition but does resort to it when there is no other way to represent the
sentence in terms of binary tree structures. Note that both Clark, who practices
the least invariance under paraphrase, and Norman and Rumelhart, who practice
the most, both advocate semantic decomposition.

The arguments for semantic decomposition take two forms. The first claims
that it is only possible, or at least easier, to compute similarity relations, make
inferences, etc., if we represent sentences in a decomposed form. The second
claims that there is empirical evidence that subjects do represent sentences in a
decomposed form. There is no cogent evidence for the first claim. Any behavior that can be computed from inspecting semantic primitives can be computed
with the aid of "meaning postulates" that interpret more complex semantic units.
This follows from the theorem in Section 1.2 (page 11) that any representation
can mimic the behavior of any other, provided they impose the same equivalence
class on their inputs. There is also no reason to suppose that procedures utilizing
a decomposed representation will be more efficient than procedures involving a
nondecomposed representation.

The current empirical evidence also gives little support to the decomposition
notion. Clark (1971) reports that subjects are slower with complex terms like
absent rather than lexically simple terms like *present,* but his tests (as noted
earlier, page   ) are tests of utilization of linguistic information rather than comprehension (that is, parsing). In contrast, Kintsch has reported no effect of lexical
complexity in his attempts to tap the comprehension process.

There are a number of arguments that can be made against semantic decomposition. First, semantically decomposed representations are complex and complexity
is to be avoided if it does not accomplish anything. Second, no one has proposed
an adequate set of semantic primitives. Suggested candidates like "transfer" or
"possess" strike many as hardly primitive but rather capable of decomposition
into more primitive concepts. The third reason is that it would seem to be more
plausible psychologically to allow the comprehender to have the option of decomposition. So, for instance, given the statement "Mary gave Fido to Bill" the
system would or would not (depending on the circumstances) make the inference
"Bill has Fido." The fourth reason for not having semantic decomposition is an
argument given by Kintsch. That is, it seems very bizarre to propose that language
has complex relational terms like *buy* but that these terms have no corresponding
concepts in memory.

Proliferation of Propositional Theories

There is little basis for choice among the four propositional theories reviewed
in this chapter. In addition to these four propositional representations there are

those of Crothers (1972), Frederikson (1972), Meyer (1974), Schank (1975), and Collins and Quillian (1972) in psychology proper. Furthermore, there are direct borrowings from linguistics, logic, and computer science in the psychological literature. The general psychological community is being forced to absorb an apparently endless parade of formalisms without really gaining anything from the new additions. One is tempted to call for a conference that would legislate once and for all what the standard propositional representation should be. However, there are a number of factors that make this impractical—besides the personal pride of the individual researchers involved. An important factor is that the representations do change in response to new problem domains and new empirical findings. So, even if the researchers were in agreement about an initial representation, this standard representation would rapidly evolve into many different representations once the researchers returned to their individual laboratories.

In logic and linguistics, there is also a very wide variety of representational structures, but there does not seem to be the disarray that I perceive currently in psychology. This is largely because there are a few standard representations which have emerged in those fields. Other representations and newcomers can be classified with reference to the standards. Which representational systems became standard is both a matter of historical accident and a matter of which were most tractable and useful for various purposes. Hopefully, some standard propositional representations will emerge for work in psychology. Until then, I only hope that the general psychological community will be tolerant of the current confusion and that those who work with propositional theories will try to minimize unnecessary communication barriers.

REFERENCES

Abrahamson, A. Review of human associative memory. *American Scientist,* 1974, **62,** 947.

Anderson, J. R. Verbatim and propositional representation of sentences in immediate and long-term memory. *Journal of Verbal Learning and Verbal Behavior,* 1974, **13,** 149–162.

Anderson, J. R., & Bower, G. H. *Human associative memory.* Washington: Winston, 1973.

Baylor, G. W., & Gascon, J. An information processing theory of aspects of the development of weight seriation in children. *Cognitive Psychology,* 1974, **6,** 1–40.

Bransford, J. D., Barclay, J. R., & Franks, J. J. Sentence memory: A constructive versus interpretive approach. *Cognitive Psychology,* 1972, **3,** 193–209.

Carpenter, P. A., & Just, M. A. Sentence comprehension: A psycholinguistic processing model of verification. *Psychological Review,* 1975, **82,** 45–73.

Chase, W. G. and Clark, H. H. Mental operations in the comparison of sentences and pictures. In L. Gregg (Ed.), *Cognition in learning and memory.* New York: Wiley, 1972.

Clark, H. H. *The chronometric study of meaning components.* Paper presented at the CRNS Colloquia International sur le Problèmes Actuels de Psycholinguistique, Paris, December, 13–18, 1971.

Clark, H. H. The language-as-fixed-effect-fallacy: A critique of language statistics in psychological research. *Journal of Verbal Learning and Verbal Behavior,* 1973, **12,** 335–359.

Clark, H. H. Semantics and comprehension. In R. A. Sebeok (Ed.), *Current trends in linguistics.* Vol. 12. The Hague: Mouton, 1974.

Clark, H. H., & Chase, W. G. On the process of comparing sentences against pictures. *Cognitive Psychology,* 1972, **3,** 472–517.

Clark, H. H., & Haviland, S. E. Comprehension and the given-new contract. In R. Freedle (Ed.), *Discourse production and comprehension*. Hillsdale, New Jersey: Lawrence Erlbaum Associates, 1976, in press.

Collins, A. Review of human associative memory. *Contemporary Psychology*, 1974, **19**, 643–645.

Collins, A. M., & Quillian, M. R. Experiments on semantic memory and language comprehension. In L. Gregg (Ed.), *Cognition and learning*. New York: Wiley, 1972.

Crothers, E. J. Memory structure and the recall of discourse. In J. B. Carroll & R. O. Freedle (Eds.), *Language comprehension and the acquisition of knowledge*. Washington, D.C.: Winston, 1972.

Frederiksen, C. H. Effects of task induced cognitive operations on comprehension and memory processes. In R. Freedle & J. B. Carroll (Eds.), *Language comprehension and the acquisition of knowledge*. Washington, D.C.: Winston, 1972.

Gomulicki, B. R. Recall as an abstract process. *Acta Psychologica*, 1956, **12**, 77–94.

Fillenbaum, S. Memory for gist: some relevant variables. *Language and Speech*, 1966, **9**, 217–227.

Haviland, S. E., & Clark, H. H. What's new? Acquiring new information as a process in comprehension. *Journal of Verbal Learning and Verbal Behavior*, 1974, **13**, 512–521.

Huttenlocher, J. Constructing spatial images: A strategy in reasoning. *Psychological Review*, 1968, **75**, 550–560.

Kaplan, R. A general syntactic processor. In R. Rustin (Ed.). *Natural language processing*. New York: Algorithmics Press, 1973.

Kay, M. The MIND system. In R. Rustin (Ed.), *Natural language processing*. New York: Algorithmics Press, 1973.

Kintsch, W. Models for free recall and recognition. In D. A. Norman (Ed.), *Models of human memory*. New York: Academic Press, 1970. Pp. 307–373.

Kintsch, W. Notes on the semantic structure of memory. In E. Tulving & W. Donaldson (Eds.), *Organization and memory*. New York: Academic Press, 1972.

Kintsch, W. *The representation of meaning in memory*. Hillsdale, New Jersey: Lawrence Erlbaum Assoc., 1974.

Kintsch, W., Kozminsky, E., Streby, W. J., McKoon, G., & Keenan, J. M. Comprehension and recall of text as a function of content variables. *Journal of Verbal Learning and Verbal Behavior*, 1975, **14**, 196–214.

Kintsch, W., & van Dijk, T. A. Recalling and summarizing stories. *Language*, 1976, in press.

Lakoff, G. Linguistics and natural logic. *Synthese*, 1970, **22**, 151–271.

Martin, E. A. *Hamming it up*. Unpublished manuscript, Dept. of Philosophy, Indiana University, 1975.

Meyer, B. J. F. *The organization of prose and its effect on recall*. Doctoral dissertation, Cornell University, 1974.

Newell, A. Productions systems: Models of control structures. In W. G. Chase (Ed.), *Visual information processing*, New York: Academic Press, 1973. Pp. 463–526.

Newell, A., & Simon, H. *Human problem solving*. Englewood Cliffs, New Jersey: Prentice-Hall, 1972.

Norman, D. A., Rumelhart, D. E., & the LNR Research Group. *Explorations in cognition*. San Francisco: Freeman, 1975.

Olson, D. R., & Filby, N. On the comprehension of active and passive sentences. *Cognitive Psychology*, 1972, **3**, 361–381.

Ortony, A. Review of human associative memory. *Journal of Educational Research*, 1974, **68**, 396–401.

Pachella, R. G. An interpretation of reaction time in information processing research. In B. Kantowitz (Ed.), *Human information processing: Tutorials in performance and cognition*. Hillsdale, New Jersey: Lawrence Erlbaum Associates, 1974.

Paivio, A. *Imagery and verbal processes*. New York: Holt, Rinehart & Winston, 1971.

Polson, P. G. A review of human associative memory. *American Journal of Psychology*, 1975, **88**, 131–139.

Posner, M. The memory system. *Science,* 1974, **183,** 1283–1284.

Pylyshyn, Z. W. What the mind's eye tells the mind's brain: A critique of mental imagery. *Psychological Bulletin,* 1973, **80,** 1–24.

Rosenberg, S., & Simon, H. A. Modelling semantic memory: Effects of presenting semantic information in different modalities. CIP Working Paper #270, Carnegie-Mellon University, 1974.

Rumelhart, D. E., Lindsay, P., & Norman, D. A. A process model for long-term memory. In E. Tulving & W. Donaldson (Eds.), *Organization of memory.* New York: Academic Press, 1972.

Sachs, J. Recognition memory for syntactic and semantic aspects of connected discourse. *Perception and Psychophysics,* 1967, **2,** 437–442.

Schank, R. C. Conceptual dependency: A theory of natural language understanding. *Cognitive Psychology,* 1972, **3,** 552–631.

Schank, R. C. *Conceptual information processing.* Amsterdam: North-Holland Publ., 1975.

Schubert, L. K. *Extending the expressing power of semantic networks* (Tech. Rep. TR 74-18). Department of Computer Science, University of Alberta, 1974.

Simmons, R. F. Some semantic structures for representing English meanings. In R. Freedle & J. B. Carrol (Eds.), *Language comprehension and the acquisition of knowledge.* Washington, D.C.: Winston, 1972.

Tulving, E., & Donaldson, W. *Organization and memory.* New York: Academic Press, 1972.

Tversky, A., & Kahneman, D. Belief in the law of small numbers. *Psychological Bulletin,* 1971, **76,** 105–110.

Wanner, H. E. Review of human associative memory. *Contemporary Psychology,* 1974, **19,** 641–643.

Wicklegren, W. A. Subproblems of semantic memory: A review of "Human associative memory." *Journal of Mathematical Psychology,* 1976, in press.

Winograd, T. Understanding natural language. *Cognitive Psychology,* 1972, **3,** 1–191.

Winston, P. H. *Learning structural descriptions from examples.* MIT Artificial Intelligence Laboratory Project AI–TR–231, 1970.

Woods, W. A. What's in a link: Foundations for semantic networks. In D. G. Bobrow & A. Collins (Eds.), *Representation and understanding: Studies in cognitive science.* New York: Academic Press, 1975.

Woods, W. A., Kaplan, R. M., & Nash-Webber, B. The lunar sciences natural language information system: final report. BBN Report No. 2378, Bolt, Beranek, and Newman, 1972.

3

Models of Procedural Knowledge

The basic idea of a stimulus-response association or connection is close enough in character to the concept of set membership or to the basic idea of automata to make me confident that new and better versions of stimulus-response theory may be expected in the future and that the scientific potentiality of theories stated essentially in this framework has by no means been exhausted.

PATRICK SUPPES

3.1 THE ROLE OF PROCEDURAL KNOWLEDGE

The propositional models reviewed in the previous chapter were principally concerned with representing *declarative knowledge*—that is, knowledge of facts about the world. This chapter will be concerned with two models of *procedural knowledge*—knowledge about how to do something. These two models are stimulus-sampling theory (Estes, 1959) and the Newell (1973) PS system. The distinction between declarative and procedural knowledge is analagous to the computer science distinction between program and data. Any complete psychological model obviously needs both types of knowledge. However, there is room for disagreement about what to represent procedurally and what to represent declaratively. Both theories reviewed in this section have opted for representing most knowledge in a procedural format. In contrast, ACT makes what might be called an "even division" between representing information procedurally and representing information declaratively. There is also room for disagreement about how different the formalisms should be that represent declarative and procedural knowledge. Norman and Rumelhart (Section 2.4, this volume) opted for a system in which there are no formal differences between the representations for the two types of knowledge. In contrast, ACT will opt for a system which makes a fundamental distinction between the representations for these two types of knowledge.

I do not want to present detailed arguments for ACT's options on these issues until the next chapter. However, to summarize, ACT's options are not empirically discriminable from the other options. Once again we run into the indeterminacy of issues about internal structures and processes. Rather, it will be argued that it is conceptually easier to organize the existing data if we make a basic distinction between procedural and declarative knowledge. A warning should be given to the reader about the procedural–declarative distinction. Besides the two issues of what to represent declaratively and what to represent procedurally and of how different to make the procedural and declarative representations, there is the uncertainty introduced because it is not always clear what to regard in a model as procedural representation and what to regard as declarative. Thus, the procedural–declarative distinction, although valuable, can be very vague and imprecise. I have sharpened it in ACT by equating declarative knowledge with information encoded in the propositional network, and equating procedural knowledge with information in the production system. However, we will see (Section 7.3) that there still are circumstances where it is uncertain where a piece of knowledge resides—in the network or in the production system.

A Stimulus–Response Model versus a Production System

Stimulus-sampling theory is being reviewed in Section 3.2 because it is the most rigorously developed of the stimulus–response (S–R) theories. An S–R theory postulates that underlying behavior are connections between observable (or potentially observable) stimuli and responses. If an S–R bond exists, then the organism, when presented with S, will respond (perhaps only with a certain probability) with R. Stimulus–response theories have the notable virtue of being extremely simple and elegant but the unfortunate drawback of being inadequate to account for certain complexities of human behavior. A production system has the power to account for these complexities. However, it has a remarkable superficial similarity to S–R theory. It proposes that underlying behavior are productions which consist of conditions and actions. The condition is a specification of some features that must be true of the internal cognitive environment and the external environment. The action is a specification of some internal and external operations. These are like stimuli and responses except that they do not just refer to external observables. They can refer to internal objects and they can be abstract specifications.

One might think that production systems grew out of frustration with S–R theory—that someone just generalized on the S–R structure to create a more powerful computational medium. I doubt that this was the history that led Newell to his formulation. The origins of production systems are to be found in the ideas of formal automata theory (for example, Post, 1943). However, my personal intellectual evolution has advanced from S–R theory, through a grey period of uncertainty about how to model procedural knowledge, to production systems. Therefore, it is an important personal exercise for me to reason through why S–R theory is deficient and to see how production systems repair the deficiencies. I have made this ''personal exercise'' public in this chapter because of the belief that there are others who would profit from it. Those for whom the inadequacies of S–R theory need no explanation and/or who are intolerant of further discussion of the theory should skip Section 3.2.

The Atomistic versus Faculty Approach
to Procedural Knowledge

Stimulus–response theory and production systems represent an approach to procedural knowledge which has not been very popular in cognitive psychology. They attempt to analyze all procedural knowledge into a fixed set of primitives. These primitives are the atoms out of which a great variety of cognitive behavior is constructed—language comprehension, language generation, inference making, question answering, problem solving, executing instructions, etc. If such a set of primitives can be found, this would seem to constitute an enormous advance because the few principles that describe these primitives could be used to account for all of cognitive behavior.

I have dubbed this the *atomistic approach* and contrast it with an approach which I call, for want of a better term, the *faculty approach*. The faculty approach gives a separate analysis of the procedures underlying each paradigm and only makes minimal effort to find general principles. That is, the faculty approach views our procedural knowledge as consisting of a large number of "faculties" for performing separate tasks. The dominance of the faculty approach in current cognitive theorizing is exemplified by the heavy use of flow charts. A flow chart specifies for a particular paradigm the exact sequence of operations that will occur and the times associated with each operation. However, there is no way to transfer the principles for one flow chart to construction of a flow chart for another paradigm. A second problem with the use of a flow chart is that it does not specify how the control of behavior gets in and out of the flow chart. The implication of a flow chart, if we took it literally, is that the person is forever stuck recognizing words or judging whether sentences are true of pictures (or whatever the task was that the flow chart represents). It is a serious weakness of current cognitive theories that they provide us with no understanding of the general control of behavior.

A related criticism of the use of flow charts has recently been made by Newell (1973). He complains that they are an informal medium for expressing procedures and that there are no principles about what may be put in a box. As a consequence one may find operations like "comprehend sentence" occurring as unanalyzed operations in a flow chart. Such operations cry out for decomposition into more primitive terms. Another consequence of the lack of an atomistic theory of procedural knowledge is that it is not possible to tell when two different flow charts are variants of one another and really describe the same processing mechanisms.

The principal argument for the faculty approach over the atomistic approach is the claim that it is not possible to achieve a tractable set of primitives in terms of which all cognitive behavior can be analyzed. For instance, few people would doubt that there would be across-task generality of principles if we reduced cognitive theory to the laws of physics that govern the nervous system. However, also few people would believe that a tractable analysis of cognitive phenomena exists at this level. It is an open question whether there is a useful atomistic model of procedural knowledge. Newell's PS and my ACT are attempts to create such models. However, it is too soon to tell whether either of these attempts will be successful.

3.2   STIMULUS-SAMPLING THEORY

The purpose of this section is to expose some of the inadequacies in S–R theory. Anderson and Bower (1973) argued that S–R theories suffer fundamental inadequacies in their account of human behavior. This is because of the *Terminal Meta-Postulate* implicit in any S–R theory. This refers to a restriction on S–R theories as to what kind of objects may be referenced by the theory. The restriction asserts that the theory may only refer to observable or potentially observable events like stimuli and responses. There can be no abstract objects in the vocabulary of the theory.

To establish rigorously that all S–R theories are inadequate one would have to prove a theorem of the following sort:

> *Consider any theory that is constructed from a vocabulary of only stimuli and responses*. Such a theory claims humans are capable of some behaviors and not capable of others. Each such theory predicts that humans are not capable of some behavior of which they are capable.

This theorem cannot be proved because it is not clear what is meant by a theory that refers only to stimuli and responses.

This section considers a specific example of an S–R theory, stimulus-sampling theory (Estes, 1959; Neimark & Estes, 1967), and points out inadequacies in it. These inadequacies do not seem to be unique to stimulus-sampling theory but rather problems that might be established with any existing S–R theory, were that theory as rigorously specified as stimulus-sampling theory. Suppes (1969a) attempted to show that stimulus-sampling models can be conditioned so that they behave identically to finite state machines (FSMs). The significance of this is that it might serve as a refutation of claims (for example, Chomsky, 1959; Chomsky, 1965; Katz & Postal, 1964; Bever, Fodor, & Garrett, 1968) that S–R theories are in principle incapable of producing the complexities of human behavior. That is, Suppes would show that S–R theories are capable of a complex class of behaviors (that is, the class of behaviors that can be computed by FSMs).[1] How-

---

[1]There are some who would argue that man is more complex than a FSM—that he is effectively equivalent to a Turing Machine. However, this argument requires the assumption that man has an unlimited supply of memory, which is never true. Perhaps in some situations it could be argued that man is equivalent to a linear-bounded automata. These are machines (see Hopcroft & Ullman, 1969) whose memory is limited by the size of the problem. Linear-bounded automata are intermediate in computing power between FSMs and unrestricted Turing Machines. In any case, if it can be shown that a stimulus-sampling theory cannot mimic an arbitrary FSM, it certainly cannot mimic an arbitrary member of the more powerful classes. This is what will be shown here, in contrast to Suppes.

ever, it will be argued in this section that Suppes fails in his attempt to prove this equivalence—that, in fact, stimulus-sampling models are equivalent only to a restricted class of FSMs. Furthermore, it will be shown that there are even difficulties in getting a stimulus-sampling model to mimic one of these restricted FSMs in a reasonable number of learning trials. In establishing these points I will take advantage of the structure that Suppes set up to relate stimulus-sampling theory to modern notions of computability. I will also trace out his argument about the equivalence between stimulus-sampling theory and FSMs.

Objects of the Theory

The basic objects of stimulus-sampling theory are a set S of stimuli and a set R of responses. On any trial a subject is presented with a subset of the stimuli. He samples a subset of this subset and his response is determined by this sampled subset—hence, the term stimulus-sampling theory. There is another principal class of objects in stimulus-sampling theory. These are connections between stimulus elements and responses. The total set of connections at any point in time defines a state of conditioning. The symbol C refers to the state of conditioning of the organism.

Axioms of Stimulus-Sampling Theory

The assumptions of stimulus-sampling theory are usually set forth as a series of axioms. The stimulus-sampling axioms are conventionally partitioned into sampling axioms, conditioning axioms, and response axioms. It is assumed in these axioms that the organism's life is divided into discrete moments. These moments are called "trials" (a classic example of the importation of laboratory terminology into psychological theory). Presumably this discretization is thought of as an approximation to the continuous flow of stimuli and responses.

Sampling Axioms

(S1)   On any trial n a nonempty set of elements is presented. Call this sample t_n.

(S2)   A sample s_n is selected from t_n. If the same presentation set t is presented on two trials the probability of any sample s being selected is the same on those trials.

(S3)   The probability of a particular samiple s_n being selected given a presentation set t_n is independent of the particular pattern of events that led up to t_n.

Conditioning Axioms

(C1)   On every trial each stimulus element in the set S is conditioned to at most one response in the set R. It may be conditioned to none.

(C2)   A response on a particular trial may or may not be reinforced. The response reinforced need not be the emitted response. If a response is reinforced, there is a probability c that any element in the sampled set, s_n, not conditioned to the response, will be conditioned. This probability is independent of the response, the stimulus element, trial number, or preceding pattern of events. If the stimulus element is already conditioned to the correct response it stays conditioned.

(C3)   If no response is reinforced, the conditioning of all elements stays the same.

(C4)   The conditioning of unsampled elements does not change.

Response Axioms

(R1)   Let m be the number of elements in the sampled set s_n conditioned to any response. Let m_i be the number of elements conditioned to response r_i. Suppose $m > 0$. Then the probability of response r_i is the ratio m_i/m.

(R2)   If no sampled stimulus is conditioned to any response (that is, $m = 0$), then the probability of response r_i is a constant p_i independent of the trial or pattern of events.

Identification with a Finite-State Machine (FSM)

Table 3.1 displays the correspondences made by Suppes between the objects of the stimulus-sampling organism (SSO) and the objects of an FSM. An FSM consists of four objects: $\mathcal{K}$, a set of states; $\mathcal{I}$, a set of input elements; $\mathcal{R}$, a set of responses; and $\mathcal{T}$, a set of transitions. An SSO consists of three objects: S, a set of stimuli; R, a set of responses; and C, a set of conditioned connections. Two of Suppes' correspondences are fairly obvious. He identifies $\mathcal{R}$ with R, and $\mathcal{T}$ with C. We will soon see just how these correspondences work.

TABLE 3.1
Correspondence Between Stimulus-Sampling Theory
and a Finite-State Machine

Finite state machine	Stimulus-sampling theory
$\mathcal{K}$ (states) ⟶ R (responses)	
$\mathcal{R}$ (responses)	
$\mathcal{I}$ (input vocabulary) ⟶ S (stimulus elements)	
$\mathcal{T}$ (transitions) ⟶ C (state of conditioning)	

A critical decision is what in stimulus-sampling theory corresponds to $\mathcal{H}$, the set of states. States seem to be abstract, nonobservable objects. They seem to be just what the Terminal Meta-Postulate would not permit. Suppes' solution is to identify $\mathcal{H}$ with R, the set of responses. We will see later that this is not an entirely satisfactory solution. It means that SSOs can only mimic FSMs in which there is a one-to-one correspondence between elements of $\mathcal{H}$ and elements of $\mathcal{R}$.

It turns out that it is also not a trivial question how to identify $\mathcal{I}$, the input vocabulary for the FSM, with S, the set of stimulus elements. Suppes chooses to identify these with patterns consisting of the current input and the past response. As will be argued, this choice is not without negative implication for the explanatory power of stimulus-sampling theory. Therefore, it is worthwhile considering some more obvious choices and see why these will not work.

Consider the obvious choice where $\mathcal{I} = S$. To see that this will not work, consider the FSM whose transition network is displayed in Fig. 3.1. In that figure the identity between responses and states has been incorporated by labeling each state with the response associated with it. This machine is in either one of two states, r_1 or r_2. When a 0 comes in, it stays in that state, when a 1 comes in it changes that state. As a simple example, this machine might describe the behavior of an organism running a maze. Let r_1 be equivalent to turning left and r_2 equivalent to turning right. Let the input 0 correspond to a choice point being painted white and let 1 correspond to a choice point being painted black. Then this transition network would generate the behavior of an organism which did the following: Assume the maze runner starts to make a left turn (state r_1). After this, if the choice point is white the maze runner would turn in the same direction as he had at the previous choice point. If the choice point were black, he would switch.

Under the assumption that $S = \mathcal{I}$ there is no SSO that will behave like the FSM in Fig. 3.1. The reason is that, depending on what the last response is, the FSM will respond differently to the same stimulus. For instance, if the last response was r_1 the machine would respond with r_1 to 0. However, if the last response was r_2 it would respond with r_2 to 0. By assumption (Axiom C1) a particular stimulus element can be conditioned to at most one response. There

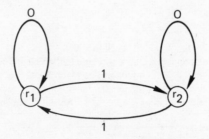

FIG. 3.1   An example of a finite state machine.

is just no way, given the present framework, to have 0 evoke r_1 in one context and r_2 in another.

Response Aftertraces

A basic problem for the SSO with $S = \mathcal{I}$ is that it has no memory for its previous responses. This has been a classic problem in the development of S–R theory and it has an equally classic solution (e.g., Hull, 1952). Assume that the stimuli impinging on the organism in trial n include not only the overtly presented elements (i.e., an element of $\mathcal{I}$) but also aftertraces of the response made on the previous trial. So, in our example of the FSM of Fig. 3.1, the stimuli would be 0, 1, S_{r1}, S_{r2} where S_{r1} and S_{r2} are the aftertraces of the subscript responses. The presentation set on a particular trial will be a pair consisting of either 0 or 1, depending on the overt stimulus, and either S_{r1} or S_{r2}, depending on the previous response.

It can be shown that no SSO with this stimulus set can mimic the desired FSM. This can be done by showing there is no state of conditioning of the after-trace S_{r1} that will yield perfect mimicry. Assume the organism has just emitted (on trial $n - 1$) response r_1. Suppose S_{r1} is conditioned to r_1. If we present stimulus 1, the organism must respond with r_2 (consult Fig. 3.1). Even if the stimulus 1 were conditioned to r_2 there would only be a ½ probability of the organism responding with r_2 (see Axiom R1). Therefore, s_{r1} cannot be conditioned to r_1. Similarly, S_{r1} cannot be conditioned to r_2 because the organism must respond with r_1 if 0 is presented.

The only other possibility is that S_{r1} might be conditioned to no response. To respond correctly on trial n, the stimulus 1 must be conditioned to r_2 and the stimulus 0 to r_1. Suppose we present 1 on trial n and the organism responds appropriately with r_2. Consider his predicament on trial $n + 1$. Suppose we present him with 1. He must now respond with r_1. Since 1 is conditioned to response r_2, even if s_{r2} is conditioned to r_1 the probability of a correct response on trial $n + 1$ is ½. Therefore, the organism cannot perfectly mimic the finite state machine with s_{r1} unconditioned. Since this is the last possibility for the conditioning of s_{r1}, there is no state of conditioning that will lead to successful mimicry. The basic problem, which this argument exposes, is that the organism must respond to the *pattern* of last response and current stimulus. In this formulation the SSO was responding to the elements in the pair individually.

Patterned Stimuli

Two possible identifications have been considered and rejected for the objects in S of the stimulus-sampling theory. The purpose of this extensive discussion was to motivate Suppes' decision to identify S with response–stimulus patterns. For the FSM in Fig. 3.1, S consists of the four possible patterns—$S = \{\langle s_{r1} - 0 \rangle,$ $\langle s_{r1} - 1 \rangle, \langle s_{r2} - 0 \rangle, \langle s_{r2} - 1 \rangle\}$.

For this stimulus set, unlike the previous two, there is a state of conditioning that leads to the desired behavior. It may be represented schematically:

$$\langle s_{r1} - 0 \rangle \rightarrow r_1$$

$$\langle s_{r1} - 1 \rangle \rightarrow r_2$$

$$\langle s_{r2} - 0 \rangle \rightarrow r_2$$

$$\langle s_{r2} - 1 \rangle \rightarrow r_1$$

However, it should be emphasized that this choice of a stimulus set is not without serious implications for the generality of stimulus-sampling theory. The organism does not directly receive such patterns. Some mechanism within the organism must merge the stimuli and responses into patterns. One might conceive of a cascading of SSOs with one encoding the elements into patterns and the other taking these patterns as inputs and appropriately responding. However, it can be shown that no SSO can be built which will take individual elements as input and produce pattern elements as outputs.[2] So Suppes is placing in stimulus-patterning an operation which is fundamentally beyond the power of stimulus-sampling theory. Thus part of the "computational task" of mimicking the FSM is being accomplished by the pattern producer rather than the SSO.[3]

We have shown that, assuming patterns, there exists a state of conditioning which will lead to mimicry of the FSM in Fig. 3.1. One might ask whether it is possible to construct a similar set of patterns and state of conditioning for all FSMs. As we will see, it is possible to mimic only a subset of FSMs in which states and responses can be identified uniquely with one another. Also one might ask whether there is a reinforcement schedule which is guaranteed to get the organism from an unconditioned state to the desired state of conditioning. The most significant technical accomplishment of the Suppes paper was to prove that there always exists such a reinforcement schedule.

The reader is advised to consult the Suppes' papers for the details of that proof, but the reinforcement schedule outlined in the proof can be easily described: At any point in time it is possible to know what stimulus pattern is impinging on the SSO. Just observe the last response and the current input element. Consult the final state of conditioning desired for the SSO. Reinforce the response specified

---

[2]The logic of the proof of this claim would be identical to the logic used earlier to show that there was no direct conditioning of the elements 0, 1, S_{r1}, and S_{r2} that would yield mimicry of the target FSM.

[3]As an empirical aside, animals can apparently be conditioned to respond to patterns (see Rescorla and Wagner, 1972). This fact has always been a sore point for S–R theories. Suppes' use of patterns in 1969 was hardly the first use in stimulus-sampling theory (Neimark & Estes, 1967). However, whenever patterns are used in a stimulus-sampling theory an important part of the information processing is left unexplained.

by that state of conditioning for the current S–R pattern. Provided each possible pattern has a nonzero probability of occurring (which Suppes proves) all patterns will eventually be conditioned.

In addition to the problems with pattern formation there are two other objections to Suppes' attempt to establish an equivalence between SSOs and FSMs. First, the number of trials required to train an SSO to behave like an interesting FSM would be enormous. Second, the class of FSMs which SSOs can mimic are a subclass of all FSMs.

Number of Patterns Argument

Arbib (1969) argued that an enormous number of patterns would have to be conditioned to be able to reproduce any interesting class of behavior. For instance, to reproduce a simple TOTE hierarchy of the variety proposed by Miller, Galanter, and Pribram (1960), Arbib computes that 655,360 patterns would have to be conditioned. This would require three years' work even if a new pattern were learned every minute of a 10-hour day. Since many thousands of TOTEs would be required to reproduce the complexities of human behavior, the learning task would seem impossible. Suppes' (1969b) reply to this criticism is that it is unclear if (a) TOTEs are the appropriate way to model human behavior and (b) the appropriate way would require anything like 655,360 patterns. Thus, Arbib fails to set lower bounds on the number of conditioned patterns required to reproduce some complex human behavior. However, this can be done by the following example.

Consider this task: A human is read a series of 10 English words and must decide if the second five words are the mirror image of the first five. An example string would be *eat, tooth, hug, very, lamp, lamp, very, hug, tooth, eat*. Humans can perform moderately well in such a task. After the first five words the human must be in a different state for each possible 5-tuple since he will respond differently to the subsequent 5-tuple depending on the first five. The way Suppes must encode such state information is by patterns. Thus, the organism must be processing a different pattern for each possible 5-tuple. This requires a liberalization of the meaning of a pattern. Now a pattern not only encodes past response and current stimulus, it also encodes the past five stimuli. However, let us grant stimulus-sampling theory this liberalization. Without it, it cannot explain the behavior. How many patterns are required?

It is reasonable to suppose that we are capable of using 10,000 English words. Consequently, at least $(10,000)^5 = (10)^{20}$ patterns are required for successful performance. To behave correctly in this situation the correct pattern of responding must be conditioned to each pattern. This requires at least 10^{20} conditionings. Assuming one pattern is conditioned per second, this would take on the order of 10^{12} years to learn. The interesting point is that a human can learn to perform this task after a minute of instruction and without a detailed conditioning history.

Of course, the above argument is not airtight. It cannot be because it is not clearly specified how stimulus-sampling theory will apply to this situation. It is interesting to consider two ways in which it might get out of the bind. First, it might posit a pattern-encoding process that transformed all 10^{20} acceptable 10-word strings into one pattern and the remaining $(10^{40} - 10^{20})$ strings into another pattern. It would then only have to condition a "yes" response to the first pattern and a "no" response to the second. The number of required conditionings has been reduced from 10^{20} to 2. Hopefully, the absurdity of this tack is apparent to all. It serves to highlight, however, my uneasiness about permitting stimulus sampling to posit patterns.

Another tack would be to propose that the adult which can perform such a task is already a very complicated FSM. An FSM can be built which takes an abstract description of another machine and mimics it. However, the minimum number of states of the mimicker would have to be larger than minimum number for the mimickee. Since an SSO encodes state information in the conditioning of its patterns, a mimicking SSO would require that at least 10^{20} patterns be already conditioned.[4]

Identification of States with Responses

Another weakness in the Suppes' formulation derives from his one-to-one identification between machine states and responses. The more general definition of an FSM (for example, Gill, 1962) permits a different response to be associated with each transition leaving a state (or, equivalently, more than one state to have the same response). Unlike a general FSM, the behavior of a Suppes FSM is totally predictable from the last response made. The way to capture the significance of this difference is with the concept of variability. Suppose one observes that a Suppes FSM, having emitted response r_1 and being presented input X, responds with r_2. Then one knows that this FSM will respond in all other circumstances with r_2 when it has emitted r_1 and is presented with X. In contrast, a general FSM can respond variably to X after emitting r_1. Clearly, human variability indicates we need the more general model.

Arbib (1969) alluded to this limitation of the Suppes theorem, but Kieras (1976) brought home the import of this limitation. He wrote:

Automata with a many–one output function must not be regarded as bizarre or pathological; indeed, they are more representative of ordinary behaving systems, both animals and machines, than S-machines (a Suppes FSM). For example, the ordinary computer can have many billions of states, yet its output at any point in time can be one of only a few symbols. In a psychological context, a subject in a Sternberg experiment makes only a binary response, but his internal

---

[4]Of course, it could be argued that the conditionings of the mimicking SSO are encoded genetically, but this would mean that stimulus-sampling theory would have to give up all pretense of explaining behavior.

state space is extremely complex, representing the stimulus list, the test item, and supporting a complicated memory scanning mechanism.

Suppes' proof establishes that an SSO can come to mimic an FSM with a state-response correspondence. However, one might wonder whether there was not some way in which an SSO could also come to mimic a more general FSM. Kieras (1976) has provided the requisite proof that SSOs cannot mimic the more general FSMs.

There might be a way for Suppes to get around this difficulty of a one-to-one correspondence between responses and states. He could propose that there were responses which were identical overtly, but which had covert differences. Thus, there might be a number of possible left turns. Each could correspond to a different state of an FSM. Provided there could be arbitrarily many versions of the same response, any FSM could be mimicked by an SSO. The problem is that, since the various versions of the response are not overtly distinguishable, there is no way to apply a reinforcement schedule to shape the desired behavior.

3.3   NEWELL'S PRODUCTION SYSTEM

The previous section illustrated some of the difficulties encountered by S–R theory in attempting to accommodate the complexity of human behavior. One purpose of this chapter is to show why production systems do not have those difficulties. Another purpose will be to describe the production system, PS, of Allen Newell. This was the source for the ACT production system, which, however, is considerably different from PS. Therefore, it will be very useful in understanding ACT to be able to make comparisons with PS.

Both PS and ACT are rather specialized notions of a very general idea proposed by Emile Post (1943). It is worthwhile considering the general Post concept before plunging into the details of Newell's PS. Post proposed a symbol manipulation system which both proved to be extremely powerful computationally and which has served as the basis for some recent ideas about psychological models of procedural knowledge. These are called *production systems*. Production systems as originally proposed by Post consisted of a set of rules, called productions, for rewriting strings of symbols and a specification of some initial strings, called axioms. So, for instance, consider the following simple production system:

Axioms a, b, aa, bb

Productions   (P1) $\$ \rightarrow a \$ a$

(P2) $\$ \rightarrow b \$ b$

This is a system for writing palindromes, strings that read the same forward and backward. The axioms consist of the shortest palindromes and the two productions allow these initial strings to be written into longer ones. The symbol "$" is a variable that may match an arbitrary string. So by taking a as the initial string and applying Productions (P1), (P2), and then (P1) we obtain $a \rightarrow aaa \rightarrow baaab \rightarrow abaaaba$.

As another example consider the production system which will generate parenthensized arithmetic expressions involving the variables $a, b,$ and c:

Axiom (   )

Productions	(P3)	$\$_1$ ( ) $\$_2$ $\rightarrow$ $\$_1$ (( ) + ( )) $\$_2$
	(P4)	$\$_1$ ( ) $\$_2$ $\rightarrow$ $\$_1$ (( ) $-$ ( )) $\$_2$
	(P5)	$\$_1$ ( ) $\$_2$ $\rightarrow$ $\$_1$ (( ) $\div$ ( )) $\$_2$
	(P6)	$\$_1$ ( ) $\$_2$ $\rightarrow$ $\$_1$ (( ) $\times$ ( )) $\$_2$
	(P7)	$\$_1$ ( ) $\$_2$ $\rightarrow$ $\$_1$ a $\$_2$
	(P8)	$\$_1$ ( ) $\$_2$ $\rightarrow$ $\$_1$ b $\$_2$
	(P9)	$\$_1$ ( ) $\$_2$ $\rightarrow$ $\$_1$ c $\$_2$

The following gives the derivation of $((a + b) \div a)$:

Axiom (   )

Production (P5)   ((   ) $\div$ (   ))

Production (P3)   (((   ) + (   )) $\div$ (   ))

Production (P7)   ((a + (   )) $\div$ (   ))

Production (P8)   ((a + b) $\div$ (   ))

Production (P9)   ((a + b) $\div$ a)

Such production systems can be shown to be equivalent to Turing Machines in their power (for example, Minsky, 1967). There is a loose sense in which one can regard these production systems as models for psychological processes. Note that the production rules consist of rewrite rules of the form $\alpha \rightarrow \beta$, where α specifies certain structural features about the string and β specifies a change in the string. Rather than specifications about strings, one can think of these as specifications about "states of mind." A production rule, $\alpha \rightarrow \beta$, could then be interpreted as specifying that whenever the mind is in state α it should be followed by state β. Thus, a production system might be used as a means for specifying what states of mind follow each other.

Of course, the two examples above do not really illustrate this possibility. That is, we cannot really think of palindromes or arithmetic expressions as states of mind. In fact, it is quite unintuitive to think of a state of mind as being represented by a string of symbols. Also the systems above are entirely internally driven, whereas a psychological system must have the capacity to respond to incoming stimuli. Fortunately, one can adapt production systems to remedy these initial obstacles to their use as psychological models. This is what Newell (1973) has done and what has been done in the ACT system. There have been a good number of recent attempts to use production systems as psychological models of procedural knowledge (Baylor & Gascon, 1974; Hunt & Poltrock, 1974; Klahr, 1973; Moran, 1973; Newell, 1972, 1973; Newell & Simon, 1972; Waterman, 1974, 1975; Young 1973). The ACT system involves another attempt. This section will focus on Newell's PS. Published descriptions of PS (Newell, 1972, 1973) are filled with many technical details that seem to obscure the essence of the system. Therefore, the PS system described in this section has undergone considerable notational simplification over the Newell descriptions. Hopefully, these simplifications have not lost any essential aspects of the PS system.

A Simple Example

The best way to learn about PS is to watch it perform a simple task such as the Sternberg (1969) memory scanning task. This example introduces many of the major features of PS except its use of "chunks." By examining the weaknesses of this incomplete system we will be in a better position to appreciate why the chunking assumptions are critical to the successful performance of PS.

PS consists of two parts—a long-term memory (LTM) and a short-term memory (STM). Short-term memory contains the string of symbols to which the productions apply. The contents of short-term memory are limited to a fixed number of symbols. In his examples Newell often assumes seven symbols to be the size of STM. This is a classic notion about the limitation of short-term memory which was popularized by Miller (1956). For instance, it has long been noted that we can immediately repeat back about seven digits but not many more. The long-term memory of PS consists of a set of productions, which transform the contents of short-term memory. Newell and Simon speculate whether long-term memory need contain anything other than productions. This section contains a demonstration that a PS can achieve the logical power of a Turing Machine with no long-term memory other than productions.

An example of a production system is given at the top of Table 3.2. This is a very simple system that will suffice to produce successful performance in the Sternberg (1969) task. One should think of these productions as being mixed in with many more that would be needed to generate the full variety of human performance. Table 3.2 is divided into two sections. At the top is a list of five productions that are required to produce the performance. Below is a history of the transformation of the contents of STM as these productions apply. Before

TABLE 3.2
An Example of a Newell Production System

Productions[a]

(PD0)	Response X $\$_1$	$\rightarrow$	Ready Response X $\$_1$
		$\Rightarrow$	Press X Button
(PD1)	Ready $\$_1$	$\rightarrow$	Ready $\$_1$
		$\Rightarrow$	Read positive set
(PD2)	n Probe $\$_1$ n $\$_2$	$\rightarrow$	Response Yes n Probe $\$_1$ n $\$_2$
(PD3)	n Probe $\$_1$	$\rightarrow$	Response No n Probe $\$_1$
(PD4)	$\$_1$	$\rightarrow$	Probe $\$_1$
		$\Rightarrow$	Read Probe digit

History of STM configurations

STM 1: Ready X1 X2 X3 X4 X5 X6

$\downarrow$ PD1

STM 2: 1 9 4 Ready X1 X2 X3

$\downarrow$ PD4

STM 3: 4 Probe 1 9 4 Ready X1

$\downarrow$ PD2

STM 4: Response Yes 4 Probe 1 9 4

$\downarrow$ PD0   Press Yes

STM 5: Ready Response Yes 4 Probe 1 9

$\downarrow$ PD1

STM 6: 6 2 8 1 4 Ready Response

$\downarrow$ PD4

STM 7: 5 Probe 6 2 8 1 4

$\downarrow$ PD3

STM 8: Response No 5 Probe 6 2 8

$\downarrow$ PD0   Press No

STM 9: Ready Response No 5 Probe 6 2

[a]Note: A single arrow, $\rightarrow$, specifies a change in STM while a double arrow, $\Rightarrow$, specifies an external action.

explaining the productions or their effect on STM, it would be useful to explain some of the terms that occur in the productions:

Response ⎫
Ready   ⎬ These are control elements that serve to key the system into what production should be evoked at a certain point in time.
Probe   ⎭

X   a variable that will match any element in STM.

n a variable that will match any digit in STM.

$\$_1$, $\$_2$ variables that match arbitrary strings of elements in STM.

Consider the five production rules on the top of Table 3.2. Each consists of a condition (left-hand part) and an action (right-hand part). The conditions specify certain properties that must be true of STM for that production to apply. As an example consider the condition of Production (PD0). The first symbol is Response, a control element. The next symbol, X, is a variable which refers to the next symbol in STM. The variable $\$_1$ matches the remainder of STM. Since X and $\$_1$ match anything, the only real requirement in STM is that its first symbol be Response.

The right-hand part of a production, its action, specifies what should take place should the condition be satisfied by the contents of STM. The rule (PD0) has two actions (as do Productions (PD1) and (PD4)). That pointed to by the single arrow, →, specifies that change in STM. In (PD0) the element *Ready* is inserted before other elements. The action pointed to by the double arrow, ⇒, specifies an action to be taken. In this case button X is pressed. The single arrow actions correspond to the transformations in Post production systems. The double arrow actions provide a means for allowing the mental state (that is, the contents of short-term memory) to affect behavior. External events can also influence the contents of STM by causing elements to be inserted into STM. We will see how this can happen in the Sternberg example.

The bottom portion of Table 3.2 demonstrates the production system in action. The line prefixed STM 1 gives the initial contents of STM. The productions are examined for the first one which matches the contents of the STM 1. PD0 does not match because the first element of STM is not Response. The condition of PD1, on the other hand, is matched. Therefore, it is selected. In matching PD1 to STM 1, the variable $\$_1$ is set to be equal to the string, "X1   X2   X3   X4   X5   X6." No change is made directly to the contents of STM (the single arrow part of the action). However, PD1 (the double arrow part) causes the positive set to be read into STM from some external display. Thus, the next state, STM 2, is changed from STM 1 by the insertion of these elements.

The rule (PD4) is the only one which matches STM 2, and therefore is selected. Production (PD4), consisting only of $\$_1$, will always match the contents of STM. It inserts the control element PROBE into STM and causes the probe digit to be read. This results in STM 3. The conditions of three rules, (PD2), (PD3), and (PD4), now match the contents of STM 3. However, (PD2) is selected because it is first in the ordering. In matching (PD2), n is a variable which matches any digit. It is matched to "4," $\$_1$ is matched to "1   9" and $\$_2$ to "READY X1." The action of (PD2) causes "RESPONSE YES" to be inserted into STM. The resulting short-term memory configuration is given in STM 4. Production (PD0) now applies to STM 4 and it causes the Yes button to be pressed. The reader may follow the course of the system in Table 3.2 from STM 5 to STM 9 to see how a negative response is generated.

No one would claim that the system in Table 3.2 is a psychologically adequate model for the Sternberg task. It is only intended to illustrate how a PS system works. There are some important features that should be noticed in this example regarding PS systems:

1. There are variables like n which can be matched to elements in a restricted class. Implicitly the production system is being given the machinery to perform class recognition.

2. There are rules like (PD1) and (PD4) which can cause the contents of STM to be transformed by means of external injection of elements.

3. The successful functioning of the system depends on the ordering of the productions. For instance, if (PD3) were allowed to apply before (PD2), the system would respond No to all probes.

4. The contents of STM stays constant at seven. New elements enter from the left and cause old elements to be ejected from the right. Often in Newell's system elements matched in a production will be brought forward to prevent their being lost.

5. Elements tend to be kept in STM after they have outlived their usefulness. (PD2) could have been formulated as n Probe $\$_1$ n $\$_2$ → Response Yes $\$_1$ n $\$_2$, in which the probe digit and its control element are deleted. However, Newell seems to be operating on the assumption that elements cannot be simply deleted from STM. They must be pushed out by interfering elements.

6. Note how elements like Probe, Response, and Ready are inserted by one production to guarantee that the next production selected is the correct one. These are *control elements* and play an important role in directing information processing.

7. Newell claims that PS has the possibility of modeling some elements of human distractability. If a random element erroneously enters STM from the environment the whole line of processing can be thrown off.

In Table 3.2 the order of elements in STM is critical, as it is in the original Post production systems. That is, elements must be in a specified order for a production to apply. In the PS Newell (1973) describes, however, this is not the case. Productions in that system do not specify the order of the elements in STM for a match. I have chosen not to include this order-free property in the examples because of the expository complications that it causes. Apparently in the current version of the PS system running at Carnegie-Mellon (Newell & McDermott, 1974) it is an option for the user to specify whether order of elements in the condition is important or not.

Reaction Time Hypothesis

The Sternberg paradigm naturally suggests reaction time predictions. Newell proposes that it should take a constant amount of time to apply each production and this time should be independent of (a) the number of productions in the system; (b) the contents of STM; and (c) the complexity of the condition of the production. Assumption (a) is particularly important. As Newell (1973) writes:

> . . . In writing a production system we only put down a few of the conditions to which the subject is presumably sensitive and could respond to if the situation (i.e., the contents of STM) warranted: a wasp lighting on the apparatus, the smell of smoke, an irrelevant remark in the background, turning off the lights and so on, any of which would surely evoke a noticing operation and subsequent alteration of the contents of STM. While reaction to such conditions might be somewhat longer, in no way could the subject be imagined to iterate through all such possible conditions taking an increment of time per possibility [p. 479].

Newell proposed that reaction time is independent of the number of productions because the productions are accessed in unlimited-capacity parallel manner. It is hard to imagine a mechanism that would serially order productions but at the same time access them in parallel in a time independent of number. However, despite this difficulty, Newell's hypothesis can be unambiguously used to derive predictions about reaction time. The production system in Table 3.2 predicts that reaction time should be independent of positive set size since the same number of productions applies for all set sizes. This prediction is known to be false. The second production system we examine later will predict the true effect of positive set size.

PS as Equivalent to Finite-State Machines

The PS as we have developed it so far is a seriously limited version of what Newell has in mind. The important thing to note about PS is that the next production it chooses is entirely determined by the current state of STM. The next state of STM is determined by the current content of STM, by the production that is applied, and by any input from the environment. Realizing these two facts it is but a short step to show that PS models, as developed so far, are equivalent to finite state machines (FSMs). Below I provide technical expositions of how to get an FSM to mimic an arbitrary PS and vice versa. The fact that there is this equivalence between PS models, as developed so far, and FSMs is not in itself damning. After all, the most powerful computer is just an FSM. The difficulty is that a distinct STM configuration is required for each state of a reduced state FSM.[5] With seven slots in which m distinct symbols may occur there are m^7 STM configurations. This means that the minimum number of symbols to mimic an n state reduced FSM is $\sqrt[7]{n}$. A very large number of states is required to mimic human cognitive functioning. In Section 3.2 I showed that a minimum of 10^{20} states was required to mimic a relatively simple human performance—to recognize mirror image string of words. One can increase the number of states by considering another task. Presumably, a subject could, with enough training, learn a serial list of 100 words. Suppose that man has a 10,000-word vocabulary, to be conservative. That means there are approximately 10^{400} possible 100-word strings. Since a subject could learn any of these strings he is capable of entering at least 10^{400} possible states. That is, having learned any such string constitutes a different state since the subject would display a different pattern of answers to questions about the string. This means given the production system developed so far, $\sqrt[7]{10^{400}}$ (which is greater than 10^{50}) different symbols would have to exist. We will shortly see how chunking deals with this problem of numbers of symbols.

Building an FSM to Mimic a PS*

As defined in the previous section an FSM consists of $\mathcal{K}$, a set of states; $\mathcal{I}$, a set of input elements; $\mathcal{R}$, a set of responses; and $\mathcal{T}$, a set of transitions. To prove that one can build FSMs to mimic PS systems one must how how to identify objects in a PS with these four sets that define an FSM:

1. Create a distinct state in $\mathcal{K}$ for each possible configuration of STM. If STM has 7 slots and m symbols may fill each slot, then there are m^7 possible configurations and hence m^7 possible states.

2. Create a new element in $\mathcal{I}$ for each distinct input that might enter STM. If only one element can enter STM at a time, $\mathcal{I}$ is simply to be identified with the symbols that can enter STM. If multiple symbols may enter STM at once, then the elements of $\mathcal{I}$ will be all ordered strings up to length 7.

3. The elements of $\mathcal{R}$ are the behavioral responses associated with the production rules (double arrows).

4. The transitions of $\mathcal{T}$ specify that if the FSM is in a state k_1 and an input i comes in, the machine will transit to state k_2 and emit response r. Such a transition may be represented by a 4-tuple $\langle k_1, i, k_2, r \rangle$. This transition will be added to $\mathcal{T}$ iff the following holds: when the contents of STM are the configuration corresponding to k_1 and the input corresponds to i, STM is changed to have contents corresponding to k_2 and response r is emitted.

The proof that the FSM constructed as above will mimic the PS is trivial.

[5] A reduced FSM is one with no redundant states.

Building a PS to Mimic an FSM*

The PS will be given a distinct symbol for each state and input of the FSM. If $\langle k_1, i, k_2, r \rangle$ is a member of $\mathcal{T}$, create the following production:

$$i \, k_1 \, \$ \rightarrow k_2 \, i \, k_1 \, \$$$

$$\Rightarrow r$$

Thus, the first one or two slots in STM will keep track of the information about current state and input. At the beginning of a cycle STM will contain a sequence of the form "$k_1 \ldots$" No production will apply since they all require the first element to be an input symbol. When input i comes in it will be inserted at the front transforming STM to "$i \, k_1 \ldots$" Then the above production will apply transforming STM to "$k_2 \, i \, k_1 \ldots$" and emitting response r. Then the PS will remain dormant until the next input. It is trivial to prove that a PS, so constructed, will mimic the FSM.

Production System with Chunking

We saw that the earlier production system was equivalent to an FSM and, further, that an enormous number of distinct symbols is required to successfully mimic human performances. As a consequence of the number of distinct symbols required that version of PS loses all credibility as a psychological model. However, one way to avoid this difficulty is to enable more than one symbol to occupy a slot in STM. That is, one can have a concatenation of symbols in one slot. With relatively few distinct primitive symbols it is possible to create a large number of concatenations. This is what Newell accomplishes with the use of chunks. Thus, in addition to whatever motivation the notion of chunks might have in understanding particular empirical phenomena, they have the important general purpose of removing from PS the impossible restrictions of directing behavior on the basis of information contained in a seven-symbol short-term memory.

The notion of a chunk was first introduced by Miller in 1956 to explain how subjects seemed to free themselves of limitations in an information-theoretic sense. Since then it has become a venerable part of cognitive psychology's explanatory hardware. Chunks are learned configurations of symbols which come to act as a single symbol. As a consequence it is reasonable for Newell to propose that they occupy only one position in STM. So, for instance, while we can hold only seven random letters in STM we can hold seven 10-letter words.

Table 3.3 provides an example of a production system working in the Sternberg task with chunks. The chunks are represented by strings of symbols contained in balanced parentheses. The list of elements in the positive set is encoded as a nesting of chunks. For instance, a five-element positive set would have the form (set 1 (set 6 (set 2 (set 5   3)))). This is one chunk consisting of the elements, set, 1, and the subchunk (set 6 (set 2 (set 5   3))).

TABLE 3.3
A Production System That Unpacks Chunks

Productions

(PD0)	(Response X) $\$_1$	$\rightarrow$	Ready (Old(Response X))
		$\Rightarrow$	Output X
(PD1)	Ready $\$_1$	$\rightarrow$	Ready $\$_1$
		$\Rightarrow$	Read Positive Set
(PD2)	(Probe n) $\$_2$ (Set $\$_3$ $\$_4$)$\$_5$	$\rightarrow$	(Probe n) $\$_2$ $\$_3$ $\$_4$ (Old (Set $\$_3$ $\$_4$)) $\$_5$
(PD3)	(Probe n) $\$_1$ n $\$_2$	$\rightarrow$	(Response Yes) (Old(Probe n)) $\$_1$ n $\$_2$
(PD4)	(Probe n) $\$_1$	$\rightarrow$	(Response No) (Old (Probe n)) $\$_1$
(PD5)	$\$_1$	$\rightarrow$	$\$_1$
		$\Rightarrow$	Read Probe Digit

History of STM configurations

STM 1:   Ready X1   X2   X3   X4   X5   X6

$\downarrow$ (PD1)

STM 2:   (Set 1 (Set 9   4))   Ready   X1   X2   X3   X4   X5

$\downarrow$ (PD5)

STM 3:   (Probe 4) (Set 1 (Set 9   4)) Ready   X1   X2   X3   X4

$\downarrow$ (PD2)

STM 4:   (Probe 4) 1   (Set 9   4) (Old (Set 1 (Set 9   4))) Ready   X1   X2

$\downarrow$ (PD2)

STM 5:   (Probe 4) 1   9   4(Old (Set 9   4)) (Old (Set 1 (Set 9   4))) Ready

$\downarrow$ (PD3)

STM 6:   (Response Yes) (Old (Probe 4)) 1   9   4 (Old (Set 9   4)) (Old (Set 1 (Set 9   4))

$\downarrow$ (PD0)

STM 7:   Ready (Old (Response Yes)) (Old (Probe 4)) 1   9   4 (Old (Set 9   4))

Let us follow the short-term memory configurations from STM 1 in Table 3.3. The first rule to apply is (PD1) which causes the positive set to be read in as a single chunk. Next (PD5) applies, which causes the probe digit to be read in. Rules (PD3) and (PD4), which detect a match or mismatch, require the chunked positive set to be broken down into its component digits. Therefore, rule (PD2) is applied twice to unpack the two levels of the positive set chunk. This leaves short-term memory in the configuration depicted in STM 5. Then the production rules apply as they did in Table 3.2 to determine a response. Note that the memory sets are tagged with the prefix OLD after being unpacked. Such prefixing can be used to prevent control elements from continuing to dominate the selection of productions. Thus, (PD2) does not apply over again to the same chunk to cause it to be unpacked a second time.[6]

Note that the production system in Table 3.3 predicts that processing time should increase with positive set size. With each additional element added to the positive set another level of embedding is required in the memory chunk which encodes the positive set. Therefore, an additional application of (PD2) will be required to unpack the set. This system also predicts that reaction time should be the same function of the positive set whether the probe element is or is not in the memory set. These predictions about the Sternberg task are known to be generally true. The production system in Table 3.3 is close to the final one offered by Newell (1973) for the Sternberg task.

The reader may be puzzled about why it is necessary to take in the memory set as a chunk and then unpack it. Could not the memory set initially be read in as three digits? Newell argues that STM is an unreliable storage medium and that elements would tend to be lost from it. This would happen because interfering elements would enter into STM, pushing out elements in the memory set. Packaged into a single chunk the information only occupies a single slot and can be kept near the front of STM.

Chunks serve as one variety of long-term memory. Putting elements into a chunk amounts basically to interassociating them. There is something very peculiar about Newell's use of chunks, however. He is conveying upon the subject the power to pack an arbitrary string of digits into a chunk. This runs counter to the current interpretation of a chunk as a familiar configuration of elements. This indicates something fundamentally wrong with the conception of long-term memory which is embedded in PS. This is a point to which I return later. Another difficulty with Newell's unrestricted use of chunks is that it makes a farce out of the limited capacity notion of short-term memory. Since arbitrarily long chunks can reside in short-term memory and since productions can act on any part of a chunk, Newell might as well allow arbitrarily many slots in STM. That is, in his use of chunks Newell seems to be abandoning one of the fundamental facts about human memory—that we have immediate access to only a few elements at a time.

However, Newell could have proposed very severe restrictions on the access to the contents of chunks and still achieved a very powerful system. For instance, one might argue that a PS should only be able to check the identity of the first element in a chunk. That is, a condition of a production might only be able to specify tests like $(3\ \$_1)$, where a test can be made whether the first symbol is 3 but where the identity of the remainder of the chunk cannot be tested. It can only be bound to

---

[6]Note that the use of an OLD tag would be unnecessary if elements could simply be deleted from STM. However, the only way to eject elements from STM is to have them pushed out by other elements. Some mechanism such as OLD tagging is required if the contents of STM control behavior but it is not possible to simply delete elements from STM. In ACT, I will deal with this by making flow of control dependent on variable bindings rather than the contents of STM.

$\$_1$. Conditions could not further specify the contents of chunks as they might with patterns like $(3 \ \$_1 \ 2)$ or $(3 \ (2 \ \$_1))$, etc. It will be shown in the following technical section that PS, even with this very restricted access to the contents of chunks, can be made to mimic an arbitrary Turing Machine (TM). It follows then that less restricted versions of PS also have this feature of achieving maximum computational power. After this technical section I will turn to the question of the consequences of this result for PS's status as a viable psychological model.

Mimicry of a TM by a PS with Chunks*

A TM consists of a finite-state control structure plus an infinite tape memory (Minsky, 1967). It has already shown how an FSM can be mimicked by a PS. A similar device will be used in this instance to simulate the finite state control of a TM. The chunk feature will be used to obtain the power of the TM's infinite tape. Figure 3.2 illustrates the basic cycle of any TM which the PS must mimic. A TM starts in a state S1 looking at some symbol E2 on a tape. The TM transition function $\mathcal{T}$, specifies a change in the symbol, a change in state, and a move either to the left (L) or right (R). Examples of left and right transitions are given by branches

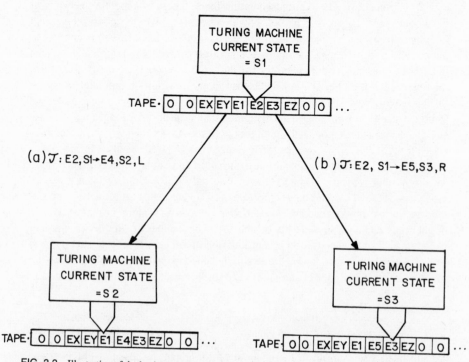

FIG. 3.2   Illustration of the basic move of a Turing Machine. The transition in (a) represents a Turing Machine which moves left when in state S1 and faced with symbol E1. The transition in (b) represents a different machine which moves right.

(a) and (b). To be able to mimic this TM, the PS needs to encode the starting configuration of the TM. That is, it must encode in STM all the nonzero symbols on the tape, the position of the TM, and its state. The nonzero symbols to the left of the TM will be encoded as one chunk. This will be the first element in STM; the second element will be the state of the TM; the third, the element currently scanned; and the fourth, a chunk to encode the nonzero elements to the right of the scan point. Thus, the starting configuration in Fig. 3.2 would be encoded as (E1 EY EX) S1 E2 (E3 EZ). Note only four STM elements are needed. Note also that the elements in the left chunk are encoded backward so that the element furthest to the right will be most accessible. The transitions of the TM will be represented by productions. The production for a left move (Branch a) would be written as

(a) $(X \, \$_1) \, S1 \, E2 \, (\$_2) \rightarrow (\$_1) \, S2 \, X \, (E4 \, \$_2)$.

The production for a right move (Branch b) would be written as:

(b) $(\$_1) \, S1 \, E2 \, (X \, \$_2) \rightarrow (E5 \, \$_1) \, S3 \, X \, (\$_2)$.

Note that (a) simulates the move to the left by taking X (X is a variable which matches any element) out of the left chunk and making it the focal element. Simultaneously it takes E4 (which is written in place of E2) and puts it in the right chunk. A move to the right is accomplished by production (b) in a similar manner. Note that these productions only operate on the element furthest to the left in a chunk. Thus, STM is limited in access to seven elements at a time.

So, to translate a TM into a PS one production is introduced for each transition of the TM. A final technical production is required: The right and left chunks contain all (but only) the nonzero portions of the tape. They cannot contain all the left and right portions because chunks, while arbitrarily long, are finite. The right and left halves of the tape are infinite but have only finite nonzero portions. It is therefore possible that the TM might read to the end of the finite nonzero portion. Then the left or right chunk in the mimicking PS would be of the form ( ) with no elements. It is necessary to insert another zero on the tape so rules like (a) or (b) can apply. Therefore, the following production rule is needed:

(c) $\$_1 \, (\;) \, \$_2 \rightarrow \$_1 \, (0) \, \$_2$.

Consequences of Equivalence between a TM and a PS

It has just been shown that a PS could be made to mimic an arbitrary TM. Can a human do this? Note that the PS was performing this mimicry "in its head" without the use of external memory. One can try to get a human to mimic a TM in his head. This requires that he commit the transition rules of the machine to memory, which is equivalent to acquiring the production rules of the mimicking PS. The person must also commit to memory the finite nonzero portion of the TM tape. Using myself as a subject with simple TM (for example, the one in Fig. 3.3) I can report that all this is possible. However, I inevitably falter as I try to simulate the movement of the TM over the tape. That is, eventually I lose track of my position on the tape, the contents of the tape, or both.

This strange mental exercise serves as a clear refutation of the psychological validity of any PS which can be shown to perfectly mimic a TM. As noted, most versions of a PS with chunking will have this difficulty. To accommodate this problem Newell would have to propose a model to explain why errors in memory can occur for chunk contents. In other words, a fundamental problem with the current PS models is that they offer no account of loss from long-term memory. A PS system augmented with the feature of a forgetful memory would pass the empirical test at hand. Such a PS would predict that a human could simulate an arbitrary TM, but with errors. From self-observation I am led to the conclusion that this prediction is correct.[7]

Productions as the Storage Medium

In the production systems we have been examining there are two types of long-term memory. The first is provided by the productions themselves and the second is the internal structure of the chunk. Newell (1973) admits that there might be other kinds of long-term memory, but manages adequately with these. An intriguing question is whether chunks are really necessary. Would it be possible for productions to serve as the sole long-term memory storage medium. In the technical section to follow I will show how a TM could be mimicked by a production system using productions as its sole storage medium.[8] This result is relevant to the issue of whether knowledge should be encoded in declarative or procedural form—discussed at the beginning of this chapter (page 78). It shows that we do not need a declarative format to achieve maximum logical power. The question remains open, however, whether the best psychological model can be achieved by these means.

Mimicry of a TM by a PS Using Production for Storage*[9]

Rather than stating the general principles for creating a PS to mimic a TM, an illustration will be given of how a simple TM can be mimicked by a PS. This will

[7]Note that one of Newell's motivations for introducing chunks in the Sternberg task was to make STM more reliable. However, as this example shows, chunks should not be made too reliable a storage medium.

[8]Newell and Simon (1972) have written: "Possibly there is no LTM for facts distinct from the production system—that is, no basic distinction between data and program; rather LTM is just a very large production system. If this were the case, the act of taking a new item into LTM would be equivalent to creating a new production (or productions) [p. 805]." Thus, it is not clear that they are aware that their use of chunks provides another long-term storage medium.

[9]The production system developed in this section contains productions which create other productions. This rather elegant idea has been used by Waterman (1974) in his work on production induction.

STATE DIAGRAM

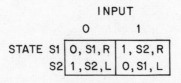

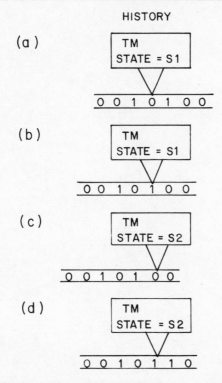

FIG. 3.3   An illustration of three moves of a simple Turing Machine.

illustrate the principles for creating a mimicking PS in a somewhat more concrete and comprehensible way. Figure 3.3 presents the simple TM that must be mimicked. The table in Fig. 3.3 gives the state diagram of a TM and illustrates in Parts (a)–(d) three moves by the TM and the resulting changes in configuration. The state diagram gives for each input-state pair the symbol to be written on the tape, the next state, and the direction of the move (L or R).

Table 3.4 shows a PS that will mimic this TM and illustrates its simulation of the three TM moves. The first line under STM shows the STM configuration which corresponds to the TM configuration in Fig. 3.3a. G1 is a single element

TABLE 3.4
A PS to Simulate the Turing Machine in Fig. 3.3

Original productions

(PD1)	G1 L $_1$	→	L I A $_1$
(PD2)	$_1$ R G2	→	$_1$ A I R
(PD3)	L L $_1$	→	L 0 A $_1$
(PD4)	$_1$ R R	→	$_1$ A 0 R
(PD5)	$_1$ U A X Y Z	→	$_1$ X U @
		add '$_1$ R @	→ $_1$ A Y Z'
(PD6)	U X Y A Z $_1$	→	@ X Z $_1$
		add '@ L $_1$	→ U Y A $_1$'
(PD7)	$_1$ S1 0 $_2$	→	$_1$ S1 0 R $_2$
(PD8)	$_1$ S1 1 $_2$	→	$_1$ S2 1 R $_2$
(PD9)	$_1$ S2 0 $_2$	→	$_1$ L S2 1 $_2$
(PD10)	$_1$ S2 1 $_2$	→	$_1$ L S1 0 $_2$

Added productions

(PD11)	G3 L $_1$	→	G1 0 A $_1$
(PD12)	G4 L $_1$	→	G3 1 A $_1$
(PD13)	$_1$ R G5	→	$_1$ A I R

History of STM configurations

(a)
G1 S1 0 G2
→ (PD7)
G1 S1 0 R G2
→ (PD2)
G1 S1 0 A I R
→ (PD6)

(b)
G3 S1 1 R
→ (PD8)
G3 S2 1 R R
→ (PD4)
G3 S2 1 A 0 R
→ (PD6)

(c)
G4 S2 0 R
→ (PD9)
G4 L S2 1 R
→ (PD12)
G3 1 A S2 1 R
↓(PD5)

(d)
G3 S2 1 G5

104

which can be unpacked into the nonzero portion of the tape to the left of the TM, S1 is the current state of the TM, 0 is the current symbol scanned, and G2 can be unpacked into the nonzero tape to the right of the TM. In this example there is just one nonzero element to the left and right of the tape. Therefore, both G1 and G2 will unpack in (1).

The right half of Table 3.4 gives the productions. (PD1)–(PD10) are the productions with which the system starts out. (PD11)–(PD13) are later added to encode changes in the tape and the position of the TM. (PD7)–(PD10) simply encode the state diagram of the TM. A similar set of productions could be used to encode the state diagram of any TM. Rules (PD1) and (PD2) are used to unpack the symbols G1 and G2. These two productions define the contents on the nonzero portions of the tape to the right and the left of the TM. A similar set of productions could be used to encode any TM tape. Rules (PD3) and (PD4) are added to handle the case when the machine runs off the finite nonzero portion of the tape, either to the left or to the right. Rules (PD5) and (PD6) cause new productions to be created to encode tape changes. Rules (PD3)–(PD6) would be part of the simulation of any TM.

Let us follow the three productions in Table 3.4 that simulate the move from (a) to (b) in Fig. 3.3. In state S1 and with symbol 0, (PD7) is selected. Production (PD7) encodes the fact that when the TM is in state S1 and reads 0, it stays in state S1, leaves the 0 unchanged, and moves to the right. This means that the next symbol to be read is the next element in the right portion of the tape, and the current symbol is added to the left portion. Rule (PD2) is evoked to unpack "R G2" into "A 1 R." The symbol A is put into STM to trigger the packing of 0 with G1. Rule (PD6) is the first rule which now matches the STM configuration. Its antecedent matches that STM configuration with the following assignment of variables: $U = G1$, $X = S1$, $Y = 0$, $Z = 1$, and $\$_1 = R$. Production (PD6) creates a new production rule (PD11): "G3 L $\$_1$ → G1 0 A $\$_1$." This rule uses a *new* symbol G3 which is put in the left slot of the STM configuration in place of G1. The rule (PD11) will allow the PS to unpack G3 into G1 and 0. In this way it can retrieve the 0 added to the left portion of the tape. Note that (PD5) and (PD6) use the symbol @ to stand for the creation of a new symbol.

The STM configuration in (b) represents the situation after rule (PD6) has operated. The three production rules leading from STM (b) to STM (c) simulate the move to the right of the TM in Fig. 3.3 from (b) to (c). The reader is invited to examine these productions in detail for himself. They serve to create another production rule (PD12) which packs a new element into the left portion of the tape. The symbol G4 now stands for the left portion of the tape.

In state S2 with symbol 0, rule (PD9) is selected to apply to STM (c). Production (PD9) introduces "L" into STM to signal a left move. Production (PD12) which has just been created is used to unpack the leftmost symbol of G4.[10] Production

---

[10]For this production system to properly work, the new productions (PD11)–(PD13) must be ordered before (PD7)–(PD10).

(PD5) is then evoked to create G5 for the new right-hand tape and to pack 1 onto that tape. Rule (PD13) is created to unpack G5. The STM configuration (d) encodes the TM configuration (d).

3.4   CONCLUSIONS ABOUT PRODUCTION SYSTEMS

Flexibility of PS Systems

It has been shown that a PS system could be produced that would generate any input–output relations (that is, any behavior) definable by a TM. It is not clear whether PS systems can be made to predict any time relation in behavior, but they do have considerable flexibility in predicting time relations. For instance, we have seen two production systems for the Sternberg task. The first did not predict an increase in reaction time with positive set, while the second did. Other models could be produced which predicted other time relations. Thus, it seems that PS systems are too flexible because some PS system could be proposed to account for almost any behavior, human or nonhuman, and because there is no way of specifying beforehand the correct PS. Thus, the PS model does not seem to be falsifiable.

One could regard PS as a medium like stochastic models for constructing theories without any empirical commitments. If so, then their flexibility would be a virtue. However, it seems that Newell has greater aspirations for his PS than just providing a medium for psychological modeling. Therefore, it is necessary to specify some principles for predicting ahead of time what the productions will be for a paradigm. Newell (1973) proposes to select the PS for a particular task according to the *principle of adaptation*. As he states this principle: "Other things equal, the subject will adopt that production system that more closely obtains his goals [p. 494]." He argues that subjects will tend to select the system that operates most rapidly and in the most error-free manner. This was the motivation for the PS in Table 3.3, that uses chunks to encode the positive set, over the PS in Table 3.2, that does not. Newell argued that STM is unreliable and there is less possibility of error if the positive set is chunked. However, Newell needs a more explicit model of the performance characteristics of STM and other aspects of his production system model if he is going to use these features to decide the correct PS model.

This difficulty in selecting the correct production system is also a problem for ACT. In working with ACT I have tried to choose production systems that seemed optimal given the performance characteristics of ACT. Thus, I, too, have adopted a principle of adaptation. Unfortunately, like Newell, I have not progressed to the point where I can prove the optimality of the production system selected. The other tack I have followed in ACT is to try to develop a theory of how productions are acquired and organized. In the last chapter of this book I report on what progress I have made so far in that attempt.

Problems with PS

There are a number of difficulties associated with the PS system which account for my decision to develop a rather different production system. Some of these difficulties have the status of true weaknesses while others have more the status of theoretical taste. However, it seems worthwhile to list them all as a prelude to ACT.

STM. As discussed earlier, Newell had some difficulty in imposing the appropriate immediate memory limitations on his system. If he did not use chunks, there was not enough information in short-term memory to model human behavior. If he did allow chunks it was difficult to prevent an unlimited amount of information from being available. I think these difficulties are symptomatic of the problem in dealing with an n-slot model of STM. Rather, I will propose that STM can in part be conceived of as an active partition of an associative network.

Chunk structure. The structure of a chunk is basically that of a tree. However, it seems that to model human long-term memory one needs the more general graph structure of an associative network. Also it would seem to be useful to impose a propositional structure on that network. (See Chapters 4 and 5 for arguments on these points.) Newell and Waterman (personal communication) have suggested that one could model an associative network via a production system.

Performance limitations. The only performance limitations on PS involve the limited size of STM and the fact that only a single production can be applied in a unit of time. In terms of accounting for memory factors, the STM limitations do not seem sufficient. Subjects suffer errors of memory over longer periods than can be attributed to loss from STM. In terms of the time characteristics of human behavior, it also seems unlikely that the time for a response to occur can be understood solely in terms of the number of productions that must be executed. There is considerable evidence (see Chapters 8 and 9) that the time for productions to apply is critically affected by the speed at which information can be activated in long-term memory. One of the goals of ACT is to model the nonreliability of memory and the speed with which information can be retrieved from memory.

Parallelism. The Newell system is an interesting mixture of parallelism and seriality. While all the available productions can be tested against STM in an unlimited capacity parallel manner, only one production can be executed in any unit of time. This seriality is particularly inconvenient in a task domain like language processing in which it seems desirable to pursue many levels of analysis at once. Therefore, ACT has been given the capacity to apply multiple productions in parallel. Of course, there are some tasks (for example, inference making, see Chapter 9) that require a high degree of seriality. ACT can always fall back on a serial control structure as a degenerate case of its parallel control structure.

Readability. As the reader has no doubt discovered, it is very difficult to understand the productions that define a PS system for even a simple task—despite the fact that they underwent some notational simplification in my exposition. This contrasts unfavorably with other procedural formalisms such as flow charts and the augmented transition networks (ATNs) of Woods (1970), which are reasonably easy to follow. In part, this is an unavoidable consequence of the precision with which production systems specify the information processing. For instance, if one investigated the arc encoding of ATNs rather than the diagrammatic representations of the flow of control, one would find ATNs no more readable than PS encodings. A high priority in my development of ACT has been to convey to its production systems some of the readability associated with other formalisms. In the next chapter I provide a network representation of the flow of control in ACT's production systems that seems as readable as ATNs. In Chapter 6 I will also be concerned with developing a subroutine structure for productions which will permit one to replace a set of productions by a call to a subroutine. This will then convey upon ACT the possibility of representing macrooperations as in a flow chart. However, unlike the flow chart formalism these macrooperations are analyzable into the basic primitives of the system.

Production Systems as Computational Mediums

Newell's PS is only one particular production system of many that are currently in use. Besides the various psychological systems mentioned earlier (p. 91) there have been attempts to use production systems as programming formalisms in artificial intelligence applications (for example, Shortliffe & Buchanan, 1975; for a general review of uses of production systems see Davis & King, 1975). It is worth noting those features which seem true of all the available production systems and which seem to distinguish production systems as computational mediums. Unlike most programming languages there are no special facilities for storing control information—no separate program counter, pushdown stack, etc. All control information must be stored in the same data base (in PS this data base is STM) that serves to store the input and output of the computation. Intuitively, it strikes me as a reasonable psychological claim that humans do not have separate storage mechanisms for control information.

A number of features of production systems follow from this unity of control and data store. Because the control information is in the data store, in each cycle of the production system there must be a reevaluation of the consequences of the current knowledge state for the control of behavior. Production systems can thus react immediately to any changes in the knowledge state. Thus stimuli which come in and change the knowledge state (for example, add an element to STM) can have immediate effects on behavior. This gives production systems a quality I refer to as *data driven*. Because each production makes reference to a data base common to all productions and no production makes reference directly to other productions, production systems are highly *modular* models. That is, if a particular production is added, deleted, or changed, the basic performance of the system tends to remain relatively unaffected. The modularity of productions seems a desirable property for modeling human behavior.

Two other features that seem common to all uses of production systems are that there is a rather restricted format for expressing the productions and that each production has the status of a relatively primitive act. These features are desirable in practical applications because it becomes easy to extend a system without having to engage in extensive restructuring of the program. The psychological motivation for these features is that they facilitate the formulation of principles to predict behavior. That is, if the variations in the format of a production are few, then few principles need be articulated in describing the variation in performance of productions. The great variation in observed behavior can be explained in terms of a concatenation of these primitive units.

Advantage of Production Systems over Stimulus–Response Theory

Finally, I would like to turn to the question of why production systems constitute an advance over stimulus–response theory:

Pattern and structure.   Recall that one of the difficulties with stimulus-sampling theory is that it could not uniquely respond to a pattern of elements. Rather it had to postulate the existence of a pattern producer which delivered a pattern as a single element. In contrast, a condition of a production could specify that a particular configuration of elements be present. Thus, for instance, a production system could be built which would respond when a stimulus was *large and black* or *small and white,* but not otherwise.

In addition, a production need not regard the elements as coming from an unordered set, but rather can make reference to structural relations among elements. In the original Post production systems, the only structure is adjacency of elements in a string. In the PS system structure is provided by adjacency in STM as well as by chunk structure. In the ACT system it will be possible to refer to the structure of a relational network. Thus, it is easy to get a production system to respond to specific relations among elements but difficult to get a stimulus–response theory to do so. For instance, it would be difficult for a stimulus–response theory to respond differentially to a star above a plus versus a plus above a star without postulating a perceptual process that mapped each configuration onto a single different stimulus element. To do this would be to pass the explanatory burden once again on to the perceptual system.

Memory.   An S–R system has no memory for its past beyond memory for its last response. In contrast, production systems can have auxiliary storage mediums. In the original Post production system, the string being rewritten served as auxiliary memory. In the PS system, auxiliary memories were available in the form of short-term memory, chunk structure, and productions. In the ACT system, an associative network will serve as an auxiliary storage medium.

As we saw in the PS system, if there were no bounds on the size of memory, it would be possible to obtain computational power equivalent to a Turing Machine. This is true of many production system formalisms, including ACT. It is probably unreasonable to assume that there is no limit at all on the amount of memory we have. Assuming some (albeit astronomical) limit on memory, then production systems are equivalent to *very* large finite state machines. The problem with stimulus–response theories like stimulus-sampling theory is that they propose that the human has no more states than he has responses. Because of their auxiliary memory, production systems are capable of entering many more states than they have responses. So, even if a production system does not have unlimited memory it is still more powerful than stimulus–response theories.

Variables.   Production systems make extensive use of variables. For instance, it is possible to have a production rule like *If X is the probe and X is on the list, respond yes.* It is not necessary to have a separate rule for each object which the variable *X* can represent. This yields a great economy in the representation of knowledge. Recall that one of the traditional problems with S–R theory is that an enormous number of conditionings of specific links are required to produce many interesting behaviors. This is particularly a problem in the learning of language. An important aspect of our language comprehension abilities is that they extend to novel sentences beyond the sentences with which we were trained. As I will document in Chapter 12, this ability to generalize experience with the language can be nicely captured through the use of variables. It is also shown in Chapter 7 that use of variables greatly increases the ability of the ACT system to express complex quantificational relations.

SUMMARY OF CHAPTER 3

This chapter is concerned with reviewing two models for procedural knowledge— a stimulus–response (S–R) model and a production system. Production systems can be viewed as generalized and more powerful versions of S–R models. Both represent atomistic approaches to analysis of procedural knowledge and both view the organism as constantly responding to changes in its internal and external environment. They try to reduce all procedural knowledge to a few primitives and they contrast with "faculty" approaches to procedural knowledge which give separate analyses to the procedures underlying different cognitive behaviors.

In Section 3.2 I took stimulus-sampling theory as an explicit rigorous S–R model, and investigated Suppes' (1969a) attempt to show that stimulus-sampling models are equivalent to finite state machines. It is shown that stimulus-sampling models are in fact equivalent to only a limited subset of finite state machines. Even to achieve this limited equivalence it is necessary to place some of the computational burden outside of the stimulus-sampling model in a pattern formation process. Also the number of trials to condition a stimulus-sampling model to mimic certain human performances is astronomical.

In Section 3.3 I reviewed Newell's PS as a prototype of a production system. PS consists of a long-term memory of productions and a short-term memory of symbols to which the productions apply. Short-term memory consists of a limited number (for example, seven) of slots in which chunks may be placed. Long-term memory capacity is provided by the ability to use chunks and productions as storage mediums. It is shown that one of these two storage mediums—chunks or productions—is necessary to get a powerful enough system to mimic humans. With either long-term storage medium, PS can be shown capable of simulating an arbitrary TM without errors. This is a problem for PS because humans seem only capable of TM simulation, with errors.

A number of difficulties are noted with Newell's PS. He uses chunks to encode nonfamiliar configurations of elements—counter to current usage of chunks in cognitive psychology. PS seems too flexible and capable of explaining any behavior. There is not any effective limitation on the amount of information immediately available in STM. There are not adequate models of the performance limitations due to memory failure and processing time limitations. It is not possible to represent the processing of multiple options in parallel as seems necessary for language. Finally, PS models are very difficult to read and understand.

Certain features are noted which are generally true of production systems and which make them desirable as psychological models. There are a number of features which are unique to them: They have a single memory for both control information and general data. They are data driven and can respond immediately to changes in the environment. They are modular and relatively little affected by changes to the production set. They make use of a restricted format for expressing productions and each production has the status of a relatively primitive act. There are a number of features that put production systems at an advantage to stimulus–response models: They can take advantage of patterns and structure in the data base. They have auxiliary memories. Finally, by use of variables they can state knowledge in a more general format.

REFERENCES

Arbib, M. A. Memory limitations of stimulus–response models. *Psychological Review,* 1969, **76,** 507–510.

Anderson, J. R., & Bower, G. H. *Human associative memory,* Washington: Winston, 1973.

Baylor, G. W., & Gascon, J. An information processing theory of aspects of the development of weight seriation in children. *Cognitive Psychology,* 1974, **6,** 1–40.

Bever, T. G., Fodor, J. A., & Garrett, M. A formal limitation of associationism. In T. R. Dixon &

D. L. Horton (Eds.), *Verbal behavior and general behavior theory*. Englewood Cliffs, New Jersey: Prentice-Hall, 1968.

Chomsky, N. Verbal behavior (a review of Skinner's book). *Language,* 1959, **35**, 26–58.

Chomsky, N. *Aspects of the theory of syntax*. Cambridge, Massachusetts: MIT Press, 1965.

Davis, R., & King, J. An overview of production systems. Computer Science Department, Stanford University, 1975.

Estes, W. K. The statistical approach to learning theory. In S. Koch (Ed.), *Psychology: A study of a science*. Vol. 2. New York: McGraw-Hill, 1959.

Gill, A. Introduction to the theory of finite-state machines. New York: McGraw-Hill, 1962.

Hopcroft, J. E., & Ullman, J. D. *Formal languages and their relation to automata*. Reading, Mass.: Addison-Wesley, 1969.

Hull, C. L. *A behavior system: An introduction to behavior theory concerning the individual organism*. New Haven: Yale University Press, 1952.

Hunt, E. B., & Poltrock, S. E. The mechanics of thought. In B. H. Kantowitz (Ed.) *Human information processing: Tutorials in performance and cognition*. Hillsdale, New Jersey: Lawrence Erlbaum Assoc., 1974.

Katz, J. J., & Postal, P. N. *An integrated theory of linguistic descriptions*. Cambridge, Massachusetts: MIT Press, 1964.

Kieras, D. E. Finite automata and S–R models. *Journal of Mathematical Psychology,* 1976, **12**, in press.

Klahr, D. A production system for counting, subitizing, and adding. In W. G. Chase (Ed.) *Visual information processing*. New York: Academic Press, 1973.

Miller, G. A. The magical number seven, plus or minus two: Some limits on our capacity for processing information. *Psychological Review,* 1956, **63**, 81–97.

Miller, G. A., Galanter, E., & Pribram, K. H. *Plans and the structure of behavior*. New York: Holt, Rinehart, and Winston, 1960.

Minsky, M. L. *Computation: finite and infinite machines*. Englewood Cliffs, New Jersey: Prentice-Hall, 1967.

Moran, T. P. The symbolic imagery hypothesis: A production system model. Unpublished Ph.D. Dissertation, Carnegie-Mellon University, 1973.

Neimark, E. D., & Estes, W. K. *Stimulus sampling theory*. San Francisco: Holden Day, 1967.

Newell, A. A theoretical exploration of mechanisms for coding the stimulus. In A. W. Melton and E. Martin (Eds.), *Coding processes in human memory*. Washington, D.C.: Winston, 1972. Pp. 373–434.

Newell, A. Production systems: Models of control structures. In W. G. Chase (Ed.), *Visual information processing*. New York: Academic Press, 1973. Pp. 463–526.

Newell, A., & McDermott, J. PSG Manual System version PSG2, Carnegie-Mellon University, 1974.

Newell, A., & Simon, H. *Human problem solving*. Englewood Cliffs, New Jersey: Prentice-Hall, 1972.

Post, E. L. Formal reductions of the general combinatorial decision problem. *American Journal of Mathematics,* 1943, **65**, 197–268.

Rescorla, R. A., & Wagner, A. R. A theory of Pavlovian conditioning: Variations in the effectiveness of reinforcement and non-reinforcement. In A. H. Black and W. F. Prokasy (Eds.), *Classical conditioning II: Current research and theory*. New York: Appleton-Century-Crofts, 1972.

Shortliffe, T., & Buchanan, B. A model of inexact reasoning in medicine. *Mathematical Biosciences,* 1975, **23**, 351–374.

Sternberg, S. Memory-scanning: Mental processes revealed by reaction time experiments. *Acta Psychologica,* 1969, **30**, 276–315.

Suppes, P. Stimulus-response theory of finite automata. *Journal of Mathematical Psychology,* 1969, **6**, 327–355.   (a)

Suppes, P. Stimulus-response theory of automata and TOTE hierarchies: A reply to Arbib. *Psychological Review,* 1969, **76**, 511–514.   (b)

Waterman, D. A. Adaptive production systems, CIP working paper #285. Psychology Department, Carnegie-Mellon University, 1974.

Waterman, D. A. Serial pattern acquisition: A production system approach. CIP working paper #286, Psychology Department, Carnegie-Mellon University, 1975.

Woods, W. A. Transition network grammars for natural language analysis. *Communications of the ACM,* 1970, **13,** 591–606.

Young, R. M. Children's seriation behavior: A production-system analysis. Unpublished doctoral dissertation, Department of Psychology, Carnegie-Mellon University, 1973.

4
Overview of ACT

I never faced a problem which was more than the
eternal problem of finding order. I never attacked
a problem by constructing a Hypothesis. I never
deduced Theorems or submitted them to Experimental Check. So far as I can see, I had no preconceived model of behavior—certainly not a
physiological or mentalistic one and, I believe,
not a conceptual one.

B. F. SKINNER

4.1 PREDISPOSING BIASES

The shape of the ACT theory has been strongly influenced by preconceived
notions that I have about the nature of cognitive functioning. The purpose of this
initial section is to identify some of these predisposing biases and to try to motivate them. My reliance on preconceived biases in constructing ACT contrasts with
a more conservative methodology for theory construction in which one attempts
to construct a theory by means of simple generalization from data.[1] There are two
justifications for my approach over simple generalization. The first is that there is
reason to suspect that a procedure of simple generalization is not the optimal way
to develop a theory of broad generality. Simple generalization is just one procedure of many for inducing a scientific theory: it involves starting with no theory
and then developing the assumptions of the theory as the data come in. My
approach is to start with my best guess and modify that as data come in. It can
be shown (see Chapter 12) that no induction procedure is uniformly better than
any other; it is just that different procedures are better for inducing different
theories. Simple generalization would provide a better induction procedure only if
my preconceived biases were largely incorrect assumptions about the human. As
I do not think they are, it is obviously rational for me to start with a theory that

---

[1]This is basically the contrast between methodological rationalism and methodological empiricism
that was set up by Anderson & Bower (1973). As my theory construction is also very responsive to
data I think it might better be referred to as neoassociationism—a term Anderson and Bower introduced
for a mixture of those two methodologies.

conforms to these biases. In a Bayesian inductive scheme, this would essentially correspond to giving one's prior probabilities their appropriate weighting.

The second justification for using preconceived biases is that the correct cognitive theory is not unique and one has to have some means of selecting from among the equivalent theories. One might as well select a theory from the equivalence class that most closely corresponds to his ideas about cognitive functioning.

Before stating these biases I should emphasize some disclaimers: The biases are not precisely defined nor is it precisely known how they influence theory construction. However, their influence is undeniable. Also these biases do not completely specify the ACT theory. They basically provide the skeleton of the model which I have had to try to flesh out with assumptions that would enable ACT to fit the data. When ACT proves wrong on some score, it is the "fleshing-out" assumptions that are first to be sacrificed. Also, since these biases are about mental structures and processes, and since we are only considering behavioral data, it is not possible to establish that such assumptions are uniquely correct. There are undoubtedly other configurations of different assumptions identical in their predictions to these. However, it may well be that my basic assumptions cannot (without postulating a very complicated set of auxiliary assumptions) yield an adequate characterization of human behavior. That is, while they cannot be shown to be uniquely correct, they can be shown to be wrong.

The following are two very general biases that I have: First, cognition involves a good deal of parallel processing. Second, there is a fundamental distinction to be made between procedural and declarative knowledge. In addition to these two, there are a number of biases about the nature of declarative knowledge and about the nature of procedural knowledge.

Parallelism

The human brain is clearly a parallel-computing device in that at any point of time there is simultaneous activity in millions of neurons. It would seem foolish to fly in the face of this neurophysiological fact and not incorporate the potential for parallelism into one's psychological model. In addition to this physiological argument there are a number of teleological arguments which support the belief that cognition should have a parallel-processing component. First, it is argued (for example, Arbib, 1964) that information processing can be much more reliable if there are multiple components performing the same computation. If the "average answer" is used, then the occasional error in any particular component will not have serious consequences. Second, if rapid processing time is important, one can respond more rapidly if independent computations are performed in parallel rather than sequentially ordered. The third advantage has to do with the problem of selecting and directing the course of cognition in response to a changing environment. For instance, Newell's PS in Section 3.3 had to select a new production in each cycle of time. As Newell notes, it would be absurd to suppose that each of the thousands of productions is serially tested each unit of time. It is necessary to suppose there is a parallel examination of the total set of productions and a selection of one.

There are three principle arguments that are made for the assumption that cognition is serial. The first is that tasks like inference making demand a good deal of seriality. One computation must be complete before another can be started because the course of the second depends on the outcome of the first. However, the mere fact that some tasks require a high degree of seriality is no argument against parallel processing. A parallel processor can always act like a serial processor when necessary. The second argument for seriality (for example, Newell & Simon, 1972) is that there are many examples of tasks which we seem unable to perform in parallel. For instance, Newell and Simon note that we cannot simultaneously divide two numbers (e.g., divide both 35642 and 69416 by 7). However, difficulties in achieving such parallelism can be accounted for by the fact that the requisite parallel processes would make excessive demands on a limited short-term memory.

The third argument for seriality is everyone's introspective experience. We seem only able to report a single line of thought although we may feel that we are conscious of multiple things at one time. Everyone has had the experience of trying to think about two things at once and ending in utter confusion. On the other hand, there are occasions when we are undeniably processing multiple things simultaneously, such as when we both drive a car and carry on a conversation. The suggestion has been made by some (e.g., Neisser, 1963) that we are only capable of thinking through one main conscious line of processing but can maintain a number of well practiced processes in parallel at a subconscious level.

Perhaps the reason why we have such poor ability to report parallel aspects of cognition is that the process of reporting is, itself, a serial activity. While we are reporting one aspect of cognition, we may forget others that are progressing in parallel. The results of Sperling (1960) are worth mentioning here. He showed that there was much more available in a briefly presented image than subjects could report. For instance, subjects presented with a brief flash of 12 letters, arranged in 3 rows of 4, can report back only 4 or 5 letters. However, if signaled after the brief exposure which row to report they are almost perfect at recalling any row. Similarly, the limitation we suffer in reporting many parallel aspects of cognition may be a function of the reporting procedure.

Procedural versus Declarative Knowledge

The ACT model makes a fundamental distinction between procedural knowledge and declarative knowledge—between knowing how and knowing that. Procedural knowledge is represented in terms of productions whereas declarative knowledge is represented in terms of a propositional network. This is in contrast to Newell and Simon's suggestion in Section 3.3 that all knowledge, procedural and declarative, is represented in terms of productions; or Norman and Rumelhart's (1975, see Section 2.4 of this book) system where all knowledge is represented in their active structural network.

There are three features which are commonly used to distinguish between procedural and declarative knowledge. All three of these were noted by Gilbert Ryle (1949) in *The Concept of Mind*. The first is that declarative knowledge seems possessed in an all-or-none manner whereas procedural knowledge seems to be something that can be partially possessed. As Ryle writes: "We never speak of a person having a partial knowledge of a fact or truth, save in the special sense of his having knowledge of a part of a body of facts or truth. . . . On the other hand, it is proper and normal to speak of a person knowing in part how to do something, i.e. of his having a particular capacity in a limited degree [p. 59]." A second distinction is that one acquires declarative knowledge suddenly by being told whereas one acquires procedural knowledge gradually by performing the skill:

> Learning how or improving an ability is not like learning that or acquiring information. Truths can be imparted, procedures can only be inculcated, and while inculcation is a gradual process, imparting is relatively sudden. It makes sense to ask at what moment someone became apprised of a truth, but not to ask at what moment someone acquired a skill [p. 59].

A final distinction is that one can communicate verbally one's declarative knowledge but not one's procedural knowledge: "A well trained sailor boy can both tie complex knots and discern whether someone else is tying them correctly or incorrectly, deftly or clumsily. But he is probably incapable of the difficult task of describing in words how the knots should be tied [p. 56]."

It should be emphasized that no piece of knowledge necessarily requires a procedural representation or a declarative representation. For instance, while a procedural representation would seem more appropriate, one can represent knowledge of how to ride a bike as a series of declarative statements. One could imagine an "interpreter" which would take these statements and transform them into the action of riding a bike. Similarly, although it might seem more appropriate to represent the knowledge that "George Washington was the first president of the United States" as a declarative statement, one could imagine this knowledge embodied in a set of procedures which would enable performance of the various actions (such as verbal reports) which manifest knowledge of this fact.

The issue of what knowledge to represent procedurally and what knowledge to represent declaratively is a current controversy in artificial intelligence. Winograd (1975) describes the controversy:

> It is an artificial-intelligence incarnation of the old philosophical distinction between "knowing that" and "knowing how." The proceduralists assert that our knowledge is primarily a "knowing how." The human information procesor is a stored-program device, with its knowledge of the world embedded in the programs. What a person (or robot) knows about the English language, the game of chess, or the physical properties of his world is coextensive with his set of programs for operating with it. . . . The declarativists, on the other hand, do not

believe that knowledge of a subject is intimately bound with the procedures for its use. They see intelligence as resting on two bases: a quite general set of procedures for manipulating facts of all sorts, and a set of specific facts describing particular knowledge domains. In thinking, the general procedures are applied to the domain-specific data to make deductions. Often this process has been based on the model of axiomatic mathematics. The facts are axioms and the thought process involves proof procedures for drawing conclusions from them [p. 186].

Computationally, any knowledge can be represented procedurally or declaratively. The computational power of a system that is almost totally procedural, such as Newell's PS which used productions for storage (page 104), is equivalent to the computational power of a system that is almost totally declarative, like resolution theorem proving (see Section 9.1). Both can be shown to be equivalent to general Turing Machines and so capable of any well-specified behavior. The issue in artificial intelligence is not whether a specific behavior can be achieved one way or another, but in which way it can be best achieved. It seems that certain knowledge can be best represented declaratively and other knowledge can be best represented procedurally. It is much more economical to represent declaratively that knowledge which is subject to multiple, different uses and that knowledge whose eventual use is uncertain. This is because we can represent it just once in the data base without having to anticipate its uses and without having to incorporate the knowledge into all the necessary procedures that will use it. As a declarative fact it can be accessed and used by many different interpretative procedures. Knowledge like *George Washington was the first president of the United States* is the sort of knowledge that one would think could benefit from a declarative representation. In ACT all knowledge acquired from sentences is represented declaratively. On the other hand, knowledge used over and over again in the same way, for example, how to generate sentences, would seem to be better represented in a procedural format in which it can be applied more rapidly. The distinction between having knowledge in the declarative versus procedural form corresponds roughly to the distinction between having an interpretive versus compiled program.

In ACT declarative knowledge is represented in the propositional network while procedural knowledge is represented as productions. Productions may examine, test, and add to the contents of the propositional network but they may not operate on themselves. As a consequence procedural knowledge is specific to the circumstances where it is intended to apply and is not generally reportable. A relevant example here concerns telephone numbers. When we first learn a phone number it is something we can report and which can be used to dial a number by means of a general telephone-dialing procedure which takes that telephone number as data. That is, it initially has a declarative form. However, some people (including myself) report that if they dial a number often enough, they lose the ability to verbally recall the number. The only way to retrieve that number is to dial it. In fact, that knowledge can be specific to a particular telephone. For example, there was a time when my ability to recall the Michigan Computer number was specific to my home touch-tone phone. This epitomizes what is meant by the inaccessibility of procedural knowledge.

Presumably, our knowledge of our native language is another case of procedural knowledge. That knowledge is so unreportable that linguists are making a profession trying to propositionalize the knowledge by painstaking self-observation. It is interesting to note that our knowledge of a new language, taught by classroom techniques, often seems declarative in that its rules can be reported. Introspectively, it seems that this class-taught knowledge is being applied by general interpretative procedures. Not surprisingly, application of this knowledge is much slower than the procedurally encoded knowledge of our own language. Eventually a foreign language can become as well entrenched as our native language. Then we often forget the rules of the foreign language. It is as if the class-taught propositional knowledge has been "compiled" into a procedural form.

Another personal example involves learning to drive. I am particularly aware of this because my wife recently taught me how to use a stick shift. One of the questions I asked her was whether I should take my foot off the gas when shifting gears. She said that I should keep my foot on the gas, but we did not like the results. So she took the driver's seat and we both watched what she did when she shifted—she did take her foot off the gas. Here was a case where procedural and declarative knowledge were in direct conflict. The only way to tap the procedural knowledge was to observe oneself performing the procedures. When I first shifted it was very much declarative knowledge that I was using—I retrieved from memory the instructions and followed them (sometimes saying to myself the steps). Now after a few months' practice I am less able to report what is involved in shifting although my performance is much smoother.

The remaining biases in this section will be classified according to whether they pertain to the nature of our declarative knowledge or to the nature of our procedural knowledge. Declarative knowledge is the sort of information that memory researchers such as myself have studied. In fact, when I use the term "memory" it is usually intended to reference only declarative knowledge. Therefore, it should not be surprising that I have developed a more articulate set of biases about the nature of declarative knowledge than procedural knowledge.

Biases about Declarative Knowledge

Nonerasable Memory

ACT assumes that memory is nonerasable. This follows from the observation that it is impossible to simply forget something. Also it is assumed that it is not possible to write over information in human memory. (The only exceptions to this assumption about the permanence of memory are the variables whose bindings can be changed.) This assumption means that almost all forgetting must be due to retrieval failure. In Chapter 8 I will develop how this retrieval failure can be attributed to associative interference.

It should be stressed how strong are the assumptions that memory is nonerasable and nonoverwritable. No existing programming language has these features. This is partly because memory is more precious in a computer than it seems to be in the human head. However, another reason is that it often leads to more efficient processing to get rid of old information rather than leaving it to trip up subsequent processing. So, if a proposition proves false, it might seem foolish to leave it stored in the data base. However, it does not seem that we forget facts once they prove false. Rather we remember them, but now with the tag that they are false.

Referential Character of Memory

It is assumed that all elements of our declarative knowledge are referential. Translated into the ACT propositional network, this means that all nodes of the propositional network can be taken as referring to something. When it is said all nodes have a referent, this does not imply that it is obvious what the reference is of all the nodes—only that it is meaningful to speak of the reference of the nodes. It also does not mean that nodes only refer to concrete, particular objects. In addition to concrete objects, nodes in ACT can refer to abstract objects, to sets, to concepts of sets, to relations, and to situations (see Chapter 7).

This bias means that it is not possible to represent variables within the propositional network because variables have no fixed reference. It is hard to see how one would represent some kinds of information without the use of variables. In particular, variables are required to represent sentences with complicated scope relations such as *All universities require some students to read all of Shakespeare's works*. As a consequence, it is necessary in one way or another to resort to ACT's production system to represent certain sentential information with complicated quantificational relations (see Chapter 7).

Propositional Nature

All declarative knowledge is represented in ACT in terms of propositions. Propositions have three important features—they are abstract, have truth values, and have rules of formation. Their abstractness means that our declarative knowledge is not tied to the modality, language, situation, etc., of acquisition. So we can report in English what we learned in French or we can write about what we have seen. The feature of having a truth value allows all our declarative knowledge to enter directly into inferential processes (see Chapter 9). The rules of formation enable us to relate network structures to their meanings (see Section 7.1).

Nonambiguous Character of Memory

Another feature of the propositional network is that it is a nonambiguous representational medium. That is, it is not possible to have two semantic interpretations of a particular network structure. This contrasts with a symbolic system like natural language where there is ambiguity, but this is similar to more formal systems such as the predicate calculus. This assumption is motivated by the observation that when we comprehend an ambiguous sentence and commit it to memory we seem to commit to memory a specific sense of the sentence. If we note the ambiguity we may commit more than one sense to memory. However, it never seems that we comprehend a sentence, later recall it, and only then disambiguate it.

Subject–Predicate Construction

Another bias of mine is that predication is the basic mode of representing information—that we store properties that are true of objects. This bias is carried over from the HAM model. In Chapter 5 I present an extensive discussion of the subject–predicate construction and alternatives. To preview, the conclusion of that discussion will be that there is very little concrete basis for choosing the subject–predicate construction—or any of the other alternatives.

Biases about Procedural Knowledge

I feel that there was considerable truth in the old S–R concept of behavior, although it is clear that this concept is not adequate to account for all the complexity of human behavior. The correct aspects of S–R theory should be incorporated into more powerful models of procedural knowledge. Those biases that I have about procedural knowledge basically reflect the desire to maintain what I perceive to be the truths of the S–R position.

Data Driven

As noted in Chapter 3, in production systems each subsequent action is selected after a reevaluation of the current data base. This gives to production systems a control structure which I refer to as *data driven*. They share this with S–R theories and differ in this property from most AI programming languages. In most AI programs various cognitive functions—inference making, question answering, parsing—run off following preset internal logics, with only occasional consultation of the environment. I strongly believe that human cognition is directed by constant consulton of the data base. In S–R theory this data base consisted of only the external stimuli impinging on the organism. However, in ACT's production systems this data base is provided by the propositional network. This propositional network records past memories, current goals and drives, as well as the current stimuli. Therefore production systems, while data-driven, are much more flexible than S–R theories. Like S–R theories they can immediately respond to important changes in the environment. However, this capacity for immediate response also extends to internal drive states or the revival of important past memories.

The data-driven character of production systems also accounts for the associative character of thought. That is, the current data base can select a production which will alter the data base. This altered data base will select another production which will again alter the data base, and so on. Thus, one state of mind directly leads to another, which leads to another, etc. Note under this conception that the associative train of thought does not involve a single idea following another idea but rather configurations of ideas following each other.

Simple and Modular Character of Procedural Units

ACT embodies the assumption that the basic units out of which procedures are constructed are relatively simple and modular. In no sense does ACT contain complex programs which cannot be divided up into many independent subparts. This embodies the traditional wisdom of S–R theory that human cognition achieves its complexity from combinations of relatively simple units.

Acquisition of Productions

I also believe in the old S–R wisdom that we learn to do by doing. That is, productions are set up to encode actions that have proved successful in response to the data base. This contrasts with the idea that we can analyze a task in the abstract and emerge with a set of procedures for the task without having actually tried out and performed the procedures.

4.2   ASSUMPTIONS OF THE ACT MODEL

Before stating the assumptions of the model it would be useful to provide a one paragraph picture of the operation of the ACT system: Memory is a propositional network of interconnected nodes. A small portion of this network is active at any one time. Activation can spread down network paths from active nodes to activate new nodes and paths. To prevent activation from growing continuously there is a dampening process which periodically deactivates all but a select few nodes (on the Active List). There is also a set of productions which provides the system's procedural component. The condition of a production specifies that certain features be true of the active portion of memory and the actions specify certain changes to memory. Each production can be conceived of as an independent "demon." Its purpose is to see if the memory configuration specified in its condition is satisfied in the active portion of memory. If it is, the production will "fire" and cause changes to memory. In so doing it can allow or disallow other productions which are looking for their conditions to be satisfied. It is assumed that there are "external interfaces" that translate the input into network representations and which can translate the activation of network structures into responses. ACT provides no model of these interfaces but rather of the cognitive processing that intervenes between the interfaces.

ACT is a sufficiently complex model that I have felt it necessary to build a computer program that would simulate it. This program is intended as a proof of the internal consistency of the model. The following assumptions are intended to specify the structure of that simulation program:

Technical Assumption

0. *Discrete Time Assumption.* For reasons of simulation it is useful to suppose that time progresses in discrete units of time. The ith unit of time will be denoted t_i. These units of time are Δt sec long.

Assumptions about the Memory Structure

1. *Representation Assumptions.* The structure of information in memory is a propositional network of nodes and links of the HAM variety. The specifics of the ACT network will be set forth in Chapter 5.

2. *Activation.* Each memory node and each memory link is either in the active state or not. If a link is in the active state then the two nodes that the link connects are active. However, two nodes can be active without their interconnecting link being active.

3. *Strength of Links.* Each link emanating out of a node has a strength, s, associated with it.

4. *Spread of Activation.* Let x be an active node and let l be a nonactive link linking x to y. Let s be the strength of l and let S be the total strength of all nodes attached to x. There is a probability $1 - e^{-s/aS}$ that activation will spread from x to activate l and y (if y is not already active) in the next unit of time. The parameter a is a time scale parameter reflecting rate of spread of activation.

5. *Active List (ALIST).* A maximum of 10 nodes may be designated as part of the Active List (ALIST). Nodes in ALIST are not deactivated during dampening. Global variables can only be bound to nodes that are on the ALIST. The ALIST serves much the same function as a short-term memory. Items can be removed from ALIST only by displacement. Items are displaced from ALIST on a first-in, first-out basis.

6. *Dampening.* After D units of time, activation will be dampened throughout the network. This means that all links and all nodes not on the ALIST are deactivated. Some such dampening process is required to prevent activation from continuously growing to the point where all of memory becomes active.[2]

Assumptions about the Production System

7. *Structure of Productions.* All productions are condition–action pairs. The condition specifies a conjunction of features that must be true of memory. The

---

[2]This dampening process has been likened to throwing a bucket of water on the system. One might have thought it more natural to have a system in which the level of activation of links varied continuously and that activation gradually decayed away over time. However, it proves difficult to adjust the decay rate so that the total activation of memory is not growing continuously over time while still assuring that structure will remain active long enough to be of use. Another complication with the level of activation idea is that one would have to propose how time for activation to spread varied with level of a link and how probability of a production matching varied with the level of activation of a structure.

action specifies a sequence of changes to be made to memory. Section 6.1 specifies the details of production structure.

8. *Strength of Productions.* Each production has a strength s associated with it.

9. *Selection of Productions.* The process by which productions are chosen is a two-stage affair. There is an initial *selection phase*. In each unit of time all the productions are tested against memory to see which might be applicable. This initial selection phase takes no time but also involves only a partial test of the productions. The exact tests made in this selection phase will be specified in Section 6.1. All productions which pass this initial preprocessing are placed on the APPLY LIST.

10. *Application of Productions.* The productions on the APPLY LIST are tested to see if their conditions are totally satisfied in long-term memory. It takes a certain amount of time to perform this test. The speed at which the test is performed varies inversely with n, the number of productions on the APPLY LIST, and the probability of completing this test in any unit of time is $1 - e^{-s/bn}$. The parameter b is a time scale parameter reflecting rate of production application. The production will be executed if its condition is satisfied at that time, and deleted from the APPLY list if it is not. It takes no time to execute the action of a production. The action can cause new memory structures to be built. All nodes and links in these memory structures are initially active. The links in these memory structures are established permanently with probability p.

11. *Strengthening.* Each production and link in memory has initial strength 1. The strength of a production is incremented by one unit every time it is executed, and the strength of a link is incremented by one unit every time it is used in matching the condition of a production.

Status of the Theory

Assumptions 0–11 were meant to be a complete, concise statement of the assumptions of the theory. Admittedly, they lack total rigor and precision. However, they are better than a listing of the program itself. A version of this program is running on the SUMEX computer at Stanford. A documented listing of this program can be obtained by writing to me. Hopefully, we will shortly have a "user's manual" available for those who want to import and use the ACT system. The program itself computes the spread of activation over the network, the dampening of activation, and the dynamic change in the strength of links. It tests the condition of productions that apply. The user must provide the system with an initial set of productions and an initial memory structure.

The model has relatively few parameters. There is a, the parameter governing rate of the spread of activation; b, the parameter governing the speed of production application; D, the time between dampening; and p, the probability of encoding a link. Unfortunately, there are serious obstacles to simply estimating these parameters and using them to make predictions. First, to derive predictions one must make many ad hoc assumptions about the exact structure of the memory network and about the exact set of productions available, since the predictions depend on these details. Thus, before the computer simulation program could be a truly effective predictive device, one would have to develop a complete and explicit set of principles for specifying the initial structure of the program. Deriving such a set of principles would not be easy. The second obstacle is one of economics. Because of the probabilistic nature of the processes (which we will see is necessary—see Chapters 6–10), it would take thousands of simulations to get accurate estimates of expected performance. It is currently not possible economically to perform those thousands of simulations.

Neither of these obstacles may be insurmountable and I am currently pursuing at least partial solutions to both.[3] However, for the time being, they prevent the computer program from being an effective predictive device. Instead, a set of approximating assumptions has evolved for analyzing various paradigms. These involve simplified notions for representing the memory structures and productions and more tractable characterizations of the basic processes like spread of activation. The degree to which these simplifying assumptions approximate the actual ACT system is uncertain, which is less than a totally satisfactory state of affairs. However, it is the best that is available to date.

Activation of the Network

The concept of spreading activation in a network is central to ACT. This concept has been used elsewhere, most notably in the work of Collins and Quillian (for example, 1972). The conditions of an ACT production can inspect only the active portion of memory. This gives the system a way of focusing attention onto that portion of the network which is currently relevant. Recently, Posner and Snyder (1975) have proposed a model that involves the incorporation of a spreading activation process that serves a similar role as that in ACT. They propose the existence of an "automatic pathway activation" which occurs without intention or conscious awareness. Its function is to facilitate the availability of various kinds of responses. Posner and Snyder contrast this with a conscious, strategic component that directs the course of cognition. This is analagous to the distinction between the procedural and declarative components in ACT.

4.3   EXAMPLES OF ACT PRODUCTION SYSTEMS

The best way to get a sense of ACT's production systems is to consider some examples. These will be the first of many productions systems that will be pre-

---

[3]I am contemplating Monte Carlo explorations into the effects of variations in the structure of the propositional network. This should give some sense of how structural variations influence predictions. A partial solution to the economic problem might be creating running versions of ACT for a dedicated laboratory computer.

sented throughout the book. The total set of conventions for expressing productions will not be developed until Chapter 6, but I will try to briefly explain those features used here. One question that might be asked of the production systems proposed in this book is whether they actually work and perform the actions ascribed to them. These production systems constitute "programs" and need to be debugged. I have found that it is never the case that I can write correctly on first attempt a production system of any complexity (for example, 10 productions). However, it has also turned out to be the case that I have not had to make drastic changes in debugging the initial systems. In this book I will indicate which production systems have been debugged and which have been successfully implemented. Unless otherwise indicated the reader should not assume the productions have been so tested. All the examples in this chapter have been tested.

A typical production system example consists of from one or two to many dozens of productions. The reader should think of these productions as being mixed in with many other productions. In fact, all the examples in the book could be mixed together to achieve one grand set of productions. However, the existence of those other productions is irrelevant for modeling a particular task since they will not be selected in the context of that task.

The Sternberg Task

First, to aid comparisons to Newell's PS consider the following ACT system for the Sternberg task. To construct such a system one needs to specify what propositional network structures will be used to represent the information and to specify a set of productions that will operate on this network. ACT will represent the positive set by a set of propositions of the form "List contains digit." Figure 4.1a shows an encoding of the positive set, 7 9 4. The conventions for this network representation are somewhat different than HAM; the details will be explained in the next chapter. Basically, we have three network propositions, one to encode the appearance of each digit in the positive set. Figure 4.1b shows how the probe digit is encoded. It assumes that the appearance of a digit on the screen causes a proposition of the form "Digit is on screen" to be constructed. All nodes and links in this proposition are initially active.

Table 4.1 gives a production system consisting of four productions which will generate the desired performances in the Sternberg task.[4] Each production consists of a condition separated from the action by a double arrow. The condition consists of a sequence of tests of memory, segmented by "&." Similarly, the action side consists of a sequence of subactions segmented by "&."

Consider the first production, (P1). It consists of a test of whether the value of the variable Vcon is the node READY. In general, variables are denoted in ACT

---

[4]For purpose of readability I have taken the liberty of slightly transforming the form of the productions from their specification in the ACT simulation program.

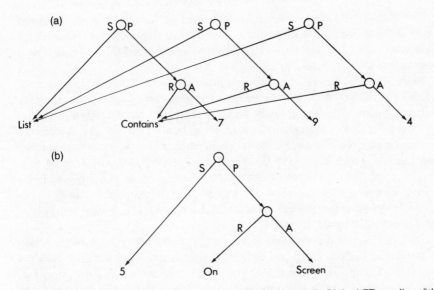

FIG. 4.1   (a) An ACT encoding of the positive set in the Sternberg task; (b) An ACT encoding of the probe digit.

by terms beginning with a capital V. Vcon is a control variable that enables the system to keep track of what state it is in. When it has the value READY, in Table 4.1, ACT is waiting for the input of a probe digit. In the action part of (P1) we find the variables Vcon and Vlist. This serves as a request to rehearse the value of these two variables. Vlist has as its value the node that contains the digits in the memory set, that is, LIST in Fig. 4.1a. The values of Vcon and Vlist are on the ALIST, the list of ten nodes to be kept active after each dampening. The effect of the rehearsal in (P1) is to bring the values of these variables (that is, READY and LIST) to the

TABLE 4.1
A Debugged Production System for Performance in the Sternberg Task

	Condition		Action
(P1)	(Vcon = READY)	⇒	Vcon & Vlist
(P2)	(Vcon = READY) & (Vprobe * (on OF screen))	⇒	(Vcon = TEST) & Vprobe
(P3)	(Vcon = TEST) & (Vlist * (contains OF Vprobe))	⇒	(Vcon = READY) & (PRESS YES) & (UNBIND Vprobe)
(P4)	(Vcon = TEST) & (ABS (Vlist * (contains OF Vprobe)))	⇒	(Vcon = READY) & (PRESS NO) & (UNBIND Vprobe)

front of the ALIST and prevent them from being lost. Recall that productions can only test the active portion of memory. Therefore, if READY or LIST were ever pushed off the ALIST and deactivated through dampening, ACT would no longer have access to these values of the variables.

Production (P1) will be constantly elicited and executed during the interval of waiting for the probe. It is assumed that the presentation of a probe causes a memory structure like that in Fig. 4.1b to be active. Production (P2) tests for the appearance of such a structure in memory. It will be selected and applied when the control variable Vcon has value READY and when the memory structure appears encoding the probe digit. The construction (Vprobe * (on OF screen)) is a linearized specification of the memory pattern being sought. The details of interpreting such linearized specifications will be given in Section 5.3. In this construction Vprobe is initially an unbound variable which will be bound to the probe digit after matching the condition.

There are two subactions in the action part of Production (P2). First, the action (Vcon = TEST) changes the value of the control variable Vcon to TEST. Now the production system is in a state ready to test whether the probe is in the memory list. The second subaction, denoted by the listing of the variable Vprobe, causes the value of Vprobe to be put on the ALIST and rehearsed.

The third and fourth productions in Table 4.1 test for whether the probe digit is in the memory set. The linearized construction (Vlist * (contains OF Vprobe)) in the condition of Productions (P3) and (P4) specifies a memory proposition like those in Fig. 4.1a. It specifies that Vlist (= LIST) contains a digit which has the value of the variable Vprobe. Production (P3) will be satisfied if this pattern is active in memory while Production (P4) will be satisfied if this pattern is not active in memory. To specify that absence of the pattern is desired, Production (P4) embeds the target pattern in a construction prefixed by ABS. The actions of (P3) and (P4) are identical except that (P3) causes the YES button to be pressed and (P4) causes the NO button to be pressed. Both set the value of the control variable Vcon back to READY to wait for the next probe digit. Both unbind the value of the variable Vprobe so that it can be bound to the next probe digit that is presented.

The production system in Table 4.1 is quite simple. However, it is often hard to follow the flow of control among the productions given a linear encoding like that in Table 4.1. Therefore, a schematic network structure has been developed like that in Fig. 4.2 to illustrate the flow of control. States of the system are indicated by circles containing the bindings of the control variable Vcon. In this simple case there are just two values, READY and TEST. Productions appear as arrows between states. At the root of an arrow is an indication of the condition that will cause the production to be elicited. Thus, in Fig. 4.2 if nothing happens P1 will cause the system to cycle in the state (Vcon = READY). The appearance of the probe digit will elicit (P2) and the system will transfer to state (Vcon = TEST). If the probe digit is on the list (P3) will be evoked, and if not, (P4) will be evoked. In

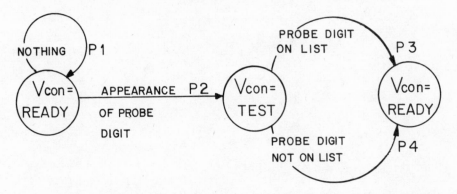

FIG. 4.2 A transition network illustrating the flow of control within the production system in Table 4.1 for the Sternberg task.

either case the state of the system returns to (Vcon = READY). There are two circles containing (Vcon = READY) in Fig. 4.2. This is only for the sake of readability. The two circles denote the same state.

This model predicts that reaction time will increase the more elements there are in the positive set because of increased time needed to apply Productions (P3) and (P4). The condition of (P3) will not be satisfied until the memory structure encoding *LIST contains digit* is active. The variable Vlist (= LIST) is kept active by (P1) and Vprobe (= digit) is active due to (P2). However, at the point of presentation of the probe the remaining structure specified in (P3) may not be active yet. If so, activation must spread from the two sources, Vlist and Vprobe, to cover the entire proposition. The speed at which this activation will spread is affected by the fan of experimental links out of Vlist = LIST (Assumption 4 in Section 4.2). As can be verified from Fig. 4.1a the more elements in the positive set the greater the fan from LIST. As will be developed in Section 8.1, the operation that detects absence in Production (P4) will also be affected by memory set size.

Note that, in contrast to Newell's PS model, this model does not attribute the reaction time increase in the Sternberg task to an increase in the number of productions that must be applied. Rather, it attributes the increase to a delay in the activation process. In general, the activation process will play an important role in determining the timing characteristics of the ACT system. A careful analysis of the activation process will be presented in Chapter 8.

Interfacing Assumptions

It should be noted that in this production system it is assumed that some perceptual parser delivers an encoding of the probe digit in network form. The process which accomplishes this perceptual parsing must be at least partially not an ACT produc-

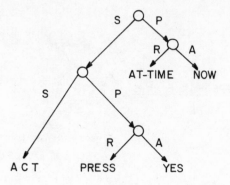

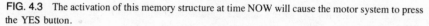

FIG. 4.3   The activation of this memory structure at time NOW will cause the motor system to press the YES button.

tion system. The reason is that ACT production systems can derive network structures from network structure, but they cannot derive a network structure from a sensory array. A similar interface is required on the action side. Note that Productions (P3) and (P4) contain elements (PRESS YES) and (PRESS NO). These are not direct specifications of actions but rather specifications of propositional structures of the form *ACT press YES* or *ACT press NO*. Figure 4.3 shows a memory network encoding for one of these. Note that the proposition is tagged with a time element to keep it distinct from propositions encoding past button presses. It is assumed that there exists a motor interface which will respond to the activation of such a structure with the correct response.

It is possible to incorporate a lot of hidden power into assumptions about the nature of the sensory interface and the motor interface. As in the case of Suppes' (1969) use of patterns (see Section 3.2) it is possible to place the real computational work in these interfaces. To avoid this pitfall, I have tried to keep the operation of these interfaces as mundane and simple as possible.

The Memory Span Task

It would be useful to consider an ACT system for a memory span task. The memory span task is a very simple test of mental capacity. A subject is given a sequence of unrelated items (e.g., digits) and is asked to hold them in memory for some period of time and then repeat them back in order. Subjects can perform almost perfectly provided the sequence of items is of length 7 or less. During the interval between hearing the digits and recall, subjects report rehearsing the sequence of digits, over and over again, to themselves.

The first decision in constructing an ACT system for this task is to specify how the to-be-remembered sequence is encoded. It is assumed that the first digit in the sequence is specially tagged as the first. Figure 4.4a illustrates how this would be encoded in ACT, supposing the first digit were a 3. A token, X, of the digit 3 is

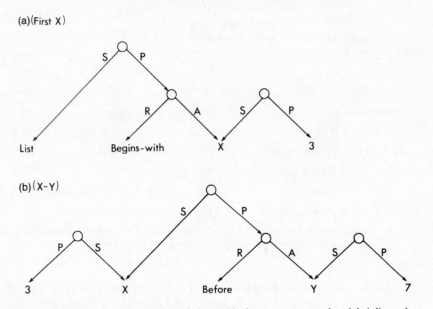

FIG. 4.4 Examples of memory structures to be used in the memory span task and their linear shorthand encodings.

set up and it is asserted the list begins with it.[5] This structure will be represented by the linear shorthand (FIRST X) in the production system in Table 4.2. The remaining elements in the sequence will be encoded according to their adjacency relations. Figure 4.4b illustrates how the subsequence, 3 7, would be encoded. This will be represented by the shorthand (X–Y) in the production system, where X is the token of 3 and Y is the token of 7.

Table 4.2 illustrates the production system for this task. Linear shorthand expressions have been used for memory structures to reduce the complexity of the expressions. It is assumed that the perceptual system delivers an encoding of the to-be-memorized sequence in the formalism illustrated in Fig. 4.4. It is also assumed that the system begins with an initializing control element, START, as the value of variable Vcon. The flow of control in this production system is illustrated in Fig. 4.5. The appearance of the first digit causes Production (P1) to be elicited and control to transfer to state (Vcon = CE). In matching the pattern (FIRST Vnumb) the variable Vnumb will be bound to the first digit. The action (Vfirst = Vnumb) in (P1) causes both Vfirst to be bound to the first digit and places that digit on the ALIST. With the input of each subsequent digit, Production (P2) will be satisfied.

[5]The token X would have been connected with an ε link to 3 in HAM. In Chapter 5 I will detail why subject–predicate constructions are now used to indicate membership.

TABLE 4.2
A Debugged Production System for Performance in the Memory Span Task

	Condition		Action
(P1)	(Vcon = START) & (FIRST Vnumb)	⇒	(Vcon = CE) & (Vfirst = Vnumb) & Vnumb
(P2)	(Vcon = CE) & (Vnumb–Vnew)	⇒	Vcon & (Vnumb = Vnew)
(P3)	(Vcon = CE) & REHEARSE	⇒	(Vcon = CR) & (Vlast = Vnumb) & (Vnumb = Vfirst)
(P4)	(Vcon = CR) & (Vnumb–Vnew)	⇒	Vcon & (Vnumb = Vnew)
(P5)	(Vcon = CR) & (Vnumb = Vlast)	⇒	Vcon & (Vnumb = Vfirst)
(P6)	(Vcon = CR) & RECALL	⇒	(Vcon = CD) & (Vnumb = Vfirst) & (SAY Vnumb)
(P7)	(Vcon = CD) & (Vnumb–Vnew)	⇒	Vcon & (Vnumb = Vnew) & (SAY Vnumb)
(P8)	(Vcon = CD) & (Vnumb = Vlast)	⇒	(Vcon = START) & (UNBIND Vfirst Vlast Vnumb)

To illustrate the action of Productions (P1) and (P2) suppose the first digits of
the sequence were 3   7   4. Upon the input of 3, Production (P1) would be satisfied and bind a token of 3 to both Vfirst and Vnumb. Upon the input of 7, the
condition of Production (P2) will be satisfied, with Vnumb bound to be a token of
3 and Vnew bound to a token of 7. The subaction Vcon causes the value of Vcon to
be rehearsed on the ALIST. The subaction (Vnumb = Vnew) causes the value of
Vnumb to be set to the new digit token and this digit token to be put on the ALIST.
Then, upon the input of 4, the condition of Production (P2) will be satisfied again,

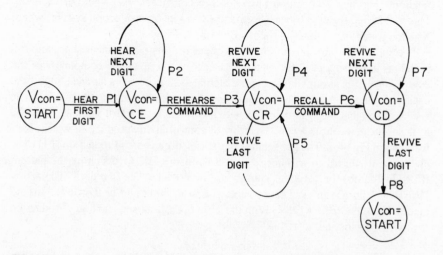

FIG. 4.5   A transition network illustrating the flow of control within the production system in Table
4.2 for the memory span task.

this time with Vnumb bound to a token of 7 and Vnew bound to a token of 4.[6] It serves to put 4 on the ALIST. Production (P2) will continue to operate, putting incoming elements on the ALIST until the last digit is received.

Upon receipt of the last digit it is assumed the command REHEARSE is given. This causes the element REHEARSE to be activated in memory which allows Production (P3) to be satisfied. The action of (P3) causes Vcon to be set to a new control node, CR. This will prevent Production (P2) from being satisfied again. It also sets Vlast to Vnumb, the last encoded digit. Finally Production (P3) sets Vnumb to the value of Vfirst, the first digit in the sequence. This serves to initialize the rehearsal process.

The rehearsal of the sequence is performed by Productions (P4) and (P5). Production (P4) rehearses all the digits in the sequence. The pattern (Vnumb–Vnew) in the condition serves to retrieve the next digit in the memory encoding. The action (Vnumb = Vnew) serves to set Vnumb to the next digit so that (P4) can reapply and to rehearse that digit on the ALIST. When the end of the sequence is reached, Production (P5) will be satisfied which will cause the rehearsal to begin over again from the start of the sequence. One might wonder why this rehearsal is necessary. The digits have already been put on the ALIST during encoding. Is this not enough to guarantee their final recall? The problem is that other elements can enter the ALIST due to accidental elicitation of other productions and so push the to-be-remembered digits off the ALIST. Thus, the rehearsal process serves to keep the digits at the front of the ALIST.

Upon the appearance of the command RECALL Production (P6) will be satisfied. It causes the variable Vcon to be reset to the control node CD, the variable Vnumb to be set to the value of Vfirst. The action (SAY Vnumb) causes the first digit to be output. Since the value of Vcon has been changed, Productions (P4) and (P5) will no longer apply and Production (P7) takes over, causing the digits to be generated in order. It operates like Production (P4), reviving the digits one at a time. The final production, (P8), is elicited after the last digit has been output. It resets the control variable Vcon to START and unbinds the variables Vfirst, Vlast, and Vnumb so that a new memory span list can be processed.

In performing this task there can be up to three control elements, CE, CR, and CD on the Active List. This means that if ACT can hold 7 digit tokens successfully it must have an Active List of length 10—hence, the estimate in Assumption 3. If a digit token falls off the ALIST it does not necessarily mean that ACT will lose memory of it. ACT may be able to recall that digit through long-term memory associations encoding the memory span list. However, these long-term memory

[6]Note that although Vnew had the value 7 in the previous matching of (P2) it can be bound to the value 4 in the next matching of (P2). This is because Vnew is a *local variable* and its binding is not remembered from one application of a production to a next. Its binding is only remembered within the application of a single production. This contrasts with Vcon, Vfirst, Vlast, and Vnumb which are *global variables*. Their values are remembered across production applications. In Chapter 6 I discuss the difference between global and local variables.

associations have only been made permanent with a probability p (see Assumption 10). This is realized in the current simulation by the following procedure: Whenever, any node is deactivated any recently acquired associations involving that node are lost with probability $(1 - p)$. Thus, new associations are available as long as their nodes are active but can be lost once their nodes are deactivated.

Noun Phrases

As another example of an ACT production system, consider the system in Table 4.3 to parse noun phrases. Figure 4.6 shows the network equivalent of shorthand expressions being used in that table. Figure 4.6a shows that the shorthand (WORDCLASS X Y Z) encodes that the word Y, of which X is a token, is a member of the word class Z. Figure 4.6b shows that (X W Y) encodes X is an idea attached to word Y. Figure 4.6c shows that (X * Y) encodes that Y is a predicate of X. It is assumed that a noun phrase, like "The tall young man" is encoded according to adjacency relations as were the sequences for the memory span task in Table 4.2. Therefore, this production system also uses the shorthands (FIRST X) and (X–Y) which were defined in Fig. 4.5.

Figure 4.7 illustrates the flow of control among the first four productions of Table 4.3. As can be seen, the appearance of the first word elicits P1 and causes control to transfer from state (Vcon = START) to (Vcon = NPO). The appearance of a determiner elicits (P2) and control is transferred to state (Vcon = NP). Production (P3) cycles in this state taking in adjectives. The appearance of a noun

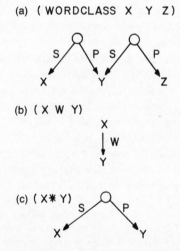

FIG. 4.6   Examples of memory structures to be used in the noun phrase parsing task and their linear shorthands.

TABLE 4.3
A Debugged Production System for Parsing Noun Phrases

	Condition		Action
(P1)	(Vcon = START) & (FIRST Vtok)	⇒	(Vcon = NP0) & Vtok
(P2)	(Vcon = NP0) & (WORDCLASS Vtok Vword DETERMINER)	⇒	(Vcon = NP) & (Vadv = NEXT) & Vtop
(P3)	(Vcon = NP) & ((WORDCLASS Vtok Vword ADJECTIVE) & (Videa W Vword))	⇒	(Vcon = NP) & (Vadv = NEXT) & (Vtop * Videa)
(P4)	(Vcon = NP) & ((WORDCLASS Vtok Vword NOUN) & (Videa W Vword))	⇒	(Vcon = START) & (Vtop * Videa) & (UNBIND Vtok Vtop)
(P5)	(Vadv = NEXT) & (Vtok − Vnew)	⇒	(Vtok = Vnew) & (UNBIND Vadv)

will elicit Production (P4) which completes the noun phrase and transfers control back to the state (Vcon = START). Note that Production (P5) is not illustrated in Fig. 4.7. It is an example of a production that is not felicitously represented in a state diagram like Fig. 4.7. The purpose of (P5) is to advance the variable Vtok to the next word token in the word string. It is called after Production (P2) or (P3) has processed the current word.

The effect of the productions in Table 4.7 is to take a network encoding of a string of words and create a network encoding of the meaning of this string. Figure 4.8 shows the network encoding of the string "The tall young man." Figure 4.9 illustrates the applications of the productions which build up the meaning of this string. Figure 4.9a illustrates the situation with nothing built yet in memory to represent the meaning of the noun phrase. The beginning of the phrase will cause Production P1 to apply with Vtok bound to the token of *the*. Then Production (P2)

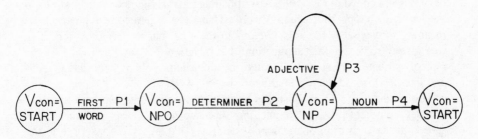

FIG. 4.7   A transition network illustrating the flow of control within the production system in Table 4.3 for the noun phrase parsing task.

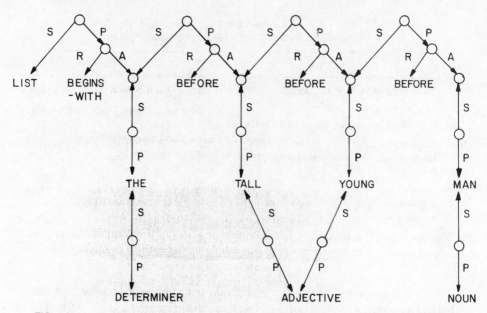

FIG. 4.8   A propositional network encoding the input of the string of words "THE TALL YOUNG MAN."

will apply since *the* is in the DETERMINER word class. The action (Vadv = NEXT) in (P2) calls for advancement of the word token. The action Vtop in (P2) creates a node to represent the topic of the noun phrase and binds this to Vtop. Figure 4.9b represents the state of the memory encoding at this point.

Production (P5) will then apply to change the binding of Vtok to the token of *tall*. Now Production P3 can apply. The condition of (P3) will match Videa to the idea corresponding to *tall*. Production (P3) predicates this idea of the topic by the action (Vtop * Videa). The state of the meaning structure after application of (P3) is illustrated in Fig. 4.9c. Also illustrated in this figure are the bindings of the variables Vtop, Videa, and Vword. That network structure represents the meaning conveyed by the adjective *tall* in the noun phrase. The next adjective *young* results, via another application of Production (P5) and then (P3), in the memory structure in Fig. 4.9d. Finally, the noun *man* results, via production (P5) and then (P4), in the memory structure in Fig. 4.9e.

This production system illustrates better than the previous two how the ACT production system principally functions to create new memory structure in response to the activation of memory structures. That is, ACT's response to the appearance of the string encoding in Fig. 4.8 is to create the network encoding in Fig. 4.9e.

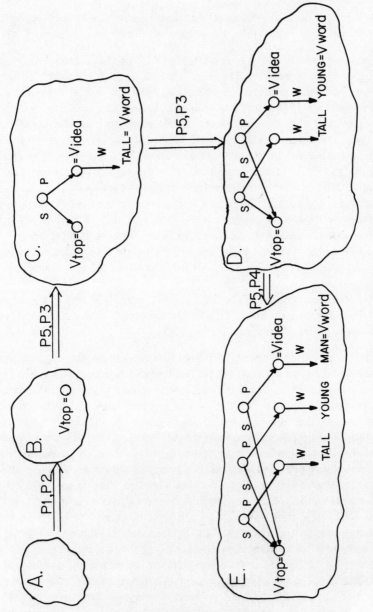

FIG. 4.9 An illustration of how the productions in Table 4.3 operate in sequence to build up the meaning of "the tall young man."

137

Performance Limitations

The ACT system has a number of factors limiting how rapidly and successfully it can perform. It is worthwhile to note each of these.

1. *Spread of Activation.*   The conditions of ACT productions can only inspect the active portions of memory. Therefore, the rate at which activation can spread to activate a structure required in a production condition is a basic limitation on how fast productions can apply. The time taken to activate a structure will depend on the complexity of that structure—the further activation must spread the longer it will take. Activation time will also be affected by the strength of the links in that structure relative to the strength of other links. The dampening process serves to magnify the effect of activation time. If a structure is not activated before dampening, the activation process will have to start over again.

2. *ALIST.*   The ALIST places a strict limitation on the number of nodes that can survive the dampening process. It serves in part as ACT's STM.

3. *Production Application.*   Another important factor is the time taken to test a production on the APPLY LIST. This will depend on the number of other productions simultaneously on the APPLY LIST and on the strength of that production.

4. *Encoding Probability.*   The links created in an ACT action are only encoded with a certain probability. This fact puts a premium on redundancy in the memory traces being set up (see Section 10.2).

These four limitations prevent ACT from being an omnipotent machine. As in the case of humans, some tasks will prove more difficult than others, and like a human there will be many ways of approaching a task, some better than others. The important question, of course, is whether the pattern of difficulties encountered by ACT corresponds to the human pattern.

One thing that may seem lacking in the ACT model is the absence of explicit limitations on how complex a production can be. Thus one can have arbitrarily many tests in the condition and arbitrarily many subactions in the action. While there are no "legal" limitations on how complex a production can be, there are some practical factors which serve to limit the complexity of a production. Productions are induced from past activation patterns in memory (see Section 12.3). Since dampening and the size of the ALIST put limitations on how widespread the activation pattern can be in memory, there is a limitation on the complexity of the productions that can be induced from these patterns. Also since the condition of the production must be matched to active memory, there are limits on how complex the condition can become and still be capable of being matched. In Section 8.4 we will come across some inference tasks where it is necessary to break down complex conditions into subconditions tested by separate productions. In the tasks for which I have developed productions, limitations on the complexity of a condition serve as limitations on how complex a useful action can be. For instance, in writing a parsing system as in Table 4.3, the size of the portion of the sentence that can be inspected by a condition puts a limitation on the amount of information that can be added to the meaning structure representing the sentence.

Strategy-Invariance

In the construction of HAM (see Section 2.2) a strong emphasis was placed on creating a strategy-free memory component that behaved according to the same principles in all tasks. All of the ACT model has this feature of strategy invariance, both the memory system and the production system. The "strategy" for performing a task resides not in the principles for memory operations or in the principles for interpreting productions, rather it lies in the logical character of memory structures and productions set up to perform the task. This feature of strategy invariance is not terribly unique—it is to be found in any programming language where the interpreter operates on an instruction in the language the same way regardless of the task. While the feature of strategy invariance is not unique, it still is desirable to have in a psychological model.

Comparisons to Newell's PS

It is useful to note the differences between ACT and Newell's (1973) PS (see Section 3.3). There is the very gross difference due to the fact that ACT makes use of a propositional network over which an activation process is defined. Another difference concerns the two models' different perceptions of the nature of short-term memory limitations. Despite the fact that both PS and ACT acknowledge a basic limitation by creating a special storage medium, the use made of the storage mediums is quite different. The STM of PS is the basic holder of data for all cognitive operations. It can hold complex chunks. The order of the elements can be tested and can play an important role in application of productions. In contrast, the order of elements in ACT's ALIST is not available for inspection by the productions. Order is important only in that it determines which elements will be lost first. The true function of the ALIST is to permit the system to keep some nodes active beyond dampening. The data structure being tested by the ACT production system is not the ALIST, rather it is the active partition of memory.

There is a significant difference in the predictions of ACT versus PS because of their different interpretation of the memory span limitation. PS predicts that it should always be possible to report out the 7 ± 2 items in STM. This is because STM can be inspected by productions—indeed, that is all productions can inspect. In contrast, ACT predicts that it is generally not possible to report the items on the ALIST. It is only when some of these items happened to be serially structured in memory, as the elements are in a memory span task, that it is possible to report some of the contents of the ALIST. If the reader will introspect a bit, I think he will agree that it is generally difficult to report out the 7 ± 2 elements in his immediate awareness. This introspective test is certainly gross, but it is as decisive as the memory span test. Just as the memory span test indicates a rather constant limitation on our immediate memory, so does this instrospective test indicate that the elements in this limited memory are not generally open to systematic inspection.

Another difference between ACT and PS is that PS only applies a single production in a unit time whereas ACT can apply multiple productions per unit time. This parallel aspect of ACT is particularly useful for modeling domains like language comprehension (see Chapter 10), in which it seems multiple parallel levels of analyses are needed. ACT productions also have strengths associated with them which means that they can vary in the amount of time needed to apply. In Section 6.2 I report on a set of effects which strongly suggest a strength-like mechanism is required. Newell uses a concept different from strength but related—the order of a production in the production list. This serves to resolve ties, should multiple productions apply. With its capacity for parallel application of productions, ACT does not need a tie-breaking capacity. It avoids the counterintuitive aspect of PS that the selection of productions is serially ordered but time for selection is not affected by the number of productions.

One feature required by a model of procedural knowledge is the capacity to rapidly modify its goal structure. This is achieved in ACT by the capacity to change the values of the control variables. This capacity of ACT gives it a simple erasable memory, in contrast to the propositional network which is not erasable. When this capacity for erasable memory is applied, for example, to the control structure governing the parse of a noun phrase (see Table 4.3), it carries the implication that we do not have memory for our various control states in processing a sentence. This prediction seems to be usually true. The PS system achieves this capacity for rapid modifiability by reordering elements in STM and by tagging control elements as old. It is not clear whether this tagging operation implies a memory for past control structure because it is not clear what happens to tagged elements after they are pushed out of STM.

Another difference between ACT and PS lies in ACT's probabilistic assumptions about formation of memory links. This contrasts with the Newell and Simon (1972) theory of a constant and slow rate of writing information into long-term memory. It is not clear, but I think this constant writing notion is supposed to extend to Newell's PS. In Section 10.2 I review memory data on depth of processing that supports ACT over the Newell and Simon hypothesis.

4.4   THE COMPUTATIONAL POWER OF ACT

One of the problems noted for PS was to properly adjust its computational power so that it matched human capacity. Without something like chunk structure it was too weak and with chunk structure it seemed too powerful in that it was then able to generate an error-free simulation of a Turing Machine (TM). The purpose of this section is to explore similar questions about the computational power of ACT. In the following technical subsection I consider how ACT might be made to simulate a Turing Machine. Then we will consider the difficulties in achieving an error-free simulation and the significance of the simulation.

Mimicry of a TM by ACT*

The first step in showing how ACT might simulate a TM is to decide how to encode the TM tape. The finite nonzero portion of the tape will be encoded by the same sort of structure used to encode adjacency in the noun phrase (see Fig. 4.8). Figure 4.10 shows how the nonzero portion would be encoded if it consisted of 1   0   1 (for convenience of visual representations in Fig. 4.10 items have been repeated such as *tape* and *before* which should be a single node). Note that there are two values out of the middle cell, a 0 and a 1. The proposition encoding the value 1 has been tagged as *false*. The 1 was a value which was subsequently overwritten by the TM with a 0. Since ACT's memory cannot be overwritten or erased, it is by use of such false tags that ACT will mimic the effect of overwriting in a TM. If this 0 is subsequently overwritten, it will be tagged as false also.

To obtain mimicry of the TM, we must convert every transition of the TM into an ACT production. A Turing Maching transition I × S1 → J × S2 × D encodes the rule that if the TM is in state S1 and symbol I is in the cell currently being scanned, then the TM should overwrite the I with a J, change to state S2 and move in direction D (either left or right). Table 4.4 shows a set of productions that would mimic a right move. A similar set of productions could be constructed to mimic a left move.

In this production system it is assumed that variable Vcell is bound to the current cell the TM is reading and Vcon is bound to the current state of the TM. Production (P1) tests whether the current state is S1 and whether the cell is a token of the symbol I. If (P1) is satisfied, Vprop will be bound to the proposition node which encodes that Vcell is a token of the symbol I. The action of (P1) sets the control node Vcon to RIGHT to call for a right move; it sets Vcon1 to S2 to remember the next state of the TM; it tags as false Vprop which encodes the old value of Vcell, and it encodes the new value of Vcell as J. Because Vprop is tagged as false, it can no longer match the condition of (P1) (see Section 6.1).

If Vcell is not the last cell encoded on the tape, Production (P2) will apply, which sets Vcell to the next cell to the right. It also sets Vcon to the TM state stored on Vcon1 (for example, (P1) had set Vcon1 = S2). If Vcell is the last cell, Production (P3) will be elicited to grow another cell to the right and to write 0 into that cell. After (P3) has applied, (P2) can apply. After application of (P2), ACT is in a position to simulate the next move by the TM.

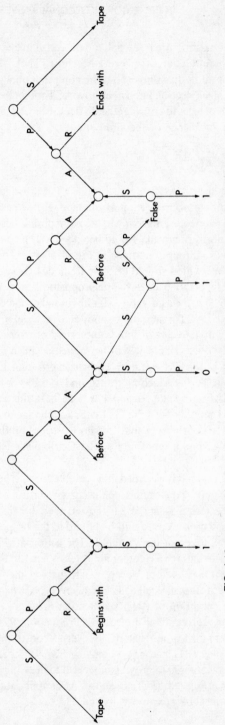

FIG. 4.10 A propositional network encoding of the finite nonzero portion of a Turing Machine tape.

TABLE 4.4
A Debugged Production System for Simulating a Move to the Right by a Turing Machine

	Condition		Action
(P1)	(Vcon = S1) & (Vprop = (Vcell * I))	$\Rightarrow$	(Vcon = RIGHT) & (Vcon1 = S2) & (Vprop * false) & (Vcell * J)
(P2)	(Vcon = RIGHT) & (Vcell − Vnext)	$\Rightarrow$	(Vcon = Vcon1) & (Vcell = Vnext)
(P3)	(Vcon = RIGHT) & (Vprop = (LAST Vcell))	$\Rightarrow$	Vcon & (Vnext * 0) & (Vcell − Vnext) & (Vprop * false) & (LAST Vnext)

Significance of Simulating a Turing Machine

As noted in Chapter 3, a Turing Machine is generally assumed to be capable of performing any well specified procedure. Therefore, if some system can simulate a Turing Machine it can be established to be of maximum computational power. The above demonstration would seem to indicate that ACT is of Turing Machine power. However, some major qualifications must be made to temper this conclusion. First, it should be pointed out that the brain has finite memory,[7] whereas this ACT simulation of a TM assumes that an unlimited number of nodes can be recruited to grow the finite nonzero portion of the TM and to overwrite the values of TM cells. A truly accurate ACT model would have to assume some bound on the numbers of possible nodes. It may well be the case that human memory is so large that it would not be exhausted in a lifetime of simulating the TM. Still, this fact does not negate the abstract point that human memory is really finite. Therefore, this demonstration really shows that ACT is equivalent to some *very* large finite-state machine.

Second, there would be some practical difficulties in getting ACT to actually be successful in its simulation. First, as the value of a cell is written over multiple times there would be considerable interference to activating and retrieving the current value of the cell. This is because ACT simulates overwriting by adding new propositions and tagging old ones as false. Therefore, the ACT simulation would start to grind very slow as interfering values became associated with cells.

Third, this simulation assumes that control nodes and other elements can be kept on the ALIST so that they will survive dampening. However, if ACT were a practical model of a human, the TM mimicking productions would be embedded among many others to perform other of life's tasks. These other productions might be accidentally evoked, placing other elements on the ALIST and displacing the

[7]It is not hard to make plausibility arguments for the claim that human memory is finite if very large. For instance, it is hard to imagine how the human brain could be capable of more states than configurations of its atoms (or perhaps some more primitive physical element set). Since there are finitely many atoms in the human head, there must be finitely many configurations and hence finitely many states.

items required for mimicry of the TM. Thus, it is conceivable that ACT could be distracted from simulating a TM.

Fourth, this model assumes that all propositions added to memory by ACT productions will actually be successfully encoded. However, there is some probability that any individual link will not be established. Therefore, it might not be possible to later recall the information on the tape. It is possible to imagine a version of the ACT system that avoided most of the failures of recall by encoding information redundantly. That is, suppose there is a probability q of failing to encode a proposition. If n copies of the proposition are formed, that probability can be reduced to q^n. By choosing n large enough, the probability of failure to encode information could be made arbitrarily small. However, after m steps the TM would have encoded m values. The probability of at least one error after m steps would be $1 - (1 - q^n)^m$. So, no matter how small q^n, there will be a value of m for which the probability of an error after m steps will be near 1. So, it is a virtual certainty, even with redundant encoding, that ACT's simulation of a TM will eventually suffer a failure of recall. Hence, error-free performance by an ACT system is not possible. In this way it differs fundamentally from the formal automata against which logical power is usually measured.

So we can say that ACT predicts that humans are capable of performing any task a TM can perform with the following qualifications: (1) they will fail if the task makes a *very* large demand on memory; (2) they may be very slow at the task; (3) they can be distracted from the task; and (4) there is a nonzero chance of random error due to failure of memory. As far as it goes, this seems an accurate prediction about human abilities. What is important and yet undecided is what ACT predicts about the relative difficulty of various tasks in terms of processing times and error rates. Deriving a characterization of performance limitations is the traditional task of psychology and it will occupy much of the remainder of this book.

SUMMARY OF CHAPTER 4

A set of predisposing biases is given which strongly influenced the shape of the ACT theory. These biases are that cognition is basically parallel; that there is a fundamental distinction to be made between procedural and declarative knowledge; that memory is nonerasable; that memory only involves referential nodes; that it represents information in terms of nonambiguous, subject–predicate propositions; that cognition is data driven; that the units of cognitive procedures are simple and modular; and that they are acquired in the course of performing a procedure. Use of these preconceived biases in theory construction is justified by the fact that they will probably lead to more rapid development of a correct theory. The ACT model embodies these biases. There are also additional assumptions to flesh out the theory. It consists of a propositional network over which activation spreads and productions which can be elicited by the active portion of the network. The theory is embodied in a computer program. This program basically serves as an "interpreter" for programs written with ACT productions. Examples are given of ACT production systems to perform the Sternberg task, to perform the memory span task, and to parse noun phrases.

ACT can be shown to be capable of mimicking the moves of an arbitrary Turing Machine and so is capable of performing any well-defined behavior. However, it suffers a number of basic performance limitations on the speed and accuracy with which it can perform a behavior. The speed and success with which productions can be elicited is limited by the requirement that they only have access to the active portion of memory. The size of this active portion is limited by a periodic dampening process which deactivates all the network structure except a select few nodes. It is also limited by the speed at which activation can spread through memory. The speed with which productions can apply is also limited by the strength of a production and by the number of other productions that are simultaneously being applied. A final performance limitation on ACT comes from the fact that it encodes associations in memory with only a certain probability.

REFERENCES

Anderson, J. R., & Bower, G. H. *Human associative memory*. Washington: Winston, 1973.

Arbib, M. *Brain, machine, and mathematics*. New York: McGraw-Hill, 1964.

Collins, A. M., & Quillian, M. R. How to make a language user. In E. Tulving & W. Donaldson (Eds.), *Organization and memory*. New York: Academic Press, 1972.

Neisser, U. The multiplicity of thought. *British Journal of Psychology,* 1963, **54,** 1–14.

Newell, A. Production systems: Models of control structures. In W. G. Chase (Ed.), *Visual information processing*. New York: Academic Press, 1973. Pp. 463–526.

Newell, A., & Simon, H. *Human problem solving*. Englewood Cliffs, New Jersey: Prentice-Hall, 1972.

Norman, D. A., Rumelhart, D. E., & the LNR Research Group. *Explorations in cognition*. San Francisco: Freeman, 1975.

Posner, M. I., & Snyder, C. R. R. Attention and cognitive control. In R. L. Solso (Ed.), *Information processing and cognition*. Hillsdale, New Jersey: Lawrence Erlbaum Assoc., 1975.

Ryle, G. *The concept of mind*. London: Hutchinson, 1949.

Sperling, G. A. The information available in brief visual presentation. *Psychological Monographs,* 1960, **74,** Whole No. 498.

Suppes, P. Stimulus–response theory of finite automata. *Journal of Mathematical Psychology,* 1969, **6,** 327–355.

Winograd, T. Frame representations and the declarative-procedural controversy. In D. Bobrow & A. Collins (Eds.), *Representations and understanding*. New York: Academic Press, 1975.

5
ACT's Propositional Network

With this system Anderson and Bower have been able to make impressively rapid progress in analyzing the way in which people retrieve from memory information concerning relatively complex verbal material. But rapid progress always involves a price, and in this instance the price has been the necessity of postulating de novo many elaborate properties of the memory system.

WILLIAM K. ESTES

5.1 PROPOSITIONAL NETWORKS AS PSYCHOLOGICAL MODELS

This section will define and motivate propositional networks. The next section describes ACT's propositional network, which is similar to the HAM representation. The final section presents a formalization of the syntax for the ACT network.

Finite Labeled Graphs

Propositional networks are a special case of *finite labeled graphs*. A finite labeled graph is most precisely represented as an ordered triple:

$$G = \langle R, N, A \rangle$$

where R is a finite set of relations, N is a finite set of nodes, and A is a finite set of links in the graph.

The members of A are represented by triples of elements denoted $\langle a \quad X \quad b \rangle$. In the pictorial representation that is so natural for graphs, a and b are nodes connected by a link and X is a relation labeling the link. As a simple example, consider the graph in Fig. 5.1 of some family relations. It would be encoded by the following: $\langle \{$wife-of, husband-of, son-of, mother-of, sister-of, daughter-of, cousin-of,$\}$ $\{$John, Mary, Harry, Bill, Jane$\}$, $\{\langle$John, husband-of, Mary$\rangle$, $\langle$Mary, wife-of, John$\rangle$, $\langle$Mary, sister-of, Harry$\rangle$, $\langle$Mary, mother-of, Bill$\rangle$, $\langle$Bill, son-of, John$\rangle$, $\langle$Bill, cousin-of, Jane$\rangle$, $\langle$Jane, cousin-of, Bill$\rangle$, $\langle$Jane, daughter-of, Harry$\rangle\}$. As Anderson and Bower (1973) wrote of this formal encoding of labeled networks—"It brings home the point that a picture is worth a thousand words."

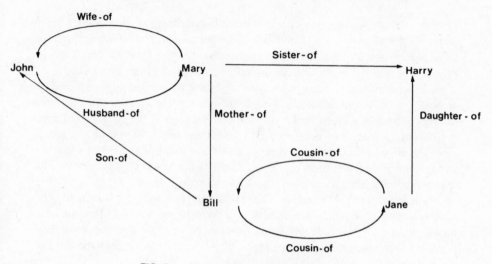

FIG. 5.1   An example of a finite relational graph.

It does serve to make the information contained in Fig. 5.1 excruciatingly precise and devoid of all excess meaning. Without this set encoding one might be tempted, seeing Fig. 5.1, to make something of the curvature or length of the arrows. These excess meanings are not preserved in the set encoding. However, the set encoding does indicate that the direction of an arrow and its label are important. An arrow in one direction may or may not be accompanied by an arrow in the opposite direction. If it is, the reverse arrow need not have the same label. Despite this advantage of preciseness, set-theoretic representations will not be used. This one example of a set-theoretic representation should indicate how the more comprehensible pictorial representation should be interpreted.[1]

The nodes in a network such as ACT are intended to represent "ideas" in the traditional British associationist sense of that term. The links represent access relationships or associations among these ideas. That is, the links represent which ideas can lead to (elicit) each other. As such, a network like ACT's is just a formal embodiment of an associative analysis of the contents of the human mind. The use of such networks makes no theoretical claims and should not be the source of controversy. Such a network only constitutes an attempt to set down on paper what ideas are connected and the relations that connect them. Networks would be

[1]Despite the fact ACT uses propositional networks, it is doubtful whether formal results from graph theory (for example, Harary, 1969) will have useful applications to the analysis of ACT. It is true that graph-theoretic notions like distance, in-degree, and out-degree play a significant role in the theory. However, one does not have to study graph theory to appreciate their application in ACT. What is doubtful is whether any of the deep and important results of graph theory can be applied to ACT (for example, the results concerning the linkage differences that underlie planar versus nonplanar graphs).

controversial and wrong if they claimed that all possible connections among ideas could be specified by a *finite* network. Such a claim would be wrong because there is a creative component to associative thought such that ideas are capable of entering into relations with an unlimited variety of other ideas. However, modern network theories have conceded this point by permitting procedures of elaboration, deduction, induction, etc., to operate on these network structures and to create new connections in the network. Productions in the ACT model give the system a capacity to generate new connections beyond those in any initial network. Given this liberalized conception of a network it is hard to see what strong empirical claims it makes. Rips, Shoben, and Smith (1973) contrast set-theoretic approaches with network approaches, but as Hollan (1975) pointed out, these are just notational differences. Network representations just amount to convenient notations for representing knowledge. Whether networks will remain with us will depend on how convenient they prove to be—that is, whether or not they turn out to be cumbersome in some applications. So far, they seem to be serving psychology rather well.

Propositional Networks

A propositional network is more than just a finite labeled graph. There are sub-configurations in the network that correspond to propositions. These subconfigurations refer to situations external to the network, have truth values, and are structured according to syntactic principles. As an example, consider the ACT representation in Fig. 5.2. The configuration of associations interconnecting *John, hit, Mary, x, y, z, u,* and *v* corresponds to the proposition *John hit Mary.* This asserts something about the external world and is either true or false. Also

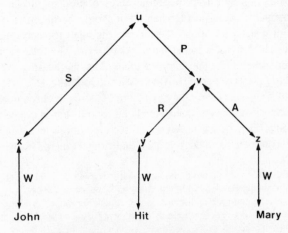

FIG. 5.2   An example of an ACT proposition.

there are rules in ACT about what constitutes an acceptable structure. For example, it is not possible to have a subject (S) link and relation (R) link emanating from the same node in such a structure.

Such propositional networks, in a sense, are rich in theoretical claims in a way finite labeled graphs are not. They are attempts to set forth a language of the mind, a "mentalese" in which all knowledge is to be represented. However, as argued in Section 1.2, I doubt that these representational assumptions can be shown to be empirically correct or wrong. It is only when they are interfaced with process assumptions that they gain empirical force. As shown in Section 1.2, very different representations can probably be made to yield identical predictions if they are interfaced with different process assumptions. Thus, one must take ACT representations like that in Fig. 5.2 with a certain grain of salt.

Propositional network models are attractive for two reasons. First, a set of processes has been developed which enable them to predict a number of interesting empirical phenomena concerning processing of linguistic material. Many of these processes were expounded in Anderson and Bower (1973) and Norman and Rumelhart (1975). Others will be developed in the remainder of this book. Other representational formalisms may also be able to explain these phenomena, but so far explicit process models involving these formalisms have not been proposed. The other reason for preferring propositional networks is that they appear to have advantages as computer data bases in information retrieval tasks. I would like to devote the remainder of this section to discussing why propositional networks lead to efficient computer information retrieval systems and noting those properties of the computer system that seem similar to human memory. Because such network systems have human-like properties and because they lead to efficiencies in information processing, I would claim that a network model (a) constitutes a viable psychological model and (b) is an important component to human intelligence. For a somewhat different discussion of propositional networks as computer models, see Woods (1975).

Until recently psychologists had not thought realistically about how humans manage the large data base of facts stored in their memory. Efficient search through a large data base is a serious obstacle to the success of many artificial intelligence applications in areas such as theorem proving, problem solving, and language understanding. There is a tendency for a particular fact to become increasingly inaccessible as these systems have to deal with more facts. It could be the case that humans do not suffer such difficulties. However, it is easy to demonstrate (see Chapter 8) that learning new information does interfere with retention of old information. On the other hand, it could be the case that humans have no means of making their search of memory efficient. For instance, to retrieve a particular fact they might simply have to serially search through all the facts they know. Again it can be shown that this is not the case. There are a number of efficiencies used in propositional networks which humans also seem to use:

Indexing by Concepts

Each node in a propositional network represents a concept and attached to that node are all the facts we know about the concept. This conveys upon propositional networks a feature I term *indexing by concept*. That is, if we can retrieve a concept's location in memory we will find at that location all the facts we know about this concept. This contrasts with a number of memory schemes in current computer models where one must serially scan through all the facts the system knows. There is no way to selectively focus on the facts relevant to a particular concept.

Double-Linked Structures

Note that the links in Fig. 5.2 are double-arrowed. This is meant to indicate the double-linked character of network structures. There are independent paths going in both directions in the network. This means that it is as easy to retrieve an answer to *Who did John hit?* where one searches from *John* to *Mary* as it is to retrieve an answer to *Who hit Mary?* where search goes in the opposite direction. Because of its double-linked character, the memory structure can be accessed with equal facility from any point in the network. Independence of access is an important feature of memory. All network structure in the ACT model is double-linked (although the links will generally be indicated by unidirectional arrows).

Indifference to Recombination

Another feature of propositional networks is that each proposition is "more or less" *self-contained,* and can enter into different combinations: Suppose the subject heard the following series of sentences:

(1)   John is a tall lawyer.

(2)   The lawyer owned a dog.

(3)   John kicked a model.

(4)   The model's name is Jane.

(5)   The model John kicked owns a car.

After hearing this information, a subject might set up the information structure like that illustrated in Fig. 5.3. Now he would be able to respond to questions like

(6)   Did a lawyer kick a model?

(7)   What does Jane own?

(8)   Did a dog-owner kick a car-owner?

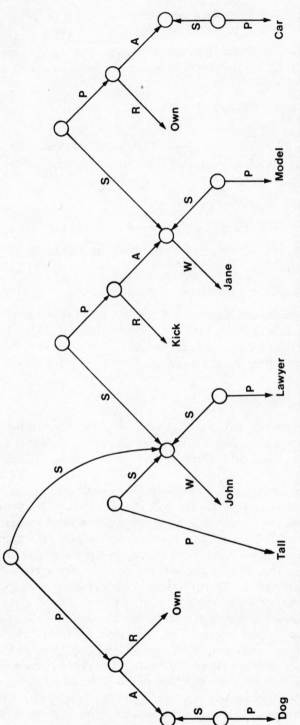

FIG. 5.3 An ACT network encoding a set of related propositions. This representation ignores most of W links between concepts and words and simply represents the concept by the word. This is done to simplify the network. The convention is used extensively throughout the book. Also, words like "own" have been duplicated for pictorial simplification.

151

etc., which requires that the subject access this information in new combinations. It permits the subject to answer these questions as quickly as one like

(9)   Is John a tall lawyer?

which queries an old fact.

Indifference to recombination seems a basic feature of human memory. In the famous work of Bransford and Franks (1971) they had subjects study sentences like

(10)   The rock crushed the hut.

(11)   The tiny hut was beside the woods.

After studying these, subjects would think they had heard new recombinations like

(12)   The rock crushed the tiny hut.

This indifference to recombination is not always found in human memory (for example, Anderson & Bower, 1973, Section 11.3; Kieras, 1974; Anderson & Hastie, 1974), but is found in many circumstances. It is important to the intelligent and efficient utilization of our memories.

Type–Token Distinction

Propositional networks make use of a type-token distinction. When using a concept in a particular proposition it is not necessary to write into that proposition all the information known about or defining that concept. Rather, just a pointer (token) is introducted to that concept (type) in memory where the definition of the concept is stored. So in representing *John kicked Mary* it is only necessary to introduce a pointer to the *Mary* concept (see Fig. 5.2) and not necessary to represent all the facts known about *Mary*. If one wants to retrieve information about the person, *Mary,* mentioned in the proposition one only needs to go to the location pointed to by the token. It is not necessary to actually incorporate this information into the proposition. In this way, propositional networks (and presumably human memories) can represent information about a concept without being bogged down by the complexity of the concept.

There are two other distinctions in propositional networks which are sometimes also called type–token distinctions. One is the relation between general concepts and individuals that instantiate the concepts. So, in Fig. 5.3, the specific *dog* that John owns is separate from the general concept *dog*. This distinction is necessary so that one can keep straight which facts are true of which exemplars of the dog class. The other distinction is between words and the concepts they reference. This distinction is necessary to keep separate facts about the word (for example, John can't spell *geography*) from facts about the concept (for example, John studies geography).

Uniqueness of Nodes

An attempt is made in propositional networks to use just one node to represent each concept, individual, relation, proposition, etc. This is very helpful because it means that it is only necessary to look at one place in the network for information relevant to each semantic object. However, there are difficulties in always assuring that each semantic object has but one representation. For instance, in reading a detective novel I may not know that the murderer and the butler are one and the same. Therefore, a distinct node would be set up to represent the butler and another to represent the murderer. When I learn of their identity I must somehow revise my memory to accommodate this fact. So it is impossible to guarantee the uniqueness of nodes. However, propositional networks try to achieve a maximum of uniqueness.

Anderson and Hastie (1974) performed an experiment that looked at what happened when subjects were induced to set up two nodes that referred to the same individual. They had subjects learn a set of facts referring to individuals by name (for example, James Bartlett) or by profession (for example, the lawyer) such as

(13)   James Bartlett rescued the kitten.

(14)   The lawyer sold the necklace.

Either before or after learning these facts subjects were told that the name and the profession referred to the same person. Subjects who only learned of the identity afterward were considerably slowed in a reaction time task where they had to affirm of one label a predicate learned of the other, for example,

(15)   The lawyer rescued the kitten.

Subjects who had learned about the identity before were as fast to affirm such statements as they were to affirm statements that were actually studied.

Invariance Under Paraphrase

Another feature of propositional networks, similar to identity of nodes, is the attempt to achieve invariance under paraphrase. This refers to the attempt to use a single representation for all sentences of identical meaning. As discussed in Section 2.5 this has considerable advantages in computer implementation since inference rules need only be framed for one representation rather than redundant rules for many different representations. Psychological evidence for invariance under paraphrase comes from the research showing that subjects have difficulty remembering which of a number of paraphrases they heard. However, as also shown in Section 2.5, invariance under paraphrase cannot always be possible. It would place impossible burdens on the comprehension system to expect it to give identical representation to all paraphrases. So, much like identity of nodes, invariance under paraphrase is a goal of propositional networks which can only be partially met.

Use of Relational Information

Note that the links emanating from a node are labeled with different relations. As an example, the node for the individual *Jane* in Fig. 5.3 has emanating from it a W link, an A link, and two S links. It is easy to construct a computer program that takes advantage of this relational information. For instance, in searching for a proposition related to an individual by an S link it need only consider those links labeled with S. This can result in a considerable savings in search time. However, the human system apparently does not take advantage of this fact. I have shown that subjects' searches of memory are as much slowed down by links with different relations as by links with the same relation (Anderson, 1975). This fact and many others will be used in Chapter 8 as evidence for a diffuse activation search along the lines of Quillian (1969), rather than the logical serial search proposed by Anderson and Bower (1973).

5.2   REPRESENTATIONAL ASSUMPTIONS

This section will explain and motivate the structural assumptions underlying the ACT propositional network. To illustrate this notation and the ACT network, examples of ACT representations will be given for the meanings commonly associated with English sentences. However, by so representing these sentences, I am not implying that subjects in a typical memory experiment represent sentences as I prescribe. Certainly the interpretation a subject gives to a sentence varies as a function of context, the subject's knowledge, and other random factors. As I will argue in Chapter 10, subjects elaborate and expand upon a sentence's core meaning. The ACT formalism developed in this section can represent any of these elaborations. However, for illustrative purposes I will use it to represent the core meaning associated with certain sentences. I assume this core meaning is common to all subjects, but that their elaborations can differ wildly.

This section assumes the reader is familiar with the HAM representation which was explained in Section 2.2. HAM will be frequently used for comparison in explaining ACT representations. Some of HAM's representational formalisms have been kept, some eliminated, and there are new additions. Those aspects of HAM that were redundant with other aspects were eliminated. It seemed an unnecessary complication to have more representational assumptions than were needed to express the information. Additions were made to enable ACT to represent certain conceptions that were not representable with the HAM formalisms. Also some additions were made to allow ACT to represent simply certain propositions that could only be represented by complex structures in HAM. These deletions and additions, then, are motivated by two of the criteria set forth in Section 1.3 for a cognitive theory—that is, parsimony and broad generality.

There are certain conventions for representing ACT networks which should be stated at the outset. Links in ACT networks point from one node to another. Usually, but not always, the pointed-from node is above the pointed-to node. *Terminal nodes* only have links pointing to them. *Nonterminal nodes* have links pointing from them. *Root nodes* only have links pointing from them. There is a certain significance to the directionality of the links in that the higher nodes are defined in terms of the nodes to which they point. However, it should also be appreciated that the ACT networks are really double-linked structures. That is, if there is an association from node A to node B labeled with relation R, there is an association in the opposite direction labeled with R-inverse. Thus, even though links are represented only in the one direction in the figures, there are links in both directions according to the theory.

In this section I discuss the meaning of various network configurations as well as the permissible network structures. To discuss meaning I use various set-theoretical concepts. I realize that such use has a tendency to "put off" some readers since it is unnatural to think of the meaning in terms of set-theoretical constructs. Therefore, it needs to be emphasized that the set-theoretical terminology is being used to achieve a precise way of specifying meaning. I do not mean to endorse any unfortunate metaphysical connotations that this usage might have.

Subject–Predicate Structures

The central representational structure in ACT is the subject–predicate construction, a carry-over from HAM. Figure 5.4 illustrates how the subject–predicate construction can be used to represent some simple sentences. The root node represents the proposition. The proposition takes the node pointed to by the P link and predicates it of the node pointed to by the S link. The set-theoretical interpretation of such a construction is that the subject is a subset of the predicate. This subject–predicate construction will be the only one in ACT that bears a truth value.

The proposition node is critical to permit modification of a proposition by such properties as false, probable, fortunate, etc. For instance, Fig. 5.5a represents the proposition *It is fortunate Caesar is dead*. The proposition node is also important for the purpose of subsequently qualifying the truth of a stored proposition. Suppose a subject initially believes that *It is fortunate Caesar is dead* and stores a proposition like Fig. 5.5a. Later he might change his mind. Since memory is nonerasable he cannot just remove that proposition from memory. What he can

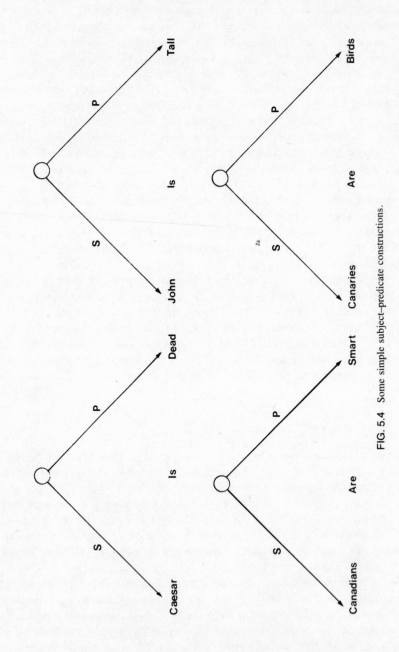

FIG. 5.4 Some simple subject–predicate constructions.

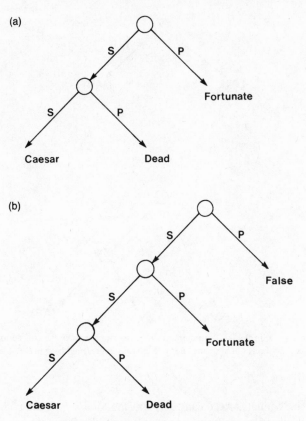

FIG. 5.5 Examples of truth qualification.

do is illustrated in Fig. 5.5b where a *false* tag is attached to the original structure. So it is essential when structures like these are initially stored that a proposition node is set up to permit later truth qualification.

Relation-Argument Structures

It is possible to define concepts relationally in ACT. Thus, we can have the concept of "lovers of Mary." Figure 5.6a shows how this would be represented in ACT. A node, X, is set up which points by an R arrow to the relation node *love* and an A arrow to the argument *Mary*. This node represents the concept of "all lovers of Mary." There was really no way to express this concept in HAM. Figure 5.6b shows the best that we were able to do. In that HAM structure the node X represents some people that love Mary, but it does not necessarily represent all the people that do. It is important to have a means for distinguishing between the concept of all the individuals that bear a particular relation to a concept and a subset

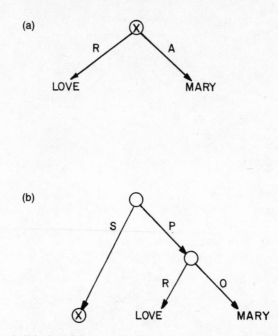

FIG. 5.6 The node X in the ACT structure in Fig. 5.6a can represent the concept of all lovers of Mary. The node X in the HAM structure in Fig. 5.6b only represents the concept of some lovers of Mary.

of all these individuals. ACT can represent the total set by the node X in Fig. 5.6a and the subset by the node X in a structure like Fig. 5.6b (except that the ACT structure would have an A link rather than a 0 link).

Figure 5.7 illustrates some ways that the relation-argument structure can appear in ACT. In Figures 5.7a and 5.7c it appears as the subject of a predicate. These examples are propositions that it was not possible to represent in HAM. For instance, Fig. 5.7c represents *Defenders of liberty are heroes* where *all defenders of liberties* is intended. HAM could only represent (via a structure like Fig. 5.6b) *Some defenders of liberty are heroes*. Figures 5.7b and 5.7d represent the relation-argument construction as predicate. These are very similar to the representations that were common in HAM and similar to the deep structures proposed by Chomsky (1965) where the sentence is rewritten as noun plus verb phrase and the verb phrase is rewritten as verb plus noun.

It is something of a misnomer to refer to the relational terms in Fig. 5.7 and elsewhere as relations. They are better thought of as functions in that they map one concept, their argument, onto another concept, the meaning of the relational structure. It is more conventional in logic to think of relations as mapping their arguments onto propositions or truth values.

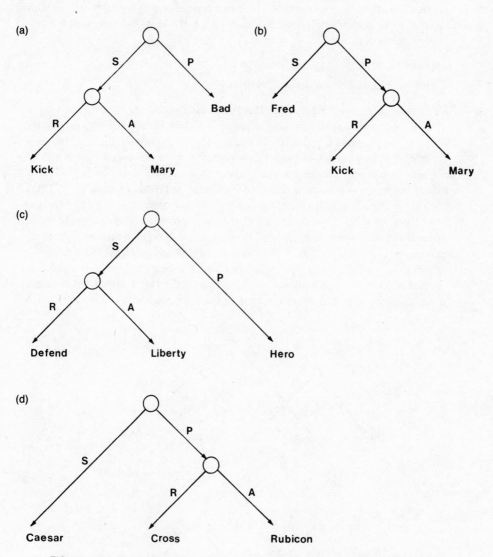

FIG. 5.7   Some examples of the use of ACT's relation-argument structures in propositions.

Multiargument Structures

In HAM we restricted facts to containing only two arguments—a subject and a predicate. This meant that there was no direct representation for propositions with three or more arguments. Figure 5.8 shows how HAM would represent the following sentences:

(16a)   John gave the book to Mary.

(16b)   John opened the door with a key.

This amounts to unpacking such multiargument sentences into a number of simple propositions. This solution is unsatisfactory basically because of the complexity of the representation. Complexity in a representation is something to avoid as a general rule. However, it is particularly bothersome in this case because it does not seem that *John gave the book to Mary* is that much more complex than *John hit Mary* which has a much simpler representation in HAM. Therefore, ACT has been given the capacity for multiargument relational structures. Figures 5.9a and 5.9b show how ACT would represent the two sentences in question. In these examples two argument links, A_1 and A_2, are created to point to the two arguments in the predicate. In general, if there are n terms in the predicate we would use relations $A_1, \ldots, A_n$. Thus, the relation A which appears in Figs. 5.6 and 5.7 is equivalent to A_1. In our work on language processing (see Chapter 11) we have never needed more than two argument links. It seems unlikely that more than

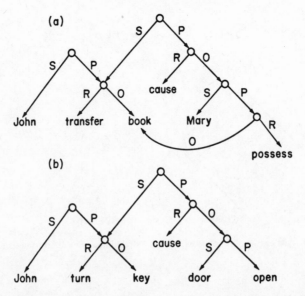

FIG. 5.8   How HAM represented multiargument sentences—(a) *John gave the book to Mary* and (b) *John opened the door with a key.*

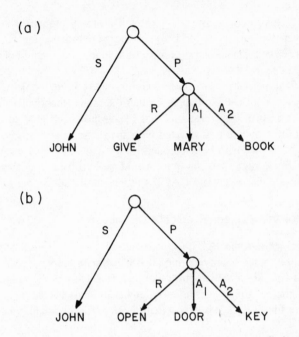

FIG. 5.9   How ACT represents multiargument sentences—(a) *John gave the book to Mary* and (b) *John opened the door with a key.*

three or four will ever be needed. The semantic interpretation of the relational nodes created in these multiargument structures is just a generalization of the one-argument case. For instance, the relational structure in Fig. 5.9a represents *all people who give Mary books.*

Anderson and Bower made three arguments against the option of multiargument relations. First, they argued that such structures did not capture certain inferences. For instance, Fig. 5.9a does not represent that *Mary has the book,* whereas Fig. 5.8a does. However, all structures fail to represent certain valid inferences. For instance, the HAM representation in Fig. 5.8a does not represent the inference *John used to have the book* or the probable inference that *Mary physically contacted the book,* etc. One can in the ACT framework define productions that will make these inferences and add them to memory as well as the structures in Fig. 5.9. So, it is not the case that ACT is prevented from encoding such inferences; rather, it is optional whether or not ACT does so.

A second criticism of Anderson and Bower was that structures like Fig. 5.9 increase the number of link labels required. However, the increase seems unlikely to be more than three additional labels. After experience working with structures like those in Fig. 5.8 versus those in Fig. 5.9, I can report the simplification in network structure seems well worth the increase in number of labels. The third argument given by Anderson and Bower was that it was easier to take advantage of partial overlaps in encoding propositions if a binary branching structure was used. However, we will see (page 178) that there are independent reasons for rejecting the use of overlap among propositions to reduce the amount of information to be encoded.

One might wonder why case relations (Fillmore, 1968) like object, instrument, and recipient were not used in Fig. 5.9 rather than the semantically neutral terms $A_1, A_2, \ldots$. The principle reason is that I have not been able to discern any rigorously defined meaning associated with such case relations. For instance, it seems that what it means to be a recipient (or dative) can vary greatly depending on the verb. Such vague case notions would be an obstacle to developing the semantic analysis that is given of ACT's representational system in Chapter 7.

Motivation for the Subject–Predicate Distinction

It might seem strange that ACT has maintained a subject–predicate distinction in its representation while abandoning the use of binary branching structure. Why not have an n-ary relational structure like Fig. 5.10a where the proposition node is directly connected to subject, relation, and arguments? What is the motivation for a structure like Fig. 5.10b where there is an extra predicate node? There are

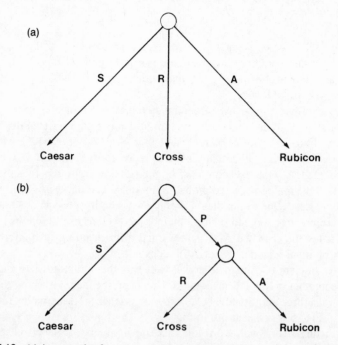

FIG. 5.10   (a) An example of an n-ary relational structure. (b) The corresponding ACT structure.

five arguments that can be made for maintaining the subject–predicate distinction. Only the first two have any real force. The other three will be reviewed because they have been made elsewhere.

1. *Parsimony in representation.*   Because of its subject–predicate construction ACT can give similar representations to statements of the form:

(17)   Caesar crossed the Rubicon.

(18)   Caesar jumped.

(19)   Caesar was emperor.

(20)   Caesar was smart.

(21)   The murderers of Caesar were evil.

In each of these cases the subject would be asserted by a subject–predicate construction to be a subset of the predicate. It is hard to see how one would represent all these examples in an *n*-ary relational network without introducing further network complications.

2. *Quantificational power.*   One of the frequent problems with network representations is that it is difficult to express quantificational relations within them (for example, see Chapter 2). This is particularly the case for *n*-ary relational structures where it is hard to represent the difference between universal and existential quantification and to express conventions concerning the scope of various quantificational terms. On the other hand, the ACT subject–predicate construction and relation-argument construction come with an explicit quantificational interpretation. The subject is asserted to be a subset of the predicate. The concept created by a relation-argument construction is defined to be the set of all objects that bear the relation to that argument. Combined with other, to-be-introduced, ACT conventions, the ACT network achieves considerable quantificational power.[2] The quantificational power of ACT is thoroughly discussed in Chapter 7.

3. *Universality of subject–predicate constructions.*   A strong argument for the subject–predicate construction would be that it is a universal distinction made in cognition and language. There is a long philosophical tradition going back to Aristotle which argues for the centrality of that distinction. However, the philosophers are hardly agreed on this issue (see Loux, 1970; Ramsey, 1931; Russell, 1911–1912). Chomsky's (1965) aspects reinforced the tradition in linguistics to ascribe a subject–predicate representation to language. Since then other linguists (Fillmore, 1968; McCawley, 1970) have argued against the subject–predicate distinction as primitive. Even more recently there have been further arguments on

---

[2]However, there are certain quantificational relationships expressible in natural language which are not really expressible in the ACT network. In Section 7.3 I show how these can be dealt with using the production system.

the other side (Culicover & Wexler, 1974). The philosophical and linguistic debate on the universality of the subject–predicate distinction, then, has become quite murky. In linguistics particularly, it depends on technical issues of transformational grammar representation—which I cannot properly evaluate. Basically, the issue of whether, "deep-down," cognition is subject–predicate seems too abstract to be decided on the basis of empirical data.

4. *Economy of representation.*   Anderson and Bower (1973) argued that the HAM binary structure permitted certain efficiencies in representation. In retrospect, these arguments about economy of storage are not compelling for a number of reasons. First, elsewhere within the HAM model Anderson and Bower propose that subjects use distinctly noneconomic representations in semantic memory experiments and paired-associates experiments. Second, the one attempt to show that subjects could economize on redundancy within propositions (Anderson & Bower, 1973, Section 8.2) failed. Finally, in the ACT analysis of the memory phenomena surrounding depth of processing, it proves important to postulate that there is no limitation on the amount of information that can be stored (see Chapter 10). Therefore, there seems to be little motivation for economy of representation within ACT.

5. *Long-term memory data.*   Note that in the ACT representation of subject–verb–object sentences the verb and object are closer to each other than either is to the subject. Thus, one might expect to see greater contingency in the recall of verb and object than verb and subject or subject and object. That is, verb and object should tend to be better prompts for recall of each other and tend to be recalled together in an all-or-none fashion. An early experiment (Anderson & Bower, 1973, Section 10.2) confirmed these predictions but a later experiment (Section 10.5) gave just the opposite result. Another prediction is that subjects should be faster retrieving a connection between verb and object than between verb and subject because the former are closer together. This can be tested by presenting the subject with pairs of words and asking them to decide whether the pair came from the same sentence. ACT would seem to predict that subjects should be faster making this judgment about verb and object than other pairs. In unpublished experiments, I have failed to find evidence to support this.

In retrospect, it seems naive to have expected such effects. The experiments suppose that when subjects study sentences like *In the park a hippie touched a debutante,* they set up a nice, tidy representation of just the information in the sentence. Subjects always told us that they did a lot more, elaborating the sentences in many unspecified ways, introducing all sorts of extra and uncontrolled connections among elements. Thus, they might elaborate the given sentence with:

The *hippie* was at a love-in in the *park.* The *debutante* was attending a classical concert in the *park.* The attenders at the love-in were running about *touching* people in the *park.* The *hippie* was *touching* everyone. The *hippie* saw the *debutante* in her beautiful gown. The *hippie* ran up to *debutante* and *touched* her. The *debutante* was upset because she did not want to have her gown *touched*.

Note that these extra sentences have introduced extra connections between each *pair* of elements in the sentence. Clearly, a proximity metric based on supposed closeness of object and verb is going to be worthless if a subject goes through anything like this elaborative process. Since subjects do, I do not think one can use sentence recall data to directly decide issues of representation. The effects of such elaborations will be discussed further in Chapter 10.

Elimination of HAM Features

It is worth noting the deletion of a number of representational features that were part of the HAM representation and explaining why these deletions have occurred. There are no longer special conventions for representing the context (time + location) of a fact. Such contextual information can be represented in ACT as propositions true of an embedded proposition. Figure 5.11a illustrates how such information was represented in HAM and Fig. 5.11b illustrates how it is represented in ACT. Besides yielding a reduction in the number of representational primitives, ACT's option does away with the HAM inelegance of having two distinct types of truth-bearing nodes—the proposition node and the fact node. (What was the fact node in HAM becomes the proposition node in ACT.) Another virtue of the deletion of the context subtree is that it is now possible to qualify the truth of the contextual elements independent of the truth of the main fact. For example, it becomes easy in ACT to represent something like "It probably was in the park that the hippie touched the debutante." Note that there are three proposition nodes in Fig. 5.11b. Any of these can be subsequently qualified with an "is false" tag. Thus, we can separately represent:

(22)   The hippie did not touch the debutante.

(23)   It was not in the park that the hippie touched the debutante.

(24)   It was not at night that the hippie touched the debutante.

Terminal Quantification

In HAM, as in ACT, new propositions are set up to assert new relations among existing concepts. In HAM there were four ways of relating new propositions to existing nodes (concepts). One way was just to have various terminal nodes in the propositions take the form of existing long-term memory nodes. The other three ways related nodes in the proposition to existing concepts through *terminal*

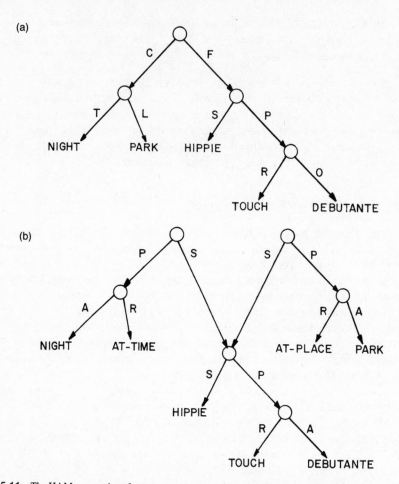

FIG. 5.11   The HAM conventions for representing time and location in (a) have been replaced by the ACT conventions in (b).

quantification. Two of these varieties of terminal quantification have been eliminated in ACT, and the other has undergone some modification.

One of the types of terminal quantification involved use of the generic operator (∀). It was used to predicate something of all individuals in a class. For instance, Fig. 5.12 shows how HAM represented *All dogs chase cats*. A node corresponding to a prototypical or generic dog is created and connected to the class concept by a generic link. This was intended to provide the expressive power of universal quantification. The generic link was inadequate as a means of achieving universal quantification in HAM and, as will be later shown, it is unnecessary in ACT. The inadequacy concerned the fact that there was no way to correctly represent propositions of the form *All black dogs are faithful*. Figure 5.12b shows the representation that would have been assigned to the sentence by HAM. A subset of dogs is created and of this subset it is predicated that all members of it are *black* and *faithful*. This is the same representation that would have been assigned to *All faithful dogs are black* although this sentence has a different meaning. Later in this section an ACT representation is given that discriminates between these two types of sentences.

The second means of terminal quantification in HAM involved relating a subset to a set by a subset link ($\subseteq$). Subset relationships are conveyed redundantly by two structures in the HAM—both by the subset relation and by the S–P construction. For instance, as Fig. 5.13a shows, in the sentence *John drew red squares,* the information that the objects are square is conveyed by subset and in *John drew square houses* it is conveyed by an S–P construction (Fig. 5.13b). Thus, HAM uses S–P constructions for adjectives and subset constructions for nouns although there is no difference in meaning. Clearly, in the interest of parsimony one construction must go. The S–P construction is needed because a

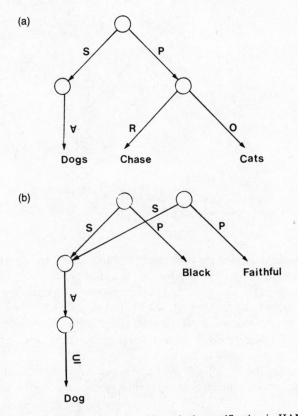

FIG. 5.12 Examples of the use of terminal quantification in HAM.

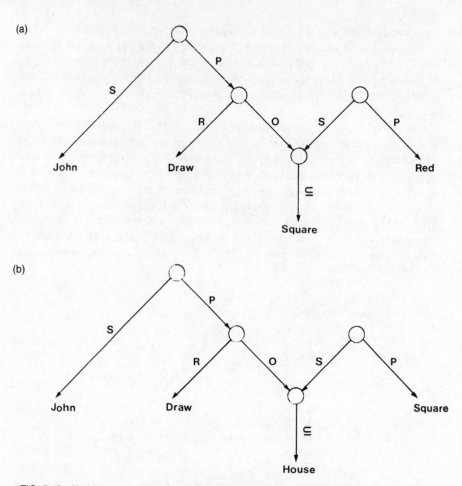

FIG. 5.13 HAM representations for (a) John drew red squares. (b) John drew square houses.

proposition node is needed for truth qualification. In fact, the ⊆ relation is defective because it conveys a proposition but does not admit of truth qualification. That is, with the subset relation, HAM might encode *A platypus is a bird*. Later information might indicate it wrong, but the ⊆ link does not have a proposition node to which an "is false" predicate might be attached. Since memory is nonerasable, HAM would be stuck forever believing this false fact.[3] Therefore the ⊆ link has been eliminated in ACT.

In ACT we can have a subject–predicate construction asserting that Spot is a dog. Since the semantic interpretation of subject–predicate constructions is that of

[3]For an inelegant way around the problem see Anderson and Bower (1973, pp. 192–193).

conveying subset information, this requires that the interpretation of Spot be that of a singleton set (that is, a set with one member) that contains the individual *Spot.* This contrasts with HAM where nodes like Spot had individuals as their interpretations. There were set-membership (∈) links in HAM connecting individuals to their sets. These ∈ links provided the third means of terminal quantification in HAM. They are no longer needed in ACT since ACT has no nodes which are interpreted as individuals.

One motivation for HAM's distinction between the subset and set-membership relations was to avoid erroneous inferences permitted by the transitive character of the subset relation. For instance, from *collies are dogs* and *dogs are animals,* it is valid to conclude *collies are animals.* However, from *Spot is a dog,* and *dog is a species,* it is not valid to conclude *Spot is a species.* One needs some way of preventing this latter inference in ACT. It has been suggested to me that the idea of dog in the first sentence, *Spot is a dog*, is not the same as the idea of dog in the second sentence *Dog is a species.* The first refers to the set of all dogs whereas the second is more abstract and refers to the classification of dog. Figure 5.14 shows how this can be represented by creating a classificatory link (labeled C) between the node DOG representing the set *dog* and the node *DOG representing the classification for *dog.*

In a sense, the HAM membership relation (∈) has been traded for the ACT classification relation (C). The classification link gives the representation the facility to encode information about the set itself rather than about individuals in the set. However, the classification node should not be taken literally as meaning the set. This is because one can have classification nodes referring to the same set but with different meanings. For instance, the sets corresponding to dodos and unicorns are both the same—that is, the null set. However, one would not want to endorse the claim that the classification *dodo* is the same as the classification *unicorn.* The classification node is taken to represent not just the set, but something more to distinguish between different concepts with the same referent. In the formal semantics for ACT networks (Section 7.1) the meaning of these classification nodes will be singleton sets whose member is just an unconstrained, abstract element.

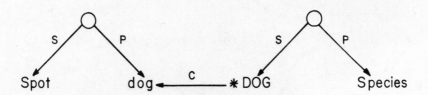

FIG. 5.14   An example of the use of the classificatory (C) link.

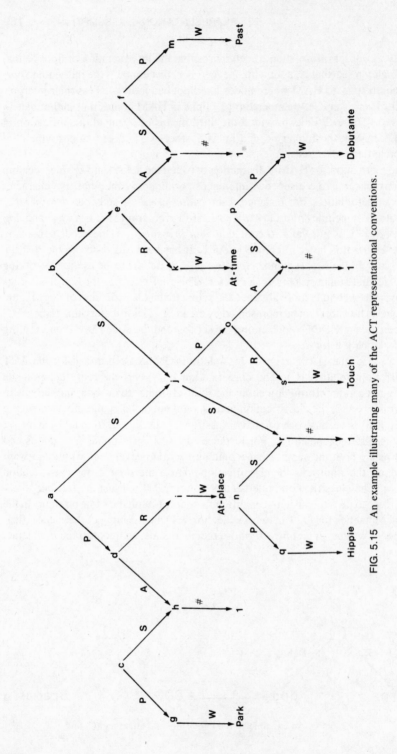

FIG. 5.15   An example illustrating many of the ACT representational conventions.

Cardinality and Word Information

It is often important to know the cardinality of a set, particularly when it is a singleton set. This is indicated by an arrow pointing from the set to a measure. This arrow is labeled with a number sign (#). Figure 5.15 illustrates its use to indicate that certain sets (nodes h, l, r, and t) are singletons. Cardinality is the sort of information that cannot be conveyed by subject–predicate construction because it is not information about the individuals in the set but rather the set itself.[4] HAM really had no means of expressing cardinality. Another example of information about the set rather than about individuals in the set is the lexical information conveyed by the W link. This is also illustrated in Fig. 5.15 (see Footnote 4).

Individual Relations?

Figure 5.15 illustrates most of the ACT conventions introduced so far in this chapter. Unlike other figures it does not simplify the true complexity of the ACT representation. It serves as a good basis of comparison with Fig. 2.5 (page 43) which provides a prototypical HAM representation. One difference between HAM and ACT, not yet remarked upon, is that ACT unlike HAM does not make a distinction between a general concept of a relation like *touch* and a particular occurrence of the relation in a proposition. The HAM distinction seemed necessary for permitting modifications like *gently touch*. However, we will see in the next section how this might be accomplished without individual relations. I find the elimination of individual relations satisfying. It never seemed that one had a natural concept of an individual touching, unlike the clear concept we have of an individual hippie.

Intersection and Union

Thus far, the HAM distinctions of context, location, time, and the terminal quantifiers have been eliminated. The additions have been the classificatory (C) link and the number (#) link. There are two further types of links that ACT possesses. These represent the intersection of two sets and the union of two sets.

The capacity to represent intersection provides ACT with expressive powers not in HAM. Consider the problematical *All black dogs are faithful*. As discussed earlier (page 167) with respect to Fig. 5.12b, HAM could not properly represent the meaning of this sentence. Figure 5.16a shows how the representation of this

---

[4]It would seem better to store the cardinality and word information as predicates of the classification node. That is, one might encode as S–P propositions facts of the order *Classification-node has-as-number n* and *Classification-node has-as-word X*. This would allow the system to change this information should it later prove that n is not the cardinality of the concept or X is not the word for the concept. ACT could qualify the propositions as false. Therefore, the use of # and W links in Fig. 5.15 is best interpreted as a temporary notational convenience.

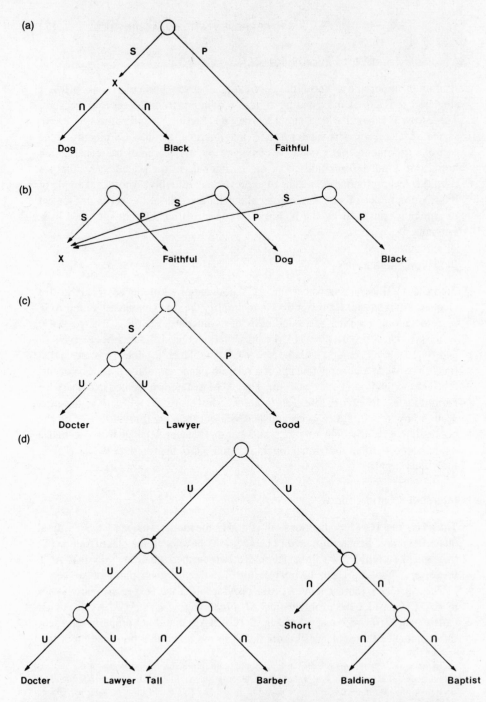

FIG. 5.16   ACT representations for (a) All black dogs are faithful. (b) There are black, faithful, dogs. (c) Doctors and lawyers are good. (d) Doctors, lawyers, tall barbers, and short, balding, Baptists.

proposition falls into place in the new ACT formalism. A set, X, is created which is an intersection of the things *black* and *dogs*. The set X is connected to these two defining sets by the intersection links, denoted ∩.

The reader should be clear on the point of the intersection construction and why Fig. 5.16b is not satisfactory. Figure 5.16b asserts, via three subject–predicate constructions, that there is a set X, all of whose members are *black, dog*, and *faithful*. It does not constrain X, however, to contain all the black dogs. It is this power that one obtains through the intersection construction. Noun phrases in language often convey intersection information.

Figure 5.16c illustrates the use of the union link to represent the sentence *Doctors and lawyers are good*. These union and intersection links can be concatenated to build up descriptions of rather complex sets. Figure 5.16d illustrates a representation for *doctors, lawyers, tall barbers, and short, balding Baptists*.

5.3   FORMAL SYNTAX OF ACT'S NETWORK

The previous section informally described and motivated ACT's network representation. This section will provide a syntax that specifies what are the acceptable network structures. The purpose of a formal syntax is to specify exactly which structures can be found in memory. Such a formalization is essential if one wants a network model to play a well-defined role in the psychological theory. A formal specification of the semantics of ACT network structures will be given in Section 7.1, after Chapter 6 in which I consider the production system. It is difficult to discuss the semantics of the propositional network without reference to the semantics of the production system.

Parts (a) through (g) of Fig. 5.17 illustrate the seven basic network structures used in ACT. Associated with each is an equivalent linear expression. It will often be more convenient to use these linear expressions rather than the network structures. Such linear structures avoid the need to draw a new network everytime we want to illustrate how ACT would represent something. Part (h) illustrates a particular "shorthand" linear structure to indicate the negation of a proposition. Part (b) of Fig. 5.17 illustrates a relational structure with a single argument—denoted $(X \text{ OF } Y)$. A relation structure with n arguments, $Y_1, Y_2, \ldots, Y_n$ would be denoted $(X \text{ OF } Y_1 Y_2 \ldots Y_n)$.

Complex memory structures can be expressed linearly by concatenating together these basic structures. Table 5.1 shows linear representations for a variety of sentences. This table follows a convention used throughout the book of replacing concepts with their corresponding words. When a word is used to refer to its concept that word is written in lower case. So, in sentence 12 of Table 5.1 *John* is in lower case indicating the concept and *Mary* is in upper case indicating the word. Table 5.1 aso follows another convention used throughout

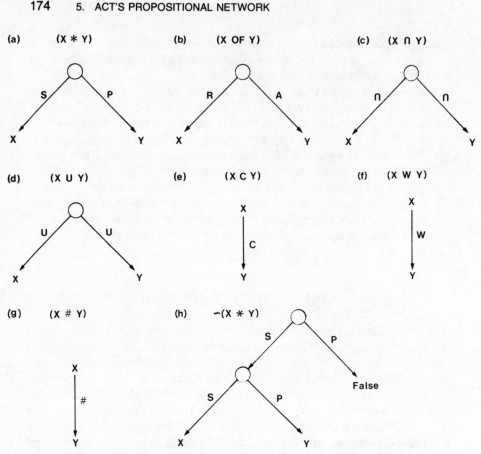

FIG. 5.17 Various network structures and their linearized equivalents.

the book of suppressing cardinality information. It is assumed that the reader knows that the sets referred to by concepts like *canary* have many members while those referred to by proper names like *John* are singleton sets. New sets are denoted by single letters. The convention is that lower case letters denote singleton sets and upper case letters denote sets which are not tagged with cardinality 1. So, for instance, h in Sentence 1 refers to a particular park, whereas A in Sentence 5 refers to some set of cats.

Example 1 gives the linear equivalent of the sentence in Fig. 5.15. It is more complicated than the other linearizations in Table 5.1. In representing it, each of the seven propositions must be separately represented. They are conjoined by "&" indicating concatenation. To represent this proposition the nodes h, l, r, and t are used to represent the individual *park, time, hippie,* and *debutante.* Two propositions are predicated of the *r touch t* proposition. To be able to represent these, the variable V1 is bound to the proposition (r * (touch OF t)). Then there

TABLE 5.1
Sentences and Their Linear Representations

1. In the park the hippie touched the debutante.

   (h * park) & (1 * past) & (r * hippie) & (t * debutante) & (VI =
   (r * (touch OF t))) & (VI * (at-place OF h)) & (VI * (at-time OF 1))

2. John loves Mary.

   (John * (love OF Mary))

3. Red-headed chickens lay eggs.

   ((red-headed ∩ chicken) * (lay OF egg))

4. It is fortunate that Caesar is dead.

   ((Caesar * dead) * fortunate)

5. Some cats are chased by dogs.

   (A * cat) & (A * (chased-by OF dog))

6. Canaries are yellow birds that sing.

   (canary * (yellow ∩ (bird ∩ sing)))

7. John did not fight Pete or Bill.

   ~ (John * (fought OF (Pete ∪ Bill)))

8. John is very happy.

   (John * (very OF (x C happy)))

9. John softly tapped the ball.

   (John * ((soft OF tap) of a)) & (a * ball)

10. The boy petted and hugged the puppy.

   (a * boy) & (b * puppy) & (a * (pet OF b)) & (a * (hug OF b))

11. John is between New Haven and New York.

   (John * (between OF (New Haven ∪ New York)))

12. John said "Mary."

   (John * (say OF a)) & (a * MARY)

are subsequent propositions predicating time and location of V1. As an exercise the reader might try constructing network equivalents for some of the other linear expressions in Table 5.1. Examples 8 and 9 show the treatment of adverbs in the new ACT representation. They become relations that take adjectives and verbs as arguments. Note in Example 8 that *very* modifies, not *happy*, but the classification happy—denoted (x C happy). This is because *John* does not bear the relation *very* to the *happy people* but to the category of happiness. The adverb *softly* in Example 9 is a higher order relation—that is, a relation which takes a relation as an argument.

Specification of Acceptable Network Structures

Now a formal specification will be given of the acceptable network structures in ACT. This specification will ignore word and cardinality links, parts f and g in Fig. 5.17. These two can be attached to any node in the network without restriction and do not figure in the later semantic analyses of ACT's representations. The rules of network formation will specify how the other five basic construction types in Fig. 5.17 may be combined—that is, types a, b, c, d, and e.

Table 5.2 specifies the rules of formation.[5] These rules make reference to the type of node. There are four types of nodes: concepts, relations, higher-order relations, and propositions. These rules specify how memory structures of certain types can be constructed from structures of various types. For instance, Rule 3 specifies how a concept structure can be constructed from a relation structure and a set of concept structures—$(R_n \text{ OF } A_1, A_2, \ldots, A_n)$. These rules are intended to be interpreted recursively. That is, a structure formed by one of these rules can enter as an element in the formation of a larger structure. Since the execution of productions is the only way that new memory structure may be added, these rules of formation serve as restrictions on the structures that may be created by the actions of productions.

As an example of how these rules specify the creation of ACT network structure Fig. 5.18 illustrates the generation of the ACT equivalent of *The hippie touched the debutante*. One starts (Fig. 5.18a) with the nodes a and b, standing for the individual *hippie* and *debutante*, as well as nodes for *hippie, touch,* and *debutante*. Figure 5.18b illustrates that from the relation *touch* and the concept b, a new concept c is constructed—as specified under the rules for constructing concepts. The proposition d is constructed from the concepts a and c—Fig. 5.18c. Then two

---

[5]Note that the grammar for the ACT network, as specified in Table 5.2, is much simpler than the network grammar given by Anderson and Bower (1973) for the HAM network. This is because (1) one can take advantage of the notational convenience of the ACT linearization; (2) simplifications to the representational assumptions; and (3) Table 5.2 is more informal than the Input Grammar defined in Anderson and Bower (1973, pp. 174–179). However, Table 5.2 can be converted into a more formally specified network grammar.

TABLE 5.2
Rules of Formation for ACT Network Structures

1. *Higher-Order Relations* If R_1^* and R_2^* are higher-order relations, then $(R_1^* \text{ OF } R_2^*)$ is a higher-order relations.

2. *Relations* If R^n is a relation that takes n arguments and R^* is a higher-order relation, then $(R^* \text{ OF } R^n)$ is a relation that takes n arguments.

3. *Concepts* If $A_1, A_2, \ldots, A_n$ are concepts and R^n is a relation that takes n arguments then the following are concepts $(X \text{ C } A_1)$, $(A_1 \cap A_2)$, $(A_1 \cup A_2)$, and $(R_n \text{ OF } A_1, A_2, \ldots, A_n)$. Also all propositions are concepts.

4. *Propositions* If A_1 and A_2 are concepts $(A_1 * A_2)$ is a proposition. The node *false* is also a proposition.

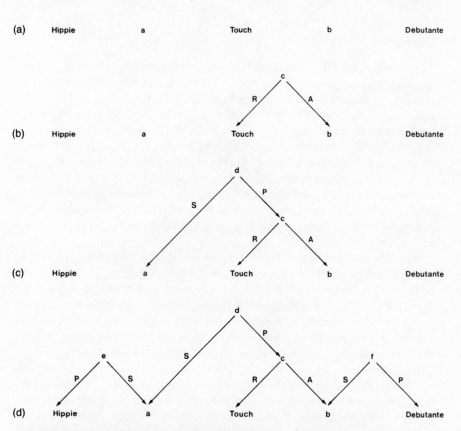

FIG. 5.18 Example of the derivation of an ACT network through the rules in Table 5.2. See text for explanation.

further propositions are constructed by joining *a* with *hippie* and *b* with *debutante* into two subject–predicate constructions—Fig. 5.18d.

An example would also be useful to illustrate the rules for creating relations and higher-order relations: Consider the sentence *John very forcefully pushed Mary*. The term *very* is one higher-order relation and it operates on *forcefully* to create a new higher-order relation—denoted (very OF forcefully). This higher-order relation operates on the relation *push* to create a new relation ((very OF forcefully) OF push). This relation then operates on the concept Mary to yield the new concept: (((very OF forcefully) OF push) OF Mary). This then is combined with the John concept to yield a proposition—(John * (((very OF forcefully) OF push) OF Mary)). Frequently, adverbs serve to select a special subset of the verbs they modify. Thus, *very forcefully push* is a special instance of *push*. However, sometimes adverbs do not do this as in the phrase *almost push*. It is for this reason that it is necessary to think of adverbs as operating on verbs to create new relations.

Comparisons with HAM

Unlike HAM, ACT does not permit more than one branch with the same label to emanate down from a proposition node. For example, whereas HAM would represent the sentence *John swam and ran* as in Fig. 5.19a where there are two P links out of the proposition node, ACT would represent this sentence as in Fig. 5.19b where there are two separate propositions. This ACT representation is preferable since it is possible to subsequently modify (for example, predicate false) one of the propositions and not the other. This is necessary should it later prove to be the case that John swam but did not run. In general, it is wiser not to try to compact multiple propositions together as in Fig. 5.19a because of the need to be able to later qualify the truth of any one proposition. This can be achieved by permitting no more than one link of a particular label to leave each proposition node.[6]

In HAM, when new structures were built it was required that all nodes above the terminal nodes be new. A similar requirement holds for ACT. Each of the root nodes in the structures in Figs. 5.17a–5.17e must be new. To understand the motivation for this requirement consider the root node in the structure in Fig. 5.17b, (*X* OF *Y*), which is defined to be the set of objects that bear the relation *X* to the objects in set *Y*. If that root node were an old memory node, then the structure would be asserting that the old memory node bore relation *X* to *Y*. The problem that might arise if root nodes could be old nodes can be seen by considering Fig. 5.20a which illustrates the situation where the relation *X* is *defeated*, the concept *Y* is *America*, and the old node is *North Vietnam*. This memory structure encodes the assertion that North Vietnam equals the set of countries that defeated America. However, this is not a desirable way to encode

---

[6]This criticism of the HAM model and suggested improvement has been made independently by Wickelgren (in press).

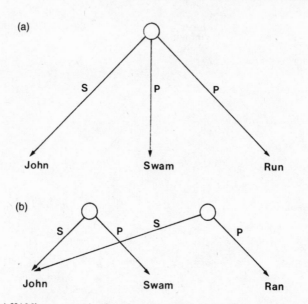

FIG. 5.19   (a) HAM's representation for *John swam and ran;* (b) ACT's representation for the same sentence.

this fact because it is not possible to modify it should it subsequently prove false (for example, after studying a Canadian text about the war of 1812). Rather, one must create a new node to encode the concept *defeat America.* The node is by definition just that set of countries that defeated America. Then, one can assert that this set is identical with North Vietnam by subject–predicate constructions. Figure 5.20b shows how this might be done. One subject–predicate construction asserts North Vietnam is a subset of the defeaters of America and the other asserts the defeaters of America are a subset of North Vietnam. By asserting that both sets are subsets of one another, it is asserted that the two sets are equal. The proposition node in these subject–predicate constructions allows for later modification of the truth of these assertions.

For similar reasons, the root node of the intersection construction (Fig. 5.17c), union construction (Fig. 5.17d), and categorization construction (Fig. 5.17e) must be new. The root node of the subject–predicate construction (Fig. 5.17a) must be new to provide a unique node to which to later attach information modifying the truth of the proposition. So, upon analysis, the reason why the root nodes of all these constructions must be unique is that memory is nonerasable and assertions must not be put in memory which are incapable of later modification.[7]

---

[7]The root nodes of these network structures are remarkably similar to the control elements proposed by Estes (1972) to account for evidence of hierarchical structures in serial learning. Like ACT's root nodes, Estes proposed new elements would be introduced to embody new connections between old elements. Like the ACT root nodes, Estes' control elements are capable of entering as base elements into further constructions.

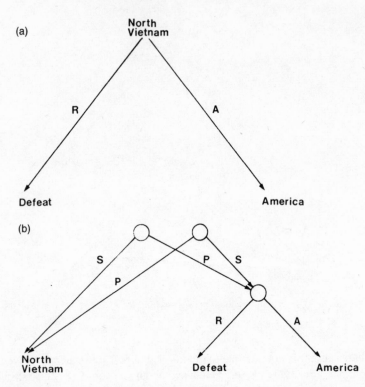

FIG. 5.20   (a) The identity between North Vietnam and the set "defeaters of America" is encoded by making Vietnam the root node of the relational structure; (b) The identity is encoded by two subject–predicate links.

SUMMARY OF CHAPTER 5

ACT uses a propositional network to represent declarative knowledge. Propositional networks lead to a number of advantages in computer implementation and it seems that human memory displays many of these advantages. The advantages of propositional networks include indexing by concept, use of double-linked structures, indifference to recombination, use of a type-token distinction, and use of relational information to direct search. Propositional networks try to use a single representation for all paraphrases.

All propositions in ACT are subject–predicate constructions where subject and predicate are concepts. Propositions can serve as concepts. In addition, it is possible to create new concepts from old ones by *union* and *intersection* constructions. One can also create a concept by applying an *n*-term relation to *n* concepts. Finally, concepts can be created by attaching classification nodes to existing concepts. There are also higher-order relations which operate on other relations to create new relations and on other higher-order relations to create new higher-order relations.

REFERENCES

Anderson, J. R. Item-specific and relation-specific interference in sentence memory. *J. Exp: Human Learning and Memory*, 1975, **104**, 249–260.

Anderson, J. R., & Bower, G. H. *Human associative memory*, Washington: Winston, 1973.

Anderson, J. R., & Hastie, R. Individuation and reference in memory: proper names and definite descriptions. *Cognitive Psychology*, 1974, **6**, 495–514.

Bransford, J. D., & Franks, J. J. The abstraction of linguistic ideas. *Cognitive Psychology*, 1971, **2**, 331–350.

Chomsky, N. *Aspects of the theory of syntax*. Cambridge, Mass.: M.I.T. Press, 1965.

Culicover, P., & Wexler, K. The invariance principle and universals of grammar. Social science working paper #55, University of California, Irvine.

Estes, W. K. An associative basis for coding and organization. In A. W. Melton and E. Martin (Eds.), *Coding processes in human memory*. Washington: Winston, 1972.

Fillmore, C. J. The case for case. In E. Bach and R. T. Harms (Eds.), *Universals in linguistic theory*. New York: Holt, Rinehart, and Winston, 1968.

Harary, F. *Graph theory*. Reading, Mass.: Addison-Wesley, 1969.

Hollan, J. D. Features and semantic memory: Set-theories or network model? *Psychological Review*, 1975, **82**, 154–155.

Kieras, D. E. Analysis of the effects of word properties and limited reading time in a sentence comprehension and verification task. Unpublished Ph.D. Dissertation, University of Michigan, 1974.

Loux, M. J. The problem of universals. In M. J. Loux (Ed.), *Universals and particulars*. New York: Doubleday, 1970.

McCawley, J. English as a VSO language. *Language*, 1970, **46**, 286–299.

Norman, D. A., Rumelhart, D. E., & the LNR Research Group. *Explorations in cognition*, San Francisco: Freeman, 1975.

Quillian, M. R. The teachable language comprehender. *Communications of the ACM*, 1969, **12**, 459–476.

Ramsey, F. P. *Universals. The foundations of mathematics*. New York: Harcourt Brace, 1931.

Rips, L. J., Shoben, E. J., & Smith, E. E. Semantic distance and the verification of semantic relations. *Journal of Verbal Learning and Verbal Behavior*, 1973, **12**, 1–20.

Russell, B. On the relations of universals and particulars. *Proceedings of the Aristotilian Society*, 1911–12, **12**, 1–24.

Wicklegren, W. A. Subproblems of semantic memory: A review of "Human Associative Memory." *Journal of Mathematical Psychology*, 1976, in press.

Winograd, T. Understanding natural language. *Cognitive Psychology*, 1972, **3**, 1–191.

Woods, W. A. What's in a link: Foundations for semantic networks. In D. G. Bobrow & A. Collins (Eds.), *Representation and understanding: Studies in cognitive science*. New York: Academic Press, 1975.

6
ACT's Production System

The wrong way to conceive of it is with the
Production System as the active net-interpreter
and with the semantic net as an associative data
structure. The right way is that the production
system is the associative structure itself.

ALLEN NEWELL

The purpose of this chapter is to present a detailed analysis of ACT's production system. The first section describes the principles of operation of the production system. The second section describes how a subroutine structure may be imposed on productions. Such subroutine structure is useful in modeling complex tasks and is also used to guide the induction system (see Section 12.3). The third and final section reports on a pair of experiments that serve to display some properties of the production system.

6.1   PRINCIPLES OF OPERATION

Figure 6.1 illustrates the basic control cycle of both ACT, the program, and *ACT*, the theory. The system starts after a dampening with the set of nodes, called ACTIVE, equal to just those ten on the ALIST. This ACTIVE set will increase for D increments of time and then dampening will reoccur and ACTIVE will be reset. During each of these D increments three operations occur:

1. ACTIVE is expanded. In Chapter 8 I describe how activation can spread from active nodes to activate additional memory structures. Also perceptual processes can cause network configurations to become active. A final way for activation to increase is by means of executing productions whose actions can activate new structures.

2. During each increment of time all productions are scanned to see if any are relevant. This selection phase involves a quick partial test of the conditions of productions to see if any might be satisfied in long-term memory. A production will be selected if its condition is able to be satisfied, but the test is sufficiently indiscriminate that productions will be selected whose conditions may not be satisfied. Any production selected is placed on the APPLY LIST unless that produc-

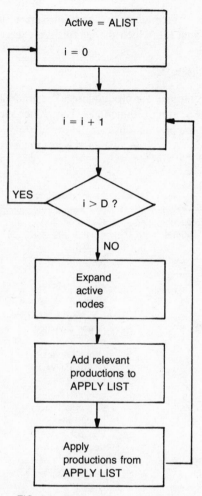

FIG. 6.1   Basic control cycle of ACT.

tion is already on this list. There can be only one copy of a production on the APPLY LIST at a time.

3.   During each increment of time there is a certain probability that each production on the APPLY LIST will be applied. This probability depends on the strength of the production and on the number of other productions on the APPLY LIST. If a production is applied, its condition is completely tested against the active portion of long-term memory. If the tests specified in the condition are satisfied, the action of the production is executed. Whether the condition is satisfied or not, that production is removed from the APPLY LIST.

Subsequent subsections of this section will concern themselves with describing (a) the structure of productions; (b) the process by which they are initially selected; (c) the process by which their conditions are tested in the application phase; and (d) the manner in which the actions are executed.

Structure of Productions

Table 6.1 specifies a grammar for productions. The grammar is specified as a set of rewrite rules for generating productions. The reader should keep distinct the rewrite rules defining the productions and the productions which are types of rewrite rules themselves. A rewrite rule in the grammar is specified as a non-

TABLE 6.1
A Grammar for Productions

(1)	Production	:	:	Condition $\Rightarrow$ Action
(2a)	Condition	:	:	Condition & Condition
(2b)		:	:	Property
(2c)		:	:	ABS (Property)
(3a)	Property	:	:	Node
(3b)		:	:	(Var = Node)
(3c)		:	:	(Pattern)
(3d)		:	:	(INTERSECTING Node Node)
(4a)	Action	:	:	Action & Action
(4b)		:	:	Node
(4c)		:	:	(Var = Node)
(4d)		:	:	(UNBIND Var)
(4e)		:	:	(Pattern)
(4f)		:	:	External
(5a)	Pattern	:	:	Pattern & Pattern
(5b)		:	:	Proposition
(5c)		:	:	Concept
(5d)		:	:	Relation
(6a)	Proposition	:	:	(Concept * Concept)
(6b)		:	:	(Var = (Concept * Concept))
(7a)	Concept	:	:	Node
(7b)		:	:	(CStructure)
(7c)		:	:	(Var = CStructure)
(8a)	CStructure	:	:	(Concept $\cap$ Concept)
(8b)		:	:	(Concept $\cup$ Concept)
(8c)		:	:	(Relation OF Concept . . . Concept)
(8d)		:	:	(Concept * Concept)
(8e)		:	:	(Node C Concept)
(8f)		:	:	(Node W Concept)
(8g)		:	:	(Node # Concept)
(9a)	Relation	:	:	Node
(9b)		:	:	Rstructure
(9c)		:	:	(Var = Rstructure)
(10a)	Rstructure	:	:	(Relation OF Relation)
(11a)	Node	:	:	Var
(11b)		:	:	LTM NODE
(12a)	Var	:	:	Vatom1, Vatom2

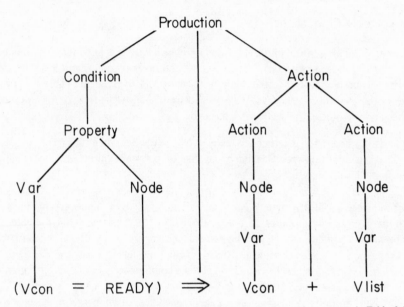

FIG. 6.2   An example of a derivation tree for a production according to the grammar in Table 6.1.

terminal symbol on the left of double colons (:   :), which is rewritten as the string to the right of the double colon. So, Rule (1) states that a production consists of a condition, followed by a double arrow, followed by the action.

The condition can be a conjunction of conditions (Rule 2a). Each individual condition can specify a property (2b) or the absence of a property (2c). A property can specify that a node is active (Rule 3a), that a variable has a certain value (Rule 3b), that a network pattern is active (Rule 3c), or that there is an intersecting path of activation between two long-term memory nodes (Rule 3d). The action part of a production can consist of a sequence of actions (Rule 4a). Each individual action can activate a node (4b), or set a variable to a value (4c), or unbind a variable from its value (4d), or perform some operation external to the memory system (4e),[1] or build a memory structure according to a pattern specification (4f). A pattern may be rewritten as sequence of patterns (5a), a proposition (5b), a concept (5c), or a relation (5d). Rules 6–10 specify how these different types of patterns may be constructed. They basically follow the rules set forth in Table 5.2 (page 177) for permissible network structures. The only thing noteworthy about these is their capacity to set a variable equal to the root node of a binary structure defining a proposition, a relation, or a concept. Rule 10 indicates that nodes may either be long-term memory nodes or variables. Rule 11 indicates that variables are expressed as terms preceded by V. As a simple example of the way Table 6.1 generates productions, Figure 6.2 gives the derivation tree for a production (P1 from Table 4.1, page 127).

[1]In this case the action actually builds a memory structure which is interpreted by some motor routine to generate the action.

Selection of Productions

The selection phase is an unlimited capacity parallel process in which a number of quick, partial tests are performed to see if the condition of a production is relevant to the current contents of active memory. Note from Rules 3a–3d (Table 6.1) that individual conditions can have one of four forms. Following is a specification of what is done during the selection phase for each form:

1. If it is a test for whether a node is active (Rule 3a), then that test is made.
2. If the condition specifies that a variable has a certain value (Rule 3b), then a test is made of this.
3. If it is a specification that a memory pattern be active (Rule 3c), there is a partial test to see if that pattern could be satisfied in active memory. This partial test involves an inspection of the long-term memory nodes specified in the pattern or bound to variables specified in the pattern. If there are no long-term nodes in the pattern, the production is rejected. If any of the long-term memory nodes are inactive the production is rejected. If the pattern contains only one long-term memory node, it passes the partial test and is put on the APPLY LIST. If it contains more than one long-term memory node, it passes the partial test if there is an intersection of activation along some path connecting two of the long-term memory nodes. All these tests made during this selection phase are necessary but not sufficient conditions for the pattern to match the active partition of long-term memory in the application phase.
4. The final possibility for an individual condition (Rule 3d) is that it specify a path of activation between two nodes in memory. A test is made of whether this is the case in the selection phase.

The above paragraph specifies what is done in the case of a positive condition. However, it is also possible to specify a condition that looks for the absence of one of these four properties (Rule 2b in Table 6.1). In this case a condition will pass the selection phase if a certain amount of time has passed without the embedded property being "partially satisfied." By "partially satisfied" I mean whatever degree of test would be adequate to get the property to pass the selection phase if that property were positively stated in a condition. This waiting process model for noting an absence is developed extensively in Chapter 8.

The philosophy behind the tests assigned to the selection phase is that they constitute a quick, easy-to-compute means of screening productions for the APPLY LIST. Particularly important in this selection stage are the tests of whether certain nodes are active and whether variables have as values certain nodes (Rules 3a and 3b). The nodes interrogated in these tests will be referred to as *control nodes*. These control nodes are inserted in the conditions of productions to provide an easy way for the selection process to weed out irrelevant productions. Almost all practical productions should make reference to some control node that specifies the context in which that production is relevant.

The preferred way of inserting control nodes into a production is via tests of the form (Var = Node) rather than testing for the activation of a node. A production which has such a test can be easily invalidated for selection by changing the value of the variable. In contrast, there is no way to simply deactivate a node. It is important to have a sure way to prevent productions from applying. For instance, if the system has gotten itself into an "infinite loop" of productions, it needs a way to prevent the execution of a production in the loop.

Matching Conditions

In each cycle of the production system there is a certain probability that the production will be applied. If there are n productions on the APPLY LIST and a production has strength s, it has probability $1 - e^{-s/bn}$ of being applied in that unit of time. Therefore, a production will reside on the APPLY LIST an approximately[2] exponentially distributed amount of time before being applied. I am uncertain whether to conceive of this waiting time as meaning that it takes this long to complete the test of the condition or as meaning that the system waits this long before testing the condition.[3]

The mean time to apply a production will be bn/s. This means that the time to match a condition will decrease with the strength s of a production and increase with the number of alternative productions, n, being applied. This reflects the hypothesis that the time to apply a production will be independent of the total number of available productions but will be adversely affected by the number of relevant productions. The strength variable has two important consequences. First, it enables ACT to model the process whereby a subject gradually performs the task more rapidly. Second, the strength variable serves as an important concept in properly modeling the induction of productions (see Chapter 12). A production is strengthened whenever it is successfully applied. By initially inducing productions with little strength, ACT has a means of protecting itself from mistaken inductions because these will not be strengthened. This process by which productions are strengthened is similar to the ideas about the development of automaticity of LaBerge and Samuels (1974) and of Posner and Snyder (1975).

It is currently assumed that the time to compute whether there is a match between the condition and long-term memory does not depend on the complexity of the condition. This assumption is being made for analytic convenience, but there is no experimental evidence available, one way or another, to support it.

The select phase tested the conditions involving whether a node was active (3a in Table 6.1), whether a variable had a particular value (3b), and whether

---

[2]The exponential distribution is approximate because n, the number of productions in the APPLY LIST, can change with time.

[3]This feature of the program is projected rather than implemented. Currently, the program computes whether the condition is matched in the same cycle that the production is selected.

there was an intersection of activation between two nodes (3d). These conditions are retested in matching a production to make sure that they are still satisfied. The condition (3c) involving whether a pattern was matched in active memory was only partially tested. This is thoroughly tested during the application phase.

I will explain the logic of the test for whether the memory pattern is matched. A pattern in a condition specifies a network structure to be built up for matching. A pattern can contain a number of variables. Some of these variables are *global* and are already bound to long-term memory nodes. In constructing the pattern structure these global variables are replaced by their long-term memory values. Other variables are *local* and have no value. These are replaced by new *pattern* nodes. Any other non-long-term-memory nodes involved in the pattern are also assigned new pattern nodes. The pattern structure is built up of these long-term memory nodes and pattern nodes. Since the bindings of the variables can change from one time to the next, it is the case that the same pattern can specify different network structures. The process by which the pattern is matched to memory is basically the MATCH process of the HAM model (Anderson & Bower, 1973). The MATCH process attempts to make a graph correspondence between the pattern structure and a portion of the active partition of long-term memory. The nodes in the pattern must be put into one-to-one correspondence with the nodes in memory such that:

(a) All long-term memory nodes in the pattern correspond to the same long-term memory nodes in memory.
(b) The labels on the links between the pattern nodes match the labels on the links between the corresponding nodes in memory.

Figure 6.3 illustrates how this correspondence is computed. It illustrates the match made between the pattern (V2 * (Before of V3)) and a memory configuration (X * (Before of Y)). In making this match it is assumed the variable V2 is global and bound to X but V3 is local and therefore not bound. The pattern structure built up is illustrated in Fig. 6.3a. It involves the long-term nodes, X and *Before*. The other nodes in the memory pattern are pattern nodes. These are nodes *a, b,* and *c*. Note that node *c* is assigned as the temporary value of variable V3. The long-term memory structure that will match this is illustrated in Fig. 6.3b. In making the match the following correspondences will be made: X = X, Before = Before, *a* = 1, *b* = 2, and *c* = Y. Note that these correspondences satisfy the specified criteria (a) and (b). As a result of making this correspondence, variable V3, which had the pattern value *c,* can be bound to the long-term memory node Y.[4]

---

[4]Note that the MATCH process cannot detect partial matches as it could in the HAM model. A partial match is not sufficient reason for the condition of a production to be considered satisfied. If there is a particular partial overlap that ACT should respond to, a special production can be built to look for that partial overlap. In programming HAM it proved difficult to obtain usable service out of the program because it was constantly distracted by irrelevant partial matches. ACT, by only responding to the partial matches specified in the conditions of productions, achieves an ability to pick and choose which partial overlaps it will respond to.

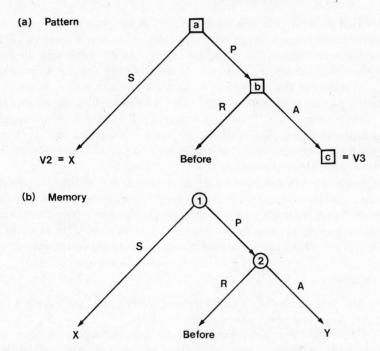

FIG. 6.3 An example of the correspondence made between a pattern and a memory structure by the MATCH process.

One qualification needs to be made about the pattern-matching process. It is not possible for a proposition node which is not embedded in another structure to match a memory node which is or vice versa. Thus, node *a* in Fig. 6.3a could not have matched node 1 in Fig. 6.3b if node 1 had predicated false, true, possible, etc., of it or if it were embedded in some other construction like "John says that...." The reason for this restriction on ACT is that it should not regard as automatically true propositions in memory which are embedded within other propositions.

In HAM it was proposed that the reaction time to make a match was principally a function of the time to compute this correspondence. As will be reviewed in Chapter 8, the current hypothesis is that it essentially takes no time to compute this correspondence and what is important is the time to activate the corresponding structure in long-term memory. I could have hypothesized that processing time was determined by both the activation rate and the time to compute the correspondence. However, the assumptions about activation rate by themselves serve to account for all the available data. Moreover, there is data which the HAM match process cannot explain but which the activation process can (see Chapter 8).

All long-term memory links used in matching a pattern have their strength increased by one. Stronger links can be more rapidly activated. This is a reasonable heuristic for increasing the strength of those links which are likely to be relevant. That is, those links that have served to match patterns in the past are likely to serve that function in the future. In HAM links were ordered on GET-lists with their availability determined by recency. In ACT this strengthening mechanism makes availability a function of frequency. In Chapter 8 I produce evidence to show that frequency is an important variable as well as recency.

In matching a pattern to memory, ACT may bind some of the local variables in the pattern to memory nodes. These local variables will retain their value throughout application of the production. However, unless made global, they will lose their values after application of the production, and their values will not be available to other productions.

There may be more than one active long-term memory that will match a pattern. For instance, in Fig. 6.3 there may have been more than one memory structure of the form (X * (before OF ?)) (that is, memory structures which only differ in the node they assign to ?) that matched the pattern (V2 * (before of V3)). The current MATCH process selects randomly from among these equivalent structures.

Absence Detection

Absence detection during the application phase works just as the inverse of the tests for the properties whose absences are being queried. That is, the absence test is satisfied when the queried property is not satisfied. It is particularly important to appreciate the implications of this fact in the case when the test specifies the absence of an intersection or a pattern. If the absence condition is satisfied, this does not mean that there is not an intersecting path between the nodes in memory or that the pattern is not in memory—only that the intersection or pattern is not in active memory. It would lead to a strange system if the test for the presence of a pattern could only access active memory, but the test for the absence of a pattern could inspect all of memory.

The capacity to test for the absence of a pattern or an intersection is a critical component of ACT. It is essential for a system like ACT to be able to recognize when it does not know something and to be able to respond to its lack of knowledge. For instance, the only way ACT can recognize foils as new in a recognition experiment would be by means of such an absence detection.

There is a potential for interaction of the pattern matching condition and the absence condition. Consider the following condition pair:

$$(V2 * (before OF V3)) \& (ABS (V3 = Y))$$

If this pair appeared in the condition of a production, the condition might fail to be satisfied even if there was (as there is in Fig. 6.3b) a memory structure to match (V2 * (before OF V3)) because that memory structure involves setting V3 to Y. That production would fail but might be selected again in the next cycle and reapply. This time the pattern might match a different memory structure that does not involve the assignment of V3 to Y. Then the production would successfully match.

Execution of Actions

If the condition of a production is successfully matched then the action of the production will be executed in that cycle of time. Again, purely for simplicity, it is assumed that it will take no time for the actions to be executed. As Table 6.1 illustrates, the action side of a production consists of a sequence of subactions which can be one of five varieties:

1. The subaction (Rule 4b in Table 6.1) can simply specify a long-term memory node (either by directly naming the node or by naming a variable bound to the node). The node is made active and put on the front of the ALIST. If the node is referred to by a variable, that variable is also given global status so that it can communicate with other productions.

2. The action (Rule 4c) can specify that a variable be set to a specified value. Such an action will cause the variable to be set, the variable to be made global, and the value to be made active and to be put on the ALIST.

3. The action (Rule 4d) specifies that a variable be unbound. This causes the value to be removed from the variable and the variable to return to having a local status. The capacity to set and unbind variables conveys upon ACT the capacity for rapid modifiability of its goal structure.

4. Another possibility is indicated by (4e) in Table 6.1. This is the capacity to cause an action to be taken external to memory. This is accomplished by activating some memory structure which is then interpreted by a motor program. This facility is mimicked in the ACT simulation by permitting the production system to execute LISP functions, and is limited by the restriction that these functions cannot modify memory and so their results cannot be directly read by ACT. Thus, this facility does not give the simulation hidden computational power. One could imagine, however, that the actions would cause information to be written on some external memory medium like a piece of paper and that perceptual processes would read this external medium and transform its contents into a memory encoding. So in this roundabout way these external actions could increase the computational power of ACT. It seems to be a fact about humans that the possibility for actions external to their memory greatly increases the computational complexity of the behavior of which they are capable. For instance, it is frequently observed in linguistics and psycholinguistics that complex sentences which cannot be understood upon being heard can be understood if the listener has a pencil and paper to write down the sentence and work on it.

5. The final type of memory action is to build up memory structures specified by a pattern. Examples of such actions can be seen in Table 4.3 (page 135) which gave a production system for parsing sentences. The patterns in Table 4.3 are of the form (Vtop * Videa) where Vtop is bound to the topic of the noun phrase and Videa is bound to some predicate. One of the complications in these structure-building actions involves avoiding building redundant information. Suppose it is already known that *John is tall* and the action involves building the

proposition *John is tall*. Then there is no need to build a new structure. Whenever a memory action specifies that two long-term memory nodes be connected by a root node, and they already have that connection in memory, there is no need to build new structures. In fact, it is desirable not to build a new structure in order to avoid having multiple nodes (the root nodes of these structures) with the same meaning.

Figure 6.4 shows a more elaborate example of how redundancy is avoided in building network structures. Figure 6.4a shows a pattern that specifies that the production system should encode the fact that *Tall lawyers cheat dumb Russians*. Figure 6.4b shows a hypothetical memory structure before execution of this action. Among other things it has encoded the facts that *Tall lawyers are dishonest* and *Americans cheat dumb Russians*. Since the structures *tall lawyers* and *cheat dumb Russians* are in memory there is no need to encode these. The top nodes of these structures can be used in encoding the new information. As Fig. 6.4c shows, all that is necessary to encode is a subject–predicate construction interconnecting *tall lawyers* and *cheated dumb Russians*.

For one subtree to match another all terminal nodes must be identical. In general, whenever a subtree in the to-be-encoded pattern matches a subtree in memory, the memory subtree is used. The one exception to this rule involves propositional subtrees. If a pattern specifies a propositional subtree with something predicated of it, ACT may not replace it by an unmodified subtree from memory. If it did, the memory subtree would no longer be regarded as automatically true because it would now be embedded in another subconstruction. Conversely, if a pattern specifies an unmodified propositional tree, it may not be replaced by a modified propositional tree from memory.

In HAM an attempt was also made to avoid redundancy in memory, but this often led to difficulties. For instance, if HAM heard *A hippie touched a debutante* and had stored in memory that *A hippie touched a debutante,* it would assume the same hippie and debutante were intended and use the existing memory structure to encode the sentence. However, it would have made a mistake if the same debutante and hippie were not intended. ACT does not fall prey to this difficulty. Suppose it were asked to execute a memory action asserting this information. This action could be expressed in a production as (V1 * hippie) & (V1 * (touch of V2)) & (V2 * debutante) where V1 and V2 represent the individual hippie and individual debutante, respectively. Figure 6.5a shows the to-be-built memory structure specified by this pattern. Since V1 and V2 are unbound variables, new memory nodes (X and Y) have been assigned to them. Figure 6.5b shows a memory structure already in memory which encodes that a hippie touched a debutante. No subtree in the pattern (Fig. 6.5a) matches a subtree in the memory (Fig. 6.5b) and therefore all of the pattern structure must be built anew. For instance, the proposition subtree (X * hippie) in Fig. 6.5a does not match the subtree (A * hippie) in Fig. 6.5b because the terminal node X does not match

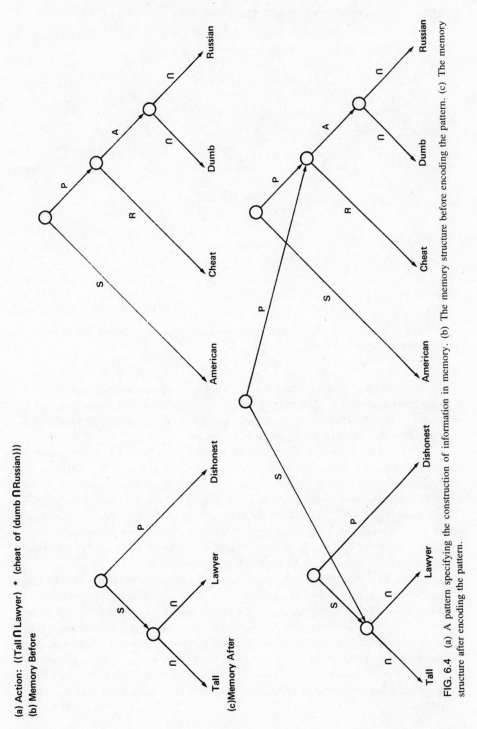

(a) Action: ((Tall ∩ Lawyer) * (cheat of (dumb ∩ Russian)))

(b) Memory Before

(c)Memory After

FIG. 6.4 (a) A pattern specifying the construction of information in memory. (b) The memory structure before encoding the pattern. (c) The memory structure after encoding the pattern.

193

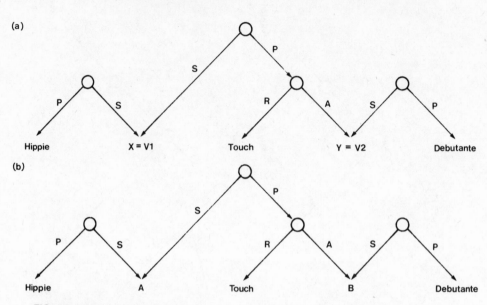

FIG. 6.5 The to-be-built structure in Fig. 6.5a cannot be replaced by the memory structure in Fig. 6.5b because there is no overlap of subtrees.

the terminal node A. The general rule is that a tree structure in long-term memory may be used to encode a tree in the action only if all the terminal nodes of the long-term memory tree match the action tree. Then any node above these terminal nodes must have the same meaning in the two trees.

It is possible, of course, that the same individuals were intended in the tree in Fig. 6.5a set up by the action as in the memory tree of Fig. 6.5b. If this is so, ACT could encode the fact that these two nodes referred to the same individuals by means of subject–predicate constructions. So, to encode the identity between X and A in Fig. 6.5 ACT could add the propositions (X * A) and (A * X). Because of the nonerasable character of ACT's memory, it is better to initially fail to identify that two references are to the same individual than to erroneously treat two references as referring to the same individual.

All links created by structure-building actions are only encoded with a certain probability, p. This probability feature is critical in accounting for why imperfect memory is displayed. For instance, it explains why a human, in mentally simulating a Turing Machine (see Table 4.4, page 143), would show failure in trying to remember what he had written on his mental tape. The notion of an imperfect memory also explains the advantage of redundancy in encoding (see Section 10.2). There are probably other ways to achieve imperfect memory besides the gross measure of failing to encode associations, but I have not worked out any others.

Note that the order of actions in a production is important. As an example contrast the effect of the sequence (UNBIND Vtop) & (Vtop * tall) & (Vhold = Vtop) versus (Vhold = Vtop) & (Vtop * tall) & (UNBIND Vtop). Assume that Vtop is bound to some value at the start of the sequence. Then the first sequence would unbind that value, predicate *tall* of a new node, and set Vhold to have the value of the new node. The second sequence will set Vhold to the old value of Vtop, predicate *tall* of that old value, and then remove the value of Vtop.

Interactions among Productions

Interesting interactions, intended or not, can occur among productions on the APPLY LIST because of their order of application. The mean time for a production to apply will depend on its strength. However, because application of productions is a probabilistic affair, any order of production application is possible. Productions on the APPLY LIST which match successfully and execute can enable or disenable the match of later productions. The importance of order of application is particularly clear in the case of contradictory productions. For instance, a child may have two productions for uttering the plural of foot:

(a)   (Vcon = CONTROL1)   ⇒ (say Vword 'S)
      & ((Vtop * Videa)   & (Vcon = CONTROL2)
      & (Vtop # plural)
      & (Videa W Vword))

(b)   (Vcon = CONTROL1)   ⇒ (say FEET)
      & ((Vtop * foot)   & (Vcon = CONTROL2)
      & (Vtop # plural))

Production (a) is a general production for pluralization. (It is assumed Vtop is bound to a to-be-expressed object.) Production (a) asserts if the topic, Vtop, is a subset of Videa—(Vtop * Videa)—and if Vtop is of plural number—(Vtop # plural)—and of Vword is the word for Videa—(Vword W Videa)—then say Vword 'S. This would incorrectly generate *foots*. The second rule asserts that if Vtop is a subset of *foot* and is of plural number, say *feet*.

There is evidence that children actually have both productions at certain points in their language development (Brown, 1973). Both productions, however, cannot be executed simultaneously. If one applies first it will change the control node (bound to Vcon) and so prevent the other from applying. Roger Brown documents that there are periods in child development when the child vacillates between the two forms of a morphemic rule. This is evidence that both productions apply in parallel but that sometimes one production is satisfied first and sometimes the other. Thus, we have a race between productions. More analytic experimental evidence for this "race" conception of production application will be presented in the third section of this chapter.

6.2 SUBROUTINE STRUCTURING FOR PRODUCTIONS

It is sometimes useful to chunk a set of productions into a subroutine. This makes it easier to understand the interactions involving that set of productions and others. As will be seen in Chapter 12, the induction routine for production systems can be made quite powerful by taking advantage of the subroutine idea. Before discussing further the nature of the advantage of a subroutine structure, it would be useful to have an example. Table 6.2 gives a set of productions to parse simple subject–verb–object sentences with possible relative clause modifiers of the noun phrases. Examples of sentences would be

(1)   The hippie touched the tall debutante whom the nasty sailor liked.

(2)   The fireman shot a lawyer.

(3)   The lawyer who sued the doctor who mistreated a patient married the widow.

This production system is purely for illustration purpose. A more adequate production system for parsing is discussed in Section 11.3. The productions have been divided into those concerned with processing main sentences, those concerned with noun phrases, and those concerned with relative clauses. Figure 6.6 illustrates the flow of control within these three sets of productions.

Consider first the productions for parsing noun phrases. These serve as a subroutine that may be called upon anywhere in sentence processing to deal with a noun phrase. As a subroutine it expects there to be certain data available for its use. Variable Vtop is supposed to be bound to the topic of the noun phrase and variable Vtok to the first word of the noun phrase. If the control variable Vcon1 is also bound to NP and if the word is a member of the determiner word class, Production (N1) will be satisfied and processing of the noun phrase will begin. The expression (WORDCLASS Vtok Vword DET) is a shorthand expression that checks whether the current word is a member of the determiner word class. The network equivalent for this was given earlier in Fig. 4.6 (page 134). If Production (N1) is satisfied variable Vcon1 is changed to control node NP1 to set expectations for what might follow a determiner.

Also variable Vadv is set to the value NEXT. This serves to call upon the production for word advancement (Production (A1) in Table 6.2). Production (A1) uses the notation (Vtok–Vnew) which is shorthand for a network structure encoding that Vtok is adjacent to Vnew (illustrated in Fig. 4.4b, page 131). The effect of the production for word advancement is to change the binding of Vtok to the next word in the sentence.

The other two productions for the noun phrase, N2 and N3, are quite similar to each other. Production N2 checks whether the next word is an adjective and, if it is, predicates of Vtop the idea, Videa, that corresponds to the adjective. Production (N2) can be called upon many times allowing for unlimited numbers of

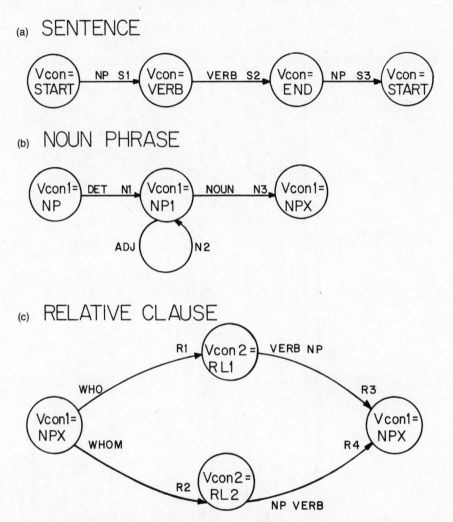

FIG. 6.6   The flow of control among the productions in Table 6.2 for parsing (a) the main sentence, (b) noun phrases, and (c) relative clauses.

preceding adjectives. Production (N3) analyzes a noun. It sets variable Vcon1 to NPX which signals the end of the noun phrase matrix. If the next word is *who* or *whom* the relative clause productions will be evoked to analyze subject or object relatives.

Now consider how the productions operate for the main sentence analysis. It is assumed that Vcon must be set to the control node START for processing of a sentence to begin. Production (S1) will be activated if Vcon is so set and if the first word of the sentence is presented (for the network equivalent of the short-

TABLE 6.2

A Debugged Production System for Parsing Sentences

Condition		Action
Productions for main sentence		
(S1) (Vcon = START) & (FIRST Vtok)	⇒	(Vcon1 = NP) & (Vcon = VERB) & Vtok & (Vhold = Vtop)
(S2) (Vcon = VERB) & (Vcon1 = NPX) & (ABS Vcon2) & ((WORDCLASS Vtok Vword VERB) & (Videa W Vword))	⇒	(UNBIND Vtop) & (Vhold * (Videa OF Vtop)) & (Vcon1 = NP) & (Vadv = NEXT) & (Vcon = END) & (UNBIND Vhold) & Vtop
(S3) (Vcon = END) & (Vcon1 = NPX) & (ABS Vcon2)	⇒	(Vcon = START) & (UNBIND Vtop)
Productions for noun phrase		
(N1) (Vcon1 = NP) & (WORDCLASS Vtok Vword DET)	⇒	(Vcon1 = NP1) & (Vadv = NEXT)
(N2) (Vcon1 = NP1) & ((WORDCLASS Vtok Vword ADJ) & (Videa W Vword))	⇒	(Vcon1 = NP1) & (Vadv = NEXT) & (Vtop * Videa)
(N3) (Vcon1 = NP1) & ((WORDCLASS Vtok Vword NOUN) & (Videa W Vword))	⇒	(Vcon1 = NPX) & (Vadv = NEXT) & (Vtop * Videa)

Productions for relative clause

(R1) $(Vcon1 = NPX) \& (Vtok = WHO)$ $\Uparrow$ $(UNBIND\ Vcon1) \& (Vcon2 = RL1) \& (Vadv = NEXT)$

(R2) $(Vcon2 = RL1)$ $\Uparrow$ $(Vtop * (Videa\ OF\ Vhold1)) \& (Vtop = Vhold2)$
$\&\ ((WORDCLASS\ Vtok\ Vword\ VERB)$ $\&\ (Vadv = NEXT) \& (Vcon1 = NP)$
$\&\ (Videa\ W\ Vword))$ $\&\ (UNBIND\ Vcon2)$

(R3) $(Vcon1 = NPX) \& (Vtok = WHOM)$ $\Uparrow$ $(Vcon1 = NP) \& (Vcon2 = RL2)$
$\&\ (Vhold1 = Vtop) \& (UNBIND\ Vtop)$
$\&\ (Vadv = NEXT) \& Vtop$

(R4) $(Vcon2 = RL2) \& (Vcon1 = NPX)$ $\Uparrow$ $Vcon1 \& (Vtop * (Videa\ OF\ Vhold1))$
$\&\ ((WORDCLASS\ Vtok\ Vword\ VERB)$ $\&\ (Vadv = NEXT) \& (UNBIND\ Vcon2)$
$\&\ (Videa\ W\ Vword))$

Production for advancement

(A1) $(Vadv = NEXT) \& (Vtok - Vnew)$ $\Uparrow$ $(Vtok = Vnew) \& (UNBIND\ Vadv)$

Special rehearsal productions

(P1) Vcon $\Uparrow$ Vcon

(P2) Vhold $\Uparrow$ Vhold

(P3) Vhold1 $\Uparrow$ Vhold1

hand, (FIRST Vtok), see Fig. 4.4a, page 131). Production (S1) sets variable Vcon1 to NP to start processing of the noun phrase. It sets variable Vcon to VERB to encode the expectation that the next main sentence constituent after the noun phrase will be a verb. Production (S1) also rehearses Vtok to make it a global variable and set Vhold to Vtop, the topic of the noun phrase. The variable Vhold will serve to remember what was the topic of the main sentence. Note that there is a special rehearsal production (P2) to keep the subject of the sentence, Vhold, active during the processing of the noun phrase. Similarly, there is a rehearsal production (P1) to keep the value of Vcon active, which marks the position in the main sentence.

Production (S2) will be activated upon completion of the noun phrase. It checks that the current expectation is for a verb—(Vcon = VERB), that the noun phrase has been completed—(Vcon1 = NPX), and that it is not in the midst of an incomplete relative clause—(ABS Vcon2). Production (S2) also checks that the current word is in the verb class and binds Videa to the idea corresponding to that word. The actions of Production (S2) are:

(a)   (UNBIND Vtop): unbinds the variable Vtop which had pointed to the topic of the noun phrase.

(b)   (Vhold * (Videa of Vtop)): builds the structure to encode the subject–verb–object main clause. Variable Vtop is made the object of the clause.

(c)   (Vcon1 = NP): sets Vcon1 to NP to initiate analysis of the noun clause describing the object, Vtop.

(d)   (Vadv = NEXT): advances the current word.

(e)   (Vcon = END): after the object noun phrase, there are no more expectations in the noun sentence.

(f)   (UNBIND Vhold): it is no longer necessary to remember the subject of the sentence.

(g)   Vtop: rehearses Vtop to make it global.

Upon completion of the object noun phrase, Production (S3) will be called upon to reset the system to begin parsing the next sentence.

Obviously, the parser outlined is quite crude when compared to all the complexities of natural language processing. However, it does serve to illustrate how an ACT production system can be constructed to perform a relatively complex task. It also shows how productions can partition themselves into subroutines which perform rather self-contained tasks. There were three subroutines in Table 6.2. Their features are summarized in Table 6.3. Each subroutine has a well-prescribed action to perform, which is specified in the second column of Table 6.3, and has a calling signal. This involves some control variable, having as value

TABLE 6.3
An Analysis of the Subroutines in Table 6.2

Subroutine	Action	Calling signal	Data input	Data output	Leaving signal
Sentence	Build up conception for SVO sentence	(Vcon = START)	—	—	(Vcon = START)
Noun	Analyze descriptors of noun	(Vcon1 = NP)	Vtok = current word Vtop = topic	Vtok = current word Vtop = topic	(Vcon1 = NPX)
Relative	Analyze subject relative or object relative	(Vcon1 = NPX)	Vtok = current word Vtop = topic	Vtok = current word	(UNBIND Vcon2) and (Vcon1 = NPX)

some control node. Also each production expects certain variables to have as values information which it can use as data. This is given under *Data Input* in Table 6.3 Under *Data Output* we have the information the calling subroutines expect to see as the values of certain variables upon completion of the subroutine. Finally, under *Leaving Signal* there are the bindings of variables which indicate that the subroutine is complete. Note that the Relative subroutine must leave two signals. By unbinding Vcon2 it signals that the relative clause is complete. By setting Vcon1 to NPX it signals that the noun phrase is complete.

An important feature to note about such subroutines is that they have autonomy from the context in which they are called. Hence the same productions can be used at multiple locations in the sentence analysis. For instance, the noun phrase subroutine can be called upon to parse main subject, main object, or a noun phrase in a relative clause. Thus, an efficiency in representation of procedural knowledge is obtained. This is one reason why it is desirable to impose a subroutine structure on a production system. In Fig. 6.6 where call to a noun phrase intervenes between two states of the main sentence routine, an "NP" labels the arc transiting between the states.

It is possible to simplify the exposition of production systems by use of these subroutine chunks. Thus one might write (S1) as:

$$(\text{Vcon} = \text{START}) \ \& \ (\text{FIRST Vtok}) \ \Rightarrow \ (\text{Vcon} = \text{VERB}) \ \& \ \text{Vtok}$$
$$\& \ (\text{Vhold} = \text{Vtop})$$
$$\& \ (\text{CALL NOUN})$$

where the subroutine NOUN can be roughly specified according to what it does, what data it requires as input, and what it gives as output. Then it would not be necessary to specify the actual productions that analyze the noun phrase. It would be assumed that such productions could be developed, if ever required, for psychological analysis. Or one could write out the productions for the noun phrase, but replace Production (N3) by:

$$(\text{V1} = \text{NP1}) \qquad\qquad \Rightarrow \ (\text{Vcon1} = \text{NPX})$$
$$\& \ ((\text{MEMBER Vtok Vword NOUN}) \qquad \& \ (\text{Vtop} * \text{Videa})$$
$$\& \ (\text{Videa W Vword})) \qquad\qquad \& \ (\text{Vadv} * \text{NEXT})$$
$$\& \ (\text{CALL RELATIVE})$$

where a subroutine to analyze relative clauses is assumed.

However, there can be dangers in using such subroutine calls to replace sets of productions. For instance, the above call to the relative clause would seem to indicate that ACT could parse an infinite embedding of relatives. Humans seem able to handle long embeddings of subject relatives but not object relatives. That is, while the following sentence is fairly comprehensible,

(4)   The boy who hit the girl who liked the cat who chased the mouse ate a lollipop.

the following sentence is definitely not comprehensible:

(5)   The mouse whom the cat whom the girl whom the boy hit liked chased ate a lollipop.

The reason for this is obvious when we consider the productions in Table 6.2 for subject versus object relatives. The object relative (R3) requires that the topic of the relative clause be held in memory until the verb is encountered. It is stored as the value of variable Vhold1 (which is rehearsed by Production (P2)). By embedding an object relative within an object relative, the original value of the variable Vhold1 is lost. Thus, one embedding of an object relative is comprehensible, but more are not:

(6)   The mouse whom the cat chased ate a lollipop.

The problems posed for ACT by center-embedding is discussed more thoroughly in Section 11.3. However, this example serves to show that the attempt to impose a subroutine structure on ACT productions systems can only be approximate. It is really all one big production system and there can be interactions among separate productions that are not in keeping with one's normal, modular conception of subroutines.

Subroutine Approximation

One advantage to subroutine analyses is that they can be used as excuses for ignorance. Consider, for instance, how one might approach modeling a subject in the task that will be discussed in the third section of this chapter. Part of the task required subjects to decide whether certain people were strong on the bases of various predicates he heard about them. He might hear:

(7)   Fred lifts 200 lb weights.

(8)   Jack runs 100 ft every day.

(9)   Tom is a star linebacker.

It is virtually impossible to know exactly what productions the subject is using to make decisions about these statements. He may have some productions encoded directly for making these inferences about such predicates. For example, he might have stored the production

((Vper * (lift OF Vweight)) $\Rightarrow$ (Vper * strong)
& (Vweight * (weigh OF Vpound))
& (Vpound * (greater OF 100 lb)))

which asserts that if Vper lifts something that weighs over 100 lb, then Vper is strong.

Or, he might have stored in propositional form

(1)   ((lift OF heavy) * strong)

(2)   (200 lb * heavy)

These encode the facts that people who lift heavy things are strong and 200 lb is heavy. The subject might represent the sentence as

(3)   (Fred * (lift OF 200 lb))

He might also have stored the very general inference rules

(4)   ((V4 * V5) & (VR OF V4)) $\Rightarrow$ ((VR OF V4) * (VR OF V5))

(5)   ((V1 * V2) & (V2 * V3)) $\Rightarrow$ (V1 * V3)

With the Propositions (1)–(3) active and Productions (4) and (5) the subject could make a series of inferences that would lead to the conclusion *Fred is strong.* Production (4) could apply to (2) and (3) with the following binding of variables:

V4 = 200 lb

V5 = heavy

VR = lift.

It would yield (6) as an inference[5]

(6)   ((lift OF 200 lb) * (lift OF heavy))

Then, Production (5) could apply to (3) and (6) with the following binding of variables:

V1 = Fred

V2 = (lift OF 200 lb)

V3 = (lift OF heavy)

This would yield the following inference:

(7)   (Fred * (lift OF heavy))

The production (5) could apply to (1) and (7) to yield the inference

(8)   (Fred * Strong).

It is possible to propose many other ways besides these two in which a subject can conclude *Fred is strong.* The exact productions evoked will depend upon the

[5]For this production to apply, some other production would have to preassign V4, V5, or VR to one of these categories. This would serve to anchor the match process to a long term memory node which could then bind the other variables.

subject's experience in the world and consequently what propositions and productions he has acquired. Moreover, there is no reason to suppose the operations that decide *Fred lifts 200 lb weights* implies *Fred is strong* will have very much in common with the operations that decide *Tom is a star linebacker* implies *Tom is strong*. Therefore, as a cover for ignorance, I will propose a subroutine called STRONG which tests whether an individual is strong. Its calling signal is (Vconstrong = START) and its leaving signal, if successful, is (Vcon = STRONG). It is assumed to consist of a set of productions which may apply differently depending on the task. It will be assumed that if this subroutine does not establish that the individual is strong it will not give a leaving signal. This subroutine will make reference to a great deal of pre-experimental information encoded in the form of productions and propositions. The signal (Vconstrong = START) initiates use of this preexperimental knowledge base.

This subroutine and three others will be proposed to model the experimental task in the next section. Predictions for that task can be derived just from the knowledge that these subroutines consist of ACT productions. It is not necessary to know the exact structure of these subroutines.

6.3 EXPERIMENTAL TESTS
OF THE PROPERTIES OF PRODUCTIONS

There are a number of performance characteristics that have been ascribed to productions, and it would be nice to provide some experimental evidence for these properties. These characteristics include the strengthening of productions, their unlimited capacity parallel selection, and their limited capacity parallel application. This section reports two experiments that test predictions from these properties. To test for these properties it seemed necessary to create a new experimental paradigm. One wants a task at which the subject must make nontrivial computations that should not be of a motor or perceptual nature, but rather of a cognitive (higher-level mental process) nature. This is to guarantee that ACT productions would be performing the computations. Also one wants a task that can be performed with data stored in long-term memory as well as immediately presented data. Further, one would like a task in which there is the potential for a number of computations to apply in parallel. This is in order to be able to perform tests of predictions deriving from the parallel application of productions.

The experimental task which I settled on and which seemed to satisfy all these criteria was one in which we had subjects judging whether particular predicates were kind, strong, bright, or dishonest. They were asked to respond with a button press by one hand if the predicate was *kind* or *strong* and with a button press by the other hand if the predicate was *bright* or *dishonest*. Example predicates are

(1)   was always willing to listen to the problems of his colleagues,

(2)   lifted the 200 lb weights in order to impress his girlfriend,

(3)   found a technique for long-range weather forecasting,

(4)   tried to lie about his age to the draft board investigator.

Subjects could also see predicates which were both *kind* and *strong* and predicates which were both *bright* and *dishonest*. Examples of these would be

(5)   helped the elderly lady move her furniture,

(6)   developed a foolproof method to cheat the IRS.

The expectation was that subjects would be able to respond more rapidly to these redundant predicates because either of two procedures (for example, one for deciding kindness and one for deciding strength) could initiate a press of the same button. Although the two procedures apply in parallel, the time for each will be variable and the faster of two will have mean time faster than either one.

Another manipulation was whether the subject was responsible for two or four of the judgment classes. In one block of trials (a two-block) the subjects were told that they would be responsible for two of the four predicates (for example, strong and bright) while in another block (a four-block) they were told that they were responsible for all four judgment classes. As will be seen, the ACT model would predict that subjects would be faster in the two-block case, because fewer productions would be relevant and hence would be on the APPLY LIST. One might argue that the reason why subjects were faster in the two-predicate case was that they could more easily rehearse the response rules (for example, ''strong goes to the right'' and ''bright goes to the left'') and that there was no facilitation of the actual decision process. To deal with this criticism, we interspersed trials in which just the word, *strong, kind, bright,* or *dishonest,* would appear on the screen. The subject was instructed to respond with the appropriate button press. This task should provide a measure of how much of the facilitation in the two-block was due to a rehearsal of the response rule.

A Production System

Table 6.4 displays a production system that is adequate to make the judgments in this task. It is assumed that this production system emerges as a consequence of the subjects' comprehension of the instructions and his performance in the few practice trials that precede the beginning of the actual experiment. The flow of control in Table 6.4 is illustrated in Fig. 6.7. That diagram is somewhat different than earlier ones because of the need to incorporate the effect of unanalyzed subroutines.

It is assumed that this system models a subject responding to words as they appear on a screen. Production (P1) binds the first word in this string to Vtok. The notation (FIRST Vtok) which appears in (P1) is shorthand for a memory structure that encodes that Vtok is the first word in a string (see Fig. 4.4, page 131). The subject is assumed to be set either to process just two predicates or four.

TABLE 6.4
A Debugged Production System for the Predicate Judgment Task

(P1)	(Vcon = START) & (FIRST Vtok)	$\Rightarrow$	(Vcon = GO) & Vtok
(P2)	(Vcon = GO) & (Vtok * CHANGE) & (Vset = TWO)	$\Rightarrow$	(Vcon = START) & (VSET = FOUR) & (UNBIND Vtok)
(P3)	(Vcon = GO) & (Vtok * CHANGE) & (Vset = FOUR)	$\Rightarrow$	(Vcon = START) & (Vset = TWO) & (UNBIND Vtok)
(P4)	(Vcon = GO) & (Vtok − Vnew)	$\Rightarrow$	(CALL COMPREHEND)
(P5)	(Vcon = GO) & (Vtok * STRONG)	$\Rightarrow$	(PRESS RIGHT) & (UNBIND Vtok)
(P6)	(Vcon = GO) & (Vtok * KIND)	$\Rightarrow$	(PRESS RIGHT) & (UNBIND Vtok)
(P7)	(Vcon = GO) & (Vtok * BRIGHT)	$\Rightarrow$	(PRESS LEFT) & (UNBIND Vtok)
(P8)	(Vcon = GO) & (Vtok * DISHONEST)	$\Rightarrow$	(PRESS LEFT) & (UNBIND Vtok)
(P9)	(Vcon = DONE) & (Vset = TWO)	$\Rightarrow$	(CALL STRONG) & (CALL BRIGHT)
(P10)	(Vcon = DONE) & (Vset = FOUR)	$\Rightarrow$	(CALL STRONG) & (CALL KIND) & (CALL BRIGHT) & (CALL DISHONEST)
(P11)	(Vcon = STRONG)	$\Rightarrow$	(PRESS RIGHT) & (Vcon = START)
(P12)	(Vcon = KIND)	$\Rightarrow$	(PRESS RIGHT) & (Vcon = START)
(P13)	(Vcon = BRIGHT)	$\Rightarrow$	(PRESS LEFT) & (Vcon = START)
(P14)	(Vcon = DISHONEST)	$\Rightarrow$	(PRESS LEFT) & (Vcon = START)
(P15)	Vset	$\Rightarrow$	Vset

His set is encoded by the variable Vset, which is rehearsed by Production (P15). The set in this production system can be changed by presenting the word *change*. If the presented word is *change*, Production (P2) or (P3) will change the value of Vset to the other value. If Vtok is followed by another word, (P4) will apply which calls upon the subroutine COMPREHEND to comprehend the predicate. The subroutine COMPREHEND uses the leaving signal (Vcon = DONE) to signal that it is complete. Productions (P5)–(P8) allow for immediate response should the word on the screen be *strong, kind, bright,* or *dishonest*. Upon completion of the comprehension of the predicate, initiated by (P4), either (P9) or (P10) will apply depending on the binding of the variable, Vset.

Production (P10) calls upon four subroutines to test whether the predicate is strong, kind, bright, or dishonest, but Production (P9) only calls upon two to test for strong and bright. Each subroutine, if successful will deposit STRONG, KIND, BRIGHT, or DISHONEST as the value of variable Vcon. Depending on which is first deposited in Vcon, one of Productions (P11)–(P14) will be evoked.

The subroutines STRONG, KIND, BRIGHT, and DISHONEST are set up by the subject to process these four judgment categories. I find it difficult to speculate as to the exact contents of these subroutines since it seems that what might be done

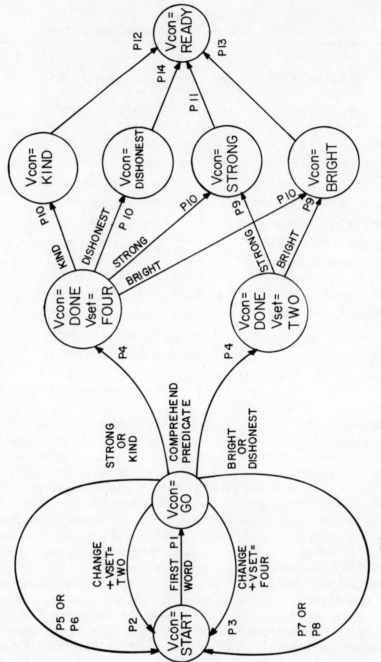

FIG. 6.7   The flow of control among the productions in Table 6.4 for the predicate judgment task.

208

to test for these various categories could be quite idiosyncratic to the subject. Undoubtedly, they would require considerable reference to preexperimental productions and propositions encoding the subject's knowledge about what these properties mean. Examples of this would include the propositions and productions described earlier with respect to the strong judgment (page 203). In addition to evoking these preexperimental productions, these subroutines would have to contain some experimental productions to direct the information processing toward the result required for the experiment.

Experimental Details

Thirty-two subjects were tested in this experiment. The experiment consisted of eight blocks of trials, alternating between blocks in which only two response alternatives were relevant and blocks where four response alternatives were relevant. Sixteen subjects went through the sequence 2 4 2 4 2 4 2 4, and 16 went through the sequence 4 2 4 2 4 2 4 2.

Altogether 60 predicates were used—10 each that were kind, strong, bright, dishonest, redundantly kind and strong, and redundantly bright and dishonest. We had a pilot group of subjects judge these 60 predicates (and some others) on the four dimensions. We selected predicates that most subjects agreed exemplified the four properties. We also took the reaction time of subjects to decide whether a predicate exemplified a particular property. This was taken as an index of how easy it was for the subject to decide about that predicate. The predicates were chosen so that the mean judgment time for nonredundant predicates on the relevant dimension was equal to the mean judgment times for the redundant predicates.

There were 50 reaction-time trials in a four-block which can be classified into ten types of tests with five trials per type. Five nonredundant predicates of each of the four classes were tested as well as five predicates of each of the two redundant classes. In addition, the four-block consisted of five trials on each of the four words (*kind, strong, bright,* and *dishonest*). There were 30 trials in a two-block which can be broken down into six types with five trials per type. Two predicate classes were designated to be tested in a two-block. These same two were tested in all two-blocks. These two predicate classes will be referred to as the *privileged classes*. There were four possible choices for privileged predicates— kind and strong, kind and dishonest, strong and bright, and strong and dishonest. Each combination was used with eight subjects. In the two-block, five non-redundant predicates of each of the two privileged classes were tested as were five predicates of the two redundant classes. Also there were five trials on each of the two words corresponding to the privileged predicates. Different predicates were tested in the two-block versus the four-block. (Five predicates of each nonprivileged class were not used for a subject.) The assignment of predicates from the six classes to be tested in the four-block and two-block or not to be tested was determined randomly for each subject, as was also the order of trials within a block.

A particular predicate was tested either in all four two-blocks or in all four four-blocks. Thus each predicate was tested four times across the experiment. It is important to note that particular privileged and nonprivileged predicates were tested equally often, but that twice as many privileged predicates were tested. This means that differences that appear in the four-block between privileged and nonprivileged predicates are due, not to the frequency of seeing particular predicates, but to the extra practice at making the privileged judgment in the two-block.

The exact procedure that a subject went through may be described as follows: He sat in front of a CRT screen with index fingers resting on response buttons. On the screen would appear the response categories. If he was in a four-block, four categories would appear. The one or two categories assigned to the left hand appeared on the left of the screen and the others on the right of the screen, where they remained for five seconds to enable the subject to prepare himself for the trial. Then either a predicate or a word appeared on the screen and the subject made his response. Feedback was given on the screen as to whether the subject had been correct or not.

Results of Experiment 1

The results from Experiment 1 are displayed in Fig. 6.8. Table 6.5 gives the error rates for the conditions displayed in Fig. 6.8. We will concentrate on the reaction times. The error rates generally reflect the trends seen in the reaction times.

The first thing to note is that there is a considerable improvement over the course of the experiment in the speed with which subjects are able to judge the predicates. The mean time in Pass 1 is 2103 msec, contrasted with 1433 msec in Pass 4. This 680-msec gain contrasts with a 63-msec gain obtained over the four passes in word identification. This difference of differences is quite significant ($t_{961} = 12.64; p < .001$) and indicates that the speedup observed in the predicate judgments largely reflects a change in the speed of the judgment process and not a general speedup over the experiment. ACT predicts this effect because the productions required for these judgments would be strengthened with practice. ACT's strength mechanism also predicts that the privileged judgments should be made more rapidly in the four-block than nonprivileged judgments because the privileged judgments are practiced more often. The data confirm this prediction, with mean reaction time for the privileged predicates being 1700 msec and mean time for the nonprivileged predicates being 1875 msec ($t_{961} = 5.46; p < .001$).

ACT predicts that subjects should react faster in the two-block to privileged and redundant predicates than in the four-block. This is because fewer productions will be on the APPLY LIST and they will be able to apply more rapidly. This prediction is confirmed: The mean time for these predicates in the two-block is 1586 msec, whereas it is 1669 msec in the four-block ($t_{961} = 3.93; p < .001$). ACT also predicts that the difference between these four-block and two-block predi-

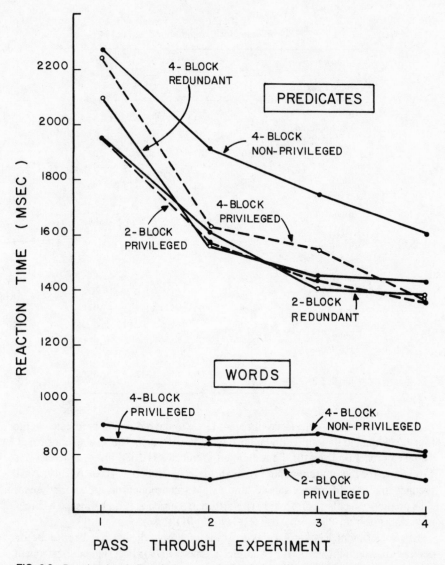

FIG. 6.8   Reaction time in Experiment 1 as a function of pass through the experiment and type of judgment. The top five curves are reaction times for word judgment and the bottom three curves are for word identification.

cates should diminish as they become strengthened. This prediction derives from the fact that the mean time to apply a production is nb/s where n is the number of productions on the APPLY LIST and s is the strength of each production. This prediction is also confirmed: The mean difference on Pass 1 is 223 msec, whereas it is 30 msec on Pass 4 ($t_{961} = 3.23$; $p < .001$).

TABLE 6.5
Error Rates for Experiment 1

	Pass			
Predicates	1	2	3	4
4-Block nonprivileged	.081	.059	.053	.053
4-Block privileged	.050	.025	.038	.025
4-Block redundant	.047	.044	.019	.009
2-Block privileged	.028	.028	.028	.044
2-Block redundant	.047	.019	.028	.038
Words				
4-Block nonprivileged	.069	.053	.050	.047
4-Block privileged	.044	.016	.034	.028
2-Block privileged	.013	.009	.012	.012

ACT predicts that subjects should react faster to the redundant predicates in the four-block than to the nonredundant privileged predicates. This is also confirmed: The mean reaction time for the redundant predicates is 1638 msec, whereas it is 1700 msec for the nonredundant predicates ($t_{961} = 2.08; p < .05$). Finally, ACT predicts that this difference should diminish as the productions are strengthened. This prediction is also confirmed: The difference on Pass 1 is 145 msec, whereas it is -60 msec on Pass 4 ($t_{961} = 2.43; p < .01$).

This experiment has similarities to some of the work that has been done on perceptual judgment tasks (for example, Garner, 1974). In a typical experiment subjects might be shown objects which may vary by shape (square or circle) and color (red or blue). The subject is asked to classify the objects by one dimension—perhaps shape. Interest concerns what happens with variation on the other dimension. That dimension can be correlated with the criterial dimension. So, for example, all squares are red and all circles are blue. In the constant condition, the irrelevant dimension is kept fixed. In the noncorrelated condition all combinations of the two dimensions occur. The typical result is that subjects react fastest in the correlated condition, next fastest in the constant condition, and slowest in the uncorrelated condition. Our contrast between redundant and nonredundant predicates is very much like the contrast between the correlated and constant conditions. Another result in this literature is that subjects are faster when there are fewer dimensions that are relevant to this decision (for example, Egeth, 1966). This is analogous to the result that subjects react faster when there are fewer predicate classes.

It is also well understood in the perceptual literature that neither of these results necessarily implies a parallel model. Both are easily predicted from a serial model. It is also the case that the results from my experiment can be predicted by a serial model. Suppose subjects scanned productions serially looking for a match. Then they should react faster, on the average, to a redundant predicate because they will find a relevant production sooner in the search. They should react faster in the two-condition because there are only two productions rather than four that need to be scanned. The speedup effects observed over the course of the experiment can be attributed to an increase in speed of scan. The fact that there are serial and parallel models which will mimic each other is just what is to be expected from the results about nonidentifiability in Section 1.2.

Experiment 2

The previous experiment showed that the procedural knowledge underlying the predicate judgment displayed evidence of the ACT properties of production strength and limited capacity parallel application of productions. However, that experiment did not investigate the relations proposed between the production component and long-term memory. Since the predicates were presented on the screen their memory encoding would presumably be active throughout the trial. The purpose of the second experiment was to create a situation in which the subject would have to activate the predicate from long-term memory. This experiment had the subject learn predicates true of individuals. Then the subject was presented with an individual's name and had to judge whether he had learned some predicate about that individual, which could be classified as kind, strong, bright, or dishonest.

A manipulation in this experiment was whether subjects learned just one relevant predicate to the individual or one relevant and two irrelevant predicates. The irrelevant predicates were ones that could not be judged on any of the four dimensions. The effect of these irrelevant predicates should be to slow down the rate at which the relevant predicate could be activated. The productions to test for predicate classes would not be able to apply to this predicate until it was activated. Therefore, there should be a slowing down of reaction time. However, this slowing down should be independent of whether the subject is being tested in the two-block or four-block and independent of whether he is being tested with a privileged or nonprivileged predicate. That is, factors that affect production application should be independent of factors that affect activation of memory. These two classes of factors should be additive. Thus, this experiment can be seen as a test for the separation of procedural and declarative knowledge.

Experimental Details

Thirty-two subjects were tested. The experiment consisted of three phases: an initial study phase, a test-study phase, and a reaction time phase. In the initial study phase subjects learned 48 facts about 24 individuals referred to by class names like *the lawyer, the German, the hippie,* etc. Twelve individuals had just one relevant predicate. The other 12 individuals had one relevant and two irrelevant predicates. For each subject the predicates were randomly assigned to individual names within the constraints of the experimental design. The subjects studied the individual sentences at a 20-sec rate. To force the subject to process each sentence meaningfully and to improve their memory subjects were asked to write some rationalization of why the predicate was true of the individual. Thus, a subject might be asked to rationalize why a lawyer would lift 200 lb weights in order to impress his girlfriend. The subject might generate the rationalization *because he felt insecure about not being in a he-man profession.* The order of presentation of the sentences in this phase was randomly determined for each subject.

After this study phase, a test-study phase followed which was intended to make sure that the subject had learned the material. He was given the predicate and was asked to recall the person of whom it was true. If he could not recall the correct name, he was told the answer and given another opportunity to study the answer. The sentences were tested in the same sequence as they had been studied. A dropout procedure was used such that each predicate was dropped out of the test sequence after the subject had successfully recalled the individual to it in two successive sequences.

The reaction time phase consisted of four repetitions of one of two sequences— a two-block judgment task, a four-block, and then a verification task, or a four-block, a two-block, and then a verification task. Again two predicate classes were assigned to the privileged treatment for each subject. There were no redundant predicates used in this experiment. The two-block consisted of the presentation of four individuals exemplifying each of the privileged predicates. Two of the four individuals in a predicate class had only a relevant predicate associated with them and two had one relevant and two nonrelevant predicates. Tests of the first type of individual will be referred to as the no-fan condition and tests of the other type as the fan condition. In addition to judging individual names, there were two tests using each of the privileged predicate words. The four-block presented four individuals in each of the four predicate classes—two in no-fan and two in the fan condition for each predicate class. There were two trials using each of the four predicate words. Each individual name was tested either in the two-block or the four-block. Over the course of the experiment the name would be tested four times.

The verification phase involved presenting subjects with sentences ascribing predicates to individuals. These sentences could either be true, ascribing predicates that had been learned of that individual, or false, ascribing a predicate learned of some other individual. All 48 sentences learned in the study phase were tested as true probes and all 48 predicates and 24 individuals were tested as false probes. Thus, there were 48 sentences tested as true and 48 tested as false in the verification phase. One purpose of this verification phase was to keep rehearsed in the subject's memory the irrelevant predicates.

The order of the material in the two- and four-judgment blocks and in the verification phase was randomized for each subject. The procedures in the reaction-time test were similar to the procedures in Experiment 1.

Results

The data can be classified according to three factors: Whether they came from a judgment task, a true verification test, or a false verification test; whether they involved an individual tested in a two-block, a four-block with a privileged predicate, or a four-block with a nonprivileged predicate; and whether the individual only had a relevant predicate (no-fan) or also irrelevant predicates (fan). Figure 6.9 presents the data classified according to these three factors. In each of the four passes through the experiment, there were only four observations per subject for each condition in Fig. 6.9. This contrasts with the 10 observations obtained in each pass of Experiment 1. The reason for the fewer observations was the need to have the subject memorize all the material. To achieve 10 observations per pass it would have been necessary to have the subjects memorize two and one half times as many sentences, which seemed far too many. To get stable reaction times, Fig. 6.9 collapses the four passes into a single mean observation. Table 6.6 reports the error rates for the conditions in Fig. 6.9.

The abscissa of Fig. 6.9 gives the predicate types in their expected order of difficulty in the judgment task. As may be confirmed, the order of difficulty was

TABLE 6.6
Error Rates for Experiment 2

	Predicate type		
	2-Block	4-Block privileged	4-Block nonprivileged
Judgment, no fan	.045	.040	.096
Judgment, fan	.110	.142	.167
True, no fan	.058	.050	.048
True, fan	.054	.054	.058
False, no fan	.043	.035	.046
False, fan	.035	.027	.039

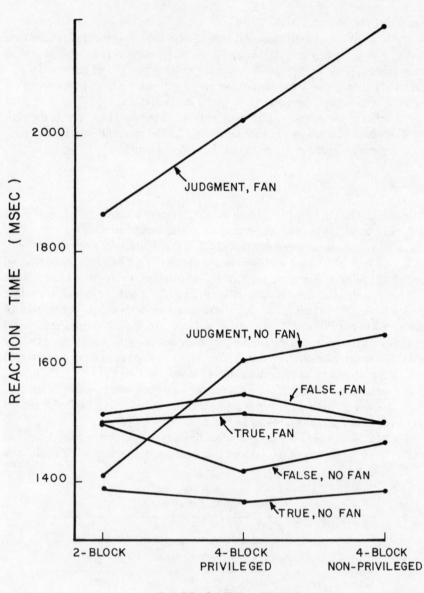

FIG. 6.9   Reaction time in Experiment 2 as a function of predicate type, fan, and type of response required.

as expected. Collapsing the fan and no-fan conditions, the mean reaction times are 1637 msec in the two-block, 1818 msec in the four-block with privileged predicates, and 1921 msec in the four-block with nonprivileged predicates. This trend is highly significant ($F_{1,527} = 41.60; p < .001$), and basically replicates the result of Experiment 1. The reaction times for word identification (not reported in Fig. 6.9) are 823 msec for the two-block, 880 msec for the four-block privileged, and 921 msec for the four-block nonprivileged. The extreme effect for word identification is 98 msec compared with 284 msec for predicate judgment. So, once again the effect for predicate judgment cannot just be in rehearsal of the response rules. Also it can be seen in Fig. 6.9 that there is no effect of predicate type on true or false verification. The reaction time averaged over true and false and over fan and no-fan are 1477 msec for two-block, 1463 msec for four-block privileged, and 1461 msec for four-block nonprivileged.

There are effects of fan for all three response types. Subjects are 471 msec slower in the fan case for the judgment task ($F_{1,527} = 198; p < .001$); 129 msec slower for true verifications ($F_{1,527} = 14.84; p < .001$); and just 32 msec slower for false verifications ($F_{1,527} = .92; p > .2$). Reaction times in such verification tasks will be considered at great length in Chapter 8. Basically, a true response in the verification task depends on activation intersecting from the subject and predicate of the to-be-verified sentence. This will be slowed down by fan out of the subject because activation will spread less rapidly down the correct path. The analysis of false judgments in Chapter 8 also expects an effect of fan. Fan should have a very large effect on the judgment task because activation must spread from the subject to activate the predicate. The effect of fan should be larger than in the case of true verification because in the verification task the slowness of spread from the subject is somewhat compensated for by the spread from the predicate.

The critical concern of this experiment is whether there is an interaction between predicate type and fan for the judgment task. A test for interaction is, in fact, not significant ($F_{2,527} = 1.01; p > .2$). There is some indication of a possible interaction in Fig. 6.9 in that the rise from four-block privileged to four-block nonprivileged is considerably steeper in the fan condition (166 msec) than in the no-fan condition (41 msec). Unfortunately, the standard error of these reaction times (44 msec) is such that such a difference of differences is not significant. Inspection of Table 6.6 indicates that some of this nonsignificant interaction could be due to a speed–accuracy tradeoff. That is, the error rate in the four-block privileged condition is lower than any other condition. So there is little evidence for an interaction between fan and predicate type. If one accepts that these data do not indicate an interaction, then they support ACT's hypothesis about the independence of the activation of the memory network and predicate application. This is also support for the basic separation made in ACT between procedural and declarative knowledge.

SUMMARY OF CHAPTER 6

ACT uses a set of quick, partial tests each cycle to see if any production should be added to the APPLY LIST. Once on the APPLY LIST, a production will wait an exponentially distributed amount of time before its condition is tested against active memory. The time waited depends on the strength of the production and the number of other productions on the APPLY LIST. The tests specified in a condition include whether a node is active, whether a variable has a particular value, whether a pattern is active, and whether there is activity intersecting between nodes. Tests in conditions can also specify the absence of these properties. If the properties specified in the condition of a production are satisfied, the action of the production is executed in the same cycle of time as the condition is satisfied.

Sets of productions can be chunked into subroutines which are called upon by setting a control variable to a certain value. They expect to be given data as values of certain global variables and return data as values of global variables. They signal their completion by setting a control variable to a certain value.

Subroutine structure is useful both to the scientist in trying to understand ACT and to ACT in trying to perform tasks. It is useful to the scientist because it makes it easier to understand the interactions among a set of productions and because subroutines can be used in place of having to specify all the productions performing a subtask. It is useful to ACT because it permits the same productions to be used in multiple contexts and because the induction system can take advantage of subroutine structures to develop systems for well-defined subtasks. However, productions, not subroutines, are the basic units of procedural knowledge. Therefore, subroutine structure may not always be appropriate and it is possible for subroutines to interact in nonmodular ways.

A subroutine structure was used to model an experimental task in which subjects decided whether various predicates exemplified strong, kind, bright, or dishonest characteristics. A rich set of predictions was derived from the knowledge that these subroutines consisted of ACT productions. It was not necessary to understand the internal structure of these subroutines. Experiment 1 supported the ACT predictions that productions should become more rapid with use, that productions are applied more rapidly when fewer are on the APPLY LIST, and that reaction time will be faster when there are two subroutines rather than one to execute a response. A second experiment supported ACT's prediction that the process of activating the network was independent of the process of applying productions.

REFERENCES

Anderson, J. R., & Bower, G. H. *Human associative memory*. Washington: Winston, 1973.
Brown, R. *A first language*. Cambridge, Massachusetts: Harvard University Press, 1973.

Egeth, H. E. Parallel versus serial processes in multidimensional stimulus discrimination. *Perception and Psychophysics,* 1966, **1,** 245–252.

Garner, W. R. *The processing of information and structure.* Hillsdale, New Jersey: Lawrence Erlbaum Assoc., 1974.

LaBerge, D., & Samuels, S. J. Toward a theory of automatic information processing in reading. *Cognitive Psychology,* 1974, **6,** 293–323.

Posner, M. I., & Snyder, C. R. R. Attention and cognitive control. In R. L. Solso (Ed.), *Information processing and cognition: The Loyola Symposium.* Hillsdale, New Jersey: Lawrence Erlbaum Assoc., 1975.

7
Formal Semantics of ACT Representations

While the types of semantic theories that have been formulated by logicians and philosophers do a reasonable job of specifying the semantics of complex constructions, they fall down on the specification of the semantics of the basic "atomic" propositions.

WILLIAM WOODS

Semantics is a term with many meanings. In this chapter it refers to a formal analysis of the meaning of ACT expressions. It is not "semantics" as that term is most often used in cognitive psychology. That is, semantics in this chapter is not a psychological theory about how subjects comprehend sentences, represent meanings, or reason about meanings. Rather it is a metatheoretical enterprise. The semantics in this chapter has the same relation to a psychological theory as does the formal study of stochastic processes. That is, it provides us with a tool to study ACT, which is the psychological theory.

The semantics developed in this chapter provides a tool that is useful in many ways. Such a tool was badly needed by the propositional theories reviewed in Chapter 2. One use for a formal semantics is that it permits one to assess the expressive power of a formalism. For instance, in Section 2 of this chapter I prove that the ACT representational system is at least equivalent in expressive power to the predicate calculus. A second reason for producing a formal semantics is to provide a clearer criterion of whether a network structure appropriately expresses a conceptualization. Until now I have been producing network structures and asserting that they are equivalent to certain English sentences. The semantics provides a means of partially checking my claim. One can ask whether the meaning formally associated with the network matches our intuitive sense of the meaning of the sentence. A third motivation for a formal semantics is to permit one to explore properties of inference systems associated with ACT (see Chapter 9). In particular, it permits one to determine whether various sets of inference rules are sound and complete.

In the first section of this chapter I present a model-theoretic semantics for the ACT network and for a subset of the production system. In the second section

I show that the propositional network and the production subset have, *combined,* the expressive power of predicate calculus. It is really not possible to get the total expressive power of the predicate calculus into the network itself. This is potentially bothersome given that one wants to express all declarative knowledge in terms of network constructions. In Section 7.3 I give examples of how it is possible to circumvent the limitations on the expressive power of the network. This involves putting into the propositional network symbols whose meaning can be interpreted by productions. One can then use these symbols to enrich the expressive power of the network.

Section 1 of this chapter and Section 2 in particular are quite technical. The third section is mainly devoted to illustrating how natural language concepts can be represented in ACT. Some readers may want to skip this chapter or skip to the third section. While I think the developments in this chapter are important, other chapters are not dependent upon them.

7.1 A MODEL-THEORETIC SEMANTICS FOR ACT

The semantics used here is an adaptation of the model-theoretic semantics that one encounters in modern logic (for example, Church, 1956; Mendelson, 1964). Model-theoretic semantics will probably seem strange to those who are mainly familiar with the attempts to formalize semantics in linguistics. However, I have chosen the logicians' approach because of serious conceptual problems in the linguistic developments. In linguistics, semantic analysis takes the form of trying to represent the meaning of a sentence as some symbol structure that is supposed to make the meaning more transparent than the original sentence. For instance, in their classic paper, Katz and Fodor (1963) propose to represent one sense of *The man hits the colorful ball* as ''[some contextually definite] → (physical object) → (human) → (adult) → (male) → (action) → (instancy) → [Strikes with a blow or missile] → [some contextually definite] → (physical object) → (color) → [[Abounding in contrast or variety of bright colors] [having globular shape]]'' where each element in this list is a primitive semantic marker or a distinguisher.

Sentences are just concatenations of arbitrary symbols and so have no meaning in and of themselves. The important thing to realize, however, is that abstract structures, like the above, are also just concatenations of symbols and have no meaning in and of themselves. Thus, translating from one symbol structure to another will never expose the meaning of either symbol structure. It may be easier to perform a semantic analysis on the abstract structure rather than the original sentence. Therefore, these abstract structures may be useful intermediate steps in performing a semantic analysis. However, they should not be thought of as constituting a semantic analysis in and of themselves.

Therefore, I will not attempt to develop the semantics of ACT networks or productions by reducing them to some set of primitives or some other abstract structures. These networks are already abstract and it is hard to imagine what could be gained by translating them into another structure. The model-theoretic approach will identify the meaning of an ACT expression with a set of procedures that will allow one to identify the referent of the expression in a model. By "model" is meant a set of objects (of various degrees of abstraction) with interrelations specified among the objects. Each possible set of objects and interrelations among them provides a distinct model. For instance, the real world provides one possible model. The semantic rules are formulated in a sufficiently abstract way that one can determine the reference of an expression in all possible models. It is assumed that the rules of reference are known in each model for primitive expressions and procedures are given for determining the references of complex expressions from the references of the simpler expressions. In terms of the ACT system, it will be assumed that the referents are known for various nodes representing primitive concepts and relations. Then, it will be explained how to interpret the reference of structures constructed from these.

Suppes (1971, 1974) has been engaged in an effort to apply a model-theoretic semantics to the analysis of natural language. He is very adamant about the superiority of this semantic approach to others. As Suppes (1974) writes:

> It is not my objective to be controversial and dialectical in this lecture, but I want to emphasize from the beginning my conviction that when it comes to semantical matters, the tradition of model-theoretic semantics that originated with Frege (1879) in the nineteenth century is *the* serious intellectual tradition of semantical analysis, and the recent offshoots by linguists, to a large extent conceived in ignorance of this long tradition, have little to offer in comparison [p. 103].

Suppes' use of model-theoretic semantics is different than my own in a number of ways. First, he applies it to natural language whereas I am applying it to the ACT formalisms. Second, he intends, apparently, to make that semantics an integral part of a psychological theory of natural language. I make no such claim for my semantics. The function of the model-theoretic semantics in ACT is to permit analysis of the objects of the theory, not to actually be part of the theory.

Semantics of Network Expressions

The semantics of the ACT network structures will be specified with respect to semantic models that consist of three sets of objects—a set I of individual objects, a set S of situations, and a set H of classifications. These three sets are disjoint. Their union will be referred to as D for domain of the model. The elements of the set I can be thought of as the basic objects of the universe—people, animals, rocks, planets, societies, rivers, etc. All propositions have as their reference an element of the set S. It is somewhat a misnomer to call the elements of S "situations" because some propositions do not refer to situations in the conventional sense of that term. For instance, it is strange to speak of universal propositions (for example, All collies are dogs) as referring to a situation. Similarly, it is strange to speak of a false proposition (for example, McGovern won the 1972 election) as referring to a situation. Of course, other propositions (for example, A hippie touched a debutante) can be seen as referring to "situations" without too much strain on the term. In any case, my use of the term "situation" must be taken as somewhat different than the conventional sense. I chose the term largely because it seemed no more inappropriate than any other. It is necessary for ACT's semantics to have some way of denoting the reference of each proposition. The final set H of classifications consists of the elements representing the reference of abstract classification nodes connected to concept nodes by a C link.

To further develop the meaning of ACT structures it is necessary to specify the meaning of each relational term in ACT. The meaning of an n-term relation will be a set of $(n + 1)$ tuples of elements from D. So if the relation were *is married to*, the meaning of the relation would be the set of all pairs $\langle x, y \rangle$ where x is married to y. If the relation were *gives* it would be the set of all triples $\langle x, y, z \rangle$ where x gives y to z. The meaning of complex relations (that is, a higher-order relation applied to a lower-order relation) is similarly defined. For instance, the meaning of *vigorously hit*, represented in ACT by (vigorously OF hit), is the set of all pairs $\langle x, y \rangle$ where x vigorously hits y. The meaning of complex relations will not be defined in the proposed semantics with respect to the meaning of their simpler subparts. Thus, the meaning of (vigorously OF hit) bears no necessary relation to the meaning of *hit*. In this case, it might seem that a subset relation would be an appropriate semantic analysis. However, there are other complex relations like (almost OF hit) where this subset interpretation will not work. Therefore, from the point of view of the formal semantics each complex relation can have its distinct meaning, unconstrained by the meaning of simpler relations.

The nature of a model-theoretic semantics is to specify the meaning of certain basic expressions in the system and provide operators which will specify the meaning of expressions concatenated from the basic expressions. There are two such operators defined for the ACT model. There is the operator V which gives the reference of all ACT expressions and the operator T which assigns truth values to some ACT expressions. Table 7.1 defines these operators for the various ACT constructions.

Rule (S1) assigns as the meaning of each primitive concept (that is, one not constructed out of other concepts) a set of objects (that is, a subset of D). If it assigns a single object to the concept, then the concept corresponds to an individual object (for example, The Rock of Gibraltar or Gerald Ford). Rule (S1) can also assign no object to the concept (for example, in the case of a unicorn). Rule (S2) applies to each relation R^n, whether that relation is simple or complex. It makes the meaning of R^n an $n + 1$ relation. The referent of the *false* symbol is the set of nonexistent situations (Rule S3). Rules (S1)–(S3) provide the interpretation of the basic symbols. The remaining rules specify how to interpret ACT network constructions built from these. Rules (S4) and (S5) give the obvious interpretation of the intersection and union of concepts. Rule (S6) asserts that the

TABLE 7.1
Rules of Semantic Interpretation for ACT Network Expressions

(S1)	If A is a primitive concept, then $V(A) \subset D$
(S2)	If R^n is an n-term relation, then $V(R^n) \subset \underbrace{D \times D \times \cdots \times D}_{n+1}$
(S3)	$V\text{(false)} \subset S$
(S4)	If X and Y are both concepts, $V(X \cap Y) = V(X) \cap V(Y)$
(S5)	If X and Y are both concepts, $V(X \cup Y) = V(X) \cup V(Y)$
(S6)	If R^n is a relation and $A_1, A_2, \ldots, A_n$ are concepts, $V(R^n \text{ OF } A_1, A_2, \ldots, A_n) = \{X_0 \mid \langle X_0, X_1, \ldots, X_n \rangle \in V(R^n) \text{ and } X_1 \in V(A_1), \ldots, X_n \in V(A_n)\}$
(S7)	If X is a classification node, $V(X) \subset H$ and is a singleton set
(S8)	$T(X * Y) = T$ if $V(X) \subseteq V(Y)$ $T(X * Y) = F$ if $V(X) \nsubseteq V(Y)$
(S9)	If $T(X * Y) = T$, $V(X * Y) \subset S - V\text{(false)}$ and is a singleton set If $T(X * Y) = F$, $V(X * Y) \subset V\text{(false)}$ and is a singleton set

concept defined by a relation-argument construction $(R^n \text{ OF } A_1, A_2, \ldots, A_n)$ is the set of all objects which bear the relation R^n to objects in the sets $A_1, A_2, \ldots, A_n$. Rule (S7) assigns to each classification node a singleton subset of the set H.

Rules (S8) and (S9) deal with propositions. Rule (S8) asserts a proposition is true if and only if the subject is a subset of the predicate. Rule (S9) assigns a true situation to the proposition if the subject is a subset of the predicate, and assigns a false situation otherwise. The term $S - V\text{(false)}$ which appears in Rule (S9) refers to the set S of situations minus those false situations. These will be the true situations. Every well-formed proposition has a referent, independent of whether it is true or not. Note that the reference of a proposition is defined with respect to the symbol structure X and Y and not with respect to the semantic interpretation (references) of these structures. Thus, it is possible that there can be concepts, X, X', Y, Y', such that $V(X) = V(X')$, $V(Y) = V(Y')$, but $V(X * Y) \neq V(X' * Y')$. As an example, consider $X = $ Richard Nixon, $X' = $ the most dishonest president in America's history, $Y = $ deceived the American people, and $Y' = $ deceived the most sophisticated electorate in the world. Suppose, that X and X' have the same reference as do Y and Y'. Still we would not want to claim that the following two sentences had the same meaning:

$(X * Y) = $ Richard Nixon deceived the American people.

$(X' * Y') = $ The most dishonest president in America's history deceived the most sophisticated electorate in the world.

If our semantic analysis assigned the same reference to these two statements, it would not be possible to explain why one of the following propositions could be true and the other not:

(Fred * (believes OF $(X * Y)$))) = Fred believes Richard Nixon deceived the American people.

(Fred * (believes OF $(X' * Y')$))) = Fred believes the most dishonest president in America's history deceived the most sophisticated electorate in the world.

The only way for these two propositions to have different truth values in ACT is for the objects of Fred's believing (that is, $(X * Y)$ and $(X' * Y')$) to have different referents. This is the motivation for rule S9 which treats the referents of propositions as independent of the referents of the subpropositional units. This is one way that ACT will attempt to deal with the opacity of natural language.

It is tempting to make the interpretation of the classification node a singleton set containing the set which is the interpretation of the classified node (that is, the concept node connected to the classification node by a C link). However, as noted earlier (page 169) the problem with this tack is that it would make identical in meaning classifications which happen by accident to denote the same set (for example, dodo and unicorn). One way around this would be to conceive of a "possible worlds" semantics (for example, Hughes & Cresswell, 1968) in which a classification node would have different interpretations (that is, sets) in different possible worlds. Since there are possible worlds where *dodo* and *unicorn* have different referents, their classification nodes would not have the same meaning. Development of a possible worlds semantics may also be a better way to deal with the opacity of propositions just discussed. However, I do not feel technically competent to develop a possible worlds semantics.

An Illustration

To illustrate these rules of semantic interpretation, Fig. 7.1 provides a simple model consisting of six objects. Table 7.2 shows the values of the semantic operators, V and T, applied to various constructions describing this domain. The six objects will be referred to by the characters A–F. We need some way to denote situations. Each proposition (true or false) about this domain has a situation referent. I will adopt the convention of denoting a situation by a lower case s, subscripted by an integer to keep it separate from other situations. Thus, the situations are denoted by s_1, s_2, etc. Lines (a)–(e) in Table 7.2 give evaluations of simple concepts like *square, large,* and *triangle,* and of simple relations like *touch* and *above.* Lines (f)–(i) give the referent of some higher-order relations concatenated on the basic relations.

Examples (j) through (n) illustrate how the semantic evaluations of various expressions are calculated. Example (j) illustrates relation-argument; Example (k)

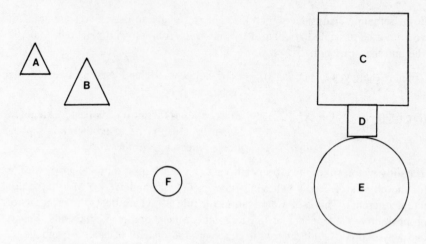

FIG. 7.1   A simple model to illustrate the semantics of the ACT network.

a true proposition; Example (1) a false proposition with negation; Example (m) a higher-order relation-argument combined with intersection; and Example (n) the truth valuation of a proposition. The reader might try to convince himself that all the valuations in Table 7.2 are correct.

TABLE 7.2
Value of Various Expressions Referring to Fig. 5.19

(a)	$V(\text{square}) = \{C, D\}$
(b)	$V(\text{large}) = \{C, E\}$
(c)	$V(\text{triangle}) = \{A, B\}$
(d)	$V(\text{touch}) = \{\langle C, D\rangle, \langle D, C\rangle, \langle D, E\rangle, \langle E, D\rangle\}$
(e)	$V(\text{above}) = \{\langle C, D\rangle, \langle D, E\rangle, \langle C, E\rangle\}$
(f)	$V(\text{opposite OF above}) = \{\langle D, C\rangle, \langle E, D\rangle, \langle E, C\rangle\}$
(g)	$V(\text{opposite OF touch}) = \{\}$
(h)	$V(\text{nearly OF above}) = \{\langle A, B\rangle\}$
(i)	$V(\text{nearly OF touch}) = \{\langle A, B\rangle, \langle B, A\rangle\}$
(j)	$V(\text{touch OF square}) = \{C, D, E\}$
(k)	$V(\text{square} * (\text{touch OF square})) = \{s_2\}$
(l)	$V(\tilde{\ }(\text{square} * (\text{touch OF square}))) = \{s_1\}$
(m)	$V(((\text{opposite of above}) \text{ OF square}) \cap \text{large}) = \{E\}$
(n)	$T((((\text{opposite of above}) \text{ OF square}) \cap \text{large}) * \text{circle}) = T$

Use of Network Semantics

With a formal semantics one can address questions in a way that was not previously possible. There is now a way to decide whether a network representation correctly expresses a sentence. We can compute the semantic interpretation associated with a representation and ask ourselves whether that is consistent with our interpretation of a sentence. An example of this was to be found in Fig. 5.16 of Chapter 5 (page 172). There we had two representations, (a) and (b), that one might think represented *All black dogs are faithful*. With the semantics it is possible to determine that only (a) has this meaning and that (b) really means *There are black, faithful dogs*. It is critical that, if we are going to propose network representations for sentences, we have a way of deciding if these representations are semantically correct.

Another issue that this semantics allows us to examine is the question of invariance under paraphrase. As noted in the review in Section 2.5 some theorists have claimed to have developed propositional representations in which no two different constructions had the same meaning. However, there was no precise way to put this claim to test for past theories. On the other hand, it is very easy to address in ACT this question of whether there exist different propositional structures with the same meaning. If we take ''same meaning'' to mean having the same situation referent, it is possible for any two propositional structures to have or not have the same meaning. This is because different models can arbitrarily assign situation referents to propositions (Rule S9 in Table 7.1). However, a better and more conventional interpretation of ''same meaning'' would be that two propositions are true in the same models. In this case, it is easy to show that there exist synonymous ACT network structures. For instance, the ACT proposition $(X * (R OF (Y \cup Z)))$ is synonymous with $(X * ((R OF Y) \cup (R OF Z)))$. Examples of these abstract schema would be (Fred * (kick OF (John $\cup$ Bill))) and (Fred * ((kick OF John) $\cup$ (kick OF Bill))). That these have the same truth values can be seen by consulting the semantics of Table 7.1. It can also be seen more informally by considering the synonymy of the English equivalents:

(1)   Fred kicked John or Bill.

(2)   Fred kicked John or kicked Bill.

Such synonymous structures run rampant in ACT. Therefore, ACT can make no pretense of achieving invariance under paraphrase.

Model-Theoretic Semantics of Productions

A model-theoretic semantics treats the meaning of expressions in terms of their reference in the external world. The total production system as developed in Section 6.1 is not amenable to such a treatment. Many expressions that appear in productions, such as the absence test, have no external referent at all. They only have meaning within the memory system. Also, unlike propositions, it is never meaningful to think of productions as having as meanings situation referents. However, there is a subset of the production system for which it is meaningful to speak of truth values. To be able to formally explore the expressive power of the ACT system it is necessary to define the truth conditions of this production subset.

Table 7.3 defines the subset of the production system in Table 6.1 (page 184) that will be subject to semantic analysis. This is the subset for which it is meaningful to specify truth conditions. It is worthwhile to note the features of productions which have been excluded from this subset and to explain why they are not amenable to a specification of truth conditions: Omitted from Table 7.3 are the tests for the absence of properties in active memory and the test for the occurrence of an intersection of activation in memory. These are conditions that test for properties of the memory system. However, the success of these tests implies nothing about the external world to which truth conditions make reference. For instance the absence of a proposition in memory does not imply the proposition is false, only that the system is ignorant on this score. Similarly, the occurrence of an intersection of activation between two nodes implies nothing about the referents of these nodes in the external world.

Other features missing from the conditions of this subset include the facility to detect whether a node is active, to test the binding of a variable, or to check whether a nonpropositional memory structure (for example, a relation–argument structure) is active. All these kinds of tests served the function of providing control structure—that is, of allowing productions to apply only in certain contexts.

TABLE 7.3
A Grammar for a Subset of the Production System

(1a)	Production	:	:	Structure $\Rightarrow$ Pattern
(2a)	Structure	:	:	Var & Structure
(2b)		:	:	(Pattern)
(3a)	Pattern	:	:	Pattern & Pattern
(3b)		:	:	Proposition
(4a)	Proposition	:	:	(Concept * Concept)
(5a)	Concept	:	:	Node
(5b)		:	:	(Concept $\cap$ Concept)
(5c)		:	:	(Concept $\cup$ Concept)
(5d)		:	:	(Relation OF Concept)
(5e)		:	:	(Concept * Concept)
(5f)		:	:	(Node C Concept)
(6a)	Relation	:	:	Node
(6b)		:	:	(Relation $\cup$ Relation)
(6c)		:	:	(Relation $\cap$ Relation)
(6d)		:	:	(Relation OF Relation)
(7a)	Node	:	:	Var
(7b)		:	:	LTM Node
(8a)	Var	:	:	V1, V2, etc.

All the production system examples I have considered so far have made good use of these features. They are very desirable features because they serve to keep useless productions off the APPLY LIST and so permit speedy application of the useful productions. However, these efficiency promoting features have no affect on the truth value of productions.

The only specifications of conditions that Table 7.3 permits are unbound variables and propositions. The unbound variables will serve a technical quantificational function to be explained shortly. The appearance of a proposition in a condition serves as a test for the truth of that proposition. The assumption is that if a proposition is stored in memory it is true.

Many possible types of actions permitted in Table 6.1 are not permitted in Table 7.3. These include commands that control the external behavior of the system. These are too unspecified to be subject to careful analysis. Also omitted are the commands that serve to set the value of variables and activate nodes. These commands guide the system's control structure and, as already stated, control structure is irrelevant to specifying truth conditions. The only permissible actions are those which cause propositions to be constructed.

As examples of the sort of productions allowed in this subset consider the following:

(P1)   (Jane * (hit OF John))   ⇒   (John * (hit OF Jane))

(P2)   (V1 * hippie)   ⇒   (V1 * dirty)

(P3)   (V1 * (right OF V2))   ⇒   (V2 * (left OF V1))

(P4)   (V1 * (brother OF V2))   ⇒   (V3 * (father OF V1))
                                            & (V3 * (father OF V2))

(P5)   Vr & (V1 * V2)   ⇒   ((Vr OF V1) * (Vr OF V2))

Production (P1) asserts that if the network propositions (Jane * (hit OF John)) is active in memory, that proposition (John * (hit OF Jane)) should be added to memory. Thus, it can be seen as encoding the proposition, *If Jane hits John then John will hit Jane*. Production (P2) encodes that if there is active in memory that someone (the variable V1) is a hippie, then add to memory that he is dirty. This basically encodes the proposition that *If someone is a hippie he is dirty* or *All hippies are dirty*. This, incidentally, is equivalent to the ACT network proposition (hippie * dirty). Production (P3) encodes that if V1 is right of V2, then V2 is left of V1. Production (P4) encodes that if V1 is the brother of V2, then there is someone (V3) who is their father. Finally, (P5) encodes that if V1 is a V2, then for any relation Vr, the set of things that bear relation Vr to V1 are a subset of the set of things that bear relation Vr to V2. As these examples illustrate, the productions in this subset do seem to be asserting propositions (in the logician's sense of propositions).

One consequence of the restrictions on the actions in this subset is that there is no way to create global variables. (Variables can only be made global in an action by occurring in isolation or by occurring in a construction of the form *Variable* = *node*.) Certain interpretative complications are posed for this subset by the fact that only local variables can occur in the condition of productions. Consider, for instance, the following production, which can appear as part of the subset:

(P6)   ((V1 * V2) & (V2 * V3)) ⇒ (V1 * V3)

This production would permit one to infer from *Spot is a dog* (Spot * dog) and from *dogs are animals* (dog * animal) that *Spot is an animal* (Spot * animal). The problem is that it cannot apply unless at least one of the three variables in the antecedent has been bound to a long-term memory node—V1 to *Spot,* V2 to *dog,* or V3 to *animal.* One cannot match a pattern structure that consists of no long-term memory nodes. Another example of the same problem can be seen in the following production:

(P7)   V1 & (V2 * blind) ⇒ ~ (V2 * (see OF V1))

This encodes that if V2 is blind, V2 cannot see anything. It would allow us to infer from the fact that Fred is blind that he cannot see George. However, for this inference to actually occur *George* must be bound to the variable V1. Thus, while we can analyze the meaning of such productions within this subset, to conceive of them actually being applied it is sometimes necessary to assume that some production, outside of their subset, has made one of the variables global and bound a value to it.

Truth Conditions for Productions

To examine the meaning of productions and to facilitate the discussion in the next section on ACT's expressive power, it will be helpful to introduce some further notation to denote truth relations. If an ACT proposition P is true (that is, $T(P) = T$) in a model, M, this will be denoted $M \models P$. If an ACT proposition is true in all possible models, this will be denoted $\models P$. If a set of propositions P_1, $P_2, \ldots, P_n$ are true in a model, M, this can be denoted $M \models P_1 \& P_2 \& \cdots P_n$. Essentially, $P_1 \& P_2 \& \cdots \& P_n$ can be regarded as a single proposition which is true if and only if all the conjoined propositions $P_1, P_2, \ldots, P_n$ are true. Similarly, then, one can define $\models P_1 \& P_2 \& \cdots \& P_n$.

Now we are in a position to define the truth conditions of a productions $C \Rightarrow A$. Let Var(C) be the set of all the variables that appear in the condition and let Var($A - C$) be the set of all variables which appear in the action but not the condition. These variables will be interpreted as ranging over nodes in the network. We say that a production $C \Rightarrow A$ is true in a model M, denoted $M \models C \Rightarrow A$, iff the following is true:

For any substitution of nodes for variables in Var(C) such that $M \models C_s$, there exist substitutions for the variables in Var($A - C$) such that $M \models A_s$ where C_s and A_s denote the condition and action after substitutions.

Note that under this definition, the ACT production connective "$\Rightarrow$" bears considerable similarity to logical implication. Also, in terms of traditional logic, the variables in the condition appear to be universally quantified and the variables in the action appear to be existentially quantified. This connection between the ACT productions and the traditional predicate calculus can be made more explicit: Let $P_1, \ldots, P_n$ be the propositions in C and let $Q_1, \ldots, Q_m$ be the propositions in A. Let $V_1, V_2, \ldots, V_i$ be the variables in Var(C) and let $V_{i+1}, \ldots, V_{i+j}$ be the variables in Var($A - C$). Then the interpretation being assigned to $C \Rightarrow A$ is very similar to the interpretation assigned to the predicate calculus formula:

$$(\forall V_1)\,(\forall V_2) \cdots (\forall V_i)\,[P_1 \,\&\, P_2 \,\&\, \cdots \,\&\, P_n$$
$$\supset (\exists V_{i+1}) \cdots (\exists V_{i+j})\,(Q_1 \,\&\, Q_2 \,\&\, \cdots \,\&\, Q_m)]$$

Before concluding this section it would be useful to introduce some further notation. If a production $C \Rightarrow A$ is true in all possible models this will be denoted $\models (C \Rightarrow A)$. Let Δ be a collection of propositions and productions. It is useful to have a way of denoting that a proposition, P_1, or a production, $C \Rightarrow A$, is true in all the models for which the elements of Δ are true. This will be denoted $\Delta \models P$ and $\Delta \models C \Rightarrow A$. These expressions indicate that P and $C \Rightarrow A$ are logical consequences of the ACT expressions in Δ. This notion of logical consequence will play a critical role in the next section which establishes that ACT can express the formulas of first-order predicate calculus.

7.2   EXPRESSION OF PREDICATE CALCULUS IN ACT

One would like to show that the ACT representations are of rich expressive power—that one is not going to be able to come up with human conceptions that ACT cannot express. The purpose of this section is to show that ACT is at least equivalent in expressive power to the first-order predicate calculus which is a rich formal language. Previous propositional theories in psychology (see Chapter 2) have not been able to capture all the quantificational relations that can be expressed in predicate calculus. There are logical systems more advanced than first-order calculus such as modal logic and the higher-order predicate calculi. However, it does not seem to be the case that these logics contain any feature which cannot be incorporated into the first-order logic by various conventions.[1] These advanced logics only allow one to express certain notions more directly. ACT also allows

---

[1]I suspect that one can establish conventions in the first-order predicate calculus to make it simulate a Turing Machine. This involves having formulas of the form TM (a, b) which are true iff b is the output of the Turing Machine input a. A set of axioms can be added to make the formula TM (a, b) correspond to any particular Turing Machine. So in this sense it is possible to mimic in the first-order predicate calculus any computable logic. However, the means I have seen for incorporating modal logic and second-order predicate calculus are much much more direct and much less bizarre than this.

many notions to be expressed much more directly than the first-order predicate calculus. However, felicity of expression is not at issue here. The issue is whether there is any feature in these logics that cannot be captured in ACT. Since the features of the advanced logics can be captured in first-order predicate calculus, it would seem adequate to establish that ACT can express first-order calculus. This would show that all the expressive power of logical languages is contained in ACT.

From showing that ACT is as powerful as formal logics it does not follow that all features of natural language and human conception are expressible in ACT. There may be features of human conception not capturable in these formal logics. However, there has been sufficient experience in trying to express natural language concepts in formal logic to know that a large portion of natural language can be so represented. Therefore, it would be a significant step to show that ACT has at least the power of these logics. Also it does not follow from the fact that there may be properties of natural conception not capturable in formal logics that these properties are not capturable in ACT. This section only shows that ACT has the expressive power of predicate calculus; it does not show that predicate calculus has the expressive power of ACT. There are many features of the ACT representation that are not directly expressible in predicate calculus, such as the distinction between a concept and its classification, higher-order relations that take relations as arguments, and propositions that can take propositions as arguments. These features might be expressible in first-order predicate calculus, but only with much circumlocutory use of conventions. Also there are other features of the production system such as tests for absence, tests for intersections, and use of control structure which seem only expressible in predicate calculus by simulating the ACT program (see Footnote 1, page 231). To conclude, the goal is to establish that ACT has the expressive power of natural language and human conception. Since these are not formally defined objects, this section will attempt to show that ACT is at least equivalent to a formally defined subset of natural language—the first-order predicate calculus.

Expressing Predicate Calculus

Up to this point the notion of what it means for ACT to express first-order predicate calculus has been left somewhat vague. I will propose here an algorithm that will translate any expression in the first-order predicate calculus into an equivalent ACT expression. To specify the notion of equivalence meant here it is necessary to introduce some further notation. If P is a predicate calculus formula, then P^T is its ACT translation under the algorithm. Similarly, if Δ is a set of predicate calculus formulas, Δ^T is a set of ACT translations. I will regard as a criterion for equivalence the following:

CRITERION FOR EQUIVALENCE: *P is equivalent to P^T if and only if for all Δ,* $\Delta \models P$ *iff* $\Delta^T \models P^T$.

In the above it is assumed that the symbol "$\models$" has been defined for first-order predicate calculus analogously to the definition for ACT. (Definitions may be found in any of the standard texts on logic (for example, Mendelson, 1964; Robbin, 1969.)

This is not as strong a notion of equivalence as one might like. One might like to have the criterion that the predicate calculus expression and its ACT translation are logically equivalent or true in the same models. However, it is not possible to make formal sense out of these criteria. Since P and P^T are in different formal languages the notion of logical equivalence cannot be applied. Also since they are different formalisms, models for one are different from models for the other. The above definition makes formulas equivalent if the translation algorithm preserves logical consequence. That is, if P is a logical consequence of the formulas in Δ, then P^T is a logical consequence of the formulas in Δ^T. This avoids the need to directly relate P to P^T as would be required to show logical equivalence. It also avoids the need to make identical the models for P and for P^T, as would be necessary to show truth in the same models.

There is a behavioristic justification for accepting preservation of logical consequence as an adequate criterion for equivalence. Consider how we might ascertain as psychologists whether a black box (containing ACT) was adequately representing predicate calculus formulas that we were giving it. The only basis we would have would be whether the box's judgments of logical consequence were correct. That is, we would give it formulas and ask it to judge what followed from these formulas. Provided its judgments were correct we would have no basis to assume it was not correctly representing the formulas. Since there is no behavioral test to show that a representation preserving logical consequence is inadequate, such a representation would be good enough for psychological purposes.

To reiterate: An algorithm will be displayed for translating predicate calculus formulas into ACT expressions. This translation algorithm preserves logical consequence. Logical consequence is an adequate criterion to conclude that the ACT translations are equivalent to the original formulas.

Thus far in this section, I have provided a general discussion of the equivalence proof. The remainder of the section provides a sketchy but technical development of that proof. It will be difficult to follow for those without some training in formal logic because I have omitted, for brevity's sake, proper development of many requisite concepts. However, enough detail has been given so that, hopefully, the properly trained reader can judge the correctness of the proof.

First-Order Predicate Calculus*

Defined below is the first-order predicate calculus that will be translated into ACT. The basic alphabet of the predicate calculus consists of the following:

(1) A set of individual variables x, y, z; V_1, V_2, ... and individual constants a, b, c, ...

(2) A set of functions $f_1, f_2, \ldots$
(3) A set of predicates $p_1, p_2, \ldots$
(4) A set of logical symbols including $\sim$, $\supset$, &, $\vee$, false, $\forall$, $\exists$

The symbol "$\sim$" stands for "not"; "$\supset$" stands for "implies"; "&" for "and"; "$\vee$" for "or"; "false" for "false"; "$\forall$" for "for all"; and "$\exists$" for "there exists." There are two basic levels of expressions in the predicate calculus—those referring to individuals or terms and those referring to propositions or well-formed formulas:

Definition of a Term

(a) Each variable or constant is a term.
(b) If $t_1, t_2, \ldots, t_n$ are terms and f_i is an n-place function, then $f_i(t_1, t_2, \ldots, t_n)$ is a term.

Definition of a Well-Formed Formula (wff)

(a) *False is a wff.*
(b) *If $t_1, t_2, \ldots, t_n$ are terms and P is an n-place predicate, P $(t_1, t_2, \ldots, t_n)$ is a wff.*
(c) If A and B are wffs, $A \supset B$, A & B, $A \vee B$ are wffs.
(d) If A is a wff and x a variable, $(\forall x)A$ and $(\exists x)A$ are wffs.

The formulas defined by (a) and (b) are known as atomic formulas. A formula of the form $(A \supset \text{false})$ asserts that A is not true and will be abbreviated $\sim A$. The following are some examples of wffs:

hit(Jane, John) $\supset$ hit(John, Jane)
$(\forall x)(\text{hippie}(x) \supset \text{dirty }(x))$
$(\forall x)(\forall y)(\text{right}(x, y) \supset \text{left}(y, x))$
$(\forall x)(\forall y)(\text{brother}(x, y) \supset (\exists z)(\text{father}(z, x)$ & father $(z, y)))$
$(\forall x)(\forall y)(\text{blind}(x) \supset \sim (\text{see}(x, y)))$

Note that all variables appear within the scope of a quantifier. Formulas with all appearances of variables bound within the scope of a quantifier are referred to as closed wffs or sentences. Formulas with free variables are basically relations and not statements about which it is meaningful to judge true or false. The goal here is only to translate closed wffs into ACT. Note that all variables in an ACT expression are implicitly within the scope of a quantifier.

Translation of Predicate Calculus into ACT*

The strategy will be to take an arbitrary expression of the predicate calculus and translate it into a special predicate calculus form called *production normal form* (PNF). Then it will be shown that there exists a set of ACT productions equivalent to these PNF formulas. This will be a brute force demonstration of equivalence.

The translation procedure is rather complicated and it will sometimes transform predicate calculus expressions into more complicated ACT constructions. It should not be assumed that the ACT construction so obtained is the best translation of the predicate calculus expression. Often ACT translations exist which are much more natural than the one prescribed by the translation algorithm. All this demonstrates is that at least one translation exists. There can also exist other, more natural, translations. Table 7.4 provides an outline of the major steps in the translation.

A formula is said to be in *prenex normal form* if it is written $(Q_1V_1)(Q_2V_2) \cdots (Q_nV_n) M$ where each (Q_iV_i) is a universal or existential quantifier and M, the *matrix*, contains no quantifiers. It is known (for example, Mendelson, 1964; Proposition 2.31) that there is an effective procedure for taking any formula A not in prenex normal form and translating it into a formula B in a prenex normal form such that A and B are logically equivalent, that is, it is provable A *iff* B.

The formula in prenex normal form can then be translated into Skolem Standard Form. Any predicate calculus form can be so translated and I will not reproduce the procedure here. A formula in Skolem Standard Form has the structure

$$(\forall V_1) \cdots (\forall V_i) M$$

This involves replacing all existential variables by Skolem functions. That is, if the variable X_j is existentially quantified it is replaced throughout the matrix by a Skolem function f of all the universal variables that preceded X_j. This encodes the dependence of X_j on the variables that preceded it. As an example, consider

TABLE 7.4
Major Steps in Translating an Expression of the First-Order
Predicate Calculus into an Equivalent ACT Representation

1. Take original formula.

2. Translate to prenex normal form.

    $(Q_1V_2)(Q_2VC_2) \cdots (Q_nV_n) M$

3. Eliminate all existential quantifiers by Skolem functions. Formula is now in Skolem Standard Form.

    $(\forall V_1) \cdots (\forall V_i) M$

4. Translate matrix M to production normal form (PNF).

    $(\forall_1 V_1) \cdots (\forall V_i) (A \& B \& \cdots \& N)$
    where each conjunct is atomic, negation of an atomic formula, or of the form
    $(P_1 \& P_2 \& \cdots \& P_n \supset P_{n+1})$.

5. Translate total formula to production normal form.

    $(\forall V_1) \cdots (\forall V_i) A \& (\forall V_1) \cdots (\forall V_i) B \& \cdots \& (\forall V_1) \cdots (\forall V_i) N$

6. Translate each $(\forall V_1) \cdots (\forall V_i) A$ into ACT productions.

the following prenex normal form expression:

$(\forall x) (\exists y)$ (philosopher $(x) \supset$ (book (y) & read $(x, y)))$

This can be replaced by the following Skolem Standard Form:

$(\forall x)$ (philosopher $(x) \supset$ (book $(f(x))$ & read $(x, f(x)))$

where the Skolem function $f(x)$ encodes the dependence of the books read on the philosopher. The Skolem Standard Form translations of prenex normal form expressions are not logically equivalent, but they do preserve logical consequence (see Chang & Lee, 1973). ACT has considerable capacity to express existential quantifiers without the use of Skolem functions. However, there are some uses of existential quantifiers which it cannot handle (within the production subset of Table 7.3)[2] without resorting to Skolem functions.

The next step in translating a predicate calculus formula into ACT is to translate the matrix of a Skolem Standard Form expression into what I want to call *production normal form* (PNF). The matrix is said to be in PNF if it has the structure $(A \& B \& \cdots \& N)$ where each of the individual conjuncts is an atomic formula, or the negation of such, or of the form $(P_1 \& P_2 \& \cdots P_n \supset P_{n+1})$. In the last case each of the P_i must be an atomic formula or the negation of such. There is an algorithm that will produce a logically equivalent production normal form to any unquantified matrix:

Algorithm. By definitional substitution we will replace all connectives in M except implication $(A \vee B \equiv\, \sim A \supset B, A \& B \equiv\, \sim (A \supset\, \sim B), \sim A \equiv A \supset \text{false})$. Let M_1 be this substituted form of M. If M_1 is atomic or the negation of an atomic proposition it is already in PNF. Otherwise M_1 is of the form $A \supset B$. This can be translated to a formula $M_2 = C \supset D$ where the consequent D is atomic. If B is not atomic already, it is of the form $(E \supset F)$. That is, $M_1 = A \supset (E \supset F)$. This is logically equivalent to $A \& E \supset F$ in which the consequent F is shorter. By continuing this operation of shortening the consequent iteratively one will achieve $M_2 = C \supset D$ with D atomic. The antecedent C can be replaced by an equivalent formula in *disjunctive normal form* (Chang & Lee, 1973). A formula is in disjunctive normal form if it is a disjunction of conjunctions of atomic propositions or negations of atomic propositions—for example $(p_1 \& p_2) \vee (q_1 \&\, \sim q_2 \& q_4) \vee (\sim r_1 \& r_2)$. Therefore, we can rewrite M_2 as the equivalent formula M_3:

$$[(P_1 \& P_2 \& \cdots P_i) \vee (R_1 \& R_2 \& \cdots \& R_j) \vee \cdots \vee (S_1 \& S_2 \& \cdots \& S_k)] \supset Q$$

where Ps, Rs, Ss, Qs, etc., are atomic propositions or negations of such. It is a simple exercise in propositional calculus to show that M_3, written as above, is equivalent to M_4:

$$((P_1 \& P_2 \& \cdots \& P_i) \supset Q) \& ((R_1 \& R_2 \& \cdots \& R_j)$$
$$\supset Q) \& \cdots \& ((S_1 \& S_2 \& \cdots \& S_k) \supset Q)$$

---

[2]The reader may write to me for an exposition of how existential quantifiers can be handled without Skolem functions by expanding the production subset in Table 7.3.

Thus, the matrix has been converted to the form $(A \, \& \, B \, \& \, \cdots \, \& \, N)$ where each conjunct is of the form $(P_1 \, \& \, \cdots \, \& \, P_n \supset P_{n+1})$. This is the desired production normal form unless $P_{n+1} = \text{false}$. In this case and if $n > 1$, convert to the equivalent expression $(P_1 \, \& \, \cdots \, \& \, P_{n-1} \supset \sim P_n)$. If $n = 1$, then we have the negation of an atomic formula, $\sim P_1$, which is also acceptable.

To summarize thus far, the original predicate calculus formula has been converted into the form:

$$(\forall V_1) \, \cdots \, (\forall V_i) \, (A \, \& \, B \, \& \, \cdots \, \& \, N)$$

which can be converted to the form:

$$(\forall V_1) \, \cdots \, (\forall V_i) \, A \, \& \, (\forall V_i) \, \cdots \, (\forall V_i) \, B \, \& \, \cdots \, \& \, (\forall V_1) \, \cdots \, (\forall V_i) \, N$$

where A through N are atomic formulas, negations of atomic formulas, or of the form $P_1 \, \& \, P_2 \, \& \, \cdots \, \& \, P_n \supset P_{n+1}$. Quantified expressions of this form are said to be in production normal form.

Translation from Production Normal Form into ACT*

I will now show how to translate each of the conjuncts, $(\forall V_1) \, \cdots \, (\forall V_i) \, A$, in this PNF expression into ACT. If each conjunct can be translated then the complete expression can be translated.

Individual constants of the predicate calculus will be translated by singleton nodes. The ACT translate of a constant, a, will be denoted a^T. The $(n+1)$-place predicates of the calculus will be translated by ACT subject–predicate constructions where the predicates decompose into n-place relations plus their n arguments. The n-place ACT relation corresponding to an $(n+1)$-place predicate, P, will be denoted P^T. One-place predicates will be represented by simple ACT concepts. The ACT concept corresponding to a 1-place predicate P will be denoted P^T. Finally, n-place functions will translate into ACT as relational structures consisting of n-place relations and n arguments. The root node of such a relational structure will be tagged as a singleton set. The n-place ACT relation corresponding to an n-place function, f, will be denoted f^T. The procedure for showing that each conjunct can be translated will be as follows: It will specify ACT translations for constants, functions, and predicates. Then it will specify how predicate calculus expressions composed from constants, functions, and predicates can be translated by ACT compositions of the ACT translations for the constants, functions, and predicates. In addition to giving the translation procedure, a correspondence will be made between models for the predicate calculus expressions and models for the ACT translations. Basically, it will be shown that for each predicate calculus model there is a corresponding ACT model in which the ACT translations display the same pattern of meaning as the original predicate calculus formulas did in their model. This correspondence will be used to establish that the ACT translation preserves logical consequence.

A model M for the predicate calculus consists of specifying an interpretation for the individual constants, function letters, and predicate letters. Let I denote the function that gives this interpretation. It corresponds to the function V for ACT. Each possible I specifies a different model just as each V specifies a different model for ACT. It can be shown that for each model M for the predicate calculus there is a distinct model M_A for ACT. This can be done by defining V in terms of I, that is, for constants $V(a^T) = I(a)$, for functions $V(f^T) = I(f)$, and for predicates $V(P^T) = I(P)$. Similarly, for every ACT model, M_A, there is a distinct predicate calculus model, M.

Consider an n-place function and its arguments $f(t_1, t_2, \ldots, t_n)$ where each t_i is a term containing no variables. Let t_i^T be the ACT translate of each term. Then this expression will be translated by the ACT expression $(f^T \text{ OF } t_1^T t_2^T \cdots t_n^T)$. It can be shown that for any predicate calculus model M and corresponding ACT model M_A, the following is true:

$$V((f^T \text{ OF } t_1^T t_2^T \cdots t_n^T)) = I(f(t_1, t_2, \ldots, t_n)).$$

To prove this one would have to use induction on the number of function letters embedded within each other.

Consider a 1-place predicate and its argument, $P(t)$, where t is a term that contains no variables. This will be translated by the ACT expression $(t^T * P^T)$. Consider an $(n+1)$-place predicate and its argument, $P(t_1, t_2, \ldots, t_{n+1})$. This will be translated by the ACT expression $(t_1^T * (P^T \text{ OF } t_2^T \cdots t_{n+1}^T))$. For convenience, denote the translation of any atomic formula (that is, a predicate and its arguments) F by F^T. It can be shown for all models M for the predicate calculus that $M \models F$ iff $M_A \models F^T$.

Consider a predicate calculus expression of the form $\sim F$ where F is an atomic formula. This will be translated in ACT by $\sim F^T$. For all M for the predicate calculus $M \models \sim F$ iff $M_A \models \sim F^T$. Let $P_1 \& P_2 \& \cdots \& P_n$ be a conjunction of n atomic formulas or their negation. The ACT translation is $P_1^T \& P_2^T \& \cdots \& P_n^T$. Again, $M \models P_1 \& P_2 \& \cdots \& P_n$ iff $M_A \models P_1^T \& P_2^T \& \cdots \& P_n^T$. Let $P_1 \& P_2 \& \cdots \& P_n \supset P_{n+1}$ be a predicate calculus expression with no variables where each P_1 is a predicate or negation of one. This will be translated in ACT by $P_1^T \& P_2^T \& \cdots \& P_n^T \Rightarrow P_{n+1}^T$. Again it is easy to show that $M \models P_1 \& P_2 \& \cdots \& P_n \supset P_{n+1}$ iff $M_A \models P_1^T \& P_2^T \& \cdots \& P_n^T \Rightarrow P_{n+1}^T$.

Consider a predicate calculus expression of the form $(\forall V_1) (\forall V_2) \cdots (\forall V_n) P$ where P is a predicate or negation of one. This will be translated by the ACT expression $V_1 \& V_2 \& \cdots \& V_n \Rightarrow P^T$. It will be proven for all M for the predicate calculus that $M \models (\forall V_1) \cdots (\forall V_n)P$ iff $M_A \models V_1 \& \cdots \& V_n \Rightarrow P^T$. Assume $M \models (\forall V_1) \cdots (\forall V_n)P$ and suppose it were not the case that $M_A \models V_1 \& \cdots V_n \Rightarrow P^T$. Let S denote a substitution for $V_1, \ldots, V_n$ and let P_s denote the formula after this substitution. Similarly, define substitutions for the ACT expression and define P_s^T. For all S, $M \models P_s$ but there is an S' such that $M_A \models P_{s'}^T$. Let P' be the predicate calculus equivalent of $P_{s'}^T$. P' differs from P only by substitution of values for $V_1, \ldots, V_n$. So $P' = P_{s''}$ for some substitution S''. Since it is not the case that $M_A \models P_{s'}^T$ then it is not the case that $M \models P_{s''}$. This contradicts the fact that for all S, $M \models P_s$. Therefore, $M_A \models V_1 \& \cdots \& V_n \Rightarrow P^T$. Similarly, we can show that it leads to a contradiction to suppose $M_A \models V_1 \& \cdots \& V_n \Rightarrow P^T$ but not $M \models (\forall V_1) \cdots (\forall V_n)P$. Therefore $M_A \models V_1 \& \cdots \& V_n \Rightarrow P^T$ iff $M \models (\forall V_1) \cdots (\forall V_n)P$.

Finally, consider a predicate calculus expression of the form $(\forall V_1) \cdots (\forall V_i)$ $(P_1 \& P_2 \& \cdots \& P_n \supset P_{n+1})$. This will be translated by the ACT expression: $V_1 \& V_2 \& \cdots V_i \& P_1 \& P_2 \& \cdots \& P_n \Rightarrow P_{n+1}$. By similar means as in the above paragraph we can establish $M \models (\forall V_1) \cdots (\forall V_i) (P_1 \& \cdots \& P_n \supset P_{n+1})$ iff $M_A \models V_1 \& \cdots \& V_i \& P_1 \& \cdots \& P_n \Rightarrow P_{n+1}$.

We have now shown how to translate all the conjuncts in a PNF expression of the predicate calculus. Let C be the expression and C^T be its ACT tranlation. It has also been shown that for all M for the predicate calculus, $M \models C$ iff $M_A \models C^T$. It only remains to show that this translation preserves logical consequence. Let Δ be a set of conjuncts from PNF expressions and let C be another conjunct. Let Δ^T be a set consisting of the translations of Δ and let C^T be the translation of C. Then to show that the translation preserves logical consequence we must show $\Delta \models C$ iff $\Delta^T \models C^T$. Suppose $\Delta \models C$ but not $\Delta^T \models C^T$. Then there is a model for ACT, M_A, such that for each $C_i^T \in \Delta^T$, $M_A \models C_i^T$ but not $M_A \models C^T$. We know then that for the corresponding predicate calculus model, M, for all C_i, $M_p \models C_i$ but not $M \models C$. This contradicts the assumption $\Delta \models C$. Similarly, it leads to a contradiction to suppose $\Delta^T \models C^T$ but not $\Delta \models C$. Therefore, $\Delta \models C$ iff $\Delta^T \models C^T$.

Example of Translation

To help make more concrete the translation procedure, consider the sentence *All universities require that some books be read by all of their students.* This would be represented in the predicate calculus by

$(\forall x)(\text{University}(x) \supset (\exists y)(\text{Book}(y) \& (\forall z)(\text{Student}(z) \& \text{At } (z, x)$
$\supset \text{require-to-read}(x, z, y))))$

The first step would be to translate this to prenex normal form:

$(\forall x)(\exists y)(\forall z)(\text{University}(x) \supset (\text{Book}(y) \& (\text{At}(z,x) \& \text{Student}(z)$
$\supset \text{require-to-read}(x, z, y))))$

Next the matrix is to be converted to Skolem Standard Form:

$(\forall x)(\forall z)(\text{University}(x) \supset (\text{Book } (f(x)) \& (\text{At}(z, x) \& \text{Student}(z)$
$\supset \text{require-to-read}(x, z, f(x)))))$

and then to production normal form:

$(\forall x)(\forall z)((\text{University}(x) \& \text{At}(z, x) \& \text{Student}(z) \supset \text{require-to-read}(x, z, f(x)))$
$\& (\text{University}(x) \supset \text{book}(f(x))))$

Then the entire formula can be converted to production normal form:

$(\forall x)(\forall z)$(University(x) & At(z,x) & Student(z) $\supset$ require-to-read $(x,z,f(x))$)
    & $(\forall x)(\forall z)$(University(x) $\supset$ book$(f(x))$)

This consists of two conjuncts which will be expressed by the following two productions:

Vx & Vz & (Vx * University)	$\Rightarrow$	(Vx * (require-to-read
& (Vz * (At OF Vx))		OF Vz (f OF Vx)))
& (Vz * student)		
Vx & Vz & (Vx * University)	$\Rightarrow$	((f OF Vx) * book)

The variables Vx and Vz in these two productions correspond to the variables x and z in the predicate calculus expression. These two productions can be somewhat tidied up over their prescribed translations by deleting separate mention of variables in the condition:

(Vx * University) & (Vz *	$\Rightarrow$	(Vx * (require-to-read
student) & (Vz * (At OF Vx))		OF Vz (f OF Vx)))
(Vx * University)	$\Rightarrow$	((f OF Vx) * book)

7.3 ACT REPRESENTATIONS
FOR NATURAL LANGUAGE CONCEPTS

The previous section provided a formal demonstration of the expressive power of the ACT system. It showed that any part of natural language expressible in the predicate calculus could be expressed by ACT. However, a problem with that demonstration was that it relied heavily on the production system to provide adequate translations. It is hypothesized to be a prime feature of productions that they cannot be directly inspected or reported upon. Thus, we do not want to translate natural language assertions into production system format because natural language information can be reported from memory. It is necessary to find some way to translate all natural language assertions into the propositional network, and still achieve full expressive power. This can be done by allowing the network representation to make use of representational symbols for which there are production system interpretations. This would permit the natural language assertions to reside in a reportable form—the propositional network, but still take advantage of the expressive power of the production system. The purpose of this section is to illustrate how the production system might augment the power of the network to represent natural language concepts.

Quantification

Consider a simple example sentence:

(3)   All philosophers read all books.

This information can easily be represented as a production:

(P1)   (V1 * philosopher) & (V2 * book) $\Rightarrow$ (V1 *(read OF V2))

but there is no way to directly represent this as an ACT network proposition. However, it would be possible to encode the sentence into an ACT network notation that involved special conventions which could be interpreted by productions as indicating the desired quantificational relation. One bizzare but workable solution along this line would be to store a set of propositions encoding the exact string of words in this sentence: "*All* is before *philosophers* which is before *read* which is before *all* which is before *books*" (see Fig. 4.8 for an ACT encoding of such a string, page 136). Interpretative productions could be defined which took this string and used it to make the correct inferences.

I suspect word strings are not the basis of our memory for such quantified expressions. Probably, subjects studying such sentences will show confusions indicative of a more abstract representation. For instance, they might confuse memory of *All philosophers read all books* with *All books are read by all philosophers*. I suspect the correct network representation for this sentence is something more like:

(Philosopher * ((universal OF read) OF (x C book)))

where a single proposition asserts that all philosophers bear the higher-order relation (universal OF read) to the classification of books. The higher-order relation *universal* applied to a lower-order relation like *read* causes the argument of the lower-order relation (the book classification) to be interpreted in a universal sense.[3] There needs to be in addition an interpretative production giving the meaning of the higher-order relation *universal* as applied to a lower-order relation like *read:*

(P2)   ((Vgroup1 * ((universal OF Vrel) $\Rightarrow$ (Vind1
          OF (Vclass C Vgroup2)))   * (Vrel OF Vind2))
          & (Vind1 * Vgroup1)
          & (Vind2 * Vgroup2))

This production asserts that if one group, Vgroup1, bears a universal relation to a classification of the second group, Vgroup2, then all individuals in the first

---

[3]Note that the universal relation must apply to the book classification and not to the book concept itself. If the universal relation applied to the book concept, the proposition would only be asserting a fact about some books. The classification node provides a means to force the relation to apply to all books.

group bear the relation to all individuals in the second group. An important feature of this interpretative production is that it is general and need not be encoded when the actual sentence is learned. The sentence may later be qualified as false but this interpretative production will not be affected and will still apply to other propositions. Also other general interpretative productions can be defined that would take the network encoding as data and use it for other activities like generating a memory report, making character judgments about philosophers, finding the location of books, etc. None of this could be done easily if the information were stored directly in the form of productions like (P1).

I would like to present some more illustrative examples of how complex semantic notions can be stored in the propositional network with the aid of general interpretative productions:

Implication

There is no primitive semantic structure in the ACT network which has the function of implication whereas implication is directly encoded in a production (see Section 7.2). Still it is possible to store in network form information which can be interpreted by productions as having the meaning of implication. This can be done by using *implies* as a relation linking propositions. Then, *John hits Mary implies Mary hits John* could be encoded as ((John * (hit OF Mary)) * (imply OF (Mary * (hit OF John)))). In addition one would need the following network production to interpret all such structures:

(P3)   (((Vsubj1 * Vpred1)   ⇒   (Vsubj2
          * (implies OF (Vsubj2   * Vpred2)
          * Vpred2))) & (Vsubj1 * Vpred1))

This production asserts that, whenever one subject–predicate proposition implies another and the first is active in memory, then the second should be added to memory.

Transparent and Opaque Reference

The distinction between transparent and opaque references is a subtle semantic distinction which HAM has been criticized for not being able to properly reflect (for example, Ortony and Anderson, 1974). Consider the sentence *John is looking for the best lawyer in Chicago*. This sentence is ambiguous. It may mean John is looking for someone particular, who happens to be the best lawyer in Chicago. This interpretation is called its transparent sense. The other interpretation, called the opaque sense, is that John is not looking for some one in particular, but whoever happens to fit the specification *best lawyer in Chicago*. It is worthwhile to consider how ACT would handle these two senses. The first, the transparent meaning, can be represented by the following propositional structure:

(John * (looking-for OF (best OF (x C (lawyer ∩ (in OF Chicago))))))

This is a relatively complex expression so I will try to work through its meaning. The most embedded construction, (lawyer ∩ (in OF Chicago)), represents the lawyers in Chicago. The next most embedded construction (x C (lawyer ∩ (in OF Chicago))) represents the classification of lawyer in Chicago. The relation *best* does not apply to the individual lawyers in Chicago but rather to their classification. Thus, the construction (best OF (x C (lawyer ∩ (in OF Chicago)))) picks out the best lawyer. The full proposition above asserts that John is looking for this individual.

The difference between the opaque meaning and the transparent meaning is that, under the opaque sense, John is not looking for a particular individual but rather anyone who fills the bill. This can be represented in ACT by having John looking not for the individual but rather the classification, *best lawyer in Chicago*. This could be represented as follows:

(John * (looking-for OF (y C (best OF (x C (lawyer ∩ (in OF Chicago)))))))

The difference between the opaque and transparent senses could be reflected by productions which would generate distinct inferences to the opaque and transparent senses. For instance, the following pair of productions captures one difference between the two senses:

(P4)	(V1 * (looking for OF Vind)) & (ABS (Vind C Vgroup))	⇒	(V1 * (knows OF Vind))
(P5)	(V1 * (looking for OF (Vclass C Vind)))	⇒	((V1 * (knows OF Vind)) * improbable)

Production (P4) encodes that if V1 is looking for Vind in the transparent sense, then V1 knows the identity of Vind. Production (P5) encodes that if the opaque sense is being used, then V1 may well not know the identity of the person for whom he is looking.

Modal Operators

One of the more advanced aspects of natural language that has been put to extensive logical study are the various modal expressions (for example, Hughes & Cresswell, 1968). The two best understood modal operators are *necessity* and *possibility*. These and other modal operators can be represented in ACT as predicates on propositions. It is possible to incorporate the various axioms and rules of inference defining these modal operators as productions. For instance, the following productions serve to unpack some of the meaning of necessity and possibility:

(P6)	(Vprop * necessary)	⇒	~ (~Vprop * possible)
(P7)	(Vprop * possible)	⇒	~ (~Vprop * necessary)

(P8) $((Vsubj * Vpred) * necessary)$ $\Rightarrow$ $(Vsubj * Vpred)$

(P9) $(Vprop * necessary)$ $\Rightarrow$ $(Vprop * possible)$

Production (P5) encodes the fact that if a proposition is necessary, then its negation is not possible. Production (P6) encodes the fact that if a proposition is
possible, then its negation is not necessary. Production (P8) is particularly noteworthy. If proposition $(Vsubj * Vpred)$ has *necessary* predicated of it, (P8) will
store a separate copy of $(Vsubj * Vpred)$ without the predication of *necessary*.
Recall that if a condition of some other production is tested for a proposition like
(Canadians * good), it would not achieve a match with ((Canadians * good) *
necessary) because the target proposition was embedded in another. So Production
(P8) serves to "disembed" the proposition. Finally, Production (P9) encodes the
fact that if a proposition is necessary it is also possible.

Definition of Verbs

To a certain extent the ACT model embodies an "antidecomposition" point of
view in that it permits semantically complex verbs to be represented and does not
necessarily decompose them into primitives. So *John kicked Bill* is represented as
(John * (kick OF Bill)) with no attempt to represent the fact that *kick* involves
forceful movement of a foot, possible pain, etc. Anderson and Bower (1973)
proposed that associated with the verb *kick* was stored in memory a network of
information conveying all this. This network could be used to make such inferences when necessary. Figure 7.2 shows the HAM representation proposed by
Anderson and Bower for this sentence example. Note the verb *kick* is connected
to a structure giving part of its meaning. Since the HAM network never had a
formal semantics, it is totally unclear whether the structure in Fig. 7.2 really does
convey part of the meaning of kick. In any case, interpretive rules would have to
be specified to permit this network structure to be used in making inferences.
Another route to expressing this information would be to have it directly encoded
as productions: For example, the following production encodes the relation between kicking and moving one's foot:

(P10)   (Vsubj $\Rightarrow$ (Vsubj * (possess OF Vinst)) & (Vinst
    * (kick OF Vobj))   * FOOT) & (Vsubj * (MOVE OF Vinst))
    & (Vinst * (TOUCH OF Vobj))

The production, as stated, would, upon activation of the proposition *John
kicked Bill*, add to memory the further propositions *John possesses a foot, John
moved the foot, The foot touched Bill.* This would produce, effectively, semantic
decomposition in that all the implications about *kicking* would be stored whenever
a proposition using kicking is asserted. However, by use of control nodes one
could limit the application of this production to when it was needed in inference
making. So, the use of productions to encode verb meaning does not commit one
on the issue of semantic decomposition.

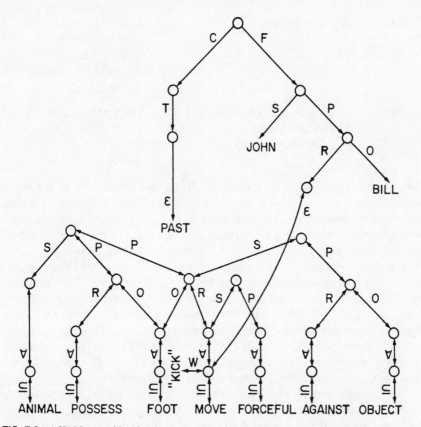

FIG. 7.2 A HAM propositional network representation proposed by Anderson and Bower to encode the meaning of *kick*.

One potential problem with storing information about verb meaning in production rather than in network form is that information in productions is hard to report. This would seem to contradict the fact that people are capable of reporting what *kick* means. One way around this obstacle is to have redundantly stored in the propositional network information about what the verb, *kick,* means. This is probably the source of much of our knowledge about verb meanings. However, another not unreasonable possibility is to assume that subjects decide what the verb *kick* means by seeing what inferences their production system makes about the verb. Consider the following sketch of a production system which will retrieve verb meaning to questions of the form *What does kick mean?*:

(P11)   ((What-does-Vverb-mean?)   ⇒   (Vdummy1 * (Videa OF
      & (Videa W Vverb))   Vdummy2)) & (Vcon =
                                         NEXT) & Vdummy1
                                         & Vverb & Videa

(P12)   (Vcon = NEXT)   ⇒   (SAY "IF SOMEONE
                                    VverbS SOMEONE
                                    THEN") & (Vcon =
                                    NEXT1) & Vdummy1 &
                                    Videa

(P13)   (Vcon = NEXT1) & (Vdummy1   ⇒   (SAY (Vdummy1 * (Vrel
         * (Vrel OF Vobj))   OF Vobj)) & (Vcon =
         & (ABS (Vrel = Videa)))   NEXT1) & Vdummy1
                                                & Videa

This sketch ignores many of the complications that would arise if this was a general workable system but it does give a sense of how ACT might go about observing its own inferences. Production P11 responds to the appearance of a string encoding the question. It retrieves the meaning corresponding to the verb and constructs a proposition involving that relation and two dummy arguments, Vdummy1 and Vdummy2. This causes a new proposition involving kick to appear in memory. Let us denote this by (dummy1 * (kick OF dummy2)). Production (P12) serves to begin generation of the answer "If someone kicks someone then. . . ." The system then waits for other productions to apply and draws inferences in response to the appearance (dummy1 * (kick OF dummy2)). For instance, Production (P10) defined earlier would generate the inference (dummy1 * (move OF dummy3)) & (dummy3 * foot). Production (P13) would match this inference and generate the continuation "he moves his foot."

This example shows how, by a process of self-observation, it is possible to retrieve information locked in productions. That is, one can define a second set of productions that will inspect the output of a first set of productions and so infer the information that must have been in the first. So information locked in productions is not totally unreportable. However, it is only by such contortions to achieve self-observation that it is possible to report the information.

Adverb Definitions

Adverbs in ACT are treated as higher-order relations that take verbs as arguments or as relations that take adjectives as arguments. In the semantics section, 7.1, there was little constraint placed on what might be the interpretation of a higher-order relation. However, it is possible to encode into the production system the appropriate interpretation of particular higher-order relations. This was already illustrated earlier with respect to the *universal* relation (page 241). I would like to provide a couple of additional examples here involving the adverbs *angrily* and *almost*. Consider the sentence *John angrily threw the ball*, represented in ACT by (John * ((angrily OF throw) OF x)) & (x * ball). There are a number of inferences possible from the adverb *angrily*. Some of these are embodied in the following general interpretive production:

(P14)   (Vsubj   ⇒   (Vsubj * angry) & (Vsubj * (Vrel OF Vobj))
           * ((angrily OF   & ((Vsubj * ((forcefully OF Vrel)
           Vrel) OF Vobj))   OF Vobj)) * probable)

This production would permit the inferences that *John is angry, John threw the ball,* and *It is probable that John threw the ball forcefully.* Note that this production is very general in that it will apply to any subject–verb–object encoding involving the adverb *angrily.* Consider now the productions that would be needed to properly draw inferences from *John almost threw the ball:*

(P15)   (Vsubj   ⇒   ~ (Vsubj * (Vrel OF Vobj)) & ((Vsubj
           * ((almost   * (intend OF (Vsubj * (Vrel OF Vobj))))
           OF Vrel) OF   * probable)
           Vobj))

This production encodes the inferences that *John did not throw the ball* and *John probably intended to throw the ball.*[4] Note that the adverb *angrily* implies *John threw the ball* whereas the adverb *almost* implies the opposite. It was for this reason that it was not possible in Section 7.1 to impose a constant semantic interpretation on the adverb. Rather each adverb requires a set of interpretative productions such as the above to specify its meaning.

Meaning of Nouns

Information about the meaning of nouns can similarly be encoded in the propositional network or in the production system. For instance, consider the definition of human as a biped mammal that can speak. This can be stored as the following set of propositions:

(human * mammal) & (human * biped) & ((human * speak) * possible)

Or one could have an equivalent production:

(P16)   (V1 * human)   ⇒   (V1 * mammal) & (V1 * biped)
                                        & ((V1 * speak) * possible)

I am inclined to believe a propositional representation is more appropriate for nouns.

An interesting question is how a subject would answer a question like *Is Trudeau human?* The simplest and most likely procedure is to simply test whether

---

[4]The second inference is only valid for relations that are intentional verbs. It does not follow from *John is almost taller than Fred* that *John intended to be taller than Fred.* Therefore, Rule (P15) should be constrained only to apply to intentional verbs.

it is stored in memory that Trudeau is human. Anderson and Bower (1973) advocated this as the principal means for making such semantic memory decisions. However, if the information is not stored one might be able to calculate from the properties stored with *Trudeau* and with *human* whether it is likely that Trudeau is a human. Rosch (1973, 1974), Rips, Shoben, and Smith (1973), and Smith, Shoben, and Rips (1974) suggest that subjects normally decide such questions by means of these computations. It would be interesting to sketch out a production system that would perform such computations. See Table 7.5.

Figure 7.3 attempts to illustrate the flow of control among these productions. This productions system assumes that a question like ''Is Trudeau a human?'' has been analyzed into a network proposition of the form (Speaker * (ask OF (Trudeau * human))). The activation of this proposition causes Production (P17) to be fired which initiates the interrogation of memory. A counter (variable Vevid) is initially set to 0. It will accumulate evidence for a *yes* response. Productions (P18) and (P19) retrieve facts about Vpred (= human in this example). Production (P18) retrieves properties that are always true about humans and Production (P19) facts that are frequently true. If the property is always true of Vpred and also of Vsubj, Production (P20) will increment the evidence counter by 2. If the property

TABLE 7.5
A Set of Productions for Making Semantic Memory Judgments

	Condition		Action
(P17)	(Speaker * (ask OF (Vsubj * Vpred)))	⇒	(Vcon = PRED) & Vsubj & Vpred & (Vevid = 0)
(P18)	(Vcon = PRED) & (Vpred * Vprop)	⇒	(Vcon = SUBJ1) & Vprop & Vsubj & Vpred
(P19)	(Vcon = PRED) & ((Vpred * Vprop) * probable)	⇒	(Vcon = SUBJ2) & Vprop & Vsubj & Vpred
(P20)	(Vcon = SUBJ1) & (Vsubj * Vprop)	⇒	(Vcon = PRED) & (Vevid = Vevid + 2) & (UNBIND Vprop)
(P21)	(Vcon = SUBJ2) & (ABS (Vsubj * Vprop))	⇒	(SAY NO) & (UNBIND Vcon)
(P22)	(Vcon = SUBJ2) & (Vsubj * Vpred)	⇒	(Vcon = PRED) & (Vevid = Vevid + 1) & (UNBIND Vprop)
(P23)	(Vcon = SUBJ2) & (ABS (Vsubj * Vprop))	⇒	(Vcon = PRED) & (UNBIND Vprop)
(P24)	(Vcon = PRED) & (Vevid * (greater OF criterion))	⇒	(SAY YES) & (UNBIND Vcon Vevid)

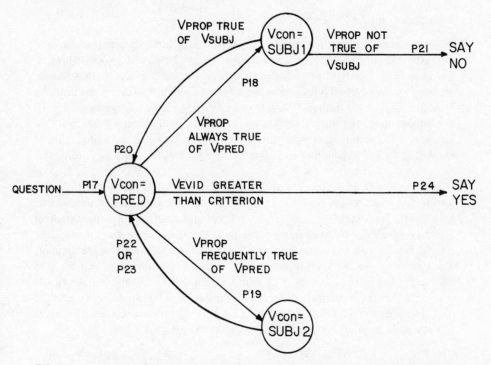

FIG. 7.3 A transition network illustrating the flow of control among Productions (P17)–(P24) in Table 7.5 for computing judgments in the semantic memory task.

is always true of Vpred but not of Vsubj, (P21) will generate a *no* response. If the property is frequently true of Vpred and true of Vsubj, (P22) increments Vevid by 1. If the property is frequently true of Vpred but not of Vsubj, then no change is made to Vevid. If Vevid ever exceeds the criterion a *yes* response will be emitted by (P24).

This exemplifies a decision by overlap of attributes. Note that this procedure is much more complex than coming to the decision on the basis of simply retrieving the fact that *Trudeau is human*. This would require the following simpler and much quicker production system:

(P25)   (Speaker * (ask OF (Vsubj * Vpred)))   ⇒ (Vcon = TEST)
                                                                          & Vsubj & Vpred

(P26)   (Vcon = TEST) & (Vsubj * Vpred)   ⇒ (SAY YES)

(P27)   (Vcon = TEST) & (ABS (Vsubj * Vpred))   ⇒ (SAY NO)

Therefore, ACT makes the clear prediction that, whenever a subject must decide by means of overlap of attributes, he should take much longer.

Information about Disjoint Sets

A good deal of human knowledge has a rather strong hierarchical structure to it. For instance, we know leopards and cheetahs are cats, cats and dogs are mammals, and mammals and fish are animals. Much of the early research in semantic memory was concerned with seeing the effects of this hierarchical structure (for example, Collins & Quillian, 1969; Bower, Clark, Lesgold, & Winzenz, 1969). One of the interesting features is that we seem to know that many of these classifications are disjoint—that something cannot be both a cat and a dog. At the same time we know that other classifications are not disjoint—that something can be both a cat and pet.

It is unreasonable to suppose that we have stored with each pair of disjoint sets the fact that they are disjoint. There are just too many things that are disjoint. Moreover, I suspect that we can decide leopards and cheetahs are disjoint without ever having previously encountered that fact. Thus, we can make this decision even if there was no opportunity to have encoded that the two sets are disjoint. The following propositional representation and production system will serve to encode and use information about disjoint sets. The idea is to store that the classification leopard is an example of the classification cat. This would be represented ((x C leopard) * (type OF (y C cat))). The following production would interpret this structure as implying leopards are subsets of cats:

(P28)   ((Vclass1 C Vgroup1) *   ⇒   (Vgroup1 * Vgroup2)
         (type OF (Vclass2 C Vgroup2)))

and the following productions will allow the system to make inferences about disjoint set:

(P29)   ((Vclass1 C Vgroup 1)   ⇒   ~ (Vind * Vgroup3)
         * (type OF (Vclass2 C Vgroup2)))
         & ((Vclass3 C Vgroup3)
         * (type OF (Vclass2 C Vgroup2)))
         & (ABS (Vgroup1 = Vgroup3))
         & (Vind * Vgroup1)

Production (P29) encodes that if Vgroup1 and Vgroup3 are distinct types of Vgroup2, then they are disjoint; that is, if Vind1 is in Vgroup 1 it is not in Vgroup3.

SUMMARY OF CHAPTER 7

A model-theoretic semantics has been developed to permit formal study of the ACT network and a subset of the production system. This semantics identifies the referent of network structures with objects in semantic models. It also provides conditions for deciding when propositions and productions are true in a particular model. This model-theoretic semantics is used to show that ACT is at least equivalent in expressive power to the first-order predicate calculus. This proof involves providing a procedure which will translate any predicate calculus expression into an equivalent ACT representation. By "equivalent" it is meant that the representation preserves logical consequence. The model-theoretic semantics is called upon to prove that logical consequence is preserved. Establishing that ACT can express first-order predicate calculus is important because this predicate calculus is known to be rich in expressive power. This proof relies heavily on using the production system to express complex concepts. It is argued, however, that complex natural language conceptions can also be directly represented in the propositional network if there exist some general productions to properly interpret the network representations. It is desirable to represent natural language conceptions in the network because only network information is directly reportable. This technique for representing natural language expressions is illustrated for quantification, implication, transparent and opaque reference, modal operators, verb definitions, adverb definitions, noun definitions, and disjoint sets.

REFERENCES

Anderson, J. R., & Bower, G. H. *Human associative memory*. Washington: Winston, 1973.

Bower, G. H., Clark, M. C., Lesgold, A. M., & Winzenz, D. Hierarchical retrieval schemes in recall of categorized word lists. *Journal of Verbal Learning and Verbal Behavior*, 1969, **8,** 323–343.

Chang, C., & Lee, R. C. *Symbolic logic and mechanical theorem proving*. New York: Academic Press, 1973.

Church, A. *Introduction to mathematical logic*. Princeton, New Jersey: Princeton University Press, 1956.

Collins, A. M., & Quillian, M. R. Retrieval time from semantic memory. *Journal of Verbal Learning and Verbal Behavior*, 1969, **8,** 240–247.

Frege, G. Begriffschrift: Eine der arithmetischen nachgebildepe Formalsprache des reinen Denkens. Halle, Germany: L. Nebert, 1879.

Hughes, G. E., & Cresswell, M. J. *An introduction to modal logic*. London: Meuthen, 1968.

Katz, J. J., & Fodor, J. A. The structure of a semantic theory. *Language*, 1963, **39,** 170–210.

Mendelson, E. *Introduction to mathematical logic*. New York: Van Nostrand, 1964.

Ortony, A., & Anderson, R. C. *Encoding definite descriptions*. Unpublished manuscript, University of Illinois, Urbana-Champaign, 1974.

Rips, L. J., Shoben, E. J., & Smith, E. E. Semantic distance and the verification of semantic relations. *Journal of Verbal Learning and Verbal Behavior*, 1973, **12,** 1–20.

Robbin, J. W. *Mathematical logic: a first course*. New York: Benjamin, 1969.

Rosch, E. H. On the internal structure of perceptual and semantic categories. In T. E. Moore (Ed.), *Cognitive development and the acquisition of language*. New York: Academic Press, 1973.

Rosch, E. H. Universals and cultural specifics in human categorization. In R. Breslin, W. Loner, & S. Bochner (Eds.), *Cross-cultural perspectives*. London: Sage Press, 1974.

Smith, E. E., Shoben, E., & Rips, L. Comparison process in semantic memory. In G. H. Bower (Ed.), *Psychology of learning and motivation*. New York: Academic Press, 1974.

Suppes, P. *Semantics of context-free fragments of natural languages*. (Tech. Rep. 171). Stanford: Institute for Mathematical Studies in the Social Sciences, Stanford University, 1971.

Suppes, P. The semantics of children's language. *American Psychologist*, 1974, **29,** 103–114.

8
The Activation of Memory

The effect of size of positive set on mean RT is linear. Another way of saying this is that the addition of an item to the positive set has the same effect, regardless of the size of the set. This kind of additivity suggests that each item in the positive set corresponds to a (sub) stage between stimulus and response.

SAUL STERNBERG

Of central importance to the ACT system is the process by which activation spreads through the memory network. Productions are evoked by having their conditions match the active partition of long-term memory. I have done considerable research in a paradigm that studies the spread of activation through memory as directly as possible. This paradigm is referred to as *fact retrieval*. In this chapter I present a fact-retrieval experiment and an ACT model for that experiment and contrast this with an older model for that paradigm (Anderson, 1974; Anderson & Bower, 1973; Thorndyke & Bower, 1974). I will also review some of the data favoring the new model, present a set of detailed tests of ACT predictions, and then discuss the generality of the model. Each of these tasks will occupy one section of this chapter.

8.1   AN ACT MODEL FOR FACT RETRIEVAL

In this section I consider the original fact-retrieval experiment (Anderson, 1974). The methodologies of all the other experiments are similar. Therefore, I describe the methodology generally, illustrating it with the details of this experiment.

Methodology

Materials.   The study material always consists of a set of sentences, though in different experiments the types of sentences studied are different. In the Anderson (1974) experiment the sentences studied were of the form *A person is in the location.* Examples are presented in Table 8.1. Subjects studied 26 sentences of this form. Individual words like *hippie* or *church* occurred in one, two, or three of these sentences. This was the means by which we varied one variable of concern:

TABLE 8.1
Examples of Experimental Material

	Subject studies		True test probes
1.	A hippie is in the park.	3–3	A hippie is in the park.
2.	A hippie is in the church.	1–1	A lawyer is in the cave.
3.	A hippie is in the bank.	1–2	A debutante is in the bank.
4.	A captain is in the park.		.
5.	A captain is in the church.		.
6.	A debutante is in the bank.		.
7.	A fireman is in the park.		False test probes
	.		
	.	3–1	A hippie is in the cave.
	.	1–2	A lawyer is in the park.
26.	A lawyer is in the cave.	1–1	A debutante is in the cave.
		2–2	A captain is in the bank.
			.
			.

the number of propositions about a concept. We called this the *propositional fan* variable.

Test probes are constructed from the study sentences. In all experiments the subject was instructed to respond *true* to sentences he had seen during study and false to all other sentences. False sentences were created by re-pairing words from the study sentences to create new test sentences. Examples of true and false test sentences are given in Table 8.1. The subject's task was basically one of sentence recognition, that is, he had to decide whether he had studied each particular combination of words in a test sentence.

Note that the test probes can be classified by the number of propositions learned about each content word in the probe. The test probes in Table 8.1 are prefixed by two digits which indicate this classification. The first digit indicates the number of propositions studied about the person and the second digit the number of propositions studied about the location. So, for instance, *A hippie is in the cave* is a 3–1 test probe because three propositions have been studied about *hippie* and one about *cave*. Anderson (1974) manipulated, for both true and false probes, the number of propositions about the person from one to three, and orthogonally the number of propositions about the location from one to three.

In general, a set of materials such as this is generated separately for each subject. This is accomplished by creating new combinations of words for study and test sentences. In the Anderson (1974) experiments the same set of persons and locations were re-paired to create different study sentences for each subject.

Procedure.   The basic procedure for these experiments can be broken down into three phases. There is an initial study phase where subjects see the sentences and are encouraged to study them meaningfully. Meaningful study is both a good technique for learning the sentences and helps ensure that the subjects commit to memory meaningful propositions and not strings of words. This is important because I want to be able to generalize these results to natural situations where people hear and remember verbal communications (for example, a news report) or study written material (for example, a textbook). In these situations it is certain that subjects do not treat the sentences they receive as strings of unrelated words.

To ensure meaningful processing a variety of techniques has been used in my experiments. Sometimes subjects are asked to write phrases that are logical continuations of the sentences. Other times they are asked to create a visual image of the situation described in the sentence. In the Anderson (1974) study subjects were just told to "try to understand fully the meaning of these sentences because this is the best way to remember them." Subjects' reports indicate that they do follow instructions. Most subjects claimed to have created a fictional world of people and places. More than one subject has joked after leaving an experimental session that he felt he was leaving old friends. The results of the experiments do not seem to vary with the particular variety of meaningful learning instructions employed. This is probably because subjects have a natural tendency to treat sentential material meaningfully and the instructions reinforce an already strong tendency.

After having studied the sentences, subjects enter a study–test phase in which their memory of the sentences is checked. This usually involves a cuing procedure in which subjects are presented with part of a sentence and try to remember what other elements went with that part. In Anderson (1974) subjects had to correctly recall answers to questions of the form *Who is in the park?* and *Where are the hippies?* If the subject makes any errors, he is given the opportunity to study the correct answer. Later he is tested on that same question again. He is not permitted to begin the reaction time phase of the experiment until he can correctly recall the answers to all such questions. In this way we are able to ensure that the material is well learned.

In the reaction time phase the subject sits in front of a screen. The test probes consisting of words from test sentences are presented on a screen before him. His right and left index fingers are on *true* and *false* buttons. He is instructed to regard as true only those sentences which he originally studied. The subject is instructed to respond as fast as is compatible with keeping his accuracy above 90%. Reaction times are measured from the presentation of the sentence to the button press. Subjects are given feedback as to their correctness after each response.

Data Analysis.   Varying numbers of subjects (usually in excess of 20—in this experiment 63) are run in particular experiments. For each subject-by-condition combination a mean reaction time is computed. For instance, in the experiment illustrated in Table 8.1 there are 18 conditions for each subject (3 numbers of propositions per person $\times$ 3 numbers per location $\times$ 2 truth values). Any trial on which a subject makes an error is excluded in calculating the mean time for a condition. The mean times of subjects for a condition are averaged to get

TABLE 8.2

Person—Location Experiment (A hippie is in the park)—Mean Verification Times and Error Rates for Trues and Falses

	Trues Number of propositions per person				Falses Number of propositions per person			
Number of propositions per location	1	2	3	Mean	1	2	3	Mean
1	1.111 (.051)	1.174 (.042)	1.222 (.046)	1.169 (.046)	1.197 (.019)	1.221 (.042)	1.264 (.030)	1.227 (.030)
2	1.167 (.065)	1.198 (.056)	1.222 (.060)	1.196 (.060)	1.250 (.014)	1.356 (.037)	1.291 (.044)	1.299 (.032)
3	1.153 (.063)	1.233 (.044)	1.357 (.054)	1.248 (.054)	1.262 (.042)	1.471 (.079)	1.465 (.051)	1.399 (.057)
Mean	1.144 (.059)	1.202 (.048)	1.267 (.054)	1.204 (.053)	1.236 (.025)	1.349 (.053)	1.340 (.042)	1.308 (.040)

an overall mean for the condition, which are the reaction time data that I will report. I will also report the percentage of errors under different conditions.

Effects of Propositional Fan

One of the basic questions that one might ask is what is the effect on the reaction times of the number of propositions studied about a content word. Table 8.2 shows the results from Anderson (1974). The reaction time data are given in seconds. The data are classified in that table into two matrices according to whether the probe was true or false. Within each matrix the data are classified by rows according to number of propositions associated with the location in the probe, and by columns according to the number of propositions per person. Note that responses are slowed down as the number of propositions increases for trues or falses. The average effect of an increase from one to three propositions is approximately the same for persons (114 msec) as it is for locations (127 msec). These data illustrate two facts that have been shown in many other experiments. First, as the number of propositions associated with a content word increases, reaction times increase. Second, this increase is approximately equal for all content words in the probe.

An example of the same effects is presented in Table 8.3 where the data are from an experiment in which subjects studied propositions of the form *The person is adj;* for example, *The captain is tall.* The number of propositions about the person and the adjective was varied from 1 to 4. The data are classified according to those concepts which had just one proposition versus those which had more than one (that is, 2–4). This is done because the frequency of items with 2–4 propositions is much less than with one. Again an increase in either dimension for trues or falses results in an increase in reaction time. Table 8.4 shows the data from yet another experiment in which subjects studied sentences of the form *In the location the person verbed;* for example, *In the church the fireman sang.* Subjects studied one or two propositions about *location, person,* and *verb.* In Table 8.4 the data are classified into *true* versus *false* and, within these classifications, according to whether one or two propositions about each element were studied. Many other experiments have found similar increases in reaction time with increases in the

TABLE 8.3
Noun–Adjective Experiment (The tailor is smart)—Mean Reaction Time

	True				False		
	$N = 1$	$N = 2$–4			$N = 1$	$N = 2$–4	
$A = 1$	881	942	912	$A = 1$	1102	1115	1109
$A = 2$–4	984	1048	1016	$A = 2$–4	1135	1252	1194
	933	995	964		1119	1184	1152

TABLE 8.4
Location–Subject–Verb Experiment (In the church the sailor sang)—
Mean Reaction Times and Error Rates (in Parentheses)

Trues

	L = 1				L = 2		
	V = 1	V = 2	Mean		V = 1	V = 2	Mean
S = 1	1220 (.034)	1183 (.017)	1202 (.026)	S = 1	1297 (.046)	1402 (.086)	1350 (.066)
S = 2	1232 (.069)	1421 (.080)	1327 (.075)	S = 2	1358 (.046)	1500 (.082)	1429 (.064)
Mean	1226 (.052)	1302 (.049)	1264 (.051)	Mean	1328 (.046)	1451 (.084)	1390 (.065)

Falses

	L = 1				L = 2		
	V = 1	V = 2	Mean		V = 1	V = 2	Mean
S = 1	1323 (.029)	1387 (.035)	1355 (.032)	S = 1	1404 (.034)	1469 (.023)	1437 (.029)
S = 2	1320 (.028)	1371 (.028)	1346 (.028)	S = 2	1488 (.023)	1511 (.063)	1500 (.043)
Mean	1322 (.029)	1379 (.031)	1351 (.030)	Mean	1446 (.029)	1490 (.043)	1468 (.036)

number of propositions about a concept. Some of these will be described in later portions of this chapter.

ACT Model for Fact Retrieval

To provide an ACT model for this task it is necessary to specify how the information is represented in long-term memory and how the subject represents the probe that is presented to him. Figure 8.1 illustrates a portion of memory encoding some of the information in the study sentences of Table 8.1. The subject just stores the propositional content of these sentences, tagged as studied in the list context. It is assumed that the probe is encoded by lower-level perceptual processes into a description of a string. This description is just an encoding of physical adjacencies: *"The* precedes *hippie* which precedes *is* which precedes *in* which precedes *the* which precedes *park."* The ACT representation for such a string encoding is

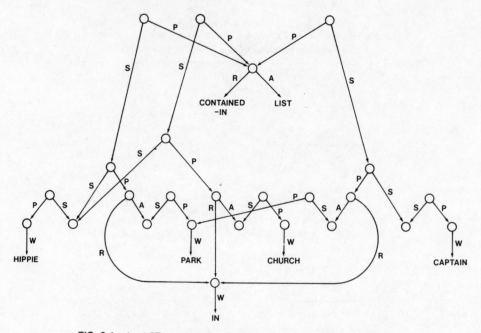

FIG. 8.1   An ACT representation for some of the information in Table 8.1.

obvious but cumbersome (see Fig. 4.8, page 136). Therefore, I will abbreviate it "The-hippie-is-in-the-park."

The perceptual system will deliver string descriptions of this form and it is the task of the productions to interface these strings with what is in memory, and evoke appropriately positive or negative responses. Table 8.5 shows a set of productions that will accomplish this task. The productions in this table appear to be

TABLE 8.5
A Set of Productions to Process the Probes in Table 8.1

	Conditions		Actions
(P1)	(Vcon = READY) & (A-Vper-IS-IN-THE-Vloc)	$\Rightarrow$	(Vcon = ENCODE) & Vper & Vloc
(P2)	(Vcon = ENCODE) & (Videa1 W Vper) & (Videa2 W Vloc)	$\Rightarrow$	(Vcon = TEST) & Videa1 & Videa 2 & (UNBIND Vper Vloc)
(P3)	(Vcon = TEST) & (INTERSECTING Videa1 Videa2)	$\Rightarrow$	(Vcon = READY) & (PRESS TRUE) & (UNBIND Videa1 Videa2)
(P4)	(Vcon = TEST) & (ABS (INTERSECTING Videa1 Videa2))	$\Rightarrow$	(Vcon = READY) & (PRESS FALSE) & (UNBIND Videa1 Videa2)

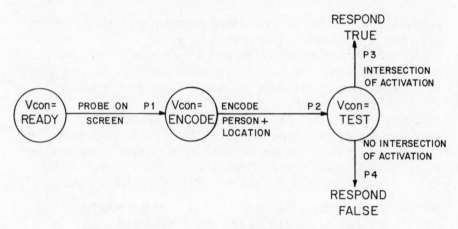

FIG. 8.2   The flow of control among the productions in Table 8.5.

the simplest set that would work. The flow of control among them is illustrated in Fig. 8.2. Production (P1) is evoked upon activation of the perceptual encoding of the probe. It binds Vper to the person in the string and Vloc to the location and rehearses these. Production (P1) also sets Vcon to the control element ENCODE. This evokes Production (P2) which retrieves the meanings of the words Vper and Vloc and binds these meanings to Videa1 and Videa2, respectively. Production (P2) also sets Vcon to the control element TEST. With the control variable so bound, either (P3) or (P4) can apply. Production (P3) will apply if there is an intersection of activation between Videa1 and Videa2 and (P4) will apply if there is not.[1] Shortly, I will turn to the question of the timing characteristics of these two productions, but first it is worth highlighting some features of this system. This system is much simpler than might seem acceptable. First, the system does not bother to comprehend the sentence. Rather, it uses its knowledge of the sentence structure to pick out the critical items, Vper and Vloc. This reflects my belief that subjects in these experiments are operating under a task-specific set of procedures. Presumably, a subject, cold off the street, would first submit the sentence to his language comprehender and try to match the output of the comprehender to long-term memory. This would take much longer than the procedure in Table 8.5. Therefore, I assume the practised subjects of this experiment use the more specific procedure in Table 8.5, although they can fall back on the more general strategy. One piece of evidence for this focused strategy is that subjects show little memory for the probes they have seen—in contrast to what one would expect if they comprehended and remembered the probes. For instance, in one experiment I

---

[1]The test "INTERSECTING" that appears in Productions (P3) and (P4) will not be satisfied by the activation intersecting between Vper and Vloc through the string encoding. The intersection test is only sensitive to activation in long-term memory and not to intersections among the encodings of sensory events.

found that subjects showed no effect of being retested on an old false probe versus a new false probe (constructed out of old study words).

Another highly focused aspect of the production system in Table 8.5 is that it does not check whether the intersection obtained between Videa1 and Videa2 actually corresponds to the asserted proposition. For instance, if the subject had stored in memory *The hippie owned a park,* this production system would generate a true response if tested with *The hippie is in the park.* We will see some evidence in the King and Anderson experiment (page 280) that subjects do display such false alarms. It is possible to amend this production system so that it will not display this defect. For instance, Productions (P3) and (P4) could look for a specific pattern of activation. For example, (P3) could be formulated as

(P3′)   (Vcon = TEST) & ((Vind1   ⇒   (Vcon = READY)
         * Videa1) & (Vind1 * (in OF   & (PRESS TRUE)
         Vind2)) & (Vind2 * Videa2))   & (UNBIND Videa1 Videa2)

This production, like (P3), would be selected only after activation had intersected between Videa1 and Videa2, but would avoid false alarming because it would only apply if the correct pattern were in memory. The production systems in this chapter differ in that they tend to rely on intersection operations such as (P3) in Table 8.5 rather than tests of specific patterns as in (P3′) above. The reason is that the tasks in this chapter usually only require the subject to respond to whether a connection is in memory. In contrast, in other experiments like the inference-making tasks of Section 9.4, subjects are required to make judgments that depend on the exact information stored in memory.

It is possible to conceive of a number of somewhat more complex production sets than this one. However, all the variations I have been able to think of have a common characteristic that an important aspect to their timing is the occurrence of an intersection of activation. The concern of this chapter is with the timing characteristics of this activation process. So, if subjects were operating under these other production sets they would also show the pattern of behavior predicted from Table 8.5. The simplicity of Table 8.5 highlights the importance of the INTERSECTING process in this fact-retrieval experiment.

One might wonder how the production system in Table 8.5 is set up. I assume that the outcome of the subject's comprehension of the experimental instructions is a set of declaratively (that is, propositional network) encoded procedures which the subject can obey by means of a general instruction-following interpretative program. The production set in Table 8.5 emerges as a consequence of the subject performing in the first few trials of the experiment. The first 10 or 20 trials of each experiment are practice trials and are not analyzed or reported. However, informal observation of the reaction times indicates that subjects display a radical speed-up over these first trials. This speed-up reflects the process by which the interpretative network procedures are compiled into a production form like that of Table 8.5.

Emission of a True Response

The principle assumption underlying my use of this paradigm is that reaction times[2] to true probes will directly reflect the rate of spread of activation through memory. A model will be presented that describes the relation of the activation process to the emission of a true response: Let T_1 be the time to activate and to execute Production (P1), T_2 be the time for Production (P2), and T_3 the time for Production (P3). It is assumed that times T_1 and T_2 will be independent of condition, but T_3 will vary with condition. The time T_3 will consist of a component $T_{3,s}$ to initially select the production and a component $T_{3,e}$ to apply the production. It will be assumed that $T_{3,s}$ varies with condition but not $T_{3,e}$. The component $T_{3,s}$ depends on the time for activation to intersect between Videa1 (the idea corresponding to the person) and Videa2 (the idea corresponding to the location). Let $T_a = T_{3,s}$ be the time for this intersecting of activation. Then the total time to respond to a true may be represented:

$$T(\text{true}) = B + T_a \tag{1}$$

where $B = T_1 + T_2 + T_{3,e}$ which are the time components that do not vary with condition. What follows is an analysis of how T_a will vary with condition.

The analysis to be given of the activation process involved in T_a will only be an approximation to the process as it was described in Chapter 4. These approximations are being made to produce a model that is mathematically tractable. I have only been able to obtain predictions from the model set forth in Chapter 4 for special paradigms—and only by means of costly simulation. The model that will be offered here has the advantage that it can be applied to the activation of any memory structure and its predictions may be calculated by hand. Thus, in terms of the criteria set forth in Section 1.3 for a cognitive theory, it scores well on effectiveness.

Consider Fig. 8.3a which shows a rather complete ACT representation for the sentence "A hippie is in the park." For production PTRUE to be selected activation must intersect between Videa1 (the hippie concept) and Videa2 (the park concept), along the sequence of nodes a, b, c, d, e, f, g, and h. Figure 8.3a identifies the relevant structural variables determining the timing of this activation:

1. C—the number of links that must be activated along the intersecting path. In this case that number is 7. This variable will be referred to as C, the *complexity* of the to be activated structure.
2. K—the strength of the preexperimental links. The rate at which activation will spread down the relevant path will be related to the strength of the alternate paths leading out of Videa1 and Videa2. A critical factor here will be the strength of preexperimental paths. There are paths going from the con-

---

[2]For an analysis of how speed of responding might be related in this paradigm to accuracy of responding, see King and Anderson (1975).

(a)

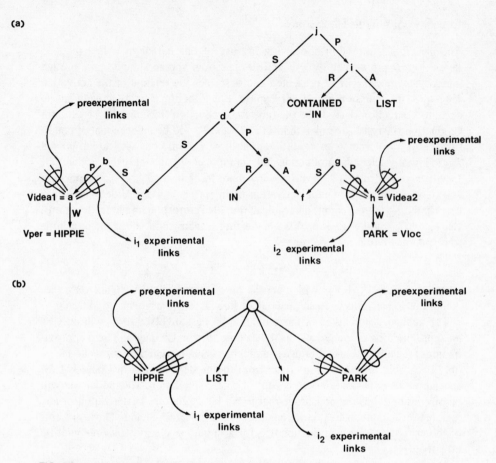

(b)

FIG. 8.3   (a) A complete ACT representations of the to-be-intersected memory structure in the experiment of Table 8.1; (b) an approximation to (a) for purposes of analysis.

cepts to facts learned about the concepts before the experiment. The total strength of preexperimental paths will be referred to by the variable K. It is assumed that K is the same for all concepts. This clearly is an approximation since preexperimental strength would vary with amount of exposure to a concept.[3]

3. i_1, i_2—interference would also be provided by other experimental links acquired in the experiment. In Fig. 8.3a we assume i_1 links associated with the person and i_2 associated with the location.

4. n—note that there is an irrelevant path leading from the proposition node d to ". . .contained-in LIST." There is also an irrelevant path leading from the

---

[3]There is evidence (Perlmutter, Harsip, & Myers, 1976) that there is greater interference from preexperimental knowledge for more frequent concepts.

predicate node e to *in*. These irrelevant paths should tend to dissipate the intersecting activation. That is, the strength of the activation coming from Videa1 and reaching d would be divided between the branch going to the "List contains. . . ." proposition and the branch going to e. The total number of such irrelevant paths is referred to as n.

A way is needed to relate these structural variables and the activation process to derive predictions for activation time. To do this, some simplifications will be made to both the structural representation and the conception of the activation process. Figure 8.3b shows a simplified structural representation of Fig. 8.3a. Figure 8.3b has *hippie* and *park* connected to a central node as well as representation of the irrelevant paths involving *in* and "list contains. . . ." It has preserved the information about preexperimental paths, experimental paths, and irrelevant paths. However, all information about the complexity of the structures has been lost.

This structural approximation will make possible the derivation of predictions. The use of an approximation serves another useful purpose—it prevents us from taking too seriously all the details in the original Fig. 8.3a. It would be a mistake to think that these fact-retrieval experiments actually tested the details of a representation like Fig. 8.3a. Subjects elaborate the sentence structure in several ways causing unspecified additions to the memory structure (see discussions on page 165 and in Chapter 10), which might introduce additional paths of intersection. Another advantage of the structural approximation is that it frees the validity of the activation analysis from the specifics of the ACT representational assumptions. Any of a large number of similar network representations would result in the same approximation and so the same prediction. Thus, the credibility of the activation analysis does not depend on the credibility of the details of the ACT representation.

General Model for Trues

Rather than deriving ACT predictions for the case of Fig. 8.3b, I will derive predictions for a more general case, and apply these general results to Fig. 8.3b. Figure 8.4 shows the general situation. There is one node connected to m (≥ 2) relevant (that is, to be intersected, active) nodes $a_1, a_2, \ldots, a_m$ and n irrelevant nodes $b_1, b_2, \ldots, b_n$. In Fig. 8.3b there were just two relevant and two irrelevant nodes. The question which concerns us is how soon will the activation from nodes a_1-a_m intersect.

The speed of spread of activation from each node, a_i, will be determined by the strength of the correct link out of a_i relative to the strength of all links. Let s_i be the strength of this link and S_i be the total strength. Then the rate of spread for node a_i is proportional to $r_i = s_i/S_i$ (from Assumption 4, page 123). As an illustration I will calculate the rates for Fig. 8.3b. Suppose each experimental link

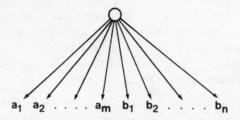

FIG. 8.4 A generalized approximate representation of a to-be-activated structure involving a_1, $a_2, \ldots, a_m$.

had strength s and the nonexperimental links had total strength K. Then the rate of spread from the person is proportional to $s/(K + i_1 s)$ and from the location it is proportional to $s/(K + i_2 s)$.

I will initially assume that all the rates, r_i, are equal and then consider the case of unequal rates. Each of the branches between the a_i and the central node in Fig. 8.4 can be thought of as really containing a number of intermediate nodes that are not preserved in the approximation. Therefore, one could in the original case consider the issue of how many nodes and links on a branch are active. However, for the approximation I will consider the whole branch to be either in a state of activation or not. A branch can be activated either by having activation spread up from the terminal node (at rate r) or down from the top node. Initially, the top node will not be active, but after the first branch has been activated it is active. Activation will spread down each of the $m + n$ branches from the top node at rate $1/(m + n)$. This reflects an equal allocation of strength to each link emanating from the top node.

It will be assumed that the time to activate a branch is exponentially distributed.[4] Initially there are m branches to be activated from the terminal nodes, each at rate r. The first completed branch will be the fastest of these m exponential processes. Assuming the m exponentials are independent, the fastest will complete in time α/mr. At this point in time the top node will become active. The remaining $m - 1$ branches can be activated either from the terminal node (rate r) or from the top node (rate $1/(m + n)$). Each branch will be activated by the fastest of these two. The fastest is also an exponential but with rate $[1/(m + n)] + r$. The complete intersection will be accomplished when the last of the $m - 1$ links is activated. The time to achieve this will be the slowest of $m - 1$ exponentials, each with rate $[1/(m + n)] + r$. The mean time for this is

$$\frac{(m + n)\alpha}{1 + (m + n)r} \sum_{i = 1}^{m - 1} \frac{1}{i}$$

Adding in the time, α/mr, for the first link to activated we obtain the following

---

[4]The assumption of exponential distributions is being made purely for analytic tractability. The available data allow no conclusions to be made about the distributions of activation time.

time to achieve a complete intersection:

$$\left(\frac{1}{mr} + \frac{(m+n)}{1+(m+n)r} \sum_{i=1}^{m-1} \frac{1}{i} \right) \alpha \tag{2}$$

One problem with Eq. (2) is that it does not take into account the complexity of the to-be-activated structure. Complexity (C) is the number of links that the activation must traverse. If the total structure has complexity C and there are m links in the approximate structure (that is, in Fig. 8.4), each link might be approximated as having complexity C/m. The quantity in Eq. (2) should be multiplied by C/m to reflect the complexity factor. This gives the final equation for T_a the time for an intersection to occur and the production to be selected:

$$T_a = \frac{C}{m} \left(\frac{1}{mr} + \frac{(m+n)}{1+(m+n)r} \sum_{i=1}^{m-1} \frac{1}{i} \right) \alpha \tag{3}$$

where α is the time scale factor (similar to a in Chapter 4, page 123). C is the complexity of the structure (in number of links), m is the number of sources of activation to intersect, n is the number of irrelevant branches, and r is the rate of activation. Substituting Eq. (3) into Eq. (1) (page 261) we get the following expression for reaction time to a true probe:

$$T(\text{true}) = B + \frac{C}{m} \left(\frac{1}{mr} + \frac{(m+n)}{1+(m+n)r} \sum_{i}^{m-1} \frac{1}{i} \right) \alpha \tag{4}$$

This equation was derived assuming the rate was the same from all m nodes. It remains to be shown how to compute a composite measure when the rates differ. Basically, we want some average rate and I will use the following equation:

$$r = \left(\sum_{i}^{m} r_i \right) \Big/ m \tag{5}$$

While Eq. (5) is quite obvious, it turns out not to be without some nonobvious empirical consequences. It predicts the *min-effect,* which will be discussed in Section 8.3.

Effect of Dampening

This analysis has ignored the effect of the dampening process on reaction time. The *true* production will be selected when activation intersects from the active nodes in the pattern. The interval between the dampenings is D time units long. The activation begins at some time during this interval. If there is not enough time left for a complete intersection, the partial path activated will be dampened except for the original active nodes in the pattern (which are on the ALIST). Activation will spread again from these original nodes after the dampening and, if the spread is rapid enough, the production will be selected before the dampening. Because the time to achieve an intersection is stochastically distributed, it is possible that an intersection might not occur during one dampening period but might occur in a later period. It is clear that the likelihood that the intersection will be stopped by dampening will increase with the mean time to achieve the intersection. If the mean time is long enough, intersections will almost never be achieved. This fact puts a clear limit on how complex a pattern in a condition may be.

The exact effect of dampening on intersection depends on the distribution of the time T_a. Just for illustrative purposes, consider the extreme case where the activation time T_a was a constant A. If $A > D$, the requisite structure will never be activated in time. If $A < D$, then there is the possibility that the activation of the requisite structure will be turned off once by dampening and then take an additional A units of time. Assume that the activation of the structure is equally likely to begin at any point in the interval D between dampenings. It will be dampened if it occurs in the last A units before dampening. Therefore, the probability of the initial activation being dampened out is A/D. The mean extra time added by this dampening is $A/2$. The expected addition to activation time because of dampening is $A/2 \cdot A/D = A^2/2D$. So the effect of dampening is to add a component that will increase with the square of A. For most assumptions about the distribution of T_a, the effect of dampening means that the true time to achieve intersection will increase more rapidly than a linear function of T_a as defined by Eq. (3).[5]

In my calculations I will use Eq. (3) and ignore the contribution of dampening. The calculated predictions will be monotonic but not linear with the true ACT predictions because of the approximation. As the above example assuming constant activation shows, the true times may increase more rapidly than the calculated values. The degree to which this approximation is a problem depends on the length of the dampening time relative to the time to achieve an intersection and on the variability of the intersection times.

Predictions for the Person–Location Experiment

Let us consider the application of Eqs. (4) and (5) to the true verification times for the case illustrated in Fig. 8.3. In this case there are two paths of activation to intersect and there are two irrelevant paths. Therefore, $m = 2$ and $n = 2$. The value of C is 7 since there are 7 links separating person and location. Let s be the strength of each experimental link. Then, the activation rate from the person node is $r_1 = s/(K + i_1 s)$, that is, the ratio of the strength of the correct link

---

[5]It is interesting that considerations of a speed–accuracy tradeoff indicate a factor which might compensate for this increase with the square. The effect of any speed–accuracy process is to principally truncate long reaction times with errors or correct guesses. This would tend to put a ceiling on reaction times and make the rate of increase with A less than linear.

to the strength of all links. Similarly, the activation rate from the location node is $r_2 = s/(K + i_2 s)$. Letting $K' = K/s$ these rates may be rewritten $r_1 = 1/(K' + i_1)$ and $r_2 = 1/(K' + i_2)$. The parameter K' reflects the strength of preexperimental links relative to an experimental link. The accuracy of predictions of the model is not very sensitive to the exact value of K'. Basically, larger values of K' just result in longer estimates of activation time but little change in the differences among conditions. Therefore, I have chosen to fix the value of the parameter at $K' = 2$ for all experiments in this chapter. It is not that unreasonable to use the same value of this parameter in all experiments because the experimental links are brought to about the same level of strength and because the estimation procedure is insensitive to values of K'. It might seem unreasonable to set K' so low because it would appear that the total strength of preexperimental knowledge should be much greater. However, larger values would result in unreasonable estimates of the activation time, and very much larger values of K' would yield estimates of activation time longer than the total reaction time. One reason why this parameter may be so low is that experimental links are very strong during the experiment, as they have been recently tested many times. After the experiment the strength of experimental links might decline relative to preexperimental links as the advantage of recency wears off. Evidence for recency effects on strength is shown in Section 8.3 (page 283). Later, in Section 8.3 (page 292) I discuss another reason why this parameter may appear so low. With $K' = 2$ the following equation gives the average activation rate, r:

$$r = \left(\frac{1}{2 + i_1} + \frac{1}{2 + i_2} \right) \Big/ 2 \qquad (6)$$

This can be substituted into Eq. (4) to predict the reaction times for the various cases in Table 8.2:

$$T(\text{true}) = B + 3.5\alpha \left[\frac{1}{2r} + \frac{4}{1 + 4r} \right] \qquad (7)$$

To derive predictions requires that we estimate B and α which can be done by means of simple linear regression. Before using Eq. (7) to derive predictions for the experiment, it would be useful to develop a model to describe the emission of a false response.

Emission of a False Response

The term "false" used to refer to negative responses is something of a misnomer that I am stuck with because of past carelessness in choosing terminology. What the subject means by a false response is not that the proposition is false but rather that he cannot recognize it. The emission of a false response, like a true response, requires Productions (P1) and (P2) from Table 8.5 to be executed, taking times

T_1 and T_2. Like the true case, we will assume these two parameters are constant across conditions. However, unlike the true case, a false response will be generated upon completion of Production (P4), not (P3).

Production (P4) consists of two time components, a time for initial selection, $T_{4,s}$, and a time for application, $T_{4,e}$. It will be assumed that the application component, $T_{4,e}$, is constant across conditions and is equal to the corresponding component for true times, $T_{3,e}$. In contrast, the time for selecting the production will vary with the condition. It is assumed that a certain time must pass before a production with an absence condition, like (P4), will be selected. During this interval there must occur no intersection of activation. The basic idea is that a waiting process is set up that waits for an intersection of activation among the nodes specified in the INTERSECTING test. If a certain period of time has passed and an intersection has not occurred, the production is selected. For this to be a sensible strategy, the waiting time must be adjusted to be longer than the mean time to achieve an intersection had the probe been true. Thus, it is assumed that the waiting time is identical to the activation time (Eq. 3) plus an additional constant, F. This additional constant, F, reflects the extra time waited just to make sure. Thus, the time to determine that a pattern is not present is given by the following equation:

$$T_{4,s} = T_{ABS} = \frac{C}{m}\left[\frac{1}{mr} + \frac{(m+n)}{1+(m+n)r} \sum_{i=1}^{m-1}\frac{1}{i}\right]\alpha + F \qquad (8)$$

There are two terms in this equation that require further specification—r and n. Calculation of the rate, r, by Eq. (4) requires that we know the rates, r_i, associated with each active node a_i in the pattern. There may be a number of experimental links associated with a_i and these may have different strengths and hence different activation rates. When dealing with true probes we are only concerned with the rate of the link involved in the true proposition. With false probes, I will use the average rate of the experimental links.

The other term whose value might not be obvious is n, the number of irrelevant links along the correct paths among the active nodes. Since there is no correct path, this quantity is basically without definition. In various paradigms it is more or less obvious how to specify this quantity. For instance, in the person–location experiment we have been considering, the value of this n is 2 since this is the value it has in all true conditions.

Equation (8) is somewhat bizarre because it presupposes that the absence process can in some way depend on all the variables that affect the occurrence of an intersection. The strongest evidence for this assumption is the fact, as we shall see in Section 8.3, that all the variables which affect true response times have the same effect on false response times.

Note that the falsification process in the person–location experiment involves all the time components as the true process plus the additional constant waiting time F. Therefore, Eq. (9) gives the prediction of the ACT model for falsification times in that experiment:

$$T(\text{false}) = B + 3.5\left(\frac{1}{2r} + \frac{4}{1+4r}\right)\alpha + F \tag{9}$$

Predictions of the Model

Equations (6) and (8) were fit to the data of Table 8.2. The three parameters estimated were $B = 531$ msec, $\alpha = 49$ msec, and $F = 104$ msec. The results of that model fitting are displayed in Table 8.6. The conditions are referred to by two digits. The first digit stands for the number of propositions associated with the person and the second digit for the number of propositions associated with the location. For comparison sake, I have included the predictions of the HAM model (see Anderson, 1974). The HAM predictions are slightly better but they involved an additional parameter.

The standard error of the reaction times in Table 8.6 is 21 msec. Thirteen of the ACT predictions are off by greater than one standard error, three of these are off by greater than two standard errors, and two of these are off by greater than four standard errors. A test can be performed measuring the significance of the size of the deviations. This test is highly significant ($F_{14,1054} = 4.82; p < .001$). So

TABLE 8.6
Predictions for the Person–Location Experiment

	Condition	Data	ACT's prediction	HAM's prediction
True	1–1	1111	1082	1115
	1–2	1167	1141	1156
	1–3	1153	1185	1182
	2–1	1174	1141	1156
	2–2	1198	1217	1216
	2–3	1233	1273	1257
	3–1	1222	1185	1182
	3–2	1222	1273	1257
	3–3	1357	1341	1315
False	1–1	1197	1186	1195
	1–2	1250	1245	1251
	1–3	1262	1289	1263
	2–1	1221	1245	1241
	2–2	1356	1321	1331
	2–3	1471	1377	1385
	3–1	1264	1289	1263
	3–2	1291	1377	1385
	3–3	1465	1445	1467

clearly, ACT's numerical predictions are not perfect, but they do capture most (83.3%) of the variance in the data. There are a number of reasons why I am not very bothered by significant deviations from predictions. For one thing, the predictive model is openly acknowledged to only be an approximation to the true ACT model. Another reason is that deviations from predictions come largely from a few peculiar data points. For instance, in this experiment the 2–3 and 3–2 falses are different by almost 200 msec whereas they should be identical according to theory. This particular perturbation has not reappeared in subsequent experiments. I am at a loss to explain the perturbation except in terms of the constraints under which material is generated—which vary from experiment to experiment. Perhaps these affect the exact manner of a subject's study of the material.

It is important to fit models to the data and to report how well the model fits relative to the standard error. However, it would be short sighted to focus on these goodness-of-fit tests to the point of ignoring the broader significance of the data and of ACT's ability to reproduce the major quantitative and qualitative trends that exist in the data. As argued in Section 1.3 the goal of accuracy must make accommodation with the goal of broad generality. What is important about this ACT fact-retrieval model is that it can make fairly accurate predictions for a wide range of experiments. This contrasts sharply with HAM which did a slightly better job of accounting for the data in Table 8.6, but fell apart completely when we tried to apply it to experiments that involved different manipulations. Recently, in an assessment of the current state of mathematical psychology, Estes (1975) has also argued that the accuracy of a model in fitting a particular experiment should not be allowed to completely override issues of the general utility of the model.

8.2 HAM'S SERIAL GRAPH-SEARCHING ALGORITHM

To provide a contrast to the ACT model I will consider the HAM serial graph-searching model proposed by Anderson and Bower (1973), Anderson (1974), and Thorndyke and Bower (1974). The HAM algorithm proposes that a subject simultaneously accessed memory from all content words in a probe. For instance, if the subject were tested with *A hippie was in the park,* he would enter memory from *hippie* and *park.* In this respect it corresponds to the intersection model. However, in contrast to the intersection model it assumes the subject begins a serial search from each concept. It also assumes that the serial searches from the different concepts in a probe proceed in parallel.

The logic of the serial search from a concept is given by the flow chart in Fig. 8.5. To explicate the flow chart, I will work through a hypothetical example. Consider a search from *thief* trying to verify whether *The thief tackled the singer* is stored in memory. Suppose stored with *thief* are the two propositions *The thief kicked the fireman* and *The thief tackled the singer.* Figure 8.6 shows a very simple

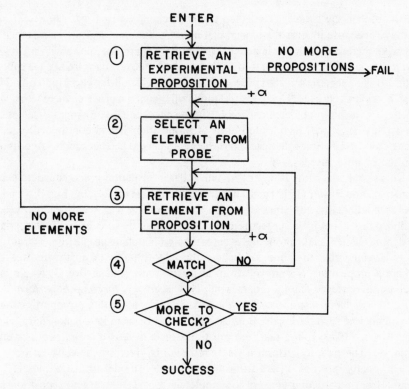

FIG. 8.5   A representation of the logic of the HAM graph-searching algorithm.

network representation of these propositions. The only purpose of this representation is to illustrate the search algorithm. The elements of the first proposition are connected to a node A. The elements of the second proposition are connected to a node B.

Now consider how the algorithm in Fig. 8.5 will effect a search from *thief* in Fig. 8.6. In Box 1 the first proposition A is retrieved. In Box 2 some element

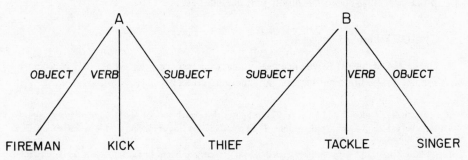

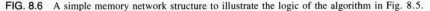

FIG. 8.6   A simple memory network structure to illustrate the logic of the algorithm in Fig. 8.5.

of the probe, say *singer,* is selected to be checked. At Box 3 *fireman* will be retrieved because it bears the object relation to A. *Fireman* and *singer* mismatch (Box 4); therefore control transfers back to Box 3. There is a failure within Box 3 to retrieve another object from A; therefore control transfers back to Box 1. Proposition B is next retrieved. Suppose *tackle* is next selected for checking (Box 2). *Tackle* will be retrieved from B (Box 3) and will match the probe element (Box 4). There is a further probe element, *singer,* to be checked (Box 5) and it is selected next (Box 2). It will match the object of proposition B and control will again transfer to Box 5. Since there are no further elements to be checked the algorithm will end with a success.

This search algorithm is described with fuller information-processing details in Anderson and Bower (1973) and Thorndyke and Bower (1974), but Fig. 8.5 bares its essential details. Note that search is self-terminating both within and between propositions. That is, a subject rejects a proposition as soon as he finds a mismatching element in the probe and accepts the first matching proposition he finds.[6] It is assumed that the time to execute this algorithm is taken up in Box 1, where a proposition is retrieved from an entry point, and in Box 3, where an element is retrieved from a proposition. That is, *time is taken up in performing long-term memory retrievals.* The time to execute the algorithm is proportional to the number of such retrievals. Both Anderson and Bower (1973) and Thorndyke and Bower (1974) found that reaction times increased as more retrievals were required. The time to perform a single retrieval is given by the constant α.

This search process differs from the Intersection model in that it requires a search from a particular concept to completely recover the target proposition in memory. It is not possible for processes from different concepts to intersect. Search processes from different concepts are independent of one another, and search time is determined by the fastest of these independent search processes. Anderson and Bower (1973) rejected the possibility of having different search processes intersect. The reason for this was the difficulty of simulating such intersection searches. The processes checking for a match against a probe require considerable bookkeeping to keep track of partial matches on the way to a total match. This bookkeeping is made much more difficult when the various search processes must coordinate their partial matches.[7]

The GET List

In the HAM model it was not really necessary to consider what other preexperimental propositions might be attached to concepts like *hippie* and *park.* All

---

[6]Actually, Anderson and Bower (1973) proposed that search was self-terminating between propositions but exhaustive within propositions. The Thorndyke and Bower model (1974) was self-terminating in both senses.

[7]Since the HAM book an intersection search process has been simulated. Hence, while difficult, it certainly is not impossible. If the reader is interested in the details he should write to me for a copy of the HAM.2 program.

propositions were serially ordered on pushdown stacks called *GET lists* and the experimental propositions were first on the GET lists. This was because GET lists were ordered according to recency. Therefore, in searching the GET list the subject would first search the experimental propositions. Once he had searched past the experimental propositions and began searching the first preexperimental proposition he could stop and respond *false*. It was assumed the subject could detect preexperimental propositions because they would not be tagged as having occurred in a list context.

There are two advantages to the HAM formulation over the ACT formulation in this respect. First, it was not necessary to include something like the parameter K of the Intersection model to reflect the effect of preexperimental links. The other advantage of this model is that it also provided a model for the falsification decisions without requiring additional assumptions about a waiting process. Subjects would respond false when they exhausted the experimental propositions. Unfortunately, the HAM model makes predictions about the data which turn out to be wrong. First, it predicts subjects should be able to verify experimental propositions faster than preexperimental propositions. Second, it predicts subjects should be slowed down to a greater extent by the number of experimental propositions with false probes than with true probes. Both predictions are wrong. The HAM model could only be fit to the fact-retrieval data (for example, in Table 8.6) by permitting different α parameters to be estimated for true and false reaction times. Clearly, it is less than satisfactory if one must assume that the search rate is different for the true and false probes.

8.3 A REVIEW OF SOME FACT-RETRIEVAL DATA

It is important that the ACT fact-retrieval model described in Section 8.1 be shown to deliver reasonably accurate predictions over a wide range of experimental manipulations. The function of this section is to review a variety of experiments I have performed and see how the ACT model fares. Given that there are a number of approximations underlying the ACT quantitative predictions, it would be a mistake to place too much emphasis on the details of the model's predictions. More important is that the ACT intersection model be able to capture the qualitative trends in the data. Particularly important are those qualitative trends that distinguish ACT from other available models like HAM.

The Falsification Process

The HAM model predicts that there should be a much larger effect of the number of propositions for false probes than for true probes. This is because the subject decides "true" upon a self-terminating search whereas he responds "false" only after exhausting all the experimental propositions. For the data in Table 8.2 the HAM model predicted that the effect of the number of propositions for falses compared with trues (comparing marginals) should be in the ratio of 2.42:1. The actual ratio is only 1.37:1. It was for this reason that separate fits had to be given for trues versus falses. I argued earlier (Anderson, 1974) that this was not conclusive evidence against HAM because the falses displayed a strong relation between mean time and error rate and the trues did not. Therefore, the failure to get the expected difference in the effect of the number of propositions between trues and falses may be due to a speed–accuracy tradeoff.

More recent experiments, however, have been conducted in which there were no differential relations between mean times and error rates but in which there was still a failure to get greater effects of the number of propositions for falses than for trues. Two such experiments have already been reported. In the noun–adjective experiment (Table 8.3) the ratio of effects for falses versus trues is .9:1 and in the location–subject–verb experiment (Table 8.4) the obtained ratio is .6:1. In none of these experiments is there a much greater effect of the number of propositions for falses versus trues. In the location–subject–verb experiment there was actually a marginally significantly greater effect for trues ($p < .10$).

Sternberg's (1969) response to the failure to get 2:1 slopes for negative versus positive probes was to assume that the search for trues is exhaustive. Applied to this experimental paradigm, this would mean subjects always search all the propositions—even when the probe is true. This seems counterintuitive. It would be more reasonable to give up the assumption that the subject decides false by an exhaustive search than to assume he responds true by exhausting the list.

The notion of an exhaustive search is particularly unpalatable within the context of the HAM model because that model assumes that subjects are capable of self-terminating in two other senses. First, the model assumes that the subject terminates search of his GET-list as soon as he exhausts the experimental propositions and reaches the preexperimental propositions. It would be unreasonable to assume that subjects searched all the propositions they know about a concept like *hippie*. Second, the HAM model assumes that the subject terminates his search as soon as the first search process from a concept comes to a conclusion.

In the ACT model it is proposed that subjects respond false by waiting for a sufficiently long period that they can be fairly confident an intersection would have occurred had the probe been true. There are two gross features of the data that are suggestive of a waiting strategy. The first is that reaction times to decide false are generally slower than reaction times to decide true. It is necessary that the subject wait longer to respond false than the time it would usually take him to respond true. This reaction-time difference occurs in experiments like the person–location experiment (Table 8.2) where subject's hand is counterbalanced over response, that is, for some subjects right is true and for others vice versa. This longer time for false also occurs in experiments like Tables 8.3 and 8.4, where the subject is allowed to make his own assignment. In these situations subjects almost always assign the dominant hand to the true response. The second fact suggesting a waiting strategy is that subjects more often incorrectly judge a true probe false than they incorrectly judge a false probe true. Erroneous false responses would occur if the subject's waiting deadline sometimes came up before the intersection required to select a true production.

Multiple-Access Assumption

An important assumption of the ACT model is that the subject can simultaneously activate memory from a number of nodes and so look for intersecting activation. The assumption that memory can be "entered" simultaneously at multiple locations is called the *multiple-access assumption*. HAM involved a similar assumption—that multiple search processes could progress in parallel from a number of nodes. The multiple-access assumption implies that there should be an equal effect of the number of propositions associated with any concept in probe. This is because a response depends on the intersection of activity from all concepts. Increasing the number of propositions associated with any concept would slow the spread of activation from that concept and so delay the intersection. As may be verified from Tables 8.2, 8.3, and 8.4 there are approximately equal effects of the propositional fan of all concepts in a probe. This approximate equality of the fan effect has been obtained in all fact-retrieval experiments.

The obvious alternative to the multiple-access model—a *single-access model*—does not anticipate these equal effects. For instance, it would be more natural for such a model to predict that the subject would search memory from the first content word in the probe. Therefore, the only effective variable should be the number of propositions associated with the first word. A single-access model can predict the equal effect if it assumes the subject randomly selects a concept from the probe and searches from this concept. This requires that the subject have an equal probability of searching from each concept. This version of the single-access model has been dubbed the random-access model. The random-access model seems bizarre because it would claim that over the wide variety of probes used subjects have distributed approximately equally probability of access over all words.

Even granting that normally subjects access from all elements with equal probability, it would seem that by appropriate training one should be able to bias the point from which memory was searched. In Anderson (1974) there was an attempt to train subjects to access memory from one of the two content words in a person–location probe like those from Table 8.1. Subjects learned the material either by trying to retrieve to location cues like *Who is in the park?* or to person cues like *Where are the hippies?* If subjects could not recall all the answers they were told the correct answer and retested. Subjects who only learned with location cues should mainly access memory from the location when tested in the reaction-time phase with a probe like *A hippie is in the park*. According to a single-access model the important variable for such subjects should be the number of propositions associated with the *location*. The converse prediction holds for person-trained subjects. However, subjects with either training showed equal effects of the number of propositions associated with both person and location.

The Min Effect

The multiple-access and the random-access models make differential predictions about an interesting feature of the data. According to the random-access model there is an equal probability of searching from each concept in the probe. Therefore, reaction time should be a function of the mean number of propositions leaving the various concepts in a probe. So the random-access model predicts equal time to deal with a person–location probe in which the person occurs in three propositions and the location in one as a probe where they both occur in two propositions.

In contrast, the multiple-access model predicts the 1–3 case should be faster than the 2–2 case because reaction time should be principally a function of the minimum number of propositions attached to a concept. The basic intuition behind this prediction is that activation from a concept with lower propositional fan will tend to activate more of the to-be-activated memory structure and so make up for the slowness of activation from a concept with higher propositional fan. To illustrate this intuition more precisely, consider the case where an intersection must occur between two concepts C_1 and C_2 that are X links apart. Suppose the rate of spread of activation from C_1 is r_1 and the rate from C_2 is r_2. What we want to do is to calculate the time t at which the two sources of activation intersect. It does not matter whether we consider the time to activate a link from a source to be a probabilistic or a deterministic function of rate. Therefore, I will work the deterministic case because it is simpler. At time t when intersection occurs, assuming no irrelevant paths, the first process will have activated tr_1 links and the other process tr_2 links. Since the whole path is uncovered, we know $tr_1 + tr_2 = X$, and therefore

$$t = X/(r_1 + r_2) \tag{10}$$

This expression can be applied to the situation where there are i_1 experimental propositions attached to C_1 and i_2 attached to C_2. Then, the rate parameters are $r_1 = 1/(K' + i_1)$ and $r_2 = 1/(K' + i_2)$, where K' is the strength of the preexperimental links relative to the experimental links. Then, the expression for t can be written

$$t = \frac{X(K' + i_1)\,(K' + i_2)}{2K' + i_1 + i_2} \tag{11}$$

The reader may confirm that this quantity is greater when $i_1 = i_2 = 2$ than when $i_1 = 1$ and $i_2 = 3$. For any fixed value of the sum $i_1 + i_2$, the expression in Eq. (11) will be smaller the greater the difference between i_1 and i_2. This is the *min effect*—that is, reaction time is principally a function of the minimum propositional fan.

The ACT model generally predicts a min effect. It follows from Eq. (5) (page 265) which makes the rate parameter in Eq. (4) a function of the mean rate.

I have been able to examine this prediction of a min effect in a number of experiments. Figure 8.7 presents an analysis for a min effect in the true data of three of these experiments. Figure 8.8 presents the corresponding analysis for a min effect in the false data of these experiments. Figures 8.7a and 8.8a present analyses for the person–location experiment of Table 8.2. Figures 8.7b and 8.8b present analyses for the noun–adjective experiment of Table 8.3.[8] Figures 8.7c and 8.8c present an experiment of King and Anderson (1975). In that experiment, subjects studied subject–verb–object sentences like *The lawyer shot the fireman* and were tested whether verb–object pairs came from the studied sentences. The points in these figures are labeled with two digits to indicate the fan associated with each of the concepts.

The 1–2 point in Figs. 8.7a or 8.8a represents the case where there is one proposition associated with the person and two with the location or vice versa. Throughout Figs. 8.7 and 8.8 I have collapsed those cases that only differ in terms of which elements occurred in the various numbers of propositions. The abscissas in these figures give the mean number of propositions associated with the two concepts. The random-access model predicts reaction time should be a linear function of this variable. Straight lines connect those probes which have the same number of propositions associated with each element. The random-access model predicts the asymmetric points should be on the function defined by these symmetric points whereas the multiple-access model predicts that they should be below.

Let us first consider the true data in the three panels of Fig. 8.7. In Fig. 8.7a the asymmetric points (1–2, 1–3, and 2–3) average 15 msec below the line defined by the symmetric points, which is not significant ($t_{1071} = .86$). In Fig. 8.7b the asymmetric point (1–3) is 2 msec below the symmetric line, which is clearly not significant. However, in Fig. 8.7c the asymmetric points (1–2, 1–3, 2–3) are 26 msec below the symmetric points and this is marginally significant ($t_{3289} = 1.83; p < .05$). Next let us consider the false data in the three panels of Fig. 8.8. In Fig. 8.8a the asymmetric points are 55 msec below the symmetric points, which is highly significant ($t_{1071} = 3.11; p < .005$). The difference is 52 msec in Fig. 8.8b, which is also significant ($t_{98} = 2.41; p < .01$). The difference is 11 msec in Fig. 8.8c, which is not significant ($t_{1071} = .77$).

There is clearly a variation in the size and significance of the min effect from experiment to experiment as one would expect if there were an effect which was weak relative to the random error. The size of the min effect is expected to be small. For instance, ACT predicts only a 16 msec min effect in Table 8.6, compared to the observed min effect of 35 msec (averaging true and false). The fact that all six analyses in Figs. 8.7 and 8.8 showed positive min effects, and three

---

[8]In these figures the 2–4 case from Table 8.3 is denoted by the mean which is three propositions.

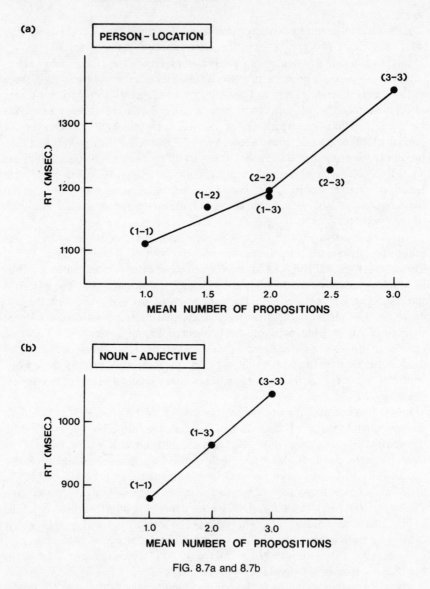

FIG. 8.7a and 8.7b

of these were significant, clearly forces the conclusion that there is a small min effect—as predicted. This conclusion disproves the single-access model and supports the multiple-access model.

Effects of Logical Relation

A difference between the HAM search algorithm and ACT's intersection algorithm lies in their sensitivity to the logical relation of a link. The HAM model

(c)

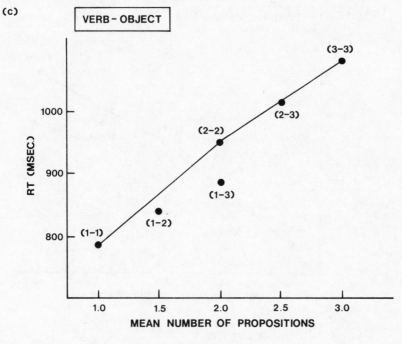

FIG. 8.7c

FIG. 8.7 Analyses for a min-effect in the true data: (a) person–location experiment; (b) noun–adjective experiment; (c) subject–verb–object experiment.

predicted subjects could use such relational information whereas the intersection model claims activation will spread down all links irrespective of their relation. Relational information is only checked in the application phase once the target proposition has been activated and the appropriate production selected. I (Anderson, 1975) have performed an experiment to test this prediction. Subjects learned propositions about political figures referred to by their last names. In these propositions the political figure could either serve the logical relation of subject or the relation of object. The question was whether subjects would be affected by the number of propositions studied using the object relation when they saw a proposition with a subject relation such as *Nixon kicked the lawyer*. The HAM model predicts no effect because of its assumption that the subject can selectively examine propositions only with the specified logical relation. In contrast, the ACT model assumes that the spread of activation proceeds down all links independent of logical relation. Therefore, adding links with any relation should slow down search equally. The results indicated an effect of the number of propositions with the irrelevant relation that was as great as the effect of the number of propositions with the relevant relation.

The experiment by King and Anderson (1975) also provides support for the

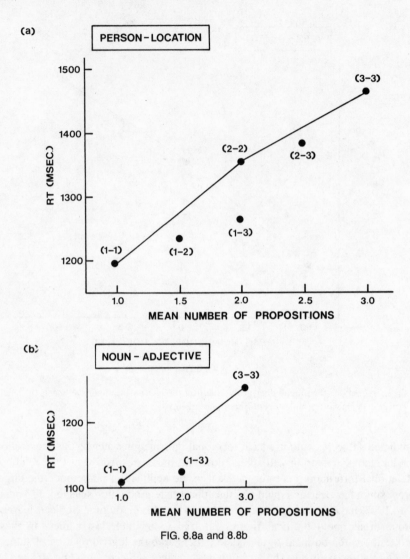

FIG. 8.8a and 8.8b

alogical character of the activation process. We had subjects study sentences like

(1)   The hippie touched the debutante.

(2)   The hippie amused the lawyer.

Figure 8.9 provides an ACT representation for such a pair of sentences. Subjects saw false probes such as *touched lawyer* in which a verb came from one sentence and an object from another. However, there is a spurious interconnection between these two elements through the common subject *hippie*. This interconnecting path might become activated upon presentation of the probe.

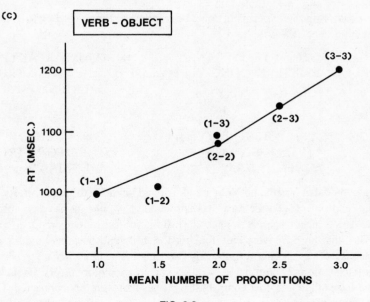

FIG. 8.8c

FIG. 8.8   Analyses for a min-effect in the false data: (a) person–location experiment; (b) noun–adjective experiment; (c) subject–verb–object experiment.

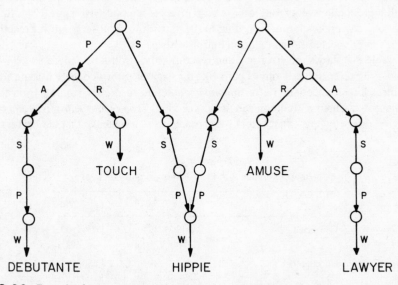

FIG. 8.9   Example of sentences used in the King and Anderson experiment. Note the spurious connection between *touch* and *lawyer*.

The subject in this experiment could be responding true according to one of two productions:

(P3a)   (Vcon = TEST)   ⇒   (Vcon = READY)
         & (INTERSECTING Vverb Vobj)   & (RESPOND TRUE)
                                               & (UNBIND Vverb Vobj)

or

(P3b)   (Vcon = TEST) & ((Vind1   ⇒   (Vcon = READY)
         * (Vverb OF Vind2))   & (RESPOND TRUE)
         & (Vind2 * Vobj))   & (UNBIND Vverb Vobj)

It is assumed that Vverb and Vobj are global and bound to the idea corresponding to verb and object. (To see how these productions would fit into a complete set for the task, consult Table 8.5, page 258). If the subject were operating according to (P3a), that is, if he were only looking for an intersection, he would generate erroneous trues every time a spuriously connected false like *touch lawyer* resulted in an intersection. Therefore, we would expect to see more errors for such connected falses than for other control false probes that were not connected. On the other hand, if the subject were operating according to (P3b) and was checking whether the path of intersection between Vverb and Vobj was a legitimate one, then there would not be a greater number of errors. However, this production would still be selected should there occur a spurious intersection between Vverb and Vobj. The production would be rejected in application stage. Because Production (P3b) would get on the APPLY LIST, it would slow down the application of the production generating a false response (Assumption 10, page 124). So if the subject were operating according to (P3b), we should observe slower reaction times to connected falses than to control falses.

Table 8.7 shows the error rate and reaction times from this experiment. *False connected* refers to verb–object pairs like the example in which there is a spurious subject interconnection. *False unconnected* refers to probes coming from two sentences without a common subject connection. *True connected* or *true unconnected* refers to verb–object pairs which came from a sentence that did or did not

TABLE 8.7
Reaction Times and Error Rates (In parentheses)

	True	False
Connected	913	1107
	(.129)	(.193)
Unconnected	917	1039
	(.142)	(.115)

share a subject with another sentence. There is no effect of connectedness on trues (and ACT predicts none) but subjects are both slower and make more errors to false connected probes than false unconnected. In King and Anderson (1975), we were able to show that there were independent effects of connectedness on speed and on accuracy—that the effect on one variable did not arise from the effect on the other variable through a speed–accuracy tradeoff. Thus, there is evidence that subjects were sometimes operating according to Production (P3a), producing an increase in error rate, and sometimes operating according to (P3b), producing an increase in reaction time. The significance of the King and Anderson experiment is that, whether subjects are responding via (P3a) or (P3b), they show a basic sensitivity to intersection of activation independent of logical relation. This outcome is predicted by ACT but was not at all expected by the HAM model.

Effect of Associative Strength

In fitting the model in Table 8.6 (page 269), we have assumed a fixed ratio of the strength of preexperimental associations to the strength of an experimental proposition. However, this should be capable of manipulation by varying the amount of study a subject gives to a proposition or by the number of test trials a subject receives on that proposition. Each time the subject receives an additional test trial about a proposition, the strength of that proposition should be incremented one unit.

Consider, for instance, the changing strengths in the location–subject–verb experiment reported earlier in Table 8.2. Through the course of the experiment subjects were tested on each proposition six times. We divided the experiment into three blocks. Let s be the mean strength of a proposition in Block 1. Then, its mean strength in Block 2 will be $s + 2x$, and during Block 3, $s + 4x$ where x reflects the increment due to one test trial. Let K be the strength of preexperimental link. Then, given the analyses on page 264, if there are i experimental propositions studied about a concept, the strength of a link from the proposition to the concept will be $s/(K + is)$ in Block 1, $(s + 2x)/(K + is + 2ix)$ in Block 2, and $(s + 4x)/(K + is + 4ix)$ in Block 3.

Figure 8.10 shows an attempt to fit the ACT model to a subset of the data of that experiment. The data are broken down into true and false probes, and probes in which all elements are unique and probes with all elements repeated. In fitting the model to the data I used the same equations and parameters that will be estimated in fitting the data in Table 8.13 (to be reported in the next section, page 300). These parameters were $\alpha = 87$, $B = 304$, $F = 167$. The strength of an experimental proposition in the first block was set at 1. I estimated approximately that the correct value of K at the beginning of the experiment was 2.65 and the value of X was .2. With these values the predictions were derived which are displayed in Fig. 8.10. As can be seen the theory and the data closely correspond. In neither

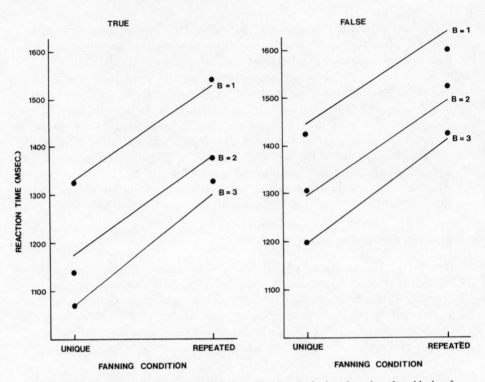

FIG. 8.10   The effect of practice on reaction time. The data are broken down into three blocks of 144 trials. The straight lines represent the predictions of the ACT theory while the dots represent actual data points.

is there much of a change in the differences among conditions across blocks although there is a considerable speed-up in reaction time.[9]

The decrement in reaction times displayed in Fig. 8.10 has been attributed entirely to an increase in the strength of the experimental propositions. One might want to argue that it is in part due to a general speedup in the subject's behavior. Therefore, another experiment has been performed in which different propositions were trained to different strengths. This permits us to contrast, during the same point in the experiment, reaction time to propositions of different strengths.

In the experiment, 24 subjects studied person–location sentences. Both words in a person–location pair either occurred in two study propositions or in four. For the two-proposition words either both propositions occurred about 50% of the

[9]Note that the relations among the conditions are holding quite constant despite the fact that K', the ratio of preexperimental strength to the strength of an experimental link, changes from 2.65 to 1.47. This is the reason for the assertation made earlier in this chapter (page 267) that the estimation procedure, which works on differences among conditions, is not sensitive to the value chosen for K'.

time, or one proposition occurred 67% of the time and the other 33% of the time. The four-proposition words either had one proposition 50% of the time and the other three 17% of the time or two propositions 33% of the time and the other two 17% of the time.

An example of the material for one subject is illustrated in Table 8.8. Each subject would see a different randomly generated set of such pairs. Consider a pair like minister–dungeon. This is a four fan pair because there are four propositions about both *minister* and *dungeon*. It has probability 50% because that particular proposition occurs 50% of the time for both *minister* and *dungeon*. Thus it is to be denoted as a 4–50% pair. Note that for true probes the same fan and probability measures apply to both noun and location. Therefore it is not necessary to examine these variables separately. The true probes will be in one of six conditions depending on the number of propositions and relative probability: 2–67%, 2–50%, 2–33%, 4–50%, 4–33%, 4–17%. False probes were constructed by

TABLE 8.8
Example of Material for Probability Experiment

Two-proposition probes		Probability (%)	Four-proposition probes		Probability (%)
baker	street	50	minister	dungeon	50
baker	tavern	50	minister	orchard	17
lawyer	street	50	minister	barn	17
lawyer	church	50	minister	park	17
farmer	tavern	50	hippie	orchard	50
farmer	church	50	hippie	tower	17
captain	factory	67	hippie	dungeon	17
captain	swamp	33	hippie	barn	17
banker	boat	67	artist	barn	50
banker	factory	33	artist	dungeon	17
fireman	swamp	67	artist	hotel	17
fireman	boat	33	artist	orchard	17
			sailor	park	33
			sailor	tower	33
			sailor	orchard	17
			sailor	hotel	17
			convict	hotel	33
			convict	park	33
			convict	tower	17
			convict	barn	17
			tailor	hotel	33
			tailor	tower	33
			tailor	dungeon	17
			tailor	park	17

randomly combining nouns and adjectives. There are four types of nouns or locations classified by their pattern of appearance in study sentences:

   50%, 50%, examples—baker, street
   67%, 33%, examples—captain, factory
   50%, 17%, 17%, 17%, examples—minister, dungeon
   33%, 33%, 17%, 17%, examples—sailor, park

All possible combinations of these nouns and locations can be constructed except
a 50%, 17%, 17%, 17% noun with a 50%, 17%, 17%, 17% adjective or a 33%,
33%, 17%, 17% noun with a 33%, 33%, 17%, 17% adjective. These cannot be
constructed because all possible combinations yield true probes. Therefore, there
are $(4 \times 4) - 2 = 14$ false conditions.

The sentences were presented in blocks. In a block those true pairs denoted
67% occurred four times, those denoted 50% three times, those denoted 33%
twice, and those denoted 17% once. In this way the true sentences preserved their
relative probabilities in each block. Thus in a block the subject saw 72 true pairs
that were presented in random order within that block. The first block served as a
study block and contained no false probes. The subject just saw true probes and
generated continuations to them. A study–test phase was dispensed with because
the dropout procedure used might upset the relative probabilities. Immediately
after the study block there were four test blocks of 144 probes each—72 true
probes and 72 false probes. The whole study and test procedure took about one
and a half hours. The order of the probes was random within a block. For each of
the six types of true probes it was possible to look at the effects of lag between
occurrences of a probe on its verification time. This is because the randomly occurring probes will naturally generate points on a lag function. This lag function
will provide us with information about the effects of recency.

There has been research on probability and recency effects in the Sternberg
paradigm (for example, Theios, Smith, Haviland, Traupmann, & Moy, 1973).
There are also a number of experiments that have looked at recency and frequency
on recognition in long-term memory (for example, Atkinson & Juola, 1973;
Murdock & Anderson, 1975; Perlmutter, Sorce, & Myers, 1975). These experiments have all found considerable strength-like effects. However, none of these
experiments has the critical design feature of this experiment. We are able to
manipulate recency and frequency of a pair independently of the recency and
frequency of its elements. Therefore, we can examine the strength of a pair independently of the strength of its component elements.

Table 8.9 presents the true data as a function of the number of propositions and
probability. The strength model of ACT predicts that reaction time should be a
function of probability and not fan. There are strong effects of probability independent of fan. One can look for an effect of fan independent of probability by
considering the 50% and 33% cases. Subjects are 44 msec faster in the two-fan
condition than in the four-fan condition ($t_{115} = 1.47$; $.10 > p > .05$). Note, how-

TABLE 8.9
True Data from Probability Experiment[a]

Probability (%)	2-FAN		4-FAN	
	Observed	Predicted	Observed	Predicted
67	1369 (.039)	1337		
50	1461 (.053)	1425	1520 (.048)	1425
33	1542 (.095)	1581	1571 (.070)	1581
17			1872 (.262)	1985

[a]Reaction times and error rates are in parentheses.

ever, that the error rate is lower in the four-fan case. So the small reaction time difference between four-fan and two-fan may be an artifact of a speed–accuracy tradeoff.

The false data from this experiment are displayed in Table 8.10. Tables 8.9 and 8.10 also include the ACT predictions. They were calculated using the earlier equations, (7) and (9), developed on pages 267 and 269 for person–location probes. These equations make reference to a rate parameter r, which was defined

TABLE 8.10
False Data from the Probability Experiment
Observed Time, Error Rate, and Predicted Time

		Location			
		50–50	67–33	50–17–17–17	33–17–17–17
	50–50	1777 (.096) 1711	1677 (.080) 1711	1845 (.116) 1818	1815 (.097) 1818
	67–33	1700 (.062) 1711	1810 (.144) 1711	1849 (.079) 1818	1858 (.115) 1818
Person	50–17–17–17	1709 (.079) 1818	1736 (.057) 1818		1984 (.163) 2009
	33–33–17–17–	1783 (.087) 1818	1766 (.100) 1818	2095 (.162) 2009	

in this experiment for true probes as

$$r = s/(K + \sum_{j} s_j) \tag{17}$$

where s is the frequency with which that proposition was tested or studied in a block. $\sum s_j$ refers to the total frequency of all experimental propositions about a concept. $\sum s_j = 6$, and K was set to 6. Thus, Eq. (17) becomes

$$r = n/12 \tag{18}$$

For false probes the rate parameter chosen for a concept was the average of the rate parameters for the individual experimental propositions. This makes the rate solely a function of fan (f). Thus the rate parameter associated with concept in the false probe with fan f can be shown to be

$$r_i = 1/(2f) \tag{19}$$

The overall rate parameter for a false probe is the average of the rate parameter associated with the person and the rate parameter associated with the location. Let f_1 be the fan from the person and f_2 the fan from the location. Then the rate is

$$r = \frac{1}{4}\left(\frac{1}{f_1} + \frac{1}{f_2}\right) \tag{20}$$

The parameter estimates obtained in fitting the model to the data were $\alpha = 32$, $B = 977$, and $F = 286$. The quality of the model's fit is reasonably good—96.3% of the variance was accounted for in the true data and 70.2% of the variance in the false data. However, the residual variance not explained in the true and false data is significant ($F_{15,414} = 1.96$; $p < .01$).

This experiment also permitted us to examine the effect of lag on reaction time. In this analysis we are only interested in true probes. The question of interest is what is the effect of the number of intervening trials since the last presentation of an item on its speed of verification? A possible source confounding this analysis is the number of intervening items that interfere with the target pair. The longer the lag since the last testing of a pair like *doctor–park* the more opportunity there is for the subject to be tested about other propositions involving *doctor* or *park*. The testing of these propositions would strengthen them at the expense of the *doctor–park* proposition. Therefore, we broke our lag data into those cases where there were 0 intervening items, 1 or 2 intervening items, and 3 or more intervening items.

The data, separated according to number of intervening items, are displayed in Fig. 8.11. The data are also separated out according to probability, collapsing over fan. The lags 0 through 2 were collapsed together, as were lags 3–16, 17–64, and lags greater than 65. Figure 8.11 is a plot of reaction times for those combinations of probability, number of intervening items, and lags where there were at least 30 observations. For 0 intervening items, there were enough observations at lags 0–2 and 3–16 and for probabilities .333, .500, and .667. For 0–2 inter-

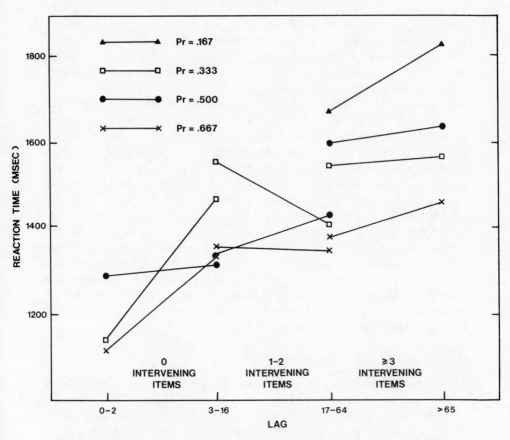

FIG. 8.11   The effects of lag, probability, and number of interfering items on reaction time.

vening items there were sufficient observations only at lags 3–16 and 17–64 and for probabilities .333, .500, and .667. For 3 or more intervening items there were sufficient observations for lags 17–64 and >65 for all probabilities.

A number of facts are apparent from Fig. 8.11. First, holding probability and number of intervening items constant, there is an effect of lag. Eight of the 10 comparisons (connected points in Fig. 8.11) confirm an increasing lag effect. The average increase over these 10 comparisons is 82 msec, which is quite significant ($t_{437} = 3.53; p < .001$). Second, holding lag and number of intervening items constant, there is an effect of probability. For instance, in all six comparisons the reaction time in the .333 case is longer than the reaction time in the .667 case. This shows a proactive interfering effect. The average difference here is 166 msec, which is highly significant ($t_{437} = 3.89; p < .001$). It is predicted by ACT since past strengthening of the interfering connection should result in greater reaction time. Such proactive interfering effects were not predicted by HAM with its GET list ordering of associations. Third, holding lag and probability constant, subjects are slower the more intervening items occur during the lag. This outcome holds for all six comparisons possible in Fig. 8.11. The average affect here is 62 msec, which is also significant ($t_{437} = 2.02; p < .05$). Such retroactive interfering effects are predicted by both ACT and HAM.

There seems to be no current mechanism within ACT to predict the lag effects observed in Fig. 8.11. The only way for the activation of a proposition to be slowed is by the strengthening of interfering links. However, the analysis in Fig. 8.11 controls for this factor. One could argue that this slowing is due to a weakening of the associations between the proposition and the experimental context due to the testing of other propositions not involving the same person and location. This was the analysis offered by Anderson and Bower (1973, Section 15.2) for all interference that is not stimulus specific. The obvious prediction of this contextual-inference model would be that the lag effects in Fig. 8.11 would be much reduced if the intervening activity had been arithmetic or some other demanding task that did not serve to strengthen associations between the context and interfering propositions. This experiment has yet to be carried out. If there is not the anticipated reduction in the lag effect it will be necessary to postulate that the strengths of links are subject to decay. Wicklegren (1974) has suggested a model for decay of strength which might be appropriate here.

Remark on the Use of Strength

The various experimental results reviewed in this section forced the development of a strength concept for describing these networks. I certainly was a reluctant convert to a strength concept. Earlier Gordon Bower and I (Anderson & Bower, 1972) had attacked the application of strength notions as they applied to word recognition judgments. It still seems implausible to attribute recognition judgments to any simple strength measure. ACT still embodies the claim of the Anderson and Bower paper that recognition judgment is based on the retrieval of patterned information from memory. However, strength enters the picture in determining how rapidly this information can be retrieved.

In being forced to accept a strength model I was a victim of the theoretical framework I set up for myself. I am sure one could propose different frameworks that would account for the strength-like results without postulating variations in strength. For instance, one might propose that the search of memory was guided by a wise, but serial, executive who chose to search memory according to various heuristic strategies which tended to favor the more frequent and recent paths. However, I have insisted on regarding the retrieval of information in these experiments as reflecting simple strategy-free processes.

Relation to Quillian's Theory

It seems appropriate to offer some acknowledgment of the similarity between the ACT concept of spreading activation and the ideas of Quillian and subsequent proponents (for example, Collins & Loftus, 1975; Collins & Quillian, 1972; Quillian, 1969). Various results, such as the ones reviewed in this section, have forced me to move away from the HAM search mechanism to a mechanism which incorporates many features of the Quillian model. Anderson and Bower (1973) criticized the Quillian model on three scores: First, it seemed unreasonable to suppose memory had an efficient hierarchical organization in which, if *Collies are dogs* and *dogs are animals* are stored *Collies are animals* will not be stored. Second, Quillian's model assumed that spreading activation was an unlimited parallel process. Third, the model failed to provide an adequate model for rejection of false probes. None of these purported deficiencies of the Quillian model is maintained in ACT's formulation of spreading activation.

In their recent paper, Collins and Loftus (1975) have criticized the first two of the Anderson and Bower criticisms—that the Quillian model implied a strict hierarchical organization and that it was an unlimited capacity parallel model. Their basic point is that the Quillian model made no clear commitments on either of these points. If true, the Quillian model gives up much of its potential for empirical falsifiability. Also, however, if this is true, the ACT model can be seen as a special case of the Quillian model—a special case sufficiently well specified to make predictions and be proven false.

Criticism of the ACT Model for Fact Retrieval

I think the ACT model advanced in this chapter does a good job of explaining in a relatively precise way the effects of a large range of experimental manipulations. However, my suspicion is that it will prove inadequate on at least one score. This concerns the ACT hypothesis that the sole determinant of activation time is the strength of a link *relative* to all others. This predicts that, if a node has a single association, the strength of that association will not affect activation time since the link always has 100% of the total strength. Intuitively this seems wrong. It is hard to test, however, because it is virtually impossible to construct an experimental situation in which it would be reasonable to hypothesize that there existed a node with just a single link.

Related to this problem is the implausibility of the ACT claim that the more one knows about a concept the harder it is to retrieve a fact about that concept. This would predict, for instance, that most subjects would be faster to verify *Birch Bayh is a senator* than *Ted Kennedy is a senator*. In a miniexperiment that I have performed to test this prediction I found that subjects took 2156 msec to verify predicates of four well-known figures and 2501 msec to verify the same predicates of four less well-known figures. It is difficult to know what to make of this result. Perhaps, the *Ted Kennedy* example is verified faster, simply because subjects were faster at encoding the *"Ted Kennedy"* graphemes. There are some experiments that have found the opposite effect of word frequency on reaction times. Dave Kieras (1974) found a weak advantage for low frequency words, and Perlmutter, Harsip, and Myers (1976) have found subjects were slower reacting to high-frequency words. These last two results notwithstanding, my intuition is strongly that the experiment could be designed showing, under some circumstances, that the more past exposure a subject has to a concept the easier it is to acquire and retrieve new information. If this can be shown experimentally, one may need to augment the notion of strength of links with the notion of strength of nodes and postulate that nodes become stronger with more exposure.

Strength of Preexperimental Links

A bothersome fact is the relatively low estimate of preexperimental strength ($K' = 2$) that is being used in fitting the fact-retrieval experiments. This implies that all the preexperimental links involving a concept have total strength equal to two experimental links. It is necessary to have a rather low estimate of K' to prevent activation time from equaling total reaction time. However, there are ways to configure a propositional network and production system to make the retrieval of experimental facts more immune to interference from preexperimental propositions. Figure 8.12 shows a propositional network structured for this purpose. A concept has been built up (made-up-for OF experiment) which identifies those concepts which appear in the experiment. It is assumed the variable Vexp has been bound to this concept. If a concept like *hippie* is used in the experiment, it is intersected with Vexp to create a new concept of hippies used in the experiment. It is to this node that the experimental propositions are attached and not to the general *hippie* concept. In contrast, the preexperimental propositions are attached to the general hippie concept.

The production system in Table 8.5 (page 258) could be modified to process such a memory structure by just changing the encoding production. Rather than P2 one would have:

(P2′)   (Vcon = ENCODE)   ⇒ (Vcon = TEST)
     & (Videa1 = ((Vgen1 W Vper) ∩ Vexp))   & Videa1 & Videa2
     & (Videa2 = ((Vgen2 W Vloc) ∩ Vexp))   & (UNBIND Vper Vloc)

This production, (P2′), binds the variables Videa1 and Videa2 to the experimental concept rather than the general concept.

The speed of application of (P2′) will be affected by the preexperimental fan. The experimental fan will affect the speed of application of Productions (P3) and (P4) in Table 8.5. The important fact about (P2′) is that it is looking for a very simple structure of 3 links. Therefore, there can be relatively high preexperimental strength and yet the total activation time for (P2) will not be great. In contrast, (P3) and (P4), which look for a more complex structure, are only affected by the experimental fan. I have estimated that the total preexperimental strength can be as great as 10 times the strength of an experimental link and still yield satisfactory fits to the data from the person–location experiment.

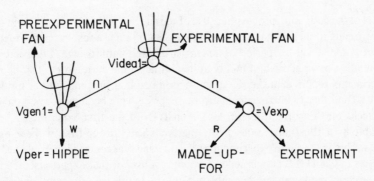

FIG. 8.12 A subconcept for hippie is constructed only relevant to the experimental context. This enables the retrieval process to partially avoid being slowed by the preexperimental facts associated with hippie.

By segmentation of a concept into subconcepts relevant to a particular experimental context it is possible to achieve a considerable reduction in the reaction time necessary to retrieve a proposition. Perhaps this accounts in part for why we are not slower than we are to retrieve facts about very frequent concepts. Perhaps, one effect of a concept's high frequency is to impose a hierarchical division of that concept into subconcepts and to evolve a set of productions that will capitalize on this hierarchical organization to enable rapid retrieval.

Comments on the Parallel–Serial Issue

ACT has been shown in numerous tests in this section to fare better than HAM. Almost every phenomenon reviewed here had the character of being something that ACT could predict and HAM could not. One is tempted to attribute this to the fact that ACT conceives of retrieval from memory in terms of a totally parallel process whereas HAM proposed a mixture of serial and parallel processes. This could be taken as evidence for the claim (page 115) that the mind is a parallel computing device. However, it is necessary to hearken back to the result in Section 1.2 that the parallel–serial issue is not discriminable on the basis of empirical data. We know that HAM is inadequate but there are undoubtedly other serial models that can handle this data.

8.4 MANIPULATIONS OF PROBE SIZE

This fourth section is devoted to presenting three similar and somewhat complex experiments. All three involve manipulation of the number of words in probes presented to subjects. These experiments serve as rather intricate tests of ACT predictions. I am very much encouraged about the basic soundness of the ACT model of the activation process because of the success it shows in predicting all the major trends in these data. The first experiment in this series was performed as a test of HAM. Over the period of a year, struggling with its data, I was led to the formulation of an activation model quite similar to the current one. (Some of the experiments reported in the previous section resulted in some further modifications.) The other two experiments to be reported have been performed basically as checks on the corrections of ACT's analysis of the first experiment.

Table 8.11 illustrates some of the materials used in the first of these experiments. This is the same experiment as the one that was reported in Table 8.3. The analysis in Table 8.3 concerned a particular subset of that experiment. Here we will be concerned with another subset. Subjects in this experiment memorized 40 sentences of the form illustrated in Table 8.11, that is, location, subject, and verb. After committing this information to memory subjects were tested with probes such as those illustrated in Table 8.11.

A subject was instructed to respond true to a probe if all of the elements from a probe came from a study sentence. As Table 8.11 illustrates, a true probe could

TABLE 8.11
Example of Materials in Experiment

Subject studies

In the winery the fireman snored.
In the bedroom the sailor danced.
In the church the hippie danced.
In the church the lawyer played.
In the bakery the hippie played.
In the bakery the lawyer smiled.
In the meadow the banker coughed.
In the meadow the warden blushed.

Types of probes

Trues

1–1–1	WINERY	SNORED	FIREMAN
2–2–2	DANCED	CHURCH	HIPPIE
1–1	WINERY	******	FIREMAN
2–2	LAWYER	PLAYED	*******

Nonoverlapping falses

1–1–1	SMILED	SAILOR	WINERY
2–2–2	DANCED	LAWYER	MEADOW
1–1	FIREMAN	BEDROOM	*******
2–2	*******	LAWYER	MEADOW

Overlapping falses

1–1–1	WINERY	SNORED	SAILOR
2–2–2	DANCED	MEADOW	HIPPIE

consist of either all three or just two content words. The three types of two-element probes were tested equally often. In two-element probes, the missing word was replaced by six asterisks. Note that the order of the words in these probes is random. We did this because we wanted to look at the effect of various types of words (that is, location, verb, and person) and so did not want to have these correlated with serial position. In point of fact, there were no significant effects of word type. For instance, a two-element probe that consisted of person and location was not verified significantly faster or slower than one which consisted of person and verb. Note also that the probes are presented without any English syntax. If we had tried to put the probes into English syntax, the three-word probes would have constituted natural English whereas the two-word probes would be awkward at best. Despite the fact that there is no syntax, it is unambiguous how a subject should assign semantic roles to the words since one is a verb, one a person, and one a location. The asterisks were introduced to equalize the length of two- and three-element probes, in the hope that these maneuvers would equalize encoding time for all the probes.

Note that some words like *danced* occur in two study propositions while other words like *snored* only occur in one. The probes can be classified according to whether they consist of words occurring in one or two study propositions. The terms 2–2–2 and 2–2 refer to probes, all of whose elements are repeated in two study propositions, and 1–1–1 and 1–1 refer to probes whose elements occur uniquely in a single study proposition. Probes were also constructed in which there was a combination of unique and repeated elements but I will not discuss these here. Some of these data are reported in Table 8.3.

The false probes are constructed by taking elements from different study sentences and presenting them in new combinations. A nonoverlapping false probe is one in which no two words come from the same study sentence. An overlapping false probe is constructed by having two of the three elements come from the same sentence. So in the 1–1–1 false WINERY SNORED SAILOR the words *winery* and *snored* come from the same study sentence.

Table 8.12 provides a set of productions to deal with the probes in this experiment, while Fig. 8.13 illustrates the flow of control among these productions. Production (P1) or (P2) will initiate processing of the probe upon its appearance on the screen. The structure (FIRST Vtok) which occurs in both of these productions is shorthand for a memory structure encoding the first element in the probe (see Fig. 4.4a; page 131). If the first element in the probe is a word, (P1) will be satisfied, and if it is a string of asterisks (P2) will be satisfied. The term "ASTERISK" in (P2) denotes a string of asterisks. If (P2) is satisfied control transfers to state (Vcon = START1) to look for the first word. Production (P3), which can execute in this state, is satisfied if the next element is a word. Production (P4), which can also execute in this state, is satisfied if the next element is another string of asterisks. Production (P4) will never be satisfied in this experiment because there are not two asterisk strings in any probe. It was put into the production

TABLE 8.12
A Production System to Respond to the Probes in Table 8.11

	Conditions		Actions
(P1)	(Vcon = START) & ((FIRST Vtok) & (Vtok * Vword) & (Vdone W Vword))	⇒	(Vcon = NEXT) & Vdone & Vtok
(P2)	(Vcon = START) & ((FIRST Vtok) & (Vtok * ASTERISK))	⇒	(Vcon = START1) & Vtok
(P3)	(Vcon = START1) & ((Vtok − Vnew) & (Vnew * Vword) & (Vdone W Vword))	⇒	(Vcon = NEXT) & (Vtok = Vnew) & Vdone
(P4)	(Vcon = START1) & ((Vtok − Vnew) & (Vnew * ASTERISK))	⇒	(Vcon = START1) & (Vtok = Vnew)
(P5)	(Vcon = NEXT) & ((Vtok − Vnew) & (Vnew * Vword) & (Videa W Vword))	⇒	(Vcon = TEST) & (Vtok = Vnew) & Videa
(P6)	(Vcon = NEXT) & ((Vtok − Vnew) & (Vnew * ASTERISK))	⇒	(Vcon = NEXT) & (Vtok = Vnew)
(P7)	(Vcon = NEXT) & (LAST Vtok)	⇒	(Vcon = START) & (PRESS TRUE) & (UNBIND Vtok Vdone)
(P8)	(Vcon = TEST) & (Vprop = (INTERSECTING Vdone Videa))	⇒	(Vcon = NEXT) & (Vdone = Vprop) & (UNBIND Videa)
(P9)	(Vcon = TEST) & (ABS (INTERSECTING Vdone Videa))	⇒	(Vcon = START) & (PRESS FALSE) & (UNBIND Vtok Vdone)

set in Table 8.12 because this set is also intended to model the later two experiments where the subject could encounter two asterisk strings in a row.

The subject reaches state (Vcon = NEXT) either by Production (P1) or (P3). Either of these productions sets Vdone to the idea corresponding to the first word in the probe. In state (Vcon = NEXT), the subject tries to retrieve the idea corresponding to another word in the probe and binds that idea to Videa. Production (P5), out of state (Vcon = NEXT), accomplishes this if the next element is not an asterisk string. If it is an asterisk string Production (P6) is evoked to advance the pointer, Vtok, in the probe string. Production (P5) advances the system to state (Vcon = TEST). In this state there is a test for an intersection of activation between Videa and Vdone. If there is such an intersection, Production (P8) will be satisfied which returns control back to state (Vcon = NEXT). Production (P8) also resets Vdone to a proposition node along the path of intersection between Videa and Vdone.[10] Now the system will try to ascertain whether there is a path of inter-

---

[10]The potential to set a variable to a node along the path of intersection is not permitted by the grammar in Table 6.1, but it has been implemented in the current ACT program. This reflects an oversight in constructing Table 6.1.

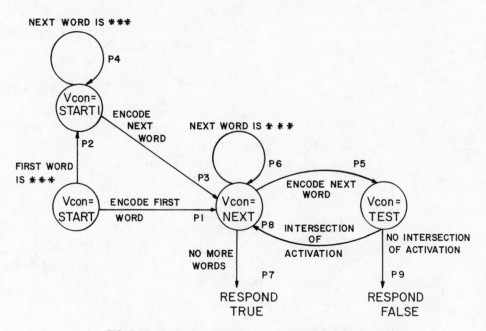

FIG. 8.13   An illustration of the flow of control in Table 8.12.

section between this node and the idea corresponding to the next word in the probe string. Production (P9) will be satisfied if there is no path of intersection between Videa and Vdone. It will cause a false response to be emitted. A true response is emitted by Production (P7). Production (P7) will be satisfied when the system is in state (Vcon = NEXT) and there are no more elements in the probe.

One important feature of this production set is that it is not restricted to the case where the number of elements in the probe set is three. It will apply no matter how many elements are in the probe and no matter in what order these elements occur. This production system just works through the probe, from left to right, making sure that each word is on a path of intersection with the other words. Therefore, this same production system will be used to model some subsequent experiments where four-element probes are used.

The current production system progresses through the probe left to right, but production systems could be constructed which progressed through the probe in other orders or randomly. The evidence from experimental data averaged over subjects is that there is not a preferred order of access. Therefore, I will not pay attention to order in deriving productions.

Predictions can be derived for this experiment given one critical assumption. That assumption is that the principal determinant of reaction time will be the time to activate that network structure which Productions (P8) and (P9) inspect for intersection. This production system involves a cycle between states (Vcon =

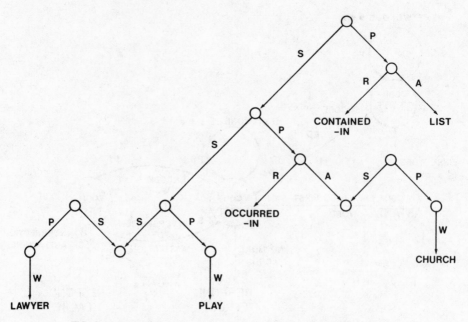

FIG. 8.14   An ACT representation for one of the sentences in Table 8.11.

NEXT) and (Vcon = TEST) as additional words are encoded and tested. Productions (P5), (P6), and (P8) which are involved in the cycle will take time to apply.
However, the assumption is that their rate of application is rapid relative to the
activation process. Therefore, to derive predictions I will estimate the time to
achieve intersection or to detect the absence of an intersection. To this I will simply
add a parameter B to reflect initial encoding and response time.

  Figure 8.14 illustrates the ACT network representation for the sentences used in
this experiment. The production system requires that activations intersect from the
words in the probes. I will first work out the ACT predictions for two-word probes,
assuming a representation like that in Fig. 8.14. There are three possible two-word
probes depending on which two words (person, verb, or location) are used. Predictions can be derived for these cases by means of Eqs. (4) and (8) developed
in Section 8.1. To apply these equations requires that we specify the complexity
(C) of the to-be-activated structure and the number of irrelevant paths (n) for each
of the three possible pairs. If the person and verb concepts are active, the complexity (C) of the structure is 4 links and the number (n) of irrelevant paths is 1.
For a person–location pair $C = 8$ and $n = 2$, while for a verb–location pair $C = 6$
and $n = 2$.[11] One could derive predictions for these three cases separately, but

[11]In reading these derivations a number of months later, it seemed to me that the value of n should
have been 3 for person–location and verb–location pairs. Apparently, I was not counting as an interfering path the link leading to "occurred-in." The consequence of a choice between these two values
for n is minor.

this would taking the details of Fig. 8.14 too literally. (The differential predictions to which Fig. 8.14 leads are not verified.) I want to simply regard it as an approximate measure of complexity. Therefore, I will use average values of C and n for the two-item case. Thus, $C = 6$ and $n = 1.67$. This leads to the following predictions for reaction time to two-word trues and falses (based on Eqs. 4 and 8):

$$\text{TIME(2-word true)} = B + 3\left(\frac{1}{2r} + \frac{3.67}{1 + 3.67r}\right)\alpha \tag{21}$$

$$\text{TIME(2-word false)} = B + 3\left(\frac{1}{2r} + \frac{3.67}{1 + 3.67r}\right)\alpha + F \tag{22}$$

To respond to a three-element true, activations must intersect from all three sources. The number of links interconnecting the three elements is 9 and the number of interfering paths is 2, that is, $C = 9$ and $n = 2$. Therefore, we can use the following equation (derived from Eq. 4) to predict reaction time to a three-element true probe:

$$\text{TIME(3-word true)} = B + 3\left(\frac{1}{3r} + \frac{7.5}{1 + 5r}\right)\alpha \tag{23}$$

The time to respond to a three-word nonoverlapping false will be identical to the time to respond to a two-word false since both can be rejected after encoding only two words. Therefore, the time for three-element nonoverlapping falses is described by Eq. (22). The time to respond to three-element overlapping falses will depend on the position of the two overlapping elements. If they are not the first two considered (as will be the case two-thirds of the time), the time to a overlapping false will be the same as the time to a nonoverlapping false. On the other hand, if the first two elements checked overlap (as will be the case one-third of the time), ACT will retrieve a path of intersection between these two words (Production P8), retrieve the next word (Production P5), and only then determine that there is no intersection between the path of intersection discovered for the first two words and the third word. It is assumed that the time to achieve the first intersection and then note an absence of intersection with the third word is equal to the time to achieve the first intersection and then the second plus the waiting constant F. That is, the time will be Eq. (23) plus the constant F. Overlapping falses will consist of a two-thirds mixture of rejection after considering only the first two words, and a one-third mixture of rejection after considering all three elements. Therefore, the appropriate equation to describe them is:

$$\text{TIME(3-word overlapping false)} = B + \frac{2}{3} \times 3\left(\frac{1}{2r} + \frac{3.67}{1 + 3.67r}\right)\alpha$$

$$+ \frac{1}{3} \times 3\left(\frac{1}{3r} + \frac{7.5}{1 + 5r}\right)\alpha + F \tag{24}$$

With these equations, predictions were derived for the ten conditions illustrated in Table 8.11. The value of r was calculated as $1/(K' + i)$ where i is the number

TABLE 8.13
Data from Subject–Verb–Location Experiment

Conditions	Observations	Error rate	Reaction time	Intersection model
Trues				
1–1–1	524	.034	1220	1299
2–2–2	524	.082	1500	1522
1–1	756	.049	1162	1126
2–2	756	.075	1391	1325
Falses non-overlapping				
1–1–1	262	.015	1275	1293
2–2–2	262	.034	1435	1492
1–1	756	.069	1289	1293
2–2	756	.103	1524	1492
Falses overlapping				
1–1–1	262	.042	1371	1351
2–2–2	262	.063	1587	1558

of experimental propositions associated with a content word and K' is the strength of the preexperimental propositions relative to the experimental propositions. The value of K' was set to 2 as in deriving predictions for previous experiments. The predictions of the model are displayed in Table 8.13. The parameter estimates are $B = 304$, $\alpha = 87$, and $F = 167$. As may be observed, the ACT model does a reasonable job of prediction for the data, accounting for 90.4% of the variance, although the unexplained variance is significant ($F_{7,812} = 3.41$; $p < .01$).

Particularly noteworthy are the ordinal relations in the data which ACT predicts. The three-element true probes are significantly longer ($t_{812} = 2.87$; $p < .01$) than the two-element probes. ACT (via Eqs. 21 and 23) predicts it should take longer to achieve intersection from three sources of activation because it is necessary to wait for the slowest of the three sources to intersect. There should be no effect of probe length on nonoverlapping falses. This is because three-element falses can be rejected by simply considering the first two elements. If anything, subjects react faster with three-element nonoverlapping falses ($t_{812} = 1.78$; $p < .10$). In contrast, as ACT expects, subjects are significantly slower reacting to three-element overlapping falses than either three-element nonoverlapping falses ($t_{812} = 4.28$; $p < .001$) or two-element falses ($t_{812} = 2.50$; $p < .01$).

Location–Name–Verb–Object Experiment

As a test of the generality of these results we performed an experiment that had subjects study four-element probes of the form *In the park Nixon kicked the lawyer*. That is, the sentence consisted of a location, the name of a famous

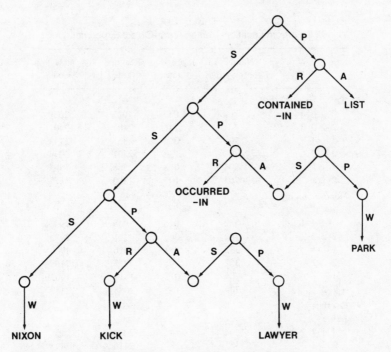

FIG. 8.15   ACT's representation for the sentence *In the park Nixon kicked the lawyer.*

person as subject, a verb, and an object. Figure 8.15 shows an ACT representation for such a sentence. Four-, three-, and two-word probes were derived from these in the same manner as in the previous experiment. Four- and three-word false probes could either be overlapping or nonoverlapping probes. (Four-word overlapping probes matched a study sentence in three words and mismatched in one.) The words in a probe either all occurred in a single proposition or all occurred in two propositions. Table 8.14 presents the data classified according to length of the probe, truth, and propositional fan.

Twenty-two subjects were run. Table 8.14 indicates the number of observations, error rate, and mean reaction time for each condition. Also included are the predictions of the ACT model based on the following equations:

$$T(4\text{-word true}) = B + 3\left(\frac{1}{4r} + \frac{11}{1 + 6r}\right)\alpha \tag{25}$$

$$T(3\text{-word true}) = B + 2.83\left(\frac{1}{3r} + \frac{8.25}{1 + 5.5r}\right)\alpha \tag{26}$$

$$T(2\text{-word true}) = B + 2.84\left(\frac{1}{2r} + \frac{4.67}{1 + 4.67r}\right)\alpha \tag{27}$$

TABLE 8.14
Data from Location–Person–Verb–Object Experiment

	Number of observations	Error rate	Reaction time	Intersection model
Trues				
1–1–1–1	704	.047	1927	2050
2–2–2–2	704	.146	2407	2401
1–1–1	704	.060	1821	1793
2–2–2	704	.138	2201	2094
1–1	704	.048	1568	1598
2–2	704	.107	1890	1877
Nonoverlapping falses				
1–1–1–1	352	.020	1949	1903
2–2–2–2	352	.060	2271	2183
1–1–1	352	.037	1916	1903
2–2–2	352	.045	2211	2183
1–1	704	.072	1813	1903
2–2	704	.135	2088	2183
Overlapping falses				
1–1–1–1	352	.145	2078	2130
2–2–2–2	352	.125	2416	2445
1–1–1	352	.071	2003	1969
2–2–2	352	.116	2318	2256

$$T(\text{4-word nonoverlapping false}) = T(\text{3-word nonoverlapping false})$$
$$= T(\text{2-word nonoverlapping false})$$

$$= B + 2.84\left(\frac{1}{2r} + \frac{4.67}{1 + 4.67r}\right)\alpha + F \qquad (28)$$

$$T(\text{4-word overlapping false}) = B + \frac{1}{2} \times 2.84\left(\frac{1}{2r} + \frac{4.67}{1 + 4.67r}\right)\alpha$$
$$+ \frac{1}{2} \times 3\left(\frac{1}{4r} + \frac{11}{1 + 6r}\right)\alpha + F \qquad (29)$$

$$T(\text{3-word overlapping false}) = B + \frac{2}{3} \times 2.84\left(\frac{1}{2r} + \frac{4.67}{1 + 4.67r}\right)\alpha$$
$$+ \frac{1}{3} \times 2.83\left(\frac{1}{3r} + \frac{8.25}{1 + 5.5r}\right)\alpha + F \qquad (30)$$

The assumptions underlying the derivation of these expressions are the same as for the previous experiment. The parameter estimates are $\alpha = 119$, $B = 473$, and $F = 306$. The quality of the predictions is quite good, accounting for 92.3% of the variance. The unexplained variance in this case is not significant ($F_{11,651}$ = 1.47).

All of the qualitative results in Table 8.13 have been reproduced in Table 8.14 except for one. In Table 8.13 there had been a nonsignificant tendency for reaction time to decrease with the size of a nonoverlapping false probe. In Table 8.14 there is a significant effect in the reverse direction (t_{651} = 2.70; $p < .01$). The production system like that in Table 8.12 would predict no effect of probe size for nonoverlapping falses because it first checks just two items. An effect would be predicted, however, by assuming the subject checked more than two words from the probe by a single production. Therefore, the false data do not serve as a strong test of the ACT model. In contrast, ACT is irrevocably committed to predicting longer reaction times to longer true probes, which the data consistently confirm.

Interaction between Probe Size and Fan

Both Tables 8.13 and 8.14 show that reaction times to true probes increase significantly with probe size. However, the HAM model of fact retrieval would predict that reaction time should decrease as a function of probe size. In the HAM model reaction time is conceived of as determined by the fastest of a number of independent search processes. The fastest time will decrease as the number of words from which to search is increased. ACT predicts the opposite effect of probe size because reaction time is determined by the last, or slowest, process to intersect. So the difference between these two models in their predictions about the effect of probe size results because one postulates independent search and the other an intersection search.

The disconfirmation of the HAM model with respect to the effect of probe size is not too damaging. One could argue that the probes with more content words took longer because of a longer encoding time, and not anything to do with the search stage. An attempt was made to equalize encoding time by making the probes of equal physical length. However, there is no compelling reason to suppose that this manipulation really equated encoding time.

There is, however, a way to test whether the probe size was affecting the encoding stage or the search stage. That is to look for an interaction with propositional fan which presumably affects the search stage. This is a simple application of the Sternberg's (1969) additive factor logic. Note that the ACT model does predict an interaction—the effect of propositional fan should be greater for larger probe size. While the exact mathematical details are somewhat complex, the intuition behind this prediction is fairly clear: It takes longer for all the sources of activation to intersect the more words there are in the probe. This time for intersection is (approximately) multiplied by a factor when the activation rate is slowed by having all words occur in more propositions. The effect of fan occurs because of this multiplication of the intersection time. With longer probes we are multiplying a longer intersection time and so we obtain a greater effect of fan.

The predicted interaction between probe size and fan is sufficiently important to work it out quantitatively. Equation (31) below restates Eq. (3) which describes the time for activations from m sources to intersect:

$$\frac{C}{m}\left(\frac{1}{mr} + \frac{(m + n)}{1 + (m + n)r} \sum_{i}^{m - 1} \frac{1}{i}\right)\alpha \tag{31}$$

The expression C/m is approximately constant for all probe sizes since C (complexity of the pattern) and m (probe size) grow approximately linearly with m. Therefore, we can consider the simpler Eq. (32):

$$X = \frac{1}{mr} + \frac{(m + n)}{1 + (m + n)r} \sum_{i}^{m - 1} \frac{1}{i} \tag{32}$$

What we are interested in is the effect of fan. Increasing fan decreases r (activation rate). So let us look at the derivative of Eq. (32) with respect to r, which indicates how intersection time varies with r:

$$\frac{dX}{dr} = -\frac{1}{mr^2} - \frac{(m + n)^2}{[1 + (m + n)r]^2} \sum_{i = 1}^{m - 1} \frac{1}{i} \tag{33}$$

This expression is negative, indicating that increasing r decreases the reaction time. Or equivalently, decreasing r (for example, by increasing fan) increases the reaction time. To find how the effect of r changes with m we take the derivative of Eq. (33) with respect to m:

$$\frac{dX^2}{drdm} = \frac{1}{m^2r^2} - \frac{(m + n)^2}{m[1 + (m + n)r]^2} - \left(\sum_{i}^{m - 1} \frac{1}{i}\right)\frac{2(m + n)}{[1 + (m + n)r]^2}$$

$$+ \left(\sum_{i}^{m - 1} \frac{1}{i}\right)\frac{2(m + n)^2r}{[1 + (m + n)r]^3} \tag{34}$$

Unfortunately, the expression in (34) will not always be negative. For small enough r it will be positive. However, in the range of values for r that I have been considering in my fits (greater than .2) this value is always negative. This means that in my fits the effect of a decrease in activation rate (r) will produce a greater increase in reaction time at larger m. The reason why the interaction between probe size and fanning reverses at low r is that the activation of a structure like the one in Fig. 8.4 (page 264) becomes principally determined by activation spreading down from the top node rather than activation spreading up from the terminal nodes. The more elements in the probe the faster the top node will be activated. This leads to the prediction that for very poorly learned material (that is, small r) the effect of the propositional fan should be less the larger the probe. This prediction has yet to be tested.

In contrast to the ACT prediction, HAM expects a smaller effect to result from fan for probes of longer length. The effect of fan in the HAM model is due to the fact that subjects will sometimes first search for the wrong proposition from the concept, slowing up retrieval of the correct proposition. In the HAM model this effect is attenuated for longer probes because of two factors. First, the more words in the probe the more likely it is that a search from one of the words will first consider the target proposition. This search process will likely result in a fast acceptance. Second, the more words in a probe the more ways it will mismatch any wrong proposition, allowing for a quicker rejection of erroneous propositions. Therefore, the process will be less delayed in getting to consider the correct proposition.

Table 8.13 shows an interaction that conforms to ACT's predictions. The effect of fan for three-element probes is 280 msec while it is 229 msec for two-element probes. However, this difference is not statistically significant ($t_{812} = .88$). The experiment in Table 8.14 offers a better test of the prediction because it reports data from four-element probes as well as two- and three-element probes. Figure 8.16a presents the true data from this experiment classified by probe length and propositional fan. As can be verified there is the predicted interaction with the effect of fan being greater for longer probes. This interaction is marginally significant ($t_{651} = 1.71; p < .05$, one tailed).

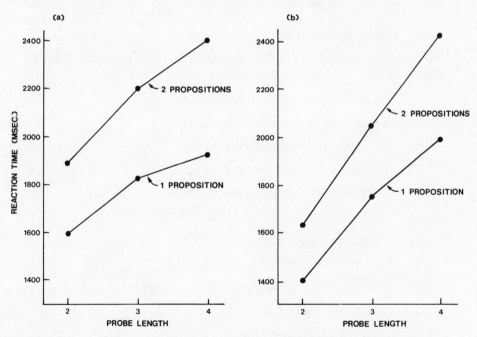

FIG. 8.16   Analyses of interaction between propositional fan and probe length: (a) for location–name–verb–person probes and (b) for person–animal–location–time probes.

A third experiment was performed to test this hypothesis. This experiment had subjects learn sentences of the form *In the office at night the janitor chased the cat.* These were sentences of the form *location–time–person–verb–animal*. The same verb *chased* was used in all sentences and was not used in the probe. Therefore, there were really four elements that varied. Four-, three-, and two-element probes were constructed from location, time, person, and animal. These probes differed somewhat from those in the previous experiments in that asterisks were not used to equalize probe length. So four-element probes were physically longer. Figure 8.16b presents the data from this experiment for the true probes. Note that the functions in this experiment are significantly ($t_{1260} = 3.31; p < .001$) steeper than the functions in the *location–name–verb–object* experiment illustrated in Fig. 8.16a. In that experiment equalizing asterisks had been used. So it seems the use of these asterisks, at least in part, had the intended effect of equalizing encoding time. Figure 8.16b again shows a marginally significant increase in the effect of fan with probe size ($t_{601} = 1.61; p < .10$, one tailed).

The three experiments reported above studied the interaction between probe size and fan for true probes. All three confirm ACT's prediction over HAM. None of these experiments has been overwhelmingly significant, but one can test their combined significance (see Winer, 1971, p. 50). This test is quite significant ($z = 2.42; p < .01$). So the combined force of these experiments is to provide strong support for the ACT model.

Effects of Memory Complexity

The experiment reported in Fig. 8.16b tested another aspect of the ACT theory. Those data came from subjects who had memorized phrases like

(3)   A janitor chasing a cat in an office at night

However, subjects also studied phrases like

(4)   A hippie chasing a chicken in a church

(5)   A fireman chasing a deer in the autumn

(6)   A lawyer in a bank during a rainstorm

(7)   A frog in a swamp during the summer

(8)   A teacher chasing a beaver

(9)   A singer in an attic

(10)   A farmer in the winter

(11)   A raccoon in a cemetery

(12)   A rabbit in a drought

(13)   A garage during a rainstorm

That is, subjects saw phrases realizing all triples, and pairs that could be realized from an original 4-tuple of person, animal, location, and time. Subjects were instructed to imagine the situation described by each of these phrases. The effect of such instructions should be to set up propositional descriptions of the situations referred to by the phrases. Figure 8.17a shows a representation for the four-tuple; Fig. 8.17b shows a representation for a triple, and Fig. 8.17c represents a pair. I have taken the liberty to somewhat simplify these figures by replacing the proposition encoding the list context by "LIST TAG."

Subjects saw pair probes derived from pair, triple, and 4-tuple study phrases, and triples derived from triple and 4-tuple phrases. They also saw 4-tuple probes derived from 4-tuple phrases. The data reported in Fig. 8.16b only concerned pairs, triples, and 4-tuples derived from 4-tuple phrases. (As mentioned earlier these probes did not contain asterisks to equalize probe length—unlike previous experiments that manipulated probe length.) One question of interest is whether reaction time to a probe of the same length will vary as a function of the size of the study sentence from which it is taken. Consider a probe "JANITOR NIGHT" taken from the sentence that resulted in the memory structure in Fig. 8.17a versus Fig. 8.17b versus Fig. 8.17c. The number of links on the path connecting the *janitor* concept and the *night* concept (that is, the variable C) is 8 in Figs. 8.17a and 8.17b but only 7 in Fig. 8.17c. Therefore, subjects should be faster in Fig. 8.17c. The number of interfering links along the path (that is, variable n) is 4 in Fig. 8.17a, 3 in Fig. 8.17b, and 2 in Fig. 8.17c. Therefore subjects should be slowest in Fig. 8.17a. This example illustrates a general point. The more complex the original sentence the more complex the path of intersection for elements in the probe and the slower the subject should be. Averaging over all possible pair probes from a 4-tuple study phrase the mean value of n is 4.5 and of C is 8.5. Averaging over all possible pair probes from all possible triple study phrases the mean value of n is 4.00 and of C is 8. The mean values for two-element study phrases are $n = 2$ and $C = 7$. A similar pattern emerges for three-element probes. Derived from a 4-tuple study phrase, the mean values are $n = 4.75$ and $C = 12.75$. Derived from triple study phrases, the mean values are $n = 3.5$ and $C = 12$. Finally, for a 4-element probe derived from a 4-tuple study phrase the values are $n = 5$ and $C = 17$.

These values were used via Eq. (4) to derive predictions for this experiment. All possible configurations were selected randomly for each subject. I could have tried to predict the differences among configurations—for example, a person–animal probe from a person–animal–location phrase versus a time–location probe from a time–location–animal phrase. This would be taking the ACT representations too literally (see discussion earlier on page 263). I am using the representations simply to get some rough index of the complexity of the structures actually set up by subjects to encode the phrases.

In obtaining predictions for this model it was necessary to introduce an additional parameter W, the time to read a word. In this experiment, unlike previous

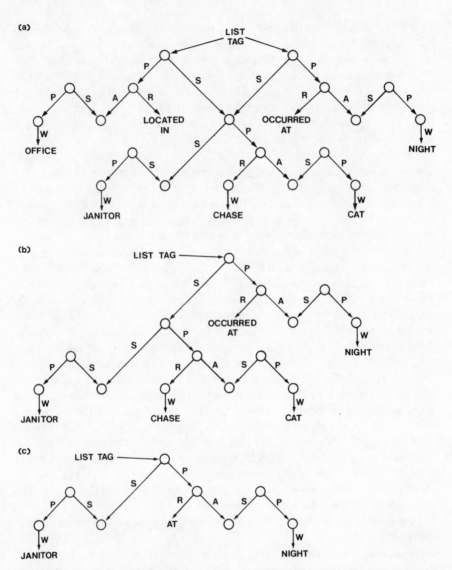

FIG. 8.17   ACT representations for (a) a 4-tuple phase; (b) a triple phrase; and (c) a pair phrase.

ones, no attempt was made to control probe length. Therefore, probes with more words were physically longer and should take longer to encode. The parameter W reflects this factor. The parameter estimates were $B = 412$, $\alpha = 64$, $W = 185$, and $F = 299$. The value of parameter W, 185 msec, is quite reasonable with this interpretation that it is the time to read a word. The data from the experiment and the predictions of the model are given in Table 8.15. The data are classified into

TABLE 8.15
Data from the Person–Animal–Location–Time Experiment

Condition	Number of observations	Error rate	Mean reaction time	Predicted reaction time
Unique true				
2S–2T	528	.057	1212	1133
3S–2T	528	.034	1343	1309
4S–2T	528	.067	1385	1379
3S–3T	528	.057	1581	1642
4S–3T	528	.030	1759	1752
4S–4T	528	.047	2002	2108
Repeated true				
2S–2T	528	.061	1356	1309
3S–2T	528	.066	1523	1539
4S–2T	528	.121	1629	1630
3S–3T	528	.080	1887	1889
4S–3T	528	.106	2050	2037
4S–4T	528	.127	2431	2438
Unique nonoverlapping false				
2S–2T	528	.049	1340	1432
3S–2T	528	.064	1537	1608
4S–2T	528	.040	1651	1678
3S–3T	264	.004	1709	1793
4S–3T	264	.015	1919	1863
4S–4T	264	.008	2095	2047
Repeated nonoverlapping false				
2S–2T	528	.161	1651	1608
3S–2T	528	.159	1846	1838
4S–2T	528	.133	1789	1929
3S–3T	264	.049	2145	2023
4S–3T	264	.034	2127	2114
4S–4T	264	.019	2481	2298
Unique overlapping false				
3S–3T	264	.083	1726	1842
4S–3T	264	.083	1975	1926
4S–4T	264	.129	2061	2227
Repeated overlapping false				
3S–3T	264	.064	2246	2078
4S–3T	264	.080	2276	2188
4S–4T	264	.121	2435	2517

true, nonoverlapping false, and overlapping false. Within this classification they are divided into unique (one study proposition per content word) and repeated (two propositions studied about each content word). Within these classifications the data are broken down according to the complexity of the study sentence from which the probe was derived and according to the length of the probe. The first value is indicated by the digit preceding S and the second by the digit preceding T. If a false probe is designated 4S, this means all the words in the probe come from sentences with four elements. The symbol S should be similarly interpreted throughout for the false probes. The data in Table 8.15 come from 22 subjects. As can be seen the predictions of the model conform quite well to the data. The model accounts for 94.2% of the variance, although the residual unexplained variance is clearly significant ($F_{26,651} = 2.34; p < .001$).

The data clearly show the expected increase in reaction time with complexity of the memory structure. For two-element true probes there is a mean difference of 222 msec ($t_{651} = 3.79; p < .001$) between those derived from four-element study sentences and those derived from two-element study sentences. There is a mean difference of 171 msec ($t_{651} = 2.91; p < .005$) between three-element true probes derived from four-element sentences versus three-element sentences. For false probes, the corresponding effects of complexity are 225 msec ($t_{651} = 3.84; p < .001$) for two-element probes and 118 msec ($t_{651} = 2.01; p < .05$) for three-element probes. The effects for falses are noteworthy in that they present another example of a variable that affects trues and also falses.

8.5   GENERALITY OF THE ACT ACTIVATION MODEL

The reason for focusing research on this fact-retrieval paradigm is the belief that the paradigm permitted somewhat direct inferences about the nature of the activation process. However, a clear implication of the ACT model is that the intersection of activation should be critical to many other tasks. In Section 4 of the next chapter I will discuss the role of these processes in inference making. In this section I consider the role of these processes in other memory tasks.

Interference with Real World Knowledge

One of the most frequent challenges to the fact-retrieval research is whether the basic phenomena are limited to laboratory learned material. A series of experiments by Lewis and Anderson (1975) are relevant to this question. Table 8.16 illustrates the materials of the experiment. Subjects studied 0, 1, 2, 3, or 4 propositions about public figures like Henry Kissinger. After learning these facts they then proceeded to a sentence recognition test. In this test they either saw experimental trues, which were sentences they studied, or preexperimental trues, which were sentences that were really true about the public figure, or falses, which were

TABLE 8.16
Examples of Experimental Materials from the Lewis and
Anderson Experiment

Subject studies

George Washington wrote Tom Sawyer.
Napoleon Bonaparte was from India.
Napoleon Bonaparte is a singer.
Napoleon Bonaparte is a liberal senator.
Napoleon Bonaparte had a ranch.

Preexperimental true

0   Fidel Castro is Cuban.
1   George Washington crossed the Delaware.
4   Napoleon Bonaparte was an emperor.

Experimental true

1   George Washington wrote Tom Sawyer.
4   Napoleon Bonaparte was from India.

False

0   Fidel Castro was a Texan politician.
1   George Washington is a swimmer.
4   Napoleon Bonaparte was a humorist.

neither true in the experiment nor true in the real world. These probes can be classified according to the number of facts learned about the public figure. Each test item in Table 8.16 is prefixed with a digit giving that information.

Figure 8.18 shows the speed of these judgments as a function of probe type and number of propositions studied about the individual. As can be seen, all probe types show an effect of propositional fan. In particular, the preexperimental trues are significantly ($p < .001$) affected by this variable. The model predicts this because preexperimental facts are attached to the same node as the experimental facts and their activation should be slowed down by the number of experimental facts.[12] Note that subjects react much faster to preexperimental trues than to experimental trues. This reflects that these preexperimental facts are much more strongly attached to the individual node. Elsewhere (Lewis & Anderson, 1975) we have presented a mathematical model showing how these data can be approximately fitted by an ACT model.

[12]Even a hierarchical model like Fig. 8.12 predicts an effect of number of experimental facts on time to verify preexperimental facts. In the hierarchical model the more experimental facts the more strength given to the branch that leads to the experimental subconcept. The stronger this branch the more interference to the preexperimental branches.

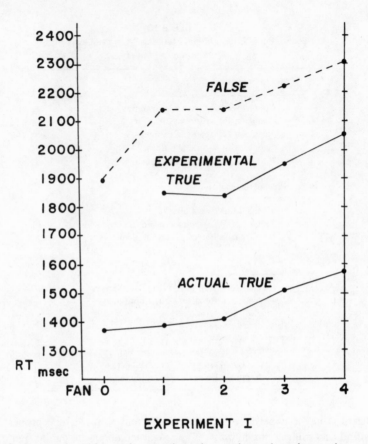

FIG. 8.18   Reaction time to false probes, experimental true probes, and actual true probes as a function of propositional fan.

Sternberg Paradigm

Sternberg (1969) has done considerable work in an experimental paradigm that has some similarity to the fact-retrieval paradigm. It has been described earlier in the book (for example Sections 1.2, 3.3, and 4.3) and is among the best researched phenomena in experimental psychology. The basic result is that the reaction time increases as a function of the size of the positive set that the subject commits to memory. This is analogous to the effect of the number of propositions. Anderson and Bower (1973) provided a model for this paradigm within the framework of the HAM model. We proposed a representation for the positive set such as in Fig. 8.19. A probe element was encoded into a propositional tree and matched against this representation. The HAM search algorithm predicted an increase in RT with positive set size because this would influence the fanning at the predicate node. In order to account for the equal slopes for positives and negatives, Anderson

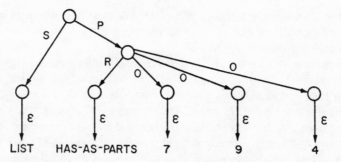

FIG. 8.19   HAM's encoding of a memory set in the Sternberg paradigm (from Anderson & Bower, 1973).

and Bower had to propose that the representation in Fig. 8.19 be searched in an exhaustive manner. This was not an intuitively satisfying assumption.

In the new intersection model a somewhat similar account of the Sternberg paradigm can be provided. The assumed representation is still basically that of Fig. 8.19.[13] Upon presentation of the probe element, it is assumed that there is an attempt to find an intersection between probe digit and the list node. This will be affected by fan for the same reason discussed with respect to fact retrieval. The waiting process model for falsification predicts the same slope effects for positives and negatives. Because the basic search process is a parallel activation looking for an intersection, rather than a serial scan, there is no reason to expect a greater effect of set size on negative judgments.

Interference Phenomena

Anderson and Bower (1973; chapter 15) also extended the HAM search model to the large literature on interference phenomena. It is important that ACT be capable of this generalization for two reasons. First, there is a rich empirical literature which should be addressed by a model claiming to be a general theory of memory. Second, it indicates a direction for practical application of this research. To show that the activation process can have an effect of a few hundred milliseconds in response time is insignificant as a practical matter. However, to show that the activation process may be responsible for failure of recall and forgetting is of great practical significance.

Interference phenomena are best described with respect to the paired-associate paradigm where they have received the most study. The basic paradigm is to have subjects study two lists of word pairs. Various paradigms include the A–B, A–C in which subjects learn responses B and C to the same stimulus A in the two lists. Typically, the subject will learn two lists of approximately 12 word pairs exempli-

---

[13]In the current ACT representation each digit would have to be encoded by a distinct proposition.

fying this relationship. Another paradigm is the A–B, D–C in which the responses to different stimuli are learned. Another paradigm is the A–B, Rest in which the subject does not learn a second list.

The strongest interference phenomena is retroactive interference. This refers to retention of the A–B pair as a function of what follows—learning A–C, learning D–C, or rest. Retention is best with rest, next best with D–C learning, and considerably worse with A–C learning. Thus learning a second response to A produced considerable interference in retention of the original response. Proactive interference refers to poorer retention of a second list pair A–C when preceded by A–B in List 1 than is retention of D–C when it is preceded by an unrelated A–B pair. Retention of a List 2 pair is best when no first list was learned—that is, in a rest, A–B paradigm.

The strong stimulus-specific interference, either proactive or retroactive, in the A–B, A–C paradigm seems related to the effect of propositional fan discussed in earlier sections. Anderson and Bower (1973) suggested that paired-associate pairs are encoded as propositions. Thus, given ''boy–dog'' to learn, the subject might form the proposition ''The word *boy* precedes the word *dog*'' or some mnemonic like ''The boy petted the dog.'' So, the argument is that if the subject learns a pair like ''boy–dog'' in List 1 and a pair like ''boy–house'' in List 2, propositional fanning will be created from *boy* in memory.

An important difference between a recall paradigm and the sentence recognition paradigm is that the subject is not simply being asked to recognize a configuration of elements. He is being asked to retrieve one element given the other. Therefore, the simple intersection procedure discussed earlier will not suffice. Figure 8.20 shows an encoding of the paired associate as the proposition ''*Boy* next-to *dog*

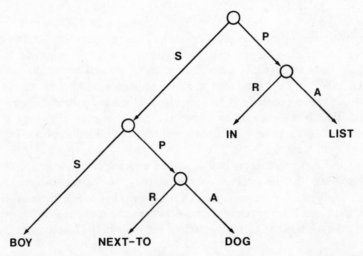

FIG. 8.20   ACT encoding for a stimulus–response pair from a paired associate list.

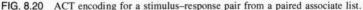

occurred in the list.'' The following pair of productions would be sufficient to permit recall from this memory structure:

(Vcon = START) &   ⇒   (Vcon = RECALL)
(Vstim * (on OF screen))   & Vstim & LIST

(Vcon = RECALL) & ((Vstim *   ⇒   (SAY Vresp)
(next-to OF Vresp)) * (in OF LIST))

In this production system it is assumed that the appearance of a stimulus on the screen causes a proposition of the form *"BOY" is on the screen* to be activated. This enables the first production above to apply. It serves to bind Vstim to the word and set Vcon to RECALL, which enables the second production to apply. The first production also activates LIST. The second production locates the memory structure defined by intersection between Vstim and LIST, binds Vresp to the object in this structure, and generates Vresp as the answer. For a number of reasons, one might expect propositional fan associated with Vstim to be a more potent variable in these recall experiments than in sentence recognition experiments. First, since LIST occurs with many pairs, the spread of activation from LIST will contribute relatively little to the intersection. Second, activation must spread down the branch to Vresp—there is no activation spreading upward. Third, because of the minimal study the links in this information structure will not be as strong as in the sentence recognition experiments.

The interesting question is why this slowing down of the intersection search should result in failure of recall. Anderson and Bower proposed, with respect to the HAM search algorithm, that there was a cutoff time within which the search process must come to a conclusion or fail. The dampening operation in the ACT model serves to provide a cutoff time, too. If the condition of the production is not totally activated within the dampening time, all nodes will be deactivated and the process will have to start all over again. If the time to achieve an intersection is sufficiently slow, it will never be achieved before the dampening time and the production will never be selected. The HAM cutoff time was motivated to prevent long and fruitless searches of GET lists, while the dampening idea was to provide some control over the spread of activation. These are two somewhat different purposes but they have the same effect in producing interference when measured by probability of recall. In the sentence recognition experiments discussed earlier, the assumption was that productions could be activated in predampening time. This was more or less assured by the prerequisite that subjects be able to recall successfully before going on to the reaction time phase of the experiment.

The analysis provided so far is designed to explain retroactive interference. That is, new associations take activation away from the old and prevent intersections from occurring before the dampening time. Proactive interference refers to the interfering effect of older associations on retention of newer ones.

An A–B connection would certainly make the acquisition of A–C harder in that it would take activation away from A–C. This negative effect on learning is referred to as *negative transfer* and is a well-established experimental phenomenon. That is, more trials are required to bring an A–C list to the same learning criterion if it has been preceded by an A–B list. Presumably, this reflects the greater strengthening of A–C required to guarantee it superdampening levels of activation in the presence of A–B.

The effect of these additional strengthening trials, however, should be to guarantee the A–C path the same rate of activation as in the case when it is not preceded by A–B. So why is A–C retained less well when preceded by A–B even if it is brought to the same level of original learning? Perhaps it is necessary to invoke some notion of decay in the strength of a link over time. We saw evidence for such a hypothesis in Fig. 8.11. Wickelgren (1974), on the basis of much research, has proposed that the rate of decay of a link decreases over time. This means that after A–C learning, the A–C link decays more rapidly than the A–B link. Therefore, the relative amount of interference of A–B to A–C grows over time. Thus, eventually, the competing A–B link may prevent recall of the A–C link.

Anderson and Bower (1973) suggested that proactive interference may actually be retroactive interference in disguise. The idea was that subjects rehearsed A–B pairs in the retention interval after A–C learning, producing retroactive interference to A–C pairs. This hypothesis was suggested by some experiments by Houston (1969, 1971) which showed that proactive interference was only obtained when subjects expected a retention test. It was assumed that only under these circumstances would subjects rehearse the A–B pairs. However, I have found in unpublished research that proactive interference is obtained even when rehearsal in the retention interval is controlled.

List Memory Experiments

A series of experiments (for example, Atkinson, Hermann, & Westcourt, 1974; Atkinson & Juola, 1973; Mohs, Westcourt, & Atkinson, 1975) has been performed on subjects' memories for lists of words. The standard procedure is to have subjects learn one or more lists of words to the criterion of perfect recital. Then subjects are required to make judgments about whether particular words occurred in a specified list. It seems that these list judgments can be accommodated by this intersection model. Figure 8.21 illustrates a network representation that encodes information about the contents of a list where the letters A through N represent different words in the list. The judgment that a word is in a list is made by an intersection between the list element and the word.

Atkinson and Juola have found that subjects are slower in responding the longer the list. This can be explained in terms of the contribution of the activation from LIST to the creation of the intersection. The more elements in LIST, the slower will activation spread from LIST to any one of them. Mohs et al. (1975) have had

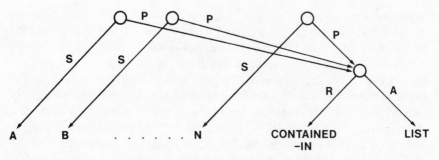

FIG. 8.21   ACT encoding for the contents of LIST.

subjects learn a number of lists, and a particular word could be in more than one list. They found that the more lists a word was in, the longer subjects took to decide whether a word was in a particular list. This can be explained by a slowing in the spread of activation from the word.

An interesting series of experiments has been performed by Perlmutter, Sorce, and Myers (1976). They had subject learn lists of paired associates, and found that both list length and a measure of preexperimental associative strength of the pair predicted the reaction time to recognize a pair. One can think of subjects recognizing the pair by finding an intersection connecting the list to the words. List length would affect the strength of the connection between the list and the words, while associative strength would affect the interconnections among the words.

SUMMARY OF CHAPTER 8

The fact-retrieval paradigm allows one to make rather direct inferences about the spread of activation through memory. This paradigm involves having subjects study sentences and later judge whether word combinations came from studied sentences. An important variable has proven to be the *propositional fan*—the number of study sentences learned about a particular word. Subjects' reaction times are slower to probes containing words of higher propositional fan. This is interpreted as reflecting a slowdown in the spread of activation due to the creation of interfering network paths. Approximately equal effects are found for true probes that consist of elements from the same sentence and false probes which do not. It is argued that subjects respond *true* upon the occurrence of an intersection of activation from all the words in the probe, and respond false after waiting a certain period without such an intersection occurring. This waiting process for falses will adjust its waiting time according to how long it would take for an intersection to occur.

The ACT model is contrasted with the HAM model for fact retrieval which assumes that serial searches proceed out of the concepts in a probe. The HAM model predicts a greater effect of propositional fan for falses versus trues whereas the ACT model predicts an equal effect. The ACT model is confirmed over HAM on this prediction. Both ACT and HAM embody what is called a *multiple-access assumption*—that memory can be accessed from all the concepts in a probe at once. The available data support ACT and HAM over a single-access assumption. HAM predicted that subjects should only be affected by logically relevant paths in memory, whereas ACT claims that spread of activation is insensitive to the logical relation on a path. Again, ACT is confirmed over HAM. ACT correctly predicts, because of its strength mechanism, but HAM does not, that reaction times to probes will be a function of the frequency of testing a probe, independent of its absolute recency of testing and independent of the number of interfering items since the last test. There is also an effect of absolute recency, independent of frequency of number of intervening items. Neither ACT nor HAM predicts this result although ACT's strength mechanism could be augmented to accommodate it.

A series of three experiments is reported in which a principal manipulation is the number of words presented in a probe. The subject's task is to decide whether all the words in a probe come from a single study sentence. The ACT model does a good job of predicting the data from these experiments. It does predict that reaction time will increase with the number of words in the probe and that this effect of probe size will interact with the propositional fan. The data also show, as ACT predicts, that the more complex the original material, the longer is the reaction time. Again these are effects that HAM does not predict.

The ACT activation is capable of predicting results in other experimental situations besides the fact-retrieval paradigm. It successfully predicts interfering effects of experimentally learned material on the speed of retrieval of real world knowledge; it predicts the results obtained in the Sternberg paradigm; it predicts the results of retroactive interference and negative transfer; and it predicts a number of the effects found in experiments where subjects learn lists of words.

REFERENCES

Anderson, J. R. Retrieval of propositional information from long-term memory. *Cognitive Psychology,* 1974, **5,** 451–474.

Anderson, J. R. Item-specific and relation-specific interference in sentence memory. *J. Exp: Human Learning and Memory,* 1975, **104,** 249–260.

Anderson, J. R., & Bower, G. H. Recognition and retrieval processes in free recall. *Psychological Review,* 1972, **79,** 97–123.

Anderson, J. R., & Bower, G. H. *Human Associative Memory,* Washington: Winston, 1973.

Atkinson, R. C., & Juola, J. F. Factors influencing speed and accuracy in word recognition. In S. Kornblum (Ed.), *Attention and performance.* Vol. IV. New York: Academic Press, 1973.

Atkinson, R. C., Herrmann, D. J., & Wescourt, K. T. Search processes in recognition memory. In R. L. Solso (Ed.), *Theories in cognitive psychology.* Hillsdale, New Jersey: Lawrence Erlbaum Assoc., 1974.

Collins, A. M., & Loftus, E. F. A spreading-activation theory of semantic processing. *Psychological Review*, 1975, **82**, 407–428.

Collins, A. M., & Quillian, M. R. How to make a language user. In E. Tulving & W. Donaldson (Eds.), *Organization and memory*. New York: Academic Press, 1972.

Estes, W. K. Some targets for mathematical psychology. *Journal of Mathematical Psychology*, 1975, **12**, 263–282.

Houston, J. P. Proactive inhibition and undetected retention interval rehearsal. *Journal of Experimental Psychology*, 1969, **82**, 511–514.

Houston, J. P. Proactive inhibition and undetected rehearsal: A replication. *Journal of Experimental Psychology*, 1971, **90**, 156–157.

Kieras, D. E. Analysis of the effects of word properties and limited reading time in a sentence comprehension and verification task. Unpublished doctoral dissertation, University of Michigan, 1974.

King, D., & Anderson, J. R. Long-term memory retrieval: An intersecting trace activation model. Unpublished manuscript, 1975.

Lewis, C. H., & Anderson, J. R. Interference with real world knowledge. Unpublished manuscript, 1975.

Mohs, R. C., Wescourt, K. T., & Atkinson, R. C. Search processes for associative structures in long-term memory. *J. Exp: General*, 1975, **104**, 103–121.

Murdock, B. B., Jr., & Anderson, R. E. Encoding storage and retrieval of item information. In R. L. Solso (Ed.), *Information processing and cognition. The Loyola Symposium*. Hillsdale, New Jersey: Lawrence Erlbaum Assoc., 1975.

Perlmutter, J., Harsip, J., & Myers, J. L. The role of semantic knowledge in retrieval from episodic long-term memories: Implications for a model of retrieval. *Memory and Cognition*, 1976, in press.

Perlmutter, J., Sorce, P., and Myers, J. L. Retrieval processes in recall, *Cognitive Psychoogy*, 1976, **8**, 32–63.

Quillian, M. R. The teachable language comprehender. *Communications of the ACM*, 1969, **12**, 459–476.

Sternberg, S. Memory-scanning: Mental processes revealed by reaction time experiments. *Acta Psychologica*, 1969, **30**, 276–315.

Theios, J., Smith, P. G., Haviland, S. E., Traupman, J., & Moy, M. C. Memory scanning as a serial, self-terminating process. *Journal of Experimental Psychology*, 1973, **97**, 323–336.

Thorndyke, P. W., & Bower, G. H. Storage and retrieval processes in sentence memory. *Cognitive Psychology*, 1974, **5**, 515–543.

Wicklegren, W. A. Single-trace fragility theory of memory dynamics. *Memory and Cognition*, 1974, **2**, 775–780.

Winer, B. J. *Statistical principles in experimental design*. New York: McGraw-Hill, 1971.

9
Inferential Processes

Much of human reasoning is supported by a
kind of thematic process rather than by an abstract logic. The principle feature of this thematic
process is its pragmatic rather than its logical
structure.

BRUNER, GOODNOW, AND AUSTIN

In the previous chapter I was concerned with the process by which subjects could
retrieve information that was more or less directly stored in long-term memory. In
this chapter I will be concerned with the situation where that information is not
directly stored but can be inferred from other information that is stored or is otherwise available. The capacity to make such inferences is a fundamental component
of human intelligence. In a certain sense, it enables us to transcend the limitations
of our experience. Therefore, it is important that ACT be shown capable of modeling, and delivering accurate predictions about, the process of making inferences.
This chapter reports what progress I have made in developing ACT models of
inference making. Inference-making tasks serve as a useful testing ground for the
production-related claims of ACT. As will be seen, ACT sometimes makes inferences by stringing together productions. More powerful tests of the character
of productions are possible when we can see the effect of a number of productions
in combination.

ACT's inference-making procedures embody a set of mechanical principles for
reasoning. Therefore, the research on theorem proving in artificial intelligence is
relevant to these inference-making procedures. In the first section of this chapter
I will provide a review of that work. Such a review should give a better perspective within which to evaluate ACT and related psychological data.

In later sections I will make a distinction between what I call *strategic inference making* and *natural inference making*. The difference between the two depends on the context in which the inferences are made. In strategic inference
making the range of possible inferences that the subject must make is severely
limited. An hypothesis of this chapter is that the subject is able to take advantage
of these constraints on the possible form of the arguments to fashion rather efficient
inference rules. Natural inference making occurs in the situation where there are
no or few constraints on the possible inferences that will be required. In this situa-

tion the subject must fall back on more general and less efficient procedures for inference making. The character of our natural inference-making system is of considerable epistemological interest. In Section 2 of this chapter I will discuss how natural inferences would be performed in the ACT system. The third section of this chapter will examine natural inference making as it occurs in syllogistic reasoning tasks. In the fourth and final section I will present an ACT analysis of strategic inference making, and ACT production systems for strategic inference making in some special experimental paradigms.

9.1 MECHANICAL INFERENCE MAKING

There has been a longstanding interest in a machine that would prove theorems, that is, reason according to the rules of logic. Leibnitz (1646–1716) proposed the creation of a "calculus ratiocinator" which would decide all intellectual issues by simple mechanical operations. Interest in mechanical logic was revived by Peano around the turn of the century and by Hilbert's school in the 1920s. A very important development occurred in 1930 when Herbrand developed a mechanical procedure for theorem proving. This has been implemented on the digital computer separately by Gilmore (1960) and by Davis and Putnam (1960). A major breakthrough was made by Robinson in 1965 when he developed a single inference rule, the resolution principle for the first-order predicate calculus. This was shown to be relatively efficient and easily implemented. Many improvements on resolution theorem proving have since been proposed.

There are a number of reviews of this work on mechanical theorem proving (for example, Chang & Lee, 1973; Green & Raphael, 1969; Robinson, 1967). In this section I will look at just a few of the significant developments. First, there is the work of Newell, Shaw, and Simon (1957) on the Logic Theorist. The Logic Theorist is hardly a real contender as a theorem prover, but it and its successor, the General Problem Solver (GPS), constitute the major attempt to develop a simulation model of human theorem proving. Second, a short exposition will be given of the significance of resolution theorem proving. Finally, I will present a review of the criticisms of theorem proving and recent attempts to develop more efficient inference-making systems.

The Logic Theorist

The Logic Theorist was an attempt to develop a program to derive theorems in the fashion of Whitehead and Russell (1935) in their book, *Principia Mathematica*. The *Principia Mathematica* lists five Axiom schema:

Axiom (1):	$(A \vee A) \supset A$
Axiom (2):	$A \supset (B \vee A)$

Axiom (3): $(A \vee B) \supset (B \vee A)$
Axiom (4): $A \vee (B \vee C) \supset B \vee (A \vee C)$
Axiom (5): $(A \supset B) \supset [(C \vee A) \supset (C \vee B)]$

In these expressions $\vee$ stands for logical *or* (inclusive) and $\supset$ stands for logical *implies*. These schema can be taken as the initial theorems of the system. Given these axiom schema new theorems can be derived by three rules of inference—*substitution, replacement,* and *detachment,* and a fourth, derived rule—*chaining*. The rule of *substitution* permits one to replace a term in a theorem by any expression, provided the substitution is made throughout the theorem wherever the term appears. So by substituting $(P \vee Q)$ for A in (2) we get:

$$(P \vee Q) \supset [B \vee (P \vee Q)]$$

The rule of *replacement* allows any connective to be replaced by its definition. Since $(P \supset Q)$ is defined as $(\sim P \vee Q)$ we can rewrite (2) as:

$$\sim A \vee (B \vee A)$$

By the rule of *detachment* if A and $A \supset B$ are theorems, then B is a theorem. This rule might be more familiar to the reader as *modus ponens*. Finally, the chaining rule says if $(A \supset B)$ and $(B \supset C)$ are theorems, then $(A \supset C)$ is a theorem.

The goal of the Logic Theorist was to produce the proofs of the first 52 theorems in *Principia*. Below I present the first of these proofs (and one of the simplest)—a proof of $(P \supset \sim P) \supset \sim P$:

1. $(A \vee A) \supset A$ Axiom (1)
2. $(\sim P \vee \sim P) \supset \sim P$ subs $\sim P$ for A
3. $(P \supset \sim P) \supset \sim P$ replace $\vee$ by $\supset$

The task Newell, Shaw, and Simon undertook was to construct a program which, when given $(P \supset \sim P) \supset \sim P$, produces this proof or some other correct proof.

To provide a standard of nonexcellence in proof finding, Newell, Shaw, and Simon (1957) consider what they called the British Museum Method. This involves taking the original axioms as a base set of theorems—call it S_0. Then a new set, S_1, is derived from this base set by applying the rules of inference. Table 9.1 shows some of the contents of S_1. Theorem 1 is the only one that derives from the rule of chaining. It comes from Axioms (1) and (2). There are no theorems available in S_1 via the rule of detachment. Theorems 3–19 are derived by replacing or ($\vee$) for implies ($\supset$) or vice versa. Then there is an infinite number of theorems that can be added by substitution. I have indicated a few that can be obtained from Axiom (1) in Theorems 20–24. Newell, Shaw, and Simon propose methods of restricting substitution to produce only a finite number of additional theorems.

TABLE 9.1
Some Contents of S_1

Theorem		Axiom
1.	$(A \vee A) \supset (B \vee A)$	(1), (2)
2.	$(\sim A \supset A) \supset A$	(1)
3.	$\sim (A \vee A) \vee A$	(1)
4.	$\sim A \vee (B \vee A)$	(2)
5–19.	replacements	(3)–(5)
20.	$(\sim A \vee \sim A) \supset \sim A$	(1)
21.	$(P \vee P) \supset P$	(1)
22.	$(\sim P \vee \sim P) \supset \sim P$	(1)
23.	$(Q \vee Q) \supset Q$	(1)
24.	$((P \supset Q) \vee (P \supset Q)) \supset (P \supset Q)$	(1)
	etc.	

By a similar move one can construct a set S_2 from S_1 and S_0, a set S_3 from S_2, S_1, and S_0; and so on. All formulas in each set S_n will be theorems. Provided that one has a means of restricting substitution so that the sets are finite, one has a workable algorithm for discovering proofs. To find a proof of $(P \supset \sim P) \supset \sim P$, just start generating sets S_0, S_1, S_2, etc., until the desired formula is found in set S_n. Then the set of formulas in $S_0, S_1, \ldots, S_n$ that led to $(P \supset \sim P) \supset \sim P$ constitutes a proof.[1]

The reader can surely see the difficulty with the British Museum Algorithm. Suppose, as a crude guess, that from each formula in S_n, 10 new formulas can be derived in S_{n+1}. Since S_0, the original set of axioms, has 5 members, there will be 5×10^n formulas in set S_n. This rapid exponential growth would make it impossible to discover proofs of any significant depth. Newell, Shaw, and Simon discuss various ways to make the British Museum Algorithm more efficient, but there is no way to avoid the exponential growth with depth of inference.

The Logic Theorist was proposed as an improvement on the British Museum Method. Rather than starting with the axioms and trying to generate the theorem it started with the to-be-proven theorem and tried to find some path that led back to the already established axioms and theorems. Thus, it reversed the direction of the British Museum Method.

However, just reversing the British Museum Method would produce no great savings. There is the same exponential explosion in possibilities going backward from a theorem as there is in going forward from the axioms. Rather, the method gains its power because it only tries those applications of substitution, replacement, detachment, and chaining which seem to bring the theorems closer to an axiom or an already proven theorem. Consider Theorem 2.02 of the *Principia*,

---

[1] This proof may be greater than n steps long as more than one formula from a set S_i may be involved in the proof.

$P \supset (Q \supset P)$. The Logic Theorist compares this with Axiom (2), $A \supset (B \vee A)$. The main connectives are the same, but the left- and right-hand sides differ. To rectify the difference on the left-hand side it substitutes P for A throughout Axiom (2) to obtain $P \supset (B \vee P)$. It now sets as its subgoal to transform this form into the to-be-proven theorem. It is necessary to replace the $\vee$ in the right-hand side with a $\supset$ but this requires that there be a $\sim$ before the term that precedes the $\supset$. Thus, it replaces B with $\sim B$ to give $P \supset (\sim B \vee P)$, and then replacing $\vee$ by $\supset$ it obtains $P \supset (B \supset P)$. This matches the to-be-proven theorem except for the B which mismatches the Q. This can be remedied by a replacement of a Q for a B. Thus, a proof has been uncovered:

$A \supset (B \vee A)$	Axiom (2)
$P \supset (B \vee P)$	substitution
$P \supset (\sim B \vee P)$	substitution
$P \supset (B \supset P)$	replacement
$P \supset (Q \supset P)$	substitution

The Logic Theorist was apparently much faster than the British Museum Method in discovering a proof to a typical theorem in *Principia*. The problem with the Logic Theorist was that it could not prove all theorems, which the British Museum Method was able to do. That is to say, the British Museum Method is complete and can prove all theorems while the Logic Theorist cannot. For instance, the Logic Theorist cannot prove $P \vee \sim \sim \sim P$. Inspecting Table 9.2, which gives a proof, one can see why the Logic Theorist might fail. This theorem is derived from Axiom (5). However, there is nothing in the to-be-proven formula to suggest Axiom (5):

> Appearances can be deceiving.
> The Logic Theorist goes by appearances.
> $\therefore$ The Logic Theorist can be deceived.

Another heuristic that is characteristic of the Logic Theorist is that it will use already proven theorems as additional axioms from which to work. In this way it

TABLE 9.2
Proof of $P \vee \sim\sim\sim P^a$

		Justification
1.	$(A \supset B) \supset [(C \vee A) \supset (C \vee B)]$	Axiom (5)
2.	$(\sim p \supset \sim\sim\sim p) \supset ((p \vee \sim p) \supset (p \vee \sim\sim\sim p))$	Substitution (1)
3.	$A \supset \sim\sim\sim A$	Previously proven theorem
4.	$\sim p \supset \sim\sim\sim p$	Substitution (3)
5.	$(p \vee \sim p) \supset (p \vee \sim\sim\sim p)$	Detachment (2, 4)
6.	$A \vee \sim A$	Previously proven theorem
7.	$p \vee \sim p$	Substitution (6)
8.	$p \vee \sim\sim\sim p$	Detachment (5, 7)

^{a}This is approximately the proof as it appears in *Principia Mathematica*.

avoids the need to rework a proof of one theorem when attempting to prove another. While this heuristic seems to have been useful in the case of the Logic Theorist, it does not necessarily increase efficiency. If the theorems it has proven are irrelevant to proving an additional theorem, considering previous theorems will slow down the operation of the system.

Altogether the Logic Theorist proved 38 of the 52 theorems in Chapter 2 of *Principia Mathematica*. Apparently, a modified version of the Logic Theorist later proved all 52 theorems (Stefferud, 1963, referred to in Hunt, 1975). So it certainly is not the case that the Logic Theorist could not be extended to handle cases like the proof in Table 9.2. As I have not been able to acquire the Stefferud report, it is unclear whether this modified Logic Theorist is complete, that is, capable of proving all the theorems in propositional calculus, or whether it just succeeded with the 52 in *Principia Mathematica*.

There were two serious deficiencies of the Logic Theorist. First, it turned out to be a bad model of how humans solve such problems. The General Problem Solver (GPS) was developed by Newell and Simon to provide a more accurate psychological model. Second, there do exist discovery procedures for proofs in the propositional calculus which are both complete and more efficient than the Logic Theorist. I will expand upon both points.

The General Problem Solver

One of the tasks to which GPS (Newell & Simon, 1972) was applied was the logic task developed by Moore and Anderson (1954). The subject's task in these experiments was to apply 12 rules for manipulating parenthesized expressions containing letters connected by dots ($\cdot$), wedges ($\vee$), horseshoes ($\supset$), and tildes ($\sim$). The connectors stand for *and, or, implies,* and *not,* respectively. The rules define various permissible transformations of the expressions. That is, they are rules of inference.

However, the subject is not told that this is a task in logic and he is not told the interpretation of the connectives. He treats the connectives entirely in terms of their syntactic properties (as defined by the rules of inference) without reference to meaning. The subject is given a set of expressions like

$$P \vee (Q \vee R)$$
$$\sim (Q \vee R)$$
$$S \supset \sim P$$

and is asked to derive from these another expression, like $\sim Q \supset \sim S$, using the rules.

Subjects in this situation seemed to display some of the features of the Logic Theorist in trying to reduce the difference between the initial formula and the final formula. However, they tended to try to transform the initial formula rather than work backward from the final formula. Therefore, Newell and Simon constructed the General Problem Solver (GPS) to work forward.

The GPS operated by a means–end procedure. As Newell and Simon (1972) describe means–end analysis:

> The main methods of GPS jointly embody the heuristic of means–end analysis. Means–end analysis is typified by the following kind of common-sense argument:
>
> I want to take my son to nursery school. What's the difference between what I have and what I want? One of distance. What changes distance? My automobile. My automobile won't work. What is needed to make it work? A new battery. What has new batteries? An auto repair shop. I want the repair shop to put in a new battery; but the shop doesn't know I need one. What is the difficulty? One of communication. What allows communication? A telephone . . . and so on.
>
> The kind of analysis—classifying things in terms of the functions they serve and oscillating among ends, functions required, and means that perform them forms the basic system of heuristic of GPS. More precisely, this means–ends system of heuristic assumed the following:
>
> 1. If an object is given that is not the desired one, differences will be detectable between the available object and the desired object.
> 2. Operators affect some features of their operands and leave others unchanged. Hence operators can be characterized by the changes they produce and can be used to try to eliminate differences between the objects to which they are applied and desired objects.
> 3. If a desired operator is not applicable, it may be profitable to modify the inputs so that it becomes applicable.
> 4. Some differences will prove more difficult to affect than others. It is profitable, therefore, to try to eliminate "difficult" differences, even at the cost of introducing new differences of lesser difficulty. This process can be repeated as long as progress is being made toward eliminating the more difficult differences. [p. 416].

The GPS would record the differences between the start and the end formulas. It would store the knowledge of which inference rules were relevant to reducing each kind of difference and would try to apply the relevant rules to the initial formulas. If it succeeded then it would have transformed the initial formulas into a form closer to the goal and it could then try to reduce the remaining differences. If the rule could not be directly applied, GPS would set as a subgoal the transformation of the start formulas so that the operator could be applied. The program, so devised, did well in simulating certain aspects of the protocols of subjects who handled these problems.

While its behavior was quite different from the Logic Theorist, GPS shared one basic principle with that program. That was an attempt to reduce the exponential search space generated by the British Museum Method by paying attention to similarities between the beginning and end of a proof. Apparently, humans also are governed by this heuristic of similarity in their solution of such problems.

One warning must be made about interpreting GPS's success in simulating human behavior in the Moore and Anderson task. It may tell us very little about human inference making as it often occurs in natural situations. Any semantic content of the connectives was hidden from the subjects. Thus, any procedures that the subjects used for directing inference making about such connectives could not be evoked. What was being studied in the Moore and Anderson task was the ability of subjects to acquire rules and apply them to symbol structures. The fact that these rules were valid rules of inference was irrelevant. This fact notwithstanding, I suspect GPS is accurate in its general conception of human proof finding and reasoning in logical tasks. In particular, there is ample evidence that humans do tend to let similarity direct their inferential processes—to the point of blinding them to possible proofs. In fact, we will see when we consider categorical syllogisms (Section 3 of this chapter) that subjects are so dominated by surface similarity that they will accept invalid conclusions.

The Resolution Method

In a certain sense, the Logic Theorist was an unnecessary enterprise because perfectly adequate methods already exist for determining whether formulas in the propositional calculus are valid. Probably the best known of these is the method of truth tables. Such procedures can also be expanded to provide proofs. Another procedure is considered here, however—the resolution method. This method is more important for its use in the predicate calculus than in the propositional calculus. It has formed the basis for a complete theorem-proving procedure in the predicate calculus, whereas the method of truth tables cannot be extended to the predicate calculus. A great many disparaging remarks have been made about resolution theorem proving—some of which will be reviewed later. This notwithstanding, it has been a central development in computer inference making and is the culmination of one of the significant intellectual developments of this century. It is important because the procedure is complete (it can achieve any deduction in the predicate calculus) and, relative to other proof procedures, it is efficient.

Resolution theorem proving is most typically used to determine if one logical formula follows from a set of premises.[2] It turns out that if one can do this, he can do a great many related tasks. For instance, to prove a formula is a tautology (or a theorem in the sense of the Logic Theorist), one simply needs to show that this formula is derivable from the null set of premises. To illustrate resolution theorem proving, consider how it might apply to the Moore and Anderson problems. In a typical problem subjects might be presented with a set of formulas like

$$P \supset Q \qquad (1)$$
$$\sim R \supset (P \cdot Q) \qquad (2)$$
$$Q \supset \sim T \qquad (3)$$
$$(P \cdot Q) \supset \sim P \qquad (4)$$

The subject's task is to see if a conclusion

$$\sim P \vee (\sim T \cdot R) \qquad (5)$$

follows from these. The resolution method adds the denial of this conclusion to the set and tries to derive a contradiction. That is, if (1)–(4) and $\sim (\sim P \vee (\sim T \cdot R))$

---

[2]This is the notion of logical consequence that was used in Section 7.2.

lead to a contradiction, then (1)–(4) must imply $\sim P \vee (\sim T \cdot R)$. All resolution proofs are *proofs by contradiction*.

The first step of the resolution procedure is to convert all clauses to *Conjunctive Normal Form*. In this form they are a conjunction of disjunctions of atomic formulas or negations of atomic formulas. Examples are

$$(P) \cdot (Q \vee \sim P)$$
$$(\sim P \vee Q \vee R) \cdot (Q) \cdot (\sim Q \vee S)$$
$$(P) \cdot (\sim P)$$
$$(P \vee \sim P)$$

It is a reasonably simple process to translate formulas into this form. For the above example from the Moore and Anderson task we would change formulas (1)–(4) and the contradiction of the conclusion to

$$\sim P \vee Q \tag{1'}$$

$$(R \vee P) \cdot (R \vee Q) \tag{2'}$$

$$\sim Q \vee \sim T \tag{3'}$$

$$\sim P \vee \sim Q \tag{4'}$$

$$(P) \cdot (T \vee \sim R) \tag{5'}$$

Now the list of formulas in (1')–(5') can be written as a set, S_0, of disjuncts of atomic formulas or their negations: $S_0 = \{\sim P \vee Q, R \vee P, R \vee Q, \sim Q \vee \sim T, \sim P \vee \sim Q, P, T \vee \sim R\}$. The resolution principle allows one to infer from this initial set of disjuncts new disjuncts, and from these, additional disjuncts, and so on. This process of forming disjuncts is continued until a contradiction is uncovered. The resolution principle states that if there are two disjuncts with the same atomic expression negated in one and not in the other, a new disjunction may be inferred by combining these disjunctions and deleting the atomic expression that appears negated in one but not in the other. So, from $A \vee B \vee \sim C$ and $B \vee C \sim D$ we may infer $A \vee B \vee \sim D$ by deleting reference to C. Applying this resolution principle to all pairs of clauses in S_0 one obtains $S_1 = \{R \vee Q, \sim P \vee \sim T, \sim P, Q, R \vee \sim Q, T \vee P, R \vee \sim T, \sim P \vee R, Q \vee T, \sim Q \vee \sim R, \sim Q\}$.[3] All the formulas in S_1 are valid inferences from S_0.

Now the formulas in S_0 and S_1 are resolved with one another to get S_2, a new set of inferences. Note that P from S_0 will be resolved with $\sim P$ from S_1. This will yield nothing in the resolvent, denoted $\square$. This signals that a contradiction has been uncovered. Thus, the addition of formula (5') to (1')–(4') has led to a contradiction. Recall that (1')–(4') were derived from the premises (1)–(4) of the Moore and Anderson problem while (5') was derived from the denial of the conclusion. Since a contradiction has been uncovered from (1')–(5') the conclusion must follow from the premises.

---

[3]$R \vee Q$ in S_1, which derives from $\sim P \vee Q$ and $R \vee P$ in S_0, is already in S_0.

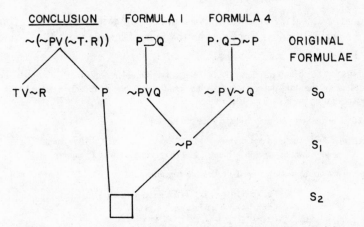

FIG. 9.1 Structure of the refutation generated by the resolution principle.

Figure 9.1 abstracts the essence of this resolution proof. It presents the original formulas (1), (4), and the conclusion (5). Formulas (2) and (3) turned out to be irrelevant. Figure 9.1 gives the disjuncts in S_0 derived from these; and also the formula $\sim P$ in S_1 derived from two formulas in S_0. The formula P in S_0 and $\sim P$ in S_1 led to a contradiction in S_2. From the information in Fig. 9.1, a formal proof can be derived.

The resolution procedure is a complete proof procedure. That is, if a proof of a formula exists, a contradiction will eventually be found as the resolvent sets $S_0, S_1, S_2, \ldots$, are formed. On the other hand, if the set S_0 is consistent, eventually there will be no further resolvents that may be found. Thus, for the propositional calculus resolution theorem proving provides an effective proof procedure. That is, it can tell whether a particular formula follows from a set of premises.

Predicate Calculus

Resolution theorem proving is more important because of its application to predicate calculus, not because of its use in propositional calculus. It would take too much space to properly develop this application here. There are some expositions of this elsewhere (Chang & Lee, 1973; Hunt, 1975; Nilsson, 1971). What I would like to do here is give a simple illustration of the method and discuss how it has been applied in a number of artificial intelligence projects. A typical predicate calculus was defined in Chapter 7 (page 233). It consists of a number of complications not contained in the propositional calculus. Propositions can be analyzed into predicates which take a number of terms as arguments. Terms can be constants, variables, or functions of other terms, and there is the potential for quantification over terms. It is much more difficult to develop proof procedures for the predicate calculus because of the fact that propositions can be decomposed into terms and it is possible to quantify over terms.

It would be useful to illustrate how various sorts of information can be expressed in the predicate calculus. Consider the following example from Chang and Lee (1973, p. 89):

PREMISES: The custom officials searched everyone who entered this country who was not a VIP. Some of the drug pushers entered this country and they were only searched by drug pushers. No drug pusher was a VIP.

CONCLUSION: Some of the officials were drug pushers.

Let $E(x)$ mean "x entered this country," $V(x)$ mean "x was a VIP," $S(x,y)$ mean "y searched x," $C(x)$ mean "x was a custom official," and $P(x)$ mean "x was a drug pusher."

The premises are represented by the following formulas:

$$(\forall x)(E(x) \cdot \sim V(x) \supset (\exists y)(S(x, y) \cdot C(y)))$$
$$(\exists x)(P(x) \cdot E(x) \cdot (\forall y)(S(x, y) \supset P(y)))$$
$$(\forall x)(P(x) \supset \sim V(x))$$

and the conclusion is

$$(\exists x)(P(x) \cdot C(x)).$$

An extension of the resolution principle we studied earlier can be used to verify that the above conclusion does follow from the premises. To do this, we must transform the premises and the negation of the conclusion into a set of disjuncts. When we do this we obtain

$$\sim E(x) \vee V(x) \vee S(x, f(x)) \tag{1}$$

$$\sim E(x) \vee V(x) \vee C(f(x)) \tag{2}$$

$$P(a) \tag{3}$$

$$E(a) \tag{4}$$

$$\sim S(a, y) \vee P(y) \tag{5}$$

$$\sim P(x) \vee \sim V(x) \tag{6}$$

The negation of the conclusion is

$$\sim P(x) \vee \sim C(x) \tag{7}$$

All variables in these disjuncts are implicitly under universal quantification. Note that the existentially quantified y in the first premise has been replaced by $f(x)$ in disjuncts (1) and (2).[4] The existential quantifier y occurred within the scope of the universal quantifier x. Thus, the person y who does the searching may vary with the person x who is searched. This dependence of y on x is captured by the function $f(x)$ which replaces y. Thus, disjunct (1) can be read "for each person (x), either he did not enter the country, or he was a VIP, or he was searched by some person (whose identity depends on him—$f(x)$)." The existentially quantified

---

[4]This is another example of the use of Skolem functions which were described in Section 7.2 (page 236).

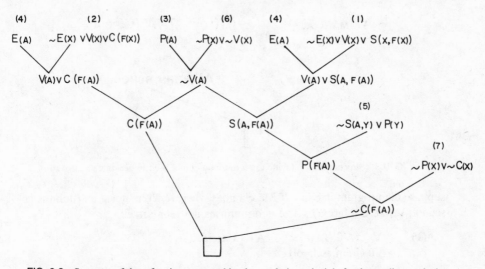

FIG. 9.2   Structure of the refutation generated by the resolution principle for the predicate calculus example.

x in the second premise does not depend on a universally quantified variable. Therefore, x is simply replaced by a constant a in disjuncts (3)–(5).

Figure 9.2 illustrates the resolutions which lead to the null clause. Note, for instance, that $P(a)$ is resolved with $\sim P(x) \vee \sim V(x)$ to obtain $\sim V(a)$. In this, the constant a is substituted for the variable x. Some of the important technical problems solved in the work of resolution theorem proving concern the conditions under which such substitutions can occur. It is because of this work on substitutions that resolution theorem proving is more efficient than earlier procedures.

Resolution theorem proving only constitutes a *semieffective* procedure. If the initial set S_0 is contradictory this will eventually be discovered. However, in some cases where S_0 is not contradictory, the procedure could go on forming resolvents forever. If it has not found the null clause at the nth level of resolvents, it has no way of knowing that the null clause would not occur at the $(n + 1)$th level—except to compute the level. Thus, the resolution procedure can detect if a contradiction exists but can never be sure that one does not exist. It is for this reason that it is called a semieffective procedure. In actual implementation a depth bound is set and computation is halted if the null resolvent does not occur by a certain level of resolvents. It can be proven for the predicate calculus that only semieffective procedures exist (Mendleson, 1964). So, on this score resolution theorem proving is not at a disadvantage to other methods.

Applications of Resolution Theorem Proving

Such theorem provers have found their way into question-answering programs and problem-solving programs (Nilsson, 1971). To provide a very simple example,

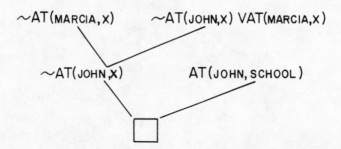

FIG. 9.3   Structure of a refutation in a resolution proof used to generate an answer.

suppose the program is told "If Marcia goes wherever John goes, and John is at school, where is Marcia?" The two premises are represented:

(1) $(\forall x) (AT (John, x) \supset AT (Marcia, x))$
(2)   AT (John, school)

To answer the question "where is Marcia?" the theorem prover is called upon to prove the formula that Marcia is somewhere:

(3) $(\exists x)$ AT (Marcia, x)

Expressions (1'), (2') represent the expressions (1) and (2) suitably transformed and (3') represents the transformed negation of (3):

(1')   AT (John, x) $\vee$ AT (Marcia, x)
(2')   AT (John, school)
(3') $\sim$ AT (Marcia, x)

Figure 9.3 illustrates a resolution proof from (1) and (2) and the negation of (3). In this resolution *school* is substituted for x, providing the answer to the question "Where is Marcia?"

Problems with Resolution Theorem Proving

The basic problem with resolution theorem proving is that it is not particularly efficient. Suppose there are n clauses in the initial level of resolvents S_0. Then there are $n(n-1)/2$ possible pairings of clauses. Suppose a proportion a of these result in resolvents. Then S_1 will consist of $a[n(n-1)/2]$ resolvents. The number of resolvents in S_0 and S_1 will be greater than $(a/2)n^2$. S_2 will be formed by combining the pairs in S_0 and S_1. Assuming a proportion a of the possible pairings result in new resolvents, S_2 will have at least

$$a \left[\frac{a}{2}n^2 \left(\frac{a}{2}n^2 - 1 \right) \right] / 2$$

members. This, together with the members of S_0 and S_1, will be greater than $(a^3/2^3)n^4$. In general, S_m will have more than $n \cdot [(a/2)n]^{2^{m-1}}$ members. This function grows exponentially as a function of an exponential function of m, the depth of the inference. Of course, the reader should be aware that the above derivation is very approximate. Complications that have been ignored could drastically change the character of this function. However, the crude mathematics do serve to illustrate the potential for an exponential growth with depth of the resolution.

Thus, it is not known whether the resolution technique avoids the exponential growth in formulas we associated with the infamous British Museum Method. The advantage it enjoys over the British Museum Method is that the rate of growth with level of inference is generally much less. There are various bookkeeping methods available for cutting down the growth factor. However, even with bookkeeping, resolution theorem proving is inordinately slow in practical applications. There are other, advanced strategies which can also further cut down on this growth factor without sacrificing completeness (see Chang & Lee, 1973). To get a proof under these strategies, however, it is sometimes necessary to compute deeper levels of resolvents than would be necessary without the strategy. Thus, in some cases these strategies can cause more resolvents to be computed.

Despite the fact that these advanced strategies may not be uniformly more efficient, they often lead to efficiencies of orders of magnitude in particular applications. It is unclear whether this is because the advanced strategies are more efficient on most problems or rather just more efficient on most problems of interest. It is interesting that the advanced resolution-theorem provers (for example, Minker, Fishman, & McSkimin, 1973) permit a large variety of higher strategies and allow the user to select a subconfiguration that he thinks will be appropriate to his task. However, even enriched by a set of higher level strategies, resolution theorem proving techniques have not really made their way into practical applications. They are still too inefficient. An open question, of some importance in artificial intelligence, concerns whether there is any way to carry out resolution theorem proving and avoid the exponential growth. An open question of much greater importance is whether there is any complete inference system for the predicate calculus which avoids exponential growth with depth of inference.

A complete system is one which will derive all valid inferences. Many theorists in AI (for example, Minsky, 1975) believe that no complete inference system can be found which would be reasonably efficient. Therefore, of late, there has been a movement in AI to abandon complete systems for more efficient systems which generate most inferences of interest. A good example of this is the PLANNER (Hewitt, 1972) programming language which has become well known in psychology because of the work of Winograd (1972) who used MICRO-PLANNER as his inference system for the blocks world.

Inference Making in Planner

PLANNER consists of a data base of simple facts plus a set of inference rules stored as procedures. Very simple assertions like *Boise is a city* are stored in the data base. However, more complicated assertions that involve logical connectives and quantifiers, like *All canaries are yellow* or *A thesis is acceptable if it is long or it contains a persuasive argument,* are stored as procedure theorems. The distinction between the data base of simple facts and procedure theorems is similar to, although not identical to, the ACT distinction between propositional versus production information.

The theorems in PLANNER are basically of the form condition–result. Thus, the above examples are encoded *If X is a canary then X is a bird* and *If a thesis is long or contains a persuasive argument then it is acceptable.* Theorems can be of the antecedent or consequent variety. Whenever incoming information satisfies the condition of an antecedent theorem it is applied. So if it is asserted *Freaky is a canary* and the above theorem about canaries were an antecedent theorem, PLANNER would add *Freaky is a bird* to the data base.

On the other hand, consequent theorems are only called when they are needed in question answering or problem solving. So, suppose the above theorem was a consequent theorem and it was necessary in some task to establish that *Freaky is a bird.* Then, this consequent theorem would be evoked and a subgoal would be set up to establish that *Freaky is a canary.* This could be established either because that fact was directly stored in the data base or by evoking another consequent theorem. Thus, consequent theorems enable one to chain deductively backward from the to-be-proven fact to already known facts. This is reminiscent of the Logic Theorist.

The distinction between antecedent and consequent theorems may correspond to a significant psychological distinction. To illustrate the distinction in a psychological paradigm, consider the circumstance of reading a paragraph and later answering questions about it. Some questions might tap facts directly stated in the paragraph and answers to these should be quite quick. Other questions might interrogate facts which had to be inferred but which were inferred in the reading of the paragraph (that is, by the psychological analog of antecedent theorems). Finally, there might be other questions which interrogated facts which were not inferred at the time of study but had to be inferred at test (that is, by the psychological analog of consequent theorems). These should take much longer than the other two types of verification.

As Winograd points out, we would not want all inferences to be made in an antecedent mode. There are a potentially infinite number of inferences possible from the assertion of any fact. We only want to store those inferences which are likely to be relevant in the future. So, for instance, upon hearing the fact that *Socrates is human* it would not be particularly useful to store the inference *Socrates has an elbow.*

The PLANNER formalism gains some of its efficiency because it contains the capacity to store task-specific information to direct the course of a deduction. That is, it is possible to store in a theorem information about what other theorems and facts are relevant. For instance, there might be a consequent theorem encoding the fact *If X is human X is fallible.* Since it is a consequent theorem it will be evoked when the goal is to prove someone is fallible. It will set up as a subgoal to prove X is human. It might add as advice to try another theorem which is of the form *If X talks then X is human.* This would be helpful advice if it were the case that in the data base, facts like *Socrates is human* were unlikely to be stored, but facts like *Socrates talked to Plato* were likely to be stored. By directing inference making in this way, the user of MICRO-PLANNER suffers the risk of missing inferences. It may be in this case that *Socrates is human* is directly stored but no fact about Socrates talking is stored. However, the efficiency gained may be worth the occasional missed inferences.

Moroever, PLANNER can be run without advice in which case it would be able to retrieve all such inferences. It is not a complete inference system, however, even in the unadvised mode. In particular, the system has no means for inferring new theorems. By inference it can only add facts to its data base. So, for instance, the following inference would be withheld from it: Suppose it had a theorem encoding *If X is red, then X is a pyramid.* It would be unable to infer the contrapositive theorem *If X is not a pyramid then X is not red.* This inability also means that there are certain types of inferences about the data base that cannot be made. So if MICRO-PLANNER is told, *Superblock is not a pyramid* then it would be unable to answer a question like *Is Superblock red*? In contrast, if told *Superblock is red,* MICRO-PLANNER would not have difficulty in deciding an answer to *Is Superblock a pyramid*? That is, one sign of MICRO-PLANNER's logical weakness is that it cannot perform inferences known as modus tollens in conventional logic while it has no difficulty with the operation of modus ponens.

The basic problem in MICRO-PLANNER is that the information in the procedural theorems is not itself open to inspection. This is similar to the ACT limitation of being unable to inspect the contents of its productions. ACT, too, is prevented from making inferences from the information contained in productions. Since implication is encoded by a production (see Section 7.2) ACT would have the same difficulty with this modus tollens example. As we will see in the next section, ACT can get around this limitation by also encoding implication in the network. I suspect a similar device could be used in the case of MICRO-PLANNER.

9.2   NATURAL INFERENTIAL PROCESSES IN ACT

A distinction was made at the beginning of this chapter between natural inferential processes and strategic inferential processes. The former operate in situations where there is little constraint on the inferences, while the latter operate in situations where sufficient constraints exist on the possible inferences that special strategies can be employed to make the inferential processes more efficient. The focus of this section and the next is on natural inferential processes. There has been a long history of interest in the origins of man's natural inferential processes and in how rational these processes are (for example, see reviews by Henle, 1962;

Wason & Johnson-Laird, 1972). By rational it is usually meant that man's inferential processes should conform to the prescriptions of logic.

There are two observations about the rationality of man's inferential processes which, in combination, seem remarkable. The first fact is that man frequently does not conform to the canons of logic in his inferential behavior—that he does not give the logically correct response to many problems. This by itself would not be that remarkable. It might mean that he simply did not understand the problems. Or it might mean that he did not subscribe to the standard logic, but rather that he was behaving according to some nonstandard logic. However, subjects can usually be made quite easily to acknowledge their mistakes. Thus it seems that subjects understand the problem and accept standard logic but they cannot apply this standard logic to reasoning problems.

A very striking demonstration of this fact comes from a series of experiments performed by Wason (for a review see Wason & Johnson-Laird, 1972, Chapters 13 and 14). Subjects in the paradigm experiment from this research had four cards placed in front of them showing the following symbols:

$$E \quad K \quad 4 \quad 7$$

They are told that each of these cards has a letter on one of its sides and a number on the other. The subject's task is to judge the validity of the following rule which refers only to these four cards.

If a card has a vowel on one side, then it has an even number on the other side.

The subject's task is to turn over only those cards which need to be turned over in order to determine whether the rule is correct. 46% of the subjects elect to turn over both E and 4 which is a wrong choice. The 4 need not be turned over since neither a vowel nor a consonant on the other side could falsify the rule. Only 4% elect to turn over E and 7 which is the correct choice. An odd number behind the E or a vowel behind the 7 would falsify the rule. Another 33% of the subjects elect to turn over only E. The remaining 17% of the subjects make other, incorrect choices. Professional logicians also are subject to the same mistakes. However, most subjects, when told the solution with a little explanation, recognize it as correct and can give a reasonable argument for the correctness of the solution.

This experiment and others suggest that humans are much better at recognizing the validity of an inference than in generating that inference. This section will discuss ACT systems for generating inferences, ACT systems for recognizing valid inferences, the origin of these two systems, and their relation to the rationality of human inferential processes.

Natural Inference System for Generation

It is possible to create mechanical inference systems which can generate all and only the inferences for a logical language. An example would be the British Museum Method described earlier. Such systems are called *complete* because they generate all valid inferences. They are called *sound* because they generate only valid inferences. As an exercise, I have created a complete and sound system for the ACT formalism. (The interested reader may write to me for a description of this system.) It requires the addition of some principles of operations foreign to the current conception of ACT. It is fortunate that the requisite principles are foreign because we would not want it to be the case that ACT were capable of becoming either a complete or sound inference-generating system. Humans are neither complete nor sound in their inference making. In this they are clearly different than the mechanical inference systems discussed in Section 9.1.

One would not want a complete inference system from a practical point of view. An infinite number of inferences is possible from any set of assertions and it would be silly for a system to set about deriving them all. The inference system must be focused on deriving only a relevant subset of the possible inferences.

There are also practical reasons for not wanting a sound system. Such a system would only make inferences if they were necessarily true. A practical inference system should make inferences if these are highly probable. There is no practical purpose in discriminating between a conclusion that has 99.9% probability of being true and one which has 100.0% probability. If a stranger comes up to me, puts a gun in my face, and asks for my wallet it is a likely inference that he wants to steal my wallet. This is in no way a necessary inference, but I would not want my system to refuse to make that inference because of the nicety of logical necessity.

When one considers how productions would be acquired to generate inferences, it is not surprising that the natural inference system is neither sound nor complete. Productions would be acquired to encode the type of contingencies that have tended to be true in past experience. There is no reason why implications which have held in the past should be sound nor why we should have had sufficient experience with all the possible types of implications to have evolved a complete system. Consider the following inference rule:

(P1)   (((Vsubj1 * Vpred1) * (implies OF   ⇒   (Vsubj1 * Vpred1)
(Vsubj2 * Vpred2)) & (Vsubj2 * Vpred2))

This embodies the common fallacy of reasoning from the consequent to the antecedent. It would, for instance, permit the following inference.

> If I was dying the doctor would be frowning.
> The doctor is frowning.
> _____
> Therefore, I am dying.

Or represented as ACT propositions:

> ((I * die) * (implies OF (doctor * frown)))
> (doctor * frown)
> _____
> Therefore, (I * die)

The production (P1), while not valid, may still arise because by chance it has worked, because it is modeled by other people, or because it works as an argument in convincing others. Whatever the source, there is no guarantee that the productions developed by ACT will be valid.

It is easy to think of inferences that ACT should make which will not always be valid. For instance, to use a fashionable example, suppose ACT encounters the sentence "Billy blew out the candles at his birthday party." It would be reasonable for ACT to make the inference that the candles were on the birthday cake and that Billy probably made a wish. This might be encoded by the following production:

(P2)   (V1 * (blows-out OF V2)) & (V1   ⇒   (V4 * cake) & (V2
       * (has OF V3)) & (V2 * candles)   * (ON OF V4))
       & (V3 * birthday party)   & (V1 * make-wish)

The origin of this production might be our frequent encoding of what happens at birthday parties. It is not a valid inference, but from the point of view of the ACT interpreter that executes productions it will be treated no differently than the following valid production which might arise from training on reasoning:

(P3)   ((Vsubj1 * Vpred1) * (implies OF   ⇒   (Vsubj2 * Vpred2)
       (Vsubj2 * Vpred2)) & (Vsubj1 * Vpred1)

Productions (P1)–(P3) give us some examples of what productions that generate inferences would be like in ACT. Note that they have the character of PLANNER antecedent theorems. That is to say, they will apply whenever the requisite patterns are active in the propositional network. If the patterns are active the conclusion is added to memory. Such productions do not wait until there is a need for the inference.

Productions for generating inferences are particularly important to prose processing. Typically prose has the character of leaving much unsaid. The unmentioned material can be important to understanding the message and must be inferred. Therefore, inference-generating productions will have an important role to play in our discussion of language processing in Chapter 11. Such productions have a predictive character in that they tend to predict the truth of other facts from the assertion of certain facts in a text. These productions also have an elaborative function and increase the redundancy of our memory representation for a text. The redundancy-producing feature will prove important in our analysis of memory for prose material in the next chapter.

Effect of Logical Training

People can become more complete and sound as inference makers in a particular domain, with training (for example, a particular field of mathematics), and ACT would predict this. The effect of this training is to set up valid productions for inference making. People can also become more efficient reasoners at a particular task domain as a function of training—again, as ACT would predict. The effect of this training is undoubtedly to evolve a set of heuristic rules like those displayed by GPS and the Logic Theorist. One of the interesting facts is that this training in one domain does not seem to generalize much to other domains. For instance, trained logicians do poorly at the Wason task—just like the rest of us. The reason for this may be the fact that the productions that evolve are specific to the partic- ular content area for which they were designed.

One way a production could be specific to a particular context is by using special nodes for the logical terms that occur in that context. For instance, suppose as a consequence of our logical training we learn the rule of modus tollens—that from *p implies q* and *not q* we can infer *not p*. This could be embodied by the following production:

$$(\text{Vprop1} * (\text{implies}_1 \text{ OF Vprop2})) \quad \Rightarrow \quad (\text{Vprop1} * \text{false})$$
$$\& \ (\text{Vprop2} * \text{false})$$

Note in this production that the relation *implies* is subscripted with a 1. This is to denote that a different concept (that is, a different node) has been set up for implication in the logic situation from the real world situation. It is plausible to suppose that we do set up distinct concepts for implication in the real world versus the logic context. The concept of implication seems to obey somewhat different truth laws in the two contexts. If the antecedent of a real world implication is false the implication seems to lack a truth value, whereas a logical implication would be true in this circumstance. Most logic texts warn the student not to regard logical implication as synonymous with the real world implication. Implication is gen- erally indicated by different physical notation in a logical expression versus a natural language sentence. All these factors would induce us to set up different concept nodes for the two implications. As a consequence productions acquired about *implies*$_1$, the logical concept, will not generalize to *implies*, the natural language concept.

Natural Inference Rules for Recognition

The preceding subsection characterized the natural inference rules for generation as a motley crew. They arise through the happenstance of experience; they are not sound, nor are they complete. Special sets of inferences—more sound and effi- cient—can be developed for special domains with special training. However, these are always somewhat restricted and cannot be generalized to "cure" the total system. It does not seem that we would really want our generated inferences to be cured in any case. While they are not always valid, as practical devices they can be very useful. However, the intellectual community requires that a distinction be made between a plausible inference and a valid inference. Therefore, as a consequence of our formal and informal training, a set of inference rules has arisen for checking the validity of inferences produced by our own generative system or inferences asserted to us by others.

Table 9.3 is an illustration of some ACT productions for the recognition of valid inferences. These productions assume that some source has asserted certain propositions (the premises) as true and is querying whether another proposition (the conclusion) is true. The productions test whether the conclusion follows from the premises asserted by the source. This source might be one's own self checking an argument he has generated. Or it might be an experimenter who is querying the subject (as it will be in the next section). In any case, these propositions are represented in memory as asserted or queried by the source. For instance, suppose it is asserted that *Socrates is a Greek, All Greeks are mortal,* and it is queried

TABLE 9.3
Some Productions for Recognition of Valid Inferences

	Condition	Action
(A1)	((V1 * V3) * (queried-by OF Vsource)) & ((V1 * V2) * (true-by OF Vsource)) & ((V2 * V3) * (true-by OF Vsource))	⇒ ((V1 * V3) * (true-by OF Vsource))
(A2)	((V1 * (V2 ∩ V3)) * (queried-by OF Vsource)) & ((V1 * V2) * (true-by OF Vsource)) & ((V1 * V3) * (true-by OF Vsource))	⇒ ((V1 * (V2 ∩ V3)) * (true-by OF Vsource))
(A3)	((V1 * V2) * (queried-by OF Vsource)) & ((V1 * (V2 ∩ V3)) * (true-by OF Vsource))	⇒ ((V1 * V2) * (true-by OF Vsource))
(A4)	(((V1 ∪ V2) * V3) * (queried-by OF Vsource)) & ((V1 * V3) * (true-by OF Vsource)) & ((V2 * V3) * (true-by OF Vsource))	⇒ (((V1 ∪ V2) * V3) * (true-by OF Vsource))
(A5)	(((V1 * V3) * (queried-by OF Vsource)) & (((V1 ∪ V2) * V3) * (true-by OF Vsource))	⇒ ((V1 * V3) * (true-by OF Vsource))
(A6)	(Vprop2 * (queried-by OF Vsource)) & ((Vprop1 * (implies OF Vprop2)) * (true-by OF Vsource)) & (Vprop1 * (true-by OF Vsource))	⇒ (Vprop2 * (true-by OF Vsource))
(A7)	((Vind1 * (Vr OF Vind2)) * (queried-by OF Vsource)) & ((Vind1 * Vgroup1) * (true-by OF Vsource)) & ((Vind2 * Vgroup2) * (true-by OF Vsource)) & ((Vgroup1 * ((universal OF Vr) OF (Vc C Vgroup2))) * (true-by OF Vsource))	⇒ ((Vind1 * (Vr OF Vind2)) * (true-by OF Vsource))
(A8)	((V1 * (not-a OF (Vc2 C V2))) * (queried OF Vsource)) & ((V2 * (not-a OF (Vc1 C V1))) * (true-by OF Vsource))	⇒ ((V1 * (not-a OF (Vc2 C V2))) * (true-by OF Vsource))

whether *Socrates is mortal*. It is assumed that you, the reader, would represent this:

((Socrates * Greek) * (true-by OF Anderson))
((Greek * mortal) * (true-by OF Anderson))
((Socrates * mortal) * (queried-by OF Anderson))

Production (A1) in Table 9.3 would apply to these propositions with the following binding of variables:

V1 = Socrates, V2 = Greek, V3 = mortal, and Vsource = Anderson.

Production (A1) would serve to add the following proposition to memory:

((Socrates * mortal) * (true-by OF Anderson))

which encodes the fact that this proposition follows from my assertions. Note all the propositions are tagged with their source. This is to prevent them from being regarded as necessarily true. We would not want ACT, after making judgments about the validity of conclusions from hypothetical premises, to emerge actually believing these conclusions and premises.

Note that the recognition productions in Table 9.3 are very much like PLANNER consequent theorems in that they consist of a to-be-proven fact—tagged by (queried-by OF Vsource)—and a set of requisite facts—tagged by (true-by OF Vsource). This contrasts with the productions for inference generation which behaved like antecedent theorems.

Production (A2) encodes that if V1 is a V2 and if V1 is a V3 then it is a V2 and V3. For example, if Canadians are tall and if Canadians are smart, then Canadians are tall and smart. Production (A3) encodes another inference about set intersection. It would allow one to infer from the fact that *Canadians are tall and smart* that *Canadians are tall*. Productions (A4) and (A5) encode two inferences possible about set union. Production (A4) encodes that if V1 is a subset of V3 and V2 is a subset of V3 then (V1 ∪ V2) is a subset of V3. Production (A5) encodes that if (V1 ∪ V2) is a subset of V3, then V1 is a subset of V3. Production (A6) encodes one inference possible from implication—that if proposition Vprop1 implies Vprop2, and if Vprop1 is true, then Vprop2 is true. Production (A7) is a relatively complicated production that will deal with universal quantification of the object (this was discussed earlier in Section 7.3, page 241). It encodes that if all of Vgroup1 have the relation Vr to all of Vgroup2, and Vind1 is in Vgroup1 and Vind2 is in Vgroup2, then Vind1 has relation Vr to Vind2. For instance, it follows from the facts that *All Canadians like all Americans, Fred is a Canadian,* and *Jack is an American,* that *Fred likes Jack.*

Production (A8) is designed to deal with negative universal statements like *No Frenchmen are Canadians* which are used in tasks on categorical syllogisms. This is represented:

(Frenchmen * (not-a OF (x C Canadian)))

where the relation *not-a* applies to the classification for the predicate, *Canadian*. The relation *not-a* must apply to the classification because Frenchmen bear this relation to the whole set and not to the individual Canadians. Production (A8) encodes the inference if no V1 are V2, then it is also the case that no V2 are V1.

The productions offered in Table 9.3 are among those which I suspect most subjects have available. My basis for deciding that these are primitive is my personal intuition and that of a number of colleagues. That is, the inferences they encode seem immediately obvious. Certainly, there could be subjects who do not have such productions and who would not find the corresponding inferences immediately obvious. Creation of these productions depends on appropriate training and some subjects may not have had that training.

There are many valid inferences that would not be directly encoded by a production. For instance, consider the premises *All collies are dogs* and *No cats are dogs* which would be encoded in ACT as:

(1)   (collie * dog)
(2)   (cat * (not-a OF (x C dog)))

There is no production in Table 9.3 that would recognize the validity of the conclusion *No collies are cats,* encoded in ACT as

(3)   (collie * (not-a OF (y C cat)))

However, the validity of this inference can be recognized if one provides ACT with the intermediate step *No dogs are cats.*

(4)   (dog * (not-a OF (y C cat)))

Production (A8) will recognize that (4) follows form (2) and then Production (A1) can derive (3) from (1) and (4). A great many additional inferences can be indirectly recognized by the productions in Table 9.3 by introducing intermediate steps. If ACT is asked whether (3) follows from (1) and (2) and only has the productions in Table 9.3, its ability to recognize this will depend on its ability to generate the requisite intermediate steps. That is, it will depend on the existence of the appropriate generative productions. Osherson (1974) has analyzed reasoning tasks performed by children in terms of the children's ability to generate the intermediate steps needed to make a conclusion obvious.

One question that one might ask about a set of validity-recognizing productions such as those in Table 9.3 is whether it is complete. The productions certainly could not recognize all valid inferences by themselves, but could they, given appropriate intermediate steps, recognize the validity of all inferences? The productions in Table 9.3 are not complete, even with intermediate steps. It is not possible to recognize all valid inferences because the logical vocabulary of the propositional network is not fixed. It is always possible to introduce new terms like ''implies'' which would require the postulation of new validity-recognizing productions to deal with these terms.

The set of validity-recognizing productions is not fixed but can be expanded with experience. Thus, while the set is not complete, appropriate training can be introduced to eliminate any particular point of incompleteness. It is also possible to have validity-recognizing productions which are redundant. For instance, it is possible to have a production which will directly recognize the validity of a subject–predicate inference from a chain of three subject–predicate premises:

$$((V1 * V4) * (\text{queried-by OF Vsource})) \quad \Rightarrow \quad ((V1 * V4)$$
$$\& ((V1 * V2) * (\text{true-by OF Vsource})) \qquad * (\text{true-by OF Vsource}))$$
$$\& ((V2 * V3) * (\text{true-by OF Vsource}))$$
$$\& ((V3 * V4) * (\text{true-by OF Vsource}))$$

However, this production is redundant with (A1) in that anything it will recognize as valid, (A1) will recognize as valid with an intermediate step.

Another question one might ask about validity-recognizing productions is whether they are sound, that is, whether they will only recognize valid inferences. There is no necessary reason that this should be so. For instance, a subject could have the following:

$$((Vprop1 * (\text{queried OF Vsource})) \quad \Rightarrow \quad (Vprop1 * (\text{true-by OF Vsource}))$$
$$\& ((Vprop1 * (\text{implies OF Vprop2}))$$
$$* (\text{true-by OF Vsource}))$$
$$\& (Vprop2 * (\text{true-by OF Vsource}))$$

This production accepts the fallacy of reasoning from the truth of a consequent in an implication to the truth of the antecedent. While such productions are possible, consideration of how validity-recognizing productions arise makes such unsound productions unlikely. That is, these productions are thought to be the result of training explicitly designed to separate valid from invalid inferences.

Another question one might ask is whether there are not also productions that will identify invalid inferences as invalid. For instance, one might have the following production:

$$((V1 * V2) * (\text{queried-by OF Vsource})) \quad \Rightarrow \quad ((V1 * V2)$$
$$\& ((V1 * V3) * (\text{true-by OF Vsource})) \qquad * (\text{true-by OF Vsource}))$$
$$\& ((V2 * V3) * (\text{true-by OF Vsource})) \qquad * \text{false})$$

This production would recognize as not valid the inference from *All criminals are evil* and *All Communists are evil* to *All criminals are Communists*. It is certainly the case that such fallacy-recognizing productions can exist and it seems that the above is one that exists for me. However, it does not seem that subjects would be as effective at recognizing fallacies as they are at recognizing valid conclusions. First, the focus of our logical training in reasoning seems to be to identify which conclusions follow rather than which do not. Therefore, there should not be as rich a set of productions for recognizing invalid inferences as there is for recognizing valid ones. Second, productions for recognizing fallacies cannot combine through intermediate steps to recognize additional fallacies. We will see in the next section that, in fact, subjects are poorer at identifying invalid inferences as invalid than they are at identifying valid inferences as valid.

The Wason Task Reexamined

It would be useful to consider how the Wason task (page 336) could be understood in terms of the distinction between generation and recognition productions. Basically, the subject in this situation is told to test the validity of *p implies q*, and is asked whether he should turn over cards with *p, not p, q,* and *not q*. Suppose the subject tries to test what follows from *p* and *p implies q*, from *not p* and *p implies q*, from *q* and *p implies q*, and from *not q* and *p implies q*. If he decides that something follows from any of these combinations he will turn over the corresponding card. This will require the use of productions for generating inferences. There are three possible productions of interest.

(P4)   (Vprop1 * (implies OF Vprop2)) & Vprop1 $\Rightarrow$ Vprop2

(P5)   (Vprop1 * (implies OF Vprop2)) & Vprop2 $\Rightarrow$ Vprop1

(P6)   (Vprop1 * (implies OF Vprop2)) $\Rightarrow$ (Vprop1 * false)
        & (Vprop2 * false)

Suppose that our typical subject has (P4) and (P5) but not (P6). This is despite the fact that (P5) is not valid and (P6) is. Then the subject will think the *p* card makes a testable prediction by (P4) (which it does) and the *q* card makes a testable prediction by (P5) (which it does not). Not having (P6), he will not think the *not q* card makes a testable prediction (which it does). So, if the typical subjects had Productions (P4) and (P5) but not (P6)—and much common observation suggests that this is so—we would see the pattern of behavior observed in the Wason task.

How is it that a subject can recognize his error when it is pointed out? Suppose he had the following recognition production:

(P7)   ((Vprop1 * (implies OF Vprop2)) $\Rightarrow$ ((Vprop1 * (implies
        * (queried-by OF Vsource))   OF Vprop2))
        & (Vprop1 * (true-by OF Vsource))   * (false-by
        & (Vprop2 * (false-by OF Vsource))   OF Vsource))

This production would enable him to see, when asked to consider the possibility of *p* on the back of the *not q* card, that this card was relevant. Also, the absence of any relevant recognition production would allow him to see that, whether *p* or *not p* had been on the back of the *q* card, the *q* card was irrelevant. Note that the possession of (P7) is not consistent with the possession of (P4), (P5), and not (P6). There is no reason why the total set of ACT productions should be consistent. It is postulated to be the nature of recognition productions that they are more logical than the generation productions and often can detect errors in these productions.

9.3   RESEARCH ON SYLLOGISTIC REASONING

The preceding section on natural inference systems made a distinction between productions for generating inferences and productions for recognizing the acceptability of purported inferences. It was argued that the former kind of inference system did not particularly obey principles of logic—that it encoded the kinds of contingencies which were probable rather than necessarily true. The recognition component is a product of formal and informal education. It tends to be more concerned with the validity of inferences. Most of the research on inferential reasoning has tended to be concerned with recognizing the correctness of inferences rather than generating inferences. Some of that research is done in such constrained experimental situations that I suspect subjects tend to create special strategic inference systems to perform in this task. Therefore, I do not think such experiments tell us anything about the character of the natural inference system. The one situation where it seems least likely that subjects set up strategic inference systems are the experiments on categorical syllogisms (Begg & Denny, 1969; Chapman & Chapman, 1959; Ceraso & Provitera, 1971; Erickson, 1974; Woodworth & Sells, 1935). The inferences required are quite difficult and subjects do not seem able to come up with any special procedures for dealing with the inference problems.

Much of Aristotle's writing on reasoning concerned the categorical syllogism. Extensive discussion of categorical syllogisms can be found in textbooks on logic as recent as that of Cohen and Nagel (1934). Modern logic has largely left the categorical syllogism behind, focusing attention on the more powerful predicate calculus and other logics modeled in that image. However, considerable psychological research has evolved around the study of categorical syllogisms.

A syllogism typically contains two premises and a conclusion which are of a set inclusion nature modified by quantifiers such as some, all, no and not. A simple example is

(A)   All As are Bs
      All Bs are Cs
      ──────────────
∴ All As are Cs

This, incidently, is a syllogism which most people correctly recognize as valid. On the other hand, they accept with almost equal frequency the following invalid syllogism:

(B)   All As are Bs
      All Cs are Bs
      ──────────────
∴ All As are Cs

The conclusion in (B) is neither necessarily true nor false, but rather is *contingent*.

In these experiments, syllogisms are typically presented just with letters in the roles of the categories. Research has been done using real words like *Republicans, conservatives,* and *morons* but it runs into the problem of interactions with the subject's biases about these concepts (see Johnson, 1972).

The general problem subjects seem to have with categorical syllogisms is that they are too willing to accept false conclusions. There are many examples like (B) above where there is no valid conclusion, but subjects accept one in any case. However, subjects are not completely indiscriminate in their acceptance of syllogisms. That is, while they will accept (B) they will not accept (C) and while they will accept (D) they will not accept (E).

(C)   All As are Bs
       All Cs are Bs
       ─────────────────
       $\therefore$ No As are Cs

(D)   No As are Bs
       No Bs are Cs
       ─────────────────
       $\therefore$ No As are Cs

(E)   No As are Bs
       No Bs are Cs
       ─────────────────
       $\therefore$ All As are Cs

To account for this pattern of errors Woodworth and Sells proposed the atmosphere hypothesis. They proposed that the terms used in the syllogism created an atmosphere which predisposed subjects to accept certain conclusions and not others. There are two parts to the atmosphere hypothesis. One part asserts that subjects would accept a positive conclusion to positive premises and a negative conclusion to negative premises. When the premises were mixed, the subjects would prefer a negative conclusion. Thus, they would tend to accept the following conclusion:

(F)   No As are Bs
       All Bs are Cs
       ─────────────────
       $\therefore$ No As are Cs

The other half of the atmosphere hypothesis concerned a subject's response to particularly quantified statements (some) versus universally quantified statements (all or no). As the above examples illustrate, subjects will accept a universal conclusion if the premises are universal. They will accept a particular conclusion if the premises are particular. So they tend to accept (G) and (H) and not (I) and (J).

(G)   Some As are Bs
       Some Bs are Cs
       ─────────────────
       $\therefore$ Some As are Cs

(H)   Some As are not Bs
       Some Bs are not Cs
       _____
  ∴   Some As are not Cs

(I)   Some As are Bs
       Some Bs are Cs
       _____
  ∴   All As are Cs

(J)   Some As are not Bs
       Some Bs are not Cs
       _____
  ∴   No As are Cs

When one premise is particular and the other universal, subjects prefer a particular conclusion. So they will accept the following:

(K)   All As are Bs
       Some Bs are Cs
       _____
  ∴   Some As are Cs

Consider the following incorrect syllogism:

(L)   No As are Bs
       Some Bs are Cs
       _____
  ∴   Some As are not Cs

It seems to compact all of the atmosphere principles into one. Unfortunately, it has not always been found that subjects prefer the particular negative conclusion, given these premises. Chapman and Chapman (1959) found the universal negative conclusion is preferred, that is, *No As are Cs*. However, Woodworth and Sells (1935) and Begg and Denny (1969) have found the atmosphere hypothesis supported on this syllogism.

The apparent illogicality of college students has not been accepted by all psychologists. There have been a number of attempts to explain away the mistakes in reasoning (Chapman & Chapman, 1959; Henle, 1962; Ceraso & Provitera, 1971). One frequent argument is that subjects misunderstand the meaning of the premises. So, for instance, they interpret *All As are Bs* to mean *A equals B*. If so, apparently invalid conclusions like (B) become valid. Ceraso and Provitera contrasted stating syllogisms in an ambiguous form versus less ambiguous form. In the less ambiguous form, *All As are Bs* might become *All As are Bs but there are some Bs that are not As*. Errors were considerably reduced by eliminating ambiguity in the statement of the premises. However, many errors were still made and these remaining errors tended to conform to the predictions of the atmosphere hypothesis.

Another argument advanced by Chapman and Chapman and by Henle is that subjects do not understand or do not accept that they are supposed to reason by the arid rules of logic. Chapman and Chapman propose that subjects continue in the laboratory experiment their everyday, probabilistic ways of reasoning. So, a subject reasons "Some *A*s are *B*s" and "Some *C*s are *B*s"; therefore, it is quite likely that "Some *A*s are *C*s."

The problem with these explanations is that subjects can (and will) recognize that they are wrong when a counterexample is pointed out. So, if the subject is asked to think of the following model—"Some women are lawyers" and "Some men are lawyers"—he quickly acknowledges that it does not follow that "Some women are men," and the subject sees that this counterexample invalidates the more abstract "Some *A*s are *C*s" example. A typical remark from a subject is— "Oh, I didn't think of that possibility." It is not "Oh, I wasn't reasoning according to your rules." The subjects understand what the experimenter means by a valid conclusion and can recognize a valid counterexample. What they cannot do is reason to the conclusion for themselves.

The other tack to account for the poor performance on syllogisms has been to attempt to understand and model the processes that underlie the errors in reasoning. This, for instance, is represented in the work of Erickson (1974). His particular model assumes that subjects interpret premises and conclusions in terms of set relations (which he represents by Venn diagrams). Errors in reasoning occur because subjects fail to see some of the set interpretations compatible with a categorically stated premise, or because they fail to see possible combinations of the set interpretations, or because they incorrectly translate from a set representation of the conclusion to a categorical expression.

An ACT Model for Categorical Syllogisms

Consider what ACT would say about performance on these categorical syllogisms. It would assume that subjects try to judge the validity of syllogisms by means of validity-judging productions of the variety discussed in the previous section (page 340). A subject would not have productions available that would identify all possible valid syllogisms. However, a subset of the valid syllogisms would correspond to existing productions. These syllogisms should be recognized rapidly. Other valid syllogisms would be identifiable if the subject could generate intermediate steps leading to the final conclusion, each step of which could be recognized by an existing validity-recognizing production. Syllogisms that can be so recognized would be recognized much less rapidly than syllogisms which did not require intermediate steps. There may be some valid syllogisms which subjects cannot recognize and for which they cannot generate intermediate steps. They should be in a state of some uncertainty about these. Subjects would also be in a state of uncertainty about how to respond to many nonvalid or contingent syllogisms. There might be productions that would recognize certain contingent conclusions as such, but it is not possible to have a set of productions that will identify all contingent conclusions. Thus, because of the incompleteness of ACT's inference system, there would possibly be some valid syllogisms and certainly some contingent syllogisms that could not be decided by validity-recognizing productions. Faced with syllogisms about which it was uncertain, ACT would have to resort to guessing strategies for decision making and might be led astray by surface features of the premises and display atmosphere-like effects. Past experiments, by insisting that the subject come to a decision on all syllogisms, have not given the subject the opportunity to indicate which syllogisms they are confident of and which they are not. The experiment to follow will allow the subject to indicate uncertainty about a syllogism.

So ACT does not predict that subjects should be able to decide the validity of all inferences. It should be emphasized that it is a general feature of all mechanical inference systems, not just ACT or humans, that they cannot decide of all purported inferences (in rich expressive languages) whether they are valid or not (see page 331). For instance, it can be proven (see Mendleson, 1964) that there is no such decision procedure for the predicate calculus. Thus, a subject's failure to perform perfectly on all syllogisms should not be regarded as a sign of irrationality. It is not logically possible to decide the validity of all inferences. However, a rational system should be able to discriminate between situations where it knows the answer about the validity of an inference and situations where it does not. In those situations where it claims to know the answer, it should be correct. This experiment was performed to see to what degree subjects are rational in this sense.

An Experiment: Recognition of Validity

One purpose of the experiment was to see if there were syllogisms that subjects found obvious and others with which they had difficulty. This experiment included five types of syllogisms—two types which were true and three which were contingent. There were nine examples of each type of syllogism. Thus, there were 45 syllogisms in all. These 45 syllogisms are shown in Table 9.4. One of the groups of true syllogisms, the *easy trues,* seemed (to myself and to my research assistant) to be immediately obvious. In terms of the ACT framework they seemed identifiable by operation of a single validity-recognizing production. The other group of true syllogisms, the *hard trues,* only seemed valid when we went through some intermediate steps, each of which could be recognized as obvious. Therefore, we expected subjects to respond much more confidently, accurately, and rapidly to the easy trues than the hard trues.

Corresponding to the easy trues were nine *easy contingents.* These had the same premises as the easy trues, but a contingent conclusion. An attempt was made to select conclusions that would be favored by atmosphere-like effects. In a similar manner nine *hard contingents* were constructed from the nine hard trues. Finally, there were nine *classic contingents.* These are contingent categorical syllogisms, which past research has shown subjects tend to falsely accept as valid. It was expected that the subjects in this experiment would display particular difficulty with these syllogisms.

Note that the range of form of the syllogisms used in Table 9.4 is wider than

TABLE 9.4
Form of the Syllogisms Used in Reasoning Task

Premise 1	Premise 2	Conclusion
Easy trues		
1. All *A* are *B*	All *B* are *C*	All *A* are *C*
2. All *A* are *B*	All *A* are *C*	All *A* are *B* and *C*
3. All *A* are *C*	All *B* are *C*	All *A* and *B* are *C*
4. Some *A* are *B*	All *B* are *C*	Some *A* are *C*
5. All *A* are *B*	No *B* are *C*	No *A* are *C*
6. Some *A* are *B*	No *B* are *C*	Some *A* are not *B*
7. All *A* are *B*	No *A* are *C*	All *A* are *B* and not *C*
8. No *A* are *C*	No *B* are *C*	No *A* and no *B* are *C*
9. All *A* are *B*	All *B* are *C*	Some *A* are *C*
Easy contingents		
1. All *A* are *B*	All *B* are *C*	All *C* are *A*
2. All *A* are *B*	All *A* are *C*	All *C* are *A* and *B*
3. All *A* are *C*	All *B* are *C*	All *A* and *C* are *B*
4. Some *A* are *B*	All *B* are *C*	All *C* are *B*
5. All *A* are *B*	No *B* are *C*	Some *C* are *A*
6. Some *A* are *B*	No *B* are *C*	No *C* are *A*
7. All *A* are *B*	No *A* are *C*	All *C* are *B* and not *A*
8. No *A* are *C*	No *B* are *C*	No *A* and no *C* are *B*
9. All *A* are *B*	All *B* are *C*	All *B* are *A*
Hard trues		
1. No *A* are *B*	All *C* are *B*	No *A* are *C*
2. All *A* are *B*	All *B* are *C*	Some *C* are *A*
3. All *A* are *B* and *C*	All *C* are *D*	Some *D* are *A*
4. Some *A* are *B*	No *C* are *A*	Some *B* are not *C*
5. All *A* are *B*	No *C* are *A*	All *A* are *B* and not *C*
6. All *A* and *B* are *C*	All *A* and *C* are *B*	The *B* are the same as the *C*
7. No *A* are *B*	No *A* are *C*	No *B* and no *C* are *A*
8. All *A* are *B* and *C*	No *D* are *C*	Some *B* are not *D*
9. All *A* and *B* are *C*	All *C* are *A* and *B*	All *A* are *B*
Hard contingents		
1. No *A* are *B*	All *C* are *B*	All *C* are *B* and not *A*
2. All *A* are *B*	All *B* are *C*	All *C* are *A*
3. All *A* are *B* and *C*	All *C* are *D*	All *D* are *A*
4. Some *A* are *B*	No *C* are *A*	Some *C* are not *B*
5. All *A* are *B*	No *C* are *A*	All *C* are *B* and not *A*
6. All *A* and *B* are *C*	All *A* and *C* are *B*	The *A* are the same as the *B*
7. No *A* are *B*	No *A* are *C*	No *A* and no *B* are *C*
8. All *A* are *B* and *C*	No *D* are *C*	Some *D* are not *B*
9. All *A* and *B* are *C*	All *C* are *A* and *B*	Some *A* are not *B*

(continued)

TABLE 9.4 *(continued)*

Premise 1	Premise 2	Conclusion
Classic contingents		
1. All *A* are *B*	All *C* are *B*	Some *A* are *C*
2. All *A* are *B*	Some *C* are *B*	Some *A* are *C*
3. No *A* are *B*	All *B* are *C*	No *A* are *C*
4. Some *A* are not *B*	All *C* are *B*	Some *C* are not *A*
5. No *A* are *B*	Some *C* are *B*	Some *A* are not *C*
6. Some *A* are *B*	Some *B* are not *C*	Some *A* are not *C*
7. No *A* are *B*	No *C* are *B*	No *A* are *B*
8. No *B* are *A*	Some *B* are not *C*	Some *A* are not *C*
9. Some *B* are not *A*	Some *B* are not *C*	Some *A* are not *C*

the four forms (*All, Some, no,* and *some not*) used in past experiments of syllogisms. The reason for this is because there are very few valid syllogisms of the traditional type and some of these few are just slight variants of one another. In addition to the 45 syllogisms used in Table 9.4, 18 more were created from the hard trues and hard falses. In these syllogisms subjects were given intermediate steps that seemed to make the conclusion more obvious. For instance, to make the fourth hard true more obvious subjects were presented with the following argument:

	1.	Some *A*s are *B*s
	2.	No *C*s are *A*s
From (1) it follows:	3.	Some *B*s are *A*s
From (2) it follows:	4.	No *A*s are *C*s
From (3) and (4) it follows:	5.	Some *B*s are not *C*s

This was called a long hard true. There was also a corresponding long, hard contingent. It had the same intermediate steps (3) and (4) as above but ended in a contingent conclusion. It was expected that the intermediate steps would help subjects recognize the validity of the true conclusions, but have no effect on the contingent conclusions.

Rather than referring to abstract *A*s, *B*s, and *C*s, the syllogisms all referred to balls which varied in color (red, blue, green), size (large, small), and pattern (spotted, striped). Subjects were asked to imagine a bunch of balls scattered on a beach and that the categorical statements described features true of these balls. The meaning of each type of statement was explained to each subject before the experiment. The following illustrates a syllogism that subjects saw in the hard, true condition:

	1.	Some green balls are dotted
	2.	No small balls are green
From (1) and (2) it follows:	3.	Some dotted balls are not small

Another issue that I wanted to explore was the degree to which subjects were able to discriminate between those situations in which he was confident of a conclusion because it was recognized by a production like those in Table 9.3 versus those situations where he was not certain of what to conclude. Almost all past experiments forced subjects to try to come to some conclusion about the validity of a conclusion. There was no way for a subject to indicate when he was confident in his decision and when he was making sophisticated guesses—if indeed such a discrimination can be made.

This experiment involved two changes designed to catch such a difference if one existed. First, subjects were told they could respond with one of three responses to each conclusion: *it follows, it does not follow, I am not certain*. Subjects were encouraged to use the *not certain* category whenever they were in doubt. Every attempt was made to make the *not certain* response respectable, to the point where it was clear to all subjects that it was a demand characteristic of the experiment that they should use the *not certain* category frequently. The hypothesis was that subjects would indicate considerable uncertainty about their decisions for all syllogisms except the easy trues. A second hypothesis is that with the *not certain* category available subjects would accept many fewer contingent syllogisms.

A second deviation from previous experiments was that we collected reaction times of subjects to make their decisions. We expected that subjects should be much faster deciding easy trues than all other syllogisms—indicating that these were being identified by the operation of single validity-recognizing productions.

A payoff scheme was instituted to insure that subjects would be careful in their decisions, and that they would be motivated to respond *not certain* whenever not certain, but that they would respond as fast as was compatible with these two previous requirements. Subjects were given 10 points for every correct decision, but were deducted 50 points for every incorrect decision. On the other hand it did not cost them anything to say *not certain*. They also were given an extra point for every second they responded correctly under ten seconds. Points could be cashed in after the experiment at the rate of 5 points to a penny. Subjects were given an initial start of 500 points. This gave them something that they would not want to jeopardize by reckless guessing.

The procedure was as follows: Subjects sat before a TV screen. Their right and left index fingers rested on buttons for "does follow" and "does not follow." To indicate "cannot decide" the subject had to move his right hand to a center button. The first two lines of a syllogism would come on the screen and remain there until the subject felt he had comprehended them. Then he would press either the right or left button. A conclusion would appear on the screen along with a statement of the lines from which it derived. The subject responded to this conclusion by *it follows, it does not follow*, or *not certain*. Reaction time was measured from presentation of the conclusion to the subject's decision. The subject was given feedback after each decision and told his current score. Past experiments have generally not given subjects feedback. It was hoped in this experiment that feedback would make the subject more discriminative in his responses and prevent him from deluding himself as to how effective he was being at identifying valid conclusions.

If the problem was a long syllogism, the first conclusion would be followed by the appearance of another on the screen—again with an indication of the premises from which it derived. Subjects had to respond to this in the same manner as the first conclusion. This was continued until the final conclusion was reached. Subjects had no way of knowing that a conclusion was final until after they responded. If it was the final conclusion the total problem disappeared from the screen and the premises for a new problem appeared.

Including the long syllogisms there were 63 problems in all. These problems were presented in a different random order to each of 40 subjects. The experiment lasted about an hour. They were paid $2.00 for the experiment plus whatever bonus points they earned (at the rate of 500 points to a dollar). Subject bonus points ranged fom −100 to 1400.

Results

Table 9.5 displays the percentage of the three choices for each of the seven types of problems, plus the mean reaction times of the correct judgments. For the long trues and long contingents, the data are presented for the last conclusion only. This conclusion is identical in form to the last conclusion of the hard trues and hard contingents. As predicted, the easy trues are found to be much easier than all other syllogisms in terms of reaction times and percent choices. Seven of the nine easy trues show a higher percentage correct than the best hard true and three of the hard trues show a lower percentage correct than the worst easy true. A simple sign test on this amount of nonoverlap in the distributions is quite significant ($p < .01$). In terms of reaction time measures, five easy trues are better than the best hard true and five hard trues are worse than the worst easy true. A simple

TABLE 9.5
Results from the Syllogism Judging Experiment

Condition	RT on Correct Responses (sec)	Correct (%)	Wrong (%)	Not certain (%)
Easy true	5.05	88.1	4.4	7.5
Hard true	8.28	69.2	9.7	21.1
Long true	8.90	83.1	2.5	14.4
Easy contingent	8.37	60.6	21.4	18.1
Hard contingent	9.81	52.2	22.5	25.3
Long contingent	11.36	37.8	23.6	38.6
Classic contingent	9.10	41.1	39.2	19.7

sign test of this nonoverlap is also quite significant ($p < .01$). The differences among the other six conditions are less marked than the strong contrast between easy trues and all other conditions.

The use of intermediate steps for the long trues considerably improved subjects' ability to recognize a correct decision. An improved percentage correct was observed on eight of the nine syllogisms ($p < .05$, sign test). However, there was a slight increase in reaction time. This was probably due to the increased scanning time to find the correct premises in a long deduction. A number of subjects spontaneously complained about the problem of searching for the correct premise in long syllogisms.

It was somewhat disappointing to observe the number of errors subjects were making with contingent syllogisms. Over the four types of contingent syllogisms, subjects averaged 26.7% errors and 25.4% use of the not certain category. So approximately one-quarter of the time subjects recognize that they are uncertain about a contingent conclusion. However, another quarter of the time they are unable to discriminate between their confidence about a contingent conclusion and their confidence about a valid conclusion. This is contrary to the hypothesis that a subject's false alarms to contingent premises were largely heuristic guesses which they could discriminate from their responses to the valid conclusions contained in the easy true syllogisms. It may be that subjects were still guessing despite instructions not to and despite a payoff which made it unprofitable to do so. After the experiment, a number of subjects reported that they had responded with *follows* when they were less than certain and that they wished they had not. However, it is unclear how much faith to put in such retrospective reports. This experiment clearly shows subjects are often uncertain about their decisions, but it has failed to provide evidence that most errors in syllogistic reasoning arise from responding under uncertain circumstances.

An interesting feature about subjects under the procedures of this experiment is that they were performing much better than subjects in past experiments. Considering only the classical contingents, where our subjects displayed their worst performance, 41.1% of their responses were correct while 39.2% were false alarms to atmosphere-favored responses. In Chapman and Chapman (1959), 19.9% were correct and 57.4% were false alarms to the atmosphere favored response. In Begg and Denny (1969) these figures were 11.1 and 56.9%. In Ceraso and Provitera, they were 35.8 and 47.9%. In Woodworth and Sells (1935) they were 34.4 and 65.6%. This indicates that subjects under the condition of feedback and instructions urging deliberation are more rational in their judgment of syllogisms than previously credited.

Conclusions from the Experiment

This experiment does not provide a very demanding test of ACT. Almost any pattern of data, including the present one, could be accommodated in the ACT theory. The performance on the true syllogisms could be modeled in ACT by positing validity-recognizing productions which identified the easy trues as valid and the hard trues as valid if inference-generating productions produced appropriate intermediate steps. The advantage of the long trues over the hard trues would be due to the provision of the intermediate steps. The performance on the contingents could be modeled by assuming subjects had in 47.9% of the cases productions that identified the syllogisms as contingent, that they had in 26.7% of the cases invalid productions that accepted the contingent conclusions, and in 25.4% of the cases neither type of production applied and subjects were not certain. The purpose of this experiment, then, was not to test the ACT model but to obtain a better understanding of the nature of subject error in syllogistic reasoning tasks. It has indicated that subjects are indeed frequently uncertain about their decisions but they are also frequently stubbornly wrong.

9.4   STRATEGIC INFERENCE MAKING IN ACT

It turns out that there is a short-cut algorithm (see Cohen & Nagel, 1934, pp. 91–94) for deciding whether categorical syllogisms are valid or invalid. However, this is quite bizarre and no subject has ever reported discovering it. Rather subjects seem to take a more diffuse approach to judging the syllogisms. This is modeled in ACT by the use of validity-recognizing productions. If a syllogism is of a form for which there is a production that will recognize it as valid or invalid the subject will identify it as such. If it can be recognized as valid through generation of intermediate steps it will also be identified. Otherwise, ACT is left in an indeterminate state and will either hazard some guess or report itself as uncertain. Thus, the ACT system for categorical syllogisms had the feature of working or not, depending on the particular problem. It should be pointed out that this was a property of any inference system for a rich language like ACT's propositional network—there are no mechanical procedures which would be able to generate or recognize all the valid inferences. It is for this reason that natural inference systems like ACT are called *noneffective*.

Because natural inference systems must be general enough to apply to a large domain of inferences they consequently will be noneffective. In contrast, for special circumscribed domains it is possible to construct generation systems which will generate all the desired inferences or recognition systems that will identify all the valid inferences. Such inference systems, built up for circumscribed domains, are called strategic inference systems.

There are some real-life situations where we seem to be performing strategic inferences. The best examples would be where we are solving a mathematical problem by a well-defined algorithm (for example, differentiation). Another situation would be where we reason about transitive relations by a simple chaining procedure (for example, if A beat B, and B beat C, and C beat D, then A will beat

D). However, it is striking to me how seldom when I am making inferences that I am proceeding according to any effective algorithm. Natural inference making was so named because it seemed more typical of man in his natural situation. In contrast, it seems many laboratory experiments on inference making study strategic inference making. This is because the types of problems subjects encounter in the experiment are often so circumscribed it is obvious how to develop an effective algorithm to deal with the problems. There are a number of experimental paradigms where it does seem that subjects have evolved special strategic inference systems to perform the tasks. As argued in Section 2.1 many of the sentence comprehension tasks have this flavor. For instance, it was shown there that subjects were much faster at verifying whether sentences describing pictures were true when they knew the type of sentences they would encounter. Another paradigm where it seems subjects are making strategic inferences is in the case of linear syllogisms (for example, Clark, 1969; Huttenlocher, 1968).

Clark's Negation Task

It would be useful to present an ACT production system that will perform a set of strategic inferences. I will present an ACT equivalent of the flow chart in Fig. 2.3 (page 33) suggested by Richard Schweickert for the Clark negation task. A set of productions that processes the sentences in the manner of that flow chart is given in Table 9.6.

In these productions it is assumed that the sentence and the picture are simultaneously on the screen and that encodings of each are active in memory. The picture need only be encoded with respect to what is at the top. Figure 9.4 illustrates the flow of control among these productions. Production (P1) encodes the sentence if it is positive and Production (P2) encodes the sentence if it is negative. These two productions both initialize the truth value of variable Vtruth to *t*, for *true*. They also both set a pair of control variables Vcon1 and Vcon. By setting Vcon = CHECKPREP, Productions (P1) and (P2) enable the execution of Productions (P3) and (P4), which check for the presence of ABOVE. If ABOVE is present, Production (P3) will be satisfied and will set Vtok to the subject of the sentence. Otherwise (P4) will be satisfied and set Vtok to the object. By also setting Vcon1 = PICTURELOOK, Production (P5) is executed in parallel with (P3) and (P4). This production binds Vword to the word that describes the object at the top of the figure.[5] Production (P5) sets the value of Vcon1 = DONE and either Production (P3) or (P4) set Vcon = CHECKTOP. Productions (P6) and (P7) can only be satisfied when Vcon and Vcon1 have these values. Therefore, they must wait for both (P5) and (P3) or (P4) to be executed. Productions (P6) and

---

[5]This is one of the few examples where we take advantage of ACT's capacity to perform productions in parallel. It is seldom the case that the logic of such inference tasks permits more than two types of information to be gathered in parallel.

TABLE 9.6
A Debugged Set of Productions for the Clark Negation Task

	Condition		Action
(P1)	(Vcon = START) & (THE-Vsubj-IS-Vprep-THE-Vobj)	⇒	(Vcon = CHECKPREP) & (Vcon1 = PICTURELOOK) & (Vtruth = t) & Vsubj & Vprep & Vobj
(P2)	(Vcon = START) & (THE-Vsubj-IS-Vneg-Vprep-THE-Vobj)	⇒	(Vcon = CHECKPREP) & (Vcon1 = PICTURELOOK) & (Vtruth = t) & Vsubj & Vprep & Vobj & Vneg
(P3)	(Vcon = CHECKPREP) & (Vprep = ABOVE)	⇒	(Vcon = CHECKTOP) & (Vtok = Vsubj)
(P4)	(Vcon = CHECKPREP) & (ABS (Vprep = ABOVE))	⇒	(Vcon = CHECKTOP) & (Vtok = Vobj)
(P5)	(Vcon1 = PICTURELOOK) & ((Vind1 * (Videa W Vword)) & (Vind1 * (top OF screen)))	⇒	(Vcon1 = DONE) & Vword
(P6)	(Vcon = CHECKTOP) & (Vcon1 = DONE) & (Vtok = Vword)	⇒	(Vcon = CHECKNEG)
(P7)	(Vcon = CHECKTOP) & (Vcon1 = DONE) & (ABS (Vtok = Vword))	⇒	(Vcon = CHECKNEG) (Vtruth = f)
(P8)	(Vcon = CHECKNEG) & Vneg	⇒	(Vcon = SWITCHTRUTH)
(P9)	(Vcon = CHECKNEG) & (ABS Vneg)	⇒	(RESPOND Vtruth) & (UNBIND Vsubj Vobj Vprep Vcon1 Vtok Vtruth Vword) & (Vcon = START)
(P10)	(Vcon = SWITCHTRUTH) & (Vtruth = t)	⇒	(RESPOND f) & (UNBIND Vsubj Vobj Vprep Vcon1 Vtok Vtruth Vword Vneg) & (Vcon = START)
(P11)	(Vcon = SWITCHTRUTH) & (Vtruth = f)	⇒	(RESPOND t) & (UNBIND Vsubj Vobj Vprep Vcon1 Vtok Vtruth Vword Vneg) & (Vcon = START)

(P7) check whether the word in the sentence matches the element on the screen. If there is no match, the value of Vtruth is changed. By setting Vcon = CHECK-NEG, control is passed to Productions (P8) and (P9). If there is no negative in the sentence, Production (P9) executes a response corresonding to the truth index, Vtruth. If there is a negative, (P8) passes control on to Productions (P10) and (P11) which generate a response opposite the truth index stored in Vtruth.

As noted in Chapter 2, this system makes the same predictions as Clark's model. A production system could also be produced whose internal workings corresponded more closely to the internal workings of the Clark model, that is, it would compare a comprehended form of the sentence with a comprehended form of the

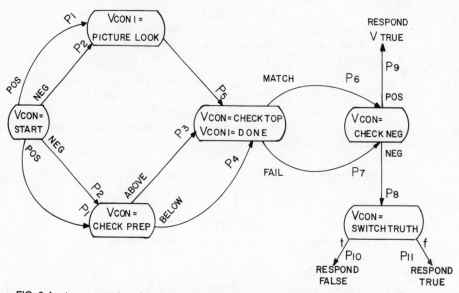

FIG. 9.4   A representation of the flow of control for the production system in Table 9.6 for the Clark negation task.

picture relation. I prefer the production system model in Table 9.6 because it is closer to my introspections about how I perform in the task.

Inference Making in Long-Term Memory

I have been involved in a number of experiments which look further at strategic inference making and which require the subject to retrieve the requisite information from long-term memory. Thus, unlike the Chase and Clark situation, the information is not immediately available. Rather it has to be activated in long-term memory before the appropriate productions can apply to it. These experiments are particularly useful because they serve to test how well the production system interfaces with the memory system. Experiment 2 in Section 6.3 was also concerned with testing how well the ACT model of memory interfaced with the ACT production system. Two experiments will be reported in this section. The first I did with David King and Rebecca Paulson. In this experiment we had subjects learn various rules about actions involving famous people. For instance, the subject might learn

(1)   People who kicked Nixon were tall.

or

(2)   People who Kissinger liked were charming.

Sentences like (1) are referred to as *subject rules* because they are rules about the subject of the verb whereas sentences like (2) are referred to as *object rules*. These sentences can be represented in ACT by the following propositional structures:

(3)   ((kick OF Nixon) * charming)
(4)   ((liked-by OF Kissinger) * charming)

The actual sentences learned were either in the unique or repeated condition. Sentences in the unique condition had person, verb, and adjective which appeared in just one sentence whereas sentences in the repeated condition had words which appeared in two sentences. So by this means propositional fan was manipulated. After learning these sentences subjects were put in a reaction time task where on a particular trial they were either given one of the original sentences to verify

(5)   People who kicked Nixon were tall.

or a two-line inference such as the following:

(6)   Fred kicks Nixon.
       Fred is tall.

The first sentence in this two-line inference could also be in the passive voice. So a subject might also see

(7)   Nixon was kicked by Fred.
       Fred is tall.

False probes were constructed by reversing subject and object. So after studying (1) a subject might see the verification:

(8)   People who Nixon kicked were tall.

or the two-line inference:

(9)   Nixon kicked Fred.
       Fred was tall.

False two-line inferences were also created by changing the adjective. Thus, a subject might see:

(10)   Fred kicked Nixon.
        Fred was charming.

Two-line inferences like (10) were inserted to force the subject to read the second sentence. Otherwise subjects could have made their decisions by only reading the first sentence of an inference. Falses created by reversing subject and object will be referred to as False 1 and those by changing adjectives as False 2.

Table 9.7 shows the productions required to perform in this task. Figure 9.5 illustrates the flow of control for this production set. Productions (P1) and (P2)

TABLE 9.7
Debugged Productions for the Action Rule Study

	Condition	Action
(P1)	(Vcon = START & ((PEOPLE-WHO-Vverb-Vper-ARE-Vadj) & (Vper * famous))	⇒ (Vcon = SUBJECT) & Vverb & Vper & Vadj
(P2)	(Vcon = START) & ((PEOPLE-WHO-Vper-Vverb-ARE-Vadj) & (Vper * famous))	⇒ (Vcon = OBJECT) & Vverb & Vper & Vadj
(P3)	(Vcon = START) & ((Vname-Vverb-(Vper) & (Vper * famous))	⇒ (Vcon = SECOND) & (Vcon1 = SUBJECT) & Vper & Vverb & Vname
(P4)	(Vcon = START) & ((Vper-Vverb-Vname) & (Vper * famous))	⇒ (Vcon = SECOND) & (Vcon1 = OBJECT) & Vper & Vverb & Vname
(P5)	(Vcon = START) & ((Vname-WAS-Vverb-BY-Vper) & (Vper * famous))	⇒ (Vcon = SECOND) & (Vcon1 = OBJECT) & Vper & Vverb & Vname
(P6)	(Vcon = START) & ((Vper-WAS-Vverb-BY-Vname) & (Vper * famous))	⇒ (Vcon = SECOND) & (Vcon1 = SUBJECT) & Vper & Vverb & Vname
(P7)	(Vcon = SECOND) & (Vname is Vadj)	⇒ (Vcon = Vcon1) & Vadj & (UNBIND Vcon1 Vname)
(P8)	(Vcon = SUBJECT) & (Videa1 W Vper) & ((Videa2 W Vverb) & (Videa2 * active)) & (Videa3 W Vadj)	⇒ (Vcon = VERIFY) & Videa1 & Videa2 & Videa3 & (UNBIND Vper Vverb Vadj)
(P9)	(Vcon = OBJECT) & (Videa1 W Vper) & ((Videa2 W Vverb) & (Videa2 * passive)) & (Videa3 W Vadj)	⇒ (Vcon = VERIFY) & Videa1 & Videa2 & Videa3 & (UNBIND Vper Vverb Vadj)
(P10)	(Vcon = VERIFY) & ((Videa2 OF Videa1) * Videa3)	⇒ (RESPOND TRUE) & (Vcon = START) & (UNBIND Videa1 Videa2 Videa3)
(P11)	(Vcon = VERIFY) & (ABS ((Videa2 OF Videa1) * Videa3))	⇒ (RESPOND FALSE) & (Vcon = START) & (UNBIND Videa1 Videa2 Videa3)

will be evoked if the probe is a single sentence. If the sentence interrogates a subject rule (P1) will set Vcon = SUBJECT; if an object rule (P2) sets Vcon = OBJECT. Productions (P3)–(P6) analyze the first sentence of an inference and detect whether it interrogates a subject or an object rule. Note that all four productions have patterns in their conditions specifying (Vper * famous). This is to distinguish the well-known figure (for example, Nixon) from the common name (for example, Fred). Depending on whether this person is the logical object or subject of the sentence, Vcon1 is set to SUBJECT or OBJECT. After Productions (P3)–(P6), Production (P7) is executed to encode the second line of the sentence. It sets Vcon to the value of Vcon1, that is, either SUBJECT or OBJECT. As may be seen from Fig. 9.5 it is at this point that the flow of control merges with the flow for noninferences. If Vcon is SUBJECT, Production (P8) will apply which retrieves the senses of the person, verb, and adjective. The construction (Videa2 *

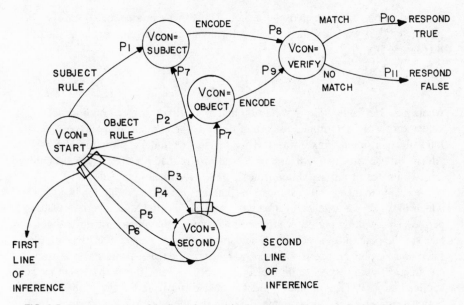

FIG. 9.5   A representation of the flow of control for the production system in Table 9.8 for the action-rule experiment.

active) serves to constrain the sense retrieved for the verb to the active sense. If Vcon is OBJECT, Production (P9) will apply to retrieve the passive sense of the verb and the senses of the other verbs. Finally, Production (P10) will identify if the matching structure is to be found in memory and Production (P11) will identify that there is no matching structure.

Reaction-Time Predictions

Predictions can be obtained for this experiment by simply estimating the times to execute the productions required for the various types of probes. For those productions that require activation of long-term memory, I will use the mathematical model developed in the previous chapter for prediction: Noninference sentences expressing subject and object rules are of equal physical complexity. Therefore, I will estimate one parameter, T_1, for the time for either Production (P1) or (P2) to execute. In inferences, the first line is shorter if it is active. Therefore, I will estimate another time T_2 for Production (P3) or (P4) (which analyze active first lines) followed by (P7) and a different time, T_3, for (P5) or (P6) (which analyze passive first lines) followed by (P7). There is an additional time, T_4, for (P8) or (P9) to apply. After (P8) or (P9), either Production (P10) will execute and generate a true response or (P11) will execute and generate a false response. The time for (P10) to execute can be divided into a component T_a for activation to intersect and the production to be selected and a time $T_{10,e}$ for the production to apply. The parameter T_a is given by the following formula derived from Eq. (3) in Chapter 8 (page 265):

$$T_a = \frac{4}{3}\left[\frac{1}{3r} + \frac{4}{1+4r}(1.5)\right]\alpha$$

where $r = 1/2$ in the unique condition and $1/3$ in the repeated condition. These values of r were determined assuming that K', the strength of preexperimental links to experimental links, was 1. This deviates from the assumption of $K' = 2$ which was used in Chapter 8. If a larger value of K' had been used, unreasonably large estimates of the activation times would have been obtained.

According to the model developed in Chapters 6 and 8, a production like (P11), which looks for an absence of a pattern, will be selected after a certain waiting period. This waiting period is adjusted to vary with the amount of time it would take for the pattern to be activated. Thus it should be selected after time T_a, defined above, plus an additional waiting constant F. False 1 and False 2 probes are identical with respect to this selection process, but differ with respect to the application of (P11). Note that False 1 probes differ from False 2 probes in that both the proper name (for example, Nixon) and the adjective (for example, tall) were connected in the memory structure. This means that the true production, (P10), would be selected for False 1 probes because of the intersection of activation between these terms but not for False 2 probes. Production (P10) will not apply because the pattern would not match memory, but its presence on the APPLY LIST would slow down application of Production (P11). Thus, Production (P11) will take an extra x units of time to apply in the case of False 1 probes. It is assumed that the time for (P11) to apply in the case of False 2 probes is the same as the time $T_{10,e}$ for (P10) to apply for true probes. The application time for (P11) in the case of False 1 probes will be $T_{10,e} + x$.

It was not possible to obtain separate estimates of T_1, T_2, T_3, T_4 and $T_{10,e}$. Rather, estimates were obtained of $T_1' = T_1 + T_4 + T_{10,e}$, $T_2' = T_2 + T_4 + T_{10,e}$, and $T_3' = T_3 + T_4 + T_{10,e}$. The parameter T_1' provides an "intercept" parameter for the noninference statements, T_2' for active inference statements, and T_3' for passive inference statements. In addition to these, three other parameters were estimated: α, the activation rate; F, the extra waiting time; and x, the extra time for (P11) to apply. With these six parameters, predictions were derived for the 16 conditions in Table 9.8. Table 9.8 presents the observed reaction times, error rates, and predictions for the conditions. In the footnote to Table 9.8 are given the six parameter estimates. The parameter F was estimated to have a negative value which was surprising. In all past experiments subjects were longer responding to falses than to trues, indicating that they waited longer before selecting a production. However, by comparing the true probes and the False 2 probes it can be seen that this is not the case in this experiment. In contrast, the False 1 probes, because of the intersection between the proper name and adjective, are a good deal

TABLE 9.8
Observed Reaction Times, Error Rates (in Parentheses)
and Reaction-Time Predictions for Action Rule Study[a]

	True	False 1	False 2
Verification unique	1700 (.026) $T_1' + 3.56\alpha = 1645$	1881 (.097) $T_1' + 3.56\alpha + F + x = 1860$	—
Verification repeated	1961 (.097) $T_1' + 4.76\alpha = 2059$	2298 (.173) $T_1' + 4.76\alpha + F + x = 2274$	—
Active inference unique	1926 (.037) $T_2' + 3.56\alpha = 1896$	2002 (.092) $T_2' + 3.56\alpha + F + x = 2109$	1858 (.062) $T_2' + 3.56\alpha + F = 1841$
Active inference repeated	2331 (.103) $T_2' + 4.76\alpha = 2308$	2520 (.147) $T_2' + 4.76\alpha + F + x = 2523$	2296 (.033) $T_2' + 4.76\alpha + F = 2255$
Passive inference unique	2102 (.059) $T_3' + 3.56\alpha = 2088$	2276 (.199) $T_3' + 3.56\alpha + F + x = 2303$	2032 (.066) $T_3' + 3.56\alpha + F = 2035$
Passive inference repeated	2494 (.145) $T_3' + 4.76\alpha = 2502$	2826 (.232) $T_3' + 4.76\alpha + F + x = 2717$	2366 (.066) $T_3' + 4.76\alpha + F = 2449$

[a]Note this model predicts no difference between subject rules like sentence (1) versus object rules like sentence (2). The divisions of data into these two classes are not given in this table. In fact, verifications and inferences based on subject rules took 2057 msec overall, and those based on object rules took 2049 msec overall. So there is little, if any, difference.
$T_1' = 417$; $T_2' = 666$; $T_3' = 860$; $\alpha = 345$; $F = -53$; $x = 268$.

longer than either true or False 2. This is attributed to the parameter x for the extra application time. Note that the three parameters, T_1', T_2', and T_3', are ordered as we would expect. T_1', the base time for a simple verification, is smallest and T_3', the base time for a passive inference, is longest. Since passive inferences are physically longer than active inferences we would expect them to take longer. The parameter, α, is much larger for this experiment than the values reported for the experiments in Chapter 8. I have frequently discovered in experiments with longer overall reaction times that the value of α for the activation rate is also longer. A possible explanation for this will be given in Chapter 13. Outside of these unexpected outcomes in the parameter estimates, the ACT model does a good job of accounting for the data (96.3% of the variance).

The Middle-Man Study

The other experiment to be reported in this section is a study I conducted with Steven Shevell. The purpose of the experiment was to have the subject encode separately in memory a large number of facts which he would later have to chain together to make an inference. Examples of the materials and the structure they defined are given in Table 9.9. The learning phase was divided into two parts. In the first part subjects learned that various people were members of various groups. There were 12 groups such as *Italians* and *lawyers*. Each group had four members in it. Individuals (like Fred) could be in one, two, or three groups. There were 48 such facts (asserting that individuals were in groups) to learn and subjects were drilled on these. Subjects were required to recall all the groups a particular individual was in and all the individuals in each group.

This proved to be a very difficult learning task. Only 10 of the original 24 subjects succeeded in it. There are at least three reasons for difficulty with this task. First, 48 facts is a large number to learn. Second, there was high fan (four individuals) out of each group and a high fan out of many of the proper names. This undoubtedly produced considerable interference. Third, the proper names used probably had a nonsense-syllable-like quality for our subjects.

The second part of the study phase passed more quickly. Subjects were told that pairs of groups formed clubs and that each club had a president. So now they learned propositions of the form *Bob is president of the lawyers and Russians*. Six pairs were composed from the twelve groups to define six clubs, each of which had a president uniquely associated with it. The club presidents were not mentioned in the first study phase.

TABLE 9.9
Sample Study Materials and Their Structure in the Inference Experiment

End Man 1	Group 1	President	Group 2	End Man 2
FRED	LAWYER	BOB	RUSSIAN	JOHN
ALAN	SKIER	JOE	BARBER	BILL
DAVE	ITALIAN	TIM	SWIMMER	PETE

PART I	PART 2
Fred is a lawyer	Bob is president of the lawyers and Russians
Fred is a skier	Joe is president of the skiers and barbers
Fred is an Italian	Tim is president of the Italians and swimmers
Alan is a lawyer	
Alan is a skier	
Dave is an Italian	
John is a Russian	
John is a barber	
John is a swimmer	
Bill is a barber	
Bill is a swimmer	
Pete is a swimmer	

The first and second parts of the study phase were intended to create a memory structure like the one at the top of Table 9.9. Note *Fred* and *John* are in the same club together. However, the material was presented in such a way that it was unlikely that subjects would have made that inference yet.

There were three testing conditions defined by the type of probe a subject would see. These three probe types are illustrated below:

1.	No Middle Man	(*A* * *C*)	FRED	****	JOHN
2.	Middle Man	(*ABC*)	FRED	BOB	JOHN
3.	Verification	(*AB**)	FRED	BOB	*****
	or	(**BC*)	*****	BOB	JOHN

All probes consisted of three words, one of which might be replaced by asterisks. The first and third words (*A* and *C*), called the *end men,* were always individuals asserted to be in the various groups. The second word (*B*), called the *middle man,* was always a club president. In the first condition, subjects saw the names of two individuals, *A* and *C*, separated by a series of asterisks. They were instructed to decide for such probes whether *A* and *C* were in the same club. They were instructed that the only way this could occur was if *A* was in one group and *C* in a different group and these groups had the same president. That is, they had to trace out in their memories a path interconnecting *A* and *C*. With respect to this network structure and the task, these problems are similar to the spy problems (Hayes, 1965). In another testing condition, the *middle man* condition, subjects also saw a probe with the president *B* to which *A* and *C* were purported to be connected. Their task was to decide if *A* and *C* were in the club of which *B* was president. In the third cuing condition they saw an individual *A* and a president *B* and had to verify whether *B* was president of a club that contained *A*. As illustrated above, these two terms were either preceded or followed by asterisks.

Orthogonal to the probe type we could manipulate the characteristics of the memory structure being interrogated. We contrasted pairs where both *A* and *B* were in three groups and hence three clubs (Fred and John are an example); in two clubs (Alan and Bill are an example); or in one club (Dave and Pete are an example). This factor is referred to as *fan*. Within each of the categories of fan we manipulated the number of paths interconnecting the two individuals. When *A* and *B* participated in three groups (3-fan case) there could be from 0 to 3 interconnecting paths. For instance, FRED and JOHN in Table 9.9 are interconnected three ways. In the 2-fan case there could be 0–2 interconnecting paths and in the 1-fan case 0–1 paths. Figure 9.6 shows the data for these various cases as a function of the number of interconnecting paths, type of probe (middle man versus no middle man versus verification), and fan. In all these cases 0 interconnecting paths indicates a probe that requires a false response.

When faced with a probe without a middle man, subjects report serially tracing paths from one of the elements trying to find a connection to the other. They respond false when all possible paths are exhausted. The data in Fig. 9.6 are con-

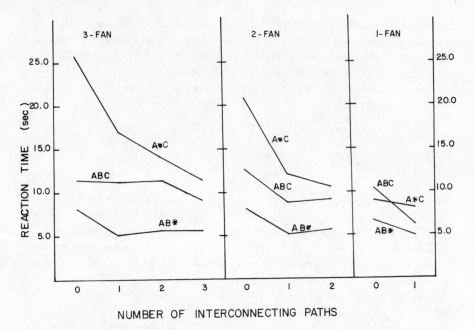

FIG. 9.6   Reaction time in the middle-man study as a study of a function of fan, number of inter-connecting paths, and probe type.

sistent with the report. First, consider the effect of fan in the no-middle-man case ($A * C$) on falses (0 interconnecting paths) versus trues with only one interconnecting path. For the falses reaction time increases from 8.59 sec for 1-fan to 25.67 for 3-fan. For the trues, the reaction time increases from 7.87 to 17.00. The ratio of these increases, 17.08 to 9.13, approximates the 2:1 ratio we would expect if subjects were conducting a self-terminating search. Another prediction from the self-terminating model is that the more redundant paths there are in the $A * C$ (no-middle-man case) the faster the subject should be. Figure 9.6 also confirms that this is the case.

In the ABC (middle-man) and $AB*$ cases, there is no ambiguity about what path should be searched since each middle man was associated uniquely with a single path. Subjects should start their searches from the middle man to prevent having to search multiple paths. Subjects report that they do just this. Note the ABC cases are much faster than the $A*C$ cases. The $AB*$ cases are even faster since the subject need only retrieve a path between one of the two end men and a middle man. Note also that subjects are much less affected by fan in the ABC and $AB*$ cases. This is consistent with the idea that they are not serially tracing paths from an end man but rather searching paths from the middle man.

Referring back to Table 9.9 one might wonder how subjects avoid a serial search in the $AB*$ and ABC cases. Consider the $AB*$ case of verifying "FRED BOB ****" in Table 9.9. There are three paths progressing out of Fred and four (only two are shown) progressing from *Bob* through *lawyer* to various instances. So it might seem that if the subject searched from *Fred* he would have to serially consider the possibilities from this node, and if he searched from *Bob* he would have to serially consider the possibilities from the *Bob* node. However, the process subjects describe is one of retrieving *lawyer* from *Bob* and then trying to recognize that *Fred is a lawyer*. In the ACT model the time for this recognition process will be affected by fan, but the process underlying the recognition judgment is a diffuse parallel activation rather than a serial search. The reason why subjects must engage in a serial search to verify that Fred and John are in the same club (the $A*C$ case) is because activation cannot spread between Fred and John in a single dampening cycle and thereby activate all the intervening structure. It can spread between *Fred and lawyer* because that is a much shorter path. So, when the memory structure becomes too complex to activate within dampening time, the subject must engage in a serial process in which he activates part of it at a time. This is a much slower process and will be much more affected by competing paths in the memory structure. Recall from Chapter 4 (page 138) that the principal factor determining how complex the condition of a production can be is the size of the structure that can be activated.

Table 9.10 shows a production system adequate to deal with these probes. The flow of control is illustrated in Fig. 9.7. As that figure indicates there are three distinct paths of control depending on whether the probe comes from the verification condition (upper path), middle-man condition (center path), or no middle man (lower path). Productions (P1), (P2), (P10), and (P20) select the correct path depending on the probe structure. Productions (P3), (P11), and (P21) serve to encode the words in the three types of probes. From this point forward the three types of probes are processed according to somewhat different logics.

If the probe is a verification probe, the subject is given the name of one club president (middle man) and one individual (end man) and he must decide if the middle man is president of a group that includes the end man. The middle man (Vpres in Table 9.10) is connected to two groups. Production (P4) retrieves one of these groups. If the end man (Vind in Table 9.10) is in that group, Production (P5) will be satisfied and a TRUE response will be emitted. If not, Production (P6) will be satisfied which passes control to (P7). Production (P7) retrieves the second group of which Vpres is president. Note in Production (P7) that there is an explicit test (ABS (Vgoup1 = Vgroup2)) to make sure that the group retrieved by Production (P7) is not the same as the group retrieved by (P4). If Vind (the end man) is a member of Vgroup2, Production (P8) is executed, emitting a true response. Otherwise Production (P9) is evoked, emitting a false response.

If the probe is a middle-man probe, the subject is given the name of the club president and both end men. The idea node corresponding to the president is bound to Vpres. The idea nodes corresponding to the end men are bound to Vind1 and Vind2. Production (P12) retrieves one group, Vgroup1, of which Vpres is presi-

TABLE 9.10
A Debugged Production System for the Middle-Man Task

	Condition	Action
(P1)	(Vcon = START) & (Vend-Vmid-***)	⇒ (Vcon = VERIFY1) & Vend & Vmid
(P2)	(Vcon = START) & (***-Vmid-Vend)	⇒ (Vcon = VERIFY1) & Vend & Vmid
(P3)	(Vcon = VERIFY1) & (Vind W Vend) & (Vpres W Vmid)	⇒ (Vcon = VERIFY2) & Vind & Vpres & (UNBIND Vend Vmid)
(P4)	(Vcon = VERIFY2) & (Vpres * president OF Vgroup1))	⇒ (Vcon = VERIFY3) & Vgroup1
(P5)	(Vcon = VERIFY3) & (Vind * Vgroup1)	⇒ (RESPOND TRUE) & (Vcon = START) & (UNBIND Vind Vpres Vgroup1)
(P6)	(Vcon = VERIFY3) & (ABS (Vind * Vgroup1))	⇒ (Vcon = VERIFY4)
(P7)	(Vcon = VERIFY4) & (Vpres * president OF Vgroup2)) & (ABS (Vgroup1 = Vgroup2))	⇒ (Vcon = VERIFY5) & (UNBIND Vgroup1) & Vgroup2
(P8)	(Vcon = VERIFY5) & (Vind * Vgroup2)	⇒ (RESPOND TRUE) & (Vcon = START) & (UNBIND Vind Vpres Vgroup2)
(P9)	(Vcon = VERIFY5) & (ABS (Vind * Vgroup2))	⇒ (RESPOND FALSE) & (Vcon = START) & (UNBIND Vind Vpres Vgroup2)
(P10)	(Vcon = START) & (Vend1-Vmid-Vend2) & (ABS (Vend1 = ***)) & (ABS (Vmid = ***)) & (ABS (Vend2 = ***))	⇒ (Vcon = MIDDLE1) & Vend1 & Vmid & Vend2
(P11)	(Vcon & MIDDLE1) & (Vind1 W Vend1) & (Vpres W Vmid) & (Vind2 W Vend2)	⇒ (Vcon = MIDDLE2) & Vind1 & Vpres & Vind2 & (UNBIND Vend1 Vmid Vend2)
(P12)	(Vcon = MIDDLE2) & (Vpres * president OF Vgroup1))	⇒ (Vcon = MIDDLE3) & Vgroup1
(P13)	(Vcon = MIDDLE3) & (Vind1 * Vgroup1)	⇒ (Vcon = MIDDLE4) & (UNBIND Vind1)
(P14)	(Vcon = MIDDLE3) & (ABS (Vind1 * Vgroup1))	⇒ (Vcon = MIDDLE5)
(P15)	(Vcon = MIDDLE5) & (Vind2 * Vgroup1)	⇒ (Vcon = MIDDLE4) & (Vind2 = Vind1) & (UNBIND Vind1)
(P16)	(Vcon = MIDDLE5) & (ABS (Vind2 * Vgroup1))	⇒ (RESPOND FALSE) & (Vcon = START) & (UNBIND Vind1 Vind2 Vpres Vgroup1)
(P17)	(Vcon = MIDDLE4) & (Vpres * president OF Vgroup2)) & (ABS (Vgroup1 = Vgroup2))	⇒ (Vcon = MIDDLE6) & Vgroup2 & (UNBIND Vpres Vgroup1)
(P18)	(Vcon = MIDDLE6) & (Vind2 * Vgroup2)	⇒ (RESPOND TRUE) & (Vcon = START) & (UNBIND Vind2 Vgroup2)

(continued)

TABLE 9.10 *(continued)*

	Condition	Action
(P19)	(Vcon = MIDDLE6) & (ABS Vind2 * Vgroup2))	⇒ (RESPOND FALSE) & (Vcon = START) & (UNBIND Vind2 Vgroup2)
(P20)	(Vcon = START) & (Vend1-***-Vend2)	⇒ (Vcon = NONE1) & Vend1 & Vend2
(P21)	(Vcon = NONE1) & (Vind1 W Vend1) & (Vind2 W Vend2) & (Vcrit * (@NUMBER OF Vend1))	⇒ (Vcon = NONE2) & Vind1 & Vind2 & Vcrit & (Vnumb = 0) & (UNBIND Vend1 Vend2)
(P22)	(Vcon = NONE2) & (Vcrit = Vnumb)	⇒ (RESPOND FALSE) & (Vcon = START) & (UNBIND Vnumb Vcrit Vind1 Vind2 Vdone Vpres)
(P23)	(Vcon = NONE2) & (Vind * Vgroup1) & (ABS (Vgroup1 * Vdone))	⇒ (Vcon = NONE3) & (Vgroup1 * Vdone) (Vnumb = Vnumb+1) & Vgroup1 & Vdone
(P24)	(Vcon = NONE3) & (Vpres * (president OF Vgroup1))	⇒ (Vcon = NONE4) & Vpres
(P25)	(Vcon = NONE4) & (Vpres * (president OF Vgroup2)) & (ABS (Vgroup1 = Vgroup2))	⇒ (Vcon = NONE5) & Vgroup2 & (UNBIND Vgroup1 Vpres)
(P26)	(Vcon = NONE5) & (Vind2 * Vgroup2)	⇒ (RESPOND TRUE) & (Vcon = START) & (UNBIND Vgroup2 Vdone Vind1 Vind2 Vnumb Vcount)
(P27)	(Vcon = NONE5) & (ABS (Vind2 * Vgroup2))	⇒ (Vcon = NONE3) & (UNBIND Vgroup2)

dent. If Vind1 is in Vgroup1 control will pass to Production (P17) through Production (P13). If Vind1 is not in Vgroup1 but Vind2 is, control will also pass to Production (P17) but by way of Productions (P14) and (P15). Production (P15) also changes the value of the variable Vind2 to the value of Vind1. (The productions after (P17) check whether Vind2 is a member of the other group under Vpres.) Finally, if neither Vind1 nor Vind2 are members of Vgroup2, Productions (P14) and (P16) will be satisfied and a false response will be emitted. If one of the individuals was found to be a member of Vgroup1, Production (P17) will apply to retrieve the other group under Vpres and bind this to Vgroup2. If Vind2 is a member of Vgroup2, Production (P18) will generate a true response. If not, Production (P19) will generate a false response.

If the probe is from the no-middle-man condition, the subject will just have the two end men (bound to Vind1 and Vind2). It is assumed that he serially searches through all the middle men attached to Vind1 to see if any are on a path leading to Vind2. The subject will respond false if he exhausts all the middle men. To do this he must have some way of monitoring when the search is complete. Therefore,

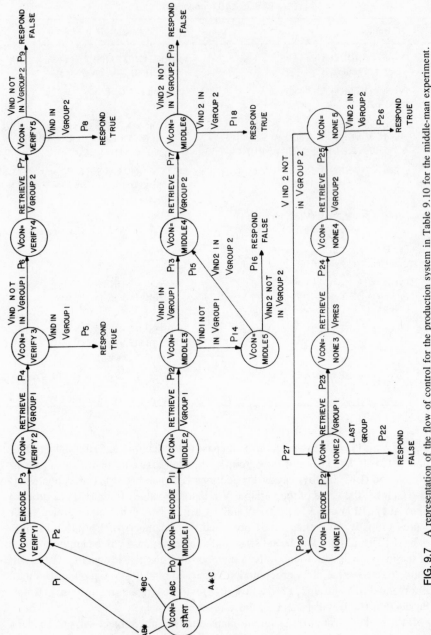

FIG. 9.7 A representation of the flow of control for the production system in Table 9.10 for the middle-man experiment.

it is assumed that the subject knows how many groups have been associated with each end man.[6] In Production (P21) he retrieves this information and binds it to the variable Vcrit. Production (P21) also sets the variable Vnumb to 0. That variable will count the number of paths tried. When Vcrit = Vnumb, Production (P22) will be satisfied causing a false response to be emitted. Production (P23) retrieves a group, Vgroup1, associated with Vind1. The list of groups tried so far are on a temporary list bound to Vdone. Therefore, (P23) checks that Vgroup1 is not on Vdone. Production (P24) retrieves the president of Vgroup1 and Production (P25) retrieves the other group, Vgroup2, associated with that president. Finally, a test is made of whether Vind2 is in Vgroup2. If it is, Production (P26) is satisfied and a true response is emitted. If it is not, Production (P27) is satisfied which passes control back to Production (P23).

Reaction-Time Predictions

The derivation of reaction-time predictions for a system as complex as the one in Table 9.10 is not tractable without a number of simplifying assumptions. We will assume that the time for Productions (P1), (P2), (P10), and (P20), which identify the probe and select the path of control, take a constant time $T1$. Production (P3) which encodes verification probes takes time $T2$, Production (P11) for middle-man probes takes $T3$, Production (P21) for no-middle-man probes takes time $T4$. Production (P22), for the no-middle-man case, which identifies that Vnumb and Vcrit are the same, takes $T5$. All other productions require accessing long-term memory. I will assume that the times for these productions to apply are determined by the time to activate the requisite long-term memory structure. The only additional time component for these will be R, the time to execute an external response.

This decision to ignore the times to apply the individiual productions and to focus on the time for memory to be activated is justified on the assumption that the rate of production application is rapid relative to the rate of spread of activation. Therefore, the time for productions to execute will be principally determined by activation process.

Productions (P5), (P8), (P13), (P15), (P18), and (P26) all involve detecting that an individual is a member of a group. Using Eq. (3) established in Chapter 8 (page 265), the time for this is given by the following expression:

$$\left(\frac{1}{2r} + \frac{3}{1 + 3r} \right)\alpha \tag{1}$$

where r is the rate of activation. In calculating r, I will assume $K' = 1$, which is consistent with the estimate given earlier in this section for the action rule study. There are five experimental paths out of the group (four to individuals and one to

---

[6]This is not an unreasonable assumption because in the learning phase the subject had to be able to recall the exact number of groups associated with each individual. This would have provided ample training in the number of groups associated with an individual.

the president) and n paths (1 to 3) out of the individual. Therefore, the value estimated for r (based on Eq. (5), Chapter 8, page 265) is

$$r = \left(\frac{1}{6} + \frac{1}{n+1}\right)\Big/2 \tag{2}$$

Productions (P6), (P9), (P14), (P16), (P19), and (P27) are attempting to detect the absence of a connection between an individual and a group. The appropriate equation here is

$$\left(\frac{1}{2r} + \frac{1}{1+3r}\right)\alpha + F \tag{3}$$

Productions (P4), (P7), (P12), (P17), and (P25) involve retrieving a group from a president. The theory developed in Chapter 8 concerned the process by which activation intersected between a number of sources. However, Productions (P4), (P7), (P12), (P17), and (P25) require activation to spread from the president to the group. It is unclear how to develop the ACT predictions for this case. As a very simple assumption, suppose that the time for activation to spread from source 1 to source 2 will increase by a factor γ with each experimental path exiting from source 1. As a consultation of Table 9.9 will verify, there are two paths leading from each president—one to each group. Therefore, it is assumed each of these productions will take a time 2γ. Production (P24) involves the retrieval of a president from a group. There are five paths leading from the group (four to individuals and one to a president). Therefore the time for (P24) is 5γ. Production (P23) involves retrieving the group from the individual. The number of groups attached to an individual varied from 1 to 3. Therefore, the time to perform Production (P23) is $n\gamma$ where n is the number of groups attached to the individual.

A number of approximating assumptions are being made in deriving predictions for this experiment. One of these is that activation does not begin spreading from the nodes in a pattern until the production which contains that pattern is appropriate. As an example of this approximation, consider a middle-man probe, *ABC*, and consider Production (P18) which queries whether one of the end men, Vind2, is in the group, Vgroup2. The time for this production to apply is estimated to be the time for activation to intersect between the nodes bound to Vind2 and Vgroup2, assuming that activation only starts spreading after completion of (P17). However, these nodes Vind2 and Vgroup2 have been active since (P11) encoded the individual words. Therefore, activation could have already intersected between these nodes when (P17) completes or there may be a partial intersection. It is quite possible that a complete intersection could have occurred and was then erased by the dampening process. The approximation being used in the predictions is equivalent to assuming that a dampening process occurs after each successful execution of a production.

There are seven parameters estimated for this model. There is the parameter T_V which represents the time ($T1$) to identify the probe, plus the time ($T2$) to encode a verification probe, plus the time R to generate a response. T_V serves as the intercept parameter for verification probes. There is a similar intercept parameter T_M for the middle-man probes. It consists of $T1$, plus the encoding time $T3$, plus R. There is an intercept parameter, T_{NT}, for the no-middle-man true probes. It consists of $T1$, plus encoding time $T4$, plus R. Finally, there is the intercept parameter T_{NF} for no-middle-man false probes which consists of $T1$, $T4$, R, and $T5$, the time to execute Production (P22). We would expect $T_V < T_M < T_{NT} < T_{NF}$. The remaining three parameters are α, the activation rate; γ, the retrieval rate; and F, the extra waiting time to detect absent patterns. Table 9.11 lists the predictions for the 27 conditions of the experiment using these equations. The data in that table are organized by row according to the number of groups associated with the individual (first digit) and the number of groups which lead to an intersection between the end men (second digit). It is organized by column according to probe type. Each cell contains the observed reaction time, its standard error, the equation for prediction, and the predicted time.

It would consume too much space to derive all the equations in Table 9.11 but I will consider one example which illustrates many of the complications. This is the case of the no-middle-man probe with 2-fan and one interconnecting path—the fourth row and third column in Table 9.11. The intercept parameter is T_{NT}. After completion of (P21) the subject begins serially searching the paths from Vind1. Production (P23) retrieves a group and takes time 2γ because there are two paths from the individual. Production (P24) retrieves the president and takes times 5γ because there are five paths from the group. Production (P25) retrieves the other group from the president and takes time 2γ. Then the subject must recognize whether Vind2 is in Vgroup2. With the experimental fan from Vind2 equal to 2 and from Vgroup2 equal to 5, $r = \frac{1}{4}$. Substituting this value of r into the expression (1) given earlier (page 371), the expected activation time for (P25) is 3.71α. If Vind2 is in the Vgroup2, a true response will have been emitted and the total activation and search time will be $3.71\alpha + 9\gamma$. However, assuming the paths are randomly ordered, there is a .5 probability that Vind2 will not be in Vgroup2. The time to determine this is greater by a constant F than the time to determine Vind2 is in Vgroup2, that is, $3.71\alpha + F$. The subject will have to return to Vind1 and trace the other, correct path. The total time to consider both paths will be $7.42\alpha + 18\gamma + F$. The average of the times for first path correct and second path correct is $5.57\alpha + 13.5\gamma + .5F$. Adding the constant T_{NT} to this we obtain the prediction in Table 9.11.

The parameters were estimated by means of multiple regression, but the best fitting model involved setting $T_V = -1.04$ sec. It seems wrong to permit a negative value; therefore, T_V was fixed at .5 sec. This had remarkably little effect on the goodness of fit, changing the amount of variance accounted for from 94.9 to 94.6%. The other parameter estimates were $T_M = 2.737$; $T_{NT} = 4.867$; $T_{NF} = 5.286$; $\alpha = .484$; $\gamma = .351$; and $F = 1.401$. As can be seen the model does quite a good job in accounting for the variance among the conditions. The cells in which

TABLE 9.11
Predictions and Data for Middle-Man Experiment
(Reaction Time in Seconds)

Fanning condition	AB* *BC	ABC	A * B
1-0	*6.35 ± .45 $T_V - 6\alpha + 4\gamma + 2F$ =7.70	10.02 ± .85 $T_M + 6.75\alpha + 3\gamma + 2F$ =9.86	*8.59 ± .77 $T_{NF} + 3\alpha + 8\gamma + F$ =10.60
1-1	4.60 ± .51 $T_V + 4.5\alpha + 3\gamma + .5F$ =4.43	*5.92 ± .39 $T_M + 7.50\alpha + 4\gamma + .5F$ =8.47	*7.87 ± 1.24 $T_{NT} + 3\alpha + 8\gamma$ =9.13
2-0	7.78 ± .82 $T_V + 7.42\alpha + 4\gamma + 2F$ =8.30	*12.56 ± 1.11 $T_M + 8.35\alpha + 3\gamma + 2F$ =10.88	*20.53 ± 2.36 $T_{NF} + 7.42\alpha + 18\gamma + 2F$ =18.00
2-1	4.98 ± .82 $T_V + 5.57\alpha + 3\gamma + .5F$ =4.95	8.68 ± .97 $T_M + 9.28\alpha + 4\gamma + .5F$ =9.33	11.89 ± 1.20 $T_{NT} + 5.57\alpha + 13.5\gamma + .5F$ =13.00
2-2	5.37 ± .62 $T_V + 5.57\alpha + 3\gamma + .5F$ =4.95	8.83 ± .97 $T_M + 9.28\alpha + 4\gamma + .5F$ =9.33	10.37 ± 1.53 $T_{NT} + 3.71\alpha + 9\gamma$ =9.82
3-0	8.15 ± .71 $T_V + 8.52\alpha + 4\gamma + 2F$ =8.82	11.47 ± 1.56 $T_M + 9.57\alpha + 3\gamma + 2F$ =11.23	25.67 ± 2.97 $T_{NF} + 12.75\alpha + 30\gamma + 3F$ =26.19
3-1	5.05 ± .51 $T_V + 6.38\alpha + 3\gamma + .5F$ =5.34	11.04 ± 1.88 $T_M + 10.63\alpha + 4\gamma + .5F$ =9.99	17.00 ± 2.32 $T_{NT} + 8.50\alpha + 20\gamma + F$ =17.40
3-2	5.53 ± .50 $T_V + 6.38\alpha + 3\gamma + .5F$ =5.34	11.23 ± 1.29 $T_M + 10.63\alpha + 4\gamma + .5F$ =9.99	14.17 ± 1.92 $T_{NT} + 5.66\alpha + 13.33\gamma + .33F$ =12.75
3-3	5.53 ± 1.00 $T_V + 6.38\alpha + 3\gamma + .5F$ =5.34	8.92 ± .94 $T_M + 10.63\alpha + 4\gamma + .5F$ =9.99	11.24 ± 1.37 $T_{NT} + 4.25\alpha + 10\gamma$ =10.43

the predictions of the model are discrepant by more than one standard deviation are starred in Table 9.11. There are six such cells out of a total 27.

Concluding Remarks about Strategic Inference Making

We have shown that the ACT mechanism can be generalized from predictions about fact-retrieval experiments to the prediction about complex inference experiments. It is the case that production systems have the capacity to provide a great variety of models. Therefore, it needs to be emphasized that the production systems proposed in this section were the ones that seemed natural for the ACT system. The systems reported are the only ones that I developed for those tasks; they were not developed by means of a trial-and-error consideration of many production systems. I hope the reader will agree that these seem natural and efficient production systems for the tasks. This serves to indicate that the ACT production system formalism may be of wide predictive potential.

SUMMARY OF CHAPTER 9

A survey is given of some mechanical inference systems, evaluating these systems on the criteria of soundness, completeness, effectiveness, efficiency, and psychological plausibility. An inference system is said to be *sound* if it makes only valid inferences. An inference system is said to be *complete* if it makes all valid inferences. An inference system is said to be *effective* if it has a means of deciding whether a particular inference is valid or not. Effectiveness is a stronger criterion which implies completeness. An inference system is said to be *efficient* if it performs within reasonable time bounds. Psychological plausibility refers to whether the behavior of the inference system corresponds to human behavior. The Logic Theorist (Newell, Shaw, & Simon, 1957) was an attempt to develop a sound inference system for the propositional calculus which avoided an exponential growth in search time with length of a deduction. However, the Logic Theorist is not complete and there do exist other procedures for the propositional calculus which are both efficient and complete. The Logic Theorist also was not a good model of human behavior. While there are effective inference procedures for the propositional calculus there are none for the predicate calculus. At best there are semieffective procedures. These are procedures which will find all valid inferences (and therefore are complete) but will fail to identify some nonvalid inferences. Resolution theorem proving is an example of a procedure which is semieffective and sound. It does not seem a realistic psychological model and it is notoriously inefficient. However, resolution theorem proving seems no more inefficient than any other complete system for the predicate calculus. Hewitt's PLANNER is an example of an inference system which is incomplete but is designed to be more efficient than resolution theorem-proving. ACT displays a number of features in common with PLANNER, and has similar incompletenesses. It is possible to formulate ACT productions for generating inferences which are like PLANNER antecedent theorems and ACT productions for recognizing valid inferences which are like PLANNER consequent theorems.

A distinction is made in ACT between natural inference systems and strategic inference systems. Natural inferential processes occur in situations where there is little constraint on the possible forms of inferences. Strategic inference systems are fashioned to take advantage of constraints on the possible class of inferences. Within the domain of natural inferences a distinction is made between systems which generate inferences and systems which recognize the validity of inferences. The inference-generating system is neither sound nor complete. Productions for recognizing the validity of inferences tend to be more sound.

The research on categorical syllogisms was reviewed as an indication of the character of the validity-recognizing productions that most subjects have. Subjects have traditionally showed considerable inability to reject as not valid contingent conclusions which bear surface similarities to the premises. ACT validity-recognizing productions would generally find it harder to identify a contingent conclusion than to identify a valid conclusion. In the situation of being unable to decide about the validity of a conclusion, ACT should be able to report its uncertainty. It was speculated that subjects would also report uncertainty when faced with difficult valid or difficult contingent syllogisms. Past experiments on categorical syllogisms have not given subjects an opportunity to indicate when they are uncertain. An experiment was performed in which subjects were urged to indicate when they were not certain on a syllogism. Subjects did frequently use the *not certain* category on hard valid syllogisms and on contingent syllogisms. However, they still frequently accepted contingent conclusions.

Strategic inference making was considered in three tasks and ACT production systems were provided for each task. Two of these tasks involved subjects making inferences with information that had to be retrieved from long-term memory. These two experiments constitute a test of the interface between ACT's production system and the memory system. These experiments showed separate effects, as ACT predicted, of complexity of the inferences and of complexity of the memory retrieval. Complexity of the inference was manipulated by the number of productions required to perform the inference. Complexity of the memory retrieval was manipulated by means of propositional fan.

REFERENCES

Begg, I., & Denny, J. P. Empirical reconciliation of atmosphere and conversion interpretations of syllogistic reasoning errors. *Journal of Experimental Psychology*, 1969, **81**, 351–354.

Ceraso, J., & Provitera, A. Sources of error in syllogistic reasoning. *Cognitive Psychology*, 1971, **2**, 400–410.

Chang, C., & Lee, R. C. *Symbolic logic and mechanical theorem proving*. New York: Academic Press, 1973.

Chapman, L. J., & Chapman, J. P. Atmosphere effect reexamined. *Journal of Experimental Psychology*, 1959, **58**, 220–226.

Clark, H. H. Linguistic processes in deductive reasoning. *Psychological Review*, 1969, **76**, 387–404.

Cohen, M. R., & Nagel, E. *An introduction to logic and scientific method*. New York: Harcourt, Brace, 1934.

Davis, M., & Putnam, H. A computing procedure for quantification theory. *Journal of the ACM*, 1960, **7**, 201–215.

Erickson, J. R. A set analysis theory of behavior in formal syllogistic reasoning tasks. In R. L. Solso (Ed.), *Theories in cognitive psychology: The Loyola Symposium*. Hillsdale, New Jersey: Lawrence Erlbaum Assoc., 1974.

Gilmore, P. C. A proof procedure for quantification theory: Its justification and realization. *IBM Journal of Research and Development*, 1960, 28–35.

Green, C., & Raphael, B. Research on intelligent question answering systems. *Proceedings of the ACM*. Princeton: Brandon Systems Press, 1969. Pp. 169–181.

Hayes, J. R. Memory, goals, and problem solving. In B. Kleinmuntz (Ed.), *Problem solving: Research, method and theory*. New York: Wiley, 1965.

Henle, M. On the relation between logic and thinking. *Psychological Review*, 1962, **69**, 366–378.

Hewitt, C. *Description and theoretical analysis (using schemata) of PLANNER: A language for proving theorems and manipulating models in a robot* (Report AI-TR-258). MIT-AI Laboratory, 1972.

Hunt, E B. *Artificial intelligence*. New York: Academic Press, 1975.

Huttenlocher, J. Constructing spatial images: A strategy in reasoning. *Psychological Review*, 1968, **75**, 550–560.

Johnson, D. M. *A systematic introduction to the psychology of thinking*. New York: Harper & Row, 1972.

Mendleson, E. *Introduction to mathematical logic*. New York: Van Nostrand, 1964.

Minker, J., Fishman, D. H., & McSkimin, J. R. The Q^* algorithm—a search strategy for a deductive question-answering system. *Proceedings of the third international joint conference on artificial intelligence, 1973*.

Minsky, M. A framework for representing knowledge. In P. H. Winston (Ed.), *The psychology of computer vision*. New York: McGraw-Hill, 1975.

Moore, O. K., & Anderson, S. B. Modern logic and tasks for experiments on problem solving behavior. *Journal of Psychology*, 1954, **38**, 151–160.

Newell, A., Shaw, J. C., & Simon, H. A. Empirical explorations of the logic theory machine. *Proceedings of the Western Joint Computer Conference*, 1957, 218–239.

Newell, A., & Simon, H. *Human problem solving*. New York: Prentice-Hall, 1972.

Nilsson, N. J. *Problem-solving methods in artificial intelligence*. New York: McGraw-Hill, 1971.

Osherson, D. N. *Logical abilities in children*, Vol. 2. Hillsdale, New Jersey: Lawrence Erlbaum Assoc., 1974.

Robinson, J. A. A review of automatic theorem proving. *Proceedings of Symposia on Applied Mathematics*, 1967, **19**, 1–18.

Stefferud, E. *The logic theory machine. A model heuristic program* (Tech. Rep. RM-3731-CC). Santa Monica, California: Rand Corp., 1963.

Wason, P. C., & Johnson-Laird, P. N. *Psychology of reasoning: Structure and content*. Cambridge, Massachusetts: Harvard University Press, 1972.

Whitehead, A. N., & Russell, B. *Principia mathematica* (Vol. 1, 2nd ed., reprinted). Cambridge: The University Press, 1935.

Winograd, T. Understanding natural language. *Cognitive Psychology*, 1972, **3**, 1–191.

Woodworth, R. S., & Sells, S. B. An atmospheric effect in formal syllogistic reasoning. *Journal of Experimental Psychology*, 1935, **18**, 451–460.

10
Learning and Retention

Memories now have attributes, organization, and structure; there are storage systems, retrieval systems, and control systems. We have iconic, echoic, primary, secondary, and short-, medium-, and long-term memories. There are addresses, readout rules, and holding mechanisms; memories may be available but not accessible (or is it the other way?). Our memories are filled with T-stacks, implicit associational responses, natural-language mediators, images, multiple traces, tags, kernel sentences, markers, relational rules, verbal loops, and one-buns.

B. J. UNDERWOOD

The study of memory data was a major component of the HAM book of Anderson and Bower (1973). We tried, with varying success, to use memory data to make inferences about the structure of information in long-term memory. This book is much more oriented to other processes and therefore only a single chapter is being devoted to the question of memory. This chapter serves two purposes. First, a number of criticisms have been made of the HAM treatment of certain memory phenomena, and I feel that I should readdress these issues within the ACT framework and respond to the criticisms. The second purpose is to apply the general theoretical framework developed in earlier chapters to analyzing some of the powerful factors that determine recall.

The most central theoretical notion in this chapter will be that subjects perform elaborations that deposit in memory more than what they are overtly required to commit to memory. These elaborations can cause memory failures, create enormous improvements in recall, and frustrate attempts to decide issues of linguistic representation. The notion of elaborative processes is not particularly unique to the ACT model, but I will take pains to show that there are mechanisms within ACT capable of performing these elaborations.

10.1 ENCODING SPECIFICITY AND ENCODING VARIABILITY

Consider the following hypothetical episode: A subject is asked "What did Mr. Lincoln do?" The subject responds, "I don't know who Lincoln is." Then the subject is asked, "What did President Abraham Lincoln do?" He responds, "Ah, now I know who you are talking about" and proceeds to tell us about Lincoln. I think such an episode would strike most as a bit improbable. However, there is considerable evidence that in some circumstances a word (for example, *Lincoln*) will be recognized in one context, but not in another.

One of the early experiments demonstrating this was performed by Light and Carter-Sobell (1970). They had subjects study homographs such as *jam*. An adjective modified these polysemous nouns to establish one or another interpretation of the noun. Thus, jam might be presented as *strawberry jam* or as *traffic jam*. The probability of recognizing the homograph was much higher if its study and test presentation suggested the same meaning of the noun. A similar experiment was performed by Winograd and Conn (1971). They determined the relative frequencies (dominance) of various interpretations for each word in a set of homographs. All homographs were studied without context; then they were tested for recognition in one of three conditions. In the first condition, a sentence context was used that selected a high frequency interpretation of a homograph; in the second condition, the contextual sentence selected a low frequency meaning; and in a third condition the test homograph was presented in isolation. Recognition was equally high in the first and third conditions, but lower in the second. The lesson of such studies is fairly obvious. When a person studies a word encoding it with one meaning, that person will not recognize it at a later test if it is encoded as having another meaning.

Most people find such results intuitive and somewhat uninteresting because they occur with polysemous words. However, strikingly similar results have been obtained in research (for example, Dapolito, Barker, & Wiant, 1972; Tulving & Thomson 1971, 1973; Watkins & Tulving, 1975) using words that are not obviously polysemous. Tulving and Thomson (1971) presented to-be-remembered words along with strong or weak associates of each word. In the weak associate condition, subjects might study pairs like *train–black,* and in the strong associate condition, pairs like *white–black*. It was found that subsequent recognition memory (for *black*) was better when the word had been studied and tested in the presence of the same associate (either high or low) rather than changing the cue word between study and test.

There is another paradigm (Tulving & Thomson, 1973; Watkins & Tulving, 1975) which demonstrates the same phenomenon in a particularly striking manner. Subjects study low associates with a target such as *train–black*. Then they are given a high associate of the word like *white* and are asked to generate four associates to the word. With relatively high probability the target word (that is, *black*) is generated. The subject is asked to judge if any of his four associates was a studied word. If the subjects generated the target word, they have a .49 probability of recognizing the word. Then subjects are given the original weak cue (that is, *train*) and are asked to recall the target. In this test, they display a .62 probability of recall. Moreover, 42% of the words recalled were not recognized in the first generate-recognize test. It had been a generally accepted idea in psychology that recognition is better than recall. This result is a clear contradiction of that idea. It serves to bring home the point that our memory performance is strongly influenced by the context of testing.

There has been some dispute about whether the encoding specificity effects obtained by Tulving and associates are real or are results of some methodological artifact (for example, Light, Kimble, & Pelligrino, 1975; Santa & Lamwers, 1974). The interested reader may refer to these sources for further discussion. I am inclined to believe they are, in some sense, "real." The important question then becomes what should be the theoretical interpretation for these results.

Episodic Theory

The interpretation favored by Tulving and associates goes under the title of *episodic theory*. It has strong Gestalt undertones. It assumes that study of a pair like *train–black* is a psychological episode which leaves a unique trace in memory. Episodic theory does not describe the structure of that trace or explain how the words *train* and *black* determine that trace. Nonetheless, the episodic trace must have certain characteristics for the theory to make sense. The trace certainly does not consist of the words *train* and *black*, existing independently, and connected by an associative bond. The trace must be a unitary Gestalt whose properties result from an interaction between the properties of *train* and *black*. The properties of this trace may be very different than the properties of a trace encoding *train* alone or *black* alone.

Tulving wants to enforce a clear separation between the memory trace we have for the event of encountering the pair *train–black* and our memory for general facts about the words *train* and *black*. Using his (1972) distinction, the former is part of Episodic Memory while the latter is part of Semantic Memory. These are postulated to be distinct systems with distinct principles. Episodic Memory encodes the moment-by-moment events of our lives, whereas Semantic Memory is our permanent, nonchanging store of knowledge about words and concepts. Retrieval in Episodic Memory operates by a Gestalt-like principle of similarity. A cue sets up an episode which, if sufficiently similar to the original memory trace, will revive the original memory. Thus, *white–black* may not revive memory of *train–black* just because the two episodes are not sufficiently similar.

Kintsch's Theory

Kintsch (1974) has proposed a theory quite similar to Tulving's. It differs principally in that he has committed himself to more specific mechanisms. He proposes that stored with each item in semantic memory is a set of phonemic, graphemic, syntactic, semantic, imaginal, and other sensory elements. In addition there may be certain episodic experiences stored with the word. When the word is presented in a list-learning experiment, it is initially represented in terms of various phonemic and contextual features. This initial representation is matched to memory. The subject then selects the various elements stored with the word plus the elements (phonemic and contextual) in the word's initial representation upon presentation. This selection of features is deposited in episodic memory as a representation of the occurrence of the word in that context.

Kintsch claims general contextual features can affect the selection of a memory code for the word in two ways. First, they can determine which representation in semantic memory is selected by the initial presentation of an ambiguous word. For instance, if the subject is thinking of *money* and is presented with *bank* he is likely to revive the sense of *bank* having to do with a monetary institution. Second, after a sense of the word has been selected, context can influence which features will be sampled from that sense. So if *fox* is in short-term memory at the time *bear* is presented, some memory episode involving a bear and a fox (for example, the bear chased the fox) might be included in the memory trace for *bear*.

The pattern-matching procedure discussed earlier with respect to Kintsch's theory (see Section 2.3, page 50) governs the recognition process. Upon seeing *bear* in a test context an episodic encoding of *bear* is constructed just as it was in the study context. If there is sufficient overlap between the encoding of *bear* in a test context and the episode in memory registering its encoding during study, it will be recognized. So it is possible that *bear,* presented in the context of *fox,* will not revive memory for *bear,* presented in the context of *park*.

The episodic-semantic distinction is important in Kintsch's model. The trace that is set up upon the presentation of a pair like *fox–bear* resides in episodic memory and cannot be accessed from the semantic memory representation of *bear*. It can only be accessed by recreating an episode sufficiently similar to the original. Note that there is an asymmetry in the access relationships. The episode *fox–bear* has access to the semantic representation of *bear,* but not vice-versa.

Elaborative Hypothesis

One can offer a slight variant of the Kintsch model which does not require the postulation of the semantic-episodic distinction. The basic idea is that the subject elaborates the study word with various propositions he has stored with the word. Suppose a subject has stored with *bear* in memory the following facts, among others:

> They include polar bears, black bears, and grizzly bears. They can be angry. They are lazy, furry, and very strong. I once saw a bear chase a fox. Bears beg for food in parks.

Suppose the subject sees a pair *fox–bear* with the instructions to remember *bear*. He may consult his memory for *bear* and store an elaborated representation in-

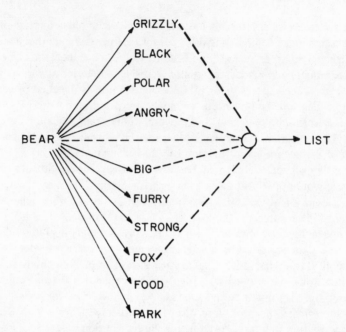

FIG. 10.1   A schematic representation of the information stored with the concept *bear*. Some of this information has been selected for inclusion in an elaboration recording that *bear* occurred in the list.

volving some of the information there. He might store in memory a series of propositions describing his elaboration such as:

> "While studying bear I thought of a large angry grizzly bear chasing a fox."

Figure 10.1 illustrates, very crudely, the state of the subject's memory after this study. The concept bear (represented by the word) is already connected to various concepts (these connections are represented by solid arrows). The effect of study experience has been to associate a number of concepts together and associate the interconnected bundle to an indication that they were thought of together in the context of the list. This is indicated by the element, LIST. The lines interconnecting the subset to LIST are dotted to emphasize that these associations may not have been successfully formed.[1]

The network in Fig. 10.1 is an approximation to an ACT propositional network. It indicates the main connections among elements without all the "clutter" of ACT propositional representation. That "clutter," while useful in accounting for

---

[1]In this elaborative model it is assumed that the subject chooses, as themes for his elaboration, information that is stored with the concept in propositional memory. As we will see in the next section (page 399), it is also possible for the subject to select his themes from information stored in the form of productions.

some phenomena, is irrelevant in analyzing this recall phenomenon. For successful recall it is simply necessary that there be an intact path from the cue to the to-be-recalled item. In this case recognition requires that the subject be able to retrieve the list tag when cued with *bear*. The network in Fig. 10.1 does preserve all the relevant paths leading to LIST. It should be kept in mind, however, that the "true" theory prescribes an ACT network in all of its complexity. The network in Fig. 10.1 is being used solely for analytic convenience.

Suppose at test, the subject is presented with *park–bear* which he elaborates as "In the park a black bear begged for food." What is the probability that this elaboration of *bear* will make contact with the memory trace that records the study of bear in the list? Recognition would only be successful if the link from *bear* to *LIST* were intact. The other concepts in the test elaboration of *bear* are not connected to LIST. In contrast, if the subject had been presented with *fox–bear* and *recreated* the study elaboration of *bear*, then recognition of *bear* would occur if the link were intact from *bear* or *grizzly* or *angry* or *big* or *fox* to *LIST*. Hence probability of recognition would be higher.[2] In general, it seems that if a word is presented in the same context at study as at test there will be greater overlap between the test elaboration and study elaboration. As a consequence there will be a higher probability of recall.

This elaborative hypothesis can be stated more abstractly and more succinctly: Connected to a concept C in memory is a set X of n other concepts. Upon presentation of a word referencing C the subject selects a subset E_i of X. The content of E_i is determined by context. Let S denote the set E_i selected on a study trial plus C itself. Similarly, the set T is defined for a test trial. The subject attempts to associate each member of S to a list marker. The probability of retrieving the list marker when prompted with C at test is a function of the number of members of T that are associated with LIST.

There is a strong similarity between Kintsch's theory and this one. However, the elaborative hypothesis does not require the postulation of separate episodic and semantic memories. That is, the memory trace encoding the study trial is not inaccessible from the concept *bear*. The concept for *bear* is directly connected to the list tag. There is failure to recognize *bear* because that connection can sometimes fail at test.

Disambiguation Hypothesis

I have been most strongly associated with a somewhat different interpretation of encoding specificity (Anderson & Bower, 1974; Reder, Anderson, & Bjork, 1974). This is an attempt to use the obvious interpretation of the Light and Carter-

---

[2]Note in Fig. 10.1 that, beside the direct path between *bear* and *list* there are indirect paths between bear and list through *grizzly, angry, big,* and *fox.* In this analysis it is assumed that if the subject's elaboration does not include these intermediate terms, he cannot use these terms to retrieve the list tag.

Sobell experiment to explain Tulving's results. Recall that Light and Carter-Sobell found poor memory for *jam* when tested as *traffic-jam* after studying *strawberry-jam*. The obvious explanation of this is that different senses of *jam* are selected by the differing contexts and that recognition judgments are being made on the basis of sense. Alternative senses are represented in the ACT model by different idea nodes connected to the same word. In the Light and Carter-Sobell experiment we propose that memory for the study trial *strawberry-jam* is attached to one idea node for *jam* but when tested with *traffic-jam*, the subject inspects the other idea node and fails to find the memory.

An obvious explanation for the Tulving result, then, lies in the hypothesis that words like *black* might also have multiple senses. As Anderson and Bower (1974) wrote:

> In the presence of *train*, one is likely to come up with the sense of *black* associated with soot and engine smoke or the sense associated with the glistening black of a polished toy train. However, in the presence of *white*, one is likely to come up with other senses of *black* such as prototypical color or the absence of light or a race of people. . . . It would seem that what distinguishes so-called homographs like *jam* from words like *black* is that the multiple senses of the former have relatively less semantic overlap. Nonetheless, the multiple senses of the "nonhomograph" are distinct, and if one sense is tagged during study, that sense must be retrieved later for successful recognition [p. 410].

The experiments by Reder, Anderson, and Bjork (1974) provide a test of these ideas. We attempted in those experiments to test for encoding specificity with a set of words which seemed to have only one sense. It seemed that low frequency words like *rhinoceros* have this characteristic. In a partial replication of the Tulving and Thomson (1971) experiment, Reder *et al.* found large detrimental effects on recognition and recall by switching associative context, but only for high frequency words. The detrimental effects for low frequency words were much reduced.

Figure 10.2 provides a network representation of the multiple-senses explanation. I have chosen the *bear* example to permit easy comparison with Fig. 10.1 representing the elaboration hypothesis. Figure 10.2 shows the word *bear* connected to some of its senses. The exact senses may differ from subject to subject. Attached to each sense node is a set of propositions specifying the meaning of each sense. These propositions are only crudely represented by arrows to some of the concepts involved. These senses are numbered. Below I have given a verbal transcription of some of the propositions attached to each.

1. A bear is a large shaggy animal feeding on berries, insects, and flesh.
2. To bear is to produce fruit.
3. A large angry grizzly bear chased a fox.
4. To bear is to give birth.
5. A black bear begged for food in the park.
6. A polar bear is strong and furry.
7. To bear is to carry.

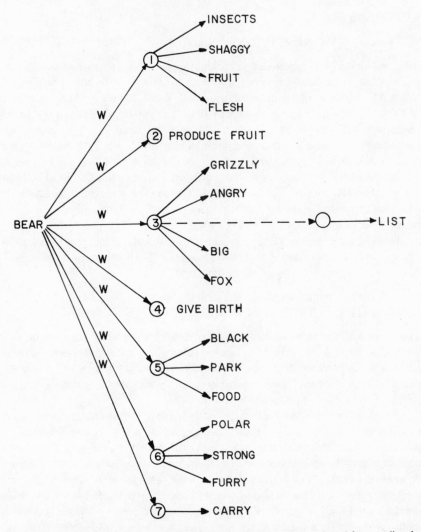

FIG. 10.2 Multiple senses attached to the word *bear*. Sense 3 has been selected for recording that *bear* occurred in the list. Compare with Fig. 10.1.

Note that some of these correspond to dictionary definitions (1, 2, 4, and 7), while others would be classified as instances of the first dictionary definition. However, they all have been attached as senses of *bear*.

The ACT model can explain how context will bias which sense is chosen. Suppose a subject is presented with a pair like *fox–bear*. There are two mechanisms for selecting a sense of *bear*. Both predict some effect of the *fox* context on the selection of a sense for *bear*. One means of encoding *bear* would be by the following production:

((Vcue − Vtarget) & (Videa W Vtarget)) ⇒ Videa

The condition of this production is looking for a memory pattern which encodes that the cue word (bound to Vcue) precedes the target word (bound to Vtarget) and that the target word is connected to an idea, Videa. For the network equivalent of (Vcue − Vtarget) see Fig. 4.4 (page 131). The variable Videa is a local variable which becomes bound to the idea node as a function of matching this pattern to memory. The action of this production simply involves a rehearsal of Videa, making that variable global and putting its value on the ALIST. In the case of a situation like Fig. 10.2, where the words are polysemous, the sense selected for Videa will be the first activated sense of *bear*. In the context of *fox,* activation can spread from that term to activate a sense of *bear*. Activation from this source would tend to select sense (3) in Fig. 10.2.

There is another way of achieving an encoding of Videa, that would much more strongly bias the encoding of *bear* to be of sense (3). This is achieved by the following production:

((Vcue − Vtarget) & (Videa W Vtarget)) ⇒ Videa
& (INTERSECTING Videa Vcue)

This constrains the sense of Videa to be one that has a path of intersection with Vcue. The typical instructions in one of Tulving's encoding specificity experiments are designed to encourage the subject to allow the first word to bias the encoding of the second. Therefore, this second production is probably a better model of the subject's encoding operation.

A number of criticisms have been privately made of the disambiguation hypothesis because it proposes that words, not traditionally recognized as polysemous, nonetheless have multiple meanings. One criticism is that there is no limit to the number of senses required because one would have to propose a different sense for almost every context in which a word may occur. This is not so. One can account for the recognition failures reported earlier by assuming only a few senses (perhaps not the same for all subjects) are attached to words. Another criticism is that it is arbitrary to embody a few interpretations as distinct senses, and ignore all others. This criticism lacks force also. I assume that these senses arise out of experience. One's experiences are arbitrary. A few arbitrary senses of a concept will be selected as a function of these experiences. These arbitrarily chosen interpretations would become embodied as distinct senses.

This disambiguation hypothesis is clearly different from the elaborative hypothesis in that it does not propose that other concepts attached to a sense will be directly attached to the memory trace encoding the word's appearance in the list. However, it is going to be very difficult to separate the two hypotheses on the basis of empirical evidence. Both predict the basic encoding specificity results. The elaborative hypothesis could predict the Reder et al. result by assuming, reasonably, that there are fewer options for elaborating low frequency words. Both predict that, having studied a pair like *train–black,* it should be better to test with *engine–black* than *white–black*. That is, if one is going to switch the cue word it is better to switch it to something semantically related. The elaborative hypothesis would claim that the word *engine* is likely to lead to the same elaboration of *black* as did *train* whereas the multiple senses hypothesis claims a greater probability of *engine* selecting the same sense of *black* as *train*. Both hypotheses identify the phenomenon of encoding specificity with the number of paths leading from a concept. Both claim that failures of memory arise because the subject at test does not take the same paths as at study.

There is no reason, within the ACT theory, to suppose that the correct explanation for the encoding specificity phenomena lies totally in the elaborative or in the disambiguation hypotheses. It would seem perfectly reasonable to propose that the correct explanation is a combination of the two. Fortunately, it is possible to provide a slightly more abstract explanation which blurs the differences between the two theories, but preserves what they have in common. I have called this the Semantic Encoding Hypothesis. This abstracted hypothesis does not lose any of the essential features of either of the two more specific theories.

Semantic Encoding Hypothesis

Connected to a term like *bear* in either Fig. 10.1 or Fig. 10.2 is a set of nodes. The semantic encoding hypothesis proposes that, during study or test, the subject will select from this set a subset which is semantically appropriate to the context of the word's presentation. This subset of nodes constitutes the word's encoding for that trial. In the elaboration hypothesis this subset is a set of associated concepts, whereas in the disambiguation hypothesis this subset is a single sense. At study these encodings will be associated to a memory structure recording the appearance of the word (represented as LIST in Figs. 10.1 and 10.2). At test these encodings will be used to try to retrieve the list information.

In this abstract hypothesis, the process underlying selection of semantically appropriate nodes is unspecified. The selection process is just as vague in the more specific elaboration hypothesis. The intersection procedure gives precision to that notion in the disambiguation hypothesis.

Related Theories

The Semantic Encoding Hypothesis bears considerable similarity to other ideas in psychology. The stimulus-sampling theory of Estes (see Section 3.2) proposed that elements were sampled from a stimulus situation to be associated with a response. One can think of a word as constituting a set of stimulus elements (as Bower has done, 1972) from which subjects select elements. One difference between stimulus sampling and Semantic Encoding theory is that in the latter, selection does not occur at random.

Martin (1968, 1971) has been developing similar ideas for application to paired-associate learning. He calls his theory *encoding variability.* In a number of the tasks Martin analyzes, the stimuli are *CCC* (three consonant) trigrams. These stimuli have the important feature that they can be divided into three elements, that is, their component letters. Martin has also considered other compound stimuli like sets of three words or stimuli that vary in a number of dimensions. He argues that in learning a response to such stimuli, subjects often attach the response to just one element or dimension. This can be shown in a number of ways. Stimuli can be presented which overlap with the original stimulus in an element. So, for instance, after studying *JXR*–dog, the subject might be tested with *JBY*. Subjects show confusion and recall to these new stimuli the response (that is, dog) learned to the original stimulus which overlaps with it. Martin is also able to show that when subjects must learn two responses to the same stimulus in two lists they will tend to select different elements of the stimulus to which to attach the response.

Martin shows that subjects will attend selectively to only certain external attributes of a stimulus. Similar ideas about stimulus selection have played an important role in the theories of Lawrence (1963), Trabasso and Bower (1968), and Underwood (1963). Martin proposes that subjects can also select from internal encodings of the words (Martin, 1975). This suggestion is very similar to ACT's Semantic Encoding Hypothesis.

The Spacing Effect

One of the earliest questions in experimental psychology concerned the effect of spacing on memory. Was it better to spend a massed amount of time studying material or was it better to space one's studies? Recently, there has been a revival of experimental interest in this question, particularly in the free recall paradigm (Glenberg, 1974; Hintzman, 1974; Madigan, 1969; Melton, 1970; Rundus, 1971; Waugh, 1970). The paradigm involves having subjects study a long list of words in which a particular word might appear twice. After list presentation subjects are required to recall as many words from the list as they can. Interest focuses on the lag between the two presentations of a word. Probability of recall increases with this variable. The improvement is quite striking on comparing the case where the two presentations are together (lag = 0, massed) with a lag of just a few inter-vening items. However, a gradual improvement in recall has been shown up to lags of 80.

It seems doubtful that this phenomena will prove to be the result of a single process, but an encoding variability analysis will probably explain part of the effect. The basic idea is that the farther two items are apart, the more variably they will be encoded. If one has two different encodings of the word, the probability is higher that an encoding of the word will be retrieved in a later free recall test than if one has just one encoding.

Striking evidence for this analysis is provided by an experiment of Gartman and Johnson (1972) on free recall of homographs. The homographs appeared twice in the list. In the *different* condition the contexts of the word's two presentations were chosen to select different meanings of the two homographs. In the *same* condition, the two contexts selected the same meaning. In a control condition, no specific inducing words were presented. Free recall of the control words showed the typical lag effect. The different words showed no lag effect but were recalled very well. The same words also showed no lag effect but were recalled quite poorly.

The encoding specificity studies of Tulving show the detrimental effects of variable encodings, in that poorer memory is found when the study and test encodings do not match. The lag studies just cited show the beneficial effects of variable encoding: When one cannot predict the encoding required at test, it is better to have multiple encodings for the required memory.

A recent experiment by Glenberg (1974) on the lag effect in paired-associate learning serves nicely to put these ideas together. As we noted earlier, in paried-associate learning it is important to have the encoding of the stimulus at test match the study encoding. (In free recall there is no stimulus so the consideration does not apply.) Glenberg looked at a continuous paired-associate task where a word is studied twice and tested once. He manipulated the lag between the two study trials and, independently, the lag between the second study trial and test. I will refer to these as study lag and test lag, respectively. Glenberg reasoned that at a short test lag a long study lag might not be beneficial. The encoding of the stimulus at test is very likely to be similar to that at the second study presentation. Therefore, it is important that the study lag be short so that encoding of the stimulus on the first study also be similar to the encoding at test. However, at a long test lag the encoding at test is quite likely to be different than the encoding at the second study. Therefore, it is important that the encoding at the first study be different than at the second study to maximize the probability that one of the encodings match the test encoding. Hence, for long test lags, long study lags should be beneficial. Glenberg found just this predicted interaction between study and test lag.

Summing Up Results on Encoding

The research on encoding phenomena has been one of the recent, significant developments in verbal learning. It does not seem to me that the explanations embodied in ACT's Semantic Encoding Hypothesis are particularly different from some of the other theories offered. The point of this section was not to show that ACT offered particularly novel insights into these phenomena. It was more to show that ACT's mechanisms embodied the current wisdom about encoding specificity and encoding variability. It was essential to do this to bolster ACT's claim to being a general model of human cognition.

Before leaving this section I think it would be profitable to inquire how significant, in a real world sense, are the phenomena of encoding specificity and encoding variability. No doubt they can produce huge effects in level of memory in a verbal learning experiment. But what about their role in everyday life? What portion of the failures and successes of memory that we experience can be attributed to encoding factors?

It seems that very little of one's typical memory failures can be attributed to encoding factors. Generally, the context is very rich in which a prompt is presented for memory. The context serves satisfactorily to disambiguate the word and achieve the desired encoding. Thus, it is unlikely that there will be failures to recognize the prompt. There is only one type of real-life circumstance in which I think I frequently encounter "memory failure" due to encoding failures. Let me relate an example episode—an exchange between my wife and myself:

LYNNE: Was Bob at the Brown Bag?
JOHN: No, he never goes—you know that.
LYNNE: What do you mean, dummy, he organizes them.
JOHN: Oh, you mean Bob Bjork, not Bob Pachella. Sure, he was there.

Note that this example is not what would be commonly referred to as "memory failure." However, many theories, including ACT, assert that the memory failure I experienced in this episode is just the sort of phenomenon that is being studied in verbal learning experiments on encoding specificity.

I also do not think encoding variability normally improves memory the way it is purported to in the lag studies. Normally, we are not trying to retrieve a word, but rather a sense of a word. Thus, if I am trying to free recall the locations I was at during the day I would not regard myself as totally successful if I recalled *bank,* indicating that I had been at the monetary institution, but forgot that I had been at the river *bank.*

Compared to most normal memory situations a verbal learning experiment is a very impoverished stimulus situation. It is for this reason that effects of encoding have proven so important. Note that this is not to say that such verbal learning experiments are not important. They are important in the same way perception experiments that study illusions under impoverished situations are important. Understanding why the system malfunctions in abnormal situations is often the key to understanding why it normally works so well. I think this is particularly true in the case of encoding effects. Successful disambiguation of words is critical to successful language understanding.

10.2 DEPTH OF PROCESSING

Everyone knows what it means to be a deep thinker but no one can tell you what it means. This situation was tolerable as long as we were just passing judgments about our colleagues, but it has now become intolerable because the notion of deep thinking has found its way into the theoretical literature on human memory. The basic result is that the more "deeply a subject processes" material the greater the probability of retaining it. Before getting into the question of theoretical interpretation, a brief description of some of the studies that make this point is in order.

Effects of orienting task.   A number of experiments (Hyde & Jenkins, 1973; Walsh & Jenkins, 1973; Till & Jenkins, 1973; Craik & Tulving, 1975) have looked at the effect of orienting task on free recall. For instance, in the Hyde and Jenkins experiment subjects studied words and were asked to perform one of the following five tasks: rate the pleasantness of a word, rate its frequency of usage, check for occurrence of the letters E or G, indicate part of speech, or decide if the word fits in one of two sentence frames. The two sentence frames were either "It is. . . ." or "It is the. . . ." They found much higher recall and better organization of recall in the first two tasks than the last three. Intuitively, it does seem that the first two involve a deeper level of processing.

Recently, Bower and Karlin (1974) have extended these findings to memory for faces. One group of subjects rated faces on a pleasant–unpleasant scale, but another group rated the faces as male or female. The first task produced better memory for the faces.

Effects of rehearsal.   It had been thought (Atkinson & Shiffrin, 1968; Waugh & Norman, 1965) that memories were deposited firmly in long-term memory simply by rehearsing them in short-term memory. However, more recent research (for example, Bjork & Jongeward, 1974; Craik & Watkins, 1973; Jacoby, 1973; Jacoby & Bartz, 1972; Woodward, Bjork, & Jongeward, 1973) has shown that there are different types of rehearsal—"deep" versus "shallow" rehearsal—and that these different types have different effects on long-term memory.

Consider the study of Bjork and Jongeward (1974). Their subjects saw for one second a pair of nouns such as "tool horn." They were then required to rehearse these for 1, 3, or 7 sec. Next, subjects would see for 1 sec a signal indicating which of the two nouns should be replaced by another new noun. The signal "gate ---" indicated that the subject was now responsible for memory of the pair "gate horn." Note *horn* was not given in the signal. For this reason subjects had to rehearse the original pair "tool horn," because they would be responsible for recall of one of these. After the second input, subjects were given 1, 3, or 7 sec of rehearsal, followed by 12 sec of an interfering digit span task, followed by a cue to recall the two words.

After a sequence of 36 such trials, subjects were asked to recall all 108 words that they had seen. This included 36 words that they were instructed to forget— *forget* words; 36 words that they rehearsed over both intervals—*both* words; and 36 words that were studied in the second interval—*second* words. Of course, subjects recalled much better in the immediate test than the delayed and in the delayed test *both* and *second* words were recalled much better than the *forget* words. However, the important result is the relative effect of the first rehearsal period versus the second on retention of *both* words. In immediate and final re-call, the length of the second retention interval produced very significant im-provement in recall, but the length of the first interval had virtually no effect. Bjork and Jongeward propose that during the first retention interval subjects are engaging in some rote rehearsal just to maintain the words in short-term memory. It is only in the second rehearsal period, when they know which words they will have to retain, that they engage in deep processing. This deep processing Bjork and Jongeward call secondary rehearsal.

Depth of comprehension.   Bobrow and Bower (1969) explored the useful-ness of sentences as mediators in paired-associate learning. Rohwer (1966) has shown that a child's memory for a noun pair is improved by providing a sentence linking them. This improvement is obtained relative to a control group which studied the paired associates without linking sentences. This is not true for adults, however. Apparently, adults spontaneously generate mediators which are as good as the provided sentence. Bobrow and Bower, however, contrasted giving the adult subject a sentence with requiring the subject to generate the sentence. Sub-jects who passively read the sentences recalled 28% of the nouns, whereas the generate subjects recalled 69%. They offer the following interpretation for this result:

> The idea is simply that recall is facilitated by S "comprehending the meaning" of the sentence, and this occurs more reliably when one has to make up a linking sentence than when one merely reads off a linking sentence that occurs in a long list of other sentences and pairs [Bobrow & Bower, 1969, p. 458].

Effect of context on memory for prose.   Bransford and Johnson (1973) had subjects study the following paragraph:

> If the balloons popped, the sound wouldn't be able to carry since everything would be too far away from the correct floor. A closed window would also prevent the sound from carrying, since most buildings tend to be well insulated. Since the whole operation depends on a steady flow of electricity, a break in the middle of the wire would also cause problems. Of course, the fellow could shout, but the human voice is not loud enough to carry that far. An additional problem is that a string could break on the instrument. Then there could be no accompaniment to the message. It is clear that the best situation would involve less distance. Then there would be fewer potential problems. With face to face contact, the least number of things could go wrong [pp. 392–393].

They contrasted memory for the paragraph with and without the context in Fig. 10.3. Having the referent picture with which to comprehend the paragraph almost doubled the level of recall. Bransford and Johnson interpret this effect in the same way as Bobrow and Bower interpreted their result—the more deeply one compre-hends a passage the better is recall.

Memory for gist versus form.   Sentences offer an interesting opportunity for study of depth of processing in that they can be subject to at least two levels

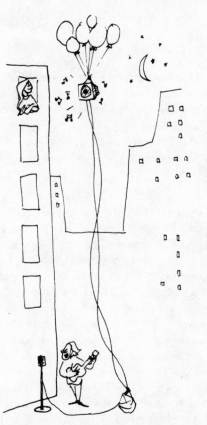

FIG. 10.3 An appropriate context figure used by Bransford and Johnson.

of analysis—their surface form and their meaning. Sentences can differ just slightly in their surface and have very different meanings. For example, contrast

(1)   The car's exhaust has polluted the air.
(2)   The car's exhaust has not polluted the air.

On the other hand, sentences can have very different surface forms, but almost identical meanings. For example, consider

(3)   The car's exhaust polluted the air.
(4)   The air has been polluted by the car with its exhaust.

One can ask whether a subject is more likely to remember the surface form of a sentence or its meaning. A depth of processing approach would predict that meaning, which presumably requires deeper processing, should be better remembered than surface form. This implies that subjects should tend to confuse pairs like Sentences (3) and (4) much more than they do pairs like Sentences (1) and (2). This basic prediction has now been verified many times (Anderson, 1974;

Bransford, Barclay, & Franks, 1972; Fillenbaum, 1966; Gomulicki, 1956; Sachs, 1967—to name just a few).

Imagery.   One of the most effective ways to have subjects learn material in an experiment is to require them to develop a visual image involving the material. The benefits of imagery can also be attributed to the deeper processing of the material it requires. There are some (for example, Paivio, 1971) who argue that imagery is effective in promoting good recall for reasons other than those that cause verbal elaboration to be effective. Anderson and Bower (1973) presented arguments against this point of view.

Mnemonic techniques.   There are many mnemonic techniques (Bower, 1970) which are remarkably effective in their ability to improve one's memory. Some of these owe their effectiveness to the simple fact that they tend to organize memories rather than leaving them disjointed. As a consequence recall is much more orderly and successful. Such techniques include the famous method of loci (Yates, 1966) and the equally famous numeric pegword technique (that is, one's a bun, two's a shoe technique—Miller, Galanter, & Pribram, 1960). Such organizational factors are easy to understand within a network model (for example, Anderson, 1972). Other mnemonic techniques work because they recode a complex novel configuration as an already learned configuration. Thus, one might try to remember the nonsense quadragram NGHT as "night without the i." As Anderson and Bower (1973, pp. 414–421) document, it is also easy to explain the effectiveness of such techniques in terms of a network model.

On the other hand, certain features of the mnemonic techniques seem to have their effect because they promote "deeper" levels of analysis. The clearest examples of this are the instructions to use visual imagery; but there are others. For example, a way to learn to spell an unfamiliar word is to make a sentence out of words whose first letters spell the desired word.

Theoretical Interpretation

We have now reviewed a rather diverse list of experimental phenomena which have two things in common. First, they involve quite large differences in level of recall. Second, these differences are all correlated with an intuitive sense that we have about level of processing. There is one paradoxical feature about many of these phenomena. The more deeply processed material often seems to involve the subject elaborating the information given with further information beyond what is stated. Thus, he would seem to be increasing the demands on his memory. At first blush, it seems paradoxical that subjects have better memory for the target material when they add further material to be remembered. I would like to go through various explanations that have been offered for the effects of depth of processing.

Motivation.   One might argue that conditions that require deep processing are more interesting to the subject and he is motivated to try harder. Such a motivational argument is virtually impossible to reject for any phenomena, but it seems implausible as an explanation for the effects of depth of processing. There is no evidence that motivation is important to learning. For instance, there is no evidence that intention to learn plays any significant role in memory (Anderson & Bower, 1972a; Hyde & Jenkins, 1973; Postman, 1964). The general outcome has been that as long as the subject is oriented toward the material and processes it at the same "depth," he will remember to the same degree regardless of whether he is trying to learn it or not.

Trace characteristics.   Kintsch (1975) proposes that in processing a piece of text we develop a series of memory traces. One progresses from sensory traces to traces of various lexical items, to traces for linguistic features (for example, phrase structures and transformations) to a representation of underlying propositions. He argues that deeply processed verbal material has a propositional representation whereas shallowly processed material tends to be represented at the level of lexical items. He proposes that propositional traces have much slower decay rates than lexical traces. Similar ideas have been offered by Wicklegren (1973) who suggests that propositional traces decay less rapidly because they suffer less interference from other memory traces. He also proposes that interference is a function of similarity and argues that propositional traces will be less similar to other traces in memory than will be more sensory traces.

These assumptions can explain a number of phenomena associated with depth of processing. First, memory for the gist of a sentence is better than memory for its form because the gist is represented in durable propositional trace whereas the form is represented in a more transient lexical trace. Instructions to process single words deeply (for example, Hyde & Jenkins, 1973) result in better memory because they increase the probability that the subject will leave a propositional trace connecting the items rather than a lexical trace.

However, there are a number of weaknesses in this explanation. First, it does not explain the advantage of elaborative instructions for sentential material (for example, Bobrow & Bower, 1969), nor does it explain the advantage of an elaborative context (for example, Bransford & Johnson, 1973). Presumably, the subjects in these experiments, under all conditions, are leaving propositional traces in memory. However, elaborative instructions leave "more deeply processed" propositional traces and these seem more memorable. If Kintsch is to maintain this tack he would have to postulate different propositional traces with different decay characteristics.

Another problem for the trace decay hypothesis is that it is not clear that lexical information decays more rapidly than propositional information. In unpublished experiments on sentence memory I have contrasted memory for lexical information (as measured by ability to retain whether the sentence voice is active or passive) with the ability to retain propositional information (as measured by ability to make truth judgments). In a test at a 30-sec delay there is poorer memory for lexical information. However, conditional on the fact that the lexical information survives the first 30 seconds, it is just as likely to be available at a later point as propositional information that survives the first 30 sec. Thus, the difficulty with information about form seems to be initially encoding the information into long-term memory, not in retaining that information.

Subject preference for deep processing.   At the Loyola Conference in 1974 (see Solso, 1975) George Mandler suggested to me that there was no real memory advantage for deeply processed memory traces. It was just that in the typical memory task (a) subjects tended mainly to form such traces and (b) success in the memory test was contingent on the existence of such deeply processed traces. So the fact that subjects tended to remember gist better than form represented a fact about what they preferred to encode. The typical sentence recall task does not really test subjects for verbatim recall of the sentence, so subjects naturally do better if oriented to process the material at a deep, semantic level. This analysis also offers an explanation of why subjects are better in a free recall test if given a semantic orienting task. Such a task causes the subjects to introduce propositions interconnecting the words. These interconnecting propositions serve to facilitate recall by introducing retrieval routes among the words. Support for this idea is the considerable evidence (see Anderson & Bower, 1972b; Kintsch, 1970) that such orienting instructions do not improve word recognition nearly as much as they do free recall. Presumably, a recognition task does not require the inter-connecting links that free recall requires.

The flaw in this argument is that it implies that subjects can, if they want to, remember any level as well as any other. For instance, while subjects normally re-tain gist well and form poorly, this could be changed by properly instructing them. Certainly, we can, if we want to, remember a passage verbatim. The problem how-ever is that it is much more difficult to learn the verbatim paragraph rather than its gist. There are a number of studies that have contrasted the effect of setting the subject to remember the gist versus the form of a linguistic message (Anderson & Bower, 1973, Section 8.3; Barclay, 1973; Graesser & Mandler, 1975). Some of these have found that subjects oriented to remember form do indeed improve their memory for form, but all the studies are consistent in showing that subjects, even when oriented to form, show better memory for gist.

Redundancy of connections.   The explanation offered by Anderson and Bower (1973) for depth processing was that when a subject processed material under instructions to elaborate, image, etc., he was likely to form many redundant interconnections between the to-be-recalled items. Therefore, there was a high probability that one of the connections would be available at the time of test permitting recall. The problem with shallow processing, then, was that it introduced few interconnections.

This explanation was somewhat problematical within the HAM framework because of the HAM assumption that there was a limited working memory in which temporary memory structures had to be held for encoding into long-term memory. This put a clear limit on how many redundant connections could be stored away in a fixed period of time. The ACT model does not assume such limitations on the number of connections that can be set up in a fixed time. Nevertheless, the redundant connections hypothesis, in its present form, runs into difficulties on another score. It provides no explanation for why similar redundant connections cannot be built up during shallow processing. For instance, suppose a subject is asked to remember the paired associate *dog–chair*. Under instructions to semantically elaborate suppose he built up the following story:

> The dog loved his masters. He also loved to sit on the chairs. His masters had a beautiful black velvet chair. One day he climbed on it. He left his white hairs all over the chair. His masters were upset by this. They scolded him.

Figure 10.4a illustrates, in a crude LNR-like notation (see Section 2.4), the approximate graph structure interconnecting the concepts in the elaboration. (An ACT structure could be provided, but it would have been a more complicated graph.) As can be seen there certainly are many redundant paths interconnecting *dog* and *chair*. However, why could not the subjects form to themselves the following elaboration:

> The word "dog" is in the book. The word "dog" is also known to be above the word "chair." The book has the word "chair" printed in large red letters. On one page, the word "dog" is larger than the word "chair." The word "dog" has its green letters printed beside the word "chair." The book tells about this. The book illustrates the word "dog."

This is a rather incoherent elaboration about the words rather than the concepts. Figure 10.4b illustrates the graph structure of connections underlying this elaboration. The reader may confirm that this graph structure is isomorphic to Fig. 10.4a. I am confident that the first "conceptual" elaboration would provide a better mnemonic to connect *dog* and *chair* than the second "lexical" elaboration. Thus, it seems that the advantage of deeper processing does not just lie in the fact that it provides a more elaborate graph structure. There is something in the semantic cohesion of the elaboration that contributes to good memory.

The elaborative production hypothesis. The difficulty with the redundancy of connections hypothesis is that it does not provide an analysis of the procedures that generated elaborations. Therefore, it has no way of explaining the differences in generating various types of elaborations. ACT productions, however, provide a medium for modeling these elaborative procedures. The basic

(a)

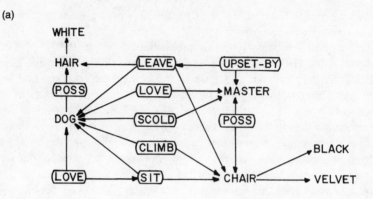

(b)

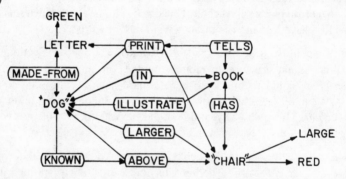

FIG. 10.4   The graph structure of the semantic elaboration in (a) is isomorphic to the graph structure of the lexical elaboration in (b).

proposal is that through experiences we have acquired productions which will, if a certain pattern of facts is active, enrich this pattern with further elaborations. So, for instance, we might have a production of the form "If a pet spoils furniture" (condition) then "the masters of the pet become angry" (action). As more such productions are applied to elaborate an input more redundant connections will be established and there will be better memory for that input. Thus, the reason why some material is more memorable than other material is that there are more productions available for elaboration of some types of material. From this viewpoint the difference between deep and shallow processing of linguistic material concerns whether the material is encoded into a form for which there is a rich set of elaborative productions. If one encodes the presentation of *dog–chair* as "*Dog* is beside *chair*" there is little that we know relevant to elaborating this encoding. In contrast, if we encode it as "The dog sat on the chair" there is much we know about how to elaborate this.

The critical feature of this hypothesis is the claim that productions exist which will create redundant connections. I think it is important to illustrate this abstract claim with an example—to show that one can write plausible ACT productions that will create redundant connections. Suppose, we present a subject with *dog–chair* and he encodes this as *The dog sat on the chair* which would be represented in ACT as the set of propositions, $(x * \text{dog}) \& (y * \text{chair}) \& (x * (\text{sit-on OF } y))$ where x and y represented the individual dog and chair. It is quite likely that we know that dogs leave hairs on chairs. This could be encoded by the following production[3]:

> (P1)   (V1 * dog) $\Rightarrow$ (V3 * hair) & (V3 * (from OF V1))
> & (V1 * (sit-on OF V2))   & (V3 * (on OF V2))

Since the antecedent of this production is satisfied in active memory, the production would execute and add the following three propositions to memory: $(Z * \text{hair})$, $(Z * (\text{from OF } x))$, $(Z * (\text{on OF } y))$ where Z represents the shedded hairs.

We also know that people are upset by the hairs on their chairs. This would be encoded by the following proposition:

> (P2)   (V1 * hair) & (V2 * chair) $\Rightarrow$ (V3 * (own OF V2)) &
> & (V1 * (on OF V2))   ((V3 * upset) * (because OF
>   (V1 * (on OF V2))))

The execution of this production would add the following propositions to memory: $(u * (\text{own OF } Z)) \& ((u * \text{upset}) * (\text{because OF } (Z * (\text{on OF } y))))$ where u represents the owner.

We also know that the original source of hairs is the cause of the hairs being on objects and that people are likely to scold what causes them to be upset. This would be encoded by the following pair of productions:

> (P3)   (V1 * (from OF V2)) $\Rightarrow$ (V2 * (cause OF
> & (V1 * (on OF V3))   (V1 * (on OF V3))))
>
> (P4)   (V1 * (cause of V2)) $\Rightarrow$ (V3 * (scold OF V1))
> & ((V3 * upset) * (because OF V2))

The effect of these two productions would be to add the following propositions to memory: $(x * (\text{cause OF } (Z * (\text{on OF } y))))$ and $(u * (\text{scold OF } x))$.

I could go on with this detail almost endlessly, showing how our knowledge encoded as productions can serve to elaborate a small data base. However, this is enough to make the point. A subject, starting with the impoverished network in Fig. 10.5a, could elaborate it via Productions (P1)–(P4) to the more redundant network in Fig. 10.5b. Ignoring paths involving loops, there are seven paths inter-

---

[3]To be an accurate statement about the real world the proposition (V3 * (on OF V2)) in the action of (P1) should be qualified as only probable, that is, ((V3 * (on OF V2)) * probable). For simplicity, I have omitted such truth modification throughout this example.

(a)

(b)

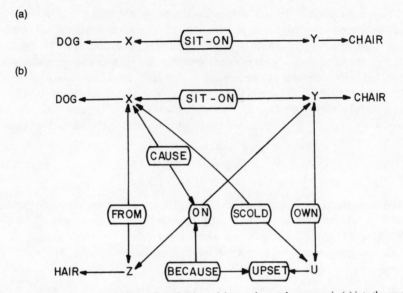

FIG. 10.5   The effect of Productions (P1)–(P4) is to elaborate the graph structure in (a) into the graph structure in (b).

connecting *dog* and *chair* in the graph structure in Fig. 10.5b whereas there is only one path in Fig. 10.5a.

There is one unfortunate aspect to this proposal. One cannot translate it into a working simulation for any of the depth of processing experiments discussed earlier. The reason is that an enormous number of facts (embodied as propositions and productions) would be required to realistically deal with the material a subject encounters in one of these experiments. The typical subject brings a lifetime of experience to bear on processing this material. It is just not possible, as a practical matter, to provide the simulation program with that background of knowledge. Therefore, one can only provide a few illustrations like those given earlier and proceed to discuss the abstract properties of this elaboration hypothesis.

An important point about the elaborative productions is that they are a product of our real-world experience with pets, furniture, etc. A member of a non-Western culture would not have these productions and might be no better able to elaborate the statement *The dog is on the chair* than the statement *The word "dog" is next to the word "chair."* The existence of elaborative productions explains the difference between the *furniture* paragraph and the *typography* paragraph (page 397) considered earlier as a counterexample to the redundancy of connections hypothesis. First, it is easier for a subject to generate the furniture paragraph because he has a rich set of elaborative productions. Second, he would be able to better remember the furniture paragraph, if given it, than if given the typography paragraph because he has productions to further elaborate the furniture paragraph.

However, in principle, it should be possible to acquire through experience the productions that would make it as easy to elaborate and to remember the typography paragraph.

There are examples where acquired familiarity with the material helps in learning a novel relation involving the material. For example, consider the sentence

(5)   The negative sentence was harder to comprehend than
         the passive sentence.

I suspect that a psycholinguist would display better memory for that sentence than the average, equally intelligent academic. Note that I make my comparison with the intelligent academic to eliminate the possibility that concepts like "negative sentence" are not known. I also have chosen a fact which I suspect few if any psycholinguists have stored. So, if they display better memory it must be their ability to elaborate upon this fact and not any differences in storing the fact per se.

There is one research area where it is well established that familiarity with the subject matter produces better memory. This has to do with the difference between skilled and nonskilled players at games like chess (Chase & Simon, 1973; DeGroot, 1965) or Go (Reitman, 1975). Here it is found that the skilled player has a much better memory for the board positions that are found in the course of a game. However, given a random board position there is very little difference. Simon and Gilmartin (1973) have proposed that skilled subjects build up subconfigurations that represent frequently encountered situations. A common board position can then be recorded in terms of these subconfigurations. The recoded board has fewer chunks and is hence easier to remember. This recoding hypothesis must be at least a partial explanation of the chess experts' success at reconstructing a board position—imagine the difference between a nonplayer and a player of chess in being able to reconstruct the opening board position. However, it is unclear to me that the recoding hypothesis explains all the success of experts. It may be that part of the experts' success lies in his ability to quickly elaborate a board position with redundant information about implications of that board position for the future course of the game.

The recoding versus elaborative strategies are very different approaches to producing memory success. The recoding approach attempts to reduce the amount of information to be remembered. Undoubtedly, it is the important component of success in some memory tasks. However, I have been unable to see how it would explain any of the depth of processing phenomena reviewed earlier. As will be shown shortly, all these phenomena can be accounted for in terms of elaborative productions. The inability of the recoding hypothesis to explain these phenomena is important because according to the Newell and Simon (1972) theory all superior memory performance must be explained in terms of recoding into fewer chunks. They propose that information can be written into long-term memory only at a constant and relatively slow rate—5 sec per chunk. Given this assumption, there is no way that a rich elaboration of the material could help. But it does. Hence, we must conclude that one of the fundamental assumptions of the Newell and Simon theory—a fixed, slow rate of information transfer to LTM—is wrong.

A better conception of buildup in memory is, I think, the one set forth earlier in the book. There is no fixed rate of writing information into long-term memory. Whenever a production is executed it can attempt to write information into long-term memory. Therefore, the amount of information written into memory during any period of time will depend on the number of productions that are executed. The execution of any particular production, however, will result only in a probability of successful encoding of information into a long-term form. Moreover, information in long-term memory is subject to forgetting due to interfering associations. Therefore, to retain a connection it is not usually sufficient to have one production executed which will encode that connection. One needs to have redundant connections and hence to have executed a number of elaborative productions.

Explanation of Depth of Processing Phenomena

I will now examine the various depth of processing phenomena listed earlier and show how the elaborative production hypothesis can explain them. First, consider the effects of orienting task on memory for words or pictures. This can be explained by assuming that the orienting task of rating for pleasantness caused subjects to encode the material in terms of its implications for a pleasantness judgment. For instance, *chair* might be encoded "as an object for hitting people with in barroom brawls" or "as an object for making love in." Given the general preoccupation with pleasure and morality, it seems likely that subjects have evolved many productions relevant to elaborating such encodings. A similar interpretation can be given to the effects of different levels of rehearsal as reported by Bjork and Jongeward. That is, secondary rehearsal causes subjects to process material at a level where elaborative productions are more available.

The Bobrow and Bower generation instructions were so very effective because they forced the subject to encode the words in a form for which elaborative productions exist. Generating a connecting sentence forces the subject to encode the sentence in a format for which elaborative productions exist since the connecting sentence is itself an elaboration. In contrast, simply giving the subject a sentence does not guarantee he will encode it into a format to which elaborative productions can apply. It is interesting to note that Bobrow and Bower report that giving the connecting sentence is very effective if subjects are further required to generate a continuation to that sentence.

A suitable context, such as those in the Bransford and Johnson experiment, serves to improve recall because it facilitates the creation of elaborations. Consider the first sentence of the Bransford and Johnson experiment:

If the balloons popped, the sound wouldn't be able to carry since everything would be too far away from the correct floor.

Only with the aid of the picture was I able to add the following elaborations:

The balloons were holding a speaker up to an upper apartment window. This permitted the sound of the serenade to be heard by the woman. It must be a fragile arrangement. If the wind blew the balloons against the apartment they might pop.

Figure 10.6 shows the graph structure without (a) and with (b) the elaboration. Clearly, the elaboration does much to interconnect the to-be-recalled concepts. There are two sources for these interconnecting elaborations. Some of them like *The balloons were holding a speaker up to an upper apartment window* were more

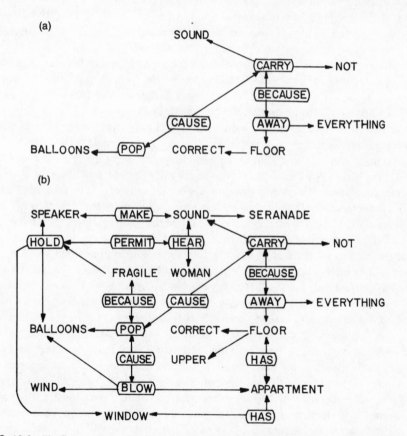

FIG. 10.6   The first sentence of the Bransford and Johnson experiment: (a) without elaboration and (b) with elaboration.

or less direct encodings of the picture. Thus, their origin would be some picture parsing routine. Others were inferences or elaborations that were permitted by the combined information in sentence and picture. For instance, the elaborations *If the wind blew the balloons against the apartment they might pop* came both from the sentence and the picture. We might think of it as being generated by the following production:

$$(V1 * \text{balloon}) \& (V1 * \text{pop}) \quad \Rightarrow \quad (V3 * \text{wind}) \& (((V3 * (\text{cause OF}$$
$$\& (V1 * (\text{near OF } V2)) \qquad (V1 * (\text{against OF } V2)))) * (\text{cause OF}$$
$$(V1 * \text{pop}))) * \text{possible})$$

This production asserts that if balloons pop, and they are near an object, a possible cause of their popping is the wind blowing them against that object. Note that two of the propositions in the condition of the production—(V1 * balloon) & (V1 * pop)—are supplied by the sentence and the other—(V1 * (near OF V2))—is supplied by the picture. Thus, we have an example of a picture and a sentence fitting together to permit an elaborative production.

Memory for gist is better than for form because we have a richer set of elaborative productions for gist. ACT would represent the form of a sentence as an encoding of the string adjacencies of the words in the sentence (see Fig. 4.8, page 136) whereas it would represent the gist as a set of propositions encoding meaning. It is unlikely that many productions would have evolved relevant to elaborating string encodings whereas many productions would exist relevant to elaborating meaning encodings. An experiment by Begg and Paivio (1969) is pertinent here. They found that the superiority of gist did not hold up for abstract sentences. One might postulate that this is because subjects have less familiarity with the semantic content of abstract sentences. Johnson, Bransford, Nyberg, and Cleary (1972) have shown that subjects did rate the abstract sentences in the Begg and Paivio experiment as harder to comprehend. The general reason that memory for the content of abstract material is poor is because we have had so little experience in elaborating such content. When sufficient prerequisite experience is given, abstract material should display the same properties as concerete material. For instance, psychologists probably display the same good memory for abstract material about their domain of research as they display for concrete material.

The facilitative effects of imagery are due to the fact that it forces subjects to encode information in a form for which elaborative productions exist. Imagery is particularly effective because it causes subjects to process material in terms of common physical properties and actions. The typical seeing subject has had a rich lifetime of experience with such properties and actions and must have many elaborative productions available. The various processing admonitions associated with mnemonic techniques can be similarly understood within the elaborative production hypothesis.

This elaborative production hypothesis is similar to the elaborative model offered in the previous section (page 381) to account for the effects of encoding specificity. In that section the notion was emphasized of the subject selecting from the set of propositions stored with a concept a number of propositions with which to elaborate the presentation of that concept. However, here we are concerned with memory for units as large as a paragraph. These units are novel and it is not going to be the case that a subject has these already represented in memory with a stock of potential elaboration stored with them. One needs some general procedures for elaboration which can apply to novel material. These are provided by the elaborative productions. It may be the case that some of the elaborations postulated to explain encoding specificity could be attributed to elaborative productions.

Similarity to Craik and Tulving

There is a striking similarity between the elaborative production hypothesis and a recent analysis of depth of processing by Craik and Tulving (1975). It is somewhat amusing to note that Craik and Tulving express their views in Gestalt terms whereas the ACT model is neo-associationist. Perhaps this is evidence that the grand contrasts, such as the Gestalt versus associationism, in psychology are vacuous. They propose that the depth of processing results can be interpreted in terms of "the idea that memory performance depends on the elaborateness of the final encoding" (Craik & Tulving, 1975, p. 291). Craik and Tulving do not provide a mechanism to explain why richness of elaboration should be helpful. Within ACT rich elaboration is critical because it produces multiple redundant paths for recall. This redundancy makes it more difficult to lose the memory trace.

In addition to this principle of encoding elaboration, Craik and Tulving propose a principle of congruity to explain why some contexts are better at producing good memory than others. A simple example of where the principle of congruity would hold is the Bransford and Johnson experiment discussed earlier. Bransford and Johnson showed that some context pictures improved comprehension and memory whereas others did not. According to Craik and Tulving this would be because the facilitating pictures formed a better unit with the to-be-remembered paragraph than did the other pictures. Within the ACT framework this principle of congruity amounts to saying that certain combinations of encodings will satisfy the conditions of existing productions while other combinations will not.

Craik and Tulving see their theory as being a rather new approach to memory in that it emphasizes, not the structure of the external material, but rather the nature of internal mental processes. As they write: "All these studies conform to the new look in memory research in that the stress is on mental operations; items are remembered not as presented stimuli acting on the organism, but as components of mental activity" (Craik & Tulving, 1975, p. 292). This is very much like the ACT interpretation which emphasizes the role of elaborative productions (that is, processes) in producing the depth of processing effects.

Frames or Scripts

A number of people have remarked upon the similarity between the ACT interpretation of depth of processing and the AI notions of frames (Minsky, 1975) or scripts (Schank & Abelson, 1975). The frames concept will be discussed more fully in the next chapter but the basic idea is that our knowledge about common, stereotypical event sequences (like a birthday party) are organized into integrated units and that these units are brought to bear in interpreting new information, particularly linguistic information. One tries to fit new information into existing frames. So if one is told that *Johnny went to a birthday party,* the *birthday party frame* would specify elaborations that involved Johnny's buying a present, the playing of games, the eating of a birthday cake, etc. The effect of using the frame is very much like the effect of executing elaborative productions.

Summing Up Depth of Processing

Unlike encoding, the effects associated with depth of processing do not seem confined to the laboratory situation. Much of our real-life success or failure at memory can be related to the depth at which material is processed. In fact, there seems to be some modest potential for the practical application of the ideas associated with depth of processing. Unfortunately, ACT's elaborative encoding of material comes from the formation of productions through tedious experience. Thus, one cannot simply ''turn on'' his deep processing and establish a rich code for some to-be-remembered material. However, what one can do is attempt to transform material from a form for which there is a paucity of elaborative productions into a form for which there is a rich set of elaborations.

This is what is done in the work of Atkinson and Raugh (1974) and Raugh and Atkinson (1975) in teaching foreign vocabulary. The foreign word is linked to a keyword in English by a similarity in sound (acoustic link) and the keyword is then linked to the English translation by a mental image (imagery link). The point of the imagery link is to translate the two English words into a format, imagery, for which elaboration is effective. In all cases, this keyword method proved to be highly effective, yielding in one experiment a final test score of 88% correct for the keyword group compared to 28% for a control. Of course, it remains an open question how useful this mnemonic technique will prove to the long-term goal of becoming totally fluent in a foreign language.

10.3 ASSOCIATIVE VERSUS GESTALT THEORIES OF MEMORY

As noted in Anderson and Bower (1973) one of the issues that motivated the construction of HAM concerned the question of associative versus configural theories of memory. Initially we thought that memory for sentences would have properties like those attributed to Gestalt wholes. A number of phenomena led us to reject that point of view and instead assert a HAM-like representation for a sentence, that is, an associative configuration of elements. These phenomena were:

1. Associative interference could be produced if multiple propositions were attached to an element. There is ample data for this claim (Anderson & Bower, 1971; 1973, Chapters 12 and 15; Chapter 8 of this book).
2. Sentences tended to be recalled partially with some elements present and others missing (Anderson & Bower, 1971; 1973, Chapters 10 and 11).
3. Independent elements of the sentence seemed to add up in their ability to prompt recall of a target sentence, as an associative model would predict. There was no evidence for "emergent information" in the configuration of a number of elements.

This associative versus Gestalt contrast as applied to sentence memory has stirred some interest. There has not really been any challenge to Claim (1) but Claims (2) and (3) have come in for careful examination by a number of colleagues. These critiques have forced me to reexamine the issues involved. One consequence of this reexamination has been a realization that the HAM model had certain deficiencies. The ACT model attempts to repair these.

Another outcome of the reexamination has been the conclusion that the Gestalt versus associative issue is not really decidable on the basis of empirical data. As we noted in Anderson and Bower (Chapters 2 and 3), there were not any clearcut theoretical issues that divided Gestalt theory and associationism. The differences largely concerned the manner of theorizing rather than the theories themselves. Since there are no well-defined theoretical differences between associationism and Gestalt theory, there can hardly be any well-defined differences in empirical predictions. It is possible to specify particularly strong versions of each theory. This is what was done in the original comparison Bower and I made between HAM and Gestalt theory. The associative and Gestalt theories that Bower and I proposed have testable differences. It turns out that both theories are wrong. However, rejecting one specific version of Gestalt theory or associative theory does not mean that all versions are wrong.

Another reason for concluding that the Gestalt–associative contrast is undecidable resides in the arguments given in Chapter 1 about the nonidentifiability of any theory that refers to properties of internal structure. I am sure that there exist fundamentally different models of internal structure, some of which would be called "associative" and the others "Gestalt," and yet these models would be identical in their predictions. Thus, the purpose of this section will not be to show that associationism is correct and Gestalt theory wrong; rather, it will be to show that ACT is one of the theories compatible with existing data. Undoubtedly, there are many other compatible theories and some of these might be called Gestalt.

Partial Recall

The basic idea underlying HAM's predictions about partial recall is that the associations encoding a sentence had only a certain probability of being formed in long-term memory. Therefore, after studying a sentence like *In the park the hippie touched the debutante,* one might have residing in memory a partial encoding of the sentence as in Fig. 10.7.

In the memory structure of Fig. 10.7 the subject has stored 11 of the 13 links required for recall of the sentence. Given such a memory structure, we should see total failure of recall when the subject is probed with *park* or *touch*. Cueing the subject with *hippie* we should see recall of *debutante* but not *park* or *touch.* Finally, cued with *debutante* we should only see recall of *hippie.* Thus, HAM naturally predicted there would be frequent partial recall of sentences, which we observed.

ACT predicts a very similar pattern of results. Indeed, the mathematical model developed in Chapter 10 of Anderson and Bower for HAM can be applied to ACT. That mathematical model described the encoding of associative networks. The model simply assumes that each link in the network has a certain probability of being formed. It was not specific to the structure or content of a network. Therefore, it does not matter that the networks proposed by HAM and ACT are different. The HAM and ACT networks are different on two scores. First, there would not be context (C) branches or membership branches (ϵ) as in Fig. 10.7. The sentence would be encoded by a large number of simpler propositions (see Fig. 5.15, page 170). Second, it no longer seems reasonable to propose that a simple net-

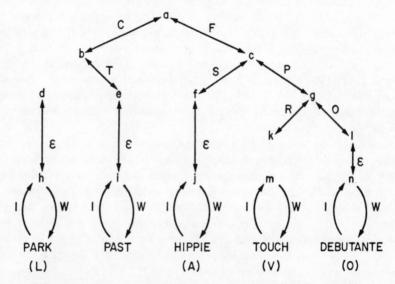

FIG. 10.7   A HAM structure illustrating the partial encoding of a proposition.

work underlies a subject's memory for a sentence. It is undoubtedly elaborated considerably in idiosyncratic ways by each subject. Such elaborations would not change the prediction, however, that there should be partial recall.

There are a couple of critical aspects to this prediction of partial recall which were perhaps lost in the mathematical developments of Chapter 10 of the HAM book. These will be highlighted here with respect to the first experiment of that chapter which involved location(L)–subject(S)–verb(V)–object(O) sentences such as the one illustrated in Fig. 10.7.

There are four possible prompts for recall. To each, the subject can recall 0, 1, 2, or 3 other words. There are three ways to recall one or two words of the three. Thus, to each of the four probes there are eight possible patterns of recall. Table 10.1 provides a classification of the data from the first experiment into the various patterns of recall for each probe. There were 41 subjects recalling 72 sentences. A quarter each of the sentences were probed with an L, an S, a V, or an O. There were 2952 observations of recall which are classified in Table 10.1. In Table 10.1 failure of recall of an element is denoted by a bar over the letter corresponding to the item. So $S\bar{V}O$ denotes successful recall of S and O but failure to recall V.

Note that 12% of the probes resulted in recall of all three elements, 11.3% resulted in recall of two items, 12.5% in recall of one item, and 64.2% of the items

TABLE 10.1
Patterns of Recall
to Location–Subject–Verb–Object Sentence[a]

Cued with							
L		S		V		O	
3 recalled							
SVO	93	LVO	87	LSO	78	LSV	95
2 recalled							
$SV\bar{O}$	17	$LV\bar{O}$	20	$LS\bar{O}$	18	$LS\bar{V}$	38
$S\bar{V}O$	33	$L\bar{V}O$	36	$L\bar{S}O$	30	$L\bar{S}V$	30
$\bar{S}VO$	33	$\bar{L}VO$	36	$\bar{L}SO$	21	$\bar{L}SV$	22
Total:	83	Total:	92	Total:	69	Total:	90
1 recalled							
$S\bar{V}\bar{O}$	41	$L\bar{V}\bar{O}$	43	$L\bar{S}\bar{O}$	24	$L\bar{S}\bar{V}$	41
$\bar{S}V\bar{O}$	23	$\bar{L}V\bar{O}$	19	$\bar{L}S\bar{O}$	16	$\bar{L}S\bar{V}$	29
$\bar{S}\bar{V}O$	37	$\bar{L}\bar{V}O$	36	$\bar{L}\bar{S}O$	30	$\bar{L}\bar{S}V$	31
Total:	101	Total:	98	Total:	70	Total:	101
0 recalled							
$\bar{S}\bar{V}\bar{O}$	461	$\bar{L}\bar{V}\bar{O}$	461	$\bar{L}\bar{S}\bar{O}$	521	$\bar{L}\bar{S}\bar{V}$	452

[a]From Anderson and Bower (1973).

in recall of nothing. Note that 76.2% of the sentences result in either recall of all or none of the elements whereas only 23.8% result in partial recall. On this analysis partial recall does not seem that prevalent. However, this contrast depends on total failure of recall which is not too interesting. The HAM model accounted for the high prevalence of complete failure by attributing it to failure of the stimulus to be encoded in the same sense at the time of test as at the time of study. That is, total failure of recall may reflect encoding problems of the sort discussed in Section 10.1.

Perhaps the more relevant contrast is to note that the probe results in partial recall twice as often as in total recall. Over a wide range of experiments it has been found that partial recall ranges from just as frequent to many times more frequent than total recall. Initially, Bower and I found this strongly unintuitive. It seemed single propositions should be stored in unitary traces.

There are two challenges that have been made to our conclusions about the existence of partial recall. The first can be gleaned from inspecting Table 10.1. Rather than considering absolute recall, consider recall of one word contingent on recall of another word. For instance, contrast recall of V contingent on recall of O [denoted $P(V|O)$] with recall contingent on nonrecall of O [denoted $P(V|\bar{O})$]:

$$P(V|O) = .637,$$
$$P(V|\bar{O}) = .073$$

Similar patterns of contingency can be obtained by considering any other pair of words. The point is that recall of one term is much higher when contingent on recall of another. Thus, it might appear that memory traces are much more unitary than would be expected by chance.

Nonetheless, the HAM model, assuming independent associations, was able to predict this pattern of contingency in the data. There are two factors in the model that allow for such contingency. First, there is the probability of failing to correctly encode the stimulus at test, producing total failure of recall. Second, we assume that subjects varied in their abilities and that they varied in the amount of effort they expended memorizing individual sentences. This meant that for some sentences for some subjects all associations had a high probability of being formed while for other sentences for other subjects all associations had a low probability. These individual differences meant that there would be more all-or-none recall than expected by chance, producing contingencies in the data. The fact that probabilities of forming links covary over individuals and sentences make it virtually impossible to reject an associative model on the basis of amount of all-or-none recall. For instance, one might propose that for some subjects and sentences associations are formed with probability 1 and for the remaining subjects and sentences associations are formed with probability 0. This extreme model of individual variation, which is not the one proposed in Chapter 10 of Anderson and Bower, would predict perfect all-or-none recall. Thus, if we permit the possibility of individual differences, no amount of all-or-none recall can be taken as conclusive evidence against the associative model. This fact supports my earlier claim about the nonidentifiability of the associative-Gestalt contrast. Of course, if we had observed perfect all-or-none recall, one might argue that it would be more parsimonious to assume a unitary trace, but we did not observe perfect all-or-none recall.

R. C. Anderson (1974) has criticized our conclusions because they come from verbatim tests of memory. That is, subjects are scored as being correct in their recall only if they get the exact word (or some very close synonym, for example, *postman* for *mailman*). R. C. Anderson has explored the all-or-none recall question under a more lax scoring procedure in which he allowed looser synonyms, superordinates (*clothing* for *sweater*), hyponyms (*sat* for *stayed*), and cohyponyms (*rifle* for *pistol*). He used simple subject–verb–object sentences. Subjects tried to recall verb and object to the subject. I will report his data in terms of recall of verb conditional on object, but the same pattern holds if one looks at recall of object conditional on verb recall. When he used a verbatim scoring procedure he found $P(V|O) = .634$ and $P(V|\bar{O}) = .084$. When he used a gist-scoring procedure he found $P(V|O) = .959$ and $P(V|\bar{O}) = .039$. Thus, Anderson found under gist scoring close to all-or-none recall as expected by Gestalt theory. A possible criticism of this analysis concerns the degree to which subjects are able to guess the correct verb given the object. For instance, suppose a subject studies *The chairman fired the pistol,* and then is cued with *chairman,* and can recall *pistol.* Then he may be able to guess the correct verb or some semantically related term. To deal with this criticism Anderson performed a norming study and found that 19% of the time semantically related guesses were made of the verb, given subject and object. This figure and data for guessing objects enables one to compute a correction for guessing. The conditional recall probabilities subject to these corrections are $P(V|O) = .951$ and $P(V|\bar{O}) = .049$. So one still has close to all-or-none recall.

Whether one is going to consider this degree of all-or-none recall as evidence for a Gestalt theory is a matter of taste. However, it is an interesting fact that such a difference in amount of all-or-none recall occurs depending on the scoring criterion. This clearly indicates that subjects store only a partial semantic specification of the concepts. What appeared to be partial recall at the sentence level is in part partial recall at the concept level. The focus of partial recall has been shifted rather than the fact of partial recall.

A perplexing feature about all this is that I have not been able to find as much evidence as Anderson for all-or-none recall using a gist-scoring procedure. In one experiment, looking at simple *SVO* sentences I found $P(V|O) = .467$ and $P(V|\bar{O}) = .021$ using a verbatim requirement, and $P(V|O) = .589$ and $P(V|\bar{O}) = .031$ using a gist requirement. There is some movement toward all-or-none recall with gist scoring but this is not overwhelming. The difference between the two studies may be related to overall level of recall. Anderson reports 31% unconditional verb recall (verbatim criterion) whereas in this experiment I found 15%. With this lower unconditional verb recall it is less likely that the conditional recall probability would go to 1, even under gist scoring.

It will require further research to determine what controls the amount of all-or-none recall. Instructions to process the sentences meaningfully do not seem to be a controlling factor. Both Anderson and I have failed to find an effect of such instructions on amount of all-or-none recall. This is interesting because, as we will see, instructions seem to be important to whether one obtains configural effects in cueing.

Conclusions on Partial Recall

ACT is compatible with the range of data reviewed. If one takes into consideration the covariance among subjects and sentences in encoding probabilities, one can account for the observed nonindependence in recall. The fact that subjects can sometimes recall only the rough concept can also be explained within ACT. This can be attributed to the situation where the subject has lost associations with the original concept but can remember his elaborations of the concept. So having studied *The chairman fired the pistol* the subject might elaborate about killing a *stockholder*. If the subject can remember the object *pistol* and this elaboration, it does much to narrow down the possible verbs.

There is another point that could be made to muddy this murky issue even further. The current ACT model would *not* have to assume partial encoding of propositions to account for the partial recall just reviewed. There are two ways ACT could account for partial recall and still assume all-or-none encoding of propositions. The first is to note that ACT assigns multiple propositions to sentences that were assigned a single proposition by HAM; so ACT represents *The chairman fired the gun* as $(x * \text{chairman}) \& (x * (\text{fire OF } y)) \& (y * \text{gun})$. There are three propositions, one corresponding to each of the three content words. So ACT could account for some partial recall of the sentence by assuming that whole propositions were forgotten. For instance, if the subject failed to encode $(y * \text{gun})$ he would be able to recall the verb but not the object to a subject.

The second way to explain partial recall without assuming partial encoding of propositions makes reference to the subject's elaborations. Suppose the subject elaborated *The chairman fired the gun* with *The chairman loaded the gun*. Further, suppose the subject could not remember the original proposition but could recall his elaboration. Then he might well be able to recall the object of the sentence but would incorrectly recall the verb as *load* or omit the verb if he knows that he did not study *load* (for example, by means of the absence of a list tag). Note that if the subject did recall *load* it would be scored as correct by Anderson's gist criterion.

So, if we took all assumptions of the ACT model as fixed except the issue of whether propositions were encoded in an all-or-none manner, there would be partial encoding models and all-or-none models compatible with the data. How then can we possibly expect to decide the issue of all-or-none encoding of proposi-tions when we do not fix the other assumptions of our memory model, that is, when we embed the issue in a question of Gestalt versus associative models?

Configural Properties of Sentence Cues

The third line of evidence Anderson and Bower gave for an associative theory concerned the effectiveness of various cues as prompts for recall. It is clear that our interpretation of this experimental evidence will have to be revised. The basic experimental paradigm is quite simple. Subjects study pairs of sentences like (5) and (6) which share a common object. These two sentences are separated in the study sequence by some number of other sentences.

(5)   The child hit the landlord.
(6)   The minister praised the landlord.
(7)   The child ... the _____. S
(8)   The ... hit the _____. V
(9)   The minister praised the _____. S_1V_1
(10)   The child praised the _____. S_1V_2

Subjects were then asked to recall the object of probes like (7)–(10). The S probe in (7) presents only subject, the V probe in (8) only verb, the S_1V_1 probe in (9) subject and verb from the same sentence, and the S_1V_2 probe in (10) subject and verb from different sentences. Note that, since S_1 and V_2 are paired with the same object, there is no ambiguity as to what the subject should recall to S_1V_2. The S_1V_1 cue is particularly important for the subsequent discussion because it pre-serves the original configuration of subject plus verb. I will variously refer to it as a *same* cue or *configural* cue. The HAM model and certain others (including our interpretation of the ELINOR model of Rumelhart, Lindsay, & Norman, 1972) made the following predictions about recall to these various cues:

$$P(O|S_1V_2) = P(O|S) + (1-P(O|S))P(O|V) \qquad (1)$$

$$P(O|S_1V_1) < P(O|S_1V_2) \qquad (2)$$

The notation $P(O|X)$ is to be interpreted as the probability of object recall given a probe of type X.[4] It is calculated by taking the average recall of all subjects to all probes of type X.

For derivation of these predictions consult Fig. 10.8 which gives the HAM representation for these sentences. It was assumed in making these derivations that the probability of traversing each W link was 1. Let a be the probability that the path is intact from the subject to the predicate node (for example, from *child*

[4]I use this notation to be consistent with past papers. However, there is a certain risk of con-fusion which deserves at least a footnote. Earlier (page 410) $P(X|Y)$ was used to denote the probability of recall of X given Y was recalled. Here and henceforth it is being used to denote the probability of recalling X given a cue of Y.

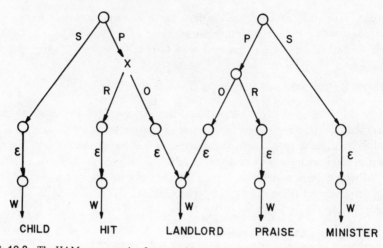

FIG. 10.8   The HAM representation for two subject–verb–object sentences sharing the same object.

to X), let b be the probability the path is intact from the verb to the predicate (for example, from *hit* to X), and let c be the probability of an intact path from predicate to object (for example, from X to *landlord*). Assuming that the probability of each path is independent of the probability for each other and asuming that the probability of recall equals the probability of an intact path from subject or from verb to object, the following equations can be derived:

$$P(O|S_1 V_2) = ac + (1-ac)bc$$
$$P(O|S_1 V_1) = (a + (1-a)b)c$$
$$P(O|S) = ac$$
$$P(O|V) = bc$$

The reader may confirm that from these equations one may derive the predictions in (1) and (2).

Prediction (2) may seem counterintuitive. One might think there is "configural information" in the $S_1 V_1$ cue which is not available from S or V singly or in the combination of S and V from different sentences as in the $S_1 V_2$ cue. Moreover, it is a frequent intuition that this configural information should play an important role in recall. Thus, a configural (or Gestalt) viewpoint might predict the opposite of Inequality (2).[5]

Equality (1) was confirmed in all the Anderson and Bower experiments. That is to say, the two values were very close to each other. Thus, it is also of interest

[5]Here it is worth noting a point made by a number of our patient critics. There are associative models which predict the configural effect. In particular, suppose in the associative account that the traversal of a link was not an all-or-none affair but rather occurred with a certain probability. Further, suppose that this probability was a function of the level of activation. (Such an assumption would not be particularly foreign to the ACT model.) Under such assumptions the probability of traversing from the predicate node to the object node would be higher with a same cue because there would be two sources of activation converging at the predicate node, increasing the level of activation.

to consider Inequality (3) which may be derived from (1) and (2):

$$P(O|S_1V_1) < P(O|S) + (1-P(O|S))P(O|V) \tag{3}$$

This prediction has the methodological advantage that it does not require use of crossed-over probes. Crossed-over probes are cumbersome methodologically for a number of reasons including the fact that it is difficult to explain to subjects how they should treat these probes. Both (1) and (3) refer to the quantity $P(O|S)$ + $(1-P(O|S))P(O|V)$. This quantity will be referred to as the *probabilistic sum* of the recall to the single-word cues.

The first two experiments of Anderson and Bower (1972a) found data that supported Inequalities (2) and (3). However, there was some doubt as to the degree to which subjects were meaningfully processing the sentences. Therefore, in Experiments 3 and 4 of that paper subjects were given an orienting task that assured that they had meaningfully processed the sentences. They were instructed to continue the sentence in some meaningful way. So, given the sentence *The minister hit the landlord,* a subject might continue it with the phrase, *with a cross*. Under these instructions, Inequalities (2) and (3) were reversed.

On the surface this seems to indicate that the S_1V_1 probe does contain configural information when the sentences are studied under instructions that force the subjects to process them in a meaningful manner. We proposed an alternate interpretation, however, by suggesting that the subject had a much higher probability of guessing his continuation to a S_1V_1 cue. That is, given the probe *The minister hit,* the subject could guess that he had generated the continuation *with a cross*. Anderson and Bower showed that subjects were much better at recalling the continuation to a S_1V_1 cue than a S or V cue. In fact, with respect to continuation recall (C), the following inequality held:

$$P(C|S_1V_1) > P(C|S) + (1-P(C|S))P(C|V) \tag{4}$$

Moreover, the size of this inequality correlated across subjects with the size of the failure of Inequality (3). We proposed in the 1972 article that the advantage of the S_1V_1 probe in recall of the continuation was mediating the advantage in recall of the object. We were so convinced of this alternate explanation that we omitted mentioning Experiments 3 and 4 from Anderson and Bower (1972a) in our book. It seemed like an unnecessary complication.

More recently, Foss and Harwood (1975) had subjects study sentences under a meaningful orienting task, but one which did not involve continuations. Subjects simply rated the sentences as to their meaningfulness. Reversals of Inequalities (2) and (3) were found here, too. Thus, it would seem that configural properties in sentence memory do not depend on whether the subjects generate continuations.

Foss and Harwood Theory

To account for this pattern of data Foss and Harwood proposed that the memory trace for a sentence consists of both an associative trace and a configural trace. The associative trace can be evoked by any of the cues S, V, S_1V_1, or S_1V_2 and obeys the relations set forth as (1)–(3). However, the configural trace has a very high probability of being evoked in the presence of an S_1V_1 cue and a low probability of being evoked in the presence of other cues. Therefore, the degree to which the S_1V_1 cue is at an advantage over the single-word cues depends on the relative importance (probability) of a configural trace versus an associative trace. The Foss and Harwood theory can also nicely account for the other facts that we listed as favoring an associative theory, that is, associative interference and partial recall. These phenomena are attributed to the associative part of the memory trace for a sentence.

According to the Foss and Harwood theory what must be varying across these experiments is the relative probability of the configural versus the associative trace. They note that recall to the single-word cues (S and V) was 38 and 40% in the two experiments of Anderson and Bower (1972a) in which no configural effects were reported. In contrast, in their experiments the level of recall was 17 and 20%. Therefore, they propose that the associative component (as measured by level of recall to the single-word probes) is what is varying across these experiments. In the Anderson and Bower experiments, the relative probability of an associative trace is high whereas it is low in the Foss and Harwood experiments. This is indicated, Foss and Harwood claim, by the level of recall to the single-word cues. Because the associative component was so high in the Anderson and Bower experiment, it washed out any configural effects. As Foss and Harwood (1975) write ''. . . Anderson and Bower were victimized by the good memories of their subjects [p. 13].''

However, there are many reasons to doubt the Foss and Harwood attempt to relate the configural effect to the level of recall. First, configural effects have been obtained at high recall and nonconfigural effects at low recall. The evidence for this is contained in the nine experiments reviewed in Table 10.2, which summarizes the data from Anderson and Bower, Foss and Harwood, and from three experiments to be reported here. The table lists the instructions used in these experiments, the mean level of recall to single-word cues, the mean level to configural (S_1V_1) cues, and the probabilistic sum of recall to the single-word cues. A configural effect is indicated by a significant difference between recall to the S_1V_1 cue and the probabilistic sum. The significant differences are starred in Table 10.2. Note that significant configural effects are found with relatively high recall (Anderson & Bower, 1972a, Expts. 3 & 4) and with relatively low recall (Foss & Harwood, 1975, Expts. 1 and 2; Anderson, this volume, Expts. 1 and 3). Nonexistent configural effects are found at high recall (Anderson & Bower, 1972, Expts. 1 and 2) and low recall (Anderson, this volume, Expt. 2).

In contrast to level of recall there is another variable in Table 10.2 which does perfectly correlate with an advantage of the configural cue over the probabilistic sum. This is whether the subjects were given some meaningful orienting instructions. Configural effects are obtained in Experiments 3 and 4 of Anderson and

TABLE 10.2
Summary of Data from Nine Experiments[a]

Experiment	Study instructions	Mean single-word recall	$P(O\|SV)$	$P(O\|S) +$ $(1-P(O\|S))P(O\|V)$
Anderson and Bower (1972), 1	None	.381	.579	.604
Anderson and Bower (1972), 2	None	.364	.584	.589
Anderson and Bower (1972), 3	Continuation	.363	.724	.597*
Anderson and Bower (1972), 4	Continuation	.429	.718	.674*
Foss and Harwood (1975), 1	Meaningfulness ratings	.173	.394	.314*
Foss and Harwood (1975), 2	Meaningfulness ratings	.200	.464	.348*
Anderson, 1	Meaningfulness ratings	.250	.543	.438*
Anderson, 2	None	.257	.468	.450
Anderson, 3	Meaningfulness ratings	.263	.512	.457*

[a]An asterisk indicates that recall to SV is significantly greater than the probabilistic sum of recall to S and V.

Bower in which subjects generated continuations; in the Foss and Harwood experiments in which instructions were used to rate the sentences as to meaningfulness; and in Experiments 1 and 3 to be reported here in which I also used meaningfulness ratings. It is somewhat surprising that Foss and Harwood did not propose to relate the magnitude of the configural effect to instruction since this is a variable many others have suggested. Perhaps the reason they ignored this variable as an explanation is that subjects typically report in all conditions, even without meaningful orienting instructions, that they treat the sentences meaningfully—that is, comprehend the sentences at study and remember the products of their comprehension at recall. So it is not the case that subjects are treating sentences as meaningless strings in one case and as meaningful sentences in the other. What meaningful orienting instructions must be doing is manipulating the *degree* to which subjects process sentences in a meaningful fashion.

ACT Theory of Configural Effects

The ACT theory, in contrast to HAM, expects an advantage of a configural SV cue. This prediction follows directly from the ACT analyses of the encoding specificity results in Section 10.1. ACT expects the sense assigned to a word to depend on context. For instance, consider the ACT representation in Fig. 10.9. All the words in that figure should be attached to multiple senses. For illustration purposes, I have indicated that *minister* is connected to two senses, U and V. The meaning U might be that of vengeful, wrath-of-god preacher and the other, V, might be a pleasant but obsequious clergyman. According to the Disambiguation

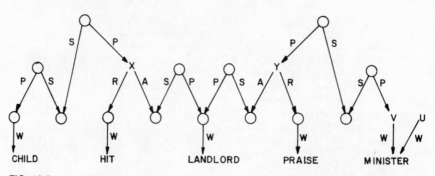

FIG. 10.9 An ACT equivalent of the representation in Fig. 10.8 showing the multiple senses attached to one of the words, minister.

Hypothesis given in Section 10.1, when subjects see the unit *minister–hit* they would be likely to encode *minister* in the sense *U;* when they study *minister–praised* they will encode it in sense *V;* and when they study *minister* alone they may encode it as *U* or *V* or in some other sense. If they do not encode a word in the same sense at test as at study, they will not recognize it nor will they be able to recall the object to it. Thus, the configural cue is at an advantage to other cues because it maximizes the probability that the subject will encode the words identically.

So, from the ACT point of view, there should always be an advantage for the configural cue in the encoding stage. In the original HAM model this encoding stage was assumed to be always successful and not to be subject to failure. The HAM analysis given earlier still applies to the retrieval stage after the encoding of the words. It still predicts that configural cues should do worse than crossed-over cues (Eq. 2) or the probabilistic sum (Eq. 3). Whether one sees an overall advantage for the configural cue depends on the importance of contextual factors in encoding. Recall from the earlier discussion of the disambiguation hypothesis (page 386) that there were two types of encoding productions available to the subject and that one produced a larger configural effect. Perhaps meaningful orienting instructions have their effect because they "disinhibit" the subject and cause him to use the type of encoding productions that produces large configural effects. Thomson and Tulving (1970) have found in their encoding specificity paradigm that the size of the configural effect can be enhanced by instructions that induce subjects to orient to the word pairs as units.

A pair of predictions follows from the hypothesis that the configural effects are occurring in the encoding stage. First, these effects should be seen in the subject's ability to recognize the cues. Second, there should be no advantage of the configured cue in recall when recall has been conditionalized on successful recognition of the cue. Experiments 1 and 2 from the series I have recently completed were designed to test those predictions. The experiments were almost identical except that Experiment 1 involved the meaningful orienting instructions of having subjects rate the sentences as to meaningfulness, whereas Experiment 2 did not involve any special instructions. The results of the experiments are reported in Table 10.3. Part (a) of that table compares object recall to the S_1V_1 cue and the average recall to the single-word cues under the two instructions. There is a significant interaction ($p < .025$) such that recall is better to the configural (SV) cue under meaningful orienting instructions but actually slightly inferior to the single-word cue under these instructions. Part (b) of Table 10.3 gives the probability that a subject can recognize a cue as coming from a studied sentence. This probability is corrected for guessing using false alarm rates to distractors. It shows a similar pattern to the object recall, that is, recognition of S_1V_1 is much better under meaningful orienting instructions. In contrast, recognition of single-word cue is slightly inferior under these instructions. This interaction is quite significant ($p < .005$).

This pattern of results is consistent with the hypothesis that the configural effect may be in the retrieval of the encodings of the words and not in the retrieval of the object from the word encodings. Table 10.3c gives the probability of object

TABLE 10.3
Results from Experiments 1 and 2
Comparing Meaningful Orienting
Instructions with No Instructions

	SV	S or V	Mean	$P(O\|S) +$ $(1-P(O\|S))P(O\|V)$
(a) Unconditional object recall				
Meaning ratings	.543	.250	.397	.438
No orienting instructions	.468	.257	.363	.450
Mean	.506	.254	.380	
(b) Corrected cue recognition				
Meaning ratings	.855	.575	.715	
No orienting instructions	.757	.585	.671	
Mean	.806	.580	.798	
(c) Conditional object recall				
Meaning ratings	.628	.454	.541	.672
No orienting instructions	.592	.421	.507	.665
Mean	.610	.438	.524	

recall conditional on recognition of the cue. Subjects perform somewhat better under meaningful orienting instructions but there is no interaction between single-word cues and the configural (S_1V_1) cues. One can look at the probabilistic sum, $P(O|S) + (1-P(O|S))P(O|V)$, for the conditional object recall. These quantities are .672 for Experiment 1 and .665 for Experiment 2. These values are above the corresponding conditional recall probabilities for S_1V_1 in Table 10.3c. Therefore, Inequality (3) is satisfied for the conditional recall probabilities.

Two warnings must be given about interpreting the conditional recall probabilities in Table 10.3c. First, they are subject to item-by-subject selection artifacts. Second, it is unclear what the subject means when he recognizes the subject–verb (SV) combination. Is he saying (a) he recognizes at least one of the subjects and verbs; or (b) that he recognizes both subject and verb as studied words; or (c) that he recognizes subject and verb as study words and that they come from the same sentences? If we are to properly calculate conditional recall probabilities and compare them to the probabilistic sum, the subject would have to mean (b). There is no guarantee in these two experiments that he was using that criterion. Therefore, the conditional recall probabilities in Table 10.3c must be taken as suggestive rather than definitive.

Experiment 3

Experiment 3 was performed to provide more definitive evidence about whether the configural effect occurred in the encoding of the individual words. This experiment involved 41 subjects studying sentences under meaningful learning instructions. As in the Foss and Harwood experiments and in Experiments 1 and 2 just reported, subjects had to rate the meaningfulness of sentences they studied. After studying the sentences, subjects were cued with subject–verb combinations. There were four types of cues defining four conditions. In condition S_OV_O both the subject and verb came from the same study sentence. In condition S_OV_N the subject came from an old study sentence and the verb was new. In condition S_NV_O the subject was new and the verb was old. Finally, in condition S_NV_N both subject and verb were new. The subject was asked to indicate separately whether he had studied the subject, the verb, and to recall the object that had occurred with the subject or the verb, if either were old. Note that with respect to object recall, the cue S_OV_O is like a configural cue (S_1V_1) in previous experiments, the cue S_OV_N is a S cue, and S_NV_O is a V cue.

In this experiment we will be able to assess the subject's ability to recognize S and V in the context of the various cues and look at their recall conditional on cue recognition. These data are reported in Table 10.4. In the first three rows are reported the probabilities for recognition of the subject, the verb, and both the subject and the verb. If the items were in fact old these raw scores constitute hits, and if not they are false alarms. With these hits and false alarms, corrections for guessing can be calculated. For instance, let $P_S(S_OV_O)$ be the probability that the subject of a S_OV_O cue is recognized in the presence of an old verb. Let $P_S(S_NV_O)$

TABLE 10.4
Recognition and Recall to Various Cues
in Experiment 3

		$S_O V_O$	$S_O V_N$	$S_N V_O$	$S_N V_N$
Subject	Raw	.850	.847	.262	.229
recognition	(corrected)	(.797)	(.802)	—	—
Verb	Raw	.764	.177	.575	.171
recognition	(corrected)	(.713)	—	(.487)	—
Subject and verb	Raw	.719	.157	.163	.054
recognition	(corrected)	(.682)	—	—	—
Object recall		.512	.287	.239	—
Object recall conditional on corrected recognition		.666	.358	.491	—

be the probability of a false alarm in the presence of an old verb. Then the following formula gives the corrected recognition, $\hat{P}_S(S_O V_O)$:

$$\hat{P}_S(S_O V_O) = \frac{P_S(S_O V_O) - P_S(S_N V_O)}{1 - P_S(S_N V_O)}$$

Similarly, equations can be given for the other corrected recognition probabilities:

$$\hat{P}_S(S_O V_N) = \frac{P_S(S_O V_N) - P_S(S_N V_N)}{1 - P_S(S_N V_N)}$$

$$\hat{P}_V(S_O V_O) = \frac{P_V(S_O V_O) - P_V(S_O V_N)}{1 - P_V(S_O V_N)}$$

$$\hat{P}_V(S_N V_O) = \frac{P_V(S_N V_O) - P_V(S_N V_N)}{1 - P_V(S_N V_N)}$$

These equations are all built on a simple high threshold guessing model (for example, Kintsch, 1970). The guessing correction for the joint probability of recognizing S and V to a $S_O V_O$ cue is less obvious. However, with some assumptions a solution can be obtained. The following equations give the true probabilities of recognizing neither S nor V, just S, and just V to a $S_O V_O$ cue:

$$\hat{P}_{\bar{S}\bar{V}}(S_O V_O) = \frac{P_{\bar{S}\bar{V}}(S_O V_O)}{P_{\bar{S}\bar{V}}(S_N V_N)}$$

$$\hat{P}_{S\bar{V}}(S_O V_O) = \frac{P_{S\bar{V}}(S_O V_O) - \hat{P}_{\bar{S}\bar{V}}(S_O V_O)P_{S\bar{V}}(S_N V_N)}{1 - P_V(S_O V_N)}$$

$$\hat{P}_{\bar{S}V}(S_O V_O) = \frac{P_{\bar{S}V}(S_O V_O) - \hat{P}_{\bar{S}\bar{V}}(S_O V_O)P_{\bar{S}V}(S_N V_N)}{1 - P_S(S_N V_O)}$$

With these values, one can obtain the desired value, $P_{SV}(S_0V_0)$, by subtraction:

$$\hat{P}_{SV}(S_0V_0) = 1 - \hat{P}_{\bar{S}\bar{V}}(S_0V_0) - \hat{P}_{S\bar{V}}(S_0V_0) - \hat{P}_{\bar{S}V}(S_0V_0)$$

The corrected recognition probabilities are reported in Table 10.4.

There are a number of interesting facts to be gleaned from Table 10.4. First, probability of recognition of the subject noun is the same in the context of an old verb as out of context. Thus, there is no evidence for a configural effect of the verb on recognition of subject. In contrast, recognition of the verb is on the order of 20% poorer in the context of a new subject as an old subject. In fact, a subject's ability to recognize that V is old in a S_NV_0 cue is almost 20% poorer than his combined ability to recognize both S and V are old to a S_0V_0 cue. So, as hypothesized, there is a considerable configural effect in encoding but it seems to be all localized in the effect of the subject on the encoding of the verb. This is not unreasonable since the sense of the verb seems much more influenced by subject context than the converse. It is much harder to imagine a "hitting" in isolation than a "boy" in isolation. There is a suggestion of a similar effect in the more traditional work on encoding specificity. Salzberg (1974) performed an experiment comparing the effect of a noun versus an adjective context on recognition of a target word. The target word suffered a greater lack of recognition if a noun context was changed. This is analogous to the stronger effect found here of noun context on verb recognition than the converse.

Table 10.4 also reports object recall. From the recall probabilities to the single-word cues, $P_{OBJ}(S_0V_N)$ and $P_{OBJ}(S_NV_0)$, we can compute a probabilistic sum. According to the HAM model derivation of Inequality (3), the probabilistic sum provides an upper bound on recall to the same cue, $P_{OBJ}(S_0V_0)$. This upper bound is .457 which is less than the observed .512. This is a significant difference ($t_{40} = 2.48; p < .01$). So once again there is configural effect in object recall, in disagreement with the HAM model. The last line in Table 10.3 reports object recall conditional on verb recognition. For the S_0V_N and S_NV_0 cues this is calculated by dividing the reported object recall by the corrected recognition scores for S and V. For the S_0V_0 cue this is calculated by dividing the probability with which the subject jointly recognizes S, V, and recalls the object (.454) by the corrected probability for recognizing both S and V. These conditional recall probabilities might be taken to reflect the probability of recall of the object given access to the encoding of the words. The probabilistic sum calculated from the conditional probabilities of recall to the single-word cues is .673 which is essentially identical to the observed conditional recall (.666) to the configured cue, $S_0\breve{V}_0$. Unfortunately, from the viewpoint of reaching a definitive conclusion, the revised ACT model expects that the probabilistic sum should be larger than the conditional object recall to S_0V_0 and the Gestalt model would predict conditional object recall to S_0V_0 to be larger.

As stated earlier, conditional recall probabilities must be interpreted with caution. In addition to potential subject-by-item selection artifacts, the probabilities are calculated from a number of separate measures, each with its own error of estimate. The error of estimate of such a composite measure is probably quite high. Further, it is possible to interpret this pattern of results as indicating that recognition of the verb is conditional on ability to recall the original sentence in which it appeared and not the converse. This is not unreasonable on an intuitive basis. It is difficult to imagine the recognition of the meaning of a verb out of the context of a sentence in which it occurred.

A possible conclusion from these experiments is that the configural effect occurs principally in the encoding of the verb. Apparently, under meaningful orienting instructions, subjects are particularly prone to let the context influence their encoding of the verb. The ACT model as elaborated in Section 10.1 is capable of predicting these effects on word encoding. However, to reiterate a theme in this section, it is not the case that Gestalt models could not predict this encoding effect too. For instance, there is Tulving's original model for encoding specificity. One cannot expect to show ACT to be *uniquely* compatible with the existing data from any paradigm. The goal is to show that it is of broad generality and captures the data from many paradigms.

10.4   EFFECTS OF LINGUISTIC STRUCTURES

In Section 10.2 I discusssed the importance of the subject's elaborative processes in establishing a redundant, durable memory. These elaborative processes take a given structure and add many new interconnections. Such elaborative processes would seem to create havoc for the logic of much of the research involving the HAM model. That research was designed to test, via recall data, detailed claims about the internal representations of linguistic inputs such as sentences. If subjects do not simply represent a sentence's meaning to themselves, but rather elaborate it, then one is not likely to see in recall data much evidence of the initial structure that represented the sentence. It will be contaminated by the elaborative structure.[6] However, one can find clear evidence for effects of linguistic structure in some experiments. This section will consider the evidence for structural effects at three levels—what Anderson and Bower call the *within-propositional level*, what they called the *between-propositional level*, and what might be referred to as the *prose level*. Structural effects can be found at the last two levels but not the first. One goal of this section is to explain why structural effects occur only at the last two levels.

---

[6]Note that these problems of elaborative structure do not provide the same interpretative difficulty for the reaction-time experiments of Chapters 8 and 9. This is because the predictions tested there did not depend on details of the internal structure but rather on the postulated processes that operated on these structures. The derivations about spread of activation (see page 263) were deliberately designed not to depend heavily on details of the network structure.

The Within-Propositional Structure

By proposition I mean the objects which are identified as propositions in the HAM model or in a model like Kintsch's. For example, the sentence *The boy hit the girl who slept in the attic* would be said to have two propositions: *The boy hit the girl* and *The girl slept in the attic*. This analysis contrasts with the ACT model or the predicate calculus, which would analyze this sentence as having five atomic propositions: *X hit Y, Y slept in Z, X is a boy, Y is a girl, Z is an attic*. The HAM model made strong claims about the internal structure of the objects it identified as propositions. For instance, HAM expected the verb and object to be closer to each other in a subject–verb–object sentence than either is to the subject. This is because they should be organized together under a predicate node in memory. Thus, HAM expected a verb to be a better cue for recall of object than of subject.

It takes some care to properly test this prediction. It might be that objects are simply better recalled than subjects, regardless of the cue. One might think also of simply seeing whether the *subject* or *object* is a better cue for recall of the *verb*. This would keep the response constant. However, this contrast has a symmetrical problem. It may be that the objects are better cues overall, regardless of what word is recalled. Thus, one must test for a contingency between verb and object over and above their general effectiveness as prompts and as responses.

This was accomplished in Chapter 10 of the HAM book where we estimated the overall effectiveness of each word in a sentence as a prompt and its overall level of recall. Then we could look at recall of object to verb and see whether it was higher than would be predicted from the average prompting effectiveness of the verb and average recall of the object. In Experiment 1 of Chapter 10 we looked at sentences such as: *In the park the hippie touched the debutante*. Here it was found that there was a slight, but significant, tendency for *touch* and *debutante* to be better prompts for each other than either was for *park* or *hippie*. This outcome was consistent with the HAM structure. However, we also noted that *touch* and *debutante* were closer together in the physical sentence. To control for this we had subjects study sentences like: *In the park the debutante during the night was touched by the hippie*. In this sentence the logical object *debutante* is closer to the location *park* than to the verb *touched*. Similarly, the verb *touched* is closer to the logical subject *hippie* than to the object. It was now found that *debutante* was a slightly better prompt for *park* than *touched* and *touched* was a slightly better prompt for *hippie* than *debutante*. These effects, while slight, were significant.

Thus, these experiments actually produced evidence for small effects of physical contingencies in the surface sentence. It seems highly implausible that subjects were just storing the physical sentence. We will see clear evidence that they do not when we consider multiproposition sentences. It may be that such physical contingencies were influencing the elaborative process, that is, subjects might tend to elaborate additional propositions about those words that occur close together in the sentence. This would introduce extra connections between the words and so produce the slight contingency in recall. It seems that whatever contingencies might be produced by within-proposition structure these are sufficiently weak that they will be overwhelmed by the subject's own elaborative processes. That is, the measurement of recall probability is not sufficiently sensitive to answer questions about within-propositional structure. There seems no way to get a subject to commit to memory a single, unembellished proposition.

Another unsuccessful study, attempting to get at within-proposition structure, was reported by Anderson and Bower in Section 9.2 of that book. There have been various studies reported as successful in the literature, but these failed to institute proper controls. Perhaps it would be worthwhile to review a couple of these attempts. Johnson (1968, 1970) has examined the effect of the surface structure of a sentence on its recall. For example, Fig. 10.10 illustrates the surface structure of one of the sentences he studied, "The tall boy saved the dying woman." Note that the elements "boy" and "saved," although physically contiguous in the sentence, are very distant in the surface structure. Johnson therefore hypothesized that there would be less joint recall of contiguous items like "boy" and "saved" that crossed major phrase structure boundaries. He measured recall contingency by the transitional error probability (TEP). The TEP is the probability that the $(n + 1)$th word is incorrectly recalled given that the nth word is correctly recalled. As Johnson predicted, TEPs are greatest at major phrase structure boundaries.

However, there is a problem in the use of the TEP as a measure of contiguity in the mnemonic representation. For instance, suppose "boy" is just an easier word to recall than "saved." Then, even if attempts to recall adjacent elements were entirely independent, one would expect to see a higher TEP between "boy" and "saved" than between "tall" and "boy." This is simply because there are more errors being made on "saved" than on "boy." Thus, transitional error

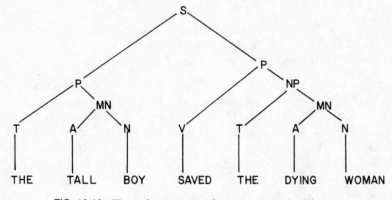

FIG. 10.10   The surface structure of a sentence used by Johnson.

probability is confounded with response availability. Indeed, in research (Anderson & Bower, 1973, Chap. 10) where independent measures have been obtained of response availability, verbs like "saved" are less available as responses than subjects like "boy."

The research of Blumenthal (1967) illustrates another attempt to use recall measures to test hypotheses about sentence representation. His research was concerned with the question of which sentential items would serve as the most effective prompts for recall of the sentence. In his 1967 experiment, Blumenthal contrasted recall of sentences like "Gloves were made by tailors" with sentences like "Gloves were made by hand." He reasoned that "tailors" in the former sentence is the logical subject and hence should be a better probe than "hand" in the second sentence which is just part of the verb phrase. His results confirmed that the words filling the more inclusive grammatical role of logical subject were better probes.

Similar to the problem in Johnson's work, there is a serious source of confounding in Blumenthal's research. He failed to control for the effectiveness of lexical items like "tailors" and "hand" as cues independent of their role in the grammatical structure. When lexical choices are controlled (Levelt & Bonarius, 1968) the effect found by Blumenthal disappears. Thus, in this kind of research we need some way to factor out the effects of response availability and stimulus effectiveness to obtain a pure measure of the structural effects of the sentence's representation in memory.

Between-Proposition Structure

In contrast to the difficulty of establishing any evidence for the within-propositional structure, there has been considerable success in showing the psychological reality of between-proposition structure (for example, Anderson & Bower, 1973; Kintsch, 1974; Lesgold, 1972; Wanner, 1968). Consider the following experiment from Anderson and Bower (1972a, Section 9.2):

(11)   The hippie who touched the debutante was tall.
(12)   The hippie who kissed the prostitute was tall.
(13)   The captain who kissed the debutante was tall.

We had subjects study lists of 16 sentences like the above. Subjects studied eight such lists. After studying a sentence like (11) in the first list, subjects might either study a sentence like (12) and (13) in later lists. Note Sentence (12) repeats the proposition *The hippie was tall* from (11). Sentence (13), while it repeats *debutante* and *tall*, does not repeat any proposition. Thus, we referred to Sentence (12) as a within-proposition repetition (WPR) and Sentence (13) as an across-proposition repetition (APR).

Over the course of the eight lists subjects could either see eight sentences repeating the first noun (N_1) and the adjective as in Examples (11) and (12) or they could see eight sentences repeating the second noun (N_2) and the adjective as in Examples (11) and (13). The HAM model predicted that subjects should be able to take advantage of the repetition of noun and adjective in the within-propositional case (that is, N_1 and A). Each trial would serve as another study for the proposition encoding the noun–adjective pair. This facilitation should not occur in the across-proposition case (that is, N_2 and A).

After each study trial subjects were cued for their memory of the 16 sentences with the adjective and the verb. Figure 10.11a shows recall of the two nouns, N_1 and N_2, for the two experimental groups WPR and APR plus two control groups. As predicted, recall of the repeated N_1 does increase across trials for the WPR group, and recall of the repeated N_2 does not increase across trials for the

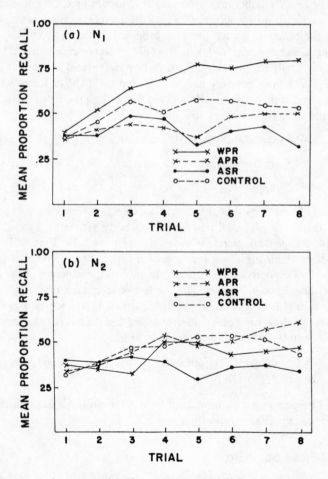

FIG. 10.11   Recall of sentences of the form ''The N_1 who VERBed the N_2 was ADJ.''   (From Anderson & Bower, 1973.)

APR group. This is evidence of the psychological reality of the proposition as a unit of analysis. Note that this contingency between N_1 and A cannot be explained in terms of physical proximity of the repeated words in the sentence. *Hippie* (N_1) is further from *tall* (A) in sentence (11) than is *debutante* (N_2). Also words were randomly assigned from the same population to N_1 and N_2. So this result is not due to any peculiarity of the words, per se, in the roles N_1 and N_2.

Other experiments (Anderson & Bower, 1973, Chap. 10) have shown that there is a strong contingency in recall of words within propositions. Such studies contrast probability of recall of a word conditional on recall of a word within the same proposition with recall of a word from another proposition. Conditional recall invariably proves to be higher in the former case.

I think a subject's elaborative processes tend to reinforce the interconnections among elements within a proposition and not the interconnections among elements across propositions. Consider the two proposition sentence *The hippie who touched the debutante was tall* which would be represented in ACT as (x * hippie) & (x * tall) (x * (touch OF y)) & (y * debutante). Note that there are four ACT propositions but only two as proposed by HAM or Kintsch. It seems quite possible that the subject will have the following productions which would elaborate the within-proposition structure:

(P5)   (V1 * (touch OF V2)) & (V1 * hippie) $\Rightarrow$ (V1 * (offends OF V2))

(P6)   (V1 * (Vr OF V2)) & (V2 * debutante) $\Rightarrow$ (V1 * (at OF ball))

(P7)   (V1 * hippie) & (V1 * tall) $\Rightarrow$ (V1 * (greater OF 6 ft))

Production (P5) encodes that if a hippie touches someone, the person will be offended (this should be qualified by a probability estimate). Production (P6) encodes that people who interact with debutantes are at balls. Finally, Production (P7) encodes that *tall* for hippie means greater than six feet. Note that the conditions of the first two productions make reference to the structure of the assertion *The hippie touched the debutante* and the last production refers to the assertion *The hippie is tall*. It is possible to have productions that cross these boundaries. For instance, the following proposition encodes that if a tall person interacts with a debutante then the debutante will look up to him:

(P8)   (V1 * tall) & (V2 * debutante) $\Rightarrow$ (V2 * (lookup OF V1))
       & (V1 * (Vr OF V2))

However, I suspect that such productions are not as probable as productions that make reference to within-proposition structure.

Effects of Prose Structure

Large units of prose tend to enter into superpropositional organization. Thus, a novel can be subdivided into episodes and the episodes into smaller event units.

One might expect to see effects of the superpropositional units on recall. For instance, a proposition should serve as a better prompt for recall of other propositions from the same episode than for propositions from other episodes. Also one might expect to see the probability of recall of a proposition more dependent on recall of another proposition from the episode than on recall of proposition from another episode. These effects could be predicted by inspecting the graph structure interconnecting propositions in the passage. Propositions from the same episode would be separated by fewer intervening links and so would be more accessible to one another. Any elaborations that the subject would perform should reinforce these contingencies. It is unlikely that he would create many elaborations providing cross-episode connections relative to elaborations providing intra-episode connections.

One problem in this research on prose is specifying precisely what are the superpropositional units in a prose passage. Recently, the attention of a number of psychologists has been given to this problem (Abelson, 1975; Crothers, 1972; Fredericksen, 1972, 1975; Kintsch, 1974; Meyer, 1974; Rumelhart, 1975; Schank, 1975). There are variations in these approaches but they have certain things in common. The to-be-analyzed text is a paragraph or a few connected paragraphs. The representation of the text is a structure interconnecting propositions. Hence, the integrity of the proposition is preserved. Third, the propositions are organized in the representations into an outline form such as a student learns to impose on a text or a lecture. That is to say, main ideas (propositions) are central and subideas (propositions) are organized under these. There can, of course, be several levels to this outline. As an example, consider the Parakeet paragraph below, taken from Meyer (1974):

> The wide variety in color of parakeets that are available on the market today resulted from careful breeding of the color mutant offspring of green-bodied and yellow-faced parakeets. The light green body and yellow face color combination is the color of the parakeets in their natural habitat, Australia. The first living parakeets were brought to Europe from Australia by John Gould, a naturalist, in 1840. The first color mutation appeared in 1872 in Belgium; these birds were completely yellow. The most popular color of parakeets in the United States is sky-blue. These birds have sky-blue bodies and white faces; this color mutation occurred in 1878 in Europe. There are over 66 different colors of parakeets listed by the Color and Technical Committee of the Budgerigar Society. In addition to the original green-bodied and yellow-faced birds, colors of parakeets include varying shades of violets, blues, grays, greens, yellows, and whites [p. 61].

I have reproduced an approximation to Meyer's representation for this paragraph in Table 10.5. I have removed from this representation her technical notation, but the outline structure of the paragraph closely approximates the hierarchy of propositions that she imposes. There are five levels of propositions, which vary from the central proposition *The wide variety in color of parakeets results from breeding patterns* to the very specific *John Gould was a naturalist.*

There is evidence that information more central in these representations is better recalled, more accurately recognized, and more rapidly verified (Kintsch, 1974;

TABLE 10.5
Meyer's Analysis of Parakeet Paragraph

Topic: The wide variety in color of parakeets results from breeding patterns.

A.   Subtopic: Wide variety in color of parakeets

1.   Wide variety in color of parakeets is available in the market today.

2.   Over 66 different colors of parakeets are listed by the Color and Technical Committee of the Budgerigar Society.

3.   There is a range of color
(a)   The original was a green-bodied and yellow-faced bird.
(b)   The varying shades include (i) violets, (ii) blues, (iii), grays, (iv) greens, (v) yellows, and (vi) whites.

B.   Subtopic: Breeding patterns

1.   There was a careful breeding of color mutant offspring.
(a)   The first color mutation appeared in 1872 in Belgium.
(i)   It was completely yellow.
(b)   A sky-blue color mutation occurred in 1878 in Europe.
(i)   These birds have sky-blue bodies and white faces.
(ii)   They are the most popular color of parakeets in the United States.
(c)   There are green-bodied and yellow-faced birds.
(i)   This is their color combination in the natural habitat, Australia.
(ii)   The first living parakeets were brought to Europe from Australia by John Gould in 1840.
(α)   John Gould was a naturalist.

Kintsch & van Dijk, 1976; Meyer, 1971). It has been shown that this structural variable is a better predictor of recall than serial position or rated importance (Meyer & McConkie, 1973). Meyer (1974) has taken the same passage and embedded it in two paragraph contexts. In one it was central and in another peripheral. Recall for the passage was better when it was central.

There seem to be at least two plausible reasons in an ACT framework why subjects should display better memory for the more central propositions. First, an ACT network structure interconnecting the proposition is going to reflect to some degree the proposed outline form. Figure 10.12 shows a tree structure equivalent of Table 10.5. I doubt whether the network structures subjects set up to represent a paragraph would be perfect tree structures as dictated by Meyer's outline form. There are undoubtedly some cross-connections between propositions producing loops. Still the tree structure representation will be approximately accurate. In this representation the central proposition tends to have less mean distance to other propositions than do the more peripheral propositions. Thus, if the subject can retrieve one proposition from the passage he will have, on the average, less distance to travel in the network to retrieve the central proposition. Therefore, there will be a greater average probability of recalling that central proposition. The

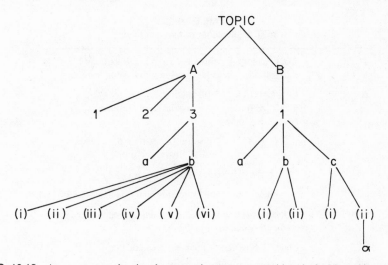

FIG. 10.12   A tree structure showing the connection among propositions in the Meyer hierarchy in Table 9.5.

second reason for the superiority of the central proposition may be attributed to subject rehearsal patterns. Subjects might call up the central proposition to help interpret the more peripheral propositions. This would constitute rehearsal of the central proposition and so improve its recall.

ACT's network representation for this paragraph preserves most of the Meyer hierarchy, but it also has other connections of a nonhierarchical nature. In Table 10.6, I have produced ACT translations corresponding to most of the units in the Meyer representation of Table 10.5. Some of the Meyer units seem so redundant with others that I have omitted representing them multiple times in Table 10.6. For instance, Subtopics A and B seem totally redundant with the Topic. However, except for these omissions, it is possible to reconstruct the tree structure in Figure 10.12 by means of overlap of concepts in the propositions of Table 10.6. Thus, the topic is connected to A1, A2, and A3 through the mention of the color of parakeets—(color OF parakeet)—and to B1 through mention of color mutation—(mutate OF color). Similarly, overlap of concepts provides the means for the other connections in the hierarchy. Note, however, that this overlap of concepts creates connections not specified in the hierarchy. So, for instance, B1C(i) and A3a are related because they both make reference to the original green-bodied, yellow-faced parakeet. Thus, ACT predicts that, while a subject's recall should display the contingencies reflected in the Meyer hierarchy, there should be other, non-hierarchical contingencies in recall because of these additional overlaps of concepts. To my knowledge, no one has looked for contingencies in recall based on nonhierarchical overlap.

TABLE 10.6
ACT Equivalents of Meyer's Units

TOPIC	$((((x\ C\ (color\ OF\ parakeets))\ *\ (wide\ OF\ variety))$ $*\ (result\ OF\ ((breed\ OF\ (mutate\ OF\ color))\ *\ careful)))$
A1	$(z\ *\ market)\ \&\ (z\ *\ (time\ OF\ today))\ \&\ ((y\ C$ $(color\ OF\ (parakeets\ \cap\ (available\text{-}on\ OF\ z))))\ *$ $(wide\ OF\ variety))$
A2	$("C\ \&\ T\ of\ BS"\ *\ (list\ OF\ U))\ \&\ (U\ *\ parakeets)$ $\&\ ((w\ \#\ \ \ (color\ OF\ U))\ *\ (over\ OF\ 66))$
A3	$((x\ C\ (color\ OF\ parakeet))\ *\ has\text{-}range)$
A3a	$((original\ OF\ parakeet)\ *\ (green\text{-}bodied\ \cap\ (yellow\text{-}faced\ \cap\ bird)))$
A3b	$((violets\ \cup\ (blues\ \cup\ (gray\ \cup\ (green\ \cup\ (yellow\ \cup\ white)))))\ *$ $(color\ OF\ parakeet))$
B1	$((breed\ OF\ (mutate\ OF\ color))\ *\ careful)$
B1a	$\alpha\ =\ (S\ *\ (first\ OF\ (mutate\ OF\ color)))\ \&$ $(\alpha\ *\ (time\ OF\ 1872))\ \&\ (\alpha\ *\ (place\ OF\ Belgium))$
B1a(i)	$(S\ *\ yellow)$
B1b	$\beta\ =\ (T\ *\ ((mutate\ OF\ color)\ \cap\ ((sky\text{-}blue\ OF\ body)\ \cap\ (white$ $OF\ face))))\ \&\ (\beta\ *\ (time\ OF\ 1878))\ \&\ (\beta\ *\ (place\ OF\ Europe))$
B1b(ii)	$\gamma\ =\ (T\ *\ ((most\ OF\ popular)\ OF\ parakeets))$ $\&\ (\gamma\ *\ (time\ OF\ today))\ \&\ (\gamma\ *\ (place\ OF\ United\text{-}States))$
B1c	$R\ =\ (green\text{-}bodied\ \cap\ (yellow\text{-}faced\ \cap\ bird))$
B1c(i)	$(Australia\ *\ ((natural\ OF\ habitat)\ OF\ R))$
B1c(ii)	$((John\ Gould\ *\ ((first\ OF\ bring)\ OF\ parakeets\ Europe$ $Australia))\ *\ (time\ OF\ 1840))$
B1c(ii)α	$(John\ Gould\ *\ naturalist)$

SUMMARY OF CHAPTER 10

Subjects in a verbal learning experiment typically encode the words they are asked to remember in some meaningful way. This encoding will involve selecting some sense of the word and building up an elaboration involving this sense. Context has been shown by Tulving to exercise a strong influence on these encoding operations. If the context at test is different than the context at study different encodings are likely to arise and the subject may not recognize the word in the test context. Such effects of context on encoding seem to be magnified in verbal learning experiments, in contrast to everyday life situations, because the context in which a word is presented in a verbal learning experiment is very impoverished. Such encoding processes also seem to play an important role in memory for isolated sentences. Subjects appear to have difficulty in recognizing the verb of a sentence when it occurs out of context. As a consequence they have difficulty in recalling a sentence in response to a verb probe. This encoding difficulty accounts for the configural effects in sentence memory observed by Anderson and Bower (1972a) and by Foss and Harwood (1975).

Subjects have acquired through experience a set of productions that permit them to elaborate certain information with additional redundant connections. They are able to display better memory for to-be-learned material if they are able to transform the material into a form for which there are many elaborative productions. The effects associated with depth of processing can be understood in terms of such elaborative productions. Such elaborative processes also have a strong influence on whether effects are obtained of linguistic structure. It is argued that these elaborative processes would tend to obliterate effects of within-propositional structure but magnify the effects of between-propositional structure and of higher level structure in a prose passage.

In general, the thrust of this chapter has not been that ACT is the only model compatible with the various memory phenomena, but rather that it was one of the models that predicted these phenomena. It was important to show that ACT could account for the various factors that had strong influences on level of recall.

REFERENCES

Abelson, R. P. Concepts for representing mundane reality in plans. In D. G. Bobrow & A. M. Collins (Eds.), *Representation and understanding.* New York: Academic Press, 1975.

Anderson, J. R. FRAN: A simulation model of free recall. In G. H. Bower (Ed.), *The psychology of learning and motivation,* Vol. 5. New York: Academic Press, 1972.

Anderson, J. R. Verbatim and propositional representation of sentences in immediate and long-term memory. *Journal of Verbal Learning and Verbal Behavior,* 1974, **13,** 149–162.

Anderson, J. R., & Bower, G. H. On an associative trace for sentence memory. *Journal of Verbal Learning and Verbal Behavior,* 1971, **10,** 673–680.

Anderson, J. R., and Bower, G. H. Configural properties in sentence memory. *Journal of Verbal Learning and Verbal Behavior,* 1972, **11,** 594–605.   (a)

Anderson, J. R., & Bower, G. H. Recognition and retrieval processes in free recall. *Psychological Review,* 1972, **79,** 97–123   (b).

Anderson, J. R., & Bower, G. H. *Human associative memory.* Washington, D.C.: Winston, 1973.

Anderson, J. R., & Bower, G. H. A propositional theory of recognition memory. *Cognition and Memory,* 1974, **2,** 406–412.

Anderson, R. C. Substance recall of sentences. *Quarterly Journal of Experimental Psychology,* 1974, **26,** 530–541.

Atkinson, R. C., & Raugh, M. R. *Application of the mnemonic keyword method to the acquisition of a Russian vocabulary* (Tech. Rept. No. 237). Stanford: Institute for Mathematical Studies in the Social Sciences, 1974.

Atkinson, R., & Shiffrin, R. Human memory: A proposed system and its control processes. In K. Spence & J. Spence (Eds.), *The psychology of learning and motivation,* Vol. 2. New York: Academic Press, 1968.

Barclay, J. R. The role of comprehension in remembering sentences, *Cognitive Psychology*, 1973, **4**, 229–254.

Begg, I., & Paivio, A. Concreteness and imagery in sentence memory. *Journal of Verbal Learning and Verbal Behavior*, 1969, **8**, 821–827.

Bjork, R. A., & Jongeward, R. H. Rehearsal and mere rehearsal. Unpublished manuscript, 1974.

Blumenthal, A. L. Prompted recall of sentences. *Journal of Verbal Learning and Verbal Behavior*, 1967, **6**, 203–206.

Bobrow, S., & Bower, G. H. Comprehension and recall of sentences. *Journal of Experimental Psychology*, 1969, **80**, 455–461.

Bower, G. H. Analysis of a mnemonic device. *American Scientist*, 1970, **58**, 496–510.

Bower, G. H. Stimulus-sampling theory of encoding variability. In A. Melton & E. Martin (Eds.), *Coding theory in learning and memory*. Washington, D.C.: Winston, 1972.

Bower, G. H., & Karlin, M. B. Depth of processing pictures of faces and recognition memory. *Journal of Experimental Psychology*, 1974, **103**, 751–757.

Bransford, J. D., Barclay, J. R., & Franks, J. J. Sentence memory: A constructive versus interpretive approach. *Cognitive Psychology*, 1972, **3**, 193–209.

Bransford, J. D., & Johnson, M. K. Considerations of some problems of comprehension. In W. Chase (Ed.), *Visual information processing*. New York: Academic Press, 1973.

Chase, W. G., & Simon, H. A. The mind's eye in chess. In W. G. Chase (Ed.), *Visual information processing*. New York: Academic Press, 1973.

Craik, F. I. M., & Tulving, E. Depth of processing and the retention of words in episodic memory. *Journal of Experimental Psychology: General*, 1975, **104**, 268–294.

Craik, F. I. M., & Watkins, M. J. The role of rehearsal in short-term memory. *Journal of Verbal Learning and Verbal Behavior*, 1973, **12**, 599–607.

Crothers, E. J. Memory structure and the recall of discourse. In J. B. Carrol & R. O. Freedle (Eds.), *Language comprehension and the acquisition of knowledge*. Washington, D.C.: Winston, 1972.

Dapolito, F., Barker, D., & Wiant, J. The effects of contextual changes on component recognition. *American Journal of Psychology*, 1972, **85**, 431–440.

De Groot, A. D. *Thought and choice in chess*. The Hague: Mouton, 1965.

Fillenbaum, S. Memory for gist: some relevant variables. *Language and Speech*, 1966, **9**, 217–227.

Foss, D. J., & Harwood, D. A. Memory for sentences: Implications for human associative memory. *Journal of Verbal Learning and Verbal Behavior*, 1975, **14**, 1–16.

Fredericksen, C. H. Effects of task induced cognitive operations on comprehension and memory processes. In R. Freedle & J. B. Carroll (Eds.), *Language comprehension and the acquisition of knowledge*. Washington, D.C.: Winston, 1972.

Fredericksen, C. H. Representing logical and semantic structure of knowledge acquired from discourse. *Cognitive Psychology*, 1975, **7**, 371–458.

Gartman, L. M., & Johnson, N. F. Massed versus distributed repetition of homographs: A test of the differential-encoding hypothesis. *Journal of Verbal Learning and Verbal Behavior*, 1972, **11**, 801–808.

Glenberg, A. M. *Retrieval factors and the lag effect* (Tech. Rept. No. 49). Ann Arbor: University of Michigan Human Performance Center, 1974.

Gomulicki, B. R. Recall as an abstractive process. *Acta Psychologica*, 1956, **12**, 77–94.

Graesser, A., & Mandler, G. Recognition memory for the meaning and surface structure of sentences. *Journal of Experimental Psychology: Human Learning and Memory*, 1975, **104**, 238–248.

Hintzman, D. L. Theoretical implications of the spacing effect. In R. L. Solso (Ed.), *Theories in cognitive psychology: The Loyola Symposium*. Hillsdale, New Jersey: Lawrence Erlbaum Assoc., 1974.

Hyde, T. S., & Jenkins, J. J. Recall for words as a function of semantic, graphic, and syntactic orienting tasks. *Journal of Verbal Learning and Verbal Behavior*, 1973, **12**, 471–480.

Jacoby, L. L. Encoding processes, rehearsal, and recall requirements. *Journal of Verbal Learning and Verbal Behavior*, 1973, **12**, 302–310.

Jacoby, L. L., & Bartz, W. A. Rehearsal and transfer to LTM. *Journal of Verbal Learning and Verbal Behavior,* 1972, **11,** 561–565.

Johnson, M. K., Bransford, J. D., Nyberg, S. E., & Cleary, J. J. Comprehension factors in interpreting memory for abstract and concrete sentences. *Journal of Verbal Learning and Verbal Behavior,* 1972, **11,** 451–454.

Johnson, N. F. Sequential verbal behavior. In T. R. Dixon & D. L. Horton (Eds.), *Verbal behavior and behavior theory.* Englewood Cliffs, New Jersey: Prentice-Hall, 1968.

Johnson, N. F. The role of chunking and organization in the processes of recall. In G. H. Bower (Ed.), *Psychology of language and motivation,* Vol. 4. New York: Academic Press, 1970. Pp. 172–247.

Kintsch, W. Models for free recall and recognition. In D. A. Norman (Ed.), *Models of human memory.* New York: Academic Press, 1970. Pp. 307–373.

Kintsch, W. *The representation of meaning in memory.* Hillsdale, New Jersey: Lawrence Erlbaum Assoc., 1974.

Kintsch, W. Memory representations of text. In R. L. Solso (Ed.), *Information processing and cognition.* Hillsdale, New Jersey: Lawrence Erlbaum Assoc., 1975.

Kintsch, W., & van Dijk, T. A. Recalling and summarizing stories. A French translation of paper to be published in *Language,* 1976.

Lawrence, D. H. The nature of a stimulus: Some relationships between learning and perception. In S. Koch (Ed.), *Psychology: A study of a science.* Vol. 5. New York: McGraw-Hill, 1963.

Lesgold, A. M. Pronominalizations: A device for unifying sentences in memory. *Journal of Verbal Learning and Verbal Behavior,* 1972, **11,** 316–323.

Levelt, W. J. M., & Bonarius, M. Suffixes as deep structure clues. *Heymans Bulletins, Psychology Institute, R. V. Groningin,* 1968, No. 22X.

Light, L. L., & Carter-Sobell, L. Effects of changed semantic context on recognition memory. *Journal of Verbal Learning and Verbal Behavior,* 1970, **9,** 1–11.

Light, L. L., Kimble, G. A., & Pelligrino. J. W. Comments on "Episodic Memory: When recognition fails," by Watkins and Tulving. *Journal of Experimental Psychology: General,* 1975, **104,** 30–36.

Madigan, S. A. Intraserial repetition and coding processes in free recall. *Journal of Verbal Learning and Verbal Behavior,* 1969, **8,** 828–835.

Martin, E. Stimulus meaningfulness and paired-associate transfer: An encoding variability hypothesis. *Psychological Review,* 1968, **75,** 421–441.

Martin, E. Verbal Learning theory and independent retrieval phenomena. *Psychological Review,* 1971, **78,** 314–332.

Martin, E. Generation-recognition retrieval theory and the encoding specificity principle. *Psychological Review,* 1975, **82,** 150–153.

Melton, A. W. The situation with respect to the spacing of repetitions and memory. *Journal of Verbal Learning and Verbal Behavior,* 1970, **9,** 596–605.

Meyer, B. J. F. Idea units recalled from prose in relation to their position in the logical structure, stability, and order in the passage. Unpublished master's thesis, Cornell University, 1971.

Meyer, B. J. F. The organization of prose and its effect on recall. Unpublished doctoral dissertation, Cornell University, 1974.

Meyer, B. J. F., & McConkie, G. W. What is recalled after hearing a passage? *Journal of Educational Psychology,* 1973, **65,** 109–117.

Miller, G. A., Galanter, E., & Pribram, K. H. *Plans and the structure of behavior.* New York: Holt, Rinehart & Winston, 1960.

Minsky, M. A Framework for Representing Knowledge. In P. H. Winston, (Ed.), *The psychology of computer vision.* New York: McGraw-Hill, 1975.

Newell, A., & Simon, H. *Human problem solving.* Englewood Cliffs, New Jersey: Prentice-Hall, 1972.

Paivio, A. *Imagery and verbal processes.* New York: Holt, Rinehart, and Winston, 1971.

Postman, L. Short-term memory and incidental learning. In A. W. Melton (Ed.), *Categories of human learning*. New York: Academic Press, 1964.

Raugh, M. R., & Atkinson, R. C. A mnemonic method for the learning of a second language vocabulary. *Journal of Educational Psychology*, 1975, **67**, 1–16.

Reder, L. M., Anderson, J. R., & Bjork, R. A. A semantic interpretation of encoding specificity. *Journal of Experimental Psychology*, 1974, **102**, 648–656.

Reitman, J. S. Skilled perception in GO: Deducing memory structures from response times. Paper presented at the Psychonomic Meetings, 1975.

Rohwer, W. D., Jr. Constraint, syntax and meaning in paired-associate learning. *Journal of Verbal Learning and Verbal Behavior*, 1966, **5**, 541–547.

Rumelhart, D. E. Notes on a schema for stories. In D. G. Bobrow and A. M. Collins (Eds.), *Representation and understanding*. New York: Academic Press, 1975.

Rumelhart, D. E., Lindsay, P., & Norman, D. A. A process model for long-term memory. In E. Tulving & W. Donaldson (Eds.), *Organization of memory*. New York: Academic Press, 1972.

Rundus, D. Analysis of rehearsal processes in free recall. *Journal of Experimental Psychology*, 1971, **89**, 63–77.

Sachs, J. Recognition memory for syntactic and semantic aspects of connected discourse. *Perception and Psychophysics*, 1967, **2**, 437–442.

Salzberg, P. M. On the generality of encoding specificity: Grammatical class and concreteness of cues. Unpublished doctoral dissertation, University of Colorado, 1974.

Santa, J. L. and Lamwers, L. L. Encoding specificity: Fact or artifact? *Journal of Verbal Learning and Verbal Behavior*, 1974, **13**, 412–423.

Schank, R. C. The structure of episodes in memory. In D. G. Bobrow & A. M. Collins (Eds.), *Representing and understanding*. New York: Academic Press, 1975.

Schank, R. C., & Abelson, R. P. Scripts, plans, and knowledge. Paper presented at the 4th International Joint Conference on Artificial Intelligence, Tbilisi, USSR, 1975.

Simon, H. A., & Gilmartin, K. A simulation of memory for chess positions. *Cognitive Psychology*, 1973, **5**, 29–46.

Solso, R. L. Discussion: Section III, *Information processing and cognition*. Hillsdale, New Jersey: Lawrence Erlbaum Assoc., 1975.

Till, R. E., & Jenkins, J. J. The effects of cued orienting tasks on the free recall of words. *Journal of Verbal Learning and Verbal Behavior*, 1973, **12**, 489–498.

Thomson, D. M., & Tulving, E. Associative encoding and retrieval. Weak and strong cues. *Journal of Experimental Psychology*, 1970, **86**, 255–262.

Trabasso, T., & Bower, G. H. *Attention in learning*. New York: John Wiley, 1968.

Tulving, E. Episodic and semantic memory. In E. Tulving & W. Donaldson (Eds.), *Organization of memory*. New York: Academic Press, 1972.

Tulving, E., & Thomson, D. M. Retrieval processes in recognition memory: Effects of associative context. *Journal of Experimental Psychology*, 1971, **87**, 116–124.

Tulving, E., & Thomson, D. M. Encoding specificity and retrieval processes in episodic memory. *Psychological Review*, 1973, **80**, 352–373.

Underwood, B. J. Stimulus selection in verbal learning. In C. N. Cofer & B. S. Musgrave (Eds.), *Verbal behavior and learning: Problems and processes*. New York: McGraw-Hill, 1963.

Walsh, D. A., & Jenkins, J. J. Effects of orienting tasks on free recall in incidental learning: "Difficulty," "Effort," and "Process" explanations. *Journal of Verbal Learning and Verbal Behavior*, 1973, **12**, 481–488.

Wanner, H. E. On remembering, forgetting, and understanding sentences: A study of the deep structure hypothesis. Unpublished doctoral dissertation, Harvard University, 1968.

Watkins, M. J., & Tulving, E. Episodic memory: When recognition fails. *Journal of Experimental Psychology: General*, 1975, **104**, 5–29.

Waugh, N. C. On the effective duration of a repeated word. *Journal of Verbal Learning and Verbal Behavior*, 1970, **9**, 587–595.

Waugh, N. C., & Norman, D. A. Primary memory, *Psychological Review*, 1965, **72**, 89–104.

Wickelgren, W. A. The long and the short of memory. *Psychological Bulletin*, 1973, **80**, 425–438.

Winograd, E., & Conn, C. P. Evidence from recognition memory for a specific encoding of unmodified homographs. *Journal of Verbal Learning and Verbal Behavior*, 1971, **10**, 702–706.

Woodward, A. E., Bjork, R. A., & Jongeward, R. H. Recall and recognition as a function of primary rehearsal. *Journal of Verbal Learning and Verbal Behavior*, 1973, **12**, 608–617.

Yates, F. A. *The art of memory*. Chicago: University of Chicago Press, 1966.

11

Language Comprehension and Generation

> Clearly, if there is to be progress in psycho-linguistics, we must avoid formulating the goals of the discipline in ways that presuppose the general psychology of the organism.
>
> FODOR, BEVER, AND GARRETT

Psychologists largely ignored language until the last twenty years. It was once thought that verbal learning research would lead to an understanding of natural language because this research was supposed to identify the laws of verbal habit formation. The various learning theory approaches to language (Mowrer, 1960; Osgood, Suci, & Tannebaum, 1957; Skinner, 1957; Staats, 1968) claimed that simple habit formation underlay language comprehension and use. However, it has since become clear (Bever, 1968; Bever, Fodor, & Garrett, 1968; Chomsky, 1959, 1968; Fodor, 1965; Garrett & Fodor, 1968; McNeill, 1968) that this is not so. Except for these learning-theory-based approaches, almost the only analyses of language had been diary accounts of child language acquisition and word count studies (see McCarthy, 1954, for a review).

In contrast to past inactivity in the field, research on psycholinguistics is a very active field today. The stimulus to this current research activity has been the success of other fields, particularly linguistics, in providing formal frameworks for studying properties of language. The type of linguistics that has influenced current psychology is structuralism. Chomsky was trained in the structuralist school and most of the subsequent research in linguistics that has developed in reaction to his work is structuralist in nature. This means that language is identified as a static object which has certain formal properties. Psycholinguists have taken various structural features of these formal analyses, like transformational complexity or markedness, and have attempted to correlate these features with human performance. Such correlations are not very satisfactory. One would like to have a process model which explained why these correlations arose. Recently, psychologists have been looking to artificial intelligence for some ideas about such process models. The principle purpose of this chapter is to look at various computer models of language processing with an eye to understanding human language processing. The first section will attempt to overview the past 25 years of computer models for language comprehension. The second section will take an intensive and critical look at augmented transition networks which are currently being promoted as psychological models for language comprehension. The third section will outline the ACT production system model for language comprehension and generation.

11.1 COMPUTER MODELS OF LANGUAGE PROCESSING

Computers have been applied to natural language processing for 25 years, resulting in a succession of major reconceptualizations of the problem of language understanding, each of which constitutes a clear advance over the previous conceptions. However, any realistic assessment would concede that we are very far from a general language understanding system of human capability. The argument has been advanced that there are fundamental obstacles that will prevent this goal from ever being realized (Dreyfus, 1972). These arguments are imprecise and lacking in rigor. The best (for example, Bar-Hillel, 1964) has to do with the extreme open-endedness of language, and asserts that an effectively unbounded variety of knowledge is relevant to the understanding process. It is boldly asserted, without proof, that it is not possible to provide the computer with the requisite background knowledge.

Machine Translation

The first intensive application of computers to language was concerned with translation. Compared to the initial projections of success, this massive effort turned out to be a dismal failure (for summary assessments see ALPAC, 1966; Bar-Hillel, 1964; Kasher, 1966). Today, it is fashionable (for example, Simmons, 1970; Wilks, 1973) to attribute the failure to the impoverished conception of language that prevailed in the 1950s and early 1960s. The language translation procedures worked much the way a student translates in a language class—but it missed something. The words of a sentence in one language were looked up in a dictionary for the corresponding words of the other language. Then the grammar of the second language was consulted for the sentential form with which to express the translation. The problem is that these programs did not have the conceptual constraints that a human has in translating sentences. Consider an example from Winograd (1974): The sentences *The fish was bought by a cook* should receive a very different translation in Japanese than *The fish was bought by a river*. This is because *cook* is agent whereas *river* is locative and Japanese uses different means for differentiating between these two noun roles. However, the decision that *cook* is agent and *river* location depends upon general conceptual and real-word knowledge and not knowledge of dictionary equivalents or of the grammar. Recent work on machine translation (for example, Wilks, 1973) has attempted a more sophisticated conceptual approach. It remains to be seen if there is any greater success.

Interactive Systems

The now popular task domain for applications of computers to language is in constructing systems that can interact with the user in his own language. Question-answering systems are the most common; the user can interrogate the program about knowledge in its data base and input new knowledge. Such systems depend critically for their success on three aspects of their design—their parser, the representation of information, and the inference system. The task of the parser is to analyze natural language input and translate it into a form compatible with the internal representation. If the input is something to be remembered by the system, it will be translated into an internal representation and stored in that form. If the input is a question, the parser will analyze it into a form that can be used to guide an interrogation of the data base for the answer. The inference system is critical in the answering of questions since many answers will not be directly stored but will have to be inferred from what is in memory. Both parsing and inferencing run into *time* problems.

The central time problem in parsing has to do with the extreme syntactic and lexical ambiguity of natural language. Let us say each word in a sentence admits of m syntactic and semantic interpretations where m on the average may be as high as 10. If there are n words, m^n interpretations must be considered although only one is intended. The fact that language is so ambiguous was a discovery of the early machine attempts at parsing (for example, Kuno, 1965). Thus far, no heuristics have been demonstrated that change in general this exponential function of sentence length to something closer to a linear function. Even for context-free languages, the best general parsing algorithm that has been developed still takes n^3 time (Younger, 1967). The human seems to be able to use general context to reduce ambiguity to something approximating the linear relation.

There is also an exponential growth factor in the task of drawing inferences. Suppose there are m facts in the data base and the desired deduction is n steps long. Then, there are something like m^n possible combinations of facts to achieve the desired deduction. This suggests that very deep inferences (that is, high n) are difficult to achieve and this seems true of our everyday reasoning. However, it also suggests that inferences should become more difficult as we know more facts (that is, high m) which is clearly not the case. In Section 9.1 I discussed some of the computer science efforts to develop efficient inference systems that avoided this exponential growth.

Although there are potentially serious time problems both in parsing and inferencing, these problems often have not surfaced as much in the past programs as one might have expected. This is because these programs have all been rather narrowly constrained. Their language systems only needed to deal with a small portion of the possible syntactic constructions and a small portion of the possible word meanings. Also, because of restrictions in the domain of discourse, only a restricted set of inferences is needed.

First Generation Language Understanding Systems

Winograd (1974), in a review, points out that there seem to have been two generations of interactive, language understanding systems. The first generation really did not attempt serious language understanding but rather focused on the goal of producing the appearance of understanding in a constrained domain. There were programs like ELIZA (Weizenbaum, 1966) and PERRY (Colby & Enea, 1968) which attempted to simulate human personalities. ELIZA was a strict Rogerian psychotherapist and PERRY a paranoid patient. Despite the fact that these programs made no serious attempt at language understanding, they had some success in convincing users that a human and not a machine was typing the answers at the other end of the terminal.

Consider a typical exchange with ELIZA:

    human: I am very lonely.
    ELIZA: How long have you been lonely?

ELIZA is looking for any pattern of the form "I am ..." and whenever it sees it, it types back "How long have you been ... ," substituting the actual phrase. When these programs made serious errors of language understanding it was difficult for a naive user to reject the possibility that these might just be manifestations of the strong personalities of the simulation. One test of Colby's program involved presenting protocols from it and from actual paranoid patients to trained psychiatrists. The psychiatrist's task was to guess which was paranoid. Most picked the true paranoid although some were fooled by PERRY. Some volunteered, because of PERRY's apparent language errors, that it may have been misclassified as paranoid and really was brain damaged.

Other first generation programs made a more serious attempt at language understanding but were only adequate in their particular restricted task domain. These were question-answering programs and they had to sufficiently analyze assertions to properly store them in the data base and sufficiently analyze questions to retrieve the correct answers. Raphael's (1968) SIR and Slagle's DEDUCOM (1965) dealt with simple set inclusion problems; Green, Wolf, Chomsky, and Laughery (1963) with baseball questions; Lindsay (1963) with kinship terms; Kellogg (1968) with data management systems; Woods (1968) with airline schedules; and Bobrow (1964) and Charniak (1969) with word arithmetic problems.

Second Generation Language Systems

After it became clear that programs could be written that looked successful in limited domains, concern shifted from giving the appearance of language understanding to modeling the basic mechanisms of language processing. Less concern was given to what the output of the program looked like and more concern to the correctness of the program's internal processing. The programs of Anderson and Bower (1973), Quillian (1969), Norman, Rumelhart, *et al.* (1975), Schank (1972), and Simmons (1973) all fall into this particular category. These programs were concerned with understanding the memory process, inferential processes, and parsing required for language understanding. The programs did not really have a task domain.

The two second generation programs with well-specified task domains are Woods' LUNAR (Woods, Kaplan, & Nash-Webber, 1972) and Winograd's (1972) SHRDLU. LUNAR was designed to answer questions about mineral samples brought from the moon by astronauts. The grammar formalisms developed by Woods will be discussed at length in Section 11.2. Winograd's SHRDLU converses with a person about manipulations it is performing in a simple world of toy blocks.

Winograd has combined good task analyses, programming skills, and the powers of advanced programming languages to create the best language understanding system extant. It has been claimed that the Winograd system could be extended to become a general model of language understanding. What would be needed is to program into it all the knowledge of an adult and extend the parsing rules to the point where they handled all English sentences. Admittedly, this would be a big task requiring hundreds of man-years of work, but, it is argued, no greater than the work that goes into writing big operating systems. However, this argument is faulty if only because SHRDLU does not deal with the time problems in general inferencing and general parsing. Further, it is unclear whether human language understanding can be captured in a fixed program. One might also question whether SHRDLU can manage the bookkeeping necessary to properly integrate all the specific pieces of knowledge and have them interact in the intended ways. Our linguistic competence is not a fixed object. It changes over the period of years as we learn new grammatical styles, new words, and new ways of thinking. There are also probably changes in our linguistic processes over short spans of time. That is, the way humans seem to deal with the time problems inherent in parsing and inferencing is to adjust the parsing and inferencing according to context.

The Nature of Question Answering

There are a number of reasons for the current popularity of question-answering programs. First of all, question-answering programs have the promise of some practical applications. Second, they pose a reasonably demanding test of a linguistic theory. However, another class of reasons for their popularity is that it is possible to avoid too demanding a test of one's ideas. For instance, it is possible to restrict the program to a particular task domain. As a consequence, one need only encode into the program mechanisms to deal with that task domain. Also one can use heuristics which might not be generally valid but which are true in that particular domain.

Another reason for the popularity of question answering is that it is user controlled. The language processing program has no goal except to answer questions. Consequently, the program is freed from dealing with some of the most problematical aspects of human language processing. That is, the program is not trying to use language as a tool to satisfy complex motives. It does not generate spontaneous speech to entertain the user, get information from the user, get the user to help it, deceive the user, etc. It simply receives sentences and stores them in the data base in a form suitable for retrieving answers. In response to a question, it generates sufficient information to provide an answer and nothing more. The only questions it asks of the user are those needed to disambiguate the sentences and questions it receives. As a consequence, the language comprehension part of the program is always much more sophisticated than the language generation part.

Another advantage of question answering is that it is a disjointed task. In one line typed to the program the informant can be talking about one topic and in the next line he might switch to a completely different topic. The program has to be able to follow this jumping about from topic to topic. This means one cannot take advantage of the contextual redundancy that characterizes much conversational and written prose. This is an advantage because these programs do not have mechanisms to use such redundancy. Since the redundancy does not exist in a question-answering domain the performance of these programs will not compare unfavorably to that of a human in the same situation.

I think the decision in artificial intelligence to work on question answering was extremely judicious. It would have been impossible to work on all of language understanding. Question-answering tasks provide a limited, but still sufficiently ambitious, domain in which to work out ideas about language comprehension. There has been considerable progress because of this choice of domain. However, one must also realize how restricted question answering is compared to human language usage.

Third Generation Programs (?)

It seems that artificial intelligence work on language comprehension is in a state of transition again (Charniak, 1972; McDermott, 1974; Minsky, 1975; Rieger, 1974; Schank & Abelson, 1975; Winograd, 1975). There is a growing realization that programs, even those as sophisticated as Winograd's, do not adequately mimic the way specific pieces of knowledge influence the language comprehension process. Consider the following passage:

Jane was invited to Jack's Birthday Party. She wondered if he would like a kite. She went to her room and shook her piggy bank. It made no sound.

Most readers understand that Jane wants money to buy a kite for a present for Jack but that there is no money to pay for it in her piggy bank. None of these facts is directly stated. The reader is required to integrate his knowledge about birthday parties and piggy banks into the semantic processing of the passage. Unfortunately, the computational mechanisms suggested so far to achieve this integration are at best vague.

A current set of proposals revolves around the idea of a frame (Minsky, 1975). Frames have been called other things by different researchers. For instance, Abelson (1973) refers to them as *scripts*, but the underlying idea is the same. The basic idea is to have a set of information stored with various stereotyped situations like a child's birthday party. Attached to each frame are several kinds of information. Some of this information is about how to use the frame, some about what to expect in the situation, and some about what to do if these expectations are not confirmed.

The term *frame* is a current catchword in artificial intelligence. What frames are, however, has not been very well worked out yet. The following description from Winograd (1974) is about as good as any for summarizing the central ideas behind the frame representations:

> The basic object in the system is a frame, which can be thought of as a collection of facts and procedures associated with a concept. It is a bit like one of the nodes in the semantic nets, or like an independent actor. It does not correspond to a "single fact" like in a formal logic representation, but is a chunking of information around a single concept. Figure 3.6 (see below) gives an example parts of the frames for the concepts "give" and "pay," in a simplified form. The system contains a hierarchical network classifying the concepts as "further specifications" of others. So "give" is a kind of "act." If we know that every act must have a time and place, then we know automatically that every "give" has a time and place. Similarly, "pay" is a kind of "give,"

> GIVE isa ACT
>
> >   ACTOR: person
> > BENEFICIARY: person
> >   OBJECT: physical object
>
> PAY isa GIVE
>
> >   OBJECT: money
> >   REASON: debt

> Associated with each frame is a set of *important elements*, or imps. These are labeled as being of central importance to the properties of the frame. Among the many possible facts about a concept, only certain ones will be relevant for a given purpose. A central set will be most likely to be relevant. In the case of giving, the ACTOR doing the giving, the BENEFICIARY receiving it, and the OBJECT being given are of primary importance. In paying, the OBJECT is further specified as being money, and the reason (which in general is an imp for any act) is further specified as being some kind of debt. The frame from "donate" would have a different further specification for its reason.

> In addition to the hierarchical structure of "isa" links and the presence of imps, frames have an explicit indexing mechanism for finding the facts relevant to a frame in a particular context. If we are looking for a connection between "pay" and "Friday," we might want the fact that payday is Friday. In a semantic net, there would be some sort of path through this connection.

In a frame system, the indexing mechanism should allow us to ask "Do you have anything stored under the association between these two concepts?", which would retrieve the desired fact, possibly along with others.

In addition, each frame has procedures associated with it. For example, if we are trying to decide whether a particular act is a payment or not, a general procedure might cycle through the imps seeing if they could be filled in appropriately for the given example. Or instead, the system could have a special procedure for efficiently deciding whether some act was a payment. The procedure would be attached to the "pay" frame, and would take precedence over the more general mapping procedure.

The flow of control in a frame system can be directed by specific procedures attached to frames, or handled more generally by a mapping mechanism which tries to view something as an instance of a frame, and control the process by looking through the important elements. Retrieval is based on a separate index, or association mechanism, and matching is done more generally than with a syntactic pattern matcher. To match two elements, a kind of general mapping or analogy like that of Merlin is used. The result of applying a particular frame may be to trigger specific procedures in a top down way, or may be simply adding this new description and seeing whether it is an element in some still larger concept which applies.

I want to reiterate that this system has not been worked out in detail. The attempt is to provide a system with enough facilities to do the things which other representations allow, but to do it within a coherent framework for putting things together. Simple facts are represented in a straightforward declarative way. If specific procedures are called for, there is a way to attach them in a way which allows the control structure to move back and forth between more general and more specific processes without having to pre-decide just how each piece of information will be stored or used [pp. 61–62].

I must confess to strong doubts about how much the frames notion has to offer, particularly with respect to what it can offer psychology. However, I must also confess to an inability to present much in the way of cogent criticisms of the frames notion (see also Feldman, 1975, for a criticism of frames and the difficulties in criticizing frames). The frames concept is still a rather vague notion. Frames seem to be sufficiently elastic to perform almost any operation. Currently there are attempts underway to implement framelike ideas as working computer systems (for example, by Bobrow and Winograd at Xerox). Apparently, implementing a frames system is far from a trivial task, but hopefully it can be accomplished. The output of such research efforts will be a higher-level, "theory-laden" programming language on the order of Hewitt's (1972) PLANNER (see page 333), or Newell's (1973) PS (see page 89), or ACT. Like any such programming language it is going to be easy to perform certain operations and harder to perform others. If the claims about the virtues of frames are correct, then we should find it easier to carry out the kinds of operations associated with human intelligence such as prose comprehension. The ease with which these operations can be performed will be the basis for judging the value of the frames theory. Note that the issue will not be whether an operation can be performed in the frames formalism but rather the ease with which the operation can be programmed and debugged and the efficiency with which it will run. Presumably, the frames system will have the power of a Turing Machine and will be able to perform all specifiable operations, but some clumsily and others with ease.

Until we have a concrete, running frames system with which we can experiment, it is impossible to evaluate with any rigor the notion of frames. Nonetheless, this has not prevented many from being enthusiastic about it (consider the recent proceedings by Schank and Nash-Weber, 1975) or a few from being negative. Below are some criticisms expressing my discontent with frames. These are not devastating criticisms because there currently exists no concrete object to criticize. However, they reflect my suspicions about problems with frames when they become concretized as a running system.

Advocates of frames point out that certain information and procedures must be stored with concepts and stereotypic situations in order to be able to properly deal with them. This is certainly true but hardly seems the culmination of 25 years of research on computer language processing. If there is some claim of substance in the frames approach it must be that there is an advantage to a static partitioning of our knowledge about concepts and situations into a finite set of chunks. This view would contrast with a network model where information is more diffusely organized and can form different chunks depending on the current situation we face. There are at least two problems with this static partitioning. First, it is difficult to know with which frame(s) to store a particular fact. Second, it seems unlikely that any fixed set of frames will be appropriate to all possible situations. As an example of the first problem consider the fact that *Birthday parties involve the giving of presents*. What frame does that belong to—A birthday frame, a party frame, a present frame, a birthday party frame, a frame about children's pleasures, a frame about toy manufacturers, etc.? It seems that the fact is relevant to a great many situations (and hence, frames). If it is only going to be stored with a few frames, how does one decide which ones? How do other frames communicate with these when they need that knowledge? The second problem reflects the fact that each situation is somewhat unique, and the best constituted frame to process it will not be the same as the best constituted frame to process any other situation. However, if there is only a fixed set of frames one has to choose one from the set no matter how inappropriate it is and no matter how much better it would be to recombine information from a number of frames. It is this problem among others that bothers Feldman (1975), who writes:

Try to introspect as you slowly read the following sentence:

"Imagine yourself walking into a room; it is the master bedroom of a quiet Victorian house, in a slum of Bombay, which has just had a fire and been rebuilt in modern style, except for the master bedroom which is only half remodeled having its decorative panelling intact but badly visible because of the thick smoke."

The sentence above causes several shifts and refinements of the image. The question is, of course, where are the frames. It is possible that there are a very large number of *room* frames embodying all the combinatorial possibilities hinted at above. Alternatively, there could be a single *room* frame that incorporated all these possibilities. Neither of these alternatives strikes me as plausible. What seems to happen is that we build our model dynamically as we process the sentence. The anti-frame hypothesis here is that the connections, which are most important (heavily used, etc.) are not specifiable in advance [p. 103].

Problems with Computer Language Systems

Current computer systems are far from adequate psychological models of language processing. Some of the deficiencies could *perhaps* be dealt with in an ACT production system of the variety proposed in the third section of this chapter. Whether they actually can or not remains an issue for further research. In any case, I will state what the difficulties are with current computer models of language and why I think ACT may provide at least a partial solution. The difficulties I will point out for current approaches are of two varieties. One has to do with their power as intelligent systems and the other with their suitability as psychological models. Difficulties of the second variety are not failings of the models as artificial intelligence efforts, but rather barriers to their becoming psychological models.

a. Information-Processing Limitations. One problem with current systems is that they are, in some ways, too powerful. For example, they can deal with linguistic structures that humans would find extremely difficult or impossible to understand, such as multiply center-embedded sentences. The ACT production system, however, comes with a model of human information-processing limitations. At least to some degree these limitations impose on ACT the same deficiencies in language processing that humans display.

b. Language Acquisition. It may well be impossible, as a practical matter, to provide a program with all the requisite information to become a language user. A better approach may be to develop a learning program which will acquire a linguistic competence just as humans do. Many current artificial intelligence formalisms do not seem particularly adapted to a learning approach. In contrast, production systems seem rather well adapted in that the learning program may acquire, one by one, the requisite productions. The next chapter will be concerned with the induction of procedural knowledge in general and the induction of language-processing systems in particular.

c. Mixing of Levels of Analysis. Winograd's program is an example of a syntax-driven program. That is, options are suggested to the program by syntax. Conceptual constraints and semantics are used to edit these possibilities. Schank's (1972) program is an example of a semantics-driven program. That is, options are suggested by semantic and conceptual sources and then checked for syntactic correctness. However, as Winograd (1974) points out, both types of processes must occur in parallel. The correct understanding of "skid, crash, hospital" will only be suggested by a conceptual analysis. The correct analysis of "Then the other one did the same thing to it" will only be suggested by syntax. No system has been proposed which is driven in parallel by syntax and semantics. However, the possibility for this is inherent in the control structure of an ACT production system. This is because multiple productions can be performed in parallel and so it is possible to simultaneously pursue many levels of analysis.

d. Disambiguation. One of the problems with all current models is that they run into difficulties when they must deal with multiple word senses or multiple syntactic possibilities. The production system formalism permits a model in which multiple parses can be pursued in parallel. The notion of strength of production allows a facility for weighting a particular parse over others. The spreading activation model provides the potential for associative context to prime a word's meaning. These parallel, strength mechanisms in the production system and the network are hard (although by no means impossible) to simulate on a computer, but this difficulty is irrelevant to the question of their psychological validity.

  e. Associative Priming.   The spreading activation provides more than just a model for word disambiguation. It also provides a model for the selection of information relevant for analysis of a current sentence. Intersection of activation from concepts in the sentence would serve to narrow down relevant information. Consider the two-sentence passage: "Jane was invited to Jack's birthday party. She wondered if he would like a kite." There is an intersection in memory from *kite* via *toy* to *birthday party*. This intersection involves the fact that *toys are given at birthday parties* and *kites are toys*. This intersection could be used to indicate the appropriate inference for the second sentence—that Jane intends giving the kite as a birthday present to Jack. Such spreading activation allows one to dynamically reconfigure the relevant information (frame?) for interpreting the passage depending on the concepts referenced in the passage.

  f. Brittleness.   One frequent criticism (for example, Winograd, 1974) of the second generation language understanding programs is that they were quite brittle. For instance, they were difficult to modify. One modification would produce interactions throughout the program with often unwanted consequences. Another aspect of their brittleness is that they overreact to small defects in the incoming sentence. They may fail to derive any meaning from a sentence because of one small ungrammaticality. The systems may even "crash" and be unable to process subsequent perfectly normal sentences. Also if the user does not carefully design his flow of control it is possible for the program to either get into an infinite regress in its pursuit of possiblities or to spend extraordinarily long periods of time enumerating and pursuing an exponential space of obviously wrong possibilities.

  It would appear to be *easier* to avoid this sort of brittleness in an ACT production system. This is not to say, if one was perverse enough to want to, that he could not construct an ACT system which was very brittle. This is also not to deny that with enough effort the points of brittleness could be avoided in other systems. One reason why it is easier to avoid brittleness in ACT is because each cycle of the production system involves a reevaluation of the consequences of the current knowledge state (that is, active partition of memory) for the control of behavior. For instance, in processing a message, the production system would in each cycle test its productions against the latest portion of the message to come in. Thus, even if the current portion of a message is ungrammatical or otherwise incomprehensible, it is easy to arrange to have a production system that would pick itself up and begin processing the input once it becomes meaningful. Another feature of production systems that can be used to provide some protection against brittleness is the strength properties associated with declarative information stored in the network or with procedural knowledge in the production system. Such knowledge is initially encoded weakly and will have minimal or nonexistent effects in the information processing unless frequently found useful and strengthened. This would prevent the occasional addition of a mistake from producing disastrous interactions throughout the production system.

Summary Assessment

This section has argued that, despite splendid advances, there are still major difficulties with current language-processing formalisms, especially if they are construed as psychological models. I have also argued that production systems offer solutions to some of these difficulties. The proof of this second claim is to display operating production systems that deal with these difficulties. That is a current, ongoing research project. However, even if successful, I do not think this would establish the unique suitability of production systems as models of human language processing. To repeat the indeterminist theme of this book: There are undoubtedly many equivalent and satisfactory ways to model human language comprehension. For the present, the difficulty is discovering one of them.

11.2   AUGMENTED TRANSITION NETWORKS

There has been remarkably little transfer from the many artificial intelligence programs for language comprehension to psychological models. There are many reasons for this: Psychologists working on process models for language comprehension are often not acquainted with computer models. Those who have inspected the computer models often find it hard to see how to translate them into psychological models. There are many details of these programs that are obviously not meant to be taken as serious psychological claims. Programs that deal with restricted task domains often have their programs specialized to that domain. It is hard to see how to generalize the program to predictions about sentences outside of its domain. Another problem is that the program may lack any general principles for language comprehension. An example of this difficulty can be seen in the analysis system written by Riesbeck (1974) for Schank's system MARGIE. The general philosophy in that system is to treat each word as distinct, requiring its own set of tailor-made computational mechanisms. Each word has a set of programs associated with it, and there are no apparent constraints on the form of these programs. These programs will execute only if conditions associated with the program are satisfied by the sentence, general context, and the analysis of the sentence so far completed. One effect of executing a program is to add to a conceptual dependency representation of the sentence. However, the program can have other effects like changing conditions and variables and so permit other programs to execute by satisfying their conditions. Thus, in this analysis system, not only is each word unique to itself but the same word can have different effects in different contexts. There appear to be no general principles about the language comprehension process. It is hard to design interesting tests of a language analysis system which allows each situation to be unique unto itself.[1]

One exception to the nonpsychological character of computer formalisms is the Augmented Transition Network (ATN). The ATN system was developed through the work of Thorne, Bratley, and Dewar (1968); Bobrow and Fraser (1969); Woods (1970, 1973); and Kaplan (1973). The use of ATNs has been adopted by Norman, Rumelhart, *et al.* (1975) and by myself (Anderson, 1975, 1976). Eric Wanner and Ronald Kaplan have begun performing experiments to test predictions of an ATN model.

The basic idea behind the ATN model exploits the fact that sentences can be divided into clauses and phrases. For instance, the sentence *The old train left the station* is divided into two noun phrases *The old train* and *the station*. Figure 11.1 shows a simple example of a pair of networks that will handle this sentence and others. The sentence network specifies that the sentence consists of a noun phrase, a verb, and a noun phrase. The Noun Phrase Network specifies that a noun phrase consists of a determiner, an optional sequence of modifiers, and a noun.

In trying to parse a sentence an attempt is made to find some path through the network which will accept the total sentence. Consider the sentence *The old train left the station*. The ATN processor will begin analysis of this sentence at initial state S_0 with its attention focused on the first word of the sentence. The only arc leaving S_0 bears the lable SEEK NP. This label indicates that this arc can be traversed only if the sentence begins with a noun phrase. To determine if this is the case control transfers to the NP network. This transfer of control is referred to as a SEEK. (A SEEK operation is referred to as a PUSH in Woods' descriptions of ATNs.) The execution of a SEEK requires three operations:

1. Any partial results in the network with the SEEK arc are stored so they can be used when control returns from a SEEK.
2. The identity of the SEEK arc is stored so processing can pick up from where it left off in the SEEKing network.
3. Control is transferred to the initial state of the network called in the SEEK.

---

[1]Schank's ideas have stirred some experimental interest in psychology (for example, Thorndyke, 1975) because of his claims that the comprehension of a sentence should be represented in terms of a conceptual dependency diagram. His conceptual dependency diagrams provide a semantically decomposed representation for a sentence. Certain psychological predictions seem to follow from such a representation. However, Schank has not made similar general claims about the nature of the comprehension process per se.

Sentence Network:

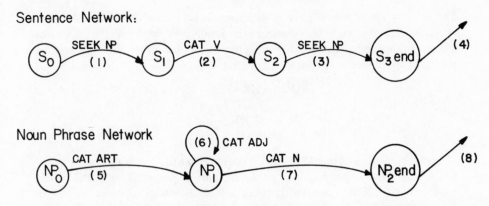

FIG. 11.1   A simplified ATN grammar. The following actions are contained on the arcs in the network:

Arc	Action
1	ASSIGN SUBJECT to current phrase
2	ASSIGN ACTION to current phrase
3	ASSIGN OBJECT to current phrase
4	ASSEMBLE CLAUSE
	SEND current clause
5	ASSIGN DET to current word
6	ASSIGN MOD to current word
7	ASSIGN HEAD to current word
8	ASSEMBLE NOUN PHRASE
	SEND current phrase

The first arc in the noun phrase network requires that the current word be an article. The initial word *the* meets this criterion. The action associated with this arc assigns *the* to the label DET (for determiner). Then control is transferred to NP_1 and attention is shifted to the second word in the sentence (*old*).

There are two principle types of arcs in an ATN. The first arc in the Sentence Network illustrates the type that transfers control to another network. The first arc in the Noun Phrase Network illustrates the type which performs some test on the current word, and performs an action, and then assigns the next word in the sentence as the current word.

There are two arcs (6 and 7) emanating from NP_1. These arcs are considered serially to see if any are satisfied by the current word in the network. Arc 6 is tried first and succeeds since "old" is in the adjective category. The action associated with network NP_1 is to assign the label MOD (for modifier) to *old*. Control is transferred back to NP_1 with the current word now *train*. *Train* is not an adjective; therefore, Arc 6 fails, but Arc 7 succeeds because *train* is a noun. The term *train* is assigned to the label HEAD and attention is shifted to *left*.

The only arc out of the NP_2 end is Arc 8 which has no conditions and does not cause the current word to be advanced. The action associated with the arc causes a noun phrase to be assembled by putting together all the pieces built up along the way. The assembled noun phrase can be represented

[NOUN PHRASE
    DET = the
    MOD = old
    HEAD = train]

Upon completion of the ASSEMBLE operation a SEND operation is executed which makes the assembled noun phrase the current phrase of the SENTENCE network. (The SEND operation is called a POP in Woods' descriptions of the ATNs.) Control is also transferred from the NP network back to Arc 1 of the SENTENCE network from which the SEEK command was initiated. Since the SEEK action has succeeded in identifying an NP network, Arc 1 is considered successful and the action associated with Arc 1 is performed. This action ASSIGNs the function label SUBJECT to the current phrase.

The next word, *left,* is recognized as a verb on Arc 2 and assigned the label ACTION. Arc 3 caused another SEEK to the Noun Phrase network which succeeds and returns

[NOUN PHRASE
    DET = the
    HEAD = station]

as the current phrase which is assigned the functional label OBJECT.

Control is transferred to State S_3 end. The analysis of the sentence is regarded as successful because this state has been reached with no more words to analyze. The final Arc 4 has the effect of bundling together all the components into CLAUSE. The final output of the comprehension process may be represented as follows:

[CLAUSE
    SUBJECT = [NOUN PHRASE
              DET = the
              MOD = old
              HEAD = train]
    ACTION = left
    OBJECT = [NOUN PHRASE
              DET = the
              HEAD = station]]

One might protest that this is too much like a surface structure, and the product of comprehension should be some deeper, more semantic representation. There are two different responses to this complaint. The first is to note that ATNs can be used to build up less syntactic characterizations of sentences. This occurs in the work of Norman and Rumelhart and in my own work with them (Anderson, 1975, 1976). Thus, ATNs are not committed to deriving surface structure. The second response is to note that the output of the ATN need not be taken to be the final product of comprehension. There can be comprehension processes which will take the output of the ATN and make further modifications—perhaps in response to the context of the sentence. We saw the use of such comprehension processes in the MEMOD model of Norman and Rumelhart (page 63).

Power of an ATN

This simple example does not illustrate the full power of an ATN. It is possible for one network to directly or indirectly call itself. Thus, a noun phrase network may call a network for a relative clause which may call a noun phrase network. This gives to ATNs the recursive self-embedding powers associated with a context-free grammar. However, ATNs in their most general form are much more powerful than that. Although the example in Fig. 11.1 involves rather simple conditions and action on arcs, it is permissible to perform arbitrary computations in evaluating a condition or action. This ''arbitrary computation'' aspect gives the machine computational power equivalent to a Turing Machine.

The Distinction between Processor and Network

There is a clear distinction in the literature on ATNs between the networks themselves and the processor that interprets the network. It is the processor that knows how to perform actions, check conditions, pass control and information between networks, etc. The processor is basically language free. We could build separate networks for French and English. A single processor could use the French network to comprehend a French sentence and the English network for English sentences (see Anderson, 1976).

One of the important features of the processor is its ability to ''back up''; that is to reparse a sentence. Suppose the following sentence was encountered:

(1)   The old train the young.

The first attempt to parse this sentence might identify *The old train* as a noun phrase. The system would have to back up and decide to treat *old* as a noun. Then *the old* would be the noun phrase and *train* the verb. To permit such backup ATNs must be capable of storing at each point where they made a decision in parsing what the other options were. An *agenda* is kept of all the untried options in parsing the sentence. There must also be a scheduler which *dictates* which option to attempt next should the current one fail.

Attractive Features of ATNs

ATNs have a number of features to commend themselves as realistic psychological models. They process a sentence in a left-to-right fashion. Other sorts of parsing systems (for example, Anderson & Bower, 1973; Riesbeck, 1974) do the same, but the graphical representation of transition networks makes perceptually salient the left-to-right dependencies in language processing.

Another attractive feature of the ATN formalism is that it can be used with equal facility to model comprehension or generation. The facility for generation has not been exploited as often as it has for comprehension. However, Simmons (1973) developed an ATN for generation and I have managed to use one network for both comprehension and generation (Anderson, 1975). Thus, ATNs capture the intuition that the linguistic knowledge underlying comprehension and the knowledge underlying production are not entirely separate.

Another advantage claimed for ATNs (for example, by Wanner & Maratsos, 1975) is that they provide a model for the segmentation of sentences into clauses. There is little doubt that humans are capable of a phrase structure analysis of sentences. It is less clear, however, what role phrase structure analysis plays in the normal comprehension of sentences. Thus, while one would like to model a subject's ability to perform phrase structure analysis, it is uncertain whether that model should be made part of a model for normal sentence comprehension.

Experimental Evidence

In addition to such global properties one would like to have evidence that more detailed features of ATN computation are reflected in human behavior. That is, one would like to have some traditional experimental evidence. Ronald Kaplan (for example, 1975) and Eric Wanner (for example, Wanner & Maratsos, 1975) have embarked on a series of experiments to try to collect such evidence.

These experiments involve a test of what is called the *HOLD hypothesis*. To understand the HOLD hypothesis consider how an ATN might process the following pair of sentences:

(2)   The witch whom sorcerers despised frightened little children.
(3)   The witch who despised sorcerers frightened little children.

The first contains an object relative clause modifying *witch* and the second a subject relative clause modifying *witch*. In interpreting the relative clause an ATN must assign *The witch* to the role of object or subject within that clause.

The question of interest concerns how the ATN decides which role *the witch* plays. One key is the use of the relative pronouns *whom* versus *who*. However, Wanner and Maratsos assume that subjects would not be sensitive to this piece of evidence. Rather, they propose that the key to an object relative is the missing object in the relative clause and similarly the key to the subject relative is the missing subject. The interesting question concerns what the ATN mechanisms are that use these keys to assign the main noun phrase (that is, *the witch*) to its correct role within the relative clause. One might propose that the noun phrase was immediately assigned to the subject role upon entry into the relative clause. This assignment would be later disconfirmed in the case of an object relative sentence. In this case the system could back up and start over or more simply it could reassign the main noun phrase to the object role. Either way of dealing with the disconfirmation would predict object relative sentences to be harder than subject relatives. The strategy has been mentioned in previous writings (for example, Woods, 1970) on ATNs to deal with the temporary ambiguity about whether a sentence is active or passive.

Kaplan and Wanner propose to use another ATN mechanism, however, called the HOLD list. They propose that the subject store the main noun phrase on a HOLD list until the point of disambiguation. Then the noun phrase is assigned to the correct role. There is a difference between object relatives and subject relatives with respect to the HOLD list. Wanner and Kaplan propose that in the subject relative the main noun should be assigned to the subject role between the relative pronoun and the verb (that is, between *who* and *despised*); whereas, in the object relative the main noun should be assigned between the relative clause verb and the main clause verb (that is, between *despised* and *frightened*). Thus, information must reside on the HOLD list longer for object relatives. It is for this reason that differential predictions are made about object relatives and subject relatives.

The general prediction is that keeping items on the HOLD list will produce a performance decrement. This prediction has been tested and confirmed using a phoneme monitoring task (Kaplan, 1975) and using a short-term memory task (Wanner & Maratsos, 1975). In the Wanner and Maratsos test subjects were presented with the sentences one word at a time on a screen. At a certain point the sentence was interrupted and the subject was presented with five first names. There were three points in interruption, as indicated below:

(4)   The witch whom sorcerers [1]/ despised frightened [2]/ little children [3]/
(5)   The witch who despised [1]/ sorcerers frightened [2]/ little children [3]/

Note that for subject relative sentences the main noun will be removed from the HOLD list by Position 1, whereas it will not be removed from the HOLD list until Position 2 for object relatives. Therefore, it is predicted that there will be poorer retention of the list of names when they are inserted in the object relative at Position 1 than a subject relative at the same position. There is no ambiguity for either type of sentence at Positions 2 and 3. Therefore, there should be no difference in recall of the names. This is almost exactly what Wanner and Maratsos found.

One might wonder why keeping information on the HOLD list should cause so much difficulty. An ATN is holding many partial results. For instance, in the object relative sentence, as soon as *the witch* is removed from the HOLD list it must be stored somewhere else and assigned to the *object category*. Thus the amount of information to be stored does not change, only the location of storage. Wanner and Maratsos propose that once a label is assigned to a noun phrase it becomes integrated with the total structure being built up. They propose that this meaningful integration makes the material more memorable.

This experimental evidence for ATNs is not very compelling for two reasons. First, these experiments test one relatively peripheral feature of ATNs, the HOLD mechanism, without testing many of the features that seem more central to the ATN notion. Second, in deriving this prediction we are asked to accept a number of assumptions that are not adequately motivated. Some of these are the following: (1) the ambiguity in an object relative will not be resolved until the late point prescribed by Wanner and Kaplan; (2) the ambiguity will be handled by the HOLD mechanism rather than any other possible ATN mechanism; (3) there is a particular difficulty in storing information on the HOLD list (rather than elsewhere); and (4) this will interact with the short-term memory task. All these assumptions may well be true, but it is going to require a larger range of converging experiments to make these assumptions convincing.

The basic problem with a complex model like an ATN is that it was not originally designed as a psychological model. There are two features which make it difficult to simply derive and test predictions about the model. First, it was designed with many options so that the computer user could have maximum flexibility in formulating a linguistic model; yet all these options must be specified to derive psychological predictions. Second, the model makes a great many different types of resource allocations. It utilizes memory resources to keep track of information on the HOLD list, functional names assigned, SEEK arcs to be returned to, and entries on the agenda. Computational effort can be expended attempting arcs, taking arcs of different types (CAT, SEEK, SEND, JUMP), updating the agenda, assigning names, revising name assignments, and checking additional conditions.[2] To make any predictions it is necessary to specify the psychological costs of all these operations. This gives the model a great many degrees of freedom in predicting any piece of data. If the research on ATNs is to free itself from criticisms of "ad hocery" it will be necessary to seek a larger data base than just that concerned with the HOLD hypothesis. Apparently, Wanner and Kaplan are engaged in a research effort to do just that.

Criticisms of ATNs

For reasons enumerated earlier (page 454), I feel that ATNs have attractive features as models of language processing. I have used them in some of my own research (Anderson, 1975, 1976). However, I have decided against continued use of these computational formalisms for a number of reasons. They evolved in a

---

[2]This list comes from Kaplan (1975).

nonpsychological context and it is not completely clear how to transform them into psychological models. The basic problem with ATNs is that their primitives are much too powerful to provide a realistic model of human information processing. Kaplan and Wanner seem to have opted for the strategy of associating psychological costs (and perhaps limits) with each type of operation. On the face of it, this research strategy seems unlikely to achieve a workable model. It seems implausible that one can take a basically too powerful model and properly constrain it by a lot of local patches and bandages. I suspect the outcome will be a very unsystematic and complex set of assumptions. Of course, it remains to be seen what the actual outcome of the Kaplan and Wanner efforts will be; one would not want to argue with success.

I would like to conclude this section by enumerating some of the difficulties that seem to arise in properly limiting the power of ATNs. My criticism of ATNs are quite lengthy, but I do not want that length to be misinterpreted. It does not reflect how bad I think ATNs are. Rather it reflects the amount of thought given to the appropriateness of ATNs. The decision about the appropriateness of ATNs was an important development in the evolution of ACT.

SEEK and SEND.   A very powerful facility is the ability to SEEK a network and return by a SEND to the same network. This gives the model the power of a context-free grammar and therefore it should be able to comprehend such center-embedded sentences as: *The cheese that the mouse that the cat chased ate pleased Eloise.* There is ample evidence that humans cannot process unlimited center-embedding characteristics of a context-free grammar. On the other hand it seems we can follow right-embedded sentences of the form: *Eloise was pleased by the cheese that was eaten by the mouse that the cat chased.* (Sentences with such right-branching structures (or left-branching) need only a finite state grammar for description, and not a context-free grammar.) So it seems that a fundamental problem with ATNs is that they have no way to bridle their potential for recursive, self-embedding.

Wanner and Maratsos propose that center-embedded sentences such as the above are difficult because it is hard to keep more than one noun on the HOLD list. However, this cannot be the total explanation. It would imply that when there are no noun phrases to be kept in HOLD lists, center embedding would cause no trouble. However, this is not so. Center embedding always poses enormous strains on comprehension. Consider the sentences:

(6)   The man called the girl who put the singer who threw money around down up.

(7)   The problem the author of the play about women's rights from Chicago invented was written up in the New Yorker.

(8)   The way in which Kennedy complained that Krushchev had claimed that the United States would not be first on the moon in Pravada on American television bothered me.

I do not think the capacity for recursive self-embedding is a feature of any aspect of human cognition, certainly not of language comprehension. An obvious means to account for the difficulty of these center-embedded sentences would be to put a limit on the depth to which ATN networks can be embedded. The problem with this limitation and others like it is that it would predict that right-embedding to depth n would be as difficult as center embedding to depth n. This is not the case. For instance, compare the above sentences with their right-embedded equivalents:

(9)   The man called up the girl who put down the singer who threw money around.

(10)   The New Yorker wrote up the problem invented by the author from Chicago of the play about women's rights.

(11)   I was bothered by the way in which Kennedy complained on American television that Krushchev had claimed in Pravada that America would not be first on the moon.

It would be complicated, although not impossible, to arrange in ATNs a mechanism that would have difficulty with the center-embedded sentences but not the right-branching sentences. It would be complicated because in both cases a SEEK would be required to an embedded network. Why should a SEEK be more expensive when calling a center-embedded network?

While complicated it would be possible to devise an ATN-like model that does display the right pattern of difficulty for center-embedded versus right-embedded sentences. In a sense, one can view this as what has been done with ACT in the next section. However, to do this would seem to require doing considerable violence to the ATN mechanisms by which one network passes control to another. In my view this is the central ATN feature and to change these mechanisms to any significant degree is to create a new computational formalism.

The ASSEMBLE command. The ASSEMBLE operation, which takes place upon leaving a network, constructs a description of the phrase by integrating all the pieces of structure built up through the course of the network. As there is no limit to the length of a network, there is no limit to the number of pieces of information that must be remembered for an ASSEMBLE command. This is clearly unrealistic. It will be necessary to place some limitation on the amount of information that can be held at one level of a network. There may well prove to be difficulties in coordinating this assumption with ideas about the amount of information held at other levels of the network, as well as other memory requirements. That is, we might expect that the amount of information that can be held at one level of the network will depend on the amount of information being held elsewhere.

Backup. ATNs have the capacity, if one parse fails, to back up and search for alternate parses. To accomplish this, at each syntactic choice point in parsing a sentence, the system must record the options. There can be arbitrarily many choice points and options. It seems unrealistic to assume that all these choice points and options are remembered. Consider the following sentences:

(12)   The cat scratched the man who hit the girl who kissed the sailor who shot the lawyer who laughed at the foreman with its claws.

(13)   The man hit the cat who scratched the girl who kissed the sailor who shot the lawyer who laughed at the foreman with its claws.

(14)   The man hit the girl who kissed the cat who scratched the sailor who shot the lawyer who laughed at the foreman with its claws.

(15)   The man hit the girl who kissed the sailor who shot the cat who scratched the lawyer who laughed at the foreman with its claws.

(16)   The man hit the girl who kissed the sailor who shot the lawyer who laughed at the cat who scratched the foreman with its claws.

Note that only for Sentence (16) is it semantically permissible to associate *with its claws* with the last clause. In other cases it is necessary to back up and search for some other location to place the modifier. Sentences (13)–(15) are very difficult, if not impossible, to process on a single hearing. Sentence (12) is difficult, but perhaps possible. Thus, it seems that subjects have not stored all the intermediate choice points in their analyses of these sentences. In these examples they have stored only the last choice point and perhaps the first.

Turing computable power.   As noted earlier, ATNs have the potential to compute arbitrary conditions and actions. This potential conveys upon them Turing computable power. However, to have viable psychological models Kaplan and Wanner will have to jettison the capacity for arbitrary conditions and actions. Otherwise, ATNs would make no falsifiable predictions since these arbitrary conditions and actions could produce any behavior. However, with this potential for arbitrary computation eliminated, it seems difficult for ATNs to account for some of the linguistic processes of which humans are capable. I will enumerate three such examples:

First, ATNs would have difficulty retrieving any meaning from partial sentences. Consider, for instance,

(17)   The boy hit the

Humans on hearing such a string of words recognize that it is incomplete but at the same time derive an interpretation of it. ATNs would not derive a representation of the main clause because they would have to wait until the completion of the clause before assembling a meaning representation. A second difficulty concerns gathering any meaning from an expression like

(18)   skid, crash, hospital

Because this is ungrammatical it would be rejected by the parser. Since this would not pass the first syntactic level, it would not be possible to bring to bear higher levels in attempting to get an analysis of the sentence. A third type of expression ATNs would not be able to handle are sentences where elements are dislocated from main phrases and placed in embedded phrases. Such examples do not occur in grammatical English but are frequent in highly inflected languages with freer word order. For instance, sentences like *The best girls that the boys saw ran away* are sometimes expressed in Latin using the following word order:

(19)   The girls that the boys best saw ran away

in which *best* is dislocated. There is no way for ATNs, without recourse to special actions, to move a term from an embedded phrase and analyze it as part of the main phrase.

So it seems Kaplan and Wanner are in a double-bind situation. They could handle all these language examples (and any others) if they kept their arbitrary condition and action aspect of the model, but this would be disastrous from the point of view of having a falsifiable model.

11.3   AN ACT PRODUCTION SYSTEM MODEL FOR LANGUAGE PROCESSING

It seems possible to formulate with the ACT production system formalism a model of language processing which has the following merits:

1. It maintains the positive features of ATNs—namely, left-to-right processing, the clarity of a network representation, and the organization of linguistic knowledge into phrase structure units.
2. It is simultaneously more flexible than ATNs and is not as powerful. The information-processing limitations which restrict the power of ACT are few in number and general.
3. The mechanisms of the language system are constructed from the same primitives as are other procedures such as those for inference making.
4. It can represent the parallel application of multiple levels of processing (for example, lexical, syntactic, semantic, and conceptual).
5. It appears to make the correct predictions about the processing difficulty of various types of embeddings of syntactic constructions.
6. Very similar systems can be built for comprehension and generation.

In this section I will try to illustrate how these virtues can be displayed within an ACT system.

The LAS Project

I have been engaged in a project to develop a computer simulation model, called LAS, for language acquisition. The early work was done within an ATN framework and is reported in Anderson (1975, 1976). Successful models of language analysis and generation were developed in the ATN framework. The work on the induction model had advanced to the point where simple grammars for English and French had been acquired and the program was able to translate between the two languages. Rather than continuing to evolve the abilities of the ATN-LAS I decided to switch over into the ACT framework both because it seems a more realistic model of human abilities and because it is difficult to handle some language examples from English and other languages (page 460) with ATNs. Paul Kline, Clayton Lewis, and I are currently engaged in the project of applying the ACT model to language acquisition. A significant subgoal in this project is to work out how ACT should apply to language understanding and generation. This involves the hand-coding of various sets of productions for processing language subsets, comparing various hand-codings, and deciding on the principles that define a good production system for language processing. It is necessary to get a sense of what the mature language system should be like before beginning to concern ourselves with the mechanisms that will acquire that system. The current stage of the project is that of developing ideas for a mature language system. Some of these ideas I will be reporting in this section. Only very preliminary exploration has been performed of mechanisms for induction. The current belief is that we will be able to implement similar induction mechanisms as those used earlier for the ATN version of LAS, but that belief has not in any serious way been put to the test of actual implementation. Some ideas about induction in general and language acquisition in particular will be reported in the next chapter.

The semantic domain for LAS is a world like that of a young child. This selection of semantic domain is somewhat arbitrary since LAS is thought to be a model of the adult learning a second language. The environment for LAS is a house consisting of a kitchen, a bedroom, and a bathroom. There are only three people in this world—LAS, Mommy, and Daddy. Besides the rooms and people the only other objects are manipulables (dolly, soap, candy, and ball) and containers (box, drawer, bed, and sink). The manipulables and containers can vary in color, number, and size.

There are various relations possible among people and objects. People may *possess* manipulables and containers. Manipulables may be *in* containers and rooms. People and containers can be *in* rooms. It is also possible to have relations like (give, take, put, go, etc.) that assert changes in these basic relations.

We want LAS to be able to deal with a language of assertions, questions, and commands about this semantic domain. We are not decided as to the exact extent of linguistic constructions that we want LAS to be able to process. However, the rewrite rules in Table 11.1 provide a grammar for a potential language subset with which we might want to deal. Compared with the total complexity of English, this subset is quite small. However, when we consider how many production rules are required to process it, this subset is very ambitious. There are a great many bits and pieces of information acquired over a lifetime which permit language processing. It does not seem possible to attempt to hand-code this knowledge for

TABLE 11.1
Grammar for LAS's Linguistic Environment[a]

SENTENCE	→	DECLARATIVE
	→	IMPERATIVE
	→	INTERROGATIVE
DECLARATIVE	→	PERSON ACTION
	→	PERSON {has, is} PPROPERTY
	→	MANIPULABLE {is, are} MPROPERTY
	→	ROOM {has, is} RPROPERTY
	→	CONTAINER {has, is} CPROPERTY
IMPERATIVE	→	ACTION
INTERROGATIVE	→	Does PERSON ACTION
	→	{has, is} PERSON PPROPERTY
	→	{is, are} MANIPULABLE MPROPERTY
	→	{has, is} ROOM RPROPERTY
	→	{has, is} CONTAINER CPROPERTY
	→	WHO ACTION
	→	WHO {has, is} PPROPERTY
	→	WHAT {is, are} MPROPERTY
	→	WHAT {has, is} RPROPERTY
	→	WHAT {has, is} CPROPERTY
PERSON	→	{Mommy, Daddy, Lassy} ({who ACTION, who{has, is}PPROPERTY})
MANIPULABLE	→	{a, the} (number) (size) (color) {soap, dolly, candy, ball} ('s) (that {is, are} MPROPERTY)
ROOM	→	the {kitchen, bedroom, bathroom} (that {has, is} RPROPERTY)
CONTAINER	→	{a, the} (size) (color) {box, drown, bed, sink} (that {has, is} CPROPERTY)
size	→	small, large
color	→	red, blue, green
number	→	one, two, three
ACTION	→	Give(s) PERSON MANIPULABLE
		Give(s) MANIPULABLE to PERSON
		Receive(s) MANIPULABLE from PERSON
		Take(s) MANIPULABLE from {PERSON, ROOM, CONTAINER}
		Put(s) MANIPULABLE in {ROOM, CONTAINER}
		{Come(s), Go(es)} (into ROOM) (from ROOM)
PROPERTY	→	given MANIPULABLE by PERSON
		MANIPULABLE taken by PERSON
		MANIPULABLE
		in ROOM
MPROPERTY	→	given to PERSON by PERSON
		taken from PERSON by PERSON
		put in {ROOM, CONTAINER} by PERSON
		owned by PERSON
		in {ROOM, CONTAINER}
		{color, size}

(continued)

TABLE 11.1 *(continued)*

RPROPERTY	→	entered by PERSON
		left by PERSON
		{PERSON, CONTAINER, MANIPULABLE} in it
		{color, size}
CPROPERTY	→	MANIPULABLE in it
		in ROOM
		{color, size}

*a*Brackets— { } —indicate a set from which one member may be taken. Parentheses — ( ) — indicate an optimal element.

This grammar is specified as a set of context-free rewrite rules. However, there are a number of context-sensitive aspects that are implied and left up to the reader's "good sense." For instance, if number is chosen in the rewrite rule for MANIPULABLE, then the noun must end with plural. Similarly, in the rewrite rule, DECLARATIVE → PERSON {has, is} PPROPERTY, whether *is* or *has* is chosen depends on how PPROPERTY is written. If it is written "given MANIPULABLE by PERSON" then *is* should be used and if it is written "the MANIPULABLE taken by PERSON" then *has* should be used. These context-sensitive dependencies were omitted to simplify the specification of the language that LAS is supposed to learn.

all of language, but it is possible, although not a simple matter, to work with such a subset.

I will provide fragments of an ACT production system to deal with this subset.[3] Table 11.2 provides a set of productions to handle declarative sentences involving the verbs *give* and *receive*. Figure 11.2 illustrates in network form the flow of control embodied in the productions. This network has the advantages of perspicacity associated with an ATN network. These network diagrams are simpler and more conventionalized than the diagrams used in earlier chapters for illustrating the flow of control among productions. Each network represents a separate subroutine (see Section 6.2) which processes a particular grammatical structure. For instance, the network in Fig. 11.2 represents the subroutine for processing main clauses. Within a particular subroutine there is a single control variable for keeping track of what is expected next in the grammatical structure. In Table 11.2 this variable is Vcon. The various nodes in the network represent the various possible bindings of Vcon. The arcs in the network represent the transitions from one state (as embodied by the binding of a control variable) to another state. To make that transition it may be necessary for an ACT subroutine to be called to process a subphrase. In this case the name of that subroutine labels the arc. On the other hand, to make the transition it may be just necessary to process a word. If so, the name of that word or of the word class labels the arc. These conventions for representing flow of control were adopted to emphasize the similarity with ATNs.

---

[3]An interested reader may write to me for a complete listing of the most current working version of a production system for this domain.

TABLE 11.2
Some Productions for Analyzing Declarative Sentences

	Conditions		Actions
(AS0)	(Vcon = START)	⇒	(Vcon1 = NP) & (UNBIND Vtop1) & (Vcon = STARTA)
(AS1)	(Vcon = STARTA) & (Vcon1 = NPX) & (Vtop1 * person)	⇒	(Vcon = S1) & (Vsubj = Vtop1)
(AS2)	(Vcon = S1) & (Vcon2 = CLAUSEX) & (Vtok * gives)	⇒	(Vcon = S2) & (Vadv = NEXT) & (Vsubj * (give OF Varg1 Varg2))
(AS3)	(Vcon = S1) & (Vcon2 = CLAUSEX) & (Vtok * receives)	⇒	(Vcon = S6) & (Vadv = NEXT) & (Varg1 * (give OF Varg2 Vsubj))
(AS4)	(Vcon = S2)	⇒	(Vcon1 = NP) & (UNBIND Vtop1) & (Vcon = S2A)
(AS5)	(Vcon = S2A) & (Vcon1 = NPX) & (Vtop1 * person) & (Vsubj * (give OF Varg1 Varg2))	⇒	(Vcon = S3) & (Varg2 * Vtrop1) & (Vtop1 * Varg2)
(AS6)	(Vcon = S3) & (Vcon2 = CLAUSEX)	⇒	(Vcon1 = NP) & (UNBIND Vtop1) & (Vcon = S3A)
(AS7)	(Vcon = S3A) & (Vcon1 = NPX) & (Vsubj * (give OF Varg1 Varg2))	⇒	(Vcon = SX) & (Varg1 * Vtop1) & (Vtop1 * Varg1)
(AS8)	(Vcon = S2A) & (Vcon1 = NPX) & ((Vtop1 * Videa) & (Videa * manipulable)) & (Vsubj * (give OF Varg1 Varg2))	⇒	(Vcon = S4) & (Varg1 * Vtop1) & (Vtop1 * Varg1)
(AS9)	(Vcon = S4) & (Vcon2 = CLAUSEX) & (Vtok * to)	⇒	(Vcon = S5) & (Vadv = NEXT)
(AS10)	(Vcon = S5)	⇒	(Vcon1 = NP) & (UNBIND Vtop1) & (Vcon = S5A)
(AS11)	(Vcon = S5A) & (Vcon1 = NPX) & (Vsubj * (give OF Varg1 Varg2))	⇒	(Vcon = SX) & (Varg2 * Vtop1) & (Vtop1 * Varg2)
(AS12)	(Vcon = S6)	⇒	(Vcon1 = NP) & (UNBIND Vtop1) & (Vcon = S6A)
(AS13)	(Vcon = S6A) & (Vcon2 = NPX) & (Varg1 * (give OF Varg2 Vsubj))	⇒	(Vcon = S7) & (Varg2 * Vtop1) & (Vtop1 * Varg2)
(AS14)	(Vcon = S7) & (Vcon2 = CLAUSEX) & (Vtok * form)	⇒	(Vcon = S8) & (Vadv = NEXT)
(AS15)	(Vcon = S8)	⇒	(Vcon1 = NP) & (UNBIND Vtop1) & (Vcon = S8A)
(AS16)	(Vcon = S8A) & (Vcon1 = NPX) & (Varg1 * (give OF Varg2 Vsubj))	⇒	(Vcon = SX) & (Varg1 * Vtop1) & (VTOP1 * Varg1)

(continued)

TABLE 11.2 *(continued)*

	Conditions		Actions
Special productions for word advancement			
(W1)	(START Vtok)	⇒	(Vcon = START) & (Vtok = Vnew) & (UNBIND Vsubj)
(W2)	(Vavd = NEXT) & (Vtok − Vnew)	⇒	(Vtok = Vnew) & (UNBIND Vadv)
Special productions for rehearsal			
(R1)	Vcon	⇒	Vcon
(R2)	Vsubj	⇒	Vsubj

The various verbs in this domain have little in common and a separate path has been constructed through the network for each verb. If there were a larger sample of verbs, a number would share the same network paths. For instance, *show, teach, sell, throw,* etc., all have the syntactic structure of *give.* This production system associates the same meaning to both *gives* and *receives.* In fact, it maps all of the following sentences onto the same meaning representation:

(20)   Mommy gives the ball to Daddy.
(21)   Mommy give Daddy the ball.
(22)   Daddy receives the ball from Mommy.

The ACT network representation for the meaning of these sentences is illustrated in Fig. 11.3.

There are calls within the main network to a noun phrase subroutine. The

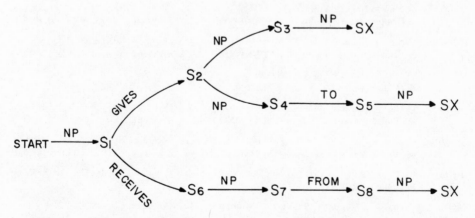

FIG. 11.2 A network representation of the flow of control in the production system for sentence analysis in Table 11.2.

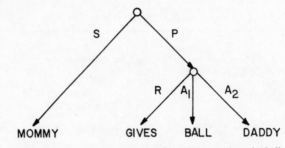

FIG. 11.3 An ACT network representation for "Mommy gives the ball to Daddy."

TABLE 11.3
Productions to Analyze Noun Phrases

	Conditions		Actions
(AN1)	(Vcon1 = NP) * ((Videa W Vword) & (Vtok * Vword) & (Videa * person))	⇒	(Vcon1 = NPX) & (Vtop1 = Videa) & (Vadv = NEXT)
(AN2)	(Vcon1 = NP) & (Vtok * a)	⇒	(Vcon1 = N1) & (Vadv = NEXT) & (Vtop1 # 1) & Vtop1
(AN3)	(Vcon1 = NP) & (Vtok * the)	⇒	(Vcon1 = N1) & (Vadv = NEXT) & Vtop1
(AN4)	(Vcon1 = N1) & ((Videa W Vword) & (Vtok * Vword) & (Vword * ADJ))	⇒	(Vcon1 = N2) & (Vadv = NEXT) & (Vtop1 * Videa)
(AN5)	(Vcon1 = N1) & ((Videa W Vword) & (Vtok * Vword) & (Vword * NUMBER))	⇒	(Vcon1 = N2) & (Vadv = NEXT) & (Vtop1 # Videa)
(AN6)	(Vcon1 = N1) & ((Videa W Vword) & (Vtok * Vword) & (Vword * NOUNSING))	⇒	(Vcon1 = NPX) & (Vadv = NEXT) & (Vtop1 * Videa) & (Vtop1 # 1)
(AN7)	(Vcon1 = N1) & ((Videa W Vword) & (Vtok * Vword) & (Vword * NOUNPLUR))	⇒	(Vcon1 = NPX) & (Vadv = NEXT) & (Vtop1 * Videa) & (Vtop1 # plur)
(AN8)	(Vcon1 = N2) & ((Videa W Vword) & (Vtok * Vword) & (Vword * ADJ))	⇒	(Vcon1 = N2) & (Vadv = NEXT) & (Vtop1 * Videa)
(AN9)	(Vcon1 = N2) & ((Videa W Vword) & (Vtok * Vword) & (Vword * NOUNSING))	⇒	(Vcon1 = NPX) & (Vadv = NEXT) & (Vtop1 * Videa) & (Vtop1 # 1)
(AN10)	(Vcon1 = N2) & ((Videa W Vword) & (Vtok * Vword) & (Vword * NOUNPLUR))	⇒	(Vcon1 = NPX) & (Vadv = NEXT) & (Vtop1 * Videa) & (Vtop1 # plur)
(AN11)	(Vcon = NPX) & ((Vtok * Vword) & (Vword * RELATIVE))	⇒	(Vcon2 = CLAUSE) & (Vtop2 = Vtop1)
(AN12)	(Vcon1 = NPX) & (ABS ((Vtok * Vword) & (Vword * RELATIVE)))	⇒	(Vcon2 = CLAUSEX)

productions for the noun phrase subroutine are defined in Table 11.3, and Fig. 11.4 illustrates the flow of control in the noun phrase subroutine. The noun phrase subroutine can call a relative clause network. I have omitted describing the structure of the relative clause. That network would be similar to, but more elaborate than the relative clause subroutine given earlier in Table 6.2 (page 196).

It is assumed in these productions for parsing that the perceptual system has delivered up a string encoding of the sentence (see Fig. 4.8, page 136, for an example). Productions (W1) and (W2) at the bottom of Table 11.2 are responsible for advancing the pointer, Vtok, that keeps track of the current word being processed. The shorthands (START Vtok) and (Vtok − Vnew) which appear in the conditions of (W1) and (W2) were defined earlier in Fig. 4.4 (page 131). Production (W1) is only executed at the beginning of the sentence and binds Vtok to the first word in the sentence. Production (W1) also serves to initiate processing of the sentence by setting Vcon = START. Thus, the routine for analyzing a sentence has the capacity to self-initiate upon the start of a sentence. Production (W2) is called whenever the variable Vadv is set to NEXT, as it often is in Tables 11.2 and 11.3. Production (W2) serves to retrieve the next word in the sentence and set this as the value of Vtok.

There are a number of features in Table 11.2 that are worth noting. First, consider how the noun phrase network is called. This always involves a pair of productions—either (AS0) and (AS1), or (AS4) and (AS5), or (AS4) and (AS8), or (AS6) and (AS7), or (AS10) and (AS11), or (AS12) and (AS13), or (AS15) and

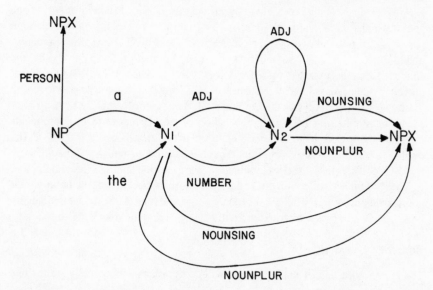

FIG. 11.4   A network representation of the flow of control in the production system for noun phrase analysis in Table 11.3.

(AS16). Consider the first such pair—(AS0) and (AS1). Note that the action of the first production, (AS0), does three things. It sets Vcon1, the control variable for the noun phrase, to NP. This permits processing of the noun phrase to begin. Second it unbinds the variable Vtop1 from whatever value it might have had before. The variable Vtop1 will be used to hold the topic of the noun phrase. The third action in (AS0), (Vcon = STARTA), sets the control node to a new value. This is to prevent the production (AS0) from reapplying. Production (AS1) applies when the analysis of the noun phrase matrix is complete (signaled by Vcon1 = NPX) and if the topic of the noun phrase is a person. It sets the value of Vcon to S1, to expect in the main phrase the constructions that can occur after the subject noun phrase. It also assigns the subject of the main clause, Vsubj, to the topic of the noun phrase, Vtop1.

Upon receipt of the verb a memory structure is built up with Vsubj in the appropriate role. As an example of this, consider Production (AS2) which applies if the verb is *gives*. There is a test in that production, (Vcon2 = CLAUSEX), to see whether any relative clause that has been initiated is complete. The production (AS2) can only apply if the relative clause is complete. Otherwise, this production might respond to the appearance of a verb in an embedded clause. On the action side of (AS2) is the construction (Vsubj * (give OF Varg1 Varg2)). This causes a memory structure to be built up with Vsubj the subject of a predicate which contains the relation *give* and two arguments, Varg1 and Varg2. Because Varg1 or Varg2 are not made global, their values will not be available to other productions.

After analysis of the verb *gives* by Production (AS2), Production (AS4) can apply, which sets the value of Vcon1 to NP to initiate processing of another noun phrase. If the noun phrase is a person (AS5) will be satisfied, and if it is a manipulable object (AS8) will be satisfied. In either Production (AS5) or (AS8), the condition contains (Vsubj * (give OF Varg1 Varg2)). The variable Vsubj is global but the variables Varg1 and Varg2 are not. Matching this structure serves to rebind these two local variables to the arguments in the memory structure built up after executing Production (AS2). In the action of (AS5) there are the commands (Varg2 * Vtop1) & (Vtop1 * Varg2). Similar commands occur in (AS8). The purpose of these commands is to build memory structures which will identify, by two S–P constructions, the node bound to Varg1 as the same as the node bound to Vtop1. This identification could not occur until completion of the noun phrase and a decision about whether the noun was a person (AS5) or a manipulable (AS8). Depending on which, Vtop1 will be assigned to the role Varg1 or Varg2.

Semantic Checking

The grammar in Tables 11.2 and 11.3 will accept many semantically anomalous constructions such as

(23)   Mommy received Daddy from a red ball.

To detect such anomalies it is necessary to have productions that will check the network structures built by the parsing routine. A production which would deal with this anomaly is

(P1)   ((V1 * (give OF V2 V3))   ⇒   (V1 * contradictory)
         & (ABS (V1 * person)))

This production encodes that if a giver, V1, is not a person then there is a contradiction involving the giver. Similar semantic checking productions can be used to detect the anomaly of noun phrase expressions like

the two red ball
a large balls.

In these expressions one element (ball, a) causes a singular number modifier to be added and another element (two, balls) causes a plural number to be added. The following production would detect the contradiction:

(P2)   (V1 # 1) & (V1 # plur)   ⇒   (V1 * contradictory)

Ambiguity

The model outlined can deal with ambiguity in many ways. One means of disambiguating the sense of a word is by associative spread of activation. For instance, consider the sentence:

(24)   The man who was carrying a money pouch went to the bank.

The appearance of *money* early in the sentence would cause activation to spread to select and activate the sense of bank associated with a monetary institution. This will be the sense selected when it comes time to interpret *bank*. Sometimes this associative priming mechanism can disambiguate the wrong meaning. Witness the difficulty we have with

(25)   The playboy who seduced women pitted the date.

Sometimes ambiguity is resolved on the basis of structural features of the sentence. Consider

(26)   John gave the money to the old bag.

The appropriate meaning of *bag* is selected, not by associative priming, but rather by the selectional restriction that requires the recipient of *give* to be animate. The following pair of productions illustrates a mechanism to enable this sort of disambiguation:

(P3)   (V1 * (give OF V2 V3))   ⇒   (V3 * contradictory)
         & (V3 * V4) & (V4 * inanimate)

(P4)   ((Vprop1 = (Vtarg * contradictory))   ⇒   (Vprop1 * false)
        & (Vprop = (Vtarg * Videa1))   & (Vprop * false)
        & (Videa1 W Vword)   & (Vtarg * Videa2)
        & (Videa2 W Vword))
        & (ABS (Videa1 = Videa2))

If the sense assigned to the recipient of *give* is animate, all is fine. However, if not, a semantic contradiction will be detected by the first production. This production is like those given earlier for semantic checking. This production tags the offending element, V3, as contradictory. This tagging serves as a cue to elicit the second production. It searches to see if attached to the offending element is a concept Videa1 which has an ambiguous word Vword to express it. If this state of affairs exists, the proposition (Vtarg * Videa1) is tagged as false and the new proposition (Vtarg * Videa2) is constructed using the other sense of this word. Thus, these two productions model a double-take process by which ACT determines if there is something wrong with its first interpretation and seeks another one.[4]

Difficulties in Comprehending Embedded Sentences

The ACT model does a rather good job of predicting the pattern of difficulty that subjects experience in processing various kinds of embedded sentences. According to ACT, subjects will experience processing breakdown because they must interrupt one subroutine to call the same subroutine. In applying the embedded routine, the variables of the routine will be filled in with new values. The values of the first call to the subroutine will then be destroyed. It will not be possible to perform any subsequent operations in the first call to the routine if they depend on the value of these variables. The sentence

(27)   The boy whom the girl hit ran away.

is manageable because the main routine is interrupted by a relative clause subroutine and not the same routine. In contrast,

(28)   The boy whom the girl whom the sailor liked hit ran away.

is not manageable[5] because the relative clause routine interrupts itself. In contrast

---

[4]One might also want to check whether the offending word occurred in the sentence or not. Otherwise, consider what the productions might do to *John gave the money to the old sack*. Supposing *sack* and *bag* to be synonymous, then the second production above would retrieve the offending sense, find it has an ambiguous word *bag* to express it, and attempt the new sense of *bag*. It would be prevented from this mistaken reinterpretation of the sentence if there were the further constraint that the ambiguous word be tagged as occurring in the sentence.

[5]One frequent remark made about such embedded sentences is that they are much more difficult to process when spoken than when written. Given the sentence written down, some paper and pencil to try out possible segmentations of the sentence, and unlimited time, sophisticated subjects can emerge with an understanding of almost any sentence no matter how complexly embedded. This observation does not contradict ACT's analysis of the difficulty of doubly-embedded sentences. The procedures

to this center-embedded sentence, the following right-embedded sentence is manageable:

(29)   The boy who hit the girl who liked the sailor ran away.

This is because one relative clause construction is complete before the next one is initiated. It is not necessary to return to the subroutine that processed *who hit the girl* after completing the subroutine that processed *who liked the sailor*. As a consequence it does not matter in Sentence (29) if the variables in the subroutine that analyzed *who hit the girl* are overwritten when the same subroutine is called to analyze *who liked the sailor*. For examples of production sets to process object relatives and subject relatives and a discussion of the overwriting of variables refer back to the discussion of Table 6.2 (page 202).

I have discussed earlier (page 457) the problems ATNs had with accounting for the difficulty of center embedding. ACT predicts whenever the same subroutine is center-embedded within itself, there will be difficulty. One level of center embedding as in Sentence (27) is not difficult because a relative clause routine is being embedded within a sentence routine. Two levels of embedding like Sentence (28) cause difficulty because they require a relative clause routine to be embedded within itself. In this regard it is interesting to note that a complement structure may be embedded within a relative clause or vice versa and still get manageable sentences:

(30)   The man who heard that the dog had been killed on the radio ran away.
(31)   The fact that the matron who killed the mouse had been raped surprised me.

ACT predicts these sentences are manageable because different subroutines would exist to process complement structures and relative clause structures. These constructions become unmanageable if another clause, either relative or complement, is embedded:

(32)   The fireman who learned that the hippie who shot the dog had grown a beard from the police ate some rice.
(33)   The fact that the minister who heard that the soldiers had been found from his neighbor had broken the window shocked the small town.

Again these become easier when expressed as right-embedded constructions:

(34)   Some rice was eaten by the fireman who learned from the police that a beard had been grown by the hippie who shot the dog.

---

subjects are using to analyze sentences in these paper and pencil tests are radically different than in normal comprehension. Subjects can use auxiliary memory on the paper to hold the information that had to be held by the variables associated with the subroutines in normal comprehension.

I fear that the reader may not always be convinced by the examples in this chapter because he is able to bring to bear sophisticated scanning strategies. Before concluding my examples are wrong I suggest reading them out loud to an unsuspecting informant.

(35)   The small town was shocked by the fact that the window had been broken by the minister who heard from his neighbor that the soldier had been found.

The one difficulty for the ACT analysis is that sometimes double embedding of complement clauses does not produce unmanageable sentences. Consider sentences (36)–(38):

(36)   The fact that Kennedy announced that America must be first on the moon over public television bothered me.

(37)   The fact that the sailor heard that the barber stabbed his friend from his father surprised me.

(38)   The fact that the shepard said that the farmer had taken the book from the child to the police was to be expected.

Sentence (36) seems quite manageable, whereas Sentence (38) is not. Sentence (37) falls somewhere in between. One reason that these sentences do not line up totally with ACT's predictions may be that subjects can use some nonsyntactic bases for comprehending these sentences. Conceptual and semantic constraints can make sentences easier. So, for instance, while the center-embedded relative construction in Sentence (28) is quite difficult, the following sentence does seem more manageable:

(39)   The question that the girl that the lion bit answered was complex.

The earlier examples, (27)–(35) in this section, were designed to avoid, as much as possible, semantic bases for comprehension.

Use of Conceptual Constraints

It is easy to model within the ACT framework how conceptual constraints can be used, as an alternative to syntax, to guide the interpretation of a sentence. Such constraints seemed to be operating in Sentences (36) and (39) above. For instance, suppose we provided ACT with the following production:

(P5)   (Vtok1 * IN) & ((V1 * Vclass1) $\Rightarrow$ (V1 * (in OF V2))
        & (Vclass1 * manipulable))
        & ((V2 & Vclass2)
        & (Vclass2 * container))

This production asserts that, whenever there is simultaneously active a token of the word IN; an instance, V1, of a manipulable object; and an instance, V2, of a container; then assert that the first instance is in the second. This would permit comprehension of the following sentences without syntax:

(40)   The ball is in the box.
        In the drawer is a candy.
        The sink has soap in it.
        Dolly is in bed.

Bottom-Up Parsing

The productions in Tables 11.2 and 11.3 exemplify a top-down parsing scheme. For instance, no attempt is made to analyze a noun phrase or a relative clause unless the production system is at a position where one is expected. However, we seem able to process and identify constituents even when they occur out of place. For instance, consider:

(41)   Daddy bought a very the large cuddly puppy.

The noun phrase, *the large cuddly puppy,* can be identified despite the fact that it occurs in an unexpected position. This suggests that the noun phrase subroutine should be capable of self-initiation just as in the main clause routine [Production (W1) in Table 11.2]. One could also have the following production which initiated noun phrase processing on the appearance of a determiner in the sentence:

(P6) $((\text{Vtok} * \text{Vword}) \& (\text{Vword} * \text{DET})) \Rightarrow (\text{Vcon1} = \text{NP})$

It seems that all routines in sentence processing should have this capacity for self-initiation. That is, each routine should be capable of being started by the appearance of a term which can occur initially in a construction that the routine is supposed to process. When a constituent like a relative clause occurs in the correct position then processing of it can either be initiated by the top-down or the bottom-up production.

There is another motivation for bottom-up parsing in addition to the fact that we can recognize constituents that are out of place. Much of the language that we hear just consists of sentence fragments. Therefore, as a practical matter, the routines for analyzing such constituents must be capable of self-initiation. One clear advantage, then, of production systems over ATNs is that production systems can exhibit the mixture of top-down and bottom-up processing which seems necessary to model natural language.

Ungrammatical Sentences

Ungrammatical sentences pose two challenges to any theory of natural language processing. First, one wants the language processor to recognize their ungrammaticality. Second, one wants the language processor not to "crash" when it encounters something that is ungrammatical but rather to be able to recover and process new input. Consider how a language understander should behave in the presence of the following two inputs:

(42)   The hippie saw the. In the church a lawyer was married.
(43)   The boy in gave the girl a book.

In (42) a sentence is not completed when another one starts up. In Sentence (43) the word *in* interrupts an otherwise acceptable sentence. We would want our language processor in Sentences (42) and (43) to note the peculiarity of the sentences. However, we would also want the processor to go on and process the acceptable sentence in (42) and recognize the meaning of the interrupted sentence in (43).

To model recognition of an ungrammatical sentence one can add productions which will announce when an unexpected construction occurs. For instance, suppose the noun phrase grammar was in the state defined by the control structure (Vcon1 = N1) between *the* and *in* in Input (42). Consider the effect of having the following production:

(P7)   (Vcon1 = N1) & (ABS ((Vtok * Vword) ⇒ (Vtok * unexpected)
        & (Vword * NUMBER))) & (ABS ((Vtok   & (Vadv = NEXT)
        * Vword) & (Vword * ADJ)))
        & (ABS ((Vtok * Vword)
        & (Vword * NOUN)))

In this state, the noun phrase routine expects a number, an adjective, or a noun. If the next word, Vtok, is none of these, the production will tag Vtok as unexpected and call for the advancement of Vtok to the next word. Similar productions could be written to handle unexpected elements at each point in the grammar.

It is also possible for ACT to successfully process Inputs (42) and (43) despite their syntactic violations. ACT would be able to process the sentence that terminates (42) because the main routine would be reinitiated by the start of a new sentence [see Production (W1) in Table 11.2]. ACT would be able to handle (43) because Production (P7), which detects an ungrammatical element, skips over the element and considers the next word. Therefore, ACT will process the sentence as if the offending *in* were not present.

Backup

It was argued earlier (page 458) that one of the psychologically unreal aspects of ATNs is that they provided the facility for unlimited backup, while it seemed that humans had great difficulty in backing up if their first parsing of the sentence is incorrect. For instance, witness the difficulty we have with

(44)   John gave the man a dog bit a bandage.

However, sometimes we can back up and recover quite easily. Consider:

(45)   I know more beautiful women than Miss America although she must know quite a few.

While it would require too extensive an analysis to specify all the information processing that goes into performing the backup in Sentence (45), it is possible to provide a partial account of how ACT might perform this. First, assume that a semantic routine notes that the interpretation of the clause *she must know quite a few* does not contrast with the interpretation initially assigned to *I know more beautiful women than Miss America*. Thus, the use of the conjunction *although* is inappropriate. ACT has in memory a record of the total sentence. The semantic interpreter could call for a reparsing of the sentence by setting Vtok to the first word in the sentence and reinitializing the main routine to process the sentence. This time, however, the parsing routines have access to knowledge about how the sentence ends and will select the correct interpretation of *more beautiful women*. Knowledge of the final clause of the sentence can be used to properly interpret the ambiguous phrase. Evidence for this claim is that we are much less likely to misinterpret when the subordinate clause comes first:

(46)   Although she must know quite a few, I know more beautiful women than Miss America.

Of course, it is not clear just how ACT would use knowledge of the subordinate clause to disambiguate the main clause. To explain this would require a relatively complex analysis of the system's knowledge about the syntactic structures involved and of the general world knowledge that is being presupposed.

It is worth noting why it is easier to backtrack in Sentence (45) than in (44). From the first analysis of Sentence (45) ACT would emerge with a correct analysis of the subordinate clause which could guide the reinterpretation of the main clause. In contrast, no interpretation is retrieved from Sentence (44) to guide a second analysis. Therefore, ACT will very likely make the same mistake in its second parse.

Note that the backup facilities being given to ACT are very much more primitive than those which exist in ATNs. ACT does not have the ability to remember its options at previous choice points and return to those choice points and reconsider its options. Rather, it can only start all over again with the chance that it can do better because of the experiences acquired and recorded in memory from the first parse. ACT could be given the facility to back up to other points beside the beginning of the sentence. For instance, it might be given the facility to reset itself back to the beginning of the last major clause. However, it is not possible in the current parsing scheme to give ACT the ATN potential to reconsider all choice points.

Look-Ahead

Because of the primitive backup facilities of ACT the program cannot deal with transient ambiguities in the same way that ATNs can. Consider the sentence pair discussed earlier (page 453) with respect to ATN mechanisms:

(47)   The old train the young.
(48)   The old train left the station.

There is an ambiguity about whether *old* is an adjective or a noun which is not resolved until the fourth word in the sentence. An ATN model would assume one option, and if this failed, it would back up and try the other option.

ACT can deal with such transient ambiguities by means of a mechanism called *look-ahead*. There is no reason why ACT need process the sentence one word at a time. It can wait and look ahead in the sentence a couple of words before deciding how to characterize the current word. The following pair of productions would suffice to process the two sentences above.

(P8)	$(\text{Vcon1} = \text{N1}) \& ((\text{Vtok} - \text{Vtok1} - \text{Vtok2})$	$\Rightarrow$	$(\text{Vcon1} = \text{NPX})$
	$\& (\text{Vtok} * \text{Vword}) \& (\text{Vword} * \text{NOUN})$		$\& (\text{Vadv}$
	$\& (\text{Vtok1} * \text{Vword1}) \& (\text{Vword2} * \text{VERB})$		$= \text{NEXT})$
	$\& (\text{Vtok2} * \text{Vword2}) \& (\text{Vword2} * \text{DET})$		$\& (\text{Vtop1}$
	$\& (\text{Videa W Vword}))$		$* \text{Videa})$

(P9)	$(\text{Vcon1} = \text{N1}) \& ((\text{Vtok} - \text{Vtok1} - \text{Vtok2}) \Rightarrow$		$(\text{Vcon1} = \text{N2})$
	$\& (\text{Vtok W Vword}) \& (\text{Vword} * \text{ADJ})$		$\& (\text{Vadv}$
	$\& (\text{Vtok1 W Vword1}) \& (\text{Vword1}$		$= \text{NEXT})$
	$* \text{NOUN}) \& (\text{Vtok2 W Vword2})$		$\& (\text{Vtop1}$
	$\& (\text{Vword2} * \text{VERB})$		$* \text{Videa})$
	$\& (\text{Videa W Vword}))$		

For some idea of how these productions would fit into a general model for processing noun phrases consult Table 11.3. Many other productions would have to be added to handle other two-word combinations which may follow the to-be-analyzed word, Vtok. As these two productions illustrate, the conditions of such productions are complex relative to the conditions normally proposed for ACT productions. I doubt that look-ahead, when it is used, exceeds more than one or two words. Otherwise the conditions would become too complicated to be activated in predampening time.

Understanding Questions

It is interesting to consider what additions would have to be made to this production system to allow it to process questions. To provide some focus I will consider what additional productions would be required to handle the following two questions:

(49)   Who gives the ball to Mommy?
(50)   Does Lassy give the ball to Mommy?

Figures 11.5a and 11.5b show how these sentences should be represented after the parser is finished with them. These questions can be handled by making some additions to the parsing productions in Table 11.2. Question (49) can be handled by simply adding a production that will accept an interrogative pronoun rather than a noun phrase in first position:

(AS17)	$(\text{Vcon} = \text{START})$	$\Rightarrow$	$(\text{Vcon} = \text{S2}) \& (\text{speaker}$
	$\& (\text{Vtok} * \text{who})$		$* (\text{wants-to-know OF Vsubj})) \& \text{Vsubj}$

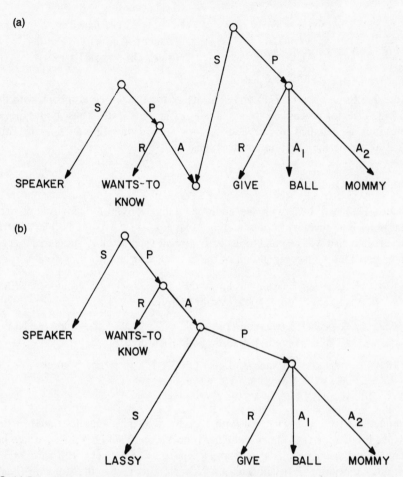

FIG. 11.5 ACT network representations for two questions: (a) Who gives the ball to Mommy? (b) Does Lassy give the ball to Mommy?

Question (50) can be handled by adding the following:

(AS18)   (Vcon = START)   ⇒   (Vcon = S9)
         & (Vtok * does)

(AS19)   (Vcon = S9)   ⇒   (Vcon1 = NP) & (Vcon = S9A)
                                & (UNBIND Vtop1)

(AS20)   (Vcon = S9A)   ⇒   (Vcon = S10) & (Vsubj = Vtop1)
         & (Vcon1 = NPX)
         & (Vtop1 * person)

(AS21)   (Vcon = S10)   ⇒   (Vcon = S2) & (speaker
          & (Vcon2 =   * (wants-to-know OF (Vsubj
          CLAUSEX)   * (gives OF Varg1 Varg2))))
          & (Vtok * give)

Note that Production (AS21) serves to merge the flow of control back with that in Fig. 11.2 for processing the remainder of the predicate. Thus, both types of questions are handled by introducing some special initial productions to Table 11.2 to handle the question constructions.

Answering Questions

Tables 11.2 and 11.3 with the addition of the above productions will parse questions into memory representations like Fig. 11.5. It is possible to write productions that will respond to the activation of such memory structures that encode questions by the generation of the correct answers:

(P8)   ((speaker * (wants-to-know OF   ⇒   (output "YES")
        (Vsubj * Vpred))) & (Vsubj * Vpred))

(P9)   ((speaker * (wants-to-know OF   ⇒   (output "NO")
        (Vsubj * Vpred)))) & (ABS (Vsubj * Vpred))

(P10)   ((speaker * (wants-to-know OF V1))   ⇒   (output V2)
        & (V1 * Vpred) & (V2 * Vpred))
        & (ABS (V1 = V2))

Productions (P8) and (P9) deal with encodings of questions illustrated in Fig. 11.5b. Production (P8) checks whether proposition (Vsubj * Vpred), which has been tagged as queried, is also encoded separately in memory. If it is, a YES is output. Otherwise, (P9) will output a NO. Note that since the structure (Lassy * (give OF Mommy ball)) is tagged as queried, it will not match the untagged structure (Vsubj * Vpred) in the condition of the production. This is because a qualified proposition cannot match a specification for an unqualified proposition. Production (P9) responds to queries like those illustrated in Fig. 11.5a, that is, it responds to questions about whether an element V1 has property Vpred. In Fig. 11.5a the variable Vpred would be bound to "gives the ball to Mommy." Production (P9) will be satisfied if there is some other element V2 (≠ V1) with property Vpred. If there is, it will output V2 as the answer.

Obviously, human question-answering procedures are much more complex than those modeled by means of the above three productions. However, these provide an indication of how question answering might progress. An adequate model for human question answering would require a book in itself (see Norman, 1973, for some of the complexities).

Measures of Transient Processing

In assessing the psychological reality of the ACT model of sentence processing, I have not yet considered any traditional experimental data. This reflects the fact that one's preexperimental data base about language processing is sufficiently rich so as to permit a very demanding set of empirical tests. That is, why should one go out to gather experimental data about language processing until he has a model which can account for what he already knows to be true about language processing?

Of course, this argument provides no justification for ignoring existing experimental data on language processing. In the abstract, there is a rich set of experimental predictions that comprehension models like ACT or ATNs make about language processing. These models specify the information processing configuration at each point in a sentence. From this specification, a good many predictions should follow. The problem, however, is that comprehension happens so fast it becomes very difficult methodologically to test these predictions.

The methodology to which I am attracted involves tests of transient information demands imposed by a sentence. This methodology usually involves looking for performance decrements in another task that must be performed in parallel with sentence comprehension. For instance, one can perform experiments like those of Wanner and Maratsos and look for decrements in one's ability to hold other information in short-term memory as a function of the demands the sentence makes on short-term memory. The logic of these experiments is that one can only keep active in short-term memory a fixed number of things. This assumption can be directly derived from the ALIST mechanism in ACT. The second type of test looks at the speed with which another process may be carried on. For instance, there is the phoneme monitoring task of Foss (1969) in which the subject must monitor a sentence for the presence of a certain phoneme such as p. The assumption behind this paradigm is that subjects will be able to respond less rapidly in the monitoring task when there is a heavy processing load at some point in the sentence. This assumption follows directly from the ACT assumption that there is a limited capacity for the parallel application of productions. Experimental evidence for this limited capacity assumption was provided in Section 6.3.

Wanner and Maratsos, using the concurrent memory load paradigm, found that subjects are poorer with object relatives than subject relatives. That is, Sentence (51) is harder than (52)

(51)   The witch whom sorcerers despised frightened little children.
(52)   The witch who despised sorcerers frightened little children.

However, this greater difficulty is only found when the memory set is presented after *sorcerers* in Sentence (51) versus *despised* in (52). Presenting the memory load later does not result in any differential effects. As discussed in the preceding section (page 455), this was attributed to the HOLD mechanism in ATNs. That is, it was proposed that it was particularly difficult to maintain unassigned noun phrases on the HOLD list. Wanner and Maratsos proposed that the modified noun (that is, *witch*) had to be maintained unassigned longer in the object relative case.

ACT also predicts the greater difficulty with object relatives. The subject of the noun phrase in Sentence (51), *sorcerers,* must be kept active until the verb comes in and is processed. This means an additional item must be added to the ALIST. In contrast, as soon as *sorcerers* is analyzed in Sentence (52), it can be assigned to its correct position in the embedded proposition. After the verb occurs in Sentence (51) *sorcerers* need no longer be maintained. So ACT predicts, as Wanner and Maratsos found, that the difficulty of object relatives is transient. However, ACT attributes the difficulty to holding *sorcerers* not *witch* in short-term memory. *Witch* must be held in the ALIST throughout the processing of the relative clause because it is required in the main clause. Thus, under the ACT analysis, the difference between the object relative and the subject relative has to do with the position of the verb. Until the verb is given, all noun phrases in the relative clause must be held in short-term memory. Once the verb occurs, they can be assigned to the proposition involving that verb.

The phoneme monitoring tasks have been used to show that a subject's processing of a sentence is hindered by various kinds of ambiguity. Foss (1970) has shown that performance in phoneme monitoring is hindered by either lexical or syntactic ambiguity. He found that there is no detriment to phoneme monitoring if the location of the critical phoneme occurs after the ambiguity has been resolved. This is clear evidence for a transient demand on sentence processing.

The phoneme-monitoring task has also been used by Hakes and Cairns (1970) to show the usefulness of relative pronouns in facilitating the processing of relative clauses. They find subjects display better performance on Sentence (53) than (54):

(53)   I admired the boy that the girl despised.
(54)   I admired the boy the girl despised.

The superiority of Sentence (53) can be seen as arising from a reduced ambiguity. In Sentence (54) the sequence *the boy the girl* could be viewed as part of a conjunction of noun phrases.

There are multiple reasons why such transient ambiguities would produce increased capacity demands on a system like ACT—or many other languages processors including ATNs. If multiple interpretations are pursued in parallel when an ambiguity occurs (as it is possible for ACT to do) then a greater number of productions must be applied per unit time. On the other hand, if only one interpretation is followed, then ACT will have to back up and attempt the other interpretation should the first interpretation prove false. This will also require the execution of more productions. In either the parallel or serial model more productions will have to be applied in the same fixed period of time. This will take capacity away from the application of productions that are performing the phoneme monitoring task during that fixed time period.

An ACT System for Generation

It is interesting to consider how sentence generation would operate in the ACT system. Tables 11.4 and 11.5 give the production systems for generating main clauses and noun phrases. Before discussing these productions systems, it is necessary to consider the input to these generation routines. They expect a set of ACT propositions tagged as to-be-spoken. Figure 11.6 illustrates the network structure that would underlie generation of the sentence *Daddy received the red ball from Mommy who was in the room*. In Fig. 11.6 the main proposition has been tagged as such and the subordinate propositions have been tagged. The topic of the sentence, Daddy, has also been tagged. This tagging is conceived of as reflecting preplanning on the part of the speaker as to what he wants to say and how he wants to say it. The tagging of the to-be-spoken propositions also serves another function: Because they are tagged they would not be regarded as necessarily true. This is good because one does not want to have a system that believes all it says.

The production systems for generation in Tables 11.4 and 11.5 follow the same general control structure illustrated in Figs. 11.2 and 11.4 for the understanding systems. This parallelism in control structure is forced on the two systems by the fact that one must generate the same word orders that the other must comprehend. The difference between the two systems concerns the contents of the conditions and actions of the corresponding productions. The conditions of understanding productions specify features true of the sentence and the actions specify additions to a network that represents comprehension of the sentence. In contrast, in speaking, the conditions specify tests of the to-be-spoken structure and the actions specify the next element to be produced in the sentence.

The specification of the next word to be spoken in Table 11.4 and 11.5 is accomplished by means of placing in the productions actions of the form (Vtok * word). For instance, in the action (GS2) we have (Vtok * GIVES). This attaches the word by a subject–predicate construction to the variable, Vtok, for the word token. The two productions, (W1) and (W2) at the bottom of Table 11.4, serve to transform this memory construction into the actual utterance of a word. Production (W1) will be elicited only to generate the first word of the sentence. It calls the subroutine (SAY Vword) to actually generate the word, and also records that the sentence begins with Vtok. The variable Vold is bound to the token of this word and Vtok is unbound. Production (W2) is designed for the remaining words in the sentence. It encodes that Vtok is the successor of Vold in the sentence, binds Vold to the value of Vtok, and unbinds Vtok. Thus, not only do these productions serve to generate the sentence, they will also build up a record of the exact sentence generated.

TABLE 11.4
Some Productions for Generating Declarative Sentences

	Conditions		Actions
(GS0)	(Vcon = START) & (Vsubj * TOPIC)	⇒	(Vcon1 = NP) & (Vtop1 = Vsubj) & (Vcon = STARTA)
(GS1)	(Vcon = STARTA) & (Vcon1 = NPX) & (Vtop1 * person)	⇒	(Vcon = S1)
(GS2)	(Vcon = S1) & (Vcon2 = CLAUSEX) & ((Vsubj * (give OF Varg1 Varg2)) * Main)	⇒	(Vcon = S2) & (Vtok * GIVES) & Vtok
(GS3)	(Vcon = S1) & (Vcon2 = CLAUSEX) & ((Varg1 * (give OF Varg2 Vsubj)) * Main)	⇒	(Vcon = S6) & (Vtok * RECEIVES) & Vtok
(GS4)	(Vcon = S2) * ((Vsubj * (give OF Varg1 Varg2)) * Main)	⇒	(Vcon1 = NP) & (Vtop1 = Varg1) & (Vcon = S2A)
(GS5)	(Vcon = S2) & ((Vsubj * (give OF Varg1 Varg2)) * Main)	⇒	(Vcon1 = NP) & (Vtop1 = Varg2) & (Vcon = S2B)
(GS6)	(Vcon = S2A) & (Vcon1 = NPX)	⇒	(Vcon = S4)
(GS7)	(Vcon = S2B) & (Vcon1 = NPX)	⇒	(Vcon = S3)
(GS8)	(Vcon = S3) & (Vcon2 = CLAUSEX) & ((Vsubj * (give OF Varg1 Varg2)) * Main)	⇒	(Vcon1 = NP) & (Vtop1 = Varg1) & (Vcon = S3A)
(GS9)	(Vcon = S3A) & (Vcon1 = NPX)	⇒	(Vcon = SX)
(GS10)	(Vcon = SX) & (Vcon2 = CLAUSEX)	⇒	(Vcon = START) & (UNBIND Vsubj Vold Varg1 Varg2)
(GS11)	(Vcon = S4) & (Vcon2 = CLAUSEX)	⇒	(Vcon = S5) & (Vtok * to) & Vtok
(GS12)	(Vcon = S5) & ((Vsubj * (give OF Varg1 Varg2)) * Main)	⇒	(Vcon1 = NP) & (Vtop1 = Varg2) & (Vcon = S5A)
(GS13)	(Vcon = S5A) & (Vcon1 = NPX)	⇒	(Vcon = SX)
(GS14)	(Vcon = S6) & ((Varg1 * (give OF Varg2 Vsubj)) * Main)	⇒	(Vcon1 = NP) & (Vtop1 = Varg2) & (Vcon = S6A)
(GS15)	(Vcon = S6A) & (Vcon1 = NPX)	⇒	(Vcon = S7)
(GS16)	(Vcon = S7) & (Vcon2 = CLAUSEX)	⇒	(Vcon = S8) & (Vtok * from) & Vtok
(GS17)	(Vcon = S8) & ((Varg1 * (give OF Varg2 Vsubj)) * Main)	⇒	(Vcon1 = NP) & (Vtop1 = Varg1) & (Vcon = S8A)
(GS18)	(Vcon = S8A) & (Vcon1 = NPX)	⇒	(Vcon = SX)

Special productions for word generation

(W1)	(Vtok * Vword) & (ABS Vold)	⇒	(SAY Vword) & (FIRST Vtok) & (Vold = Vtok) & (UNBIND Vtok)

(continued)

TABLE 11.4 *(continued)*

	Conditions		Actions
(W2)	(Vtok * Vword) & Vold	$\Rightarrow$	(SAY Vword) & (Vold − Vtok)
			(Vold = Vtok) & (UNBIND Vtok)

Special productions for rehearsal

(R1)	Vcon	$\Rightarrow$	Vcon
(R2)	Vsubj	$\Rightarrow$	Vsubj

It is not the case that the productions for generation are simply the productions for comprehension (analysis) with condition and action reversed. They often overlap in their conditions. For instance, the conditions of Production (AN1) (Table 11.3) for comprehension and Production (GN1) (Table 11.5) for generation both contain a test of whether the topic of the noun phrase is connected to a person. There are three types of information found in productions for analysis and generation: word class and other syntactic information like the test of whether the topic is a person, information about the sentence, and information about the semantic structure. The syntactic information always finds itself in the condition of a production. The sentence information is in the condition of a comprehension production and the action of a generation production. The semantic information is in the action of a comprehension production and the condition of a generation production. I have done work with ATN formalisms (Anderson, 1975, 1976) in which it is possible to use the same network arc for generation and comprehension. This simply requires changing the information in an arc specification that is regarded as condition and that which is regarded as action. This requires that two separate ATN interpreters be built, one for comprehension and one for generation. In the ACT system, with just one interpreter for all productions, it is necessary to have separate but related productions for performing the two tasks.

It is necessary for the production systems in Table 11.4 and Table 11.5 to choose between a number of synonymous constructions expressing the same semantic referent. For instance, Productions (GS4) and (GS5) decide between whether the object or the recipient of *give* should follow the verb. Whichever of these productions executes first will determine the expression. Thus the selection among synonymous structures is conceptualized as a race between competing productions, with one production winning sometimes and other productions winning other times.

Note in Table 11.5 that as the adjective and noun predicates of Vtop1 are generated [by Productions (GN4), (GN6), (GN7), (GN8), (GN9), and (GN10)], the propositions asserting these predicates are tagged as spoken. This is to prevent them from being matched and generated over and over again. Note that Produc-

TABLE 11.5
Productions for Generating Noun Phrases

	Conditions		Actions
(GN1)	(Vcon1 = NP) & ((Vtop1 W Vword) & (Vtop1 * PERSON))	⇒	(Vcon1 = NPX) & (Vtok * Vword) & Vtok
(GN2)	(Vcon1 = NP) & (Vtop1 # 1)	⇒	(Vcon1 = N1) & (Vtok * a) & Vtok
(GN3)	(Vcon1 = NP)	⇒	(Vcon1 = N1) & (Vtok * the) & Vtok
(GN4)	(Vcon1 = N1) & ((Vprop = ((Vtop1 * Videa) * sub)) & (Videa W Vword) & (Vword * ADJ))	⇒	(Vcon1 = N2) & (Vtok * Vword) & Vtok & (Vprop * spoken)
(GN5)	(Vcon1 = N1) & ((Vtop1 # Videa) & (Videa W Vword) & (Vword * NUMBER))	⇒	(Vcon1 = N2) & (Vtok * Vword) & Vtok
(GN6)	(Vcon1 = N1) & ((Vprop = ((Vtop1 * Videa) * sub)) & (Vtop2 # 1) & (Videa W Vword) & (Vword * NOUNSING))	⇒	(Vcon1 = NPX) & (Vtok * Vword) & Vtok & (Vprop * spoken)
(GN7)	(Vcon1 = N1) & ((Vprop = ((Vtop1 * Videa) * sub)) & (Vtop # plur) & (Videa W Vword) & (Vword * NOUNPLUR))	⇒	(Vcon1 = NPX) & (Vtok * Vword) & Vtok & (Vprop * spoken)
(GN8)	(Vcon1 = N2) & ((Vprop = ((Vtop1 * Videa) * sub)) & (Videa W Vword) & (Vword * ADJ))	⇒	(Vcon1 = N2) & (Vtok * Vword) & Vtok & (Vprop * spoken)
(GN9)	(Vcon1 = N2) & ((Vprop = ((Vtop1 * Videa) * sub)) & (Vtop1 # 1) & (Videa W Vword) & (Vword * NOUNSING))	⇒	(Vcon1 = NPX) & (Vtok * Vword) & Vtok & (Vprop * spoken)
(GN10)	(Vcon1 = N2) & ((Vprop = ((Vtop1 * Videa) * sub)) & (Vtop1 # plur) & (Videa W Vword) & (Vword * NOUNPLUR))	⇒	(Vcon1 = NPX) & (Vtok * Vword) & Vtok & (Vprop * spoken)
(GN11)	(Vcon1 = NPX) & ((Vtop1 * Videa) * sub)	⇒	(Vcon2 = CLAUSE1) & (Vtok * who) & Vtok
(GN12)	(Vcon1 = NPX) & ((V1 * (Vrel OF Vtop1)) * sub)	⇒	(Vcon2 = CLAUSE2) & (Vtok * whom) & Vtok
(GN13)	(Vcon1 = NPX) & ((V1 * (Vrel OF V2 Vtop1)) * sub)	⇒	(Vcon2 = CLAUSE3) & (Vtok * whom) & Vtok
(GN14)	(Vcon1 = NPX) & (ABS ((Vtop1 * Videa) * sub))	⇒	(Vcon2 = CLAUSEX) & (UNBIND Vcon1)

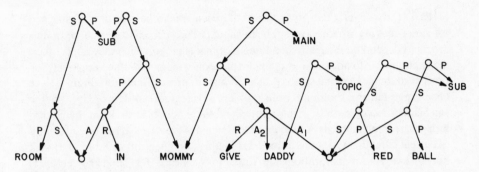

FIG. 11.6   This tagged propositional network guides generation of the sentence *Daddy received the red ball from Mommy who was in the room.*

tions (GN11)–(GN13) test for whether Vtop1 is involved in any further sub-ordinate propositions, not tagged as spoken. If it is, the CLAUSE network will be elicited to generate this proposition. If not, Production (GN14) will be elicited which signals there is no clause by executing (Vcon2 = CLAUSEX). Note that Production (GN14) tests for the absence of only one particular structure that Vtop1 might appear in—((Vtop1 * Videa) * sub). It is assumed here that before the absence of this structure is determined, the presence of one of the structures specified in (GN11)–(GN13) will have been detected. As in the production system for comprehension, the generation productions for the relative clauses have been completely omitted for the sake of brevity in this book.

In contrast to the rather extensive discussion I was able to give for the production system for comprehension, I am totally at a loss as to what to note about this generation system. With the comprehension system it was possible to suggest additions that would give the system many additional features—to perform seman-tic checking, disambiguation, conceptual production, bottom-up parsing, handle ungrammatical constructions, backup, lookahead, and question answering. There has been much less attention in the artificial intelligence literature to issues of language generation. Therefore, there has not developed a set of measurements that one can make of this generation system. Similarly, there has been less attention in psychology to tests of generation. Hopefully, as more work is done with explicit models of generation, a set of issues and questions will evolve about the language generation process.

SUMMARY OF CHAPTER 11

A review is made of the last 25 years of language processing by computers. There is clear progress discernable if we compare the early simple-minded processing with the current much more sophisticated systems best exemplified by Winograd's

SHRDLU. However, there are problems of exponential time growth in parsing and inference making which have not been solved. The success of current programs seems to depend on the restricted domain of discourse to which they apply. Also these programs do not seem to integrate past knowledge into the comprehension process to the degree that seems typical of human prose processing. Frames have been suggested as a solution for this problem of integration of knowledge, but the suggestions have yet to be implemented and there is reason to doubt their suitability once implemented. A number of deficiencies are noted about the suitability of current computer programs as models of human language processing: They lack human-like information-processing limitations, means for language learning, means for mixing semantic and syntactic levels of processing, and human-like methods of disambiguation. They are also brittle and lack resilience to flaws in the input.

Augmented Transition Networks are examined as psychological models. Of the available computer formalisms they seem to be most suited for psychological modeling. Unlike some other processing formalisms, ATNs seem to have some basic principles of operation which lead to general predictions that can be tested. They process sentences in a left-to-right fashion, use a perspicacious network representation, can be used to both model comprehension and generation, and provide a model for the segmentation of a sentence into surface structure. Ronald Kaplan and Eric Wanner have begun performing tests of predictions derivable from ATN mechanisms. The experimental evidence to date is not compelling because it tests relatively peripheral features of ATNs and because a good number of inadequately motivated assumptions must be made to derive predictions. It seems difficult to test ATNs because they involve so many separate mechanisms. A general problem with ATNs as psychological models is that they are too powerful in their language comprehension abilities. It seems difficult to properly constrain the power of these models and still retain the ATN framework. This is particularly a problem with respect to ATN's facility for recursive self-embedding.

Sets of ACT productions are introduced for analyzing and generating sentences about a special semantic domain involving a child in a house. The core set of productions is very similar to ATNs except that it does not have the same power to perform such operations as unlimited self-embedding or backup. It is easy to augment this production set with other productions which will perform such operations as semantic checking, use of conceptual constraints, bottom-up parsing, processing of ungrammatical sentences, look-ahead, understanding and answering questions. The ACT system for language analysis also seems to properly account for the difficulty experienced with various types of embedding and for the transient processing difficulties created by different types of sentences.

REFERENCES

Abelson, R. P. The structure of belief systems. In R. C. Schank & K. M. Colby (Eds.), *Computer models of thought and language*. San Francisco: Freeman, 1973.

ALPAC (Automated Language Processing Advisory Committee). *Language and machines—computers in translation and linguistics.* Washington, D.C.: National Academy of Sciences, 1966.

Anderson, J. R. Computer simulation of a language acquisition system. In R. L. Solso (Ed.), *Information processing and cognition: The Loyola Symposium.* Hillsdale, New Jersey: Lawrence Erlbaum Assoc., 1975.

Anderson, J. R. Computer simulation of a language acquisition system. In D. LaBerge & S. J. Samuels (Eds.). *Perception and comprehension.* Hillsdale, New Jersey: Lawrence Erlbaum Assoc., in press.

Anderson, J. R., & Bower, G. H. *Human associative memory.* Washington: Winston, 1973.

Bar-Hillel, Y. *Language and information.* Reading, Massachusetts: Addison Wesley, 1964.

Bever, T. G. Associations to stimulus-response theories of language. In T. R. Dixon & D. L. Horton (Eds.), *Verbal behavior and general behavior theory.* Englewood Cliffs, New Jersey: Prentice-Hall, 1968.

Bever, T. G., Fodor, J. A., & Garrett, M. A formal limitation of associationism. In T. R. Dixon & D. L. Horton (Eds.), *Verbal behavior and general behavior theory.* Englewood Cliffs, New Jersey: Prentice-Hall, 1968.

Bobrow, D. G. A question-answering system for high school algebra word problems. *AFIPS Conference Proceedings,* 1964, **26,** 577–589.

Bobrow, D. G. & Fraser, J. B. An augmented state transition network analysis procedure. *Proceedings of the International Joint Conference on Artificial Intelligence,* Washington, D.C., 1969, 557–567.

Charniak, E. Computer solution of word problems. *Proceedings of the International Joint Conference on Artificial Intelligence,* Washington, D.C., 1969, 303–316.

Charniak, E. *Toward a model of children's story comprehension.* MIT Artificial Intelligence Laboratory Mimeo, December, 1972.

Chomsky, N. Verbal behavior (a review of Skinner's book). *Language,* 1959, **35,** 26–58.

Chomsky, N. *Language and mind.* New York: Harcourt, Brace & World, 1968.

Colby, K. M., & Enea, H. Inductive inference by intelligent machines. *Scientia,* **103,** 669–20 (Jan.–Feb., 1968).

Dreyfus, H. L. *What computers can't do.* New York: Harper and Row, 1972.

Feldman, J. Bad-mouthing frames. In R. Schank & B. L. Nash-Webber (Eds.), Theoretical issues in national language processing (mimeographed conference report), 1975.

Fodor, J. A. Could meaning be an R_m? *Journal of Verbal Learning and Verbal Behavior,* 1965, **4,** 43–81.

Foss, D. J. Decision processes during sentence comprehension: Effects of lexical item difficulty and position upon decision times. *Journal of Verbal Learning and Verbal Behavior,* 1969, **8,** 457–462.

Foss, D. J. Some effects of ambiguity upon sentence comprehension. *Journal of Verbal Learning and Verbal Behavior,* 1970, **9,** 699–706.

Garrett, M., & Fodor, J. A. Psychological theories and linguistic constructs. In T. R. Dixon & D. L. Horton (Eds.), *Verbal behavior and general behavior theory.* Englewood Cliffs, New Jersey: Prentice-Hall, 1968.

Green, B. F., Wolf, A. K., Chomsky, C., & Laughery, K. Baseball: an automatic question answer. In E. A. Feigenbaum & J. Feldman (Eds.), *Computer and thought.* New York: McGraw-Hill, 1963.

Hakes, D. T., & Cairns, H. S. Sentence comprehension and relative pronouns. *Perception & Psychophysics,* 1970, **8,** 5–8.

Hewitt, C. *Description and theoretical analysis (using schemata) of PLANNER: A language for proving theorems and manipulating models in a robot* (Report AI-TR-258). MIT-AI Laboratory, 1972.

Kaplan, R. A general syntactic processor. In R. Rustin (Ed.), *Natural language processing.* Englewood Cliffs, New Jersey: Prentice-Hall, 1973.

Kaplan, R. Transient processing load in sentence comprehension. Unpublished doctoral dissertation. Harvard University, 1974.

Kaplan, R. On process models for sentence analysis. In D. A. Norman & D. E. Rumelhart. *Explorations in cognition*. San Francisco: Freeman, 1975.

Kasher, A. *Data retrieval by computer: a critical survey*. (Technical Report No. 22 to Office of Naval Research, Information System Branch.) Hebrew University of Jerusalem, January, 1966.

Kellogg, C. H. A natural language compiler for on-line data management. *Proceedings of the 1968 Fall Joint Computer Conference*, 473–492.

Kuno, S. The predictive analyzer and a path elimination technique. *Communications of the ACM*, 1965, **7**, 453–462.

Lindsay, R. K. Inferential memory as the basis of machines which understand natural language. In E. Feigenbaum & J. Feldman (Eds.), *Computers and thought*. New York: McGraw-Hill, 1963.

McCarthy, D. Language development in children. In L. Carmichael (Ed.), *Manual of child psychology*. New York: Wiley, 1954.

McDermott, D. V. *Assimilation of new information by a natural language-understanding system*. MIT Artificial Intelligence Laboratory Memo, February, 1974.

McNeill, D. On theories of language acquisition. In T. R. Dixon and D. L. Horton (Eds.), *Verbal behavior and general behavior theory*. Englewood Cliffs, N.J.: Prentice-Hall, 1968.

Minsky, M. A framework for representing knowledge. In P. H. Winston (Ed.), *The psychology of computer vision*. New York: McGraw-Hill, 1975.

Mowrer, O. H. *Learning theory and the symbolic processes*. New York: Wiley, 1960.

Newell, A. Production systems: Models of control structures. In W. G. Chase (Ed.), *Visual information processing*. New York: Academic Press, 1973. Pp. 463–526.

Norman, D. A. Memory, knowledge, and the answering of questions. In R. L. Solso (Ed.), *Contemporary issues in cognitive psychology*. Washington: Winston, 1973.

Norman, D. A., Rumelhart, D. E., & LNR Research Group. *Explorations in cognition*. San Francisco: Freeman, 1975.

Osgood, C. E., Suci G. J., & Tannebaum, P. H. *The measurement of meaning*. Urbana, Illinois: University of Illinois Press, 1957.

Quillian, M. R. The teachable language comprehender. *Communications of the Association for Computing Machinery*, 1969, **12**, 459–476.

Raphael, B. SIR: A computer program for semantic information retrieval. In M. Minsky (Ed.), *Semantic information processing*. Cambridge, Massachusetts: MIT Press, 1968.

Rieger, C. J. Conceptual Memory: A theory and computer program for processing the meaning content of natural language utterances. Unpublished doctoral dissertation, Stanford University, 1974.

Riesbeck, C. K. *Computational understanding: Analysis of sentences and context*. Stanford Artificial Intelligence Laboratory Memo AIM-238, 1974.

Schank, R. C. Conceptual dependency: A theory of natural language understanding. *Cognitive psychology*, 1972, **3**, 552–631.

Schank, R. C. *Conceptual information processing*. Amsterdam: North-Holland Publ., 1975.

Schank, R. C., & Abelson, R. P. *Scripts, plans, and knowledge*. Presented at the 4th International Joint Conference on Artificial Intelligence, Tbilisi, USSR, 1975.

Schank, R. C., & Nash-Webber, B. L. *Theoretical issues in natural language processing*. Proceedings of an Interdisciplinary Workshop in Computational Linguistics, Psychology, Linguistics, and Artificial Intelligence, 1975.

Simmons, R. F. Natural language question-answering systems; 1969. *Communications of the Association for Computing Machinery*, 1970, **13**, 15–30.

Simmons, R. F. Semantic networks: Their computation and use for understanding English sentences. In R. C. Schank & K. M. Colby (Eds.), *Computer models of thought and language*. San Francisco: Freeman, 1973.

Skinner, B. F. *Verbal behavior*. New York: Appleton-Century-Crofts, 1957.

Slagle, J. R. Experiments with a deductive question-answering program. *Communications of the Association for Computing Machinery*, 1965, **8**, 792–798.

Staats, A. W. *Learning, language, and cognition*. New York: Holt, Rinehart & Winston, 1968.

Thorndyke, P. W. Conceptual complexity and imagery in comprehension and memory. *Journal of Verbal Learning and Verbal Behavior,* 1975, **14,** 359–369.

Thorne, J., Bratley, P., & Dewar, H. The syntactic analysis of English by machine. In D. Michie (Ed.), *Machine intelligence.* Vol. 3. New York: American Elsevier, 1968.

Wanner, E., & Maratsos, M. An augmented transition network model of relative clause comprehension. Unpublished manuscript, Harvard University, 1975.

Weizenbaum, J. ELIZA—a computer program for the study of natural language communications between man and machine. *Communications of the ACM,* 1966, **1,** 36–45.

Wilks, Y. An artificial intelligence approach to machine translation. In R. Schank and K. Colby (Eds.), *Computer models of thought and language.* San Francisco, 1973.

Winograd, T. Understanding natural language. *Cognitive Psychology,* 1972, **3,** 1–191.

Winograd, T. Five lectures on artificial intelligence. Stanford Artificial Intelligence Laboratory, Memo AIM-246, 1974.

Winograd, T. Frame representations and the declarative-procedural controversy. In D. Bobrow & A. Collins (Eds.), *Representation and understanding.* New York: Academic Press, 1975.

Woods, W. A. Procedural semantics for a question-answering machine. *Proceedings of the 1968 Fall Joint Computer Conference,* 457–471.

Woods, W. A. Transition network grammars for natural language analysis. *Communications of the Association for Computing Machinery,* 1970, **13,** 591–606.

Woods, W. A. An experimental parsing system for transition network grammars. In R. Rustin (Ed.), *Natural language processing.* Englewood Cliffs, New Jersey: Prentice-Hall, 1973.

Woods, W. A., Kaplan, R. M., & Nash-Webber, B. The lunar sciences natural language information system: Final report. BBN Report No. 2378. Cambridge, Massachusetts: Bolt, Beranek, & Newman, 1972.

Younger, D. H. Recognition and parsing of context-free languages in time n^3. *Information and Control,* 1967, **10,** 189–208.

12
Induction of Procedures

Too much faith should not be put in the power of
induction, even when aided by intelligent heuristics, to discover the right grammar. After all,
stupid people learn to talk, but even the brightest
apes do not.

NOAM CHOMSKY AND GEORGE MILLER

This chapter is concerned with the processes by which procedural knowledge is
acquired. There are two aspects to this acquisition process. First, the system
must identify the procedures that are required to succeed in a particular task. This
is not a trivial problem because the procedural knowledge is not usually directly
stated to the learner. He must induce the procedures by observing examples of the
behavior the procedures are supposed to generate. This has the appearance of
being a very difficult logical task for problem domains like language acquisition.
It has seemed incredible to some that humans are able to succeed at induction
tasks like language learning. This induction problem has no real parallel in the
acquisition of declarative knowledge. Usually, we are directly told the propositions we have to commit to memory, whereas there seldom is a direct statement
of procedures.[1] Of course there are some cases where we must induce declarative
knowledge. For example, this is just the task of a scientist. However, it seems
that we go about that induction task much more awkwardly and with much less
success than when we induce procedural knowledge. Witness the fact that a generation of scientists has had so little success in identifying the principles of language understanding, but that almost all children learn to understand a language.

The other aspect of acquiring procedural knowledge is to encode the procedures
once they have been identified. Within the ACT model this means encoding productions which are the units of procedural knowledge. Here the same considera-

---

[1]Moreover, in those circumstances where we are told what the correct procedure is, it does not
seem that this direct statement serves as a basis for learning the procedure. For instance, we can be
told how to swing a tennis racket, but it seems the only way we learn is by constantly practicing the
swing. To provide a more cognitive example, studying a language from a textbook never seems
adequate enough preparation for speaking it. Rather one must observe examples of correct speech
behavior in the language and attempt to mimic these examples. So it may well be the case that the
only way to acquire procedural knowledge is through induction from examples.

tions are relevant that are involved in the acquisition of declarative knowledge. That is, we can ask if procedures are encoded gradually or in an all-or-none manner. We can ask if part of a production may be encoded just as it was asked (Section 10.3) if part of a proposition might be encoded. One can also inquire as to the retention of procedural knowledge over time.

So one can break up the acquisition of procedural knowledge into an induction problem and an encoding problem. While the encoding problem is interesting, the focus of this chapter is on the induction problem. I currently regard the induction problem as the most significant problem in cognitive psychology. It would be an intellectual accomplishment of great historical and philosophical importance to provide a set of mechanisms powerful enough to solve the induction problem while at the same time simple enough to be psychologically plausible.

This chapter does not contain a solution to the induction problem within the ACT framework. It sets up the background for the solution which I am currently pursuing. In the first two sections of this chapter I establish various logical results about induction, while in the third section I set forth some principles for an ACT induction system. However, it remains to be shown that these principles really constitute a solution to the induction problem; that is, it must be demonstrated that they will succeed at the variety of human induction tasks.

12.1   THE GENERAL PROBLEM OF INDUCTION

This section will provide a general formal analysis of the induction problem. These results are adaptations and extensions of results established by Gold in two papers (1965, 1967). The formally trained reader should consult these original papers. No one should pursue the induction problem without being thoroughly introduced to Gold's work. This work is significant because it provides a basic vocabulary of results and concepts with which to measure current attempts to produce induction systems. These results show very clearly that certain approaches to certain problems cannot work and other approaches to other problems will work only in certain senses.

The principal function of these formal analyses is to establish some facts at a level of generality that is not otherwise attainable. To appreciate the need for such a level of generality imagine the following scenario: A colleague presents us with a program theory for language acquisition. As evidence of the prowess of his theory he presents us with a demonstration of that program encountering some sentences from English, making some interesting generalizations, and then being able to recognize and generate some novel sentences. Suppose he then made some claim such as that his program could learn all possible languages. How would we be able to go about evaluating this claim? It is not practical to set about trying to have the program learn a trial language. It would be useful to have an encyclopedia of formal results about language acquisition which told us under what circumstances what kinds of language were learnable. Formal work on induction and language learning is beginning to provide us with this encyclopedia. There are probably already enough negative results about what kinds of learning problems are not solvable to be able to debunk the boastful claim of our hypothetical colleague.

One difficulty with much psychological work on induction is that it is very particulate. This criticism applies to some degree to my own work on language acquisition. Psychologists usually study a very specific induction problem, such as extropolation of a particular type of series, and try to devise a model for that particular problem. Little concern is given to whether the induction model is general or whether it will just solve that particular type of problem. The formal work on induction can serve to alert one to issues of generality. Unfortunately, this abstract work has not made clear contact with the specific problems of human induction. Still there are some helpful results. Let me list informally some of the conclusions that will be established in this chapter:

1. While it is possible for a learner to succeed at a large class of induction problems it is not possible for him to know he has succeeded.
2. It is only possible to learn a procedure if one has access to all instances of the behavior that the procedure is supposed to compute. However, one does not need to see all instances.
3. It would take an astronomically long time to learn most procedures.
4. The human induction mechanism contains strong innate specifications about natural languages.
5. It is not possible to learn an arbitrary language containing ambiguity or synonymy.
6. One cannot learn a language if he is only given examples of grammatical sentences, but he could learn the language if he is also given information about ungrammatical strings.

It is clear that these claims have psychological significance although they might strike the reader as mystical or preposterous. There is a clear and rigorous sense in which each is true. The purpose of the formalism is to transform such informal, and consequently vague, claims into precise results.

The next two sections of this chapter will at times become somewhat technical, particularly in proofs of theorems. Parts of these sections are at the same level of formality as those starred sections in Chapters 3, 4, and 7. However, I have tried to make the important points available to the general but determined reader. In particular, I have tried to state theorems as informally as possible, leaving formal technicalities in the introduction to the theorem and in the proof.

A General Framework for Induction

I will develop a formal framework for analyzing induction problems in which the elements of the induction problem are represented in terms of formal automata.

Results from the literature on formal automata and related literature will be used to establish some of the points.[2] It is generally accepted by workers in the field that any specifiable procedure can be formalized by a Turing Machine. I will frequently speak in terms of Turing Machines. I will also discuss formal automata that are weaker in computational power than Turing Machines. These classes of automata serve to formalize subsets of the specifiable procedures. The purpose of using such classes of machines to represent procedures is to achieve generality in one's conclusions.

I have borrowed from Gold techniques for analyzing a formal framework in which all induction problems can be conceptualized. Language learning is just a special case within this framework. Any to-be-induced behavior can be thought of as a relation between a class of inputs and their responses or outputs. The induction task is to identify that relation. In terms of learning to speak a language, this means learning to respond to a semantic intention with the sentence that communicates that intention. In terms of concept formation, this means appropriately labeling a stimulus array. In terms of sequence extrapolation, this means responding to an initial part of a sequence with the correct ending. In terms of playing chess, this means responding with the correct move to a board position. In terms of riding a bike, this means responding with compensatory adjustments of weight to changes in speed and vertical orientation of the bike. In terms of being a scientist, it means constructing correct theories in response to sets of data.

It will be assumed in this analysis that the only source of information about the desired relation is observation of input–output pairs exemplifying the desired relation. This assumption is not always totally accurate psychologically. In cases of chess, bike-riding, and theory construction there are principles and admonitions that are given to the learner as well as examples. Thus, the learner is given hints about what the correct relation is. However, one can question how useful these hints are to the learning process. The ACT model for induction (Section 12.3) will not make direct use of such hints. Moreover, in one very complex induction problem, language acquisition, it seems that learning relies almost totally on an exemplary information sequence. My belief is that, even when more direct instruction is available, one learns a procedure by performing examples of the behavior computed by that procedure. That is, one learns to do by doing.

Figure 12.1 provides the general framework in which to conceptualize the induction problem. The to-be-induced relation is formalized by a target machine. This target machine will generate the desired response to each input. The learner— the induction machine in Fig. 12.1—has access to the behavior of the target machine. In language learning the target machine might be an adult model. In learning chess the behavior of the target machine might be obtained by watching a master play. The final element in Fig. 12.1 is the hypothesis machine which is the learner's best guess as to the correct relation. In language acquisition the

[2]Good introductory expositions of formal automata are to be found in Hopcroft and Ullman (1969), Hunt (1975), and Minsky (1967).

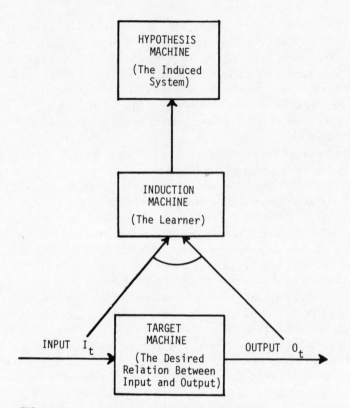

FIG. 12.1   A machine representation of the general induction problem.

hypothesis machine would be what generates the semigrammatical sentences of the learner. In chess the hypothesis machine would be the learner's current program for playing chess. It should be emphasized that the input to the induction machine is the input–output pair of the target machine. The output of the induction machine is the hypothesis machine. The induction problem is considered solved when a hypothesis machine is produced that mimics the behavior of the target machine.

The framework in Fig. 12.1 emphasizes that there are three procedures to be kept separate for purposes of formal analysis. Two of these, the induction machine and the hypothesis machine, are internal to the learner's head; the third, the target machine, is external.

There are a number of dimensions in which this induction problem can vary. One is the class of possible target machines or to-be-induced relations. Clearly, the larger this class of possible target machines, the harder it will be to induce the correct one. A second dimension is the sequence of the input–output pairs the learner sees. Is the sequence a purely random selection from the set of possible pairs (a set which is often infinite) or is it systematic in some way? Does the learner see all possible input–output pairs or only a selected subset? The third dimension is the learning algorithm embodied by the nature of the induction machine, and the fourth dimension is the criterion we choose for success. By placing rather minimal restrictions on the class of target machines, the information sequence, and the criterion for success, it is possible to prove the existence of a learning algorithm that will always succeed at a wide range of induction tasks. This algorithm provides a landmark concept in understanding the induction problem.

Nature of the Relation

There are two major possibilities about the relation between input and output. In the ahistorical case, the output at time t depends only on the input at time t. In the historical case, the output depends on the total past history of inputs. I will focus on the ahistorical case because it is more tractable and seems more representative of psychological situations that interest me (see Gold, 1965, for some analysis of the historical case). The correct interpretation of a sentence is not a function of all the past sentences encountered. Of course, it might depend on the context of the past few sentences. However, as long as the correct response depends only a bounded, finite portion of the immediately preceding inputs, the induction problem is equivalent to the ahistorical case. That finite portion of the past input can be regarded as the input at time t.

Focusing on the ahistorical case, we can ask what is the class of expected relations (target machines). One might take a restrictive view and assume the learner need only worry about learning a rather limited class such as those relations that could be generated by a finite state machine. Or, one might take a very unrestricted viewpoint and require that the learner be able to induce any relation that can be embodied by a Turing Machine. Initially, I will consider that the target machine might be any member of the class of machines that computes primitive recursive functions (see Minsky, 1967). I will call these primitive recursive automata or PRA. This is a very large class of machines but smaller than the class of all Turing Machines. The reason for selecting this class is that it is the largest set for which it is possible to show learnability. The PRA differ from Turing Machines principally in that the halting problem is always solvable for them (see Minsky, 1967) while it is not solvable for all Turing Machines.

The PRA would appear capable of performing all the behavior of which a human is capable. With respect to language, any context sensitive language can be recognized and/or generated by some PRA. There are no convincing arguments that I know of that any natural language is more complex than context sensitive. So it seems reasonable to suppose that all the linguistic feats of a human are capable of mimicry by a PRA. Therefore, if we have an algorithm which can induce a PRA, it should be capable of learning any human language.

Information Sequence

The one restriction that must be made on the nature of the information sequence is that there not be relevant input–output pairs to which the learner does not have access. That is to say, the learner could ask for and see the output for any input. This is a reasonable assumption since in most induction problems there are no input–output pairs which are in principle inaccessible to the learner. Formally, it is assumed that the information sequence, I, is a countable series of input–output pairs. The series may include repetitions but must include all input–output pairs. It may be infinite but all input–output pairs must have a finite position. Even though there may be infinitely many different pairs each can have finite position. For instance, there are infinitely many pairs in the series $(1,1), (2,2), (3,3), \ldots$ but each has finite position. An information sequence which satisfies this constraint will be called a *complete sequence*.

Criterion for Success

One cannot require that the hypothesis machine be identical to the target machine since there are different machines which will display the same behavior. Since the learner's only information is the behavior of the target machine he cannot know which of these equivalent machines is the target machine. But this is not a dilemma from the point of view of human induction. It should suffice that the hypothesis machine display the same behavior as the target machine. It is meaningless to require that it have the same form since the target machine was only a convenient fiction for formalizing the desired relation between input and output.

Let us say instead that the target machine is *identified in the limit* if, after some finite time, a hypothesis machine is constructed that mimics the target machine and the induction machine does not change the hypothesis machine thereafter. Note that there is no requirement that the induction machine announce that it has solved the problem. It can never really know it has achieved success since it is always possible it might encounter some unexpected input–output pair. This is the case with respect to language acquisition. One is never certain that he has learned all the rules of the language. (I occasionally find myself consulting Fowler's *English Usage* to get a remedial lesson.)

With these assumptions about the class of possible relations, the information sequence, and the criterion for success we are in a position to state the first theorem:

THEOREM 1: *There exists an algorithm which will identify in the limit any PRA given a complete information sequence.*

PROOF: Consider the following procedure which is called the *enumeration algorithm*. There is an effective enumeration of all PRA. By this I mean it is possible to order all PRA to correspond to the positive integers in such a way that an algorithm can be specified for generating the nth PRA. This enumeration gives an infinite sequence of PRA. For instance, the PRA could be ordered by an alphabetic enumeration of the rules which define the machines. Despite the fact that this enumeration is infinite, each PRA has some finite position in it.

The algorithm starts out considering the first PRA in the enumeration as the hypothesis and stays with it until it finds some input–output pair that is inconsistent with it. The algorithm then searches for the next PRA in the ordering which is consistent with all the existing data. It stays with that PRA until inconsistent evidence is found and then proceeds to the next consistent machine in the enumeration. Since the information sequence contains all input–output pairs it will reject any incorrect PRA after some finite time. Since the correct PRA occupies some finite position in the ordering and since each incorrect PRA preceding it will be rejected after a finite amount of information, the correct PRA will be uncovered after a finite time.   Q.E.D.

This theorem is significant. It shows that it is possible, in principle, to solve a very large class of induction problems—probably much larger than the set that humans face. I will return shortly to the enumeration algorithm identified in this proof and questions of its psychological reality. However, it would be useful to consider some variants of Theorem 1.

It is interesting to inquire whether it is possible to have identification in the limit for an arbitrary Turing Machine:

THEOREM 2:   *There exists no algorithm which can identify in the limit all Turing Machines.*

For a proof see Gold (1965, 1967). His proof relies on the notion of a *methodical informant,* which I do not want to spend time defining, and relating that to an *arbitrary informant,* the type of information sequence I have been assuming here.

I would like to establish two further theorems about identifiability of automata. These concern identification of nondeterministic automata and identification of automata with incomplete information sequences. Both theorems will prove very useful in the next section on language acquisition.

Nondeterministic Automata

Until now it has been assumed that the relation between input and output is deterministic. An interesting question concerns the situation when the relation is nondeterministic. That is, a particular input can map into a number of outputs. This is a realistic psychological situation, for instance, in the case of learning to speak a language. The same semantic intention can be expressed in a number of ways. To explore this question we must first define what we mean by a nondeterministic relation. A relation R between input and output is said to be nondeterministic if that relation can be expressed as a union of finite number of deterministic relations $R_1, R_2, \ldots, R_n$. Thus, the input pair $\langle i, o \rangle$ is in the nondeterministic relation R if any of the deterministic relations R_1–R_n map i into o. Given an input i, an automaton which computes R will sometimes have the output specified by each of the deterministic relations $R_1 \cdots R_n$. We will say an algorithm identifies a nondeterministic automaton in the limit if after some finite time it produces a hypothesis machine that will respond to each input with the same range of responses as the target machine. An information sequence will be said to be complete if it contains in finite position all the input–output pairs of the target nondeterministic automata.

THEOREM 3: *There is no algorithm which can identify in the limit any non-deterministic finite-state machine (FSM), given any complete information sequence.*

PROOF: Consider the following sequence of deterministic FSMs: M_0 is an arbitrary FSM. Let M_x be a FSM that does not map any input into the same output as M_0. M_1 is the same as M_0, except it maps 1 onto the output onto which M_x maps 1. M_2 is the same as M_1 except it maps 2 onto the output onto which M_x maps 2. Similarly, one can define the rest of an infinite sequence. M_n will differ from M_0 in that it maps inputs, 1 to n, onto the output of M_x.[3] Each M_n is an FSM.

Suppose there were an algorithm, A, that would identify any nondeterministic FSM. Let I_0 be a complete information sequence generated by M_0. A will identify M_0 after some finite time t_0. Let I_{t_0} be the finite portion of I_0 up until this point. I_{t_0} could have been generated by the nondeterministic FSM $M_0 \cup M_1$. Consider some extension, I_1, of I_{t_0} which is complete for $M_0 \cup M_1$. Then A will change its guess from M_0 to $M_0 \cup M_1$ at some finite time $t_1 > t_0$. Let I_{t_1} be the finite sequence of I_1 up until t_1. In general, we can create from $I_{t_{n-1}}$ an extension I_n which is complete for $M_0 \cup M_n$. By hypothesis A will change its guess from $M_0 \cup M_{n-1}$ to $M_0 \cup M_n$ after some finite time t_n. Thus, we also have a general definition for I_n. Define $I^* = \lim_{n\to\infty} I_n$. I^* is an information sequence which will cause A to change its guess infinitely many times. It is a sequence consistent with the nondeterministic automata $M_0 \cup M_x$ and has every input–output pair of $M_0 \cup M_x$ in finite position. Therefore, I^* is complete for $M_0 \cup M_x$. However, A will never identify $M_0 \cup M_x$ given I^*. Therefore, A cannot identify all nondeterministic FSMs.   Q.E.D.

The above theorem establishes that it is not possible to identify in the limit any nondeterministic FSM. It follows, then, that it is not possible to identify non-deterministic automata that come from larger classes of machines like the PRA.

Incomplete Information Sequences

It is possible that the learner might not have a complete information sequence. For instance, in learning a language we may not encounter sentences longer than a

---

[3]The notion of an FSM operating on integers might seem a bit bizarre to some. It might help to think of the FSM as operating on a binary encoding of the integers.

certain bound. It is possible that the rules of the language might be different than we hypothesize for these unseen sentences. Since we never encounter them we will never know. However, this platonic dilemma is really not a practical problem because we will never be tested on these unseen sentences so our deficiency will not appear.

The following theorem establishes the fact that unseen instances do not matter if they are also not tested. First, two preliminary definitions are required. An information sequence is complete for a set I of inputs if each of these inputs and their corresponding outputs occur at some finite position in the sequence. An algorithm identifies a target machine in the limit for a set I if it can induce a hypothesis machine that mimics the target machine on set I.

THEOREM 4: *There exists an algorithm that will identify in the limit any PRA for set I_1 given a complete information sequence for set I_2 iff I_1 is a subset of I_2.*

PROOF: Suppose I_1 is a subset of I_2. Then the enumeration algorithm outlined earlier will identify the PRA in the limit for I_1. This follows from the fact that there is, in the enumeration of all PRA, a first machine that mimics the target machine on set I_2. This may be a machine equivalent to the target PRA on all input or not. Because this machine has finite position and because the sequence is complete for I_2 this machine will be selected in finite time. Since I_1 is a subset of I_2, the algorithm has identified the PRA for I_1.

Suppose I_1 is not a subset of I_2. Then consider some i from I_1 but not I_2 and its corresponding output o. The target PRA, call it A_1, generates the pair $\langle i, o \rangle$. Consider a second PRA, A_2, identical to A_1 for all input except for i for which it generates output o'. Suppose there was an algorithm which could identify all PRA in the limit for I_1 given a sequence complete for I_2. Then this algorithm would identify A_1 in the limit given some information sequence I^* complete for I_2. Then its guess machine, G_1, will generate the pair $\langle i, o \rangle$. The information sequence I^* could also have been generated by A_2. Faced with A_2 as its target machine and the sequence I^* the algorithm would also guess G_1. However, G_1 does not mimic A_2 on the input I_2. This contradicts the hypothesis that there exists an algorithm which will identify in the limit for I_1 all PRA with a sequence complete for I_2. Q.E.D.

The Enumeration Algorithm

The enumeration algorithm used in these proofs is not particularly plausible psychologically. It was used to show the existence of some algorithm to solve the induction problem. It does not, of course, follow from these proofs that the enumeration algorithm is the only algorithm or even the best. The enumeration algorithm assumes that the subject searches all possible relations while looking for a correct one. There is some evidence that subjects may do something like this in a simple concept attainment task (for example, Trabasso & Bower, 1968) where there is a small, finite number of possibilities. However, this exhaustive search strategy is clearly out of the question in a situation like language learning. Nonetheless, it provides a conceptually simple procedure against which to compare other procedures.

There are two computational aspects of the enumeration algorithm that make it undesirable. Recall that it tests the behavior of the hypothesis machine against each input–output pair it observes from the target machine. If the hypothesis machine is in error it then transits to the next machine in the enumeration compatible with all the input–output so far. The first problem with the enumeration algorithm is that it is very costly to change its hypothesis. It must remember all past input–output pairs in the sequence so it can test machines subsequent in the enumeration to the rejected hypothesis machine. This places an enormous memory burden on the algorithm. Also there may be astronomically many machines between the old hypothesis machine and the first acceptable one in the enumeration. Therefore, it will take astronomically long to find the next hypothesis machine because the algorithm must check all these intermediate machines.

One can remove the requirement that the machine remember all past input–output pairs by arranging for an information sequence in which input–output pairs are repeated infinitely often. Then, whenever one adopts an incorrect hypothesis machine, information will later come in to reject it. This is what Hamburger and Wexler (1975) assume in their work on learning transformational grammars. This seems a reasonable assumption; that is, it is unreasonable to assume that we hear sentences just once in our life with no possibility of having them later repeated.[4] However, one pays a price for giving up the memory requirement. One will be much slower in finding the correct machine. Hypothesis machines which could be rejected out of hand because of memory for past information will not be rejected until the information is repeated.

It seems possible to avoid testing all the machines in the enumeration between an old rejected hypothesis and the first acceptable alternative.[5] For instance, one might be able to organize the machines according to some sort of tree structure. On the basis of one piece of evidence, a whole branch of the tree might be rejected. This sort of structuring has been done with some success with simpler machines such as finite-state machines (see Biermann, 1972; Pao, 1969). This will not reduce the number of trials to success, but will cut down on the amount of computation per trial. (A trial is an input–output pair.)

The second problem with the enumeration algorithm does not concern the amount of computation per trial, but rather the number of trials to reach success.

---

[4]For this procedure to work it is not necessary that all sentences are actually repeated. It is only necessary that the learner be able to obtain repeated information about a sentence, if he desires it.

[5]There is no reason why other induction algorithms need enumerate all possible machines in order to achieve identification in the limit. However, there is another sense in which all induction algorithms produce at least a partial enumeration of the machines. That is, we can consider as an enumeration the sequence of hypothesis machines they produce en route to the correct hypothesis.

That is, how many input–output pairs must the enumeration algorithm consider before identifying the target machine? There are an infinite number of PRAs compatible with any finite set of input–output pairs. Therefore, an arbitrary PRA will require an astronomical number of trials before it can be identified. Of course, there are a few PRAs early in the enumeration which will be identified quickly. However, almost all PRAs will take *very* long to identify. Given any finite bound on the number of trials to criterion a finite number of PRAs will be identified within that bound but an infinite number will take longer than that bound for identification. This is true despite the fact that the enumeration algorithm will identify all PRAs in finite time. Thus, one is motivated to inquire whether there is an algorithm faster than the enumeration algorithm. To explore this question we need to define the notion of one algorithm being uniformly faster than another. Algorithm A is uniformly faster than Algorithm A' if (a) A will identify all target machines for all information sequences at least as fast as A' and (b) A will identify at least one target machine faster for at least one information sequence.

THEOREM 5: *There is no algorithm that can identify PRAs uniformly faster than the enumeration algorithm.*

PROOF: Suppose there was an algorithm, A, which was uniformly faster than the enumeration algorithm, E. Then there must be some machine, M, which it identifies faster for some information sequence, I. Let n be the trial at which A first guesses M. On that trial E must guess some other machine M_1. M_1 is consistent with the information sequence so far observed. Suppose the target machine really were M_1 rather than M. Then E would identify M_1 by Trial n, given an information sequence I_1 for M_1 identical to I until trial n. Since A's guess on trial n is M, it would only identify M_1 on a later trial.   Q.E.D.

One might wonder how much of this difficulty is due to the fact that we are considering all PRA. Therefore, it is instructive to consider the corresponding theorem for finite-state machines (FSMs).

THEOREM 6: *There is no algorithm which can identify FSMs uniformly faster than the enumeration algorithm operating on an enumeration of all FSMs.*

PROOF: Identical to that for Theorem 5.

It is worth noting here that if E is faster than A on one information sequence, it is faster than A on uncountably infinitely many sequences. Let I be an information sequence for which E identifies M on trial t before A identifies M. Let I_t be the subsequence of I up to trial t. There are uncountably infinitely many ways to extend I_t, besides I, which are consistent with M. Each extension gives a different information sequence on which E is faster than A.

Given that the enumeration algorithm is so hopelessly slow, given that there is no algorithm uniformly faster, and given that humans do solve induction problems, there must be something wrong with the framework set up. There are generally thought to be two possible differences between the psychological situation and this formal framework. First, the information sequence may contain hints as to the desired target machine and the learner expects such hints and takes advantage of them. For instance, a language learner might do well to assume that the initial simple sentences he encountered provide all the basic rules of the language and that later more complex sentences derive from recursive application of the simple rules identified by the earlier sentences.

The second solution is that all target machines may not be equally likely and that the learner's hypotheses progress from the more likely machines to the less likely. For instance, suppose the machines were ordered, such that the nth machine had probability $a(1 - a)^{n-1}$ of being the correct machine. That is, there was a geometric probability density across the possible machines. Then the mean number of machines that need to be considered before the correct machine would be $1/a$. Even if the probability of a particular machine being correct is very small (for example, $a = .000001$), the mean time to success would avoid astronomical values. Horning (1969) and Feldman (1970) have proposed that machines are ordered by complexity. Chomsky (1965) has proposed that in the language learning situation the learner has a very restricted hypothesis space as to what might be possible machines and only considers these. Chomsky's proposal amounts to an ordering scheme in which there is first a set of plausible machines in the enumeration, each with finite probability, followed by a set of implausible machines each with zero probability.

Thus we have come to what is a significant psychological conclusion. We have shown that any induction algorithm which assumes nothing about the induction problems will be hopelessly slow. A successful algorithm must be prepared to process hints from the information sequence or it must incorporate assumptions about what is a plausible solution. I think humans do make rather strong assumptions about what does and what does not constitute a plausible solution. This can be seen by considering a number of induction situations and noting those relations which humans have success inducing and those at which they have difficulty. This should give some indication as to the nature of the induction algorithm they are using:

Concept formation.   The typical concept formation task is one in which a picture is presented that may vary in a number of dimensions. For instance, a picture might be presented of one, two, or three objects. The objects may be red, blue, or green; square, circle, or triangle; have 1, 2, or 3 borders. In this example there are $3 \times 3 \times 3 \times 3 = 81$ possible objects. The subject is to decide what defines a concept by seeing exemplars of the concept. Subjects (see Johnson, 1972, for a review) do better at inducing conjunctive concepts like *two squares* over disjunctive concepts like *either two objects or squares*. Subjects find great difficulty with other relations that are not really more complex. For instance, the concept might be that the number of objects and the number of borders sum to 4. Needless to say, such a concept does not readily occur to a subject.

Sequence learning. Subjects in sequence learning experiments have to learn how to extrapolate a sequence of 1's and 0's. For instance, how should one continue 1 1 1 0 1 1 1 0 1? Subjects tend to come up with rules about runs of 1's and 0's. Subjects, even with math training, are unlikely to notice that this is a sequence of Fibonacci numbers coded in binary.

Pattern learning. Suppose we had to learn to distinguish between a flower of species X and one of species Y. One is unlikely to consider whether the number of petals on flower X is prime.

Language learning. Language learners assume that adjectives preceding the subject noun modify that noun and that adjectives preceding the object noun modify it. They do not consider the possibility that adjectives in the subject noun phrase modify the object noun or vice versa.

Implications for the Rationalist–Empiricist Controversy

If one takes either solution to the induction dilemma posed by Theorems 5 and 6 one has, in a sense, taken a rationalist position. That is, one assumes that, explicit or implicit in the induction mechanism, there are some strong innate assumptions about the nature of the induction problem. The first approach, assuming hints in the information sequence, claims the learner knows these hints will be present and operates according to them. If he is faced with an induction problem that contains no hints or false hints he will fail. The second approach assumes that the learner knows what the likely relations are before he begins the learning attempt. If he is given a relation (for example, a language) that violates his initial assumptions he will either not learn it or take astronomically long to learn it.

It is worth noting that we can assume that the human learner has innate knowledge about language without assuming that he has any special language facility. We also need not assume there has been an evolutionary process in which a mechanism was evolved explicitly for language learning or other induction problems. It is possible that man came upon a set of induction mechanisms purely at random. Subsequent to the creation of these induction mechanisms and to their genetic encoding, languages evolved. Since languages must be capable of being transferred from parent to child, they needed to be ones that could be induced. Thus, it may be that randomly determined induction procedures determined the shape of natural languages. Given that most of the relations humans try to induce are man-made objects like language, it is perhaps not surprising that they have such success at the typical induction tasks they face. That is, it seems reasonable that man only creates to-be-induced objects that he can induce.

The problem of the psychologist, of course, is not to settle the question about the origin of the innate assumptions about to-be-induced objects. Rather, it is to identify what these assumptions are. That is, by looking at the behavior of subjects in induction tasks the psychologist must try to induce the hints that the learner is expecting and the assumptions he is making.

This a particularly thorny and convoluted scientific problem. The psychologist must be aware that the human subject expects the psychologist to give him certain types of problems and/or certain hints and that the psychologist probably has an implicit and hard-to-resist tendency to comply with the subject's expectation. However, the psychologist cannot identify what the subject's expectations are unless he gives the subject problems that violate these expectations. In this regard a useful function can be served by the formal framework established in this section. That is, by comparing the problems we want to pose to our subjects with the space of possible problems, we might be better able to see new ways to study induction.

Application to Scientific Induction

There is reason for a child coming into the world to be optimistic about the induction problems he will face, despite Theorems 5 and 6. This is because he knows the induction problems posed to him by his community are problems that other children like him have solved with their induction mechanisms. However, there is no reason for us, as scientists, to be so optimistic at the outset about our induction problems. The formal framework in Fig. 12.1 applies perfectly to scientific inductions. The target machine in Fig. 12.1 would be that aspect of the world we wish to explain. We can either perform controlled experiments on it or observe natural experiments. These experiments will provide us with input–output information. That is, they give information about how a particular system (for example, a human) responds to certain inputs. The hypothesis machine is our scientific theory at the current time.

There are many a priori reasons to be pessimistic about this induction task. First of all, there is no reason to assume that there are any constraints on the possible input–output relations. The number of possible input–output relations is *uncountably infinite* which is many more than the number of theories that can be described in our natural language which is countably infinite.[6] Second, even assuming sufficient restrictions on the possible input–output relationships so that they are describable, there still is no reason to be optimistic. For instance, suppose all we knew was that the to-be-induced relationship was describable by a Turing Machine. Then we know (Theorem 2) it is not possible to identify that relation.

If it were the case that any relation in nature could be described by a PRA or some machine from a smaller class like finite-state machines, then the scientific induction problem would have a solution in the limit. There are so-called "plausibility" arguments that this is the case. For instance, with respect to the psychological induction problem, one might argue from physiological considerations that

---

[6]A countably infinite set is one whose members can be put in correspondence with the positive integers. An uncountably infinite set is one which has more members than can be put into correspondence with the positive integers.

because man has finite memory he is equivalent to a finite-state machine. However, even if man were some finite-state machine and even if we could put some finite (but astronomical) limit on his number of states it would take astronomically long to identify the correct finite-state machine if it were arbitrarily chosen.

So, all in all, it is remarkable that science is possible. However, God or luck has happened to bless us with a universe where some scientific progress has been made—even a little progress has been made in psychology. This must mean that, just as in the case of the child, the scientist's induction mechanisms are fortuituously in tune with the nature of the universe. There are probably many important assumptions that permit scientific progress, but I have only been able to discern three:

Nature is simple.   There is a rough principle of parsimony in science. Consideration of theories tends to go from the simple to the complex. This manner of progression works because nature tends to admit of simple explanations. However, a universe could be constructed in which a pure principle of parsimony would be far from an optimal strategy. Scientists apparently do not exhaust all the simple theories before trying more complex ones. Evidence for this is the fact that major theoretical breakthroughs occur when someone sees how a different theory will characterize a set of data currently handled by a more complex theory. The reason scientists do not exhaust all the simpler theories first is that they have no way to enumerate systematically, in order of complexity, all the possible theories compatible with a set of data.

Failures are uniformly distributed.   Few theories explain all the relevant phenomena. There always are exceptions. However, there is an assumption that if a theory has predicted on an a priori basis 95% of the phenomena so far, it will continue to have that track record with new phenomena, and if it is off by a small amount on the remaining 5% it will tend to continue to be off by corresponding small amounts with new phenomena. This means that even if our theories cannot be correct, we can know if they are good approximations.

There are hints in the data.   As noted earlier the induction problem becomes much simpler if the information sequence contains hints as to the to-be-induced relation. One of the strongest types of hints, which seems to be applicable in many problems, is that one can uniquely identify the state of the to-be-induced system from various observational indices. For instance, when a mechanical spring is in a certain position it is always in the same state and will respond identically to various inputs (manipulations). The induction problem is much easier if we can identify the state a system is in. This is not the case for humans. The number of states in which the human system can be is much greater than manifested by its overt measurable behaviors. However, in psychology there is the hope, justified or not, that our introspections and intuitions provide hints as to internal mechanisms. This is part of the justification for allowing pretheoretical biases to influence theory construction (see Section 4.1).

If this view of scientific induction is correct it justifies numerous attitudes expressed in Chapter 1 and elsewhere. First, the nature of scientific progress is one of enumerating hypotheses looking for the correct one.[7] The speed of progress depends on one's ability to prove current hypotheses wrong and try new ones. Thus, the frequently expressed complaint about psychology, that theories are proven wrong so rapidly, is really a virtue and a sign of progress. However, we should not lose track of the fact that the correct theory is probably very far down the road in the enumeration of hypotheses. Therefore, we must be prepared to accept for temporary purposes approximately correct theories. This makes important the criterion of broad generality, because the greater the data base on which our theory has proven approximately correct the more probable it will maintain that degree of correctness elsewhere. There are two bases for constructing new theories. One is parsimony and the other is intuition or preconceived bias. Finally, the criterion for success in psychology must be that the predictions of the theory mimic the phenomena. Unique identifiability is not possible. This is particularly the case in behavioral psychology where we do not have information on the internal states of the system.

12.2   APPLICATION OF RESULTS ON INDUCTION
TO LANGUAGE ACQUISITION

The purpose of this section is to continue the formal analysis of induction of the preceding section but to specialize it for the case of language acquisition. First, we will consider some results that characterize the syntactic approach. The goal in this approach is to induce an algorithm that will be able to identify the grammatical sentences of the language and separate these from ungrammatical strings. While this syntactic approach has dubious psychological relevance it was the first formal approach and results from it can be transferred in part to a semantic approach to language acquisition. The goal of the semantic approach is to induce an algorithm which permits one to go from a sentence to a characterization of its meaning and also to go from meaning to sentence. This is clearly much closer to the psychological problem of language acquisition. A syntactic characterization of the language emerges as a by-product, only, of the *map* acquired between sentence and meaning. Ungrammatical sentences are those which do not properly map into an interpretation.

Syntactic approach

The syntactic approach can be placed into the formal framework of Fig. 12.1. The target machine in this case maps strings of words onto a binary output—grammatical versus ungrammatical. The task of the inducer is to develop a hypoth-

---

[7]Unfortunately, since this enumeration is not systematic one might worry that the correct hypothesis might be overlooked.

esis machine which mimics the behavior of the target machine. To do this is to induce a syntactic characterization of the target language.

The psychological equivalent of this abstract model is a learner who hears strings of words marked as sentence or nonsentence. It is easy to see how the human learner would receive the positive information about what is a sentence. Every time someone utters a sentence he can assume it is grammatical. It is much less clear how he would learn what are nonsentences. We might consider him trying out nonsentences and being corrected. However, this does not correspond to the facts of the matter (Brown, 1973; Braine, 1971). Language learners do not try out all combinations of words. Second, they are often not corrected when they utter a syntactically incorrect sentence. Third, they appear to make little use of what negative feedback they get. However, it needs to be emphasized that this framework assumes that the human learner gets both positive and negative feedback. Assuming positive and negative information the following theorem is true.

THEOREM 7: *There is an algorithm that will identify any primitive recursive language in the limit provided there is a complete information sequence containing all sentences and nonsentences.*

PROOF: A direct result of Theorem 1 (page 496).

The primitive recursive class of languages is very large and I know of no coherent argument that any natural language is not induced in this class. It does contain all context-sensitive languages but it does not include all languages that can be generated by transformational grammars (see Peters & Richie, 1971).

Also the results about learning time can be directly translated to the language acquisition problem. For any sequence of information about sentences and nonsentences there is no algorithm uniformly faster than the enumeration algorithm. An induction algorithm can be faster than the enumeration algorithm only if it is taking advantage of valid constraints on the possible languages or about hints in the information sequence. In this case it is not uniformly faster but is faster on the relevant problems.

Positive Information Only

One might wonder what would happen if the inducer were only given positive examples of sentences in the language. This seems to be the information that a human receives. The following theorem establishes that identification is not possible in this case. It uses the concept of a superfinite class of languages. A superfinite class of languages consists of all languages of finite cardinality (that is, languages that contain only finitely many grammatical sentences) plus one language of infinite cardinality. Most interesting classes of languages such as the finite-state languages contain a superfinite class of languages.

THEOREM 8: *No class of languages which contains a superfinite class is identifiable in the limit given only positive information.*

PROOF: The proof of this theorem is similar in abstract structure to the proof of Theorem 3. Consider a sequence of finite cardinality languages $L_1, L_2, \ldots$, etc., such that for all n, $L_n \subset L_{n+1}$ and $L_n \subset L$ where L is an infinite cardinality language. Moreover, it is required of this sequence that $L = \bigcup_{n=1}^{\infty} L_n$. Suppose an algorithm, A, exists that will identify any member of a superfinite class given only positive information. Then for any information sequence I_1 consistent with L_1 there is a finite time t_1 such that A will identify L_1. Let I_{t_1} be the finite portion of the sequence up to t_1. One can create a new sequence I_2 identical to I_1 up to t, but which is complete for L_2. By assumption, given this sequence A will identify L_2 at finite time t_2. Define as I_{t_2} the information sequence I_2 up to t_2. In a similar way one can define I_n for each n. Define $I^* = \lim_{n \to \infty} I_n$. I^* is an information sequence complete for L, but one for which A will never identify L. Q.E.D.

There are a number of circumstances in which the syntax-based approach will yield identification of the target language without negative information. All these require that stronger assumptions be made about the learning situation. Either the class of languages must be very restricted or there must be hints in the learning situation.

The work of Horning (1969) gives one example where, by assuming a rather minimal structure in the information sequence, one is able to achieve language learning with only positive information. He achieves this by assigning probabilities to grammars in the light of the observed sample of sentences. He assigns to each rule in a grammar a certain probability. One case he considers is where the rewrite rules involving a particular nonterminal are equiprobable. For instance, consider the following simple grammar and example derivation in it:

$$S \rightarrow X\ S\ Y \quad \Pr = 1/2$$
$$\rightarrow c \quad\quad\ \Pr = 1/2$$
$$X \rightarrow a\ X\ a \quad \Pr = 1/2$$
$$\rightarrow b \quad\quad\ \Pr = 1/2$$
$$Y \rightarrow b\ Y\ b \quad \Pr = 1/2$$
$$\rightarrow a \quad\quad\ \Pr = 1/2$$

$$S \rightarrow X\ S\ Y \rightarrow a\ X\ a\ S\ Y \rightarrow a\ b\ a\ S\ Y \rightarrow a\ b\ a\ c\ Y \rightarrow a\ b\ a\ c\ a$$

Each of the nonterminals $(S, X, \text{and } Y)$ is involved in two rewrite rules. Therefore, each rule has probability $1/2$. The reader may verify that the probability of this particular string, *abaca*, is $1/32$.

Horning assumes that the information sequence being observed is being produced by a stochastic grammar which is generating sentences according to a set of probabilities. His goal is to select the most probable grammar in the light of the evidence. In deciding the most probable grammar, Horning has to select the grammar G_i which maximizes the following quantity:

$$P(G_i|S) = \frac{P(G_i)P \ (S|G_i)}{P(S)}$$

where $P(G_i|S)$ is the probability of the grammar G_i given the sample $S;$ $P(G_i)$ is the prior probability of the grammar; $P(S|G_i)$ is the probability of the sample given G_i; and $P(S)$ is the prior probability of the sample. This is, of course, just Bayes Theorem. To maximize $P(G_i|S)$, an algorithm must maximize the combination of $P(G_i)$ and $P(S|G_i)$. The value of $P(S|G_i)$ can be computed from the probabilities assigned to individual rules in the grammar. It is less obvious how to measure $P(G_i)$. Horning introduces a "grammar-grammar" which generates grammars in a canonical form. By associating probabilities with the rewrite rules in the grammar-grammar it is possible to assign a probability to a grammar derived from it—just as it is possible to assign probabilities to sentences derived from a grammar. Horning proves that it is not only possible to select a correct grammar in this situation, but also to select the most probable grammar of the equivalent correct grammars.

Horning also points out that in selecting the most probable grammar he is also selecting the simplest. Here simplicity is measured by the number of rules in the grammar and the number of applications of rules needed to derive sentences in the sample. The more rules in the grammar, the lower the probability of deriving the grammar from the grammar-grammar. The more applications of rules required to derive a sentence from the grammar, the lower the probability of the sentence in the grammar. Thus, Horning's procedures can be interpreted as trying to maximize the simplicity of a grammar which is a frequently stated linguistic goal. That probability and simplicity should be related is just what one would expect from information theory.

The Semantics Approach

The importance of semantics has been very forcefully brought home to psychologists by a pair of experiments by Moeser and Bregman (1972, 1973) on the induction of artificial languages. They compared language learning in the situation where their subjects only saw well-formed strings of the language versus the situation where they saw well-formed strings plus pictures of the semantic referents of these strings. In either case, the criterion test was for the subject to be able to detect which strings of the language were well formed, without the aid of any referent pictures. After 3000 training trials subjects in the no-referent condition were at chance in the criterion test, whereas subjects in the referent condition were essentially perfect.

It was shown earlier, with respect to the syntax approach, that the induction problem was not too hopeful unless there were constraints on the problem. Successful learning could only be guaranteed given complete information about nonsentences (a very implausible assumption) and even then only with astronomical learning time. If successful and rapid language learning is to occur under the syntax approach, strong assumptions about the learning problem have to be incorporated into the induction algorithm. One might wonder how much different things are under the same semantic approach. Results like those of Moeser and Bregman have left some believing that there must be magical powers associated with having a semantic referent—that one can have rapid success under the semantics approach without the strong assumptions that seem to be required for the syntax approach. To explore this issue I have tried to put the semantics approach to a formal analysis. The outcome of these formal analyses indicates that there is no particular advantage to the semantics approach. Success here, too, will only be guaranteed if the induction algorithm incorporates strong assumptions and these assumptions are satisfied by the language learning problem. Subjects in the referent condition of Moeser and Bergman's experiment succeeded because the problems posed to them satisfied these assumptions. I have created (Anderson, 1975, 1976) referent conditions which are no more helpful than no-referent conditions.

To pursue a formal analysis of the semantics approach, I will cast language learning with a semantic referent into a formal framework like Fig. 12.1. Comprehension and generation fit differently into this framework. In comprehension we regard sentences as inputs to the target machine and semantic representations as outputs. In generation we regard semantic intentions as input and sentences as outputs. First we will consider the situation where each sentence has a unique semantic referent and each semantic referent has a unique sentence. That is, there is no real ambiguity or synonymy in the language. This is not a realistic assumption but it allows the following theorem to be proven.

THEOREM 9:   *There is an algorithm which will identify in the limit any deterministic PRA for understanding sentences or any deterministic PRA for generating sentences given a complete information sequence of sentences and their meanings.*

PROOF: This theorem follows from Theorem 4. In understanding, the learner encounters a subset of all inputs or strings, the grammatical sentences, and their corresponding outputs. However, this is also the set on which the learner will be tested. In terms of Theorem 4, the test set I_1 is identical to the presentation set I_2. Thus I_1 is a subset of I_2. Theorem 4 identifies this as a sufficient condition for identification in the limit. Similarly, in generation the learner only sees the inputs corresponding to the well-formed semantic structures. However, again this is not a problem because the test set equals the study set.   Q.E.D.

THEOREM 10:   *There is no algorithm which can identify in the limit any FSM for speaking a language with synonymy or for understanding a language with ambiguity.*

PROOF: To represent speaking a language which has synonymous sentences one needs a nondeterministic relation mapping meanings into sentences. To represent understanding a language which has ambiguity one needs a nondeterministic relation mapping sentences into meaning. By Theorem 3 such nondeterministic relations are not generally learnable.   Q.E.D.

Theorems 9 and 10 provide a rather different picture of the language learning situation under the semantics approach than Theorems 7 and 8 gave of the situation under the syntax approach. Theorem 9 shows a situation where learnability is assured given an information sequence consisting of only sentences and no non-sentences. It requires that the learner have access to all sentences and their meanings. This is a more reasonable assumption about the information sequence than the assumption underlying Theorem 7 which was that the learner had access to negative information about ungrammatical sentences. However, the semantics picture, while different, is not more optimistic than the syntax picture. Theorem 10 shows that if we make the plausible assumptions of ambiguity or synonymy in the language, there is no longer a formal guarantee of learnability. Also, even without ambiguity and synonymy, there is the problem of efficiency. Theorem 5 is valid as a qualification on Theorem 9. That is, there is no induction algorithm for the semantics approach uniformly faster than the hopelessly slow enumeration algorithm.

Another difficulty in the semantics approach is that it offers no explanation of how it is that humans are able to make judgments about the grammaticality of sentences. The information the learner receives is about sentences and their semantic interpretations. He is given no information about what to do with non-sentences. Theorem 9 provides no guarantee that his language comprehension mechanism will map nonsentences into judgments of ungrammaticality. However, the mechanisms that humans acquire to relate natural language sentences to their meanings do relate nonsentences to judgments of unacceptability.

The following is one way to conceive of how humans emerge with a syntactic characterization of the language when they are only attempting to induce a semantic characterization: Suppose that the semantic procedures humans induce have the property that they fail to map some strings of words into any meaning (that is, they are partial functions). Suppose that the strings which cannot be mapped are judged as ungrammatical. Then, the semantic routine would induce, by accident, a syntactic characterization of the language. It might seem remarkable on this account that the semantic procedures should fail to map just those strings that are ungrammatical. However, this is not so remarkable when one realizes that the linguistic community which judges grammaticality came to its definition of grammaticality by the same induction mechanisms that the new language learner must use.

A question that can be asked about the semantics approach is whether it is necessary to separately learn to speak and to comprehend or whether one can learn to do one function and simply perform the other by computing its inverse. It is always possible in principle to compute one function from its inverse. Suppose one had a procedure to generate sentences. That procedure could be used to comprehend sentences by applying it within the following algorithm: Given a sentence to comprehend one could begin enumerating semantic structures and generating sentences to express these referents. He would continue doing this until he generated a sentence that matched the to-be-comprehended sentence. The meaning of the to-be-comprehended sentence would be the last semantic structure he had generated. Obviously, this analysis-by-synthesis procedure would be impossible as a practical algorithm but it shows that there always exists at least one inverse procedure. There may also be very efficient inverses. I have worked with language processing formalisms which are neutral to the issue of generation versus comprehension and can be used with equal facility in either direction (see Anderson, 1975, 1976).

12.3   SUGGESTIONS FOR INDUCTION IN ACT

It would be useful to start out with an overview of how induction is to be conceived of within the ACT framework. ACT productions are basically specifications that the activation of a certain memory structure (the condition) should be followed by the activation of another memory structure (the action). There are other aspects to conditions and actions having to do with testing values of variables, setting variables, unbinding variables, making variables global, etc. However, these aspects are all technical means of directing the principal functions of productions which is to have the activation of one memory structure result in the activation of another memory structure. When a particular pattern of activation is followed by another pattern of activation, an ACT production is set up to encode this contingency as a condition–action pair. This is the *only* way productions are set up. This assumption embodies the classic stimulus–response wisdom that we learn to do by doing (see page 122). The original production is an encoding of the specific pattern of activation and at first is quite weak. However, by means of generalization and repeated successful applications that production will come to deal with a general class of patterns and will be strengthened.

A procedure in ACT will be correct only if it consists of the correct productions. These productions will be established only if there existed the correct contingencies of activation of condition patterns followed by activation of action patterns. Arranging for such contingencies is an important problem but will not be given much attention here. As an example of how such contingencies might be arranged, consider how a production system might be set up to perform in one of the experiments on fact retrieval or inference making modeled in Chapter 8 and Section 9.4. It is assumed that the subject encodes the instructions declaratively, that is, in the propositional network. Further, it is assumed that the subject has a general interpretative procedure (encoded in production form) that will enable him to follow these instructions. As a consequence of following these instructions, the subject creates the desired activation contingencies in memory. These activation contingencies are transformed by a production inducer into the production systems displayed in Chapter 8 and Section 9.4. In general I think experimental instructions are initially encoded declaratively but are transformed into productions as a consequence of performing the experimental task. This is why subjects are always given practice trials before beginning the experiment. The effect of these practice trials is to set up the requisite production system.

Note that this view of induction is not concerned with directly relating external patterns of stimulation to external patterns of response. Rather it is concerned with internal patterns of activation. Figure 12.2 outlines schematically how a production comes to be induced. The external environment provides some indication of the desired condition–action pairs by inputting C and A. The stimulus C will eventually be transformed to the condition of the production and A will eventually be transformed to the action. (C and A need not be distinct.) They

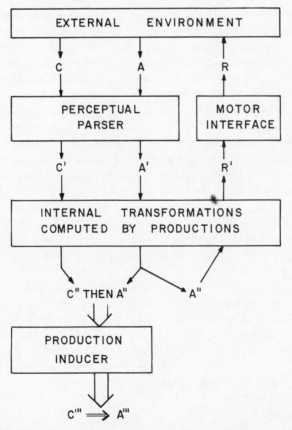

FIG. 12.2   External specifications of the condition–action pair, C and A, are converted by the perceptual parser and internal transformations into C'' and A''. From these a production is induced. Also A'' can be mapped onto an external response R.

will be transformed by the perceptual parser to network forms C' and A'. To these, various productions might apply, transforming them before the desired pairing is achieved. This transformed pair manifests itself as the pattern C'' followed by A''. The production inducer in response to this contingency creates the production $C''' \Rightarrow A'''$ which will reproduce A'' when C'' is active. Note also in Fig. 12.2 that A'' can be mapped by various productions onto a network specification of a response R'. This is in turn mapped into a response R by the motor interface.

It would be useful to instantiate the framework in Fig. 12.2 with a couple of examples. Consider the problem of teaching someone to understand a language. In that case one might present the learner with a sentence (C) and a picture (A) depicting the meaning of the sentence. The sentence would be transformed by the perceptual encoder into a network encoding (C') of the word adjacencies in the sentence (see Fig. 4.8, page 136) and the picture would also be converted into a network representation (A'). In this case, assume that there are no internal transformations so C'' = C' and A'' = A'. The production inducer then produces a production (or a series of productions) which will respond to the network encoding of a sentence by creating a network encoding of the picture. Then, if the sentence is later presented alone the induced productions would generate the picture representation as the meaning of the sentence.

As another example consider the case of a subject in the fact retrieval task of Chapter 8 after he has just committed the instructions to memory in propositional network form. In this case, the input from the external environment is a probe that is encoded according to word adjacencies. This provides the condition (C'). In this case there is no specification of the action. However, the general interpretative productions will apply the network instructions to C'. The outcome will be the activation, A'', of a network structure encoding the correct response. Thus, activation A'' is paired with C' = C''. A production is induced which will now respond to the activation of pattern C' with response A''. Note A'' in this case involves a response specification (that is, R') and will result in the emission of an external response R.

The general framework in Fig. 12.2 will require considerable specification before it can be regarded as an operative model. The directions this specification will take are discussed below under five headings. After this discussion I will provide a pair of illustrative examples of how ACT might go about the induction of simple sequential patterns. The specifications given in the following discussion and examples are highly tentative. They are provided to give the interested reader a sense of how induction might progress in ACT.

1. Effects of Preprocessing.   Note in Fig. 12.2 that the production inducer does not operate on the external objects C and A. Rather it operates on the obejcts C'' and A'' which have undergone transformations due to the perceptual parser and possibly also due to internal transformations computed by existing productions. The success of an induction routine depends upon the right description. For instance, one is much more likely to be able to solve the Fibonacci example given earlier (page 503) if he had regarded the 0's and 1's as digits (rather than arbitrary symbols) and was able to properly chunk them into units. Gestalt variables like similarity and continuity may play a strong role in the organization of the description given by the perceptual parser. Past experience also has an important role to play through the internal transformations computed by productions. The original output of the perceptual encoder may be recoded in terms of higher-order chunks. It is in terms of these higher-order chunks that the new productions will be formed. In the context of the ACT memory, it is also possible to have important effects of associative priming.

Strategies are used, and hints processed by the internal transformations (see Fig. 12.2). It is assumed that the procedures that form the actual production inducer are strategy invariant. So, in the flower identification example (page 503), if one is given the hint "Count the number of petals" this hint has its influence by transforming the output of the perceptual encoder, thus making it easier to detect the prime number of petals. The sophistication of the internal transformations probably increases with experience. This sophistication may not always be beneficial, however. For instance, in language learning, it is often remarked how children seem to be much better language learners than adults. It is also noted that adults can better learn a language in a free learning situation than a classroom situation where a teacher and text provide the learner with strong hints. A frequently suggested source of difficulty for the adult is that he attempts to encode the new language with respect to the old. Perhaps, the classroom situation exacerbates the tendency to incorrectly encode the language.

2. Production Formation.   The mechanisms for production induction will assume a number of conventions for representing ACT productions. These conventions are critically important for ensuring that the separately induced productions will work together properly. These conventions are more restrictive than those set forth in Table 6.1 (page 184) which define the syntax of ACT productions. If all productions are induced according to these conventions, then the total variety of productions allowed by Table 6.1 will not be realized. However, the ideas about production induction are still too tentative to think about revising the syntax of productions as set forth in Table 6.1.

One important convention will be that of a control variable. We will assume that at any time in processing there is a control variable in charge of processing and that the production inducer has knowledge of that control variable and its current binding. Suppose that control variable is Vcon and its binding is X. Suppose further that the production inducer is to encode the contingency between pattern C'' and A''. Then the following production would be induced:

$$(\text{Vcon} = X) \ \& \ C'' \Rightarrow (\text{Vcon} = Y) \ \& \ A''$$

where Y is a new value to encode the change of state. The production inducer is going to have to do more than just form productions that directly encode contingencies in activation patterns, but this will always be the first step.

Because of the basic architecture of the ACT production system, the condition, C″, will be a conjunction of properties. This fact will cause ACT to reproduce one of the most ubiquitous facts about human induction—that conjunctive concepts are much easier to acquire than disjunctive. For instance, it is very easy to specify the test for whether something is a *black square* as two propositions in the condition of a production: (V1 * black) & (V1 * square). However, there is no way to encode in the condition of a single production that something is black or square. This would require two productions—one testing if the object is black and the other testing if the object is square. Because disjunctive concepts require multiple productions they should take longer to acquire.

3. *Subroutine Structure*.   Many cognitive procedures are basically hierarchical in structure. This is particularly true of procedures for language processing, because of the recursive structure of language. Therefore, in acquiring procedures the learner must chunk sequences of operations into subroutines and embed one subroutine within another. It has already been shown in Chapters 6 and 11 how subroutine structures may be used profitably to encode linguistic knowledge.

There are two distinguishable subproblems in inducing subroutine structure. One is identifying which strings of operations should be chunked into a subroutine and the other is embedding one subroutine within another. The decision about what sequence of operations to regard as a chunk is made by the preprocessing operations in Fig. 12.2 that transform the input. The success of the induction task will depend on the success of these preprocessing mechanisms at correctly chunking the series. If the encoder chunks a series (100)   (110)   (011) (001), the underlying pattern might not be induced, but it would become very obvious if the pattern were chunked (1001)   (1001)   (1001).

Given a chunking by the preprocessing mechanisms, the production inducer proceeds to create a subroutine by use of the following conventions: The initiation of a subroutine is signaled by the setting of the control variable for that subroutine to an initial value. The end of a subroutine is signaled by the setting of that control variable to a final value. Thus, the first production in a subroutine must start with the control variable set to the initial value and the last production must end with an action that sets the control variable to a final value.

There must also be additions to the higher routine (let us call it the main routine) in order to embed the subroutine within it. Let Vcon be the control variable for the main routine and let Vcon1 be the control variable for the subroutine. Let U be the value of Vcon when the subroutine is called, X be the starting value of the subroutine, and Y be its terminating value. Then the following productions need to be added to the main routine:

(P1)   (Vcon = U) $\Rightarrow$ (Vcon1 = X) & (Vcon = UA)
    & (VI$_1$ = J$_1$) & $\cdots$ & (VI$_n$ = J$_n$)

(P2)   (Vcon = UA) & (Vcon1 = Y) $\Rightarrow$ (Vcon = W)

Production (P1), by setting Vcon1 = X, starts processing in the subroutine and by setting Vcon = UA halts processing in the main routine. Production (P1) also sets the global variables VI_1, VI_2, . . . , VI_n to values that will be used in the subroutine. Some of these settings will be to NIL in which case an UNBIND command should be used, that is, $(VI_x = NIL)$ is equivalent to $(UNBIND\ VI_x)$. Production (P2) will be satisfied upon completion of the subroutine. It will set Vcon to W to enable processing to pick up in the main routine.

A simple example of this would be productions to parse the subject noun phrase at the beginning of the sentence. This would require the two productions:

(Vcon = START) $\Rightarrow$ (Vcon1 = NP)
                                  & (Vcon = STARTA)
                                  & (Vtop = Vsubj)

(Vcon = STARTA) & (Vcon1 = NPX) $\Rightarrow$ (Vcon = VERB)

In this example the first production calls the noun phrase subroutine by setting Vcon1 = NP. The variable that holds the topic of the noun phrase, Vtop, is set to the value of the variable which holds the subject of the sentence, Vsubj. The second production will be executed after the noun phrase is parsed. It sets the expectation for a verb in the main sentence.

4. Generalization of Productions.   It is important for the production inducer to realize when two productions are instances of a more general production. There are many circumstances under which productions should be generalized. I will briefly discuss three. The first involves the situation where the production system has newly formed a production which has the same control node as an existing production and has memory structures in the condition and action which are isomorphic as graph structures to the structures in the existing production. For instance, the subject might already have the production for a noun phrase:

(P3)   (Vcon1 = NP1) & ((Vtok * RED) $\Rightarrow$ (Vcon1 = NP2)
          & (red W RED))   & (Vtop * red)

(In this production it is assumed Vtok is bound to the current word in the sentence and Vtop to the topic of the noun phrase.) Upon encountering the adjective *blue* he might form the production:

(P4)   (Vcon1 = NP1) & ((Vtok * BLUE) $\Rightarrow$ (Vcon1 = NP3)
          & (blue W BLUE))   & (Vtop * blue)

The memory structures in these two productions—(Vtok * RED) & (red W RED) & (Vtop * red) in (P3) and (Vtok * BLUE) & (blue W BLUE) & (Vtop * blue) in (P4)—are isomorphic as graph structures. However, they are not identical. Where the first has the word *RED* and the concept *red* the second has *BLUE* and *blue*. These structures can be merged by replacing the differing elements by variables:

(P5)   (Vcon1 = NP1) & ((Vtok * Vword)   ⇒   (Vcon1 = NP2)
         & (Vword * ADJ) & (Videa W Vword))   & (Vtop * Videa)

In forming a merged production such as (P5) the system does not destroy the individual productions, that is, (P3) and (P4), that gave rise to it. Note in forming this production a word class ADJ has been set up as a restriction on the words that may follow this rule. This word class initially will contain just the terms *red* and *blue*. Language contains rules that apply to arbitrarily defined word classes and it is necessary to form word classes when making generalizations. The creation of a word class when replacing a word by a variable may reflect a rule of induction that is specific to language acquisition. I cannot think of how it would be applicable in other situations.

The second case for collapsing productions occurs when there are two productions in a network identical except for the values of their control variables. An instance of this is illustrated in the noun phrase grammar below:

(P6)   (Vcon1 = NP) & (Vtok * the)   ⇒   (Vcon1 = NP1)

(P7)   (Vcon1 = NP1) & ((Vtok * Vword)   ⇒   (Vcon1 = NP2)
         & (Vword * ADJ) & (Videa W Vword))   & (Vtop * Videa)

(P8)   (Vcon1 = NP2) & ((Vtok * Vword)   ⇒   (Vcon1 = NP3)
         & (Vword * ADJ) & (Videa W Vword))   & (Vtop * Videa)

(P9)   (Vcon1 = NP1) & ((Vtok * Vword)   ⇒   (Vcon1 = NPX)
         & (Vword * NOUN)   & (Vtop * Videa)
         & (Videa W Vword))

(P10)   (Vcon1 = NP2) & ((Vtok * Vword)   ⇒   (Vcon1 = NPX)
         & (Vword * NOUN)   & (Vtop * Videa)
         & (Videa W Vword))

(P11)   (Vcon1 = NP3) & ((Vtok * Vword)   ⇒   (Vcon1 = NPX)
         & (Vword * NOUN)   & (Vtop * Videa)
         & (Videa W Vword))

Note that Productions (P7) and (P8) are the same except for the control nodes. One would like to merge these two productions such that whenever (P8) had been evoked, (P7) would now be evoked. Note that (P8) is evoked by setting Vcon1 = NP2 whereas (P7) can be evoked by setting Vcon1 = NP1. Therefore, one can evoke (P7) wherever (P8) was evoked by the following operation: For every production whose action involves setting Vcon1 = NP2, create another production identical to that except that its action involves setting Vcon1 = NP1. The only production in (P6)–(P11) that sets Vcon1 = NP2 is (P7). Therefore, the following new version is created of (P7):

(P7′)   (Vcon1 = NP1) & ((Vtok * Vword)   ⇒   (Vcon1 = NP1)
          & (Vword * ADJ) & (Videa W Vword))   & (Vtop * Videa)

Production (P7) is not erased but (P7′) is added. This merging process has introduced a loop into the subroutine.

A third case for generalization concerns whole subroutines. It may be discovered that there exist two subroutines which can handle the same structure. This is a cue to merge the two networks into a single network. Where these networks were called by other productions, new productions should be added calling the new, merged subroutine. Again, we do not want to eliminate the old productions, we just want to add more general ones. Noun phrases provide a good example of subroutines that need to be merged. Redundant noun phrase subroutines might be built up to handle subject position noun phrases and object position noun phrases. If subject and object noun phrases have the same grammar (as they do in English) they should be merged.

5. Principle of Strengthening. Note in the above example generalizations that the old productions were not eliminated. It is just that new, more general productions were added. One does not want to throw out the old productions because the generalized productions may prove to be overgeneralizations. A second problem is that information from the environment is not always perfect. One would not want the system to throw out a correct rule because of a random incorrect piece of information. For this reason all production rules have an initial weak strength. As they are repeatedly proven correct their strength is increased. Stronger productions will be elicited more rapidly and so come to dominate. In this way incorrect rules can be set up but will do no permanent damage to the induced system because they would not be strengthened. Section 6.3 reported evidence for this strengthening aspect of productions.

Status of these Assumptions

These five assumptions do not make a complete induction system. A current goal in the LAS research project (see page 461) is to embed these assumptions into a working computer program. I am optimistic that these assumptions or something similar can serve as the basis for a successful induction system. One reason is that assumptions very similar to these were able to serve as the basis for an earlier version of the LAS program (see Anderson, 1975, 1976) which did successfully induce augmented transition network characterizations of natural language. In the remainder of this chapter I will consider how these principles might apply to the induction of serial patterns. I will provide a hand simulation of how they may apply. This is purely to illustrate the ACT mechanisms for induction. The problem was chosen for its simplicity. Inducing a serial pattern might be seen as inducing a language generation routine that has no semantics. I do not think these hand simulations constitute a serious psychological model for serial induction tasks as studied and modeled by Greeno and Simon (1974), Kotovsky and Simon (1973), and Restle and Brown (1970). I suspect subjects in these experiments emerged with a declarative rather than a procedural characterization of the sequences. Evidence for this is the fact that they can verbally describe the sequence structure. What I will be concerned with is not inducing a declarative characterization of the sequence but rather inducing a procedure to generate the sequence. This certainly is a somewhat artificial task but it does serve to illustrate ACT's induction mechanisms.

There is, however, one task where the hand-simulations proposed in this section may have some relation to a feasible psychological model. These are the experiments by Reber (1967, 1969) on the learning of letter sequences generated by finite-state grammars. Here subjects spend many trials trying to learn various sequences generated by the grammar. They are unable to report verbally any regularities in the strings. However, they nonetheless have acquired knowledge about the regularities in the strings. This is manifested by considerable positive transfer in learning new strings generated by the grammar. Reber (personal communication) reports that maximum transfer occurs in those circumstances where subjects are least inclined to consciously look for structure in the material. It seems clear that, whatever the nature of knowledge for the structure in the sequences, it is not the same as in the more traditional serial extrapolation tasks. Rather, it displays some of the characteristics that we would expect of procedural knowledge.

Induction of Simple Periodic Sequences

We will consider the induction of simple sequences with fixed periods. Examples are:

A B A A B A A B A A ···

C X R T C X R T C X ···

D D D D D D D D D D ···

D D A D D D D A D D ···

The ACT induction system will only be successful with such sequences if it properly chunks the sequences into their periods and builds subroutines for each chunk. I will not model this preprocessing stage but simply assume that this preprocessing has been accomplished either by the perceptual encoding or by existing productions. As an example I will consider how the ACT induction system would operate on the following sequence:

A B A A B A A B A A B A ···

Assume that this sequence is chunked in periods of size 3. This means a subroutine will be set up to produce the sequence A B A. I will assume that one production will be set up to produce each item in the sequence. Each production encodes a contingency between activation patterns in memory. In the framework of Fig. 12.2, a production will be produced to link a pattern C″ to A″. In this serial extrapolation task, there is really no condition pattern, that is, no C″. The action pattern is a propositional network specifying that a letter be generated—something of the form "I say A now." I will abbreviate this memory pattern as (SAY A). Thus, the three productions to encode the first chunk are formed from the following pairings:

1. C″ = NIL   A″ = (SAY A)

2. C″ = NIL   A″ = (SAY B)

3. C″ = NIL   A″ = (SAY A)

Subroutine SUBA in Table 12.1 shows the three productions that were set up to form the subroutine. In these productions the control variable Vcon1 has been

TABLE 12.1
Production System after Studying
(A B A) (A B A)

Conditions		Actions
Subroutine SUBA		
(P1)	(Vcon1 = SUBA)	⇒ (Vcon1 = SUBA1) & (SAY A)
(P2)	(Vcon1 = SUBA1)	⇒ (Vcon1 = SUBA2) & (SAY B)
(P3)	(Vcon1 = SUBA2)	⇒ (Vcon1 = SUBAX) & (SAY A)
Subroutine SUBB		
(P4)	(Vcon2 = SUBB)	⇒ (Vcon2 = SUBB1) & (SAY A)
(P5)	(Vcon2 = SUBB1)	⇒ (Vcon2 = SUBB2) & (SAY B)
(P6)	(Vcon2 = SUBB2)	⇒ (Vcon2 = SUBBX) & (SAY A)
Main routine		
(P7)	(Vcon = START)	⇒ (Vcon1 = SUBA) & (Vcon = STARTA)
(P8)	(Vcon = STARTA) & (Vcon1 = SUBAX)	⇒ (Vcon = S1)
(P9)	(Vcon = S1)	⇒ (Vcon2 = SUBB) & (Vcon = S1A)
(P10)	(Vcon = S1A) & (Vcon2 = SUBBX)	⇒ (Vcon = S2)
Additions through generalizations		
(P11)	(Vcon = S1)	⇒ (Vcon1 = SUBA) & (Vcon = S1A)
(P12)	(Vcon = S1A) & (Vcon1 = SUBAX)	⇒ (Vcon = S2)
(P13)	(Vcon = STARTA) & (Vcon1 = SUBAX)	⇒ (Vcon = START)

introduced to ensure that the letters are generated in proper sequence. The formation of these productions from the activation pairings follows exactly the principles
set out earlier for production formation (page 515). Table 12.1 shows the set
of productions available after the system has processed the first two triplets. A
second subroutine, SUBB has been set up for the second triplet. Table 12.1 shows
these two subroutines, each of which will output a sequence *A B A,* and the
main routine which strings these two subroutines together. Production (P7) in the
main routine calls subroutine SUBA and (P8) receives control when it transfers
back from the subroutine. Productions (P9) and (P10) serve the same function for
subroutine SUBB. The format of these subroutine embeddings conforms to the
conventions set down on page 516.

Note that subroutines SUBA and SUBB are identical except for their control
variables and the values of these control variables. Therefore, in accordance with
the principles for subroutine merging (see page 519), an attempt is made to replace SUBB by SUBA. To accomplish this, a new production is added to the
main routine for each production that refers to SUBB. These new productions are
identical to the old except that reference to SUBB is replaced by reference to
SUBA. Productions (P11) and (P12) are added in this capacity as new versions of
(P9) and (P10). Note that (P7) and the newly created (P11) serve the same function
in that they serve to call the subroutine SUBB. Therefore, an attempt is made to
merge these productions. This is accomplished by creating (P13) as a new version
of (P8) in which Vcon is set to START. This follows the principle on page 518
for merging control structure. There is now a loop in the main network in which
(P7) elicits (P13) which in turn elicits (P7). This loop constantly calls the sub-

MAIN ROUTINE

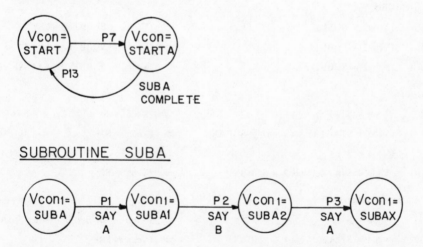

SUBROUTINE SUBA

FIG. 12.3   A representation of the flow of control among the critical productions in Table 12.1.

routine SUBA to put out three-item sequences of the form A B A. Figure 12.3 illustrates the control structure of this main routine loop and the subroutine SUBA. The productions in Fig. 12.3 will serve to generate the sequence at hand. Since these productions always will be successful they should be strengthened to the point where they come to dominate over all the other productions. At this point a solution to the induction problem will have been achieved.

Induction of a More Complex Letter Series

It would be useful to consider how ACT might go about inducing a series with a more complex structure than the preceding example. Consider the sequence A B C B C D C D E D E F ···. There is no simple sequence repeating at cycle 3, but there is a pattern with cycle 3. The sequences of three are successors in the alphabet. The first member of one sequence of three is also the alphabetic successor of the first member of the previous sequence. If ACT is going to be able to induce a production system that will generate this series the preprocessing mechanisms will have to both chunk the series into triples and notice the successor relationships.

As in the previous example we will assume that the preprocessing mechanisms recognize that the series is of period 3 and consequently subroutines will be built to handle successive strings of three elements. Thus, it will try to build a subroutine to process the first sequence (A B C). The first condition–action pair will be built to handle the generation of the output A. The condition–action for the formation of this production (see Fig. 12.2) is $C'' = $ NIL and $A'' = $ (SAY A). Therefore, the first production in the subroutine is

$$(Vcon1 = SUBA) \;\Rightarrow\; (Vcon1 = SUBA1)\ \&\ (SAY\ A)$$

For the next production we will assume the perceptual encoder notices the relationship between A and B and encodes this relationship as the condition for the formation of the next production. Thus, the next production formed is

$$(Vcon1 = SUBA1)\ \&\ (A * (precedes\ OF\ B)) \;\Rightarrow\; (Vcon1 = SUBA2)\ \&\ (SAY\ B).$$

Similarly, the third and final production of this subroutine is formed:

$$(Vcon1 = SUBA2)\ \&\ (B * (precedes\ OF\ C)) \;\Rightarrow\; (Vcon1 = SUBAX)\ \&\ (SAY\ C).$$

In similar manner another subroutine is formed to encode the next triple (B C D) and both subroutines are embedded in the main routine. The state of the production system at this point is illustrated in Table 12.2.[8] Note in Production (P3)

---

[8]Note in Table 12.2 that Productions (P6) and (P7) are not merged despite their considerable similarity. This might seem in violation of the principle stated on page 517 for generalization of productions. It would be disastrous to merge Productions (P6) and (P7) because (P7) ends the subroutine and (P6) does not. An auxiliary rule would have to be added to production generalization to the effect that one cannot merge two productions if one terminates a routine (by setting the control variable for that routine to the final value) and the other does not.

TABLE 12.2
Production System after Studying
(A B C) (B D C)

	Conditions		Actions
Main routine			
(P1)	(Vcon = START)	⇒	(Vcon1 = SUBA) & (Vcon = STARTA)
(P2)	(Vcon = STARTA) & (Vcon1 = SUBAX)	⇒	(Vcon = S1)
(P3)	(Vcon = S1) & (A * (precedes OF B))	⇒	(Vcon1 = SUBB) & (Vcon = S1A)
(P4)	(Vcon = S1A) & (Vcon1 = SUBBX)	⇒	(Vcon = S2)
Subroutine SUBA			
(P5)	(Vcon1 = SUBA)	⇒	(Vcon1 = SUBA1) & (SAY A)
(P6)	(Vcon1 = SUBA1) & (A * (precedes OF B))	⇒	(Vcon1 = SUBA2) & (SAY B)
(P7)	(Vcon1 = SUBA2) & (B * (precedes OF C))	⇒	(Vcon1 = SUBAX) & (SAY C)
Subroutine SUBB			
(P8)	(Vcon1 = SUBB)	⇒	(Vcon2 = SUBB1) & (SAY B)
(P9)	(Vcon1 = SUBB1) & (B * (precedes OF C))	⇒	(Vcon2 = SUBB2) & (SAY C)
(P10)	(Vcon1 = SUBB2) & (C * (precedes OF D))	⇒	(Vcon2 = SUBBX) & (SAY D)
Subroutine SUBC			
(P11)	(Vcon3 = SUBC)	⇒	(Vcon3 = SUBC1) & (SAY V1)
(P12)	(Vcon3 = SUBC1) (V1 * (precedes OF V2))	⇒	(Vcon3 = SUBC2) & (SAY V2) & V2
(P13)	(Vcon3 = SUBC2) (V2 * (precedes OF V3))	⇒	(Vcon3 = SUBCX) & (SAY V3)
Additions to main routine			
(P14)	(Vcon = START)	⇒	(Vcon3 = SUBC) & (Vcon = STARTA) & (V1 = A) & (UNBIND V2)
(P15)	(Vcon = STARTA) & (Vcon1 = SUBCX)	⇒	(Vcon = S1)
(P16)	(Vcon = S1) & (A * (precedes OF B))	⇒	(Vcon3 = SUBC) & (Vcon = S1A) & (V1 = B) & (UNBIND V2)
(P17)	(Vcon = S1A) & (Vcon1 = SUBCX)	⇒	(Vcon = S2)

of the main routine, the condition has encoded the successor relationship between the first letter of the two chunks. This occurred because the preprocessing mechanisms noted the relationship and made it the input for formation of Production (P3).

At this point the system is in a position to make a generalization. The productions that define the first subroutine, SUBA, can be put into correspondence with the productions that define the second subroutine, SUBB. To do this the element A in SUBA must be put in correspondence with B. Similarly, B must be put in correspondence with C, and C with D. Thus, to merge these subroutines into one the specific elements must be replaced by the variables V1, V2, and V3. The three productions (P11)–(P13) give a new subroutine, SUBC, which is a merging of SUBA and SUBB. Also it is necessary to add Productions (P14)–(P17) which serve as an alternate route through the main routine which will evoke the subroutine SUB3. Note that Productions (P14) and (P16), besides evoking the subroutine, initialize V1 and unbind V2.

Table 12.3 shows the state of the production system after it has processed the

TABLE 12.3
Production System after Studying
(A B C) (B C D) (C D E)

Conditions		Actions
Main routine		
(P14)	(Vcon = START)	$\Rightarrow$ (Vcon3 = SUBC) & (Vcon = STARTA) & (V1 = A) & (UNBIND V2)
(P15)	(Vcon = STARTA) & (Vcon3 = SUBCX)	$\Rightarrow$ (Vcon = S1)
(P16)	(Vcon = S1) & (A * (precedes OF B))	$\Rightarrow$ (Vcon3 = SUBC) & (Vcon = S1A) & (V1 = B) & (UNBIND V2)
(P17)	(Vcon = S1A) & (Vcon3 = SUBCX)	$\Rightarrow$ (Vcon = S2)
(P18)	(Vcon = S2) & (B * (precedes OF C))	$\Rightarrow$ (Vcon3 = SUBC) & (Vcon = S2A) & (V1 = C) & (UNBIND V2)
(P19)	(Vcon = S2) & (Vcon3 = SUBCX)	$\Rightarrow$ (Vcon = S3)
Subroutine		
(P11)	(Vcon3 = SUBC)	$\Rightarrow$ (Vcon3 = SUBC1) & (SAY V1)
(P12)	(Vcon3 = SUBC1) & (V1 * (precedes OF V2))	$\Rightarrow$ (Vcon3 = SUBC2) & (SAY V2) & V2
(P13)	(Vcon3 = SUBC2) (V2 * (precedes OF V3))	$\Rightarrow$ (Vcon3 = SUBCX) & (SAY V3)
Generalizations		
(P20)	(Vcon = START)	$\Rightarrow$ (Vcon3 = SUBC) & (Vcon = STARTA) & (UNBIND V2) & (V4 = A)
(P21)	(Vcon = S1) & (V4 * (precedes OF V5))	$\Rightarrow$ (Vcon3 = SUBC) & (Vcon = S1A) & (V1 = V5) & (UNBIND V2) & (V4 = V5)
(P22)	(Vcon = S1A) & (Vcon3 = SUBCX)	$\Rightarrow$ (Vcon = S1)

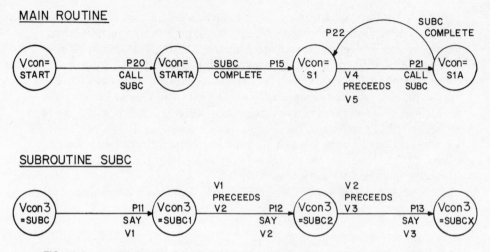

FIG. 12.4   A representation of the flow of control among the critical productions in Table 12.3.

third triple (C D E). Omitted from Table 12.3 is mention of all the structure in Table 12.2 that does not involve the subroutine SUBC. Since this one subroutine will handle all the series it will be constantly strengthened and will come to dominate. As a consequence of studying (C D E) Productions (P18) and (P19) have been added to the main routine. They call SUBC, this time with V1 initialized to C. Note that Productions (P16) and (P18) are identical except for the elements A, B, C, and the value of the control variable Vcon. By replacing these elements with variables and by using the value of Vcon in (P16), these productions can be merged to form a single production, (P21). Note that there are two variables which have been added to (P21)—V4 and V5. The variable V4 replaces A in (P16) and B in (P18). The variable V5 replaces B in (P16) and C in (P18). To permit these different bindings of the variable from one production to another, (P21) contains actions to set the value of V4 to V5 and unbind V5. To initialize V4, Production (P20) is built as a new version of (P14). It includes an action to set the value of V4 to A. Finally, Production (P22) is added as an alternate to (P17). It serves to introduce a loop in the main network so that SUBC will be called to process every chunk. Figure 12.4 illustrates the final set of productions that will serve to process this sequence. There is now a path of control in the main network that goes from (P20) to (P15) to (P21) to (P22) back to (P21), and so on. This path, which constantly calls SUBC, will serve to process the total sequence and will consequently be strengthened, becoming the main path.

General Observations about Induction Examples

The induction principles for ACT have yet to be embodied in a working program. When a working program is built there will undoubtedly be significant additions, changes, and complications that I have not foreseen. However, it is necessary to include this section in order to make it credible that induction could be handled in the ACT framework and to give some indication of how it would be handled.

The serial pattern learning task was chosen because it is a particularly simple task and consequently it is relatively easy to see how induction principles would apply to it. It also has a certain similarity to language generation. A current goal of my research project in induction is to develop a model for induction of a production system for language processing.

SUMMARY OF CHAPTER 12

The induction problem is concerned with the process by which subjects build up procedures from observing examples of the input–output characteristics of the to-be-induced procedures. A formal analysis of the induction problem is provided in which the to-be-induced procedures are defined by various abstract automata. Identification in the limit is offered as a satisfactory criterion for success in the induction problem. By this criterion a learner is considered successful if, after some finite time, he induces a procedure which mimics the behavior of the to-be-induced procedure. There exists an algorithm, the enumeration algorithm, which can identify in the limit any procedure computed by a primitive recursive automaton. Primitive recursive automata seem to be a sufficiently large class of machines that they include any procedure of which a human is capable. The enumeration algorithm is one which simply enumerates the possible procedures until it comes upon a correct procedure. The enumeration algorithm would be extremely slow to identify most procedures but there is no algorithm uniformly faster than it.

There are two types of solutions to dilemmas posed by formal results like the fact that there is no procedure uniformly faster than the enumeration algorithm. These formal results depend on two assumptions—that all solutions are equally plausible and that there are no hints as to the correct solution other than the input–output examples. Solutions to the formal dilemmas can be obtained if either of these assumptions is changed. Such solutions amount to taking, in a sense, a rationalist position on the problem of induction.

The formal results about induction can be applied to language acquisition. There are two ways to view the language acquisition problem. The first way is the syntactic approach which views language acquisition as the process of learning to make judgments about grammatical correctness. The second approach is the semantic approach which views language acquisition as the process of learning to map between sentence and meaning. To learn a syntactic characterization of an arbitrary language it is necessary to be given information both about what are sentences of the language and what are nonsentences. It does not seem reasonable, however, to assume that a language learner gets negative information about non-sentences. To learn a semantic characterization of an arbitrary language, it is necessary that there be no instances of ambiguity or synonymy in the language. It is unreasonable to assume natural languages are not ambiguous or not synonymous. Thus, both the syntactic and semantic approaches require unreasonable assumptions to guarantee successful learning. In addition, both face enormous problems of efficiency. Tractable solutions under either the syntactic or the semantic approach are only possible if we make assumptions about what are plausible languages or make assumptions about hints in the data.

In ACT a production arises as the encoding of a contingency between two activation patterns. A production inducer makes the first activation pattern the condition of the induced production and makes the second pattern the action. One important class of variables determining the success of induction in ACT is the processes (perceptual and production-computed) that determine the condition and action patterns presented to the production inducer. Appropriate preprocessing by these mechanisms can make solvable otherwise impossible induction problems. A set of conventions is specified for use of control variables, embedding one subroutine within another, and for generalizing productions. Another important aspect to the induction process is the growth in the strength of productions with successful use. This provides a means for gradually merging new productions into the system and preventing mistaken conditions from having disastrous consequences. Hand-simulations are offered of how these principles for induction might apply to acquiring a production system for the generation of sequential patterns.

REFERENCES

Anderson, J. R. Computer simulation of a language acquisition system: A first report. In R. L. Solso (Ed.), *Information processing and cognition: The Loyola Symposium*. Hillsdale, New Jersey: Lawrence Erlbaum Assoc., 1975.

Anderson, J. R. Computer simulation of a language acquisition system: A second report. In D. La Berge & S. J. Samuels (Eds.), *Perception and comprehension*. Hillsdale, N.J.: Lawrence Erlbaum Assoc., in press.

Biermann, D. W. An interactive finite-state language learner. Paper presented at First USA–JAPAN Computer Conference, 1972.

Braine, M. D. S. On two types of models of the internalization of grammars. In D. I. Slobin (Ed.), *The ontogenesis of grammar*. New York: Academic Press, 1971.

Brown, R. *A first language*. Cambridge, Mass.: Harvard University Press, 1973.

Chomsky, N. *Aspects of the theory of syntax*. Cambridge, Massachusetts: MIT Press, 1965.

Feldman, J. *Some decidability results on grammatical inference and complexity*. Stanford Artificial Intelligence Project Memo AIM-93.1, 1970.

Gold, E. M. Limiting recursion. *Journal of Symbolic Logic*, 1965, **30**, 28–48.

Gold, E. M. Language identification in the limit. *Information and Control*, 1967, **10**, 447–474.

Greeno, J. G., & Simon, H. A. Processes for sequence production. *Psychological Review*, 1974, **81**, 187–198.

Hamburger, H., & Wexler, K. A mathematical theory of learning transformational grammar. *Journal of Mathematical Psychology*, 1975, **12**, 137–177.

Hopcroft, J. E., & Ullman, J. D. *Formal languages and their relation to automata*. Reading, Massachusetts: Addison-Wesley, 1969.

Horning, J. J. *A study of grammatical inference* (Tech. Rep. No. CS 139). Computer Science Department, Stanford University, August 1969.

Hunt, E. B. *Artificial intelligence*. New York: Academic Press, 1975.

Johnson, D. M. *A systematic introduction to the psychology of thinking*. New York: Harper & Row, 1972.

Kotovsky, K., & Simon, H. A. Empirical tests of a theory of human acquisition of concepts for sequential events. *Cognitive Psychology*, 1973, **4**, 399–424.

Minsky, M. L. *Computations: finite and infinite machines*. Englewood Cliffs, New Jersey: Prentice-Hall, 1967.

Moeser, S. D., & Bregman, A. S. The role of reference in the acquisition of a miniature artificial language. *Journal of Verbal Learning and Verbal Behavior*, 1972, **11**, 759–769.

Moeser, S. D., & Bregman, A. S. Imagery and language acquisition. *Journal of Verbal Learning and Verbal Behavior*, 1973, **12**, 91–98.

Pao, T. W. L. A solution of the syntactic induction-inference problem for a nontrivial subset of context-free language (Rep. No. 70-19). The Moore School of Electrical Engineering, University of Pennsylvania, August, 1969.

Peters, S., & Ritchie, R. W. On restricting the base component of transformational grammars. *Information and Control*, 1971, **18**, 483–501.

Reber, A. S. Implicit learning of artificial grammars. *Journal of Verbal Learning and Verbal Behavior*, 1967, **6**, 855–863.

Reber, A. S. Transfer of structure in synthetic languages. *Journal of Experimental Psychology*, 1969, **81**, 115–119.

Restle, F., & Brown, E. Organization of serial pattern learning. In G. Bower (Ed.), *The psychology of learning and motivation: Advances in research and theory*. Vol. 4. New York: Academic Press, 1970.

Trabasso, T., & Bower, G. H. *Attention in learning*. New York: Wiley, 1968.

13
Provisional Evaluations

> Of making many books there is no end and much
> study is a weariness of the flesh.
>
> SOLOMON

One of the fringe benefits of writing a book is that one has the freedom of format to provide a chapter of self-evaluation. I will briefly state what I feel are the strengths of this book and of the ACT theory and then go on to a more extensive discussion of potential weaknesses. The principal contribution of this book, from my point of view, is that it offers a psychological theory of very broad generality. In this book it was applied, with moderate success, to many aspects of language, memory, inferential reasoning, and induction. It has obvious potential for extension to problem solving and indeed Greeno (1976) has done just that. It is an open question whether it can and whether it should be applied to issues of perception and imagery. With these possible and notable exceptions ACT seems capable of modeling all the tasks of concern to modern cognitive psychology.

The other contributions are:

1. Chapter 1 and subsequent chapters presented arguments for the nonidentifiability of the structures and processes of a cognitive theory. It was argued that the goal of cognitive psychology should be to produce models of broad predictive generality and not to attempt to uniquely identify models.

2. An argument was also made in Chapter 1 and elsewhere for the role of formal analysis in cognitive psychology as an alternative to data gathering. A few well chosen empirical facts can be made to go a long way in testing the validity of a theory.

3. The procedural-declarative distinction (Chapters 2, 3, and 4) was emphasized as a way of structuring theories about cognitive processes. Reviews were provided of existing ideas about propositional (declarative) knowledge and procedural knowledge.

4. A production system model (Chapters, 4, 5, 6, and 7) of procedural knowledge was integrated with a propositional network model of declarative knowledge.

5. A formal semantics (Chapter 7) was defined for the propositional network and the production system. This semantics made it possible to prove claims about the expressive power of the ACT representational system.

6. A spreading activation process was defined (Chapter 8) for the associative network, and empirically tested. The production system serves basically as the interpreter for the active portion of memory.

7. In Chapter 9 the distinction was developed between strategic inference making and natural inference making. Natural inferential processes deal with inferences in unconstrained situations whereas strategic inferences are special case rules developed to enable more efficient inferential reasoning. Empirical tests were made of both types of inference systems.

8. In Chapter 10 I provided ACT analyses of three important factors in human memory: encoding specificity, depth of processing, and prose structure.

9. In Chapter 11 I provided an ACT model for language comprehension and generation and contrasted it with other existing models, principally augmented transition networks.

10. In Chapter 12 I presented a general formal analysis of the induction problem and provided a proposal for an ACT model of induction.

THE DIFFICULTIES

The single most serious difficulty with the ACT model concerns the question of empirical testability, despite the fact that this book contains many empirical tests of ACT. R. Sternberg once described his impression of HAM when he first dealt with it as a graduate student at Stanford: It seemed like a great lumbering dragon that one could throw darts at and sting but which one never could seem to slay. No matter what embarrassing data one would uncover, it always seemed that HAM could find some explanation for it. I am afraid that this plasticity may also be a problem for ACT.

Bower and I have been challenged with respect to HAM and now I am challenged with respect to ACT to specify some set of critical theoretical assumptions that could be put to the test. E. Smith has pointed out the problems in evaluating HAM because there was no such specification. The only experiments that researchers could perform that seemed to have much consequence for HAM were reanalyses of paradigms that Bower and I had used in support of HAM. This is why the experiments of Foss and Harwood and of R. C. Anderson (see Chapter 10) seemed critical. They found, by reanalysis or slight variation of our memory paradigms, evidence that contradicted the conclusions we had made. In my own research I have been most influenced by unexpected outcomes from slight variations of paradigms that had previously yielded results in support of HAM. Data from novel paradigms seemed too open to multiple interpretations in terms of HAM and so lacked much force.

There are a number of remarks that need to be made about the empirical accountability of ACT. First, because of the fact that it is a more general theory than HAM it is more accountable. In HAM we could always assign empirical blemishes to processes we did not propose to seriously analyze, such as the parser, elaborative processes, guessing strategies, etc. One can still attribute unexpected results to such sources in ACT, but there are now ways to test if these attributions are correct. Because ACT provides models for these processes it predicts that other empirical consequences should occur if these processes were responsible for the phenomena at hand. These other predictions can be examined as converging evidence for one's post hoc explanations. Of course, there is no guarantee that ACT can ever really be pinned down. Its basic processing primitives are very flexible and one might attempt to save the model by engaging in an infinite retreat, "post-hocing" explanations for failures of prediction, then post-hocing explanations for the failures of these post-hoc explanations, etc. However, such an infinite retreat would clearly discredit the model.

Another remark that needs to be made about the empirical accountability of ACT is that one cannot seriously expect to perform a single experiment and slay ACT. If ACT makes a prediction that proves wrong, that exact version of ACT will have to be abandoned but I am obviously going to propose a slight variant of the theory with slightly changed assumptions that is compatible with those data. It would be nice if the theory could be reduced to a few critical assumptions that could be subjected to simple experimental tests. However, things just do not work that way. ACT is only going to be rejected by repeated attacks that keep forcing reformulations until the point comes when the theory becomes unmanageable with its patches and bandages.

One of the principle reasons why ACT is not subject to simple empirical test is that it is largely a model of internal structures and processes. That internal model is reasonably simple and subject to strong constraints, but there is no similarly simple and rigorous specification of how to relate the internal processes to external manipulations and observables. For example, there is no formal theory of how a sentence is to be represented, what the exact productions are that perform an inference, or how a subject will direct a search of his memory to retrieve a word in a free recall test. In the preceding chapters I have specified ACT systems for particular paradigms, but there are no general principles for analyzing situations and specifying ACT systems for them. A cognitive theory is ultimately only as good as its interface with data. Therefore, one of the high priority tasks in the development of the ACT theory is to formalize procedures that will go from the specification of an experimental paradigm to an ACT model for that paradigm.

Another comment on the empirical accountability of the ACT theory is that it is an ill-conceived goal to set out to prove the theory wrong. We know from the outset that ACT is wrong. An interesting goal is to find out in what ways ACT is in error. From this point of view, it is to be expected and desirable that tests of the theory result in reformulations of the theory rather than wholesale rejection of it.

Besides this central problem of empirical accountability there are five other issues which are potential weaknesses in the ACT theory. It is unclear at this stage how serious these criticisms of ACT are.

1. Does the procedural–declarative distinction miss a significant generalization? Earlier, in Chapter 4, I pointed out how extremely intuitive the procedural–declarative distinction was and that it seemed that declarative knowledge and procedural knowledge obeyed different laws. It was acknowledged that there undoubtedly was a way to formulate a model that did not incorporate this distinction. However, it seemed that such a model would have to be more complicated. One way to collapse the distinction might be to regard the links in the propositional network as productions themselves. That is, if there is a link going from node A to node B regard this as a production that has A as its condition and B as its action, that is, the production A ⇒ B. This is presumably what Newell had in mind in the quote at the beginning of Chapter 6. It is difficult to see how to pursue this option in detail. One would somehow have to encode the relational information in a network into productions. Existing ACT productions look for active network configurations. If there are no networks, one would have to think of some other way to encode this configurational information. It would be necessary to think of some way to formulate the principles of associative interference and spread of activation (Chapter 8) for production systems rather than networks. One would have to develop reasons for why the traditional features of propositional knowledge—reportability, rapid acquisition, poor retention—are only true of part of the production system. I still remain doubtful that there can be a parsimonious collapsing of the procedural–declarative distinction. However, there is one outcome in the evolution of the ACT model that suggests the two knowledge systems may be one. This is the evidence showing that both productions and propositional links have strength properties (Chapters 6 and 8).

2. Is ACT too atomistic a model of human cognition? ACT provides a relatively fine-grained analysis of the procedural and propositional knowledge underlying performance. The justification for this is the belief that only at this level of analysis will generalities emerge across different types of cognitive behaviors. It remains very much a question for future research how much across-task generality there is under the ACT analysis. However, even if many generalities are found it might be argued that ACT is too atomistic a model to enable tractible analysis of interesting cognitive behavior. For instance, few people doubt that there would be across-task generality of principles if we reduced cognitive theory to the laws of physics that govern the nervous system. However, also few people would believe that tractible analyses of cognitive phenomena exist at this level. Perhaps ACT has gone down the reductionist road farther than is manageable or necessary. Perhaps it would be better to have more macroprinciples for analyzing cognitive behavior.

3. Do ACT's primitives make it too flexible a model? There was much concern in developing ACT that it be in principle capable of the complexity that exists in human cognition. Therefore, there were analyses of its computational power

(Chapter 4), its expressive power (Chapter 7), and the complexity of the languages it could process (Chapter 11). It may be capable of generating any behavior a human can, but it may also be able to generate many behaviors a human cannot. I do not know of any class of behavior that ACT can generate which humans cannot, but this does not preclude such a class. It may turn out that further restrictions are needed on the class of things that ACT can do.

Some people have made the observation that ACT may be so flexible that it really does not contain any empirical claims and really only provides a medium for psychological modeling—that very different psychological theories can be created by writing different production systems for the same task. It is unclear to me whether this is true, but to the extent that it is, ACT acquires the status of a theoretical medium like stochastic models. This is certainly not what I intended in creating ACT, but nonetheless I suppose that would be a contribution.

4. Are the parameters of ACT consistent over the task domains? In the ACT model there are certain basic processing parameters that need to be estimated, such as the size of the ALIST and the rate of activation of memory. In fitting the ACT model to an experiment we are free to estimate these parameters in such a way as to get a maximally good fit. It would not do, however, to have wildly different parameter values estimated for different experiments. The one parameter for which there is enough data to explore this question is α, the activation rate. There were five fact-retrieval experiments reported in Chapter 8 and two inference experiments in Chapter 9 for which α was estimated. The value of α varied from 32 msec (probability experiment page 288) to 484 msec (middle-man experiment, page 373). The average value of α in the fact-retrieval experiments was 69 msec while the average value in the inference experiments was 415 msec. This very large discrepancy may be related to the overall reaction times in the two sets of experiments. The mean reaction time in the fact-retrieval experiments was 1617 msec whereas it was 6070 msec in the inference experiments. There is one explanation of the difference between the parameter estimates for the two types of experiments which relates this to the differences in mean reaction time. A correlation between mean reaction time and α could be predicted from what I have called a breakdown model. Suppose there is a certain probability at any point of time that a process may break down and the subject may have to begin again from the start. This could happen in the ACT model because of dampening or because a critical control node was pushed off the ALIST. Because the process has to begin again, the amount of time spent waiting for structures to be activated will be doubled. Thus, because of these breakdowns, the effect of the activation rate will be magnified. The frequency of such breakdowns will increase when the time to complete a process increases. That is, breakdowns should occur more often in experiments with long mean reaction times. Since the frequency of breakdowns magnifies the effect of activation time, a correlation will be introduced between the activation time and mean processing time.

The effect of such breakdowns is to destroy the Sternberg (1969) additive factors logic in analyzing reaction time. It allows the time estimates for independent stages to interact. When one process gets longer there will be an increase in breakdown frequency and so the time estimates for other processes will be magnified. One would hope that the probability of such breakdowns during any experimental trial would be so low that the interactions introduced would be minimal. This may be a valid assumption for experiments where mean reaction times are about 500 msec. However, it may no longer be a valid assumption when mean reaction times approach 10 sec.

5. There is considerable difficulty in communicating the content of a production system. I do not think that it is really harder to understand a procedure written in ACT productions than in other programming languages, but it is difficult. Sufficient familiarity with a programming language to read and understand an arbitrary procedure in that language only comes with the investment of an amount of time that most readers will not be willing to make. The networks illustrating the flow of control among the productions were introduced as a partial solution to the communication problem. How successful is this and other measures I have taken will remain to be seen. I am certainly open to any further suggestions for reducing the communication barrier.

PRACTICAL APPLICATIONS?

I would like to conclude this chapter with a remark about one of the ultimate goals I have set for my research efforts (see Chapter 1), that is, that it produce a theory capable of practical applications. The obvious focus for practical applications of a theory like ACT is on education. As the reader of this book has no doubt noted, there is a dearth of suggestions for such practical applications of ACT. My original naive expectations about ACT have been considerably disappointed in this regard. I had thought practical suggestions would naturally flow from the theory as it evolved. That clearly is not the case. Applying ACT to practical problems will be no different than attempting to apply ACT to a new experimental paradigm. That is, practical applications from a theory like ACT will be forthcoming only by dint of much effort.

REFERENCES

Greeno, J. G. Process of understanding in problem solving. In N. J. Castellan, D. B. Pisoni, & G. P. Potts, (Eds.), *Cognitive theory*. Vol. II. Hillsdale, New Jersey: Lawrence Erlbaum Assoc., 1976.

Sternberg, S. Memory-scanning: Mental processes revealed by reaction time experiments. *Acta Psychologica*, 1969, **30**, 276–315.

Author Index

Numbers in *italics* refer to the pages on which the complete references are listed.

Subject Index